GENTLEMEN AND OFFICERS

The Impact and Experience of War
on a Territorial Regiment
1914–1918

by
K. W. Mitchinson

The Naval & Military Press Ltd

in association with

The Imperial War Museum
Department of Printed Books

Published jointly by

The Naval & Military Press Ltd

Unit 10 Ridgewood Industrial Park,

Uckfield, East Sussex,

TN22 5QE England

Tel: +44 (0) 1825 749494

Fax: +44 (0) 1825 765701

www.naval-military-press.com

www.military-genealogy.com

www.militarymaproom.com

and

The Imperial War Museum, London

Department of Printed Books

www.iwm.org.uk

Printed and bound in Great Britain by
CPI Antony Rowe, Chippenham and Eastbourne

FOR D.H.M.

CONTENTS

Page

APPENDICES AND MAPS

Note on Maps

ILLUSTRATIONS

The plates of illustrations constituting the centre pages are largely drawn from the albums held by the Department of Printed Books, Imperial War Museum. Prints may be obtained from the Department of Photographs by quoting the relevant 'HU' number at the end of each caption.

ACKNOWLEDGEMENTS

Any work on the First World War owes a great debt of gratitude to the Imperial War Museum and to the staff of the Departments of Printed Books, Documents and Sound Archives: their help over the years of research into this book has been greatly appreciated. Particular thanks must go to Gwyn Bayliss, Mary Wilkinson, Sarah Paterson and Martin Taylor for their efforts in preparing this work for publication. Richard Bayford of the Photographic Staff has made an excellent job of reproducing the LRB photographs considering the age and condition of the prints. I am grateful to the Director-General and the Trustees of the Museum for permission to use material in the LRB collection. The Keepers of the Documents and Photographic Departments have also allowed me to reproduce items held in their respective archives. Acknowledgement is also given to the Public Record Office, the British Library Newspaper Library, the National Army Museum, the Guildhall Library, and to Peter H. Liddle for allowing access to and use of papers deposited in his 1914-1918 Personal Experience Archive. The following publishers have also granted permission to quote from their publications: William Kimber, Picardy, Constable, Penguin and the Edinburgh University Press.

Martin Middlebrook kindly made available several questionnaires which he had circulated to LRB men in preparation of his *First Day on the Somme*, and Joe Harris, the Secretary of the LRB Veterans' Association, has been of immense help and encouragement in providing contacts with former members of the regiment. The greatest debt however is owed to these ex-soldiers themselves. They were prepared to give up their time and allow themselves to be interviewed or to reply to my many letters and telephone calls. Without their help, generosity and patience, so much of the material for this book would never have been collected. The names of these men are listed separately, but special mention should be made of Sid Amatt, Maurice Howard, Basil Houle, John Sutton, 'Sunny' Jessop, and Jack Terry. Owing to the frailties of age, many of the men dictated their responses to members of their family who then despatched the answers on to me, and my thanks are of course extended to those relatives.

K.W. Mitchinson

PUBLISHER'S NOTE

I am delighted to be able to offer this new study of the London Rifle Brigade in the Great War to the public. Over a decade ago we were fortunate to acquire from the LRB association a large collection of albums, diaries, periodicals and photographs relating to the unit's history. With the assistance of my former deputy, David Nash, a young teacher began to examine this material in our reading room. It proved to be a rich mine and to my surprise, just after David Nash had left the Museum, a formidable Amstrad-generated tome arrived in the morning mail from the author, one Kevin Mitchinson. Many commuting days later I finished reading it and decided that it ought to be published - preferably by the Museum since it was based so firmly on our collection. Several barriers had to be overcome but, reinforced by the Museum historian's (Peter Simkins) equally favourable assessment, and with the vital support of the Director-General, Dr Alan Borg, we eventually surmounted the obstacles.

The printout was scanned, no easy task given its variable quality, and then re-checked edited and typeset by Mary Wilkinson, our Head of Acquisitions and Cataloguing. The final outcome is now presented hopefully as the author originally intended, with suitable illustrative material. We have striven to retain a wealth of data which we hope will be appreciated not only by students of the First World War but also by family historians. If you had a relative who served in the LRB this is the book to buy. Even if your relative did not serve in the Territorial unit, it is still worth purchasing for the vivid picture it recreates of both recruitment and life in the trenches.

Dr Gwyn Bayliss
Keeper of the Department of Printed Books
Imperial War Museum

FOREWORD

In recent years, our collective understanding of the British Army in the First World War - the biggest army in the nation's history - has been greatly enhanced by an increase in studies of its organisation and social composition. While British and Commonwealth scholars continue to make immensely valuable contributions to the debate on the High Command and civil-military relations, a growing number have turned their attention to the long-neglected socio-military aspects of the subject and are publishing detailed analyses of individual divisions, brigades and battalions. At last we are beginning to examine in depth the factors which motivated these units and ask a wider variety of questions. What effect, if any, did the social composition of a unit at a given time have on morale and battlefield performance? How quickly did units recover after major battles? Where did their casualty replacements come from? How did infantry battalions keep going after setbacks and not only avoid mass protests and mutinies but summon up sufficient resolve to win an outstanding series of victories from August 1918?

K.W. Mitchinson has already published one such painstaking battalion study in his book on the Oldham Pals - *Cotton Town Comrades* - which appeared in 1993. This present work, *Gentlemen and Officers*, focuses on a notable Territorial unit - the London Rifle Brigade - and sheds yet more useful light on the British Army of the 1914-1918 period. The author captures the essential "flavour" of the London Rifle Brigade by drawing out its particular characteristics and, in so doing, augments our knowledge of what the British Army of 1914-1918 was *really* like - as distinct from the image which we have inherited from the literature of disillusionment and *Oh, What a Lovely War!* This book is a most welcome addition to the new generation of scholarly unit studies.

Peter Simkins
Historian, Imperial War Museum
April 1994

PREFACE

This study is not an attempt to provide a straightforward account of a regiment's military activity during the Great War. Intriguing and absorbing as that would be for a regiment like the LRB, which saw such extensive action between 1914-18, another look at its engagements from the purely military aspect would not be particularly valid. In common with many other battalions, a history of the LRB was published in the early 1920's, so the student of its military history can refer to that volume for the regiment's day to day activities. These regimental histories were usually compiled from the War Diaries and faithfully recorded the exploits and battles of the respective units. Consequently, the finished books concentrated largely upon the military operations and paid little attention to the effects which those operations had upon the morale, composition and structure of the battalion. The slaughter of the big offensives and the constant drain of men during the routine of trench warfare are adequately covered and described, but these volumes remain essentially a diary of events and a chronology of the war as experienced by that particular unit. It is rare for the individual soldier, especially the NCOs and privates, to receive much of a mention as individuals. The battalion was their all encompassing home, through which the often anonymous soldiery arrived, fought, were wounded, killed, or survived, but these battalion histories usually make only scant references to social backgrounds, individuality, the hopes and aspirations of the men, the impact of new arrivals, or the loss of departed friends. Those men who are mentioned by name are generally only those who received an award or medal, or, who appeared in the monthly compilation of casualties.

The end of the 1920's and the early 1930's witnessed the publication of works based upon the reaction of individuals to the war, and former soldiers like Graves, Blunden, Sassoon and Chapman published their often bitter and ironic memoirs of their personal experience. These books, written by educated and literary-minded veterans, cast a more individual light on the everyday aspects of the war and, at the same time, threw the stark horror of the war into a perspective that the earlier reminiscences and regimental histories had not attempted. The calamity of war, the loss of friends and the dichotomy of life between the home and war fronts were revealed in some of the finest prose of the Twentieth Century, while their sometimes vituperative attitudes fostered and maintained the growing anti-war sentiments of the democracies evident in the 1930's. Books written by non-commissioned men like Manning and non-intellectuals like Richards fuelled the passions of those who believed that modern war could never be repeated and that the sacrifice of those killed during the Great War should not have been in vain. Unfortunately those beliefs were rudely shattered by the rise of the fascist dictators and, by the final years of the decade, the apparent inevitability of a future, perhaps even more cataclysmic conflict, again haunted Europe.

The years following the defeat of Hitler's Germany were filled with a new batch of memoirs and histories recalling the events of that war, but in the 1970's attention again returned to the Great War. Since then there has been a spate of books collecting information from individual survivors and concentrating upon particular battles of the war. The study of history, both social and military, had progressed to the more extensive use of both oral and written recollections, and works by Martin Middlebrook and Lyn MacDonald have opened the First World War to a new generation of readers brought up on a diet of comics and novels recounting tales of valour performed during the 1939-45 conflict. These pioneering books have been supplemented by numerous recent works by old soldiers who have refound their diaries and letters of 70 years ago, and although hardly rushing into print, have produced books of varying worth and quality.

What has been missing in the 70 years since the war ended is a study of one regiment from a social rather than a military viewpoint - an account which traces and emphasises the character of that regiment during its wartime transitions and transformations, and, above all, its motivation. Those who have studied accounts of the war know that the old Regular Army was all but destroyed by December 1914, and that the Pals battalions were so severely mauled on the Somme that the experiment of locally-raised units was not repeated. What has not been closely investigated, however, is how the survivors of those units fared during the latter stages of the war when Regular battalions were comprised of conscripts, and the Pals battalions were 'Pals' only in name.

This study attempts to rectify this omission, but for one regiment only - a Territorial unit of the City of London Regiment, known as the London Rifle Brigade. Trying to paint a social picture of a regiment 70 years after the events poses numerous problems, least of all the availability of reliable and sufficient sources. Furthermore, it is impossible to dwell solely on the personality or character of the regiment - the principal ambition of this work - because they cannot be viewed in isolation from its military history as the changes that the Regiment underwent were primarily, although not exclusively, a consequence of its activities in the field. So, although reference to the principal engagements will be made, except where they contribute to the central theme there is little attempt to relate the minutiae of plans and execution of orders to the depth a reader might expect from a more conventional military history. The reader familiar with the topography of the Western Front will recognise the areas, villages and trench systems readily enough, but there are no map co-ordinates given and trench nomenclature has been kept to a minimum. The maps in this volume should provide sufficient information for readers to identity the location of the engagements.

In view of the importance of casualties to the composition of the regiment's two active service battalions, frequent reference to fatality figures and, where possible, statistics for those wounded will be made. The whole issue of casualty figures has been a controversial one, and it is not proposed to be drawn into the debate except where figures quoted in the *War Diary* are at great variance with those calculated at a later date, or where they contribute directly to the general argument.

This attempt to analyse and discuss the varying and varied composition of the LRB must of course rely principally on primary sources. Allowance has to be made for the natural pride and affection evident in the written sources, and also to the limitations of oral history - what A.J.P. Taylor described somewhat disparagingly as 'old men drooling over their youth'. There are bound to be faults and failures of memories, confusion and misconceptions over what happened so long ago, and the impression of an engagement held by an all too frequently uninformed Rifleman, can differ radically from that of his officer. That does not mean of course that the recollections of a man privy to more detail is correct, and that of the ill-informed wrong. Both contribute to an understanding of the events as seen at the time from different perspectives. This study tries to make use of those differing viewpoints, and in that respect it is easier to do it for the LRB than for certain other regiments. By virtue of the motives underlying its original foundation and its subsequent history, the LRB attracted men from the educated classes who could record their thoughts and actions in intelligent, illustrative, and, at times, incisive prose. This has made the task of constructing a view of the regiment in the pre-war era and during the first two years of the conflict that much easier, but as the composition shifted away from the volunteer to the conscript the material becomes harder to find. However, sufficient sources have survived to provide a description of a regiment, which despite some tumultuous experiences still considered itself to be a cut above the average Territorial battalion. Its traditions were older than even some of the Regular Army units, and it was a regiment whose social composition was sufficiently narrow in scope to allow the Duke of Cambridge, the Commander-in-Chief of the British Army, to address the assembled battalion as, 'Gentlemen, and officers, of the LRB'.

THE SOURCES

After the First and Second World Wars, many former members of the LRB donated their diaries, photographs, memorabilia etc. to the Regimental Museum. In time Bunhill Row was demolished and the Headquarters of the Regiment moved to Sun Street. When this building was in turn demolished, the contents of the museum were donated to the Imperial War Museum where they are now housed. It is from this variety of sources - known simply as the *London Rifle Brigade Collection* - that much of the information used in this work has come. The principal collections used are those held in the Department of Documents and the Department of Sound Records at the I.W.M., the National Army Museum, Chelsea, the British Library Newspaper Library, Colindale, and Peter H. Liddle's 1914-18 Personal Experience Archives, now attached to Leeds University. Finally, the original questionnaires sent to 33 members of the LRB Veterans Association elicited a tremendous response. This led in turn to sheaves of letters passing between the author and the former soldiers and subsequently many tape-recorded interviews (see names supplied below).

Also included is a list of the primary and secondary sources used in this study. In the case of the former, their location is also given. It is not intended to be a bibliography of literature on the First World War as only books and papers used in this work are listed. When reference is made to a source in the text, where possible the name of that source - found in the list below - is given either before or after the reference, and thus there is no specified footnote. The reasons for this are to economise on space, to avoid constant reference to footnotes which merely give the name of a frequently used source, and because many of the personal diaries and accounts are written on un-numbered pages. There is thus little point in repeatedly giving the name of the source as a footnote when normal academic procedures cannot be fulfilled, and when it can be done more simply within the text. To maintain a uniform practice, this procedure is continued for those unpublished sources which do have page numbers. Reference to published material is made in the usual way, but the full title of the work, the publisher and date, are given in the list below, rather than in the footnotes.

Unpublished Personal Recollections and Papers, and their Location. (Unless otherwise stated the sources are housed in the LRB Collection in the IWM.

Amatt, S.A.	Tape recording. (IWM Sound Records)
Angel, R.L.	Reminiscences of an A4 Boy. (P.H. Liddle Archive)
Bates, A.S.	Correspondence April-May 1915. Operations Orders, 1916.
Borrett, H.G.	Letters. (IWM Dept. Docs. 79/35/1)
Denny, A.	Letters and reports by Addison Denny from the Ypres Salient during the Second Battle of Ypres.
Evanson, E.	The experiences of Rfn E. Evanson as a prisoner of war.

Forrow, S.V.	Papers. (Army Museum, Acc.No.7911-47)
Foster, G.M.	Letters. (P.H. Liddle Archive)
Fuller, J.	Papers. (IWM Dept. Docs. 88/1637)
Griew, B.	Letters. (P.H. Liddle Archive)
Grigg, J.S.	Papers. (IWM Dept. Docs. 84/9/1)
Harding, E.B.	Seven years in the LRB. (P.H. Liddle Archive)
Hember, V.	Letters received from Victor Hember.
Hollis, A.	Diary and papers. (P.H. Liddle Archive)
Honour, R.	Diary. (IWM Dept. Docs. 81/35/1)
Houle, B.	Black as the pit: a true account of an experience of a POW in German hands during the 1914-18 War (Family possession)
Latham, R.	Minced memories and mixed metaphors.
Lintott, R.	Letters. (IWM Dept. Docs. 86/66/1)
MacGrath, J.	Last letter, 27 June 1916.
Magnus, A.V.	Diary.
Malborough, W.G.	Papers. (IWM Dept. Docs. 86/48/1)
Mason, R.J.	Up the Rangers. (IWM Dept. Docs. Misc.250. Box 12)
Meacham, A.G.	Diary and papers. (IWM Dept. Docs. 79/29/1)
Myer, H.D.	Soldiering of sorts. (P.H. Liddle Archive)
Pocock, F.A.	From Bunhill Row to Ypres.
Polhill, A.V.	Tape. (IWM Sound Records, SR.9254)
Russel, H.	My generation, (Typed MSS IWM Dept. Docs)
Schuman, A.	Memoirs. (Army Museum)
Terry, J.W.	Diary. (Family possession)
Wallis, F.H.	The London Rifle Brigade.
Williams, H.G.R.	Saturday afternoon soldiers. (P.H. Liddle Archive, and microfilm in IWM Dept. Docs. PP/MCR/86)
Willett, W.	Typed MSS (IWM Dept. Docs. 82/1/1)
Williamson, H.W.	Tape. (IWM Sound Records, 4257/1)
Wray, F.and M.	Christmas 1914.

Other Personal Contributions.

Below is a list of former members of the LRB who replied to a questionnaire, corresponded by letter, or were willing to be interviewed and tape-recorded.

S.A. Amatt, W.A. Braine, G.A. Chambers, F. Dyer, W.M. Fry, H.W.G. Gower, F. Hadfield, R. Miller Hall, A.E. Holmes, B.E. Houle, M. Howard, E.R. Hughes, L. Jessop, G.M. Lee, R.M. Parker, S.H. Partridge, H.G. Paterson, N.M. Perolls, A.V. Polhill, H.E. Pratt, S.G. Richardson, T.R. Short, J. Sutton, J.W. Terry, A.E. Thain.

Official Papers and Publications.

Parliamentary Debates, Hansard.
Soldiers Died in the Great War. (HMSO, 1920)
War Diary of the 1st Battalion LRB, Public Record Office; WO 95/1498
WO 95/2961-2
War Diary of the 2nd Battalion LRB, Public Record Office; WO 95/3005

Newspapers and Journals.

City News, City Press, Daily Chronicle, Daily Express, Daily Graphic, Daily Telegraph, Dawlish Gazette, The Despatch, Evening News, Evening Times, Hornsey Journal, LRB Veterans' Association Newsletters, Reynold's, Sussex Daily News, Territorial Service Gazette, The Times.

Published Sources

Barrie, A. .... *The War Underground*, (Star, 1981).
Baynes, J. .... *Morale: a Study of Men and Courage*, (Cassell, 1967).
Bell, D.H. .... *A Soldier's Diary of the Great War*, (Faber & Gwyer, 1928).
Brown, M.
& Seaton, S. .... *The Christmas Truce 1914*, (Cooper, 1984).
.... *Croydon and the Great War*, (1919).
Dalbaic, P.H. .... *The History of the 60th Division*, (Allen & Unwin, 1927).
Dixon, N.F. .... *On the Psychology of Military Incompetence*, (Cape, 1976).
Edmonds, J.E. .... *Official History of the Great War*, (HMSO).
Ford, T.M. .... *Memoirs of a Poor Devil*, (Philpot, 1926).
French, J. .... *1914* (Constable, 1919).
Fry, W.M. .... *Air of Battle*, (Kimber, 1974).
Green, H. .... *The British Army in the First World War*, (Trehern, 1968).
Grey, W.E. .... *2nd City of London (R.F.) in the Great War* (HQ.1929).
Grimwade, F.C. ...... *The War History of the 4/Londons*, (HQ.1922).
Groom, W.H.A. ...... *Poor Bloody Infantry*, (Picardy, 1976).
Haldane, R.B. .... *An Autobiography*, (Hodder & Stoughton, 1929).
Henriques, J.Q. .... *The War History of 1st Battalion Queen's Westminster Rifles,*
1914-18, (London, 1923).
Herbert, A.P. .... *The Secret Battle*, (Methuen, 1919).
.... *History of the POW. Civil Service Rifles*, (Wyman & Son, 1921).
James, E.A. .... *British Regiments, 1914-18*, (Samson, 1978).
King, E.J. .... *The History of the Seventh Middlesex*, (Harrison, 1927).
Latham, B. .... *A Territorial Soldier's War*, (Gale & Polden, 1967).
Lindsay, J.H. .... *The London Scottish in the Great War*, (HQ. 1925).
Linzell, H.H. .... *Fallen on the Somme*, (M.A.Argyle, 1981).
.... *The London Rifle Brigade*, (Constable, 1921).
.... *The LRB Record, 1908-1939*.
Manning, F. .... *The Middle Parts of Fortune*, (Buchan & Enright, 1977).

Messenger, C. ....*Terriers in the Trenches*, (Picton, 1982).

Middlebrook, M. .....*The First Day on the Somme*, (Penguin, 1971).

..........................*Mill Hill School Book of Remembrance*,

Montague, C.E. ......*Disenchantment*, (Greenwood Press, 1978).

Moran, Lord ....*An Anatomy of Courage*, (Constable, 1945).

Morris, J. ....*Hired to Kill*, (Hart-Davis, 1960).

Nobbs, G. ....*Englishman Kamerad*, (Heinemann, 1918).

Price, R. ....*An Imperial War and the British Working Class*, (London, 1972).

'Private X'..............*War is War*, (V. Gollancz, 1930).

Richardson, F. ....*Fighting Spirit: Psychological Factors in War*, (Leo Cooper,1978).

Sellwood, A.V. ....*The Saturday Night Soldiers*, (Wolfe, 1966).

Simkins, P. ....*Kitchener's Army*, (Manchester University Press, 1988).

Shaw & Sons, ...*Pro Patria: Records and Extracts from Correspondence of Employees Serving their King and Country*, (1919).

..........................*A Short History of the LRB* (HQ. 1916).

Smith, A. ....*Four Years on the Western Front: being the Experiences of a Ranker in the LRB, in the 4th, 3rd, & 56th Division* (Odhams, 1922).

Spiers, E.M. ....*Haldane: an Army Reformer*, (Edinburgh University Press, 1980).

Ward, Dudley C. .....*The 56th Division*, (John Murray, 1921).

..........................*War Record of the Northern Assurance Co. Ltd.*, (1919).

Wheeler-Holohan, A. *The Rangers Historical Records from 1859 to the*
& Wyatt, G.M.   *Conclusion of the Great War*, (Harrison & Sons, 1921).

Whitehead, J. ....*Jim: Jottings and Letters from James E. Whitehead*, (privately printed, 1917).

Williamson, H.W. ...*How Dear is Life*, (Macdonald & Co., 1984 edition)

INTRODUCTION

In the mid-nineteenth century, Victorian England's greatness amongst nations seemed secure. Protected by her natural defences and her 'wooden walls', the world's foremost Power basked in the glory of her maritime supremacy and the benefits which accrued from trade and commerce. Although the period of the 'New Imperialism' was still a generation away, her Empire already straddled the globe and her warships patrolled the colonies and the expanding trade routes. Her industrial capacity far exceeded any rival's, and she had emerged from her latest entanglement with mainland Europe as a champion of the Turk against the threat of Russian expansionism. However, following her uneasy alliance with the French during the Crimean War, Britain's relationship with France reverted to its more traditional one of tension and mutual mistrust. Once again, Albion began to look suspiciously upon the colonial and maritime ambitions of her neighbour across the Channel.

Napoleon III had pledged the Second Empire to a role of expansionism and glory, but wherever the Gallic adventurer turned for conquest, he found the British lion lying menacingly across his path. Resolved on a policy of bowing to none, Napoleon paid increasing attention to the modernisation of his navy and France was soon leading the way in the construction of warships powered by steam engines and protected by armoured hulls. Fearful of this impudent competition, the launch of the *Gloire* in 1859 stung the British Admiralty into action and, in the face of what was perceived as the growing challenge from across the Straits of Dover, the Government turned its mind to how the numerically superior French Army could be defeated should it ever manage to evade the Royal Navy and land on the British Isles.

From this concern emerged the concept of the Volunteer Corps - an organisation designed to be more efficient and reliable than the old militias. Linked to the growing national interest in rifle shooting, the Rifle Volunteer Force was born in 1859 when the Secretary of State for War authorised the Lords Lieutenants of Counties to begin recruiting. In London the Lord Mayor appears to have been somewhat lax in responding to the call with the consequence that the City of London held only forty-ninth place in the new force's seniority. The name by which the first unit so raised by the City was known evolved as the London Rifle Brigade, and it thus later took as its motto, *Primus in Urbe*. So great was the enthusiasm among the middle classes to enlist, that within a few weeks two battalions were formed and thus it acquired the title 'Brigade' - a name it would retain long after the formation had shrunk to a fraction of its original size.

Despite War Office ambivalence, a growing financial crisis and periodic recruitment difficulties, the Volunteer Force in London was to exist in the same form for the next 49 years. Then, in 1908 the LRB underwent its first great transition - the conversion to a unit of the newly created Territorial Force. For the six years until the outbreak of war, the LRB established itself as one of the elite units of the Territorial

Force, maintaining its selective procedure on admissions and, although usually only about two-thirds strength, forging a name for itself in its standards of expertise at drill, musketry and marching. The band of enthusiastic middle-class volunteers provided the foundations upon which the regiment was to expand to a degree almost beyond recognition and upon which, following the cessation of hostilities, it was re-created in 1920. During the intervening years the two active service battalions had fought in some of the severest and desperate battles of the Western Front. The regiment had seen its battalions all but destroyed on five occasions, had been stunned to disbelief when one of its units was disbanded, and by mid-1918 had witnessed the transition of the surviving battalion to one barely recognisable as a unit of the LRB. Somewhere near 13,000 men passed through the ranks during the war and of this total, just under 2,000 were fatalities. Yet despite the many and varied personnel changes, the regiment retained something of the character not only of the pre-war Territorial battalion, but also of the Volunteer Force. The original social composition of the regiment had altered dramatically by 1918, but when it was reformed in the early post-war years, those who had filled the ranks both before and during the war came back to re-enlist in the regiment that was to them less of a military unit, more a way of life.

This study attempts to trace and follow the changes experienced during the regiment's war experience by looking at the social and educational backgrounds of the men, how the appearance of new drafts affected the style of command and regimental *esprit de corps*, and thus, the very character and composition of the regiment at different times of the conflict. Above all, it is an attempt to portray the impact of the war upon that character by using whenever possible the recollections of the men themselves. Their attitudes, aspirations, beliefs and reflections tell the story of the changes that occurred, and the similarities which remained. Enormous as the casualties were, there was always an adequate number of old members serving throughout the period of devastation to ensure that their dedication and loyalty to the regiment were sufficient to guide the battalions through their mutations. The enthusiasm of these longer-serving members allowed the continuance of the essential idiosyncrasies, traditions and *esprit* which had evolved during the Volunteer days, and which were to continue through the war years and on into the later reorganisations which occured both before and after World War II. It is probably not a unique story - other units of the London Regiment had similar experiences - but it is a story of bravery, depression, fortitude, disillusion, resolution and resilience. It is a social and military history of one unit, of one regiment, of the largest Army ever put into the field by Britain; a regiment and an Army that were to suffer appalling and unnecessary losses, yet emerge victorious in the most titanic of soldiers' wars.

CHAPTER I

The LRB and the Territorial Force

For the existing units of the Volunteer Force, the birth of the Territorial Force was something of a traumatic experience. The man responsible for the creation of the TF, R.B. Haldane, had originally envisaged a force different from the one which finally emerged. Prime Minister Asquith's Liberal Government was keen to reduce both the Army and Navy Estimates in order to divert spending to social welfare. This objective was to aid Haldane in his efforts to silence some of the opposition. Many Liberal supporters and MPs were initially suspicious of his proposed reforms but swung round to support them once Haldane had demonstrated that his scheme could save the Exchequer over £2m. Earlier efforts to reform the auxiliary forces and make them more efficient had foundered on hostility from within the organisations who feared that their traditions and privileges would be eroded or lost. The impetus for improvement had come from the shortcomings evident during the Boer War when failures in the Army's organisational structure had become embarrassingly obvious. It was upon the patriotism and jingoism inspired by the South African War that Haldane hoped to capitalise and thus succeed where Arnold-Foster, his predecessor, had failed. Haldane, long a student of the organisation and structure of continental armies, envisaged what he called a 'Hegelian Army' - the concept of the 'nation in arms'. This, he believed, could be founded upon voluntary service and be capable of reinforcing the Regular Army in times of crisis.[1]

Haldane's philosophy envisaged the Territorial Force becoming a vehicle to educate the nation in what he considered to be its military responsibilities. The protection of the Empire was of paramount importance, but he believed that if Britain was ever called on again to provide an army capable of undertaking a continental war, the means by which the existing standing army should be expanded was through the medium of his newly created Territorial Associations. For financial and social reasons Haldane had not, from the start, put a great emphasis on the quality of training and the military efficiency likely to be attained by the peacetime TF He believed that from a practical point of view, the insistence of any period of concentrated or protracted peacetime training would be likely to dissuade men of the commercial classes from enlisting.[2]   (The implicit understanding was that there would have to be at least six months of intensive training for the TF before its units could be expected to be posted overseas.)

This apparent acceptance of a low level of proficiency and ability to respond quickly to any national emergency was considered by some to be a fundamental handicap to the whole concept of the TF. Furthermore, sections within the War Office were known to oppose the idea of basing any future expansion of the Army on the TF rather than on the Militia. Consequently, to gain further support Haldane had ultimately to agree to leave the Militia - an organisation which he considered to be of very dubious value - outside the TF, rather than incorporating it within the new organisation. Other sections of the community opposed the reorganisation on the grounds that the TF was nothing but a subtle half-way house towards full conscription. On the other hand, the supporters of conscription considered that the experiment with the TF would fail, and that the nation would then have no option but to accept the imposition of full-blown compulsory military service. Haldane knew that he faced intense opposition from various directions, but with the help of the King and the expediency of compromise the Bill proposing the creation of the TF became law. Thus, on 31 March 1908 the Volunteer Force died and the TF was born.[3]

The LRB was dissatisfied from the outset with its allotted position of seniority in the new Territorial Force. The City of London Territorial and Auxiliary Forces Association's Committee resolved by 18 votes to two that the Secretary of State be recommended to accept the regimental numberings which it had devised.[4] The LRB's Commanding Officer, Lord Bingham, objected to the proposal because it gave the four Royal Fusilier battalions numbers one to four in the new City of London Regiment. This meant that the LRB was designated the Fifth Battalion, City of London. For the oldest Volunteer Corps in the capital, this came as a severe demoralising blow, and appears to have influenced some members in their decision not to transfer to the new Territorial Force.

Another factor which determined the strength of the reformed battalion was the embodiment clause and the imposition of fines for men who neglected their training. The issue of non-attendance at camp was a matter to which the Recruiting Committee of the TAFA frequently applied its collective mind and eventually came up with a compromise. It felt that to urge employers to grant extra days leave would be a mistake as firms would simply not be prepared to employ members of the Territorials. Instead, it was decided that the large employers of clerks - the Banks, Insurance Houses, etc. - should be encouraged to grant leave to their employees, but that any refusal by such a company would be considered adequate reason for non-attendance at the annual camp. The Stock Exchange was prepared to be cooperative, and agreed that they would do 'everything in their power' to enable men to comply with the prescribed regulations. By June 1908, over 700 firms, many of them companies who employed large numbers of LRB men, had signed a document stating that they would give men in the Territorials 'reasonable facilities' to fulfil their obligations.[5] The principal difficulty facing both employers and employees was that most of the members of the Territorials tended to be the office juniors who came at the bottom of the list when employees were being asked when they wished to take their holiday entitlement. The Recruiting Committee decided that the companies should be asked to be more flexible in allowing their juniors to take their holidays when the annual camp was taking place. Even if a company was prepared to be sympathetic to the needs of the TF, it might only allow its juniors to attend camp for one of the two weeks. Owing to pressure of office work during August, E.B. Harding, for example, was 'advised (if not actually ordered)' to take his other week's holiday during May.[6]

Even if an employee could take his full two weeks holiday at the time of camp, he also had to be prepared to use it solely for that purpose. For men with families this was a major sacrifice, and again a source of some bitterness. A member of the LRB wrote to The Daily Telegraph on 18 January 1909:

> *I only get a fortnight's holiday in a year and I feel that during that fortnight I require real rest of body and mind. I have spent many weeks under canvas or in barracks...I say that it is putting too severe a strain on the self-sacrifice of the average Englishman to expect him to give up all, or even half of the one short period in the year when life is worth living.*

This soldier went on to suggest that the annual camp be replaced by a revival of the old Easter training session and that an aggregate of weekends should be accepted in lieu of the consecutive week or fortnight. Another cause of complaint among the men was the actual venue of the camps. The LRB attended camps on the coast for three successive years at the beginning of the century, but from 1907 to 1913, only one was held in a similar location. At a meeting of the Recruiting Committee in 1911, the Commanding Officers of the City Regiment recommended that annual camps should again be held at the seaside as an inducement to recruiting. This idea was rejected by Major-General Sir A. Codrington, who feared that camps would rapidly degenerate into two weeks of pleasure and that the quality of the training would decrease as a consequence.[7] Two other factors which also affected the willingness of men to serve concerned the financial provisions while at camp. The initial complaint was that there were no Separation Allowances for married men which thus meant the possibility of financial hardship for the soldiers' dependents. Secondly, once the 1911 National Insurance Act became law, salt was further added to the wound when the Territorials discovered that National Insurance deductions would be made from the men's camp pay of one shilling per day. The War Office response to a petition from the Territorial Force representatives was merely to claim that it was beyond their sphere of responsibility, and that they could do nothing.[8]

In view of these difficulties, it is perhaps not surprising to discover that the attendance by the LRB in its early days at camp was not particularly good. In its period as a Volunteer unit, all camp expenses had to be paid for either by the individual or from regimental funds, and when the camp was changed from Easter to August there was another falling off in attendance. Once it became a Territorial unit, the camp had to be held in August, but after a poor start the attendance figures did improve as the years passed. For example, at the 1913 camp, from an effective strength of 98, 'O' Company had 89 of its men present at camp, 50 of whom were there for the full two weeks. The under-strength 'G' Company had 58 of its men present with 13 officially granted leave of absence.[9] To take account of the fact that many men could only attend for one week, the first seven days were usually devoted to section and company training, while battalion and brigade schemes were undertaken during the second week. The tactics rehearsed were not exactly imaginative, but were enjoyable. All attacks were 'frontal', with little thought apparently being given to outflanking movements, and the climax of the fortnight, the night scheme, invariably ended as a fiasco.[10]

Apart from camp itself, a new recruit was required to complete 40 drills and the musketry course within his first year. Many men had belonged to their school OTC and were thus excused the initial recruit drills and were treated as 'trained men'. Such a man had to complete only ten drills before he went to the August camp. Company drills were performed weekly, or, in some cases, fortnightly and were in addition to the monthly battalion parades. The usual drill, performed in civilian dress with a black belt and sword,[11] lasted for an hour and would often include a lecture for at least part of the time. Many of the trained, long-serving men were present at well over 40 drills each year, while the average of one Section of 'O' Company, excluding recruits in their first year, was 33 sessions.

Once the TF came into existence, the quality of the training was generally considered to have improved. This was probably a consequence of attaching to each Territorial battalion a permanent staff of Regulars. In the LRB's case, this meant the RSM and two Sergeant Instructors. These men supplemented the work of the Clr-Sgt and CQMS of each of the eight companies. These were all long-serving members who had been promoted from the ranks and thus were well accustomed to the orders of command and drill procedures. The musketry test was usually performed at Easter, either at Bisley or Hythe. This again meant that the men would lose all of their official holiday because the battalion paraded immediately after work on Thursday, and returned home on Monday evening. Other weekends were spent at the Rifle Brigade's barracks in Aldershot, and occasionally further afield. The LRB is thought to have been the first Volunteer battalion to abandon the formal, social manoeuvres which characterised the Volunteer movement in the 1880's, and undertaken the more relevant experience of spending four days in barracks.[12] The weekend schemes were taken seriously by the men, but they still maintained a close observance of good manners. For example, when Graham Williams was 'captured' by a corporal during one such exercise, his personal bicycle was damaged. The corporal insisted upon finding a repairer, even though it was a Sunday, and paying for the damage to the machine himself.

The compulsory training requirements placed a heavy burden of commitment on the men, and were thought to be an important reason why the TF was so understrength. The demands were not as onerous on the young, single clerks, but for the older, married men, such as those who had fought in South Africa, they made significant inroads into normal family life. Another handicap that the Territorial battalions had to overcome was the ridicule with which the general public had viewed the Volunteer units. To make matters worse, sections of military authority had scarcely regarded them in much better light, refusing to take the Volunteers seriously. Encouragement and assistance had come reluctantly, and on one occasion the LRB's camp had to be cancelled at the eleventh hour when the Secretary of State suddenly decided not to loan the battalion sufficient tents for the two week exercise.[13] Haldane had been acutely aware that his new creation would have a hard task in convincing both the nation and parts of the military that it was a force which should be taken seriously. He hoped that the TF would be able to bridge the traditional British gulf between Army and society and had originally intended that the Territorials should reinforce the Regular army in any future continental war. However, in addition to accepting that the Militia should remain distinct from the TF, opposition from within his own party forced Haldane to come to an even greater, and more reluctant, compromise. This further expediency meant that his entire concept of a combined British Expeditionary Force, composed initially of the Regular army and supplemented a few months later by the Territorials, had to be adandoned. Instead, Haldane was forced to accept that his new creation would be a force for home defence only. This decision was an 'illogical and retrogressive step', for the whole *raison d'etre* of the new organisation was to provide the means of expansion of the Regulars, rather than to provide a separate army.[14] Yet, disagreeable and disappointing as this reverse was, in some ways it did eventually work to Haldane's advantage. Some of the older men, who had shown a reluctance to enlist or even downright opposition to the new force, were persuaded to make the transfer from the Volunteers - who had always only been intended for home duties - to the Territorials. Furthermore, in 1909, when each of the Territorial units was allocated an area of the homeland to defend, Haldane tried to exploit and capitalise upon the feelings of local pride and identity as a positive inducement to enlistment.

Whether it was to be used at home or abroad, Haldane knew that finding sufficient recruits to the new battalions would prove difficult. The LRB had experienced something of a recruiting boom during the South African War, when a total of 150 of its men had served with the City Imperial Volunteers or City Imperial Yeomanry. This represented somewhere near one seventh of the battalion's entire strength, but it could still send 997 men to the Whitsun camp in 1900. Sufficient volunteers had poured in to warrant an expansion from the existing ten companies to twelve. However, the boom was short-lived and by 1905 the battalion had again reverted to ten companies and the total strength had fallen to under 600. In November 1906 the figure was 531, of whom only 15% were under 21 years and 55% had over five years' service. By 1908, numbers had fallen to 481, and this was at a time when most of the other units seem to have been increasing their strength. Lord Bingham, the LRB's Commanding Officer, believed that the principal reason why the LRB was so understrength was the fact that men had to pay for their own uniforms. Furthermore, since 1861 the regiment had charged an entrance fee of one guinea and an annual subscription of another 21 shillings. Half of the membership fee was refunded if a man could pass an exam based upon the manual within his first week, but by the time the TF was formed, the entrance fee and subscription had risen to 25 shillings, in addition to a company subscription of half-a-crown for privates. It was for these reasons that the LRB was regarded by the Regulars, and most of the other Volunteer units, as a 'smart lot of cranks'[15] However, the regiment always considered that it was a privilege to be a member, and thus a man should be prepared to pay for the honour. If any man could not afford to pay, he could always join the Militia or one of the ordinary Volunteer battalions. The expectation that he would have to pay for his expenses, uniform etc., naturally made the social composition of the regiment different from many others of the new City and County of London Territorials, and this difference had been reflected in the make up of the CIV. Members of the working classes could rarely afford the financial demands of the LRB and other similar Volunteer battalions, so when the CIV was formed largely from these elite battalions, the largest single occupation group was that of 'Clerk'. A recent writer has argued that the relationship between class and the willingness to join the CIV shows that the motive of patriotism was probably strongest amongst the occupational groups like clerks, who were working class in origin, but who in Edwardian Britain regarded themselves as socially superior to the labourer and artisan.[16] That patriotism remained an important reason for enlisting in the TF is clear from the memoirs. As he was about to leave Aldenham College, Graham Williams and his classmates were interviewed by the master who ran the OTC and were told by him that it was their duty to join the TF:

> *Patriotism was nothing to be ashamed of or played down...We all saw it* [i.e. the war with Germany] *coming, and, with most of my contemporary associates, I felt it was up to us to do something about it...So most young men at the time - certainly those of my social stratum felt it was 'the thing' to join the Territorials when they left school, where many had received training in the school Cadet Corps or OTC...The only threat to* [England's] *idyllic existence came from the Kaiser's Empire...so as a matter of course we joined the Territorials.*

While the concept of duty might have been sufficient for men like Williams, who had been enthused with the notion at Public School, other men needed to have their sense of patriotism aroused. Haldane campaigned across the country in 1909 capitalising on the fears awakened by the naval scare of the previous year. He was helped in his efforts when Lord Northcliffe, an advocate of full conscription, part-financed du Maurier's play, *An Englishman's Home*. Well attended, regular performances of this production also awakened sufficient interest and fear of a German invasion for men to enlist in large numbers. The LRB certainly needed the benefit of such publicity for the number of men that transferred to the TF in April 1908 was small. As its Volunteer existence drew to a close,the LRB's strength fell to only 465, and by August the total number of men who had transferred, as well as the new enlistments, only amounted to a mere 332. Because it had reached 30% of its establishment, this was sufficient for the battalion to be 'recognised' as a unit of the 2nd London Brigade, but clearly, more had to be done if the regiment was ever to achieve anything like real efficiency. Other units in the City of London Regiment were experiencing similar difficulties, and the Recruiting Committee undertook several surveys in attempts to discover why recruiting was so slow. Apart from the problems of camp attendance discussed above, the Committee also believed that the rates of pay, the apprehension of being called out more than once a year, and even merely having a 'T' on the uniform to denote Territorial all contributed to the reluctance of men to join. Several recruiting ideas were discussed at length; the possibility of displaying posters at railway stations, printing a list of the TF units in Wyndham's Theatre programme and giving early notice that the TF would line the Coronation route of 1910 were all considered.[17] Owing to the expense involved, most of the schemes came to nothing, and this was at a time when recruiting was only 38% of the previous year and some units were in danger of falling below the 30% establishment.

In other parts of the country recruiting was even slower. In the industrial heartlands of Lancashire and Yorkshire, for example, several battalions tottered on the precipice of dissolution. It has been estimated that during the final years of its existence, the Volunteer units had recruited only approximately 25% of its membership from the non-skilled classes.[18]   This was an improvement compared with earlier decades, but in areas where there were few middle-class citizenry the attraction of the Territorials seemed fairly remote.   Factory workers tended to marry earlier than their office counterparts and also worked longer hours.   This meant that there was less opportunity for them to attend parades regularly and besides, in the eyes of many of the more militantly minded workers, the Territorials were seen as yet another tool of the oppressive Establishment.   This does not mean, of course, that Territorial units were treated with a general hostility by the proletariat as a whole, for many battalions recruited in working class areas enjoyed an active and reasonably efficient existence. Yet the fact remains that in general terms, those units such as the LRB, which attracted the young, perhaps idealistic middle-class patriot, were more likely to have a strength nearer its intended establishment than those which recruited the artisan or unskilled worker.

The enthusiasm to enlist engendered by the navy scare of 1908 waned once the Admiralty and Government had agreed on an increased building programme of Dreadnoughts.   The crisis did however prove beneficial to the LRB as its strength had increased to 744 within a year of its creation as a TF unit.   Besides the desire to express their patriotism, the young clerks also joined for a variety of other reasons.   Many were attracted by the bonus offered by some firms to any employee enlisting in the Territorials.   For example, E.B. Harding spent part of his bounty on a new pair of boots, while Phillip Maddison wanted a new suit.[19]   Some joined because they had brothers or fathers already serving, and groups of young men joined together on leaving school.   Undoubtedly a major incentive to enlist was the sporting and recreational facilities offered by the class battalions like the LRB.   Bunhill Row was the largest Territorial drill hall in London and when not required for parades, could be transformed into a fully equipped gym and boxing ring.   A thriving athletic club also met there weekly throughout the winter.   While one writer's assertion that sports played little part in their military life might be true of certain Territorial units,[20] games certainly played a major role in developing battalion and company *esprit de corps* among the class battalions of the London Regiment.   The athletic team frequently met the other Territorial battalions in fierce competition, which apart from the usual events, also included an extremely prestigious half-marathon completed in full marching order.

Important as regimental *esprit* was, the soldier had a closer association and affiliation to his section and company.   When the TF was created the battalion had been reduced to eight companies - the strongest of the original sixteen survived, hence the somewhat bizarre lettering of A, D, E, G, H, O, P and Q.   Each company had been affiliated to one of the Wards of the City since 1868, so the Ward of Cordwainer, for example, had a close relationship with 'H' Company and contributed towards the prizes offered for its annual shooting and drill competitions.   These prizes were worth substantial sums - for example, 'G' Company competed for a total of £36 of prize money at its Bisley shoot in August 1913.   To further develop a sense of belonging, the companies held `Bohemian Concerts', with the men wearing dress uniform, and suppers in London restaurants in addition to the Regimental Annual Dinner.   Each company printed its own Year Book which contained the names and addresses of all members, dates of drills, results of competitions etc.   These books had originally been produced in the Volunteer days, but their publication appears not to have been a widespread practice in the other seven City battalions. As late as June 1914, the Recruiting Committee decided to recommend that grants be given to battalions in order to provide them as an aid for company commanders to keep in touch with their men.[21]

One of the most prestigious inter-company competitions was the annual march. This consisted of a 13-mile course, completed in full marching order. For any chance of victory, it had to be done in a time of well under three hours. The company marching teams practised for the event at weekends, but it was really an extension of one aspect of regimental life which the whole battalion took extremely seriously. The LRB had long prided itself on its marching, and one member recounted the story of a 28 mile march in 1877 with the Regulars. The exercise, under a broiling sun, ended with a convoy of carts filled with exhausted Regulars, but no LRB men, trailing behind the perspiring column.[22] The tradition continued into the Territorial era, when, soon after the creation of the TF, an editorial in a newspaper on the class battalions of the London Regiment suggested that it was absurd to think that men who worked in banks and offices could be physically fit enough to be of any use in an emergency. It went on to conclude that these men could not be expected to do even a 10-mile march in full kit and then be able to perform any useful duty at the end. Thus was born the idea of the London to Brighton March - a publicity and recruiting gimmick for the London Territorials.[23] Clr Sgt Dick Wallis and Lt F. Brewsher led a team which completed the march in about 18 hours in 1911. That time was, however, soon bettered by another of the elite battalions, the London Scottish. With regimental pride at stake, the LRB trained hard, and in April 1914, 60 men under Capt Ralph Husey and Wallis established a new record by completing the 52 and a half mile march in 14 hours 23 minutes. In full marching order this was no mean feat, and besides attracting the intended publicity in the national press the success of the march was often used as a means of instilling pride and *esprit* into new recruits.

Another feature of regimental life which contributed to *esprit* was the School of Arms. Originally established in 1861, the School attracted some 200 men to its weekly practice sessions of gym displays and bayonet and sabre drill. It gave an annual exhibition which was intended as a publicity event, and reached such a level of expertise that *The Standard* of 10 March 1913 thought it would be worthy of demonstration alongside those of the Regular Army and Navy at the Olympia Tournament.

The need to attract recruits was of paramount importance as the first decade of the century passed. An essential element behind the concept of a Territorial Army was the development of an identity associated with the men's county or neighbourhood. The troops would thus feel that they were a local cog in a much greater machine. The idea of fostering this sense of local identity was a sound one, but it caused greater problems for the London Regiment than in most of the Territorial units of the County Regiments. The type of man who enlisted in the class battalions of the London Regiment usually travelled into the City from the suburbs, and enlisted at an Headquarters nearer his office rather than where he lived. However, the LRB had also traditionally recruited a percentage of its men from several particular districts within the London postal area. When Ford became a member in 1876, he was posted to 'G' Company which was composed of men drawn mostly from Clapton and Hackney.[24] A few years earlier two companies of a Volunteer unit called the 12th Tower Hamlets, which had recruited largely from Stoke Newington, had been transferred to the LRB when a reduction in its numbers made it no longer viable. These three areas were well represented in the immediate pre-war battalion, as were former pupils of several notable schools. In 1905 'E' Company had absorbed a new regiment called the 4th London, which was comprised largely of men from the Grocers' Company School. The Stationers' Company and Merchant Taylors' Schools, St. Dunstan's College and the Royal Masonic School also provided a sizeable number of recruits, but the largest number from any single school was probably that from Christ's Hospital near Horsham. Harding thought that there were at least 24 'Old Blues' serving in August 1914, with the added probability of a further ten about whom he was not quite certain. The young school-leavers usually began work in the City aged 17 years, and enlisted in the T.F. battalion of their choice from that age onwards. Some lived in lodgings, but the majority appeared to have travelled from their parents' home, and attended the evening drills before returning to the suburbs. By analysing the residences of members of two companies immediately before the war, certain localities from where substantial numbers of LRB men were recruited can be detected.

In general terms, West London was poorly represented in the ranks of the LRB. Of the 176 men whose home addresses are known, only 12 came from areas like Acton, Ealing and Twickenham. Similarly, the working class districts of inner London, like Hoxton and Shoreditch, contributed only 8 members. North and North-East London are better represented, with 50 coming from areas around Palmer's Green, Stoke Newington and Leytonstone. Twenty-one came from more outlying districts in Kent and Essex such as Woodford Green and Westcliffe-on-Sea, which lay on the main commuter lines into the City. The best represented areas were those which lay south of the Thames. A total of 85 came from boroughs whose positions describe an approximate arc from Bexley, through Bromley, Catford and Thornton Heath to Wimbledon. The addresses are mainly those of tree-lined streets consisting of terraced houses with bay windows and some decoration on the porches and windows - in other words, the usual type of housing constructed in the latter half of the nineteenth century for the artisan and office worker. The addresses are those of houses rather than flats or maisonettes. Most have a house number, but there is also a good proportion which merely have a house name. This usually indicates a semi- or detached house, and as might be expected, come from the areas like Coulsdon and Sutton further to the south, which were really still almost rural villages in the early years of the century.

These districts of South London supplied the huge numbers of men needed to work in the commercial offices of the City, and competition to recruit them between both the City and County battalions of the London Regiment was intense. There does appear to have been something of a 'gentleman's agreement' among some battalions not to poach men from another battalion's most immediate or natural recruiting zone.[25] This was made more complicated by the fact that men often joined a certain battalion not because they lived in a certain area, but because they worked in a shop, office or organisation which traditionally supplied men to a particular unit. Once their own immediate areas had been scoured clean for recruits, some battalions began to target specific districts which might well be on the other side of London from their Headquarters.[26] By 1912, the competition was so intense that the Committee representing the City Battalions decided to approach its equivalent in the County organisation, with the intention of establishing mutual arrangements with regard to recruiting areas. The response from the County of London Association objected to the suggested allocation of districts, and the idea seems to have been dropped.[27]

How far the LRB itself was involved in advocating such a scheme is unclear, but it was probably intended more for the benefit of the other six City battalions rather than the LRB and the Post Office Rifles. As far as the LRB was concerned, the picture is predominantly one of a South London battalion, but one drawn from the neighbourhoods lying beyond the tenements and unadorned terraces immediately south of the river. The districts from where so many of the LRB men came were all well linked by rail to the City, and as Bunhill Row was so close to where most of them worked, it was easy for the men to call in at HQ for the evening drills, sports training or simply for a drink, and still get home without difficulty. This social aspect of regimental life was also an incentive to enlist. In its later years the Volunteers had tried, largely in vain, to ensure that the reason for joining had been patriotic desire rather than for motives of pleasure or status. The *Volunteer Service Magazine* in May 1898 admitted that there was a lot of truth in the assertion that men enlisted for pleasure, and in the case of the LRB, the facilities were a major attraction. Bunhill Row offered an excellent billiards room, and the fact of actually paying an admission and membership fee, after having found two existing members willing to sponsor a potential member, reinforced the notion that the man was joining a fairly exclusive club.[28]

What the exact strength of this military, social and sporting 'club' was in the years preceding the war, is difficult to determine precisely. That it fluctuated quite alarmingly in some years is quite obvious, but according to *The Standard* of 10 March 1913, at that time the LRB was one of the few Territorial battalions which was 'anything approaching its full strength'. The monthly return for April 1913, presented by the regiment to the TAFA, gives the strength as 22 officers and 766 men - or 6 officers and 288 other ranks under establishment.[29] 1913 was a crucial year for the TF in general as the large numbers of men who had joined it in 1909 would complete their initial four years' engagement. In the City of London Regiment alone this amounted to about 50% of the men, and another 20% of its total strength - the men who had transferred from the Volunteers to the TF on its formation - had completed their four years in 1912. Several schemes had been discussed with a view to persuading these men to re-enlist for another four years, including a bonus of £1.[30] The promise of this bounty was unlikely to convince men of the class battalions one way or the other, and none of the proposals appear to have had much of a decisive effect on retaining men. For example, the strength of 'H' Company plummeted from 101 in 1912, to a mere 69 twelve months later.

The Subscription Books of the LRB have survived, and from them, what is probably a reasonable estimate of the number of serving members can be made.[31] The books list the names, numbers, company and addresses of the soldiers, and record whether they have paid their half-year membership fee of 12s.6d. for the six months ending 31 October 1914. For those joining after war had been declared, a payment of 6s.3d. for their first quarter was required and logged. By noting those men whose subscriptions were paid for that period, it can be seen that it was not only 'H' Company that suffered a major numerical decline in 1913.

In the two months of February and March 1909, the height of the 'invasion scare', 352 men attested in the LRB, and in the course of the whole year, 459 joined.

By the time their four-year term was up in 1913, 79% of those soldiers had either already left the battalion or did not re-enlist for a further term. With this massive influx in 1909, and another 190 men joining in 1910 and 1911, battalion strength rose to 898, or only 96 men below establishment. Recruiting picked up again in 1912 and 1913, when 120 and 199 men respectively enlisted, but, to set against this intake, by 1914, 62% and 41% of the men who had joined in the previous two years, had already left. An average of 18% of the men did not serve for more than a year. Despite this drain, the July 1912 meeting of the Recruiting Committee could record with some delight that the City battalions were 87.3% of establishment, 'higher than it has ever been'. Unfortunately, the sequence of regimental numbering is not continuous in the Subscription Books. This suggests that a number was reserved for a man after his first visit, but that if he did not turn up again and thus no subscription was paid, the number was never formally issued. Similarly, there are many examples of men who seem to have attested and been issued with their number, but then left before making any subscription payment. In view of these assumptions, it is difficult to be precise, but it would seem that slightly over one in three men failed to complete their full period of engagement. This wastage was regrettable and became of even more concern to the battalions once the drain of time-expired men began from 1912.

The total number of non-commissioned men who were fully paid up members of the LRB in July 1914 amounted to 603. This is 59 fewer than a return of battalion strength dated 28 May 1914, but the difference can probably be accounted for by the inclusion in that official return of men who were still considered to be 'on strength', but whose subscriptions had only recently lapsed. The more the battalion could claim were members, the more money it could claim in grants and assistance. However, that the LRB was not considered to have been too seriously under strength when compared to the other City battalions, is suggested by the fact that it did not request the grants then available to subsidise the costs of employing a recruiting sergeant and of showing recruiting slides in cinemas. A figure of just over 600 other ranks is probably fairly accurate as the entries in the Subscription Books show that once war was declared, and the rush of enthusiastic volunteers began, 350 men had to be admitted into the regiment in order to bring it up to full establishment.

This then was the LRB on the eve of war. Somewhat understrength, but a unit which through its social composition had developed a particular brand of *esprit*, and one which had, through its marching, shooting and drill, reached a good standard of proficiency. It was a battalion which in an emergency assumed it would be doing nothing more dramatic than guarding railways, bridges and power stations dotted in and around the capital. It was a regiment in which discipline was enforced in a way that would not be understood or tolerated in the Regular Army for it was a form of discipline which had grown from an acknowledgement that the men were educated, enthusiastic part-time volunteers. In common with the rest of the TF, the fact that the men of the LRB were part-timers laid it open to ridicule. The term 'Saturday afternoon soldiers' was a stigma upon which the press and satirical magazines loved to capitalise. The reviews in Hyde Park and elsewhere were regularly treated by the nation as something of a joke, and the men were frequently caricatured and used as material for jibes. Despite what Dick Wallis believed amounted to virtually an orchestrated campaign of disparagement, Graham Williams considered that the expression 'Saturday afternoon soldiers' was not really meant in any derogatory sense. To him, it was simply more of an example of what he calls 'typical British self-denegration and understatement'.

At the beginning of August 1914, these unselfish, patriotic, part-time soldiers prepared for the annual two-week camp. That year it was to be held on the coast at Eastbourne. An advance party set off on 1 August and the remainder of the battalion was to follow the next day. The men knew that a major European crisis had developed, and that the Kaiser's army had already violated the neutrality of Luxemburg. War was a distinct possibility, but few of the LRB would have believed that within four months they would be on the continent, holding their own sector of front, and facing the formerly invincible German Army.

CHAPTER II.

The Outbreak of war and Mobilisation.

In June 1914 the Balkans provided the spark that was to ignite Europe and plunge her into war. The peninsular had long been regarded as the area most likely to cause the eruption that many had been predicting as inevitable. It was in that troublesome area that the 'armed camps' of Europe came into the closest rivalry. The activities of the various Serb nationalist groups had antagonised the Austrians, who saw the threat of an expansionist Serbia as a dagger held to her throat. The assassination of the Archduke Franz Ferdinand on 28 June, gave the 'war party' in Vienna the excuse for which they had been waiting. Egged on by the Kaiser and, more especially, the German General Staff, the Austrians presented Serbia, whom they blamed for the assassination, with an unacceptable ultimatum; the Serbs, relying on earlier Russian promises of support, refused to comply with the demands. The pressure on politicians increased as the military men of the Great Powers insisted on mobilisation. Their plans depended on exact and precise timetables, and any delay in the ordering of the commencement of the war plans would, they argued, leave them at a dangerous and perhaps fatal disadvantage.

By the end of July, the Kaiser had lost his nerve, but events had moved beyond his control; von Moltke and his Staff ruled in Berlin. Their encouragement to Conrad von Hotzendorff, the Austrian Chief of the General Staff, was the deciding factor in the Austrian policy and from the beginning of August the Great Powers either declared war, or had war declared upon them. On the periphery of the developing conflict lay Britain. Europe asked two vital questions: would Britain and her Empire, the supreme maritime power, come in on the side of the countries with whom they had until recently been vigorous colonial rivals? Or, as many in Germany believed, would she once again remain aloof from what she considered to be a purely European squabble?

It has already been noted that many English people had long believed that a titanic clash between the two foremost trading nations was inevitable, and indeed, many on both sides had long looked forward to it. The Germans, jealous of Britain's Empire and trade supremacy, sought what they considered was their rightful share of the globe; the Kaiser's whole policy of *Weltpolitik* had been undertaken for this very reason. Britain, formerly secure in her imperial glory, had awoken to the fact that in Germany she faced a bitter and perhaps deadly rival. The measures taken by Fisher at the Admiralty and by Haldane at the War Office had realigned Britain's overseas commitments and concentrated thoughts on the possibility of a European rather than a colonially-based war. But, when it came to the crunch, would she be prepared to send her small army to the continent to help the French, or could she afford to stand aside, behind her wall of ironclads, and allow the French to suffer another defeat? A further humiliating defeat of the French would surely affect the balance of power to a far greater extent than had been the case in 1870.

The Liberal Cabinet under Asquith was deeply split over the issue. The fact was that Britain had no formal alliance or agreement to aid the French, but she did have what many considered to be a moral duty to do so. Military men from the two nations had carried on unofficial informal talks on how a British Expeditionary Force could assist the French Army, and there was a more formal agreement between the respective fleets. Ultimately, Britain's dilemma was solved for her politicians by Germany's invasion of Luxemburg and Belgium. This action, necessary to the success of the Schlieffen Plan, broke the guarantee of neutrality promised by, amongst others, Britain and Prussia in 1839. The 'scrap of paper', as the Kaiser called the Treaty of London, was the means by which those who advocated action on behalf of the Entente could justify Britain's entry into the war. With the refusal of the Germans to withdraw her troops from the Low Countries, Britain's ultimatum signalled her declaration of war on the Central Powers. Her small, badly understrength Territorial Army was ordered to mobilise and prepare to prevent and repel a possible German invasion on the South or East coasts. Few of the men in the LRB expected that they would be required to do more than that. As they returned from their short excursion to Eastbourne the anticipation was for immediate posting to their war station; none of the other ranks, however, had the vaguest idea of where that might be.

When the train carrying the LRB pulled into Waterloo on the evening of Sunday 2 August, the men were a little surprised to be dismissed. They had not, in their excitement, remembered that mobilisation was a lengthy but strictly timetabled affair. There was no room for improvisation or anticipating events. Orders for mobilisation had been drafted in 1911 and once the machine was set in motion, it operated as smoothly as if it were routine. The influx of recruits, requisitioning of vehicles and the general myriad tasks of the procedure, turned the drill hall into a seething mass of humanity. All busied themselves performing their varied and assorted jobs, and, above all, making sure that the timetable was adhered to. Depending to which company they belonged, men were ordered to report to HQ in full marching order, as specified. Their haversacks were to contain a pair of socks, tooth-brush, laces, towel, soap, razor and brush, knife, fork and spoon, housewife, clasp-knife and tin opener. The soldier was responsible for providing these items himself and, when his company commander was satisfied that his kit was complete, the soldier was issued his embodiment bounty of £5 10s. The battalion would be rationed on the fifth day of mobilisation and until then each man was given a subsistence allowance of 9d.[32] The cafes and eating houses of the City did a roaring trade as the young men crowded into them anxious to grab something to eat between parades.

A major problem though concerned the acquisition of sufficient vehicles for the Transport section. Of equal importance was the difficulty of finding sufficient men who knew enough about horses to cope with the expansion of the section as it was brought up to full strength. Parties were despatched to requisition horses from the streets - the unfortunate owner of the cart being given a receipt which he could then present at Bunhill Row and obtain compensation.[33] Gradually horses and wagons were acquired and the Drill Hall filled by them. Recruits queued around and between them, officers and NCOs performed their tasks amongst them, but despite accidents the system was operating, and operating successfully. The telegrams and posters ordering the men to report had gone out, and by the fifth day the battalion was up to strength. That day it moved off to the Merchant Taylors' and the Cowper Street Schools for parades and drills. The heightening activity and speculation were obvious but, beneath the outward appearance of enthusiasm and animation, the young men were also apprehensive. The question of serving overseas had not yet been raised officially, but everyone knew that the new recruits were being asked on enlistment whether they would be willing to do so.[34] One young man, Russell Latham, who had excitedly torn open the mobilisation envelope that dropped on the mat of his home in Prospect Hill, soon found himself praying that the politicians might still find a way to secure peace.

When the men were dismissed at the end of the day, they returned home or to beds in the houses of their friends. This practice was stopped on the 10 August following what, fortunately, turned out to be a false alarm. It was the job of the police to go round to members' houses and order them to report to HQ if the alarm was raised. Unfortunately, as all the Territorial units tried to get through to the local police stations, the police switchboards became so overloaded that the system was seen to be an emphatic failure. From then on the men slept on the floors of the local schools and gradually began to acclimatise to communal living. For those members who had attended boarding school this new style of living would not prove too difficult to accommodate. Others with their middle class inhibitions found the new departure embarrassing. For example, Henry Williamson's central character, the semi-autobiographical Philip Maddison, was distressed to discover that the toilet doors ended inches short of the ground. In consequence he suffered what he felt to be a profound indignity.[35]

The LRB Regimental Band were paid professionals and, according to the regulations, had been disbanded on mobilisation. Deprived of the official musicians, the summer evenings were rounded off instead with concerts performed by the men themselves. Some of the younger members of the band had re-enlisted as ordinary members of the regiment, so their talents could be readily utilised. Similarly, many of the men were used to singing and reciting in the parlours of Edwardian England. Among the turns performing during those early days and nights of mobilisation was the younger Bassingham's rendition of *'Friend of Mine'*. Son of a long-serving member of the regiment, this 21 year old was soon to be one of the battalion's first fatalities in Plugstreet Wood.

These days at Merchant Taylors' were days of transition. The young volunteer army had to lose its easy-going civilian ways and, in a very short period of time, become one of unquestioning and obedient soldiers. At times this was difficult and tough, for the educated young men were unused to the ways of the Army - and at times the transition was almost unendurable.[36] Yet, on other occasions, there were also moments of relief and hilarity. One night, as Lt Furze crept round a tree trunk at 02.30 hoping to catch the sentry unaware, he found a recently sharpened bayonet about to penetrate just below his second button. During that night's subsequent tours of inspections, Furze could regularly be heard shouting 'Friend' in strident and certain voice.[37] The atmosphere was tense and expectant, but it was also a little like an enjoyable Scout camp; on occasions company officers were known to request that their men take the training just a little more seriously.

Who were these new recruits to the battalion, busily learning the strange ways of the army, and why had they chosen to enlist in those early days of August? For the time being, we shall leave the men as they sweated through their basic drills on school playgrounds, sang their romantic ballads and patriotic songs, and tenderly nursed the growing blisters and sores on their feet and shoulders.   In order to make some assessment of the composition of the full strength battalion, an explanation of the motives, occupations and backgrounds of the new members must be attempted.

The Regimental History, like those of some of the other London Territorial battalions, is a little coy and vague about the number of men within its ranks on the outbreak of war. As we know, the LRB was considerably understrength, but this was by no means unique amongst the London Regiments; the 4th London had gone to camp with 'about 650', The Rangers claimed about 850, 2nd London about 600, the Queen's Westmisters 511, the 'Shiny Seventh' about 600; the London Scottish, like the LRB, avoid giving any figure.[38] From the LRB's Subscription Book mentioned earlier, it can be determined when and how the battalion was brought up to its full establishment. *King's Regulations, 1912* laid down that the regimental numbers of the Territorial Force would extend to 9,999 and when that figure was reached, a new series would be commenced. The LRB reached that number on 7 August, so recruit G.N. Maskell received the new Number 1. The doors were closed to further recruits later that same day when the number 136 had been reached - men still queueing or arriving eager to enlist were turned away after their names had been taken. Thus, between the 4 August, when 18 men had enlisted, and the 7 August, when 216 were accepted, a total of 350 men were attested as members of the regiment. However, not all of this number were actually new members, for, as Haldane had envisaged, many of the 1908 and 1909 intakes came back to re-enlist when the crisis broke. We can probably assume that these men would have been given some sort of priority in the queues, and of the 350 August recruits at least 54 were re-enlistments rather than complete novices. The exact figure is impossible to determine precisely for, rather than re-issuing them with their original numbers, these men were allocated new ones within the running sequence.   Their experience and familiarity with the LRB system would prove to be an essential asset during the hectic early days of August.

The scenes in Bunhill Row were duplicated outside the Headquarters of the other London Regiments. Queues formed on hearing that a regiment still had vacancies and then came the slow shuffle towards the desk within the Drill Hall. Would-be recruits hoped that the cry of 'Full Up' would not ring out before they had managed to fill out the enlistment form. In the LRB Major Burnell found the numbers so great that he did not have time to select the men individually if the mobilisation programme was to keep to schedule. So, in order to speed up the process, and of course to ensure that the usual sort of LRB man was selected, he resorted to an expedient: being a former Rowing and Rugby Blue himself, he ordered all rowing men to leave the queue and fall in on the other side of the road; these were then marched into the Drill Hall. Next he ordered all rugby men to do the same. According to one source, these two categories appear to have provided the LRB with all the men it needed.[39]

Undoubtedly, the driving motivation of the new recruits was a mixture of solid patriotism and sense of duty, combined with the element of excitement and adventure. These were heady days as wartime fever gripped the nation; military bands played, banners flew and Musical Hall *artistes* exhorted. The young men of the City were caught up in the excitement and euphoria and, although determined to do their bit for their country, were concerned that they should do it with their friends and colleagues. This desire among the City clerks was recognised fairly early on by the War Office, as a letter from Major-General Rawlinson, the Director of Recruiting, to Major Hon. R. White demonstrates.[40] Rawlinson explained that he had heard of many City employees willing to enlist if they were assured that they could serve with their friends. He then suggested to White that he should collect the names and addresses of those who would be willing to enlist with a view to enroling them in a Service battalion of the Royal Fusiliers. Evidence from some LRB men corroborates this desire to serve with colleagues; R. Miller Hall and A. Thain joined the queues outside Bunhill Row with friends because it was known to be a class regiment and because they wanted to serve together. Gadsdon returned from his school OTC camp and was taken along by a friend, Geoffrey Richardson, who was already a member of 'P' Company. Others, like H. Gower and F. Dyer, joined because they had relatives still serving or who had recently left the regiment.[41]

Some men combined the desire to serve with friends with a more immediate one of becoming a little better off financially. Office juniors, often a long way from their home town, did not draw good pay and, if that was their only source of income, money was short. One member decided that nothing could be more uncomfortable than his existing perilous financial position and was overjoyed at finding that the Army was always thrusting money at him for one reason or another.[42]

Some of the clerks and juniors were actively encouraged to enlist by their firms, many of whom promised to pay them full salary and to keep their positions open for them while they served with the Colours. Harding, from the Sun Fire Office, was paid his full salary of £40 per annum plus rises for the duration. As time went on though, some companies decided that in view of Army Pay and Allowances half salary only should be paid.[43] The promise of an improved level of income was a strong inducement to the young men and initially, of course, joining the Territorials rather than one of the Service battalions was considered to be relatively safe as you could simply opt for Home Service. To be paid twice seemed somewhat strange but to be paid for not doing something which you had not enjoyed particularly when you had done it seemed downright bizarre. The Army had given the clerks a chance to do something else and this was not lost on one of them in a letter home. Jim Whitehead could have taken a cushy job on the headquarters Staff but refused it; 'It is only like being in an office; in fact you are a clerk, and as such I might as well be at home'.

The 350 completely new or former members of the regiment soon took it to a size never attained since its formation as a Territorial battalion. This new-found strength, however, was not a phenomenon unique to the LRB. Four months before the outbreak of war, Haldane's child, the Territorial Force, was over 5,000 officers and 150,000 other ranks short of its designed establishment of 15,977 officers and 401,556 men.[44]   Of the quarter of a million men actually serving in the various regiments and units, only 17,621 had undertaken to serve overseas if required - this amounted to five complete units.[45]   Haldane had intended that the Territorials and their County Associations should be used for any expansion of the Army in time of emergency or war. Consequently, Kitchener's decision to create the New Armies, rather than to use Haldane's existing framework, was bitterly regretted by the latter.   Many of the Territorials too, especially those who had volunteered for foreign service, felt humiliated and snubbed at this apparent rebuff. However, in his defence, Kitchener was concerned about the possibility of a German invasion and believed that in the absence of the Regulars, the Territorials would be required to fulfil their intended role. Furthermore, in mid-August, Lord Esher commented that Kitchener 'knows nothing of the organisation of our home armies', and although he was 'learning', he chose to work within a framework with which he was familiar. Thus, the Secretary of State's rejection of a massive expansion founded upon the Territorials can largely be explained on two grounds. Firstly, his initial belief that given the conditions of service within the TF there would be severe restrictions on its battalions serving overseas and, secondly, that until the threat of a German landing had receded they would be needed for home defence anyway.[46]

More salt was rubbed into the wounds of the Territorials when soon after the outbreak it became obvious that their own expansion was being seriously impeded by the creation of the New Army. Mobilisation equipment had to be obtained once the order had been received and, while the War Office was responsible for providing some items, the bulk had to be purchased or acquired by the County Associations[47] - this explains the activities of the LRB in trying to round up sufficient horses and carts from the streets around Bunhill Row. The problem was further exacerbated by the War Office failing to supply the equipment which it was required to do and by decreeing that some County Associations would be forbidden to obtain equipment from their usual contractors. The LRB managed to provide clothing and most of the equipment required on mobilisation, either from stores or local contacts. The men of the 2nd Battalion, however, had to wait a considerable time before receiving their kit and uniform.

Kitchener's decision was to be severely criticised after the war. The *Official History* complains that the intense recruiting of the New Armies had deprived the Territorials of members and this, combined with the failure to foresee that the Territorials might be used overseas and consequently suffer severe casualties, meant that when they did need reinforcements, they were not available.[48]   Because it would have provided the most cost effective method, Sir John French called the decision to raise an entirely new army rather than develop and expand existing Territorial machinery a 'great administrative mistake'.[49]   Similarly, another writer believed that if Kitchener had used the officers and NCOs who created and trained the New Armies to stiffen the existing Territorial organisation, complete Territorial Divisions could have been shipped out to France in October 1914 and the process maintained as fast as rifles could have been provided for them.[50]

Kitchener soon realised and accepted that the Territorials would in fact be needed for service overseas. In mid-August it was decreed that men who had opted for home service in units which had volunteered for overseas duty should be separated from those who were prepared to serve abroad. The bulk of the Territorial regiments of course had never made such an undertaking but it was decided that now was the time to raise the issue again. The question had been discussed on several occasions in the pre-war LRB, and on 15 August Lord Cairns, the Commanding Officer, addressed the assembled regiment on the issue. Appealing to their sense of honour and prestige amongst the Territorial Force, he urged the men to give consideration to serving overseas. The War Office had stipulated that any unit in which 75% of the men volunteered for overseas service would be sent out as a unit; this was an important factor in many men's decisions. Regimental *esprit* had developed and grown sufficiently among the new recruits since their enlistment that the break-up of the battalion would seem dishonourable. Thus, with a great deal of satisfaction, Cairns was able to inform the War Office immediately that the required 75% of the LRB had agreed. The LRB was the first battalion in the 2nd London Brigade to make the decision and this fact did not go unnoticed.

In the LRB the method of ascertaining a man's answer to the question of overseas service was for him to parade before his company commander. It was an extremely difficult decision to make as many of the older men had families, good jobs and good salaries. The younger men had fewer commitments and were more likely to be swayed by what friends in their sections and platoons decided. The London Scottish were asked individually and the decision accepted 'without comment' by the company commander.[51] The officers of the Rangers were asked confidentially by the Commanding Officer whether they would serve unconditionally or with the battalion as a unit.[52] The LRB followed a similar procedure and after another appeal at Bisley by the Bishop of London many of the waverers seem to have been convinced, and the proportion of those accepting overseas service rose.

The number of original 1st Battalion men who did eventually decide to go is a little difficult to determine accurately. Initially volunteers were required to be between 19 and 40. This upper limit would certainly rule out at least a proportion of the senior NCOs if they chose to use that as their justification. At the younger end, many of the boys were only 17 and 18. Some parents later petitioned the regiment and War Office in an attempt to get their under-aged boys returned to England, although it seems that the majority of the youngsters were accepted for the overseas contingent. Russell Latham and his cousin Jack Chappell managed to persuade their platoon commander to perjure himself about their age in return for a sudden zeal and smart appearance. Others like Harding, Johns, Gadsdon and Williamson were also under age but managed to convince the authorities that they should not be left behind.

Captain Soames claimed that 95% of 'O' Company volunteered and the 12 men who did not, declined because they were under age or had 'equally good reasons'.[53] Russell Latham thought that only 26 out of the 900-odd men did not volunteer - i.e. over 97% compared with the 'nearly 90%' claimed by the Queen's Westminsters.[54] The figure of 26 is certainly too small because 37 1st Battalion men appear in two companies alone of the newly raised 2nd Battalion. Without the necessary evidence, it can not be simply assumed that the men being transferred would be distributed evenly among the eight companies of the 2nd Battalion - that would suggest a total of about 144 or 16%, which is, however, probably nearer the mark. A clue does come from the fact that 32 men were sent from the 2nd Battalion in early October to replace men who had apparently been rejected for foreign service on medical grounds. One of these men was

Leslie Savery from Hampstead. Rejected as medically unfit when he first applied to join in April 1909, he was accepted in August 1914 only to be sent down to the 2nd Battalion, again for medical reasons.[55] Later the same month another 26 men were sent from Haywards Heath to join the 1st Battalion. It is possible that not all of the 58 men being sent from the 1st Battalion were medically unfit and perhaps significantly the dates coincide with the last appeal for volunteers made at Crowborough. Those that did make the switch from 2nd to 1st Battalions were mainly men who had re-enlisted in September. Some of these former Territorials, such as the Figg brothers, initially signed on again for one year. Ultimately, however, one of the two, except for a short time out with trench fever, was destined to serve the entire war in France. There were also certainly few others who managed to get to the 1st Battalion on the strength of service in their school OTC. and parental influence.

Richard Lintott, for example, 18 in July 1914, had attended Horsham Grammar School and Hurstpierpoint College. He was rejected by the Royal Sussex on medical grounds, the East Surrey's did not want him because his eyes were not up to scratch, and so he eventually enlisted in the Public Schools Special Corps. Quickly dissatisfied because many of his friends left to take up commissions - which left only the 'scum' - he applied again to the Royal Sussex, only to find it full up. Desperate to get into a *bona fide* unit he asked his father to approach a family friend Major Harvest, Second in Command of the 2nd Battalion LRB. Harvest replied that he would 'do my best to get him in, but cannot make any promise to make him a Field Marshal'. Harvest was as good as his word and in October Lintott joined the battalion. Not content with merely the reserve battalion, he 'jumped' at the opportunity when volunteers for the 1st Battalion were called in October and shortly found himself down with the battalion at Crowborough.

The men who made the switch in the opposite direction for one reason or another certainly did include some who were under age and who later went out as drafts to the 1st Battalion. As he was invalided home from France in January 1915, one such man, Martin, a veteran of the Brighton March, could only have spent a short time with the 2nd Battalion before changing his mind about foreign service or becoming fit. Two men at least of 'G' Company, Branch and Thomas, both pre-War members were transferred to the 2nd Battalion because they were only 17 years old. Branch, an employee of the Commercial Union Assurance Company, was to take a commission with the Devons when old enough. Others such as Wally Waldheim also eventually ended up elsewhere, in his case, the Kensingtons. Waldheim had been one of the many that had swelled the ranks of the LRB in February 1909 and had served continuously ever since. He was, like Martin, also a member of the Brighton March team, and was to be killed in October 1918.

Whatever the precise figure of those taking the General Service Obligation, it is clear that at least four out of every five of the old soldiers and new recuits volunteered for overseas duty. War caused the regiment to be brought up to strength rapidly with new blood and, although some of the older, familiar faces might not be with them when they went abroad, the composition of the unit had not altered significantly. This first great test of loyalty to the regiment had easily been passed and, once those who had decided for home service only had gone, an even more united feeling developed among the overseas volunteers. There grew a single-mindedness of purpose, a feeling that they were about to step out into a great new adventure which would demonstrate their belief in themselves, the regiment and their country. They had joined up to serve the country that had treated most of them relatively well and to fight for the maintenance of the system and way of life that had allowed them to enjoy their reasonably comfortable existence. Fifty years later the Bishop of London addressed the survivors and stressed that their motive had been the preservation of the 'British way of life' and 'a willingness to accept a personal responsibility for its protection and defence'.[56]

What they considered to be right and just was worth defending, but above all, their enlistment perhaps symbolised that essential feature of Edwardian life - the feeling of belonging to something and of being able to identify with your peers for a particular purpose or cause. The social and moral identification among the men is obvious to see, but to them, and of more immediate concern, was what military purpose they might be able to fulfil. Few believed that the Territorials would be able to do anything other than guard lines of communications if they went abroad, and even Haldane, whose faith in them was unsurpassed, had always intended that they should have six months training before being required to undertake active service. The prevailing sentiment was that the war would be over by Christmas anyway, so what danger was there to be found in guarding supply dumps and railways in France rather than England? Besides, it would probably be a lot more fun.

The majority of the men who agreed to foreign service did so during the three week stay at Bisley. The two day march gave the battalion an early opportunity to test the depth of *esprit* among the new recruits. One writer commented; 'It is safe to say that the battalion had never been more efficient or filled with greater keeness than it was at the time of mobilisation'.[57] It is a little difficult to accept that, with so many inexperienced men, the battalion was equal in efficency to the pre-war one, but what became obvious during the march was the continual development of regimental *esprit*. Such discipline and *esprit* could not have been created only since the birth of the Territorial Force. It had emanated from the Volunteer days and been carried through into the Territorial era.

In the early stages of the trek march discipline was not too good. Some of the recruits apparently nipped into a nearby fruit shop during a halt and were hauled before their company commander for an 'admonishment'.[58] The veterans of the Brighton march were concerned that everyone should keep in exact step and were constantly grumbling, 'goodnaturedly', at those who dragged or over-stepped.[59] Feet had not had time to harden and many new boots had not been sufficiently worn in to prevent blisters. Ignoring the pain as best they could, Latham recalled it was the 'pride of the Regiment which urged them doggedly on'. Drinking from water bottles was strictly controlled by the simple expedient of the officers observing the number of men standing behind the hedges during halts; when the groups dwindled, it was time to permit another drink. The route was lined for much of the way by cheering civilians, which no doubt acted as an incentive to some to stay in the column. Yet despite this, many men from the other regiments in the brigade fell out. One LRB member, with a certain amount of justifiable pride, recorded that the Post Office Rifles, drawn from a similar type of civilian as the LRB, lost 20 or 30, while the 6th and 7th London, recruited from the inner ring areas, 'left a trail scattered along the road side in hundreds - those who fell out [did so] not singly but in groups of four to a dozen at a time'.[60] Heat, blisters and exhaustion clearly affected many of the less physically robust but the Regimental History claims that only one LRB man fell out - the reason given for this exception being that he had a fit. Pocock recalled four and Williams also suggests that there were perhaps several. He comments that any man falling out 'usually found himself before the Colonel the next day to explain his action, and he had to produce a really convincing excuse backed by the MO'. No new recruit even at that early stage of his military training and experience would want to let his comrades or the regiment down by giving up; *esprit* within him had developed sufficiently highly for him to be aware that unpleasant and painful though the march might be, the opprobrium of his colleagues would be greater.

Marching stamina was again tested when the brigade left Bisley and headed south towards Crowborough. Day after day, training at Bisley had involved parades, company manoeuvres, practice attacks and weapons drill. The men sweated and tramped through the heather, while faces wan and pale from working in City offices became deeply tanned. Other discomforts had also to be faced. One of the most brutal was vaccination, which in the army was commonly believed to be performed with a hat pin at the rate of four injections per minute. The men remained in total ignorance of what their eventual fate or destination might be but contented themselves with speculation and becoming fit.

On 9 September, with many men still suffering from the after effects of vaccination, the brigade began its march to Crowborough.[61] It was billeted in Reigate overnight (long enough, according to Latham, for Pte Bell to fall in love with the owner's daughter of a tea shop in which he stayed) and then, after marching past the King, on to East Grinstead. The battalion remained here for four nights, enjoying the hospitality of the locals because the baggage had not yet arrived and there was no water laid on at the Crowborough camp. The Transport was experiencing difficulties with its tradesmen's vans and horses but eventually arrived at Camp Hill six hours after the men. The weather had broken and the facilities at the camp were virtually non-existent. Just about everything was in short supply and, although the tents had arrived, the pegs had not. This allowed Latham and Chappell to put some of their recent military training to good use - a diversionary conversation with the guard on the Colonel's tent, while the real attack went in on his rear to remove sufficient tent pegs for their own use.

This important aspect of soldiering - the 'winning' of items that are not technically yours - must have been a little alien to the respectable, decent clerks and schoolboys. In the Army, it is an essential skill, which needs to be learned as rapidly as possible. The men had cause to thank the semi-legitimate system of acquisition when a recent arrival, an expert in its operation, began to produce remarkable results. Sgt Cook 'Tootsie' Hands, a Reservist with over 20 years Regular service, was appointed with about half a dozen other old army cooks, now over military age, by Lord Cairns. The standard of food at Crowborough was universally condemned until Hands began 'winning' the items of stores which the LRB had been denied. There was an immediate and appreciated rise in the quality of the rations produced.[62] Rations apart, the remainder of the facilities at Crowborough remained primitive. The weather became progressively worse as October arrived and the camp degenerated into a sea of mud. Training continued, but there was litle real idea of what tactics the men should be adopting. The war in France was still one of movement so, although digging was practised, the importance of that skill was not yet immediately realised. The days spent on the heathlands around Camp Hill resulted in the men gaining fitness, and the route marches hardened the feet. By the beginning of the month the recruits with no previous experience had passed their firing tests and done the required forty drills which meant they had qualified as 'trained men'. Two hour runs before breakfast had been the order of the day since arriving at Bisley, and all this added exertion had played havoc with the uniforms; the green walking out uniform became the one worn during training - which left the already shabby khaki one for evening wear. This practice continued even when a new issue of service dress arrived later in the month.

Uncomfortable as the conditions were, the men still appear to have enjoyed the experience and the holiday spirit that had been evident at Bisley prevailed throughout this period. Richard Lintott, newly arrived from the 2nd Battalion, described his new comrades as 'a very nice lot of fellows' and of being 'very excited indeed'. Meanwhile, Captain Somers-Smith was still having to ask the members of 'P' Company to try to develop a more serious attitude to life in general.[63] Leave was rarely granted to the men, the general anticipation of a sudden invasion of the country by the Germans being the implied reason, but they could still communicate easily with their parents and, for the married minority, with their wives. Washing and darning was sent home regularly with newly photographed postcards of the tented camp, and uncensored letters passed back freely to London's suburbs.

Little reliable war news was reaching England from France in the early weeks of the War. The Retreat was of course under way, yet despite this temporary set-back there was no real concern about the eventual outcome. The seriousness of the Allied position was unknown and while the rumours of an impending German landing were common, the men of the 2nd London Brigade thought their future was more likely to lie in foreign fields. Turkey's declaration of war convinced some that they would shortly depart for the Middle East, while others argued that their role was to save Montenegro or Serbia from the rapacious Austrian and infidel Turk. When the Stores were rumoured to have received a delivery of sleighs and snow shoes, the destination became Russia - presumably to replace the legendary Russians who, *en route* for the Western Front, had landed with snow on their boots in Newcastle. By the end of the month though, things began to look a little more certain. Lintott wrote to his father on 30 October explaining; 'I am nearly certain we are going to France.' This thought came with the issue of new kit, uniforms and rifles, route marches on successive days in full kit, the order to despatch any excess or extra possessions home, and two anti-typhoid inoculations. Tension rose further with the advent of several 'alarms', and then, with the granting of 24 hours leave, their fate at last seemed sealed. Absence of tropical kit or snow shoes seemed to indicate France.

On 3 November, for the second time, the Adjutant, Captain Oppenheim, received embarkation orders - those received five days before having been later cancelled. The men were despatched on a few hours embarkation leave to bid farewell to families and friends and returned to Camp Hill during the late evening. The wind was blowing and, between a few light showers, the moon shone strongly. The men gathered their equipment together, speculated on what the morning would bring and wrote a few final lines home. As they settled down to a few hours rest, an air of expectancy hung over the mud and canvas camp. However much they might have thought or anticipated this moment since volunteering for foreign service, the reality of that decision was now upon them and.in the chill dark of a November evening the doubts would inevitably nag. It required courage not to have accepted foreign service, to have remained behind with the 2nd Battalion while friends and office colleagues opted to go; was it not irresponsible to have given up a secure job and salary, to leave wives and children to fend for themselves and to falsify your age because you feared more what your friends might think of you than what overseas service might bring? Irresponsible perhaps, but there was comfort in the knowledge that the battalion's *esprit* was such that whatever had to be faced, it would be done so with fortitude and faith in the traditions of the regiment. Comradeship and *esprit* were described by Perolls as being 'never greater' during this early period of service, and, while others would claim the same for other periods, undoubtedly it was to provide a cloak of security for the young men about to embark on active service.

Some mention has already been made of men who originally enlisted in the 2nd Battalion but who were to travel with the 1st Battalion to France in November. By the beginning of February 1915, a further 168 men had been drafted from the 2nd to the 1st, thus greatly affecting the personnel of the serving battalion. So, here is a convenient place to leave the men of the 1st Battalion, as they prepared to leave Crowborough and embark onto active service, in order to look at how the 2nd Battalion had originally come into existence, and at the sort of men who had flocked to join it.

Throughout the month of August 1914, recruits poured into the Territorial and New Army battalions in response to the Government's call for 100,000 men. Kitchener had requested that the Territorial Associations use their influence to secure the required number as soon as possible, but at the same time he had ordered that Territorial units at full strength were not to recruit over establishment until the initial 100,000 had been raised. Any Territorial wanting to serve overseas would be allowed to transfer to the Regular Army and his place could be filled by another in his original regiment. In other words, until the first New Army was raised, there was to be a block on further Territorial recruiting.

War Office figures record an average of about 6,000 men enlisting each day during the first three weeks of August and about 9,000 during the fourth week. On 31 August the daily figure was just in excess of 20,000 and on 3 September over 33,000 men enlisted.[64] This upsurge, which was to last until the middle of September, was the consequence of two actions taken by the War Office. One was the decision to promote the idea of the Pals battalions, and the other was to allow the formation of Reserve, or second line TF units. Any regiment in which 60% of the men had volunteered for overseas service - as had been achieved in the case of the LRB - was authorised to re-commence recruiting. Thus, once more the queues formed in Bunhill Row.

Many of the men who created the 2nd Battalion LRB in September 1914 were those who had applied to join the 1st Battalion, only to find they were too late. Their names had been taken, but rather than join one of the New Army service battalions, they had decided to wait until the Territorial Force could accept them. As soon as it became known that the doors had been re-opened, men like R.M. Parker went down to HQ in the hope of being accepted. Those who had attended public schools or who had served in OTCs were accepted straight away and directed up to the Members' Room where they were sworn in. These men had had a little more time to think about the consequences of their enlistment than their colleagues who had done so in August, but their motives were identical. The time had allowed Jack Terry, a young clerk in the parcels office of Waterloo Station, a period of 'heart-searching as to how he could best serve his country', while for others the outbreak of war and the resultant anti-German sentiment within the country had created new problems. Maurice Howard had been working for a German firm in Brighton until the war had caused its closure. Howard had never dreamed of joining the Territorials but had now to consider a fresh start. He decided that it was his duty to join and began to look forward to the prospect - the problem facing him was into which unit should he enlist. Born a Londoner, he returned to the capital and by chance met an old friend. The colleague told Howard that he had just joined the LRB so why didn't he? Howard agreed and by the time his friend, Lewis, returned from a route march, he too had been accepted.

Besides the men already noted - i.e. those who had joined the LRB since its formation as a Territorial unit but had since resigned - there were others re-enlisting who could offer the experience of having seen active service. Ranks and Hampton had both served with the City Imperial Volunteers in South Africa and A.J. McVeagh's service as a corporal in the Boer War ensured his early transfer to the 1st Battalion. Several sets of brothers, including the Vernons and the Ebbett twins, both teachers within the London County Council, enlisted during the early days of September. These were in turn followed by a group of five men from Parr's Bank who joined together and were later destined to go out together on the same draft.

Two friends and clubmates of Victor Hember, a 1st Battalion member, Eyers and Rivers, the former a French teacher and the latter a student, enlisted in September. So too did Wright, Cockerell and Terry, three men who were to have similar military careers and who were to become good friends. Another two men who were to develop a firm friendship, Aubrey Smith and Claud Vallentine-Warne, were sworn in early on the first day of recruiting, and a little later, two teachers from Bowes Park School, Wood Green, Kerry and Robinson, also took the oath. Among other men who will appear regularly in the succeeding pages are Heavingham, who left his job in the bookstall on Highgate station, Munday, whose quiet word in the ear of Wallis in 1917 defused what was potentially a very explosive situation, and a young 23 year old employee of Monkhouse, Stoneham & Co., William Marlborough.

Many of these recruits would no doubt identify themselves with Montague's description of the volunteers as being men of 'handsome and boundless illusions...straining to discharge an obligation of honour'.[65] This sense of duty and honour was certainly of great importance to a large number, while others might have identified more with the views expounded by Lloyd George in one of his great recruiting speeches of September 1914. In his 'Appeal to the Nation', Lloyd George described the conflict as an opportunity for the young men to seize the 'glow and thrill' of sacrifice and then went on to claim that the nation was undergoing a form of rebirth. This new, emerging society, he believed, was one in which class divide was already narrowing and one where the 'great flood of luxury and sloth which had submerged the land' was also fast disappearing.[66] Others were a little less sure of their motivation. Morris for example, working quite happily for a private bank in Croydon, had been left completely untouched by the national clamour to enlist and it had not occured to him to offer his services to King and Country. It was the chance encounter with a recruiting sergeant outside the Queen's Hall which persuaded him to try the London Scottish; they rejected him on the grounds of poor eyesight. Still not too sure why he was doing it, he went down to Bunhill Row. There, an over-worked medical orderly suggested that as the doctor was harrassed by the numbers turning up, he should keep his glasses on until he reached the head of the queue and then memorise as much of the card as possible. The ploy worked, but like so many of the new battalion Morris would leave it to take up a commission before it went overseas. He would, however, come across the LRB again in somewhat less pleasant circumstances two years later.[67]

The rush of would-be recruits for the LRB was so large that had permission been granted another battalion could have been formed.[68] The War Office was not yet ready to authorise the raising of a third battalion but the press of numbers meant that the regiment could be especially choosy about whom it did accept. Most of those enlisting were the usual sorts of LRB men, but there was also a group which was not exactly typical. The muster rolls of two companies, 'G' and 'H', have survived and, as they give details on 318 of the 964 men forming the limit, they provide a useful breakdown of the newly constituted battalion.

The largest single occupation of the men was that of student teacher - of which there were 58 - and it appears likely that most of these came from Islington Training College. Forty-five of them were employed by the LCC and the remainder by other Local Authorities. One of the number later remembered smarting under a sense of indignation at the recruiting posters demanding 'men' and joined his colleagues in their march to Bunhill Row. Wearing straw boaters and blazers, they arrived at HQ only to be dismayed to find a queue stretching down the street. Spotted by some alert officer, they were ordered to by-pass the queue and marched straight into the hall as a body. Following attestation and medicals, the group was posted to 'H' Company, which immediately became known as the Schoolmasters' Company.[69]

It is difficult to spot any pre-war members of the LRB who were either serving or student teachers, but these 58 new recruits would be of the same social class as the more usual recruit. The status of a state schoolmaster was similar to that of a clerk. Both groups fell within the lower middle class and both, although not as well paid as many artisans, would find themselves more at home in the LRB rather than, for example, in the Fusilier Territorial Battalions. Of the remainder, we see a more predictable breakdown; five employees from Kilburn Town Hall, five from the Port of London Authority, six from various railway depots, and three from the office of the Buenos Aires Railway Company. Twenty-five came from named banks and eleven from specified insurance or assurance companies. A further seven worked with their fathers, which probably means in a family office business rather than manual occupation, four are listed as unemployed, and three employees from the office of the Continental Type Company also enlisted in the same company. This final group elected to join the LRB rather than enlist in the 6th London, the battalion which normally attracted the skilled men from the printing trade. Finally, 68 of the number have their address and occupation recorded simply as 'City' or 'E.C.', one was discharged as medically unfit, and the remainder worked for businesses of one form or another in the City.

The residences of the men show a little more diversity and are spread over a greater area of the capital than was noticed for those of the pre-war members. However, areas that had traditionally provided a large number of LRB men still figure prominently; fifteen came from Ilford, ten from Westcliffe-on-Sea and twelve from

Leyton or Leytonstone. Similarly, the inner suburbs of North London, such as Stoke Newington, Hornsey and Stamford Hill, are well represented, as is the familiar sweep of boroughs from the south and south east of London up to the Thames. West London areas are again not common and neither are the zones lying within the inner ring north and east of the river. There are only six addresses that come from outside the London postal district, one of them being a local recruit who did not join until the battalion had been posted down to Haywards Heath. There were seven sets of brothers joining and the average age of the two companies was 23 years 4 months.

Only four of the men state their religion as Catholic and five are recorded as Jewish. All those who do not specify attendance, membership or allegiance to another church are simply entered as Church of England. Although it is impossible to be accurate this probably means that they were not particularly regular church-goers. Those who did specify other than Church of England are more likely to have regarded themselves as practising Christians; 35 claimed to be Non-Conformists, another seven identified which branch of the Free Churches they subscribed to, while one man clearly was not too sure of his faith and simply declared himself to be 'Protestant', which was probably near enough. The middle and lower middle class were really the stalwarts of religion in late Edwardian England. Church attendance brought respectability and the opportunity to mingle with, and perhaps even meet, your social superiors. The Non-Conformist churches provided, in addition to a gathering of many local businessmen, sporting and social clubs where both sexes could mix with a fair degree of informality. Yet the concept of a devout body of practising Christians does not really come through in the papers and diaries that the men of the regiment have left. That is not of course to suggest that the soldiers were anti-religious, for many men sought and found comfort in God when in the trenches. So, although it seems likely that formal religion played little part in the lives of most of the men, if asked, the majority would probably insist that they did abide by the Christian code and ethics.

By September 1915, 63% of the men from this First Reserve Battalion had been drafted out to the 1st Battalion. The bulk were to go in four main parties, all of which arrived in France before the battalion took part in the 2nd Battle of Ypres. However, it was noted earlier that some of the men from the 2nd Battalion were to travel with the 1st Battalion when it left for France in November. It is to this battalion, then preparing itself for departure overseas, that the narrative will now return.

CHAPTER III

An Arboreal Sojourn

Late in the evening of 4 November a telegram from their son Richard arrived at the Lintott household in Horsham: 'Crossing tonight..I think we are going to France'. This wire from Southampton was the confirmation the Lintotts had been expecting since Richard had returned to Crowborough following his brief few hours of embarkation leave. The family, like the men waiting to board ship at the docks, knew that the LRB was now heading for foreign shores and active service - something which few of the founders of the Territorial Force in 1908 had ever really believed a possibility.

The total number of LRB men who embarked upon the former Orient Line cattle ship *Chyebassa* varies according to which source is used. The Regimental History talks of 848 all ranks,[70] while the *War Diary* has 863 including 29 officers and one Medical Officer. Whatever the total number of other ranks, and it varied from unit to unit, the figure of 30 officers is correct as during the months of August and September the officer establishment was brought up to strength by the arrival, in particular, of six new Second Lieutenants. These men had all attended well-known public schools, including Radley and Haileybury, had all spent time at either Oxford or Cambridge, and had served in their respective Officer Training Corps. Letters of introduction from OTC colonels were usually sufficient to ensure acceptance by the regiment and these young officers would fit easily, both educationally and socially, into the existing Mess.

The outbreak of war had also brought three retired members back to Bunhill Row. Lt Slessor had originally joined in 1890 and had retired in 1903 - he now became the battalion's Intelligence Officer. A former Etonian and Oxford man, Kirby, had retired in 1912 and now rejoined 'G,' Company as Lieutenant, and Burnell, also of Eton and Oxford, returned to command 'G' Company. Finally, H.B. Price joined in August and was appointed Lieutenant on the strength of having had some military experience in Canada. What that service was is unrecorded, but only two other officers, Matthey the second in command, and the Machine Gun Officer, A.L. Lintott, could claim to have seen any active service - that having been during the South African War. Similarly, only two of the senior NCOs had been in South Africa; RSM Harrington as a Regular had served through the siege of Ladysmith, and RQMS Bate had been in the City

Imperial Volunteers. At least seven other members of the regiment travelling on the *Chyebassa* had also been in the CIV and there were of course other men with Long Service and Territorial Efficiency Medals who would provide the newer recruits with a wealth of experience and advice.

As the collection of university scholars, medical students, City clerks and erstwhile schoolboys marched out of Camp Hill, the other battalions of 2nd London Brigade paraded to see them off. The regiment could not march behind its own bugles because the band had been disbanded, but the Post Office Rifles supplied the music, and shortly the battalion entrained for Southampton. On arrival at the docks the troops embarked almost immediately and tried to settle down in the cramped holds and accommodation areas. The iron decks caused problems for the men in their nailed boots, but the vehicles and horses were swung on hoard without much difficulty. Companies were allocated particular areas, 'P', for example, being crammed in a hold with rudder chains clanking below and horses stamping above. Once under way the men were allowed to move about the ship. The *Chyebassa* was one of 14 transports being shepherded across by three destroyers on a calm sea and the troops disembarked at Le Havre early next morning. Those men who had not yet acquired the cynical attitude towards Army efficiency that more experienced troops adopt were soon given a further useful lesson when the iron rations were discovered to be missing their essential bully beef and biscuits. Further disillusion might have set in when, after the hard march up from the docks to the camp at Le Havre, insufficient tents had been allocated for the battalion. This meant that a proportion of the new arrivals spent their first night on French soil in the open. Wallis, who could usually to be relied upon to take a cheery view of events, remembered that despite the appalling conditions at the camp, 'The only bright spot to our gloom was that we were in France on active service, which made everyone cheerfully happy'. There were probably men in the battalion shivering in the cold of a frosty French night and listening to the traditional tales of horror told by old soldiers to newly arrived recruits, who might not have subscribed fully to Wallis's opinion.

The next day, 6 November, witnessed the invective against the British Army being turned instead upon the French and their railway system. The battalion, complete with its Transport, entrained for St Omer in the usual cattle trucks and endured the uncomfortable journey in cramped and cold conditions. Only one official halt was made, but the many unscheduled ones aroused the anger of the men who blamed the selfishness of the French for these apparently unnecessary delays. It was widely believed that priority was being given to French, rather than British troop trains.[71] Whoever or whatever was to blame for it, the delayed arrival at St Omer was probably advantageous in the long run because no-one at St Omer knew who the regiment was or where it was supposed to be billeted. Further delays thus ensued while accommodation was found. The French cavalry barracks eventually allotted for the night turned out to be 'a great deal filthier than their cattle trucks'[72] and the next day the battalion trudged to Wisques. Here the cold, wet and stiff battalion, 'many unclean of tongue and for the most part entirely Godless', entered a former Benedictine Convent. To Russell Latham this seemed 'a sad commentary on the state of affairs to which the world had drifted'.

For the next ten days the battalion was allotted to Army Troops and spent the time digging on what was known as the Blendeques - Aire Position. The accommodation in the Convent was again basic in the extreme; no fires, no water and only candles for lighting. It rained continually during these November days and because greatcoats were considered bad for discipline the men spent days and nights in sodden clothing, sweating and freezing in turn. Although they were not complete novices at roughing it, by now the men found the conditions trying. They might not have appreciated it at the time, but this period was to provide useful experience as preparation for the environment into which they were about to be thrown. Apart from digging, the men practised rapid loading and firing of the rifles which they had been issued just before embarkation. This training was carried out in both local chalk pits and inside the Convent itself. These rifles had been converted to take the new ammunition, unlike those used by the London Scottish on Messines Ridge a few days earlier, but even so problems with jamming frequently occured. Empty cases with wooden bullets painted red were used for practice, but occasionally, Williams recalled, live rounds were fired accidently and ricocheted dangerously around the walls of the Chapel.

The first two casualties occurred at Wisques - the first, a large Transport horse called the 'Pride of Hammersmith' died, and the second, a Private in 'A' Company. This unfortunate man was spiked through the foot by another's entrenching tool, an incident which prompted the observing Latham to recall that the 'strange mutterings' of the injured man 'suggested that the regiment was already acquiring a new and most sanguinary tongue'. On 13 November the Orderly Room received news that the battalion would be the next unit sent to the front area. The troops knew little of what was happening in the war, expecting that their families at home had more idea about what was going on, but the lack of information and the miserable conditions do not seem to have dampened Richard Lintott's spirits too much. He could still write home claiming he was having a 'very good time and enjoying it all immensely'. Some men could tolerate the damp and cold but were more nervous and unhappy when on guard duty in the Convent's crypt. The main part of the new Convent was still unfinished and was an extension to an existing site. The impenetrable darkness of the original crypt shrouded the coffins of numerous nuns and it was amongst these eerie shapes that the unfortunate LRB guards patrolled.

No-one appears to have appreciated this initial period of active service at Wisques. It was a period of limbo which was resented by men anxious to get on with the more serious aspects of war. Here they did not seem to be doing anything except get wetter and wetter and the training was carried out 'with nobody interested'. They wanted to move nearer the line and feel as if they were doing something useful. To add to the gloom and despondency, a runner from GHQ cheerily reported that all the Staff, including Sir John French, were betting that the war would be over by Christmas. Sergeant Dick Wallis thought this news was almost the last straw to their misery: 'Could it be possible that we were not going to see any fighting at all?...more depressed than ever, there was very little cheerfulness in the battalion'.

On 15 November, Wallis' prayers were answered. Orders were received that the regiment was to join 11 Brigade of the 4th Division and would leave Wisques the following day for Hazebrouck. The march of about 17 miles was done on *pave* in poor weather. The men, damp before the march began, were soaked by the time they reached Hazebrouck. Of more concern than the dampness of their bodies though, was the condition of their feet. Route marches around the Sussex lanes in September and

October had done little to prepare the feet for the uneven *pave* of Northern France and Belgium, and this, coupled with the fact that they were carrying full packs for the first time over any distance, caused great hardship. The Regimental History claims that no one fell out, and all then marched another 11 miles on the 17 November to billets in Bailleul.[73] The *War Diary* mentions that on arrival at Hazebrouck, 15 sick were sent to hospital at Blendeques and although these could have been suffering from a multitude of illnesses not directly connected with the march itself, what Latham described as 'many', were unfit to continue the march on Bailleul and went instead by train. This party endured the increasingly common discomforts of the French railways - managing ten miles in five hours - and on arrival at Steenwerck was confidently informed by the Rail Transport Officer that, to his certain knowledge, there was no such formation as the LRB in the British Expeditionary Force. Rumour then arrived that the rest of the battalion were at Merville, about 11 miles south-west of Bailleul. Thus the party optimistically climbed aboard a convoy of lorries containing the battalion's rations, and set off. On arrival at Merville the rumour was proved false. Feeling pretty fed up and unwanted, they returned to Steenwerck. Here they discovered that after spending two nights in Bailleul the battalion had marched eastwards to Romarin.

The final stage of this march towards the front ended in a blizzard in the village of Romarin a mile and a half west of Ploegsteert. Billets were found which gave some protection from the weather, but not all men could immediately take advantage of them. Pocock, a signaller, was detailed to keep an eye out for enemy aircraft. So, with a whistle to hand, he passed a 'cheerful hour' during which he could hardly see across the road, let alone spot an aircraft, before seeking the relative comfort of his billet. By the morning of the 20 November, the weather had cleared, the ground was hard but dry, and something of a 'picnicking air'[74] had returned to the regiment. Now it was within range of German guns, morale recovered quickly from the depression at Wisques. There was again a feeling of excitement and, according to Wallis, 'all our troubles vanished'.

It seems likely, and is certainly consistent with LRB philosophy, that the honour of being the first company to go into the trenches was decided by ballot. The regiment was still operating under the old eight company system, unlike the Regulars, to whom half companies would be attached for trench instruction. The idea was that the eight half companies would be mixed up with the Regulars, who could then allow some of their platoons to come out on rest. The two Regular battalions were the Somerset Light Infantry and the Hampshires, veterans of the Retreat from Mons, and consequently badly cut up during those early battles. They were grateful for any respite from the never-ending drudgery and boredom of trench life and proved good and willing teachers to the LRB. During the night of 20-21 November, the first men of the old 'E' and 'O' Companies moved up through Ploegsteert Wood and entered the trenches on its eastern side. If the men risked a peep above their parapets in the half light of a November morning, they could spot the German trenches about 100 yards away across the flat expanse of No Man's Land. The LRB could now really claim it had arrived at the war.

One of the earliest effects war in the front area had upon the battalion was its shedding of the old eight company system. In the Volunteer days it had been a two battalion regiment, so originally the sixteen companies were lettered A - Q. But, by the time the Territorial Force was formed numbers had dwindled to such an extent that only those companies which could muster anywhere near a reasonable figure survived. Those of the disbanded companies were then allocated to the remaining ones. Within three days of arriving at Ploegsteert, the War Office ordered that the regiment should adopt the four company system in order to fall into line with the Regular units to which it was attached. With the intention of returning to letters as soon as was considered practicable, and to avoid early confusion, the companies were designated 1 - 4. The re-organisation would make the pairing of Regular and LRB platoons easier, but the other, and perhaps the more important reason for the order, was that there were insufficient experienced officers to continue with the original system. Tradition could count for little in the exigencies of war.

When not in the trenches the reorganised battalion was allocated billets in Plugstreet (as Ploegsteert immediately became known) and at a farm 600 yards to the north known as the Report Centre. The initial period of instruction in the front line only lasted one day and the companies then took it in turns to patrol in the wood, becoming acquainted with its rides, clearings and reserve breastworks. It was during this period in reserve that the battalion suffered its first fatality, although the actual means of Private Jack Dunnett's death is not totally clear.

The most likely version is the one given in the Regimental History. This records that Dunnett, one of two brothers who enlisted in August, was killed by a shell while breakfasting.[75] Willie Fry, who is often a little vague on events of that period, thinks he was killed while on a fatigue party,[76] while Latham offers a detailed, but mis-dated, account. He explains that after No 2 Company had gone into the trenches one man was not accounted for at roll call. He was apparently later found at the side of the track where he had collapsed unnoticed with a bullet through the knee. Unable to move he died during the night from the effects of the wound or the severe frost that set in. Latham is probably confusing this incident with the death five days later of Pile. Dunnett was in 'D' Company rather than either 'E' or 'O', which later became No 2, but the strange sequel is that however he died Dunnett is the only man of the LRB killed during this time in Plugstreet to have his name inscribed on the Hyde Park Memorial to The Missing. He was presumably buried in the wood, but his grave was lost during later battles.

Dunnett's death only three days after the first companies had gone into the wood provided a talking point, a 'deep impression'[77] and a confirmation that the LRB were now actually facing direct physical danger from the enemy. Curiosity as to how he died and the circumstances of his death was inevitable within the battalion and it seems strange, in view of the care taken to ensure proper burial of later casualties, that Dunnett's death was not accompanied by a full burial service in one of the cemeteries already in use within the wood. However, it was not only the Germans who were causing problems to the newly arrived men of the LRB. As they wandered about the wood, stood to in the front trenches and began the routine of working parties, there was another danger that strove to trap the inexperienced soldiery.

The day before Dunnett was killed some LRB men had, on the orders of an officer of the Hampshires to whom they were attached, fired upon a party of 'Germans' trying to take them from the rear. The 'Germans' were in fact a fatigue party of Hampshires, one of whom was killed in the ensuing exchange. As well as the danger of being fired upon by friendly troops, the Germans were regularly shelling the wood. These shells occasionally took their toll, but the factor that was to cause the highest number of casualties to the battalion, as the initial period of frost turned to one of almost continual rain, was the condition of the trenches.

By the time the LRB arrived in the sector, the front lines had settled down. The Germans had a foothold in the eastern edge of the wood, but with most of their line stretched away across the flat fields, north towards Messines and south towards Warneton. The efficiency of the drainage ditches, although not yet totally destroyed by shellfire, was quickly affected by the extensive digging undertaken by the two sides. Furthermore, the combined problems of a very high water table and the fact that there was so little fall when baling or pumping was attempted, meant that trenches soon filled with water. The art of revetting had not yet been perfected so trench walls were continually collapsing and there was a constant battle against the rising level of water in the trench bottom. The front line was dug to a depth of only about two feet and then the walls were built up with sandbags. The reserve lines were more carefully built as the wood offered shelter to the working parties and the walls were consequently more substantial. The LRB was provided with pumps, in fact an untypically large number was provided by the Army, but there was not a great deal of expertise within the regiment on their use. They frequently broke down and on occasions suction and exhaust pipes were fitted to the wrong inlet and outlet valves. Lt Kirby, late of Eton and Magdalen and something of an 'engineer', set himself to design an efficient pump. This was subsequently manufactured in Britain and sent out to the battalion, but unfortunately proved no more successful in operation than those more conventionally acquired.[78]

The time spent in the front trenches by companies of the LRB was limited by the rota which attached them to the Regulars and by the need for their services elsewhere. After all, they had gone overseas expecting to be put onto lines of communication and it was in this task that they were primarily engaged. The regiment soon became known as the 'Fatigue Fifth' because, apart from the usual ration parties going nightly to the front line, most of the battalion were busily, but reluctantly, building breastworks and dugouts in one of the rides quickly christened Bunhill Row. Wallis had so enjoyed himself during his initial day at the front that it was to his 'great regret' that he had to return to the supports and work on the reserve line. The rain, which fell in steady downpours, did much to dampen their spirits, and again the feeling that they were not doing anything really useful reappeared. Important visitors, including Russians and Japanese, frequently arrived at the 'Tourist Line' - so called because it was a safe spot to view the British front - but enthusiasm for the construction of the reserve line was clearly lacking. Wallis insists that there were no complaints and 'every man was cheerfully miserable and glad to be there...(but) we hated Bunhill Row'.

The depression felt by some of the men was alleviated when the battalion was ordered to take over a stretch of trench and hold it on its own, rather than in conjunction with the Regulars. Spirits revived now that they realised the High Command had confidence in their ability to hold a sector of the front and companies prepared to move up and occupy what was known as East Lancs Trench. However, although morale might have improved, the weather certainly had not. No 3 Company moved into the thigh-deep water of the front trench on 10 December and, within two days and two nights, its strength had been more than decimated. The privations and hardship caused by the atrocious conditions resulted in Battalion HQ sending in another company to replace No 3 two days early. So many from No 3 had reported sick that Latham believed only some 40 were actually left to be relieved. During the month of December it seems likely that about 100 men of that one company reported sick and, those who did not, were suffering from dysentry and other debilitating illnesses. Even Wallis, who had been so elated at the news of holding their own stretch of front, thought 'nothing mattered - conditions could not get worse - we were all too wet to care.' The *War Diary* only records numbers of men wounded, not the number reporting sick, so the total figure is unknown. The various diaries and letters frequently mention the names of men in the respective sections who disappeared for a time to the Field Hospital at Steenwerck, or were invalided home. Many were to lose their feet as a consequence of frost-bite or gangrene which set in when feet had been constantly immersed in the water and mud of the trench bottom.

Given the circumstances into which these inexperienced troops had been thrown, a major concern was to try to make the conditions when out of the line as bearable as possible. These men were used to fairly comfortable lives and at least a third of them had never even attended a peacetime Territorial Camp. School OTC's and the time spent at Crowborough had helped the men to some extent, but life in Plugstreet was far removed from those experiences. The war had already introduced the men to extreme physical hardship in the wet of the trenches, and now, in mid-December, they were to undergo another new experience - the fear and excitement of a local offensive.

On 18 December Battalion HQ received orders that the regiment would be Brigade Reserve during an attack by the Regulars on the following day. The object of the attack was apparently to relieve pressure on the Russian Army by attempting to convince the Germans that the pause after the battle at Ypres was only temporary.[79] The Rifle Brigade and the East Lancs would try to force the Germans out of the trench that enfiladed 'Hants Trench', and drive on across the fields beyond. The LRB had already been engaged in making straw and wire-netting palliases which were designed to be thrown over the enemy wire. Two companies were then deployed in Bunhill Row in support, with the other two in reserve. The two Regular battalions attacked but met with little real success; the artillery bombardment was inadequate, but the real enemy was the mud. Towards the end of the day, the two LRB companies were ordered forward through the wood to take up positions in Hunter's Avenue. Originally they thought they were simply to man these breastworks in case of a German counter-attack, but then instructions arrived which ordered them to continue the attack.

While the main attack by the Regulars was going on, nerves among the LRB men were already fraying. Two of their own shells landed in the British trenches and the waiting LRB men could hear the screams and cries of the attacking troops as they struggled through the mud. Henry Williamson looked at his friend Baldwin's 'ashen face' and tried to get up. As his knees were wobbling he gave up the attempt and slumped prostrate again into the relative safety of the trench.[80] Greatcoats had been ordered to be left behind, and as they waited for four interminable hours, expecting any moment to be ordered forward, a hail storm blew up.

> *Conversation was impossible. We crouched in the mud cut off from intercourse with our fellows - isolated with our own thoughts. Thoughts are poor company on the eve of an attack, they inevitably*

lead into the most distressing channels - to vivid pictures of the future, of mangled bloody flesh - of many things worse than a quick death...Hour after hour of dreadful misery dragging slowly on until we almost longed to be moving into that bloody inferno which was already raging not 100 yards in front - anything to escape the creeping stupor of that deadly cold. (Russell Latham)

Fortunately for the LRB the order to continue the attack was cancelled, and parties were ordered to go out and collect the wounded. Latham's blood froze in his veins as he came across the mangled and bloody remains of the troops who had been caught in the shelling. Williamson's abiding memory of this aftermath was how one of the wounded sang '*Oh for the wings of a dove*' as he was carried back through the wood - the song echoed through the stillness of the trees as quiet settled again over the sector.[81]

As far as casualties were concerned, the battalion lost only one man, L/Cpl Roache,[82] but in terms of experience the attack marked a new watershed for the battalion. Death was not new to them by this time, but the numbers of casualties and the manner in which they were killed or wounded was. Until now the majority of deaths had been relatively clean ones caused by snipers' bullets. Now, as the men were clearing the trenches and fields following the attack, they were exposed for the first time on a large scale to the effects that modern weapons had upon the human body. An issue of warming rum was provided to steady their tremulous nerves and temporarily drive the chill from their bodies. Unfortunately, the rum in one jar appears to have been replaced with some sort of poisonous cleansing fluid; one man took a draught, swallowed it and, according to Henry Williamson, later died. Yet, despite the salutory nature of this first battlefield experience, Graham Williams was disappointed that the LRB were not ordered to continue the attack: 'we all wished to see (the honour of the LRB) distinguish itself, as had the London Scottish at Messines'.

For the companies doing their turn in reserve in the wood the regime was fairly relaxed. Richard Lintott, for example, frequently went out shooting and snaring rabbits. A more serious hunt rounded up five Germans who had been deliberately left in the wood after their comrades had retreated. Two were dressed in British uniforms, and three as farm labourers, but all suffered the same fate when despatched to Brigade. Williamson was detailed to go with another rifleman to act as a witness to a firing squad, although this may well have been for a British soldier rather than the captured Germans. The dugouts in Hunter's Avenue and Bunhill Row were acquiring a greater degree of sophistication and comfort - more like log cabins than dugouts - but the problem of the ever present adjacent pools of water, such as the 'Blue Lagoon', continued to ensure that the floors were always damp and coated with mud. Small flower patches, quaintly named 'Kew Gardens', and polite notices requesting walkers to 'Keep off the Grass', appeared with Spring, and the ruined farm houses which acted as billets for companies were gradually made more weather-proof. For the companies at rest in the village and for HQ details, accommodation was found in the homes of civilians who had decided that the front line was sufficiently far off to risk staying.

Relations between the Flemish-speaking civilians and their London lodgers were on the whole good - the Regimental History prints a glowing account by a Plugstreet host of her memories of the LRB.[83] But there were some, like Pocock, who thought the Belgians were a little too grasping; 'One day they had the impudence to tell us the black-buttoned soldiers were rich....It is a well known saying in our regiment about the Belgian people that; Manners - they have none and their customs are beastly'. The Belgians may have been concerned to get as much money from the soldiers as possible, but they trusted the men sufficiently to allow them to help themselves to drinks after the patron had gone to bed, confident that the saucer left on the bar for the cash would be full next morning.[84] The Signalling section stayed in the same billet long enough to be referred to by nicknames given them by their hosts; Pocock was 'le petit', Chappell 'le grand', Nicholson 'le gros', Kelsey 'le petit gros blonde' and Corporal Smith 'le vieux corporal'. The civilians were willing to prepare and cook meals for the men when they came out on rest, and the warmth of their kitchens and fires were of course a welcome change from the ice and wet of the trenches. Important and useful as these relationships were to the 'Saturday afternoon soldiers', it was the one which developed between them and the Regulars of 11 Brigade that was to give them the greatest satisfaction and enjoyment.

In the pre-war days, the LRB rarely had anything to do with regiments except other Territorial ones. The occasional weekend musketry shoots at Winchester had however meant some contact with the parent regiment, and it is clear that there was considerable satisfaction in being brigaded with the Rifle Brigade's 1st Battalion in Plugstreet.[85] The men of the Regular battalions and the LRB came from very different backgrounds and experience and there had been some concern within the War Office as to how the Territorials would adapt to the conditions of active service. After the war Sir John French wrote that while the Territorials fought with great gallantry during the heat of battle, once they had been withdrawn from the excitement and danger, 'a severe reaction came upon them. The heavy losses amongst their friends and comrades bowed them down with grief; for they necessarily lacked, as yet the professional training and stoicism of men whose real business is war'.[86] French was referring to the London Scottish after their defence of Messines Ridge, but the same could apply to virtually any Territorial or New Army battalion, the LRB included. The press had also concluded that the TF would find the transition to war more difficult than the more common type of army recruit because '...being more educated than the average 'Tommy' (he) finds himself cursed with a vivid realization of horrors, present and potential resulting from his more highly developed powers of imagination'.[87]

The loss of friends with whom they had worked and enlisted was bound to affect the men in these early days of the war and the Regulars of 11 Brigade appear to have appreciated this fact by not expecting too much from their new comrades-in-arms. The LRB were viewed as somewhat eccentric by the Regulars, initially because so many of the clerks wore glasses. This certainly aroused much amusement and mickey-taking, but later, when the regimental subscriptions were collected, the Regulars were downright amazed. This collection, Harding remembered, 'raised ribald laughter from the Somersets who had already found us rather comic, and could not believe that anyone could be insane enough to pay a subscription for the privilege of being stuck in the mud there'.

Strange as the subscription appeared to the Regulars, they were very pleased to see the Territorials arrive and 'seemed to be filled with admiration of the fact that we had voluntarily undertaken to be trained as soldiers during peacetime...they always went

out of their way to do anything they could for the 'London R.B.' as they called us'.[88]
Pocock too remembered that the Rifle Brigade and the Somersets were very friendly 'and
proud of us also because we had volunteered to go out and had come up to relieve them
last November when they were worn out...They respected us and would do anything for
us'. By the same token, the LRB were proud to have been put into such a famous
brigade as the 11th;

> *It has always been a source of pride to me to have served and fought*
> *as a private soldier with the old pre-1914 Regular Army...It was an*
> *education and a delight to a youth of 17 to serve in the trenches and in*
> *action with these men, real soldiers, and I used to listen spellbound to*
> *their tales and conversations...masters in the art of scrounging and*
> *could always supplement their rations somehow.*[89]

But not all the old soldiers were as welcoming to the newcomers as were the
majority: Latham first encountered his new tutor in a muddy dugout where the old
warrior had been peacefully sleeping.   On introducing himself the eager youth
discovered that the Somerset, with obvious and undisguised disapproval, regarded him
simply as 'one of those bleeding Territorials' they were expecting, and went back to
sleep.

The difference in the social class between the Regulars and the LRB was
obvious for all to see. So too was their standard of behaviour which, as would be
expected, was more 'rough and ready'.[90]   Many of the Regulars were Reservists who
had joined their battalions during or after the Retreat and, although possibly long out of
the army, had not lost their old army habits of scrounging and stoically making the most
of whatever conditions prevailed. To them lice were a fact of life, an inevitable aspect
of life in the trenches and all part of 'the game'. To the LRB, on the other hand, 'such a
state of affairs appeared as a reproach, a thing to be limited as far as possible and
referred to only in hushed whispers'.[91] Similarly, other habits of the Regulars did not
fit with what the LRB would consider to quite be the way to carry on. For example, it
was alleged that rather than be performed under the supervision of an NCO, the relief of
sentries was left to the men themselves. As only one of the Somersets at one particular
post possessed a watch, he could call his relief half an hour early and get away with it.
What Latham considered to be an apparent 'lack of discipline' was also demonstrated
when the Regulars allegedly left their posts and disappeared into the wood to brew up -
something which seemed so unmilitary that the conscientious new arrivals would not
dared to have done.

The picture of the old Regular Army instructing and fighting side by side with
the 'Saturday afternoon soldiers' was too good to be wasted for the Home Front's
propaganda machine.   Newspapers looked for stories that would demonstrate the
cooperation and respect between the old and the new armies and in January 1915 the
Weekly Journal carried one relevant to our story. The account was apparently given to
the paper by a Lance-Corporal of the Royal Engineers home on sick leave. It was later
spotted by Jack Chappell's brother in paper used to wrap up some clothes sent home by
Jack for washing. Chappell's cousins, the Latham brothers, were among a party sent out
to dig snipers' posts in advance of the line when they came under fire from both

directions. After lying flat for some time, and expecting a German attack to develop, Russell shouted to his brother Bryan; 'Latham, Latham, have you any chocolate?' This *sang froid* so impressed the RE that he concluded the account by stating; 'After that the Terriers rose highly in our estimation and we realised that, whatever the youngsters lacked in experience, they made up for in true British pluck'.

The impact of war upon the LRB during its early months did of course manifest itself in many strange forms - whether mental, moral or physical - but one of the strangest was the truce that took place between elements of the opposing armies during Christmas 1914. The event produced such a remarkable reaction amongst the participants, and was well-documented at the time, that an account of the incident provides an interesting insight into how the men of the LRB viewed the war and their enemy.

The *War Diary*'s entry for Christmas Day 1914 gives no clue to the peculiar events of the day; 'Weather was freezing. Very quiet day with practically no shelling'. In fact no mention of the incident appeared until 2 January 1915 when an order was received from Second Army that the 'informal truce' with the enemy was to cease and any officer or NCO found having anything to do on a friendly basis with the enemy would face Court Martial. This implies that the Staff had, if only tacitly, allowed it to continue for at least 8 days. The length of time that the truce did actually last in the Plugstreet sector is open to some dispute, but the fact repeatedly comes through in the memoirs that the men in the front area thought the incident had been given official sanction.

The sources agree that the initial stages of the truce began with the Germans erecting Christmas trees on their parapets and asking the troops opposite to exchange songs during the night of 24-25 December. Firing had certainly taken place during Christmas Eve because young Bassingham, the singer of *'Friend of Mine'* during the heady days of September, was sniped and killed. As night fell, a German band, which Pocock thought 'seemed to require new instruments and a good deal of practice', struck up. During evening 'stand to' Wallis believes that the Germans called over and asked if the British would stop firing on Christmas Day. The request was, according to Wallis, passed back to GHQ and sanction was apparently given.

After swopping several songs, the men settled to sleep and the remainder of the night passed quietly. On Christmas morning parties of troops began emerging cautiously from their respective trenches. Which side appeared to make the first move is not clear, but Willie Fry thinks that it was begun by a corporal in the East Lancashires who was 'outstanding in a reckless (machine gun) crew and egged on by his companions, climbed up on the front parapet'.[92] Once the initial contact had been made, the LRB and their German counterparts began heading across No Man's Land. Goode and Panton, both peacetime medical students at the London Hospital, somehow acquired a half a bottle of rum and took it with them as a present.[93] Soon, the area between the trenches took on the appearance of a 'football pitch at half-time', and Latham even talks of a spontaneous, albeit 'disorderly football match', using a dead rabbit as the 'ball' taking place. The fraternization that followed is well known and was reported back to England in the letters of the participants. Many of their parents sent the letters to their local newspapers, and although the following appeared in the *Manchester Guardian*, it is typical of the genre:

We had a splendid day yesterday under the circumstances. Our chaps were in the trenches, but some understanding was arrived at with the Germans and not a shot was fired, and the Germans came out of their trenches and we came out too, and met them halfway, and exchanged souvenirs and chatted, some of them knowing our lingo and some of us knowing theirs. They weren't half a bad lot really. You should never think we were flying at one another's throats a few hours previously. [94]

Wallis thought that the truce had not originated among the front line troops, but most of the accounts agree with Lydall and the Signaller Pocock; '...the truce was arranged verbally and unofficially between the various regiments then occupying the Front Line on either side...It was agreed that neither side should shoot during Christmas week...these revelries more or less continued until the New Year when hostilities recommenced'.

The troops, like Wallis, believed that once the truce had started, High Command was prepared to allow it to continue and even, from at least Brigade level, actually seem to have encouraged it. The opportunity was taken by both sides to collect and bury the dead who had lain out in No Man's Land since the attack of 19 December. 2Lt Johnston, who had spent some time training as a parson, recited a passage from the burial service over what some remember as a mass Anglo-German grave, while another source records that the dead were carried back to their respective lines. [95] Captain Bates, commanding No 4 Company, wrote to his sister that he had been ordered not to fire unless the Germans did, [96] but Fry remembers that there was a great deal of apprehension during the day in case the artillery had not heard that a truce was in operation. [97] He is mistaken, though, by stating that when Corble was shot in the head and killed during the afternoon the truce was brought to an abrupt end; Corble was not in fact shot until either 4 or 5 January.

There is as much confusion over when the truce actually ended as there is over how it originally began. Henry Williamson thought it lasted four days, during which time the LRB frequently came out of the wood, waved and wandered over to the German lines for a chat. [98] Some reports have it lasting less than that and cite as evidence the message received from the Germans by the officer in Hants Trench at 08.03 hours on 27 December:

Gentlemen. Our automatic rifle has been ordered from the Colonel to begin the fire again at midnight. We take it honour to award you of this fact'. [99]

The Regimental History gives the date of this message as New Year's Eve rather than the 27th and it is clear that the truce did last into the New Year. No 3 Company went into the line again on 27 December and 'for three more days a sort of truce existed. Although strongly denounced by HQ conversations were carried on at night between listening patrols who met in No Man's Land and exchanged newspapers'. [100] Whether the 'HQ' referred to was Battalion, Brigade or Division is not clear but incidents occurred during New Year's Day which appear to have again had the tacit approval of Brigade: 'A very drunken German was extricated from our wire. We relieved him of some cigars and sent him down to Brigade as a prisoner. Brigade returned him with thanks as they wanted the 'Peace' to continue until some important defensive work on the edge of the wood was completed. The German was taken to the edge of the British wire and dispatched across No Man's Land.[101]

Early on New Year's Day, Pte Brewster was apparently lolling casually and contentedly around on the fire-step. With head and shoulders above the parapet, he was more concerned with his breakfast bacon sizzling over the fire than with his safety. Suddenly, with a scream of 'I'm dying' and blood trickling from his throat, he collapsed into the trench. His comrades feared the worst but upon investigation the wound was found to be only superficial. 'Upon being told sternly not to be an ... idiot he at once seized his bacon, still happily intact, and ate with a relish which did credit to a dying man. No further firing occured so we charitably gave our friend the enemy, the benefit of a considerable doubt.'[102]

That same night a wiring party of the LRB out in No Man's Land reputedly ran out of wire, whereupon an obliging German threw over one of his reels so that the job could be finished. The German then announced that his unit, a Saxon Regiment, was being relieved in three days by the Prussians and as far as he was concerned the LRB could 'give them hell...So for yet three more days the unofficial armistice went on, an occasional rifle being fired in the air as a matter of form'.[103] The *War Diary* records two men being wounded on 2 January with the 'usual sniping and intermittent shelling', but there were certainly no deaths until that of Corble.

Neither the *War Diary* nor any other account mentions any disciplinary action or rebukes handed down following the truce. Fry put this down to the sheer number being involved as it could have been difficult to justify punishment to a few for the actions of many.[104] By the same token, punishment, in theory, would have to have been meted out to the several officers who had taken part in the fraternisation, and that would have proved embarrassing. To officers and men of the LRB the truce symbolised the attitude they held towards the war and the Germans. Wallis regarded it 'very much as a sporting fight...with no bad feeling on either side'. That did not mean, of course, that their determination to win was not assured. The atmosphere of holiday excitement still prevailed despite their introduction to trench warfare, and by indulging in a truce during the season of goodwill the LRB were merely continuing the long tradition of cease-fires between enemies during religious festivals. Such a sporting thing as conversing and shaking hands with your foe appealed to the sense of fair play and gentlemanly behaviour with which the officers had been inculcated at the better known public schools, and which the other ranks had also acquired at their less famous ones. Although Wallis, ever the correct soldier, might partly condemn the affair as an episode not to be especially proud of, even he could excuse it on the grounds that it gave them the opportunity to bury the dead. To most of the men though, it probably just seemed the natural thing to do.[105]

Once the festivities had ended, the business of trying to make life bearable in the trenches and killing the enemy recommenced. The official order of priorities was: construction of fire positions, wire etc., the safety of the garrison, and lastly, comfort of the garrison. Two new machine gun posts were in the course of construction during January and February, but both positions lay empty for some time awaiting the guns.

To try to ensure continuity in the defensive work, which was difficult when companies were only in the front positions for three days, three permanent parties were detailed for the tasks of wiring, woodwork for revetting, building etc., and pumping. Wiring had been generally done on dark nights and was not really a job that anyone fancied.[106] Three volunteers were asked for to go out every night, or four out of five, under LCpl H. Smith. In return for undertaking this task the men were excused all normal trench tours - an offer that Maurice Howard found difficult to resist . After Smith had been wounded, the party came under the command of John Stransom, who was later commissioned into the regiment and continued to serve in it during the post-war period. Although a hazardous job, particularly as the wooden posts were hammered into the ground rather than screwed as was later the case, Howard and his friend Atkins preferred it to 'swimming around in the trenches. Really we had an easy time until we moved up the line into the Salient'.

January 1915 was particularly stormy and wet. The previously small River Warnave, which ran through the LRB lines, flooded, and the trenches swam with about three feet of water. Often the wind would drop, the temperature fall and the ground freeze - then the boots froze, and the tails of the greatcoats which had been hacked off when weighed down with mud were missed. Goatskin jackets were issued which although warm gave no protection to the legs and feet. The toll of those contracting frostbite rose, and then in February cases of cerebro-spinal meningitis and scarlet fever begin to appear in the *War Diary*. At least three men of those who were sent away to No 10 Stationary Hospital died from the former disease and there is also a report of typhus in the battalion during February which necessitated the innoculation of every man.

The Germans too were doing their best to add to the casualty list.[107] The shelling and sniping were not as effective in reducing the men in the front line as were disease and the elements, but the number of dead continued to rise. The four loopholes in the LRB trench were precisely registered by the Germans and if a cap was held over the 3" aperture, it was drilled instantly. One man was reported to have been so concerned not to expose himself at the loophole, while taking a shot at the Germans, that he pulled the trigger before the muzzle was fully through the opening - the bullet struck the steel plate, ricocheted back and killed the man.[108] When the battalion tried to inflict casualties upon the Germans, the options were not as extensive as those enjoyed by the enemy. The British artillery was usually quiet owing to shell shortages, so the LRB turned its attention to improvisation. Perhaps not surprisingly, being a battalion of unskilled men, their efforts in the field of weapon technology, like that of drainage techniques, do not appear to have been too successful. 2Lt Cartwright remembered several futile attempts at home-made bombs - their only apparent success being to wound several men during demonstrations. Peter Titley appears to have been the regimental enthusiast, devising a catapult made from two growing saplings. Unfortunately, he contrived to wound himself whilst in the act of firing. No-one seems to remember any of the bombs ever being used against the Germans.[109]

Another form of warfare of which the LRB had had no previous experience was the ancient art of mining. Summer camps and lectures at Bunhill Row had not broached the subject, but the battalion were to come across this insidious and nerve-wracking mode of fighting in the Plugstreet sector.

Mining was the natural and inevitable consequence of the stalemate attained on the Western Front at the close of 1914. Both sides were exhausted but wanted to keep pressure on their opponents by small scale offensive action by exploding mines under strong points to score local successes. Occupying a trench, below which the enemy was thought to be mining, was a particularly hazardous and anxious job. Not surprisingly the troops hoped they would be relieved before the mine blew, but the incoming relief then had to endure the same worries until its tour was completed. To hear rumours that your unit was not again to go into the line where a mine was known to be and then to be told that instead of rest, another tour was imminent and, furthermore, that the RE were convinced that the Germans had finished digging and were set to fire, was a severe blow to morale. This happened to No 3 Company at the end of January 1915. Fortunately for them, their three day tour eventually passed without the expected happening, and in the event that 'mine' appears never to have been blown.

One author has written that by the end of 1914 men of the LRB were immersing an ear into the icy-water of a petrol can sunk into the trench bottom in an attempt to detect German mining.[110] One of the Wray brothers confirmed the use of this technique but does not remember hearing anything more sinister than the curses of men detailed to relieve him. Bryan Latham was convinced that mining never took place at all,[111] but Captain Burnell recalls some very noisy sappers, one of whom shouted 'Bill is down the shaft' loudly enough for the nearby Germans to hear. Whether this alerted the Germans, or whether the RE simply did not like digging in water Burnell did not know, although the British digging did cease for a while.[112] No German mine was ever actually exploded near the LRB and the only other contact the battalion had with this method of war was towards the end of their period in the wood. A shaft was dug from the corner of Somerset Trench - Bugginsville Shaft towards the German strong point known as the Birdcage. R.H. Stonnill heard Welsh voices and a lot of splashing about down in the bowels of the earth but the mine was not blown until after the LRB had left and gone north.[113]

The combination of increasingly sophisticated means of killing each other and the treacherous weather conditions could have resulted in a decline of battalion morale. Memory can exclude the nasty and uncomfortable experiences and dwell only on the better and happier times but it is remarkable that none of the extant sources ever really record the writer's genuine discomfort at having found himself thigh deep in clinging mud or consistently dodging German snipers and shells. It could be expected that letters home to parents would paint a hearty and rosy picture of things with the intention of making it appear all was well, and perhaps when in later years the men were committing their memoirs to paper they were equally selective in including only the more pleasant aspects. Whatever the reason, the surviving image is certainly one of high morale and contentment.[114]

When Wallis went on leave at the end of December he found the people at home 'refused to believe that we were enjoying ourselves more than we had ever done in the pre-war days...and it was often a matter of wonder to us why every man in England was not clamouring to get out to our wonderful war in Belgium'. Maurice Howard claims that he 'enjoyed every minute of it' and Richard Lintott recorded in his diary; 'Getting very fat with this luxurious living'. Even Jim Whitehead, who was a little more hard to please thought the advanced billets were 'very comfortable' and Gadsdon 'enjoyed this arboreous stay immensely'.[115]   Undoubtedly one reason why the men did enjoy themselves was the entertainment and meals they arranged for themselves when out of the line.   When enduring the atrocious conditions in the trenches, the abundance of parcels from home made the feasts and concerts something to look forward to.   Not surprisingly, a great deal of effort was put into their organisation.   No 4 Company's New Year's Eve concert was complete with a professionally printed programme and an avalanche of parcels supplementing the rations.   Christmas had produced a similar benevolence from home when the battalion's mail amounted to 88 mailbags.   This had taken the Divisional postal authorities by surprise and had necessitated special transport arrangements.   11 Brigade's Post Office always claimed that the LRB's mail was double that of the other four battalions put together.[116]

The parcels received contained such comforts as handkerchiefs, cigarettes, writing pads, socks, etc.   Victor Hember was so overwhelmed with his six parcels, which all arrived in one batch just after Christmas, that he became fed up with a glut of chocolate.   He requested instead that future parcels should contain fruits such as figs and raisins, a packet of salt and pepper and a box of wax Vestas.   One platoon, at least, had received parcels from the people they had been billeted with at East Grinstead, and each man in the battalion received a Christmas letter from young girls aged between eight and ten years addressed to 'our brave soldiers'.[117]   The Regular battalions of the brigade did not do nearly so well as the LRB, presumably because their dependents at home were financially less able to dispatch luxuries in such quantity.   The LRB then took great pleasure in giving many of their extra rations to their less fortunate comrades.   This did much to make the battalion feel part of the brigade and further helped to cement the friendly relations between the Regulars and the Territorials.   The number and regularity of the parcels arriving, although gratefully accepted by the Regulars, was always a source of wonder and envy to them; and the key to this bounty remained for a time a closely guarded secret.

The brainwave was supposed to have come upon a man as he peered across the cold expanse of No Man's Land one chilly night.   Knowing that some newspapers distributed cigarettes to the troops on behalf of their readers and printed the names and addresses of the donors, the LRB man collected the names for some weeks and sent off letters to them 'professing an almost pathetic gratitude for the few cigarettes... all were steeped with heartfelt thanks at having found a friend in an otherwise friendless world'.   All were signed 'No. 4697, A Lonely Soldier', who then sat back and waited for the civilians to send another few tins.   The scheme later widened by the inclusion of the original man's section.   They put it on a more commercial basis by devising a scheme of equivalents - the length and detail of the 'Thank you' letter to the donor depended on how big the parcel had been.[118]

The contents of the parcels were stuffed into sandbags and pockets for consumption when in the line, left in billets for their return or taken as snacks when on bathing parade or as tit-bits when attending a Divisional Concert.   The 4th Division's Concert Party -'Follies' - was one of the first such groups and employed two local girls nicknamed Glycerine and Vaseline.   These girls spoke no English, loved exposing their legs to the delight of the audience, and recited in charming innocence such ditties as, *'I'm feeling cold and rather funky / It's enough to freeze a brazen monkey'*.[119]   Apart from this somewhat less than intellectual entertainment, there were trips to the cinema in Armentières. In March Victor Hember complained to his clubmates;

> *I really think that someone ought to write to the RSPCA on our behalf. Here we are, over a hundred terriers who haven't seen a decent girl since leaving old England at the beginning of November, having to watch charming girls not quite out of their teens, falling in love and being loved, cuddled and kissed. It was absolute cruelty to animals. In fact it made us all dreadfully homesick.*

Homesickness does appear from time to time, for example, in the letters of Jim Whitehead: on one occasion while looking at a photograph he 'thought I was at the Club'; and on another, 'life is becoming a little monotonous...let us hope it is for not much longer, though it does seem four months since we came out here'. In the same way as complaints about the physical conditions have not survived, complaints about mental strains are also rarely mentioned. This can be ascribed to the morale of the battalion which continued to remain sound, and, although there were grouses about it at the time, one of the essential conditions for high morale is pride in a man's own appearance. Despite the appalling difficulties in trying to maintain some sort of cleanliness in the mud of "Plugstreet", the battalion made the attempt of keeping up its pre-war reputation for smartness.

Once a system had begun to operate, company bathing parades were held about every twelve days. Normally the men enjoyed the opportunity to clean up, either in Armentières or once in the brewery just south of Ploegsteert - the owner complained about the unusual use of his brewing vats and the exercise was not repeated.[120] The men were not as perturbed as the owner because, 'being neither a Regular battalion nor the unhappy Earl of Clarence we had no regrets that the vats were not being used for their legitimate purpose'.[121] Their only drawback was the depth as it meant that two rather undersized privates had to cling to the sides rather than splash around with the gay abandon of their comrades.

Other occasions were not so carefree and happy. One day in February a general and the press came to inspect how the bathing system operated. This entailed keeping 70 men hanging around in shirts and underwear until the visitors had paid their cursory visit. An understandably bitter Victor Hember complained; 'It was annoying to us, wasting our spare time in this fashion'. Another general, watching weary and mud-splattered LRB companies coming out of the line, decided they were not clean enough and reported his disgust to Battalion HQ. The order came down that when they came out of the trenches 'we should, the next day, thoroughly clean every bit of dirt off our clothes'.[122] The idea was that when out of the trenches they should look as though they had never been in, unlike the Honourable Artillery Company who 'hadn't, but always tried to appear as though they had'.[123]

Compared with their Regular comrades, the LRB considered themselves to be positively clean. Members regularly sent washing home and frequently received new items of underclothing from parents and families. Sgt Arthur Feast, a member since the Volunteer days, had received such a parcel from his home in Purley the day before No 11 Platoon paraded for a bath in Armentières. Not wishing to lose the brand new pair of underclothes just put on, he refused to hand them over at the baths; Army regulations demanded that each soldier must hand over a set, so Feast was given half an hour to 'make arrangements'. He went into town and on return handed over a parcel of frilly lady's underwear - honour was satisfied on all sides.[124]

Strange and new as all these experiences were to the LRB, the Regimental History records that the men settled down 'extraordinarily quickly'[125] to their changed situation and circumstances. However, as the winter and the Germans took their toll of the men, new faces began to appear. The battalion was beginning to undergo its first transition, but one that was not to alter its character to any significant degree. The drafts arriving were all from the 2nd Battalion; some men who had re-enlisted on the outbreak of war, and the many other eager young clerks and teachers who had responded to the hoardings, rallies and recruiting posters appearing all over London. Now, after having trained and acquired the rudimentaries of soldiering, they were being shipped out to replace those who had returned home with frostbite or wounds and the growing number who would never return.

Apart from the 58 largely ex-Territorials who had joined the 1st Battalion before it left for France, the 2nd Battalion was to furnish 464 men to its parent unit while it was in the Plugstreet sector. The largest draft, of about 200, left Haywards Heath in January and after four days at Base Camp in Rouen, the bulk joined the battalion on 1 February 1915. The men had been asked to volunteer for foreign service as there was still no compulsion for Territorials to serve overseas, and it appears that there was no difficulty in finding sufficient men to do so. The eight companies of the 2nd Battalion provided about 25 men apiece and the two young friends, Aubrey Smith and Claude Vallentine-Warne were among the 23 from 'Q' Company. Jack Terry was all set to go with 'A' Company but was forced to withdraw two days before the departure with severe dental problems. He was to remain in England until 2nd Battalion went out as a complete unit in January 1917. The two teachers from Bowes Park School, Kerry and Robinson of 'H' Company, joined the Ebbett twins, along with the bookseller Heavingham and the five men from Parr's Bank on the draft. Linzell, from Finchley, and Victor Hember's friend, Eyres, volunteered to go, along with Fulkes (who would soon have three stripes on his sleeve) and the young Charles Hudson, who had given up a scholarship at the Technical Institute to enlist. L.A. Bleaden, who had brothers in the Royal Fusiliers and the HAC, went from 'D' Company along with Charles Bradford. Bradford was to die in 1916 shortly before he was due to take a commission. The Valentine brothers who, like so many of the volunteers, had attended the Merchant Taylors' School, and the Vernon brothers, who would both be wounded by the same shell in May, also left their safe billets in Haywards Heath for the unknown discomfort of active service.

By the time the last of the several drafts had arrived at 1st Battalion in early April 1915, the *Chyebassa* men had dwindled to about half their original number. The Colonel, Earl Cairns, the Second in Command, Lt Col Matthey, and Major King were all invalided home between January and March. Capt Bates was promoted to Major and took command of the battalion. Cairns, as was the usual tradition, had been a Regular, and although not a figure well-known to the other ranks had provided them with a figure-head who appeared to know what he was doing; Latham 'knew him vaguely as the old man, the omnipotent one, who lived quite comfortably somewhere in the rear'.

From a memorable incident one night when he attempted to inspect the wire in front of the trenches with the aid of an electric torch, the men decided he was not lacking in courage, but perhaps just a little in circumspection.[126]

Of the other *Chyebassa* officers, Lt Slessor, the Intelligence Officer who had joined the LRB Cadets in 1885 and rejoined in August, was invalided home in December. Captain Cholmeley, late of Eton and Magdalen, followed him in February. Lt Kirby, the Oxford blue and 'engineer', was sniped in the head in December and would eventually die of its effects in 1917; 2Lts Kitching and the 'quiet but not over efficient'[127] Fursdon of 'P' Company returned home in February and March respectively; 2Lt Wilfred Willett, the medical student who had run foul of his family by secretly getting married just before the war, was blinded while trying to pull a wounded man to safety in December.[128]

Three officers were killed during this period: 2Lt Kenneth Forbes, of Winchester College and Amersham, was killed in February and Lt Gerard Morrison in March. Morrison had attended Harrow before reading law at Magdalen and his death was keenly felt in the battalion. Writing home Whitehead said; 'We were terribly cut up about it...He was a Britisher through and through, the most popular officer in the regiment...and was loved by us all'. The third officer to die was one of four men promoted from the ranks in February to replace some of the casualties. Two of these men were long serving members, Wallis and Cotter, both colour-sergeants in November 1914. Cotter, a member of the Brighton March team was killed just before the battalion left for Ypres. Although only joining the LRB in August after having served in the King Edward's Horse for many years, Reginald Russell was an obvious choice to become Transport Officer. The last of the four was typical of the sort of man the LRB were to promote either from the ranks of the serving or the Reserve battalions as the war continued. Rupert Flindt from Tulse Hill had enlisted after leaving Christ's Hospital and its OTC in 1911. He had then involved himself thoroughly in the activities of the regiment - marathon team, shooting team etc. - before opting for foreign service with his brother and sailing on the *Chyebassa*. Young, intelligent, sporting and enthusiastic men like Flindt were to leave for commissions in increasing numbers once the battalion had been withdrawn from the Salient in May 1915.

During this same early introduction to war, 51 other ranks were killed or died of wounds and disease. Of these, 12 were men who had originally enlisted in the 2nd Battalion but who were then drafted to the 1st Battalion between January and March. Two of the 51 died at home, three have no known grave and eight died in the hospitals of the rear areas. The remainder are scattered in the four cemeteries either inside or on the edges of Plugstreet Wood, with the majority, 21, lying in the LRB Cemetery just south of the village.

The earliest burials in the cemetery took place in December 1914 and the first LRB men were interred in January. Corble, the first post-truce fatality, was the initial LRB burial, followed shortly by Tommy Sanders from Palmer's Green. Sanders, of 11 Platoon, had been pumping in the trench when, in a moment of forgetfulness, he straightened his back at a point where the parapet was low; a sniper's bullet pushed one of his lungs through the gaping hole in his back. His body was taken back through the wood to the cemetery and his puttees arranged beneath his body to allow him to be lowered into the grave. He was left outside on the ground during the freezing night and by the time of the ceremony next morning, 3 inches of half-frozen water lay in the bottom of the grave.[129] Later in the month one of the three Daniel brothers, all of whom had enlisted in August and sailed on the *Chyebassa*, was buried. So too was Herbage, the friend of Pocock the signaller. Peppiatt, one of the Brighton marchers and marathon team and an employee of the LNWR, succumbed to wounds in early February and was buried in the regimental plot, and one of the few non-Londoners, Pike from Bradford, followed shortly afterwards.

Deep inside the wood other LRB men were buried in Rifle House Cemetery even after interments in the LRB Cemetery had commenced. Sgt Peddel, another of the Brighton March Team who had served since 1909, was sniped and killed just before he was about to take a commission in the Rangers, and the elder of the two Powis brothers, both of whom were to die before the Battle of Ypres had ended, was buried at the end of March. The earliest deaths were buried in Lancashire Cottage Cemetery, just to the south of the wood. Five LRB men lie in there, including 34 year old Sgt Evan Warner from Waddon. Warner had been in the Brighton March and his two younger brothers were both later to become officers in the LRB.

If a man was wounded and evacuated his first stop was usually Bailleul. Bevan, formerly of St Paul's School, Hammersmith, combined his pre-war membership of the regiment with that of a medical student at the Charing Cross Hospital. He was shot on 10 December and died in Bailleul two days later. Another man to die of wounds in Bailleul was 22 year old Eric Bradley from Worcester. He was well known in the regiment for always appearing with his uniform clean and boots polished and he attracted a good deal of comment for using his scanty rest periods and valuable water supply to keep his teeth sparkling white for what he called the 'good times after the war'.[130] Further afield, the young Bugler Ethelbert Garton was one of those to die of meningitis in St Omer, and another soldier from the old Volunteer days and peacetime member of the Regimental Entertainment Committee, Corporal Harry Petty, died of sickness at the Territorial Base Camp in Rouen.

On 11 April 1915, Battalion HQ received news that in six days time the regiment was to be relieved. The order was 'secret' but came as no surprise to the battalion as the news had been public property the day before in Plugstreet.[131] The days of floundering around in the mud of the wood, of showing foreign dignitaries the sights of the reserve lines, of giving initial trench instruction to Canadian and British Territorial soldiers, were drawing to a close.[132] The battalion's introduction to warfare had been muddy rather than bloody - the largest number of deaths on any one day being two - but huge numbers of men had disappeared home and new ones appeared to replace them. Even so, when the companies were relieved by the 7th Worcesters on the night of 16-17 April and marched back to billets in Steenwerck, the LRB was still the LRB. It is a bit of an exaggeration to say, as Williams does, that almost everyone knew one another, but undoubtedly the character and *esprit* of the regiment was unchanged. There was some regret at leaving the Plugstreet sector for, despite the discomforts, the stay had been an enjoyable and valuable experience. Furthermore, although unknown at the time the regiment was never again to be 'quite so closely integrated with any place as we had been with Plugstreet, or to have quite the same relationship with the inhabitants'.[133] The news that they were to be relieved had also coincided with the appearance of spring in the wood. The mating songs of thrush and blackbirds and the growing warmth of the sun were invigorating tonics to the shredded nerves and weary bodies of the men. Fresh optimism over their future appeared, 'and we felt that come what may we could face the worst with a light heart'. The new arrivals from the 2nd Battalion had refilled the ranks but, although the regiment itself had not changed in character, the war had. The hiatus which followed the First Battle of Ypres had allowed both sides to draw a little breath; the pause was now over. The battalion was about to be thrown into the fiery cauldron that was known simply as The Salient.

CHAPTER IV

Into The Fiery Furnace

All I can say is that, if hell is a worse inferno than that which the LRB was in, then it would pay one to be righteous (L/Cpl LRB)[134]

The relief of being withdrawn from the front zone, coupled with the promise of a reasonably extended period of rest, transformed the physical appearance and general atmosphere of the battalion. The haggard, unshaven faces, bearing lines of stress and fatigue, seemed to fill out and the dulled, hollowed eyes that had witnessed death and mutilation of friends once more regained their former sparkle and life. Those five days at Steenwerck gave the men the opportunity to reach a state of cleanliness long forgotten both in themselves and their increasingly scruffy and improvised uniforms. There were some schemes for company training, but the atmosphere was again more one of a holiday camp with a fair degree of general relaxation of discipline. However, it was apparent that trouble was brewing further to the north. The evening sky was often lit by the glow of fires and the swelling roll of gunfire in the daylight hours continued into the those of darkness. The men began to wonder and speculate whether the developing battle to the east of Ypres would involve the LRB or whether they would be sent to the rear areas for lines of communication duties. As the days passed, rumours swept the battalion of new and more terrible weapons of war. Wounded passing through Steenwerck spoke of the Germans using gas to break the line before infantry attacks. The increasing activity in their own area and on the roads soon convinced the LRB that before long they would be swept up into the maelstrom that was gathering momentum to the north. The boys of the LRB were thus determined to make the most of their apparently limited stay in Steenwerck.

The battalion's fears were soon realised. Following an inspection by Lt Gen Pulteney, Commander of III Corps, on 23 April, the battalion set off on a route march. Shortly after their departure a messenger arrived bringing orders instructing the regiment to 'Prepare to move at short notice'. Subsequent orders to be ready to move at three hours and then two hours notice arrived, and then on 24 April the battalion was instructed to entrain at Steenwerck for Poperinghe. The infantry of 11 Brigade collected their equipment and piled themselves into the cramped railway trucks. Although speculation was rife, there was for the time being some mystery as to their destination:

> *We didn't really know where we were being sent, but the general rumour was that we were being rushed up into the line to block a gap left by the Canadian Jocks. We'd heard that the Germans were using gas and we of course hadn't been issued with any sort of mask, so you can imagine we were feeling a little nervous.* (M. Howard)

Initially the train headed away from the front, but at Hazebrouck it turned north-east and soon 'Ypres' was on everybody's lips. The train crawled past carriages packed with frightened refugees heading in the opposite direction and it was clear that ambulance traffic on the roads alongside the tracks was heavy. Gunfire could be heard to the east as the LRB pulled into Poperinghe and began its short march to Busseboom. Here it was joined by the Transport which had travelled by road and, on being informed that the regiment was Army Reserve, was allocated billets in the farms of the village.

The following day, 25 April, the battalion tramped another three miles to the north-east and occupied a large former hop store on the main Ypres-Poperinghe road at the western end of Vlamertinghe village. Although the march distance was short, progress was slow; rows of picketed and saddled cavalry horses, constant convoys of supply and ammunition limbers rumbling eastwards on the uneven *pave* and ambulances carrying the wounded away to the rear hampered and delayed the march. When it arrived at the hop store the battalion was told it was no longer merely a Reserve unit, but had now come under the orders of V Corps. It did not matter a great deal to the men which Corps they actually belonged to as it was becoming obvious that all available troops were being rushed into the line to stem the German offensive. Meanwhile all they could do was sit, wait and observe. Men played brag to while away the time, endlessly cleaned their rifles and sorted out their equipment. They had been ordered to dispose of any surplus kit, so many of the souvenirs collected during the Plugstreet days were dumped with the Transport. Among the items deposited were cameras which, although officially forbidden, appear to have been 'fairly general' in the battalion.[135] Victor Hember unknowingly took what was to be his last shave for ten days, men wrote letters home and in melancholy mood Russell Latham spent much of the time watching the walking wounded, 'red-eyed and so utterly weary that they seemed to move automatically rather than through any conscious effort of their own'. Transport wagons and ambulances rolled past the billet, and 'for the first time', he decided, 'I knew real fear, the fear which produces a void at the pit of one's stomach'.

Other men watching the stream pass realised that among the bleeding and bandaged men were others who appeared to have no wounds upon them. Dressings lay across their faces but apart from mud their uniforms were unstained. As they were jolted along they let out rasping coughs and strange gurgles came from their throats; eyes streamed and were many shades of red. The men of 11 Brigade knew that these were the victims of the gas attacks that had been rumoured and they also knew that here they were, only a short march from the front, and still without any form of preventive measure.

At 18.15 hours, with the Hampshires in the van and the LRB bringing up the rear, 11 Brigade moved off. The march towards the front figures largely in the recollections of the men - more so in some than the subsequent fighting. The Regimental History describes it as 'very trying',[136] but to one man at least, the former NCO and recently commissioned 2Lt Wallis, the march was an uplifting experience. He records that the column soon began to sing all the old songs: 'We were all in high spirits and it's doubtful if any peacetime march have ever had such universal singing'. Whitehead, though, was clearly not feeling as content as his company commander and wrote that the 'merriment was only skin deep; our thoughts were of our home and friends'.

Apart from the disquieting knowledge that they were undoubtedly heading towards the fighting, the men were further hampered by being weighed down with extra ammunition. The night was fine but very dark, 'which made the hundreds of flashes and flares from all sides of the Salient more vivid than ever amid the deafening roar of guns and of the distant outbursts of rifle and machine-gun fire'.[137] When the column arrived on the outskirts of Ypres it was clear that it could not pass through the centre as the Germans were dropping huge shells, four at a time, onto the market square. The brigade swung to the north of the city passing the dead end of the Yser Canal at what was supposed to be the double. The ruined cloth hall and cathedral were silhouetted against the light from the raging fires behind. The destruction of the houses and streets and the streams of wounded witnessed on the way up made even the usually optimistic Wallis realise 'very fully that we were in for some bitter fighting'.

The column marched on along the shelled roads towards the small hamlet of St Jean. The troops had actually left Vlamertinghe in such a hurry that many had not filled their water bottles but Canadian soldiers obliged them as the column halted for a time in front of their medical post. Halts were frequent because the roads were choked with ammunition limbers, ration carts and pack horses. Hember surveyed the scene glowing in the light of numerous fires and later wrote: 'In parts the smell was terrible...It is impossible for anyone to understand the awfulness of an absolutely ruined village. The tremendous holes in the road, ruins, dead horses and perhaps dead bodies...I for one was feeling rather anxious'.

The hamlet of St Jean comprised a handful of houses and a church straddling a minor crossroads. Traffic and infantry were converging from four directions so targets for the German guns were easy to find. 'The whole village became a veritable inferno of earsplitting crashes and blinding sheets of red flame. From overhead rained wicked lumps of jagged iron'.[138] The church was burning fiercely, the road pitted with gaping shell holes and all around lay the putrifying carcasses of dead cattle. The men sheltered and cowered in what cover they could find and, above the scream of high explosive and the crash of burning timbers, the men realised that gas shells were also pouring into the shattered village. Eyes began to smart and men doubled up with wretching coughs; harrassed orderlies passed among the wounded trying to administer what aid they could while, incessantly, shells rained down blowing men and horses over with the force and blast of their explosions. Latham suddenly went 'cold with horror for the air seemed filled with piercing shrieks of anguish' as a huge shell screamed into another battalion in the column behind the LRB. Men picked themselves up again and wondered if he alone 'would be the one to rise'.[139]

The object of this short but tumultuous stay in St Jean was to collect entrenching tools from the Transport limbers. One wagon had been ditched on the way up which left No 3 Company very short of the implements. Once the remaining ones had been issued, the column moved forward again: 'On and on, apparently never coming to the end of this nightmare march'.[140] The battalion was making for another small hamlet, Fortuin, on the St Julien road. Amazingly, in view of the shell fire descending upon St Jean, the battalion appears so far to have taken no casualties but once it reached Wieltje, where again the devastation was almost complete, men began to receive wounds. Alan Taylor was hit in the groin and was helped down to the dressing station by his brother Fred. Taylor survived but Neville Wright, who took a piece of shrapnel through both eyes, would later die in hospital. 'Still', Howard recalled, 'that blistering march continued on':

> *Here again more shells bursting on either side of the road show up in*
> *their blinding flashes the forms of marching men so that for an instant*
> *every detail of their equipment stands out clearly against the flame,*
> *and they appear to be marching literally, as indeed they are*
> *metaphorically into an inferno. Heedless of this the companies hurry*
> *up the slope to where a grove of poplars lining the road marks the*
> *hamlet of Fortuin...hurriedly taking up a line along hedges just behind*
> *the crest of the ridge, digging in feverishly began. Crouching behind*
> *their meagre parapets, the men await expectantly the renewed fighting*
> *of the coming day.* (A. Pumphrey)

The parapets were indeed meagre. By dawn they had managed to hack through the roots of hedges and dig away the heavy wet earth to a depth of about two feet. Packs were placed above the shallow trench but, as the position had only recently been vacated by a field gun battery, the Germans continued to fire at it. Pocock, worn out by the march and nervous excitement, had been astonished at the reserves of energy he uncovered when it was 'a question of do or die'. Jim Whitehead was feeling the strain and confided that 'we were all fed up and looked very miserable'. Dawn was approaching as the men put down their entrenching tools, picked up their rifles and peered out of their hastily improvised trenches. Bryan Latham recalled: 'I think every man knew that when daybreak came we were for it, and therefore had no particular wish to hurry even that objectionable night to close before its time'.[141]

When the first streaks of dawn lightened the eastern sky on the morning of 26 April, the battalion stood to arms, but with little real idea of where it was or what or who lay in front. Captain Husey and Lt Johnson had set off ahead of the battalion from Vlamertinghe in an attempt to ascertain the situation at the front but had returned from their reconnaissance with little information as to whether the LRB were in the first or second line. Initially, given the protection offered by the hedge, the troops had imagined themselves 'pretty secure from observation' and could move around a little without immediately coming under fire. However, a German aeroplane soon discovered that the former gun site was now occupied by infantry and, as the trench had been dug straight, it soon came under both enfilade and frontal fire.

The shelling continued throughout the morning and casualties began to mount. Around noon Battalion HQ was ordered by Brigade to send a company to close a gap that was reported to exist between the left of the Hampshires and the right of the Somersets. Major Burnell undertook a reconnaissance but failed to find the left of the Hampshires. He reported that, as the area through which the company would have to pass was being heavily shelled and appeared to be under direct enemy observation, if the task was done in daylight casualties were bound to be heavy. Brigade sanctioned delay of the move until nightfall, but then ordered that the entire battalion, rather than just one company, should go.

Unfortunately, Brigade was unable to tell the battalion where the gap that the regiment had heen ordered to plug actually was. Despite the confusion, the order to move from their cramped trench was certainly received with some relief by the men who 'were all heartily glad'.[142] They had been subjected to shelling and machine gun fire and had seen the cottage housing the battalion's ammunition and spares for the machine gun blown sky high by a German shell. However, the relief at being ordered out of the enfiladed trench was soon tempered when it became obvious that no-one knew exactly where they were meant to be going. A gunner officer gave them some vague directions and information about a mixed detachment of several regiments further over to the right, and of the Rifle Brigade which was supposed to be on their left. Eventually, and really because it could find no-where else to go as dawn approached, the battalion began to dig in to the north of the small track leading from the Zonnebeke-Kansas Cross road near Hill 37. To Williams, 'It seemed that we must have spent most of the night marching aimlessly about in the neighbourhood of Zonnebeke. At one point we came upon two British 18-pounders pointing in different directions!'

It was a clear night and as the men began digging shells began to fall around them. Fortunately, the trench was dug with good traverses and went to a depth of 4' 6". However, as dawn broke, it was discovered that as it had been dug across a field of flowering mustard, the parapet was beautifully defined by the brilliance of the surrounding yellow flowers. The day itself was another fine, clear one and the new trench attracted a good share of German artillery fire. The men could do nothing but cower in the bottom and try to take what cover it afforded: 'The two days spent there were very uncomfortable, there not being room for everybody to lie down so we had to sit squashed up and keep smiling'.[143] The battalion suffered a severe blow to its morale later that day when it became known that RSM Harrington, of Ladysmith fame, had been killed in St Jean. To compound the general depression, the following day again saw the men subjected to continuous shell fire from the north, north-east, north-west and south-east. In his memoirs Aubrey Smith wrote:

> There is no need to recount in detail all the horrors and discomforts of the three days spent in that enfiladed trench shelled intermittently and unable to strike back, we lay at the mercy of the German guns on the Gravenstafl ridge. Of the enemy we saw nothing...At last on the night of 29 April, after some 170 casualties...we were ordered to quit the trench...and move to the St Julien front, where we should indeed see something of the enemy.[144]

Lancelot Jessop also remarked at the frustration of having to endure the bombardment without even yet having set eyes on a German. Russell Latham recalled 'such continuous and ferocious bombardments as we were suffering were in themselves sufficiently demoralising. They were made more so by the fact that we had not even the satisfaction of feeling that the Hun in the opposite trenches was sharing a similar fate'. The British guns were so short of shells that what few existed were kept in reserve for use against infantry attacks rather than counter-battery work.

The trenches occupied by the battalion were on the forward slope of the ridge and, even without the clarity offered by the mustard, provided easy targets for the German gunners. During the evening of 29 April - another beautiful, although hectic, day - the battalion was ordered to move down the slope about half a mile and take over some trenches currently held by another Territorial unit, the 4th Yorkshire. The relief of this bewildered and demoralised unit was conducted after dark and, despite several hitches and problems, particularly with the state of the trench, by dawn the line held by 11 Brigade was again continuous. The LRB extended and improved some of the trenches which lay a few yards to the north of the Fortuin-Kansas Cross road, roughly opposite the cottage named Hindu Cot. The sluggish Hanebeke ran parallel to the lines approximately 500 yards in front. The British trenches could be brought under enfilade fire from the east by the German guns on the Gravenstafl ridge and by direct frontal fire from those on the continuation of the ridge to the north. The battalion was to remain in these trenches undergoing infantry attacks and intense shellfire for the next four violent days.

Apart from doing what they could to improve the cover, the men could do little except take the punishment. Victor Hember in his usual cheery way talks of them being 'tickled up every day with a few shells of a fairly small variety' but did not think too many actually landed in the trench. The casualty figures seem to bear this out for, apart from those dying from wounds in the rear areas, there appear to have been no actual deaths recorded for 29 and 30 April. The *War Diary* gives 15 wounded on 29th and only one other rank the following day. However, although walking wounded were able to get away, owing to the shelling it was more difficult for those more severely wounded to be evacuated; some of these men were to die of their wounds while still in the trenches during the activity of the following day. As May Day approached and around them the ground heaved and swelled from the shellfire, many examples of courage and stoical endurance were witnessed:

> *Within a few yards of me was Pte...perhaps the bravest man I ever saw. With both legs pulped to a bleeding scarlet mess, with one arm gone and without the slightest hope, yet he retained his faculties clearly and exhorted to courage a companion wimpering from a slight flesh wound which would take him to England and comfort.* (R. Latham)

The fact that they had not yet seen the enemy, but had only been on the receiving end of his shells, was one reason why the men were experiencing some degree of demoralization. Morale seems to have been fairly low as even the news that they might have to mount an attack did not bring the 'sinking feeling common to such occasions'.[145]   They had suffered the extreme discomforts of virtually continuous gunfire and machine gun bullets but had not had the opportunity or satisfaction of returning fire.   They were repeatedly warned to keep a sharp look-out for any signs of an infantry advance, especially when the shellfire intensified, and indeed several began to welcome the prospect.   Others, like Russell Latham, decided they did not care whether they went forward or back, just so long as they could escape from the 'soul destroying inertia'.   Latham's request was soon to be answered but Richard Lintott was a little more concerned at what the future might bring: 'There is a lot of heavy fighting going on...and we are having our full share and I think we have more to come.   I am sorry my commission has not come through yet because I should like to get home to see you all again'.   Sgt Rolfe, a long-serving member who had rejoined in September, handed two postcards to Jim Whitehead - one addressed to his mother and one to his fiancee - with instructions to post them if anything should prevent his reclaiming them.

May Day passed with little activity.   Men continued digging and improving the trenches and Battalion HQ received instruction on the procedure to be followed if a withdrawal from the present positions was ordered.   According to the *War Diary*, the total number of casualties to date was 33 killed or died of wounds and 124 wounded. This represented almost one man in five of the approximately 800 who marched into the Salient, but the losses had not been spread evenly between the four companies.   For example, No 15 Platoon had sustained several direct hits and lost accordingly, whereas No 11 Platoon had suffered hardly at all.   Similarly, the Signalling Section was still virtually in one piece with, so far, only Cooper, a lone victim of a whizz-bang, having been killed.   Pocock, Chappell, Kelsey, Lewis and Pigden were told off to establish a telephone station in the trench occupied by No 4 Company.   Later, a listening patrol was sent out in advance of the line and reported that the Germans were digging in around a nearby cottage - the battalion machine gun went up and drove them off.   In the main trenches, as darkness fell, the men prepared to get what rest they could.   Sentries peered into the gloom of the night and the mist rising from the Hanebeke through increasingly bleary eyes.   Every half an hour or so a salvo of shells would come across from the German lines to hurl shrapnel and high explosives upon the dozing troops.   Exhausted, uncomfortable and nervous, the LRB, with their old comrades from the Somersets on their right and the 1st Royal Irish Fusiliers of 10 Brigade on their left, slept fitfully through the night that would herald the most dramatic and testing day yet in its history.

Early next morning the men were issued with a primitive form of gas mask which had come up with the rations during the night.   The mask consisted of what they were told was a pad of chemically treated gauze with tapes attached at the corners.   The troops were advised that in the event of a gas attack they should urinate on the pad but were warned that it would not be proof against a prolonged dose of noxious fumes.[146] The battalion was stirred into activity during the morning to fire ten rapid rounds vaguely in the direction of the Germans to support an attack by the French, which never took place.   Then, at 17.00, Germans could be seen massing in preparation for an attack on the other side of the Hanebeke valley.   'Stand to' was called and 20 minutes later, during a ferocious bombardment of shrapnel and high explosive, gas was seen to be drifting from the German trenches opposite the two left companies of the LRB and the Royal Irish further over to the west:

*I put on my mask but still got a whiff of it which immediately affected
my lungs. My eyes started running and everyone was coughing and it
seemed impossible to breathe through the mask. I think some of the
boys tore them off but after a few minutes I found I could breathe a
little easier and I saw that almost everyone was manning the parapet
and looking to their front.* (M. Howard)

When recounting the events of the attack to his club friends Hember, probably
in deference to his female readers, claimed that they wetted the gauze with water from
their bottles, and believed that only one man was actually overcome by the chlorine.
Whitehead, too, wrote that only two men, both of whom had already been wounded,
died from its effects. Although the gas itself had cleared within 15 minutes, the men
were still suffering from its effects, as well as enduring the continuing bombardment,
when the German infantry attacked. The enemy deployed south of Winnipeg crossroads
and advanced at the double. The two left companies of the LRB, Numbers 3 and 4, who
had suffered most from the gas, had their field of fire obscured by a hedge. The two
right companies, however, could bring rapid fire down upon the approaching masses of
enemy infantry. This was the opportunity for which the men had been waiting, and the
chance to utilize efficiently all those hours of rifle practice put in during drill evenings at
Bunhill Row and after. The infantry had little support from the artillery, 'perhaps one
battery which did its best', but '[we]...simply blazed away, emptying our magazines and
reloading as we had so often practised...It was most exhilarating and we thoroughly
enjoyed ourselves while it lasted feeling that, at last, we were getting some of our own
back for all the discomfort we had recently been put to!' [147] Further over to the left, No
3 Company waited until the Germans were clear of the hedge and opened up at 50 yards,
'...with a venom, which only the enemy's inhuman use of gas could have engendered we
loosed off with a withering hail of lead. So sudden and unexpected a shock produced
the utmost confusion and we laughed hysterically as the survivors stumbled and cursed
over the corpses of their comrades in a frantic effort to return to safety'.[148]

The infantry attack had lasted fewer than forty minutes but the casualties among
the LRB had been sufficient for two attached platoons of the 4th Yorkshire to be ordered
up to the front. Sniping continued while some of the wounded were being evacuated and
while rations and supplies were brought up. Owing to the exhausted condition of the
men and the lingering effects of the gas, 70 men of the East Lancs under the command
of the LRB's Captain Somers-Smith were prevailed upon to bring up 35 boxes of small
arms ammunition and then take their place in the support trench. Wallis thought their
arrival a tonic to his tired troops as they told the LRB that, 'everything was merry and
bright - that we were well on the way to Berlin etc. etc.' and happily helped their former
Plugstreet comrades in the evacuation and treatment of the wounded. Hember, in the
badly mauled No 4 Company, was also glad to see them: 'You may be sure by this time
we were all pretty tired having during the week that passed been marching and digging
every night. It was a relief to our minds when reinforcements came into the trench'.

The arrival of darkness brought no real respite from activity. Wiring parties
from each company went out although in places the Germans were only 50 yards
away.[149] Those in the trenches wearily began to rebuild the collapsed walls, cleaned
their rifles and sorted their equipment while gulping what rations they could. This was

the eighth successive night of virtually no sleep and the fourth on which digging had to be done. A flurry of excitement occurred around midnight when the smallest man in the battalion, Pte Hovil, brought in two weeping and equally small 'Prussians' as the regiment's first prisoners. The story went around that when the two had been surprised and captured one threw down his rifle, emptied his ammunition pouches, chucked down his knife and shouted, 'Comrade. Shoot nicht!'. The events of the day had clearly had their effect on the enemy's side too.[150]

To balance against the capture of the Germans, four LRB men had in turn been taken prisoner. The listening patrol sent out the night before to the vicinity of the ruined cottage in advance of the lines had stayed out during the day and nothing had been heard from them since. Corporals Jasrowski and Cannell went out to look for them but returned with the news that there was no sign of them. Jim Whitehead along with Spicer, Barnett and another man, who suffered from the LRB characteristic of poor eyesight, were sent out to the cottage as replacements. Unfortunately, the fourth member had lost his spectacles and, as he could scarcely see, spent much of the journey tripping over obstacles. At the ruin, not surprisingly, he proved totally useless as an observer. The patrol could, however, hear the Germans digging furiously. As the British artillery was incapable of doing anything to interrupt their progress, by dawn of 3 May the enemy had advanced their line to within 200 yards of the British trenches.

If any accurate maps actually existed at Brigade HQ, they should have noted that the LRB was the battalion holding the front trench. In reality, however, the 'LRB' was by now something of a hybrid unit. The four companies of the battalion had been augmented by two companies from each of the 4th Yorkshire and 2nd East Lancs. This combination of Territorials and Regulars continued to hold the line under intermittent shelling and sniping during the course of the day, but their ordeal was, for the time being, approaching an end. Orders arrived that all wounded were to be evacuated, all dead to be buried and any surplus equipment that could not be carried away should be disposed of. Casualties continued to occur during the day but the confidence inspired by the previous day's action had restored morale and done much to arouse a fierce pride in what the battalion had achieved: 'We knew we had done well, but how well only gradually became apparent as the fighting eased off'.[151] 'Everybody seemed anxious [for another German attack to develop] as we felt we should be meeting them on equal terms and would teach them a jolly good lesson'.[152] However, a withdrawal, through a new and already defended line, began after midnight. The LRB seem to have been able to get all their wounded away. This was not the case, according to a disquieted Whitehead, in all regiments: 'Some left 50 and one left 80. It seemed dreadful that these poor fellows should have to be left behind'. The *Official History* points out the difficulty faced by the operation. Although 11 Brigade was in 'such close contact with the enemy that in places the opposing sides were within a few feet, they were able to draw off under cover of darkness and the whole retirement was carried out as planned and without a hitch, favoured by the usual ground mist '.[153]

Despite the hazards of the night withdrawal - the difficulties of disengaging, the noise created by the troops overcoming fallen trees and other obstacles - the evacuation was conducted without suffering any further casualties. Whether the order that all spare ammunition and spares should be carried away was obeyed is questioned by one survivor, as is the following account from Graham Williams who claimed that the battalion marched back in fours through Wieltje:

> *Some of the 11 Brigade were there and said, 'Blimey. It's the London RB's and they're marching in step!' Then they cheered us. The cheers did not embarrass us...for we were proud that the LRB - Saturday Afternoon soldiers - were marching in step as a battalion, - or what was left of one, - when other troops, Regulars at that, were not'.*

Maurice Howard, although in a different company than Williams, scoffed at this idea:

> *Marching in step? What an imagination he must have. We were so bloody weary (I'm not sure we didn't even chuck our arms away). Can you imagine coming out after ten days like that, falling in, and in step? They'd be bloody glad to get us moving.*

Whatever the degree of march discipline, the load was lightened as they left what extras were being carried at the canal bank. It was here, Whitehead later recalled, that they began to realise how badly the battalion had been smashed up. When moving off again progress was quicker and the column began to sing - albeit in a 'half-hearted manner'. The weary battalion presented a very sorry picture as it headed towards the rear; soaked through and through, unshaven, unwashed for ten days, faces haggard from want of sleep, but 'on we went, not knowing whither'.[154] Spirits rose not only because they were marching in the opposite direction to the guns, but also when the familiar figure of 'Tootsie' Hands surrounded by the company cookers came into view. Tea and skilly - the first hot food they had eaten for nine days - worked wonders, and appreciation reached new heights when, rather than detail parties of exhausted men to do the job, the cooks themselves began to clean the dixies. But sleep and rest was not yet quite at hand. The battalion was ordered to move from Elverdinghe Chateau wood to another wood: 'We were told, or at least rumour said that it wasn't far. But by jingo we all felt that tramp'.[155] Another survivor remembered, 'it was rough work and most of us were done by the time it ended which spoke badly for our physical condition'.[156] On arrival at their new destination bivvies were erected or dug and roll call taken; the losses since marching up from Vlamertinghe seven days earlier were recorded as 16 officers and 392 other ranks - i.e. almost one in two men had already been killed or wounded.

The full impact of their losses would take some time to sink in, but a preliminary jolt came with the arrival of the mail. Although the horse lines themselves and the routes up from them were being heavily shelled, the Transport had managed to get rations and supplies up to pre-arranged dumps every night during the battle. Now in the shelter of the wood, one Transport wagon was needed to convey the mail bags of each company. Hember's company alone received 16 mail bags, but of course many parcels were for men who could never claim them. Although ravenous, it was impossible for the men to consume all the food from home. It was, therefore, agreed that each company should share out its parcels with a battalion of the brigade. The Regulars, whose families were probably less able to despatch such luxuries, were very appreciative, and the gesture once again endeared the LRB to their professional comrades - in the same way as the identical act had done in the Plugstreet days. That relationship, forged in quieter days, continued during these more violent ones and remained a source of great satisfaction to the LRB. During the first night in the Salient, Pocock had spoken to a man in the Somersets and asked him where the East Lancs were. The Somerset replied, 'We could very well do without them, and the Hants as well...the LRB, RBs and Sets were as good as any other four regiments put together'. Pocock appreciated these sentiments and welcomed the obvious respect shown by the Regulars. In return he later recalled; 'we were proud to be included in such a famous Brigade as the 11th'. Similarly, after hearing some Regulars ask, 'Who have we on our right?' - 'LRB' - 'Thank God for that', Hember wrote, 'We are all great pals'. Whitehead thought that because the regiment had acquitted itself so well alongside the Regular units, the already friendly relations had 'been doubled since the last affair'.

The immediate consequences of the battle were there for all to see. The companies had been savagely struck and many platoons were down to single figures. In Victor Hember's section there was only himself and his sergeant; Wallis's 'D' Company had only 29 of the 180 that had entrained at Steenwerck, and another had gone in 170 strong and marched out with 42. Only Dicky Richardson and Jim Whitehead were left of their section and overall numbers were reduced further as men who had survived the fighting reported sick. In No 3 Company at least eight men went off to hospital with bad feet or shattered nerves. These were the fortunate ones. Smith recalled that they had to be very ill to get sent down the line. The majority merely seem to have been given pills for their various ailments, and were then sent back to duty.[157] Rumours began to circulate that a draft of about 140 men would soon arrive from 2nd Battalion. On hearing the rumour, Sgt Denny explained in a letter to the Depot that he could do with the entire draft for his company as that would just about bring it back up to strength. Denny thought that of the 108 members of the old 'Q' Company, which had landed in France six months earlier, only 15 now remained with the battalion. The situation with regard to bringing the officers up to strength was, however, more easily rectified. Six direct commissions were granted and one of the newly-commissioned Curley Boston's first tasks was to inspect his platoon's rifle. The unit consisted of himself, Sgt Bull, one lance-corporal and one rifleman. The four commanders gave the lone man's rifle a particularly throrough inspection. It was, however, all to no avail because after the parade the man promptly reported sick.[158]

The battalion was subjected to the usual round of 'Thanks Parades'[159] from a brigadier who 'hoped he would be able to get us into a charge that we might take our revenge' - a sentiment not particularly welcomed by Jim Whitehead. These parades were probably not met with the same cynicism as would greet them in later years, but spirits certainly did rise when Major Bates, the CO, told them that whatever happened to the rest of the brigade, the LRB would not be going back to the trenches for at least four days. 'This cheered us up somewhat as the woods were pleasant and comfy..This pastoral life appealed to our fancies immensely but alas! was too good to last'.[160]

At 23.00 hours on 8 May a Captain Charles from 4th Division's Staff brought orders that the battalion was to be at the chateau in Vlamertinghe by 06.00 the following morning. It was known that the Regulars in the brigade had received drafts and the worst was feared for the LRB; 'The men sighed, said nothing, but their faces told their own tale. We had not recovered from our last dose and the thought of another so soon tickled our interiors'.[161]   However, on arrival at Vlamertinghe, it was announced they were being put to work digging in the chateau grounds and the canal bank. This was undoubtedly a better alternative than going straight back into the line, nevertheless, once they began the tasks, the battalion made the unhappy discovery that those on the canal bank still came under some shell fire. Although the efforts of the cooks in ensuring that hot food was available in the evening were again appreciated by the men, 'we weren't half getting fed up..and hope every day for relief of a real kind'.[162]

The relief was about to happen, but not the sort for which the men had been hoping. During its stay in Vlamertinghe the battalion had been issued with the new experimental gas masks comprising a flannel hood with two mica eye-holes. Also, a few men who had been only slightly wounded during the earlier engagement filtered back which increased battalion strength to about 300. The men were warned on the night of 11 May that they were to relieve another regiment in the front line trenches and the move forward took place during the evening of 12 May. The troops were detailed to carry all equipment, including tools, to the front where it would be split by companies into several positions.

As the men once more marched towards the front, a keen observer might have noticed that leading some of the platoons were men with familiar faces but wearing unfamiliar and unconventional uniforms.   Maurice Wray, one of the newly commissioned former NCOs, had managed to 'win' a khaki shirt, collar, tie, turned the top of his tunic in and used ink to put on two shoulder stars and to cover the marks of the removed sleeve chevrons.[163] Wallis, on the other hand, having been commissioned from the ranks earlier in the year, had acquired a more suitable uniform as befitted a company commander. Marching happily at the head of his company, he noted that the shelling had eased a little, and 'We were all feeling very happy and had a cheery advance'. Many of the men tramping behind him might have disagreed with Wallis's sentiment but they were probably as confident trailing in his wake as they would have been in that of any, more experienced, officer. Wallis was the ideal man to have around in a crisis. Although not as approachable as his friend Husey, and something of a martinet, which probably befitted his many years as an NCO, he was not without a sense of humour. He had proved his worth earlier in the battle by going amongst his platoon looking cheerful and joking with the men.   He gave the impression of being imperturbable and, according to Williams, had done much during the fierce engagement of 2 May to keep up the spirits of the men.

Brigade had ordered the LRB to relieve a battalion of Dublin Fusiliers in the front trenches with a minimum of 150 men. Nos 1 and 2 Companies were detailed to take on this task while No 3 was to occupy three defended posts east of Wieltje village. No 4 was to remain with HQ near Essex Farm (Wieltje Farm on later maps) half a mile behind the front. The strength of the battalion was near 290 when it moved into position and this time the infantry were told they could expect a little more help from the artillery.   The supply of shells had improved only marginally and certainly not sufficiently for Arthur Feast to overcome his natural cynicism. When a British field gun fired four shells, the first they had seen, Feast affected a slight stutter and exclaimed, 'I s..see the p..parcel p..ost has been delivered to the Gunners - we ought to see ours tonight'. Although Feast might not have been over-impressed, Hember was: 'Unlike the previous time we had plenty of guns to reply this time and they did. Between the two of them there was a hell of a row. We felt anything but happy lying at the bottom of the trench while the ground simply shook...Next morning it rained and we wondered what kind of day it would bring'.

Belonging to No 4 Company, Victor Hember was one of the more fortunate members of the battalion lying in trenches near HQ. The two companies detailed to go up to the front line had been forced to undertake a more exposed and perilous journey as the trenches lay just beyond the crest of a slight hill on which Shell Trap Farm was sited. The safest way to execute the relief was to travel by means of a ditch beside the Wieltje-St Julien road. Once having left the shelter of the ditch, the men then had to cross the skyline, silhouetted against the burning city of Ypres, before descending. The crest and slope over which the men had to double was continually swept by high explosive and machine gun fire. When they finally reached the trench, the men found it a shambles. It was so shallow and collapsed that it could not take even the reduced numbers of five platoons. (Three platoons of No 2 company had remained further back near the village). Under constant, harrassing fire, those in the front trench commenced to make the attempt to improve it as best they could.

At 04.00 on 13 May the shelling increased to become a systematic bombardment along the front and support lines. Communications were soon cut and intelligence depended upon the ability and courage of the runners to cross the shelled zones. One message carried from Brigade to Essex Farm instructed that the village of Wieltje should be held at all costs, and further advised that two companies of the 1st King's Own Royal Lancs were in support at La Brique. Twenty-two minutes later at 07.20 Brigade ordered that the reserve company, No 4, was to be sent up to the front as close support. Accordingly, the remaining three platoons of No 2 and all but 20 men of No 4 were despatched forward. The platoons went over the crest in artillery formation and suffered few casualties - unlike a battalion of Regulars who had advanced in extended order. The LRB was now, however, fully committed to the battle and with only a handful of men alongside the HQ details as reserve, Bates requested that the two companies of the King's Own be sent up to Essex Farm.

Shortly after the message was sent 30 men of No 2 Company returned from the front. They explained that the trenches were so congested and flattened that there was no room for them to shelter. Unfortunately, it was too late to recall the remainder of the company as well as the men of No 4, who had also just been ordered forward. Consequently, on arrival at the front many of the latter's men were forced to endure the incessant shell fire and drenching rain, sheltering in shell holes immediately behind what remained of the demolished trench. Despite the intense shelling and its exposed position, the LRB officer commanding the trench, Captain Somers-Smith, believed that they could hold on and a message was sent down accordingly. His confidence and the tenacity of his men were of crucial importance to the entire front. It soon became apparent that the Germans were about to launch an infantry attack. With the two companies of the King's Own having since been sent elsewhere there were no reserves behind the LRB. One of the battalion's machine guns, under the command of 2Lt Gooding, was positioned to cover the road down which the attack was expected to develop; but this was soon knocked out by enemy shelling. This meant that an undefended gap of about 30 yards existed between the right of the company just to the north of the Wieltje-St Julien road and a small party of nine men on the southern side under the command of L/Sgt Belcher.

Aware of the danger posed by this gap, Battalion HQ ordered that the other machine gun be sent up. The crew, crawling and scrambling across the shell-torn fields, dragged their gun and ammunition and managed to close the hole temporarily. Once it began to fire, the gun immediately attracted German shelling:

> *At one stage there was a cry for Stretcher Bearers and I went with three others, keeping way down in the trench and crawling along till we came across Machine Gun Sgt Birt who'd been badly hit. We couldn't move him for some time but when the shelling eased off a bit we got him out of the trench and down to the dressing station.* (M. Howard)

Whether the Germans fully realised the danger this uncovered section of road presented to the British is not known, but for the time being attention shifted to the left flank of 11 Brigade near Shell Trap Farm. Further over, the 2nd Essex suffered heavily as they re-took the farm, and when the Germans counter-attacked against the Hampshires and Somersets they were held up by wire. The British, rejoicing at the enemy's misfortune, were then reputed to have 'stood up and dared them to come on'.[164] Thwarted once more, the Germans again began searching for any gap in the British line. One such hole appeared to be developing between the right of the LRB and the left flank of 2nd Cavalry Brigade. The cavalrymen had been under heavy and constant shell fire and those who remained alive were grouped in shell holes rather than linked trenches. During the course of the bombardment some of the men climbed from their improvised shelters and began to withdraw. Drily noting the retirement, the LRB *War Diary* reports that these men were 'prevailed upon to return'. This somewhat succinct account loses some of the colour provided by a man nearer the event:

> *I couldn't see a great deal myself because I was still looking after Sgt Birt and there was so much smoke and some trees in the way, but a man further over to my right told me afterwards that he had seen Captain Husey scrambling between the shell bursts waving his revolver at the bewildered cavalrymen. Of course we couldn't hear what he was saying but it was probably something polite like, 'Get back into those trenches or else'.* (M. Howard)

The nearest LRB men to the scene was L/Sgt Belcher's party. This small group was protecting both the right flank of the LRB and that of the entire 4th Division. Smoke and trees obscured the view to the front and south but it became clear that German infantry was trying to penetrate between Belcher's group and the remnants of the cavalry brigade. Belcher, an unassuming furniture salesman from the Waring and Gillow store in Surbiton, and his men kept up a constant fire upon the approaching Germans. They were helped by Powell and another man crouching in an isolated shellhole just to the north of the road. These soldiers collected rifles from wounded men and kept them firing, hoping to convince the enemy that there were at least eight men in the hole.[165] The ruse worked and the German attack melted away. Belcher and the others had maintained such a continuous and rapid volume of fire that the Germans must have believed the line was still held in strength. For taking the lead in preventing what might have become a decisive enemy break-through, Belcher became the first non-commissioned man in the Territorial Force to receive the Victoria Cross.[166]

On Powell's left, towards the centre of the LRB, the shelling continued to take its toll. Jim Whitehead had received a shrapnel wound in the head at the commencement of the bombardment. Once attended to he helped to clean and reload his comrades' rifles until he was buried by a collapsing traverse. On being dug out he suffered contusions and lay helpless in the trench for most of the day. When the German infantry attack had been repulsed he and three other wounded sought permission to attempt to reach the dressing station. Intending to use a hedge which ran at right angles from the trench as cover, Whitehead's group was reluctantly given permission and the party set off. Crawling and scrambling as they helped each other, they managed to reach the safety of dead ground. The following morning Whitehead was being treated in a Bailleul dressing station and the day after he was comfortably ensconced in a hospital on the coast - his part in the battle over.

A few hundred yards to the rear of where Whitehead had been wounded, Victor Hember and about 20 men had lain as reserve all day in a trench near Battalion HQ. Things had been relatively quiet for this detachment - so much so that several men had even tried milking a herd of cows that had wandered innocently towards the battle. Wallis, their company commander, had gone up to the front line with the rest of the company and had kept up the spirits of his men by joking that he would rather swop places with a well-known attendant at the Holborn Baths than experience another bombardment of such ferocity.[167] However, by dusk the shelling and fighting were easing off and the LRB, to its surprise and delight, was relieved by the King's Own. The battalion of 20 officers and 218 other ranks moved back to the divisional support line and took what shelter and rest they could in a newly dug trench. 14 May was a quiet day with only one death - that of the long-serving Sgt Marshall. Rain continued to fall in torrents and, to sap their diminishing morale even further, the survivors discovered that their packs, containing the remains of the parcels from home, had been rifled.

An extremely wet, hungry and weary battalion moved further back to the second support line near Irish Farm the following day. Although they could not yet be certain of their future, the men began to speculate upon whether their part in the battle was coming to an end. Gunfire at the front continued to be heavy but with battalion strength at an all-time low many questioned what further use they could be in their present state. Expectations rose when the battalion was sent further to the rear to provide working parties. Although a great deal safer than working near the front, these fatigue parties were not without incident. Maurice Wray, still sporting his improvised officer's uniform, paraded to command a mixed group of LRB and Northumberland Fusiliers. Carrying a somewhat unconventional 'fowling piece', he attempted to give an order to one of the Fusiliers. The bewildered fusilier looked at him quizzically and asked him if he knew 'who the b.... h... he was talking to'. Later in the day, Wray did not have any more success with an extremely doubtful sergeant-major of the Rifle Brigade to whom the party was delivering ammunition.[168]

Finally, on 19 May orders arrived that the battalion was to be withdrawn from 4th Division and was to proceed immediately via Vlamertinghe to Tatinghem near St Omer. The order was received with mixed emotions because the welcome news of relief away from the dangers of the front was tinged with regret at leaving their comrades of the Regular battalions. The battalion already knew it had again won 'unstinted praise from all the Regular regiments'[169] for its part in the action of 13 May and there does appear to have been genuine regret amongst the other regiments that the LRB was leaving. Wallis said, 'We all felt a lump in our throats at being forced to leave this glorious 4th Division for the unknown GHQ troops'. However, orders were orders, so in the evening of 19 May the battalion marched back to billets in Vlamertinghe. It was only three weeks since the LRB had spent the disquietening day in the near-by hop store, watching the wounded stream away from the front. To the numbed survivors, it seemed an eternity.

A very tired and bedraggled battalion of 19 officers and 344 men - some of the lightly wounded had already returned - clambered aboard the 20 buses provided for the journey on from Vlamertinghe. The weather had cleared up and the sun broke through to warm their filthy bodies and lighten their spirits. For the present they could forget the filthy state of their uniforms and a diet of biscuits, and look forward instead to a long and deserved rest in the comfort of the rear areas. New uniforms were soon issued and on arrival at Tatinghem the mail was awaiting them. Plenty of time was provided for the men to write home and generally revive themselves and their spirits. Then, on 28 May, it was announced that the LRB was to form part of a composite battalion comprising themselves, the Rangers and the Kensingtons. This new battalion, they were told, would relieve the 6th Welsh at assorted railheads and depots behind the British lines in France. The *Official History* rather pointedly remarks that the decision was forced upon the authorities by the fact that, because the recruitment of the New Armies had 'interfered' with that of the Territorial Force, there were insufficient Territorials to fill the gaps created by the recent fighting.[170] There was perhaps something of an irony in the LRB's present position. Reduced to under half strength, having experienced both the boredom of static trench warfare and the horrors of a major offensive, the battalion was now about to be employed on the tasks for which, six bloody months before, it had believed it was originally sent to France - working on the lines of communications.

While the battalion rested at Tatinghem, wounded men, including Gadsdon of the machine gun section, gradually filtered back. Depending upon how early in the battle they had been hit, many of these men had little idea of how badly the regiment had been affected by the engagement. While in hospital some had heard disturbing rumours that it had virtually ceased to exist . For example, Pocock had been told that there were only about 40 men, excluding the Transport section, left in the battalion. Whitehead, in a similar vein, was assured by a sergeant that the total, including the Transport, was 34. Those who had remained with the regiment throughout the battle passed their time swopping experiences and trying to ascertain what had happened to friends and colleagues. Further information regarding fates was provided by the returning wounded but there was still a great deal of uncertainty, speculation and downright ignorance.

Battalion HQ were constructing a better, but by no means complete, picture. News came in of men reported to have been admitted to hospital and of those who had later died of wounds. At least seven men originally thought to have been killed were found to be alive and by the end of the month the mystery of what had happened to the listening patrol for whom Corporal Jasrowski had gone out to search had been solved; it was reported via the Red Cross that its four members were prisoners in Germany. Officers and senior NCOs also spent some of their time writing the many letters to next of kin. Sgt Denny described this duty as 'the most pathetic incident so far as I am concerned of the war'. These, often rather stereotyped letters, were frequently supplemented by more personal ones written to grieving parents and families by friends of the dead.

Neither the *War Diary* nor the Regimental History actually provide a complete picture of the final casualty list. The closest set appears in the *War Diary* of July 1916 when it compares the losses for the 1 July with those of 2nd Ypres. It gives a total for the period of 24 April - 21 May of four officers and 109 men killed, 17 officers and 295 wounded, 13 missing and two officers and 60 men sick. By using the official figures published after the war, a more thorough breakdown can be made. The final total of non-commissioned men who were killed or died of wounds as a consequence of the battle is 134. This figure divides into 62 from the original 1st Battalion and 72 from the 2nd Battalion. If these totals are added to that for the deaths which occured during the Ploegsteert period, they become 100 and 92 respectively. Thus, if the *War Diary*'s figure of 834 non-commissioned men on the *Chyebassa* is accepted, 12% of those men were dead by the end of May. Similarly of the 465 men drafted from the 2nd Battalion, a somewhat higher proportion - 20% - were dead as a consequence of their shorter, four month period of active service.

The breakdown can be taken further by using additional information given in the *War Diary*. Of the 344 other ranks who arrived at Tatinghem, 196 had landed in France on 5 November 1914. To that figure we should add another ten who were currently officers but had been serving in the ranks in November. So, only 206, or 25% of the original *Chyebassa* men were still with the battalion following their seven month period of foreign service; with the 100 known to have been killed or to have died, a total of 528 men had therefore either been wounded, had gone sick, been sent home as under age, invalided, or had returned to England for commissions. Despite this massive haemorrhage of men, however, the battalion had changed little in character or composition for only three of the 192 dead had addresses from outside the London area. A similar picture of stability of type can also be seen in the case of the serving officers.

On 19 May there were 19 officers present with the battalion. Already a total of 64 had served abroad with the regiment but only four of those at Tatinghen had actually been mobilised with the unit in August 1914. Of the original pre-war officers, three had been killed, six wounded and at least ten invalided home; but the battalion was still officered by men whom it could easily recognise. Moreover, in some respects these men were possibly more typically LRB men than those they replaced as they had come, not from Regular units or university OTCs, but from the ranks of the regiment. Of the 19 present, ten had been promoted from the ranks and three had arrived from the 3rd Battalion - the other two, excluding the LRB originals, had come from elsewhere.

Several of the men who had lost their lives in the battle around Ypres had been the backbone of the regiment for many years and the impact of their deaths would take some time to overcome. CSM Geoffrey Frank, 17 years a part-time soldier, member of the Entertainment Committee and one of the battalion's finest rapid shots, had been killed early in the battle. L/Cpl Frank Sparks, late of Whitgift Grammar School, who in the pre-war days had advocated greater training and practice with the machine gun, was found dead beside the remnants of his beloved weapon. Sparks had once described himself as a 'simple policy puncher at Lloyds': one night in the Salient had been enough to turn his dark hair, snowy white. Another long-time member, Sydney Legg, also of the machine gun section and an 'idol of the School of Arms', has no known grave. Neither does the athlete, Sgt Albany Featherstonehaugh; already badly wounded, he was killed while trying to struggle out of the trench to attack the Germans single-handed. L/Sgt Furrell, like Featherstonehaugh a Brighton marcher, and a one time member of the Kensingtons, was killed by a shrapnel ball in the temple. The same fate as befell Pte Cedric Bell, the boy who had reputedly fallen in love with the Reigate tea shop girl, Maggie Curtis, and had only recently returned to the battalion after recovering from a wound. According to Latham, Bell was killed while snoozing in the trench, but in fact died of wounds in Bailleul hospital.

Another senior NCO to die was the man who had given his postcards to Jim Whitehead for safe-keeping. Sgt Rolfe, 'a fine man' and one of the battalion's 'best sergeants', had worked in the family business. Another member from a family-owned concern was George Landsburg. It is possible that the jewellry business in Hatton Garden prevented Landsburg from sailing on the *Chyebassa* as he went out later with a draft from the 2nd Battalion. Several of the younger pre-war members had their deaths announced in the same issue of the *Hornsey Journal*. The Moore brothers, well-known participants in the Smoking Concerts, members of the Entertainment Committee and sons of teachers, died during the early stages of the battle. One of them was killed on the same day as the 21 year old accountant Arthur Pigden. This former KRRC cadet and stalwart of the Young Men's Christian Union in Stroud Green had been wounded in the hand by the same shell that had killed his fellow signaller Kelsey and two others. Pocock sent the wounded Pigden further down the trench to seek better shelter. Soon after, a shell hit the traverse he was in, blowing another man to pieces. A shaken and bleeding Pigden crawled back to Pocock's end of the trench and insisted that he could not simply cower there and do nothing. As he heaved himself across the trench to pick up a rifle, a shell splinter caught him in the stomach and finished him off.

Kerry and Robinson, the two teachers from Bowes Park School who had enlisted together and been drafted at the same time from the 2nd battalion, died within a week of one another. Another teacher, Harold Eyres, the friend of Victor Hember, was hit by a stray bullet and died in a Boulogne hospital. L/Cpl Hampton, who had served in the CIV, and another rejoined veteran, Fred Banks, one of Whitehead's platoon, both appear on the Menin Gate Memorial to the Missing. One of the Valentine twins from the Merchant Taylors' School was killed while the other survived without a wound. John Wagstaff, late of the Home Fire Department of the Northern Assurance, had only arrived on the last draft from the 2nd Battalion, but was killed on 13 May. Another clerk from an insurance office, Elliot from Gresham Life, died of wounds at Vlamertinghe - one of the few to have a known grave.

It was noted earlier that the *War Diary* recorded a total of 60 men who had reported sick during the battle. Most of these apparently departed during the period when the battalion was out of the line between 4 - 12 May. One of these men was the elder of the three Dixon brothers, Bill. He had successfully hidden the fact that he was blind in one eye but was found out and sent down the line when mud affected his good one. Besides those who went sick, nearly 300 men were actually wounded and evacuated. It was noted earlier that the machine gun section suffered badly during the course of the battle and, in addition to those already mentioned, at least four other members were wounded. Among the wounded NCOs CSM Manbey was badly injured but received a Divisional Card for his work during the battle. Sgt Addison Denny took some shrapnel in his arm but was soon back with the battalion, where he remained until returning with the cadre in 1919. L/Sgt Harvey-George, well-known in the regiment for his 'rather excitable manner and for his reputation as an originator or spreader of rumours', received a 'Blighty', and another who reached England and was later transferred to Bunhill Row for the duration was L/Cpl Gordon Clippingdale. John Stransom, wounded two days before being gazetted, 'Schumery' Doust, from Whitehead's platoon, and C.H. John were all later commissioned into the 1st Battalion but went first to the 3rd Battalion when they had recovered from their wounds. They were joined at Tadworth for a time by Lindsay, a cartoonist , who was to be commissioned on the field in July 1916. The Vernon brothers had lucky escapes - both wounded by the same shell - and eventually ended up in adjacent beds in Henley Hospital. Young Charles Hudson, the former student from the old 'Q' Company draft of the 2nd Battalion, was evacuated to the Base; as was another of that same draft, Gurnat, who left with injured feet.

Of the names which have appeared most frequently in these pages, 'China' Pocock the signaller was sent down the line; he was not too severely wounded and joined the 3rd Battalion in July where he was to stay for the remainder of the war. Bryan Latham had departed with a shrapnel wound in his leg during the first night up, and his path back to the battalion's dressing station near Zonnebeke was trodden by his brother Russell a few nights later. Both men were commissioned into other regiments on recovery and so pass from our story. E.B. Harding, who had already spent ten days in a Steenwerck hospital before acting as bearer at Tommy Sanders' burial in the LRB Cemetery, was also wounded on the first night. Harding was evacuated to the same school room in Bailleul where he had spent the night *en route* for Ploegsteert in November. He returned to England where he spent some time on recruiting duties at Bunhill Row before being posted to the 3rd Battalion. He was joined at the Depot by a former 2nd Battalion man, Leslie Bleaden, who had come away suffering from gas. Bleaden was not as fortunate as Harding, being sent out again and killed on 1 July 1916.

Maurice Howard had returned to the trenches after carrying Sgt Birt down to the aid station and was later detailed to escort a badly shell-shocked man down the line. Howard himself was still suffering from the effects of the gas attack on 2 May and remembers riding in a cart and keeping up a 'bizarre monologue' on cricket in an attempt to keep his companion quiet. On arrival at Wimereux orderlies put a surprised Howard on a stretcher and whisked him off to England along with his companion. His period of active service was over and, like Harding he spent the rest of the war with the 3rd Battalion as an Instructor.

A minority, of course endured the storms of steel and clouds of gas and suffered no more than cuts and bruises, shattered nerves and extreme fatigue. Lancelot Jessop and Victor Hember escaped without a scratch, as did the CIV veteran Sgt Henshaw, whose 'petty and tyrannical' ways had so harrassed the Latham brothers.

Henshaw had been buried twice by shell bursts but survived without injury on both occasions. The two friends Aubrey Smith and 'Kimbo' Valentine-Warne had seen their company destroyed around them but had come through unharmed and were soon to be employed together detraining the 21st Division at Audruiq.

Of the officers who lost their lives, Captain Large, a Brighton marcher, died of wounds in Boulogne. Formerly of Charterhouse and Oxford and an Underwriting Member of Lloyds, he had been promoted to captain on the field. The other four deaths were all lieutenants who had been commissioned from the ranks. The former KRRC cadet Sidney Lines was killed on 13 May, the same day as the 19 year old son of a knight, Beril Pocock from Esher. Lt Price, the stockbroker who had been commissioned on the strength of 'some military training in Canada', was killed on 3 May. Also killed that day was the 19 year old Richard Lintott - the boy who had contrived to get himself initially into the 2nd Battalion and then onto the *Chyebassa*. He had been gazetted only four days before his death and the circumstances of it were later explained to his parents in a letter from his friend Arnold Pumphrey. While lying in a hospital bed, Pumphrey, one of the battalion's few non-Londoners, wrote: 'Your son was sleeping in a dugout and the shell landed...he was a good brave soldier, a comrade and a friend of mine...his invariable cheerfulness was in this campaign one of the finest traits in a loveable character'. Pumphrey went on to finish with the usual platitudes of an instantaneous death and no disfigurement etc. The young man who had tried so hard to get himself onto active service in the shortest possible time was apparently buried where he fell at Fortuin. His grave was not located after the war and his name appears on the stone panels of the Menin Gate.

The remaining officer to fall was 2Lt Gooding. Like many of the LRB he was a Freemason and had attended St Dunstan's College in Catford. He had only been appointed Machine Gun Officer on 12 May and was killed beside the gun that had temporarily closed the gap along the St Julien road. For some unexplained reason, Gooding is unique in the LRB as he is the only member to have his name engraved on the Le Touret Memorial to the Missing.

When considering the nature of the battle and the years of subsequent fighting that followed in the same areas, it is hardly surprising that so many of the LRB men have no known grave. The positions held by the regiment in April and May all fell into German hands by the end of the battle and were to remain within enemy lines until recaptured during the Third Battle of Ypres. During the intervening years the positions held near Hill 37 and Hindu Cot were converted into major strong points by the Germans and received massive attention from the British artillery. The ground was so pulverised and churned into the morass for which the later battle is best remembered that, by the time the infantry attacked in August 1917, they were wading through a virtual swamp. Their bodies disappeared into the slough to join those of the LRB. Consequently, the names of three officers and 110 non-commissioned LRB men who fell during the battle appear on the Menin Gate. Of the remaining 32 men who died, only five are buried in known graves actually within the Salient. After the years of pounding and destruction, these were the only bodies found that could be positively identified: one is that of 2Lt Lines who is buried in Sanctuary Wood Cemetery; the remainder lie in Poelcapelle Cemetery some distance from where they fell. Another six men were buried in Bailleul, the town to which most of the wounded had been initially evacuated. The remaining 21 died in the Base Hospitals nearer the coast or at home.

For those who survived, the aftermath of the battle, whether spent in a hospital or Tatinghem, provided time to reflect on their recent experience. The memoirs produced later bear a justifiable pride in the regiment's performance and achievements in what had been its first severe test of mettle. Both the Russell brothers came through unscathed and Henry later wrote that the artists, civil servants, schoolteachers etc. all behaved 'remarkably well under very severe strain and their casualties were quite terrible'. Graham Williams, who had also come through unwounded, wrote that the cavalry on Belcher's right flank, 'trained professional soldiers, had broken, whilst the LRB, 'Saturday afternoon soldiers', never for one moment thought of leaving their position, in spite of having suffered the same shelling'. The *Offical History* too was fulsome in its praise for the stand made by 11 Brigade: 'Seldom have there been finer displays of courage'. It then went on to criticise the parsimony of the pre-war years in not providing the infantry with adequate artillery support. Later, it praises the Territorials who fought 'more than well',[171] in what it describes as a new form of battle '..in which the enemy planned that his infantry should merely have to occupy ground from which his guns had driven every living creature and in which man was not pitted against man, but against material'.[172]

If the battle had not thrown him into a deep depression, Jim Whitehead, in the Territorial Base Camp at Rouen, would probably have appreciated the accolades being showered upon the troops. He had been profoundly saddened by the death of his friend Dicky Richardson on 13 May and his depression increased as other familiar faces disappeared with wounds or for commissions. However, by the end of the month some of his old section had turned up at the Base and he could write home saying that he was now 'feeling so much better'. His spirits continued to rise and the disappointment at not having been sent home was soon replaced by an announcement that he would rather stay with the regiment than return to England for a commission. Meanwhile, those who remained learned that they were to be dispersed over the various southern railheads. As they prepared themselves for the move, they could look back with both sadness and pride at the part they had played in halting the German offensive. The Plugstreet stay had given them experience of the worst conditions of trench life, but the Battle of Ypres had blooded and almost annihilated them in the most ferocious of ways. The regiment had won a Victoria Cross, as well as several other gallantry awards, and had the satisfaction of performing feats of courage and endurance that had never originally been expected of Territorial troops. In later years Russell Latham looked back upon the battle and reflected on what it had meant to him and, no doubt, to many others who also had experienced it:

> *That was Ypres, that opposing of human flesh and bone to those steel and chemical thunderbolts, so numerous, so well directed, so often larger and much heavier than a man. That was the bravery that, far greater than any prowess in personal combat, gilds the dark memories of the Salient.*

CHAPTER V

The Rebuilding Period 1915

While the former insurance clerks, bank cashiers, schoolteachers and stockbrokers practised their new trades of coal-heaver, railway labourer and assorted odd-job men, speculation continued as to what would eventually become of them. Graham Williams realised that leaving Plugstreet had signalled the beginning of the end of the old peacetime LRB, and that Ypres had put the finishing touches to it. Because many of the senior NCOs and the various specialist sections had been so depleted, it was difficult to find more than a nucleus of any of them. What soon become clear to all was that there was no question of the regiment going back into the line without first receiving a massive influx of new men, and the time to train them. It was thought unlikely that the 2nd Battalion would be able to send any further significant number of men, and it was known that the 3rd Battalion was certainly not in a position to despatch a draft for some time. Rumours abounded as to whether they would stay permanently on lines of communication, be returned to England, or be converted into an Officer's Training Battalion.

In fact Major Bates had discussed the battalion's future with 11 Brigade's commanding officer on 15 May and had made three suggestions. The first proposal was that it should remain in the front line, and thus, in a short time, become extinct. Secondly, if the battalion received reinforcements from other units, it would lose the essential character of the LRB - this, according to Bates, 'would be a pitiable waste of exceptional material'. The third option was to return to England and be made up to strength with men from the 2nd and 3rd Battalions. This was the option which Bates himself preferred as he felt the rebuilt battalion would then be worthy of the original. Finally, a variation of the third proposal was to return the battalion to England and there re-organise it as an Officer Training Corps. The authorities in their somewhat perverse way were to come up with another suggestion a few months later - to be retrained as a pioneer battalion for the 8th Division. Not surprisingly this idea horrified Wallis, partly because the men were so ill-fitted for such an occupation but more importantly, it might be suspected, for the humilation it implied to the tradition of the regiment. Fortunately. the Army lost interest in this plan, but only after the battalion had actually begun training for such a role. For the time being, however, many of the men were turning their thoughts more to their individual futures rather than that of the unit as a whole; the New Armies training in England were desperately short of officers and the educated and now experienced men of the LRB were the ideal type to bring these units up to strength.

In December 1914 Willie Fry, still under age to be officially on active service, was asked to accept a commission in the 2nd Seaforth Highlanders but was so appalled at the thought of trying to order around these 'enormous kilted Scottish Regulars' that he declined the offer.[173] This invitation was a consequence of a War Office paper to Colonel Cairns asking if he could recommend any men for a commission. Cairns is reported to have replied that, as about 95% of his men were capable of becoming officers, it would result in the LRB becoming an OTC. So he decided to recommend none. However, although Jim Whitehead decided that he would sooner stay with the LRB, apparently 'a good number' gave in their names. Williams also recalled that in January 'some' men had obtained commissions either in the LRB or other units. It has already been noted that men such as Wallis were given direct commissions but, if a man did want to take up a commission, the more usual way in those early Plugstreet days was to apply when at home recovering from wounds or while on leave. Most COs of the forming New Armies would seize the opportunity of acquiring the services of a man from the leading Territorial units and would endorse their application immediately. This was certainly the method used by Blande who was wounded in December and then trained with the Inns of Court OTC. As Cairns appears to have been declining to release those still with the battalion, for the majority of men this was possibly the only way.

It is very difficult to determine exactly how many men left the regiment during the Plugstreet period for commissions. There must certainly have been a fairly significant drain, although clearly some men continued to resist the opportunity to return home. In January Richard Lintott's father had been trying to pull strings to get his son commissioned but Richard himself, like Whitehead, decided he would rather stay with the battalion than return to the 3rd Battalion: 'It's far better to be here and it's a lot more fun'. Among those who did leave were Monson, who was killed during the Ypres battle with the 2nd Wiltshire Regiment, and a renowned souvenir hunter and patroller of No Man's Land, Sgt Pothecary. Maurice Howard, however, thought that there was not much talk about commissions after his arrival from the 2nd Battalion in January, and believed that he did not know of any who applied for one. It is possible that no one in Howard's platoon did apply but it is certainly incorrect for the battalion as a whole. However, what is equally clear is that whatever the number of those who left *before* 2nd Ypres, it would soon be surpassed by those who would leave *after* it.

While engaged on the lines of communication, many men began requesting that their relatives at home ask commanders of the New Army battalions to apply to the LRB for their release and allow them to return to England. Major Bates seems to have been more ready to accede to these requests than did his predecessor, but his apparent willingness still did not offer a great deal of hope to those men whose families did not have any influential friends at home. This category were given the chance in July when permission was granted for men to apply direct to the Artists Rifles - a battalion of the London Regiment which had already been converted into an OTC while serving in France. After a training period of only five days the men would then be commissioned into a regiment already at the front. This method suited those who merely wanted to become officers as quickly as possible, but failed to satisfy the basic attraction of the original procedure. The advantage of the latter method was the prospect of spending a long time training at home while former comrades were still working or fighting in France. Thus, many men seem to have preferred to wait until leave came round and then apply in the usual way rather than risk being sent almost immediately to virtually any unit short of officers at the front. Others with no hope of a friendly colonel at home went off to the Cadet School at Blendecques as the year progressed. In all, at least 48 chose this route, while 73 others were recalled from home. This might have had something to do with dissatisfaction at the pioneer role recently ascribed to the battalion, or, more likely, as a consequence of friends disappearing home: for example, over 20 men from the former Transport section had taken commissions by August.

There are two figures for the total number of men taking commissions during this period. The first comes from a brief Regimental History published in October 1916 which claims that 535 men of the 1st Battalion had become officers by the time the book was being compiled.[174] This figure would include men who were commissioned after the beginning of the Somme offensive as it specifies 30 direct commissions, a figure roughly double those granted before the end of 1915. A better figure is that supplied after the war which claims that 412 *Chyebassa* men received commissions during the course of the war. This figure is probably a little too large because from other sources only 396 men can be positively identified as later becoming officers. Furthermore, some of these - although certainly a minority - are known to have taken them after the Somme battles of 1916. Whichever figure is accepted, and for this purpose the lower total will be taken, if the totals of those *Chyebassa* men who were killed by the end of May, and those who had already been granted direct commissions, are deducted, it shows that almost 50% of the original 1st Battalion had left to take a commission by the time the battalion went back into the trenches in November 1915.

To the men who either chose not to go for commissions, or perhaps were refused them, the loss of so many of the original battalion must have dealt a blow to morale. Things did improve though as more of those who had been wounded at Ypres returned to the battalion. Many of these men had spent some time with the 3rd Battalion at Tadworth and arrived with drafts from that unit. By July the rebuilding of the overseas battalion was well under way. In August, three drafts totalling 105 men had rejoined the battalion from the Territorial Base Camp in Rouen, and by October another 109, including the young NCO from Ilford, William Marlborough, had arrived from the 2nd Battalion. This unit was now so under strength that it was to provide no more drafts to the parent battalion. Thus, the bulk of the men arriving at Rouen and being posted to the 1st Battalion's expanding companies were the recruits of December 1914 - May 1915. The *War Diary* records that in three drafts of September and October, a total of 318 men joined from the 3rd Battalion, a figure which does not co-incide exactly with the figure provided by the reserve battalion itself. The difference between the totals of those men sent overseas and those arriving at Battalion HQ is 92. Although some of these might initially have been sent to other units, the majority probably joined their colleagues with the battalion a few weeks later. So, who were these men coming to replace the dead, wounded or departed originals? Why had they chosen to give up their jobs, and why, rather than join a unit of the generally better publicised New Armies, did they opt to enlist in a battalion which actually demanded they pay for the privilege? To try to construct a picture of the new battalion before it returned to the mud of the southern Salient, and to ascertain the impact the war had already made upon the recruitment and character of the regiment, it is necessary to look at the early days of the new reserve battalion currently training in England.

Permission to create the 3rd Battalion had been granted on 26 November 1914 and it began recruiting on 1 December. The purpose behind the regimental third battalions was to provide drafts to their other service battalions. Several units, though, soon discovered that finding the recruits to fill the ranks was not as easy as it had been during the earlier months of the war. Consequently, once the first great wave of patriotism and enthusiasm for enlisting in the Army had spent itself, the recruitment of suitable men took on a more mundane character. It was noted earlier that the 1st Battalion had been brought up to strength in a matter of hours by men of the same class as had been joining the LRB since its formation as a Territorial unit. Similarly with the 2nd Battalion; the clerks, office juniors, and agents etc. had flocked to join the Colours, and found themselves quite at home in the company of their social and occupational peers. As October turned into November, however, and the initial rush of willing volunteers began to wane, the newly raised 3rd Battalion discovered that it had to do more than merely open the doors of Bunhill Row every morning at nine o'clock and admit a waiting, anticipatory queue of young zealots.

The LRB was not alone in realising that something more had to be done if a Third Battalion was to provide the quality of men that the 1st and 2nd Battalions would require once they had gone overseas and had begun to sustain casualties. Other 'class' battalions of the London Regiment were also beginning to experience a similar problem. There was not thought to be an immediate shortage of suitable volunteers that might create an unexpected or embarrassing situation, but the LRB, like its counterparts, began to turn its individual mind to how it might continue to attract the sort of man, in the sort of numbers, that would be required in the future.

It was soon realised that the columns of the quality press could be utilised for publicising and advertising the various advantages of belonging to a unit that contained men of a similar social class. Following a comment in *Reynold's* of 5 December 1914, in which the LRB was reported to have acknowledged that recruiting was 'somewhat slow', a longer and more explicitly propagandist article was printed in the *Daily Telegraph* five days later;

> *Early in its history the several Companies of the battalion were officially adopted by the different Wards into which the City is divided. The corps is recruited principally from the banks and insurance offices, Lloyds, the Stock Exchange, shipping firms, wholesale houses, public companies etc. In its ranks are to be found a large number of professional men.*

No mention of the subscription was made, but it is probably safe to assume that the type of man who would read the *Telegraph*, and perhaps be attracted by the article, would know that if he enlisted in the LRB as in any of the more class-conscious units of the London Regiment he would be required to pay a sum for the privilege. After all, professional men had known of the City Territorials and their quirks for years, and although 25/- might represent a fair proportion of the annual salary of an office junior,[175] they were prepared to pay it if it meant they would not have to be too closely associated with their social inferiors. Philip Maddison was told in no uncertain terms that 'the battalion for the bobtails is the Tower Hamlets.'[176] War had since intervened, but patriotism did not over-rule everything. Basil Houle was accustomed to singing in Windsor Castle's private chapel and then to taking tea afterwards. Consequently, he and his school fellows of the Windsor Choir School, rather looked down on the Eton boys who used to 'slouch around in their frock coats'. After all, Houle had been 'mixing with royalty which had spoilt me!' and in the class-conscious Britain of the early twentieth century many, but by no means all, considered it better to stay with their peers.

The Regimental History of the Rangers candidly admits that after permission had been granted to raise its Third Battalion in January 1915, only about 25 men were recruited in the first week, 25 in the second, and although the number increased to 40 in the third, it became, 'increasingly necessary as time went on to adopt the traditional methods of recruiting'.[177] Units began to put on a 'show', raise a band, parade the regimental Colours through the streets of the capital, put up recruiting posters in the large offices and banks, and, in the case of the Rangers, serialise the regiment's history since 1780 in daily papers.

The activites of the Territorial battalions already in France and Belgium also clearly acted as an inducement to recruitment. The quickly legendary stand by the London Scottish on Messines Ridge on Halloween 1914, and the numerous letters home sent by LRB men and published in the local and daily papers on the Christmas truce, kept those two units, particularly, in Londoners' eyes. Exploiting this publicity, three members of the LRB were visiting City offices by late 1914 and obtaining on average around forty extra recruits a week.[178] By May 1915 incentives of a day's holiday were being offered to members of office staff who brought forward a recruit who was accepted by the LRB.[179] This was at a time when the 3rd Battalion was at only about half strength and the news of the 1st Battalion's activities during 2nd Ypres and of Sgt Belcher's Victoria Cross not yet known.

Steady though recruiting proved to be before 2nd Ypres, there appears to have been an element of concern over the type of man who was presenting himself for enrolment. It was all very well to insist on men of a similar background and occupation, but that in itself could cause problems for a unit suffering from a lack of equipment and expertise in anything other than office work and form filling. *The Times* of 22 April 1915 carried a report that the 3rd Battalion LRB had vacancies, 'which it is desired to fill by the enlistment of those who have practical experience of boot and shoe repairing'. The success or otherwise of this advertisement is not recorded, but there were certainly problems once men had begun to be posted overseas in finding replacements able to cope with the needs of the Transport animals.

From time to time special large recruiting rallies and campaigns were organised by the City Regiments. Covering one such event, *The Despatch* of 15 June 1915 announced that as 'Clerks, solicitors barristers and businessmen fight side by side in the LRB...(it) should certainly not want for likely men'. The regiment again took part in a joint recruiting march through London in early October.[180] These occasions gave City staffs the opportunity to see what sorts of figures their former office colleagues cut in uniform, and, more importantly, gave some of the regiments the chance to parade their Colours and bugle band through the streets.

Throughout these years the regiment remained keen to continue to attract the usual LRB man, but he need not necessarily have been a Londoner. Letters, such as the one which appeared in the *Sheffield Independent* of October 1915, were regularly sent to the provincial papers. These invited recruits from clerical workers and explained that 'there is a Regiment which caters especially for them'. While admitting that the training would be demanding and onerous, the letters pointed out that it would be '...far pleasanter if carried out with others whose civil occupation is the same'. The residences of LRB fatalities do not include any Sheffield addresses coinciding with the serial numbers of men enlisting during that period, but the LRB certainly did attract a number of men from nearby Chesterfield.

The men joining the LRB from the North of England would presumably not have been influenced by a contemporary poster appearing on the London Underground. While home on leave, Graham Williams could not understand why fellow passengers on the Underground were giving him amused glances as he sat in uniform with its LRB shoulder flashes. He discovered, on rising, that he had been sitting beneath a small recruiting poster exhorting men to 'Join the LRB; the Finest Regiment God ever made'. Williams thought this description of the LRB was in 'rather poor taste' and took a lot of living down. In 1916 the other battalions in the 56th Division soon latched onto the slogan and began referring to the LRB as 'God's Own' and 'The Heavenly Host'.

Benefical as the letters, adverts and so on may have been to recruiting figures, the two most successful methods of enlisting men remained personal contact and the 'grape vine'. In June 1915 the LRB formed a special recruiting squad based at HQ, consisting of about a dozen men under a sergeant. All the members were men who had been wounded in France and consequently had practical experience of the work done by the battalion which was by then well-known amongst the London public. The squad would visit the familiar haunts of office workers during their lunch breaks, for example, around St Pauls and the Stock Exchange, and extol the virtues of LRB life to the young men. Armed with handbills which unashamably made no bones about the requirement of the 25/- annual subscription ('payable in quarterly instalments') which, according to the bill, ensured that 'the social standing of the Regiment is maintained and provides special advantages and comforts which would otherwise be missing',[181] the recruiting team descended upon the alfresco diners. Russell Latham, a temporary member of the squad, thought that it used to pick up a 'considerable number' of recruits by this method. However, Schuman, another member of the team, remembered that despite the 'white feather' campaign and an abundance of propaganda, there were still many young men who did not appear anxious to give up a good City job and enlist.

When reviewing its recruiting methods, the Regimental History of the 12th London asserted that its 'most successful scheme of all', inaugurated in mid-1915, was the use of empty shops and offices in the West End as temporary recruiting cffices.[182] E.B. Harding, on the other hand, who had experienced recruiting methods in the LRB for a considerable period, believed that such schemes were important but that in the LRB recruitment was most successful through 'the grapevine, the old boys' network, and our HQ Staff'. The evidence of several of those who enlisted during 1915 and 1916 appears to support this contention. 'Chucks' Hadfield remembered that 'Chesterfield had at least twelve happy LRB members' and was quite content to enlist with a group of friends who travelled down to London to specifically join the LRB There were, of course, other motives too; Basil Houle finally opted for the LRB rather than one of the other London Regiments because it had the most attractive posters and was advertising more than the others, while W.A. Braine decided there was 'no particular reason' but was talked into it by a recruiting sergeant during a drive outside the Mansion House. Young men in the offices were warned by their colleagues to stay clear of these recruiting rallies unless they were ready to join up, as the pressure on them to enlist was intense and sometimes difficult to resist.

The majority of the would-be recruits to the LRB were persistent in their determination to ensure that it was the LRB they eventually joined. Despite having won his House Shooting Cup, it took G.M. Lee five attempts to pass the LRB eyesight test, and H.E. Pratt went so far as to provide references in order to be accepted. On a more mundane note, Leslie Blacking decided on the LRB simply because his initials were 'L.R.B.' and because he had relations living near where the battalion was currently stationed.[183] Attempts to recruit the ever-diminishing number of suitable, willing volunteers during 1915 were in the face of ever-increasing competition from other Regiments. The mushroom growth of New Army service battalions from August 1914 continued during the next twelve months, and each, eager to fill its quota, vied with its rivals to get up to its required strength as soon as possible. Civic pride was often at stake as mayors and councillors stomped their wards encouraging and cajoling young men to enlist and bring honour to their boroughs. Competition and rivalry were so intense that in July the Under-Secretary of State for War informed Parliament that efforts were being made to encourage some form of cooperation and mutual assistance between the recruiting agencies of the Regular and Territorial Armies. He added ruefully that both were finding it difficult to attract recruits.

The London Regiment alone had 27 battalions, including the Honourable Artillery Company, and each was recruiting its third battalion by mid-1915. Not all these units would of course attract the LRB type of man, but service battalions of the Royal Fusiliers and the Middlesex Regiment were targeting the very sorts of middle-class clerks, sportsmen etc. that the LRB preferred. The method was to insert a descriptive element in the particular battalion's title; hence the 17th and 23rd Battalions of the Middlesex Regiments called themselves 'Football', while the 10th and 26th Battalions of the Royal Fusiliers adopted the names 'Stockbrokers' and 'Bankers' respectively. These battalions were deliberately trying to attract the same sort of man who, in pre-war days, would have been likely to have enlisted in the more socially acceptable units of the London Regiment. Similarly, as most of the LRB men had attended public rather than council schools, the competition from the four Royal Fusiliers and one Middlesex Regiment battalions who described themselves as 'Public Schools' would also entice the would-be LRB recruit - especially perhaps those who might recoil from paying the regimental subscription, either from financial consideration or as a matter of principle.[184]

In addition to these units who were trying to enlist a particular class of man, there were other service battalions that sought to recruit from specific localities. The pre-war LRB was principally, but not exclusively, comprised of men from the N.E. and S.E areas of London, and in May and June 1915 three non-London regiments began raising battalions that were associated with areas from which the LRB had traditionally attracted a large proportion of members; the 13th East Surrey battalion was called the 'Wandsworth', the 11th West Kent, the 'Lewisham' and the 21st Middlesex, the 'Islington'. These were in addition to the existing pre-war Territorial units recruiting from the immediate London area - amounting to twelve battalions - which in turn doubled and then sometimes triplicated following the outbreak of war.

Competition for recruits, then, was acute and the situation was exacerbated as the rush of volunteers dwindled to an alarming trickle. A War Office memorandum of May 1915 comments that the supply of men willing to join the army of their own accord, and who could be spared from industry, was rapidly becoming exhausted. A recent appeal following the Whit holiday had produced a fair number of recruits, but the rate at which men were joining was not considered sufficient to keep the forces up to strength. The memorandum gloomily concluded: 'It seems as if the voluntary system has had its day, and that compulsory methods will have to be introduced if we are to be in a position to maintain our forces in the field'.[185]

The difficulties of finding more recruits were frequently addressed in Parliament. In June Sir J. Rolleston asked the Under-Secretary of State for War a question pertinent to the current position of the LRB as a member of a composite battalion; if it was now War Office policy that Territorial units on active service would receive no more drafts from their own units at home and that, if their strength fell below 400, they would be formed into composite battalions or attached elsewhere. He went on to assert that if this was the case, it would be 'discouraging to the efficiency of and the recruiting for the Territorial Force and will be a virtual breach of faith with individual officers and men'.[186] In reply Tennant stated that it was not the case that further drafts would not be sent, but admitted that when battalions were much reduced in numbers, 'it may be necessary to associate them temporarily for convenience of command and administration, with another battalion'. He finished his statement, on what was to become an increasingly contentious matter, by explaining that any such attachments would cease as soon as reinforcements from home became available.[187] This promise was very important to the new recruits of the 3rd Battalion who were enthusiastically learning the traditions and customs of the LRB. They had deliberately chosen to enlist in it rather than one of its competitors and the last thing they wanted was to be sent abroad to some other more mundane and less prestigious unit.

By the time the first draft of recruits left Tadworth to join the overseas battalion in August 1915 the 3rd Battalion was almost 1400 strong. March had proved the most productive month for recruits with 203 enlistments. The average for the first eight months of the year was a creditable, although not particularly excessive, 148. Perhaps more important than the actual numbers enlisting at this stage was the efficiency of the training they had undergone before being drafted. A discussion on the methods, quality and extent of home training will be found later but, for the men arriving at Battalion HQ in France by October 1915, there was a little time to have some of their most obvious deficiencies made good - and deficiencies there were. The only aspect of warfare that the men felt confidently trained in was the use of the bayonet. Rifles had been in such short supply that without the loan of former Boer Mausers and other more-or-less obsolete weapons from local schools, the men would have had virtually no musketry practice. Similarly, Lewis Gun and grenade training had been unknown, although some digging practice had been undertaken. The men had even spent two day stretches in trenches living off rations and learning trench routine, but conditions in Tadworth were to be very different from those they would find in Belgium. Perhaps the only satisfactory element of their training, apart from the fairly useless technique of bayonet fighting, was the quantity of route marches they had done. Yet these had frequently only been ordered because there was nothing else to do.

What the training lacked in expertise, the enthusiasm of the men went some way to rectify. When the battalion had arrived at Tadworth it had to erect its own tents, lay its own drains and generally develop a virgin site. Conditions remained fairly primitive but the men soon developed an *esprit* that helped to overcome the difficulties. This was aided by the fact that men who had joined together were usually kept in the same training platoons. These recruits slept, trained and messed together, and had their own platoon officer and drill sergeant. Typical of such a unit were the so-called 'Wheatley's Lambs'. Most of the 30 odd recruits were (unofficially) 17 or 18 years old, had all come from offices in the City and were of the same social class as their officer, Fletcher Wheatley. Wheatley, a 19 year old tea taster, had returned from Ceylon to enlist and, after initially joining the Artists, was commissioned into the 3rd Battalion. He appears not to have had much of a regard for authority, or for his fellow officers as he spent most of his time with his platoon in their bell tents. He was also, given his trade, tee-total - not that this was very different from the boys under his command: 'There was a beer tent in the camp, but we never dreamt of going in it. We were really very young and slow in growing up'.

The situation did improve a little with the appearance of men wounded at Ypres. Their experience with regard to wiring and trench building was put to good use, but their chief contribution to camp life seems to have been their custom at the beer tent. While waiting to be drafted back to the 1st Battalion these men were all posted to 'D' Company and the night before their departure they pulled a stunt which shocked the more naive boys of Wheatley's Lambs:

> *There were large tin basins used as urinals outside every group of tents and these lads decided to get their own back on the Colonel who had gone out with the 1st Battalion but hadn't stayed long in France. I don't know why but he wasn't very popular with them so they collected these basins which were pretty full because they'd had a good night's drinking and quietly placed them outside Colonel King's tent. Then they kicked up a great row and King came out to see what all the fuss was about. He tripped up and fell into the basins but as the boys were leaving for France before dawn next morning there wasn't time to pin anything on them. But we were terribly shocked because at that time we were in awe of all officers higher in rank than 2Lt and besides, we didn't think that sort of thing should go on. But later of course we learned differently.* (B. Houle)

Although the bulk of the men were still dispersed over many French railheads, the 1st Battalion had resumed its separate identity. Some of the specialist sections were already beginning to reform and practice their skills. The unwelcome news that the battalion had to commence training as a pioneer unit had interrupted this a little, although by 23 November, a month after the last full draft had joined the battalion, this idea had been abandoned. A week later the battalion was to go into the trenches as an ordinary infantry unit of 8 Brigade in the 3rd Division.

The boys in training were eager and keen to get on with the job, and occasionally had needed to employ a little subterfuge to get themselves on a draft to France. For example, having been discovered to be under age, Basil Houle was kept back when the remainder of 'Wheatley's Lambs' went overseas. Upset at being on his own amongst strangers he requested an interview with the colonel. King asked him if his parents had agreed to him being sent overseas and Houle happily replied that he had sought and gained their permission. The first that his father and mother knew of it was when a postcard arrived from Rouen some days later. During the training period at Tadworth Arthur Schuman had also been separated from the school friends with whom he had enlisted. However, like Houle, Schuman was able to rejoin most of them once he had been posted to France. Furthermore, when Arthur Hollis was selected for a draft, his brother Vincent applied to be sent at the same time. It was decided that Arthur should be retained until his brother had finished his training and the two left together in October 'bound for eleven different destinations, according to reliable and confidential information'.

The Hollis brothers arrived at Rouen Territorial Base Camp where they spent a month repeatedly charging a suspended sack filled with straw. They also discovered that, compared with troops from other regiments, or even anyone who had the 'slightest acquaintance with the language of a Billingsgate Market porter, their foul language was elementary' to say the least. Experience of life at the Base Camp was universally disliked - the huge training ground being variously called the 'Sahara' or 'Bull Ring' - and to most men it came as a relief to be sent up the line. Harold Morgan, arriving with the first draft, was welcomed by the Base Details with shouts of, 'Are we downhearted?' Cheerily and earnestly the draft responded, 'No!' only to be warned, 'Then you soon will be'.[188] Basil Houle soon was. Whilst trying to work a fast one by claiming that, as he was non-religious, he should be excused Church Parades, he and several others who tried the same ploy were put on filthy jobs. Consequently, Houle and his companions 'couldn't get away from there quick enough'.

Conditions at the camp were positively luxurious compared to those the new arrivals had to endure when they reached the battalion. This was a type of warfare that even the veterans of the original battalion had not experienced. Conditions in Plugstreet Wood had been grim, but the wood itself had offered shelter and allowed the construction of reasonably comfortable timber dugouts in the support lines. The front lines were frequently underwater, but the support and reserve companies could be kept fairly dry in the nearby farms or Ploegsteert village. The front held by the LRB around the St Eloi sector was very different. Although the lines in both sectors tended to be built-up breastworks rather than trenches, the quality of those in the northern sector were markedly worse. The *War Diary* continually records, 'trenches in a shocking state...parapets continually falling in...stream flooding HQ Dugout' etc., which meant that the troops were more concerned with trying to make them almost bearable than killing the enemy. The Germans too had their problems and according to Victor Hember appeared to be 'peaceably inclined'. Houle also believed that there was little actual fighting, but as he was a sniper and often not in the trenches at night, there was opportunity for activity which he might not have experienced. The casualty returns do suggest either a very quiet enemy or a tacit 'live and let live system', and the problems posed by the enemy probably did take second place to those of the elements.

The difficulties experienced in maintaining some sort of security and an element of comfort in the front lines were matched by those faced in the journey up to them. The start of the trip was not too bad as a long, winding, revetted and corduroy bottomed communication trench led from HQ towards the support line. Unfortunately, this 'splendid piece of work' disappeared before the support line was reached and the 'path' became a slush through and between water-filled shellholes. From the supports to the front it grew progressively worse - several treacherous plank bridges, running streams and mud in places waist deep. Ration parties slipped and waded across this morass - one reputedly taking five hours to complete the journey of approximately one mile. Yet even the atrocious conditions could provide lighter moments. When Sgt Foulkes, not one of the most popular of men, tripped and fell into a stinking, fetid hole with the ration sacks pinning him in the mud, the rest of the party left him struggling for about five minutes because they were too busy laughing. Hollis described the ration fatigues as 'very harrowing experiences slithering and sliding in mud and losing contact which caused more 'wind up' than the gun flashes'. The effort required to struggle across the terrain by individuals carrying personal kit or sandbags was bad enough, but the machine gun section had to start off for the front hours before the rest of the battalion as man-handling the Maxim across the swamp was so awkward.

The new members also began to learn what the Army meant by the word 'rest'. Instead of allowing a period of sleep, cleaning up and general recuperation, the Army decided that idle hands made Tommy a poor soldier, and so heaped upon him an assortment of jobs and tasks which permitted him anything but 'rest'. The most usual occupation was forming part of a working party. While commanding such a group on his very first night in the line, the young 2Lt Fletcher Wheatley was severely wounded. Common as this sort of work was, others were engaged on mining activity alongside the divisional RE. The Hollis brothers were detailed to go into Ypres Wood as Brigade miners and spent several days filling and dragging sacks of spoil underground. They were thought to be 30 feet underground, but the miners punctured a deep shell hole which flooded the tunnel and thus caused it to be abandoned. On another occasion, Basil Houle was sent alone into a listening post in the heavily mined sector of The Bluff. As he sat isolated, save for the occasional visit from a grumpy engineer, he could hear the Germans laughing while they tunnelled remorselessly towards him. After a week of this, the LRB NCO asked if the squad could be put on a working job as the listening was 'driving us all mad'. The request was granted and the six men spent the next week filling sacks with liquid mud.

Occasionally the battalion was withdrawn as far as Poperinghe, a town still relatively unscarred by war and able to offer some degree of comfort. After the mud and slime of the front area the town was almost an oasis of food, heat and shelter. For those who sought it, there was also spiritual comfort:

> *Three or four of us were walking around Poperinghe one day and three*
> *Padres approached us and said that they'd just opened a little place*

> *and would we like to come in for a cup of tea. We did and that was*
> *the beginning of Toc H. But I never knew until after the war that there*
> *was such a thing called Toc H even though I was there at the Opening.*
> (B. Houle)

Toc H offered men comradeship, spiritual and moral support and, although it was coincidence that London Regiments were in the vicinity at its inception, long after the war 'Tubby' Clayton spoke of the considerable part played by the LRB in its early development.[189]

Comforts at the front were rare - a donation of a number of sunflaps by the Bee Badminton Club presumably doing little to alleviate the hardship of winter. The general conditions were made even worse by the fact that the Divisional General was a tee-totaller and forbade the issue of rum. On rare occasions rum was put into tea dixies, much to the delight of the men who believed that it was an absolute necessity to prevent chills and cold feet. Whether the rum ever did much to prevent the onset of trench foot is open to debate, but regular massage with whale oil became a strict routine and according to Hollis was an effective antidote.

After the first few weeks in the sector, the animals of the Transport section were probably better provided for than the men. Fine brick standings and covered shelters were built for them at the Transport lines and although the men understood and agreed with the attentions paid to the animals, they wondered why the same consideration could not have been offered them. One man returning from leave wrote home: 'It was a rainy and windy day and I found our place in a turnip field with tents that had just been put up to sleep in...I call it a 'camp' because it said so on the sign board, but as a matter of fact, there were just some tents pitched amongst the heaps of slosh and lakes of mud'.[190]

The atrocious conditions must have had an impact on the battalion's strength and the Regimental History, unlike the *War Diary*, notes that 165 men were reported as 'sick' during this period. As an example of how difficult it is to assess accurately the precise number of men on the strength, some simple sums can be calculated from figures provided by various sources. The Regimental History gives a figure of 25 officers and 806 other ranks for 25 October 1915. If the totals of the drafts and the men returning to battalion from the Base Camp given in the *War Diary* are added to the 344 who boarded the buses at Vlamertinghe, the total came to 737. From that we should subtract those who are known to have gone home for commissions or to Blendecques, which amounts to 120. So, the total strength would then be 617 instead of 806 and by similar calculation, 28 officers instead of the stated 25. The figure given for the beginning of their trench tour on 23 November is 26 officers and 751 men, despite there being no mention of any further draft arriving or any other men leaving. This figure, though, is similar to that recorded as battalion strength when leaving Voormezeele to join the 56th Division; 29 officers and 761 men. According to the Regimental History, the battalion was at 'full strength'. That figure is too low for a battalion at this stage in the war to be officially at full strength, but it was fairly typical for a Territorial unit owing to the politicking going on at home over how the serving battalions should be reinforced. If the figure of 761 is accepted it means that 60% of the battalion had had no experience of active service and were to receive their baptism of fire in the breastworks and trenches of the southern section of the Salient.

The number of men recorded by the *War Diary* as having been wounded during the time at Voormezeele and St Eloi was 24. A further unspecified number, including Vincent Hollis, were taken to form part of the brigade machine gun section. The number of dead is more easily ascertained. The *War Diary* records seven killed and one man who died of wounds, while the figures published after the war include two more who died at Base Hospitals either from wounds or disease. Two battalion bombers, Bradbury and Gates, were killed early in the tour and were buried behind the parados in ground consecrated by the chaplain. Their bodies, like that of another killed shortly after, were not later identified and their names appear on the Menin Gate. The man dying of wounds must have been Cpl Stanley Groome. He was shot accidently by another man while cleaning his rifle and is buried in the huge cemetery at Lijssenthoek, south of Poperinghe. The three remaining men are all buried in Dickebush New Military Cemetery and include Frank Rivers, a friend and fellow clubmate of Victor Hember. Rivers, like many of the LRB a keen athlete, was over six feet tall. He was talking with Schuman, 'when suddenly my tunic was bespattered with his brains - they looked just like water-melon seed'. Rivers, a 20 year old from Finchley and one of the first entrants to the 3rd Battalion, was buried by the chaplain and a photo of the grave sent back to the 'club' in North London.

For the men who had enlisted in the 3rd Battalion anticipating excitement and glory, little of either was found in the mud of Belgium. The experience of war had not measured up to their expectations; instead they had endured the most appalling conditions, been subjected to gas attacks, and had been witnesses to the occasional blowing of German mines. Instead of pulsating bugle-led bayonet charges across the green sward of No Man's Land, against a cowering and frightened enemy, the men had carried out a few mud-splattered patrols which had discovered no Germans but merely the evidence of their wiring work. It had not been the anticipated introduction to warfare for the clerks, but they had been blooded and conditions could not get much worse. What they could look forward to as 1916 dawned was the great offensive which the British Army must surely launch in the coming year. Furthermore, the regiment was being withdrawn from the Regular 3rd Division and was about to spend a happy three months training as part of a unit which its original conception as a Territorial battalion had intended - a member of an elite, London, Territorial Division.

CHAPTER VI

Preparations for Catastrophe

As the new 56th (London) Division formed, there developed a keen but friendly rivalry between its constituent units of the London Regiment. Among all battalions a strong sense of *esprit* developed based upon the traditions of the regiments already implanted during their pre-war or post-mobilisation training and further fostered now in an atmosphere of competition. Frequent inter-battalion sports and matches took place, which helped the blossoming of morale and added in a friendly manner to the former traditions of competition evident in the Brighton March, tent pegging and marathon events that had dominated the pre-war days. The various regiments knew that they had the opportunity to create a division that could be second to none, undiluted as it was by any non-London unit except that of the Pioneer Battalion and a portion of the Divisional Engineers.

Esprit, an important element of high morale, became an essential consideration for all units and later became the measure of a battalion's capacity to continue in the line following a severe battle or mauling without endangering formations on its flanks. Comradeship and pride in the regiment and its past deeds had long been recognised as the roots from which sound morale grows. From the earliest days of training, the LRB did much to encourage altruism amongst the men and this was continued in the methods of discipline employed while on active service. The men were not only encouraged, but were also obliged to be smart on parade and to achieve a high standard of drill. Keen competition on bombing and musketry courses was also encouraged, and to remind members they belonged to an elite regiment, there was a regular emphasis on the Brighton March success. Frequent pre-war smoking concerts were held which, as mst of the men were unmarried, served a similar function to that of Regular soldiers messing and living together. The idea of both was to imbue the men with the sense that the regiment was a family - in the case of the working-class Regulars this often became the only family they possessed. For the Territorials, with their ready-made families at home in the suburbs, the regiment had to try to gain at least an equal share of the men's devotions. The army had to try even harder, and offer the man something in the realms of emotion and filial ties that perhaps his stiff and, in some respects, distant middle-class family atmosphere could not adequately provide.

The structured and disciplined atmosphere of Bunhill Row gave the recruits of 1914-15 a sense of belonging to a regiment already renowned throughout the London area, and, following the stand at Ypres, one that had performed deeds which bore comparison to any Regular unit in the British Army. The men rapidly developed a sense of absolute loyalty to the regiment and soon learnt definite ideas about what would be acceptable behaviour and what might show up the regiment in an unfavourable light. Self-confidence and confidence in their leaders led them towards a regimental *esprit* that was to serve the unit well in the trying times ahead. But self-confidence is a difficult element to quantify and evaluate. The men of the LRB were certainly confident in their particular battalion as a whole, and the rest of the 56th Division was composed of like-minded units. The morale of the entire division was consequently high, as witnessed by the friendly, but serious rivalries already mentioned, and by the low incidence of crime and misdemeanour. No doubt the fear of disgrace or letting their respective regiments down in the eyes of the other battalions served as a strong inducement to self-control and discipline. These ideas of loyalty, group spirit and 'playing the game' had been developed and absorbed by the men of these elite units not only during their Army training but also from their schools. These had taught that the basis of good morale and discipline grew from an awareness of a correct balance between self- and imposed control.

This important regimental confidence had been built up on a system of discipline that to the Regular army was incomprehensible. The LRB knew that educated, intelligent volunteers could not be treated in the same way as it might handle a possibly illiterate man from the working classes. 'Bull' was a meaningless method of discipline to the LRB but that did not mean to say that there was no discipline or that the unit accepted second-rate standards of turnout or behaviour. Unneccesary 'bull' can be replaced, and was, by an understanding that the men had sufficient pride in their regiment not to need colour-sergeants or drill instructors bellowing and shouting at them in the Aldershot manner. This attitude was in fact sustained for most of the war in the serving regiment; it came as a surprise to men posted to it, and was missed by those transferred from it to more orthodox regiments. Adjutants arriving from Regular units in the pre-war days were mystified as to how the battalion could operate in what appeared to an outsider such a casual system. Men did not have to stand to attention when speaking to a lance-corporal (unlike, for example, as a rifleman was required to do in the Civil Service Rifles), but new recruits soon discovered that there was an essential, anticipated element of self-imposed discipline, and should it fail, there was always that dispensed by the men themselves. The LRB was not unique in this, but it was possible for men who worked together in the city offices to meet at Bunhill Row in positions of private and officer and not suffer any embarrassment providing good sense was exercised and the good of the regiment the paramount concern.[191]

Even during wartime and the subsequent infusion of drafts from other regiments, the principle of reciprocal responsibility remained. As such a high proportion of LRB officers had been rankers, they could talk on friendly and equal terms with the men or NCOs, whom they treated as 'gentlemen'. The officers realised that if the men were to perform to their utmost, a system of hard, iron discipline was not the way. Such a method may have suited other units, particularly later in the war and from time to time even the LRB itself, but the platoon and company commanders knew that the best method was to cultivate the man's sense of honour in both himself and the regiment. This could be done by inspiring the men with his own example in battle - as was demonstrated through the calm and assured courage shown by Wallis and Husey at Ypres - or by their immaculate turnout when out of the line. The result was that the morale developed through such means was based not on control from external agencies and the fear of unpleasant reprisals, but was born of the member's own self-control and will not to let the regiment down.

Independence and initiative were encouraged from riflemen and their suggestions were frequently sought and acknowledged. Many soldiers of the First World War frequently complained in later years that they never knew what was supposed to be happening on their left or right flanks, or what their particular part in the overall plan was intended to be. They also tell of how they remained ignorant of their leaders' tactical or strategic ambitions. The educated volunteers serving in the LRB in 1916 were not mere cannon-fodder and, while they clearly were not taken into the confidence of the red-tabbed staff officers, their platoon officers and NCOs did try to explain the object of an operation as far as they themselves knew it to be. The regiment would probably have agreed with the theory later propounded by Lord Moran that if a reason can be explained for everything, discipline is not necessarily destroyed but is partially replaced by leadership and trust.[192] The concept of stressing to each man that he was an important and vital cog in a larger wheel helped to build personal as well as unit morale. Furthermore, the absence of the more usual form of Army discipline and the total reliance upon superiors, which can so easily crush initiative from ordinary riflemen, also meant that the troops acquired confidence in their own ability to get themselves out of tight spots if their section commanders were killed or incapacitated.

This less formal relationship between officer and ranker could have caused difficulties if mutual trust had been insufficient, or if regimental *esprit* had not penetrated deeply enough to ensure that should problems arise, they could be overcome without a weakening of authority or respect on the part of the officer. There does not, for example, seem to have been the difficulty experienced by Manning's central character, Bourne, in *The Middle Parts of Fortune*, when he paraded before his officer. Because they came from the same social background Bourne felt embarrassed and uncomfortable, and both characters tacitly recognized a peculiar ambiguity in their relationship.[193] Similarly, even if any of the commissioned NCOs could have been described as one of Harry Penrose's 'boot faced'[194] officers, there was no apparent friction in relations with their former friends and colleagues in the ranks. The troops were supposed to hate these officers because they had not come from the established officer 'corps'. Indeed, all the evidence suggests that relations between officers and men, and NCOs and their sections, were excellent at this stage of the war. This was in spite of the fact that the impact of war had brought changes in the composition of the battalion's officer corps by June 1916. The most significant aspect of this transformation was the disappearance of all Regular officers; this meant that for the first time in its history the LRB was completely officered by peacetime part-time volunteers or wartime commissioned men. By June 1916 Arthur Bates, who had sailed on the *Chyebassa* as one of the eight company commanders, had risen to command the battalion he had joined in 1900. His second in command was Ralph Husey, wounded at Ypres and rapidly becoming recognised as an exceptional soldier and inspirational leader of men. The Adjutant was the former Colour-Sergeant Dick Wallis - the only one of the nine senior officers commissioned from the ranks.

A study of the six men who served as company commanders before and during the coming battle shows that there is not any real difference in their educational backgrounds compared with those of their counter-parts who sailed on the *Chyebassa*. All but one had been to one of the top public schools such as Eton or Harrow, and all had been to either Oxford or Cambridge. Five had already seen active service with the LRB, while the other, de Cologan, had arrived, complete with monocle, from the Somali Camel Corps in 1915. Two of the six were to be wounded and leave the battalion before the battle opened, and of the four remaining, three had already been wounded or invalided home for a period of time.

The greatest changes though took place among the junior officers, of whom a total of 28 served with the battalion during June and the commencement of the offensive. Compared with the second lieutenants of 1914, the background and education of these 1916 soldiers were very different. Only four had attended one of the top public schools, 18 had studied at the minor ones or local grammar schools, the schools of another two are unknown and four had attended nothing more grand than the local council secondary school. None of the pre-war officers or rankers Commissioned in the Field in 1915 had attended anything less than a grammar school, so these four young officers of 1916 were new types to the LRB. Furthermore, only two of the 28 had studied at Oxbridge.

Five of the total were men who had been given direct commissions during the Battle of Ypres or immediately after, and another 17 had been commissioned from either the 2nd or 3rd Battalions of the LRB. The majority of these had only arrived at the 1st Battalion in May or June, but of the total, exactly 50% had seen active service as other ranks or newly commissioned officers at Ypres. The experience of these men would prove a valuable asset, especially to those going into the trenches for their first tour only a month before the long-awaited offensive opened. Although nine of the 28 had not originally joined the LRB but had served in some other regiment since August 1914, six had been commissioned in those other units and then later transferred to the training regiment at home. So, despite the fall in the proportion of the second lieutenants that had attended a major school, those young officers present were, in some respects, more typical of the LRB man than their 1914 equivalents. As the greater proportion had only served in the one regiment, they had advantages in that they were better attuned to regimental traditions. Furthermore, because 12 of them had been pre-1914 members, they understood and empathised with the pre-war *esprit* that had provided the mobilised battalion with its sound and essential base for later expansion. These officers were known and respected by the longer-serving members of the battalion, and from their evident pride and affection for the regiment, the newer recruits from the 3rd Battalion could soon feel they had merely swopped the family atmosphere of the training unit for the equally strong fraternal one of the serving battalion.

As they came from the same social class these officers were virtually indistinguishable from the men in the ranks. They had identical peacetime occupations and, of course, came principally from the capital or Home Counties. Like so many of the men in their platoons, they are constantly referred to in contemporary accounts as 'athletes', and they clearly shared the same attitudes to life in general, and affection to the LRB in particular, as their men. Furthermore, because they held identical philosophies about the regiment and the nature and purpose of the war, and because the *esprit* that had grown in both officer and men had developed to such an extent that the LRB itself was the very means by which those philosophies could be represented and manifest themselves, the men could speak on almost equal terms to their commanders without either party experiencing any feelings of awkwardness or diffidence.

The officers out for the first time, and particularly those who had not come through the ranks of the LRB itself, would rely heavily upon the battalion's experienced NCOs. Ypres had taken many of the pre-war non-commissioned men, and those who had replaced them as section leaders and commanders had, by and large, been the surviving pre-war members and the recruits of August 1914. There were also now some NCOs from the 2nd Battalion drafts and even one or two, such as William Marlborough, who had been promoted from those sent out by the 3rd Battalion. Stripes were not easily acquired in the LRB of 1916 and those who did earn them might, in more conventional units, have become over-conscious of the fact that those they now commanded could just as readily have been awarded them. In the LRB there does not seem to have been jealousy or recorded resentment; Smith recalled that as late as July 1917 there were about half-a-dozen 1914 men in the Transport section who were still without a stripe, but that none of them seemed to care in the slightest because there was no 'disgrace in being a private in the LRB'.[195] The easy and confident relations between the officers, NCOs and riflemen were clearly another important ingredient in establishing high morale and developing the sense of a 'family' atmosphere within the battalion.

In some units discipline was relaxed when out of the line, but again this does not appear to have been the case in the LRB, at least at this point in the war, because it was of such a relaxed nature anyway that it would have been difficult to make it any less formal. Morale was high enough for a man to do the things required of him not because he was told to do so, but because he wanted to do them. In a regiment like this where virtually all of the men could have taken commissions, the self-control was sufficient to ensure that overall discipline would not break down in the absence of more formal restraints; one of the vital elements of morale must be this correct balance between self- and imposed discipline - a balance founded in the pre-war regiment and which continued to operate successfully at this stage in the war.

In many ways of course, discipline, probably the most essential condition for any army to function effectively, is the product of its organisation and the means by which that organisation is viewed by the soldiers to whom it is applied. Unlike warriors of old these men probably had no need or desire to pledge a mutual voluntary oath declaring that they would not run or quit the ranks, but the same three factors identified by Thucydides as necessary for success still applied. These were: willingness to fight, shame at being seen to falter and obedience to superior orders. The fear of reproach is a decisive factor in many mens' minds and the opportunity to excel in a regiment comprised of men of such similar intelligence and background must have added an extra incentive to some to try just that little harder. Yet, by the same token, knowledge that they belonged to an elite unit must have been sufficient for others to feel that, providing they fulfilled the expectations required of them, they had nothing more to prove. The over-riding concern was a sense of duty, accentuated by a profound feeling of strong loyalty to the regiment and to comrades.

The discipline of any army must be to ensure that threatening and dangerous situations are met by 'fight rather than flight'.[196] In order to achieve this, the social consequences of flight must be made more unpleasant than the physical consequences of staying put. It was noted earlier how the public shame of letting down their friends and comrades had been instilled in the men of the LRB at their public or private schools. Yet, even had this not been the case, the recruits of 1914 and 1915 were still fighting a war that they thought was worth fighting. This was not perhaps for such esoteric or abstract concepts as the righteousness of democracy over the evil of tyranny, but for the preservation of their way of life and all it represented. This faith in the things they held dear could sustain many men through the hardship of static trench warfare, but even the most enthusiastic and idealistic warrior likes to see evidence of his belief that he really is superior to the enemy before the offensive opens. The fear of what the mental horrors of battle might entail and the physical retaliation that the enemy might bring to bear can breed exaggerated fears and sap morale. To try to counter this fear of the unknown, all LRB ranks attended a 'flammenwerfer' display in April, and once the preparation for the offensive began in earnest, frequent practice attacks over trenches identical with those of the Gommecourt sector were made. Familiarity with their objectives, with their own personal equipment, their own commanders and sections and, equally important, the divisional support arms, all contributed to an increasing faith in themselves and their comrades.

While close attention was paid to these mental factors which so affected morale, consideration was also given to the men's physical conditions. While the battalion trained at Magnicourt-sur-Canche, efforts were made to ensure provision of the best facilities permitted by the circumstances. Billets were found in barns and stables which, although not luxurious, were better than those they had been forced to endure at Voormezeele. *Esprit* had rapidly improved from the depression evident in January, and to consolidate this improvement the LRB, as usual, laid great store in providing regular mail deliveries. The contribution made by families at home naturally played a major part in this aspect of morale building, and to ensure that all soldiers benefited from food parcels those men whose relatives might not be able to afford as regular supplies as others had their comforts supplemented from regimental funds. The practice of charging subscriptions continued until the introduction of conscription forced Parliament, eventually, to prohibit it. Until then, however, Wallis remarked that everyone was 'anxious and willing' to pay the amount because each considered it an 'honour and privilege' to serve in the ranks of the LRB. Other battalions of the London Regiment, such as the Artists and London Scottish, also continued to charge for membership, but the practice was not perhaps as happily accepted by all men as it was by Wallis. The *Territorial Service Gazette* of 3 April 1915 recorded that it had received letters from men serving in the LRB complaining that five francs had been deducted for subscriptions and that they regarded it as 'mean to have their hard-earned pay stopped for a corps sub. when they were at the front'. No doubt some men did resent having to pay the amount, but the advantages which it allowed the men in the trenches were obvious for all to see. There is no mention in any of the memoirs or amongst the survivors which suggests that the resentment was widespread, or that it caused any damage to *esprit*.

The new arrivals to the battalion from home would soon hear of the indefatigable work done by the Transport section in getting up with the rations every night at Ypres and, similarly, of the work done by the cooks in preparing the food. As Napoleon stated, and most commanders have since reiterated, soldiers are always intimately concerned with their stomachs. The survivors of 2nd Ypres impressed upon their newer comrades that the regiment had done better than other units in the quality and quantity of the rations sent up during the battle. Every day Lt Peterson and Tootsie Hands packed up parcels of cooked fresh beef and cold bacon for each platoon or section, and afterwards Hands often proudly proclaimed; 'The only Regiment in the British Army wot 'ad fresh meat froo aht the second battle of Wipers - the LRB and thanks ter Toots!'[197] Knowledge such as this would again impress the new members and build faith and confidence in the reliability of the battalion's supporting arms and constituent parts.

Great emphasis was laid on the new men to persuade them that they 'belonged' to the regiment and although much could be done in the 3rd Battalion which could emphasise the family nature of the regiment, the transfer to the 1st Battalion meant that the process had to be developed further to take account of the changed, active service experience. Yet no matter how great the attempt was to make the regiment a home from home, ultimately, the extent to which the practice was successful lay in the degree of the individual's perception and consequently personal morale. Group morale, in other words, was only as strong as individual morale, and that in turn was dependent on how the soldier saw himself in relation to a small group such as the platoon, and to the larger battalion or regimental unit as a whole. The available evidence suggests that the re-built battalion of the LRB quickly re-established the *esprit* for which it was renowned in its pre-war days and which had helped see it through the tumultuous events of Ypres. On 2 May 1916, exactly a year since the battalion had experienced the German gas attack at Fortuin, it received orders that the division was moving to VII Corps area. Here it would prepare for the commencement of a massive combined Anglo-French offensive, which would take place later that summer.

On 28 April 1916 Lieutenant-General Sir T.D.O. Snow, Commanding VII Corps, was informed by General Allenby, Commander of Third Army, that his Corps would be required to undertake an offensive against the Gommecourt salient at the end of May. VII Corps was to comprise the 37th Division, a New Army unit already positioned in the Gommecourt area, and two First Line territorial divisions, the 46th (North Midland) and the 56th (London). Arrangements were immediately set in train to get these two divisions concentrated in the area where the attack would take place, and, following the arrival of orders on 2 May, 169 Brigade comprising the LRB, 2nd London, Queen Victoria's Rifles and the Queen's Westminster Rifles, began the march towards the front.

The re-constituted LRB arrived at Halloy on 7 May and was billeted in huts for two weeks. During this time various forms of training were conducted before the battalion then moved to St Amand, a small village five miles behind Fonquevillers. The regiment had left Magnicourt having done well in the brigade sports at Frevent and having the satisfaction of getting eleven more men through the brigade bombing course than any other battalion. Spirits were high and expectations great as the columns swung towards the front. Although some of the battalions in the division had received drafts from other regiments, the LRB was still composed of men who had enlisted and trained with the regiment. Another draft from the 3rd Battalion had joined just as the division left Magnicourt. This brought the battalion's 'total strength' up to 30 officers and 936 other ranks. However, that is just one of four totals given for 11 May; the so-called trench strength amounted to 27 officers and 719, but ration strength, which included the cooks, Transport and other details not available for the line, brought it up to 29 and 835 respectively. The final figure - effective strength - includes 3 officers and 64 other ranks on courses or leave, which brings it up to 30 and 899. The difference between that figure and total strength was made up by men in hospital and sick or wounded who had not yet been evacuated.

Chyebassa men were in the minority in the regiment as a whole, but the Transport section, disbanded after Ypres and then re-born in August 1915, did still have a large proportion of its original members. The section had in fact only suffered a total of three deaths during Ypres so there were still some 30 originals in a total of 51. Of the new members, most were men who had arrived from the 2nd Battalion before Ypres and had since managed to arrange a transfer to the section. They included the two friends Aubrey Smith and Kimbo Vallentine-Warne, while the remainder were selected from 3rd Battalion men who applied to go on a riding course. Smith had applied and was accepted into a unit which thus still had its mobilised, and to some extent even its pre-war, appearance, but the changes that had come about within the companies had left him able to count his old comrades of No 4, or 'D' Company as it was now known, virtually on the fingers of two hands.[198] Some of the original members had transferred to other specialist sections - for example Graham Williams, now a Lance-Corporal, had re-trained as a signaller - and others had disappeared off to the various brigade formations. Thirty-one LRB men, including Lancelot Jessop, had been detailed to form part of 169 Brigade Machine Gun Company in April, but 'Sunny', as he was more commonly known on account of his cheery nature, had missed his friends so much that he had contrived to get sent back to the battalion. Similarly, some men who had been temporarily detached from the companies for other duties, such as Basil Houle, rejoined their comrades in preparation for the attack.

Confidence in and enthusiasm for their respective tasks is evident from the memoirs. For example, a request for 'skilled bowlers' to volunteer for what later turned out to be bombing sections appeared in Orders. Under the leadership of 2Lt 'Curley' Boston, the men chosen grew so 'enthusiastic...over this new act that the CO had to explain that bombing alone could not win the war'.[199] Wiring parties sweated to set new records for speed and efficiency, but probably the most important factor in the preparedness of the battalion for its role in the coming battle was the fact that there were only between 100 and 110 men who had as yet not seen active service in the trenches. It is going too far, however, to assert that a 'high proportion of well-trained pre-war volunteers' remained in the ranks of the LRB by June 1916.[200] The real proportion of such men was probably only about 15% in total, and with a smaller percentage than that actually serving in the companies themselves. However, all the men serving in the 1st Battalion had joined the Army before November 1915, so even the most novice of the new arrivals had had a minimum of seven months training. The majority of the battalion, therefore, had been together since at least October 1915. This period in the trenches and what Houle described as the 'hell of a good time', while the London

Division reformed, had allowed the battalion to attain what it considered to be a thoroughly professional expertise in all arms.

That this fine battalion, and the others like it in the division, were to be squandered by attacking one of the strongest parts of the German line in an effort to divert German artillery from British attacks further south, was one of the tragedies of the war. The German position in front of Gommecourt had been developed into a virtual fortress of three major trench systems and a near-rectangle of extensive defensive works encompassing most of the village. To the west of that, the trees of Gommecourt Park hid more trench systems, many of which included dugouts up to forty feet deep. These shelters, some of which were supplied with water and even electricity, were immune to shells from all but the biggest guns; a provision in which the British artillery of all sectors was singularly short. The general lie of the land over which the British were to advance also ran in the Germans' favour. Gommecourt village lies on the top of a gentle plateau and, while the lines of the London Division lay on the opposite forward slope of a shallow valley, their communication trenches and rear areas were fortunately screened from enemy observation by the village and trees of Hebuterne. The North Midlanders did not enjoy this advantage: the land held by the 46th Division, to the north-west of the salient, was exposed to German view. Furthermore, the trenches in this part of the line were more prone to flooding than those occupied by the Londoners; a factor which would further hamper the attack of the North Midland Brigades.

General Snow did in fact request that the diversionary attack - for that was what his Corps were to be employed to do - should take place further north near Arras. General Allenby considered the proposal and then decided that as such an attack would have no bearing on the activities of the German artillery on the Somme sector, it would not fulfil its primary objective. Therefore, he insisted that planning for the Gommecourt attack should continue.[201] As the *Official History* later noted, if Snow had been given more time to prepare, he would undoubtedly have ordered mining operations to be conducted with the object of destroying some of the known German strongpoints.[202] However, as he originally expected the attack to begin by the end of May, all available man-power was necessarily utilized in digging new assembly trenches, gun pits and communication trenches. Once they were completed, what little time remained could be spent digging and training on replica trenches of the Gommecourt salient.

Apart from the depth and extent of the German defences, another major problem facing the attacking troops was the width of No Man's Land. In front of the 56th Division this extended down the slope to the valley bottom and then up towards the Park and village, a distance of about 800 yards. The attacking infantry would either have to cross this area, probably under shell fire and risk annihiliation, or try to lessen the distance by advancing the British line. This was the option taken by Snow, and thus an operation in which the LRB was to play a large part was set in train.

Stretching across the fields roughly half way between the British and German lines was a small hedge - shown on British maps as 'Z' Hedge or Patrol Wood. The LRB had relieved the 3rd London in 'Y' Sector immediately to the west of the hedge on 21 May, and two nights later, suffered its first casualties when a patrol went out to investigate the hedge. Division had ordered that new trenches should be dug behind the hedge but before the work could be done, the hedge and the surrounding area had to be secured from German patrols. Consequently, Lt Clode-Baker and 15 men went out on the night of 24-25 May, and stayed there for the next 24 hours. The difficulty was that with only a small bank protecting them from German observation the men had to lie still during the long hours of daylight. No German patrols appeared during the rest of the night and this small party was relieved the following night by another under the command of 2Lt Jerry Pogose. On the night of 25-26 May Capt Somers-Smith took over a 100 men to lie out in front of the hedge while the 416 Field Company RE of 167 Brigade taped and pegged the outlines of the new trenches. Finally, during the following two nights, another LRB party covered the troops of 167 Brigade as they dug the system, protected further by the darkness of the wet night and the deliberate clatter of transport limbers passing up and down the streets of Hebuterne.

The troops had quickly dug nearly 3,000 yards of fire trench and 1,500 yards of communication trenches. On subsequent nights, working parties were found to wire and strengthen the new system. Here lay the paradox facing the 56th Division. The idea of the diversionary attack was to tie down German troops and artillery, but this could not be done without broadcasting the fact that there was to be an attack. Yet, at the same time, the troops constructing the new front line system naturally worked in the hope that they would not be spotted and have artillery fire brought down upon them until the trenches were deep enough to offer some protection. Wallis recorded that whenever the German artillery opened up - as it did once the chalk of the new parapets was spotted - the British guns, now amassed in huge numbers, immediately replied in overwhelming force. To further persuade the Germans that an attack was being planned for the sector, the RFC secured aerial supremacy and, in cooperation with the guns, registered many of the German artillery positions, dumps and likely assembly areas etc. If General Snow was to adhere to his instructions, then the troops under his command were obliged to demonstrate, rather than obscure, their preparations.

When not manning the front trench or posts, the LRB provided working parties of roughly half company strength to continue the work on the trenches. Despite the hazardous operations conducted during the month, and the increasing German attention being paid to them, the battalion was lucky in losing only four dead and 16 wounded. Although casualties were light, the rain continued to pour almost incessantly upon the heads of the men. It drenched them as they worked on the defences, as they struggled and slipped under their burdens of barbed wire and picquets, and as they repeatedly practised the attack over the replica trenches in Halloy.

For the men who had been in the trenches at Vormezeele, the experience of this new sector, even despite the rain, was a much more enjoyable one. Although it had suffered from German shells, Hebuterne was a far more comfortable village in which to spend the war than the shattered barns and hovels of the Salient. The two companies in battalion support occupied the remains of the farms and outbuildings, with the support trenches themselves running through the nearby orchards and along the streets. Again, when approaching the support lines, instead of having to creep along at the dead of night, relieving troops came up in daylight and had interesting pieces of scenery behind the German lines nonchalantly pointed out to them as they approached. The communication trenches running from the support to the original front lines were an impressive ten feet deep. This not only allowed the easy movement of men to and from the trenches in daylight, but also meant that the cookers could be brought up to the village. Consequently, the troops in the front lines often received their food hot.

The village itself had a small dry canteen where the troops could buy tinned fruit etc. and in what little spare time they had the men cultivated the flower beds dotted around the billets and trenches begun by the previous occupants; 'Kew Gardens', 'Garden of Eden' and 'Don't pick the flowers' notices soon appeared amongst the ruins. The companies taking their turn in the original front trenches were not quite as comfortable. As there were only three dugouts allotted to the other ranks of each company, the sergeants naturally took those. Furthermore, although the trench bottom was brick-lined, these former French trenches were too wide and lacked sufficient traverses to offer good protection against shelling. This was, in addition to the endless carrying parties and revetting fatigues, yet another default for the numerous working parties to rectify. Victor Hember wrote wistfully to his 'Clubites' from Hebuterne in late May:

Before we came here we were told it was a very quiet piece of line with hardly any shelling and very few casualties. Something must have happened to upset this ideal state of things since we have been here or else 'somebody' was a bally liar as we have already had casualties every day.

Basil Houle also thought that the sector had been a quiet one before the arrival of the Londoners: 'We were told that the Germans used to come over to play cards with the French. One evening a party came over under a corporal and we potted them and killed the corporal. I rather think they were expecting a quiet game'. If such card schools had existed in earlier days, the legacy had remained for some time for the British had been in possession of the sector for many months. Houle is probably confusing the incident with an attempted raid by a small German patrol on one of the LRB posts on 18 June.

While all the preparatory work went on, there were other distractions. The Lord Mayor of London inspected the division in early June, but by the time he arrived to pass along the ranks of the LRB, the battalion had been on parade in the rain for over two hours. Not surprisingly, the visit lost something of its intention as a morale building exercise. A plethora of generals, surrounded by immaculately dressed staff officers, watched them as they practised their attacks in a variety of formations. Sometimes these went on under smoke, sometimes with full packs, but never with the amount of equipment and impedimenta they would have to carry on the actual day. At the end of the manoeuvre the generals returned to their comfortable headquarters and the men of the LRB trudged back to their bare huts and attempted to dry out as best they could. By mid-June they were back in the front line again, but the posts were held by only one company to allow the remainder to continue digging. The weather cleared up for a few days, which helped, but by the time they were relieved by the 7th Middlesex on 21 June, the men were exhausted. However, relief did not mean rest - 'D' Company was immediately detached for duties with the RE at Mondicourt, and on the subsequent four days, the whole battalion repeatedly practised the attack. Once again the weather was foul.

Meanwhile, on 24 June, the British bombardment had commenced. The Germans of course knew an attack was imminent but were not convinced as to where the blow would actually fall. The opening of the bombardment and the intense digging conducted during the previous weeks persuaded them that an attack would be made against Gommecourt and although they did engage on some limited counter-battery work, most of the German guns lay hidden and idle in splinter-proof emplacements. They had registered on the new British front line - now only 250-400 yards in front of their own - and waited until called upon by the infantry. The British had hoped to get their front advanced by another 200 yards, but the weather, and more importantly the time, had prevented the work being done. The attacking infantry would still have to advance a considerable distance once the barrage had lifted from the German front line and ensure they reached the German trench, before the enemy appeared from their dugouts. This aspect of the attack worried Lt Col Bates. He had grown increasingly concerned over the plans passed down to him from Brigade, and had eventually protested when the reserve company was ordered to provide a carrying party for the RE long after the attacking companies had gone over. Bates argued that all four companies should get across No Man's Land as quickly as possibly, unhampered by anything not needed immediately. Then, once it had been established that there were no Germans left alive, the reserve company could return to the British front and act as 'coolies'. However, Brigade appear to have held the same belief as Rawlinson, the Commander of Fourth Army, that the bombardment would destroy all German opposition and the troops would merely have to occupy the enemy trenches. This miscalculation was to cost the men of the 56th Division dear.

On paper the weight of the British bombardment appeared impressive. The divisional artillery was supplemented by Corps batteries comprising all calibres and each designated specific targets and functions. Five further 18-pdr. batteries remained directly under the Divisional General for wire cutting, and these were assisted by the three Brigades' Heavy and Stokes Mortar Batteries. Finally, if the German wire still provided an obstacle to the infantry, Bangalore Torpedoes would be fired the night before the advance.

The Germans on the receiving end of the bombardment - mainly the *55th Reserve Infantry Regiment (2nd Guard Reserve Division)* - kept a meticulous record of the damage resulting from it.[203] The *War Diary* records the intensity of the shell fire, but it was not until the second afternoon of the bombardment that a shell - a dud - managed to penetrate a dugout. As the next days passed, only another two dugouts were reported badly damaged, despite the belief that the British were firing 15-inch shells. The ground above the dugouts was of course suffering badly, with trenches blown in and shrapnel fire concentrating on roads and rear areas. During lulls in the shelling, parties went out to repair the trenches, and in the afternoon of 30 June, a number of British were taken prisoner from a small patrol inspecting damage to the German wire. After interrogating the British, a German officer reported to his superiors that there were 'No black troops present - no gas - nothing known about attack'. Other reports from the German companies manning the front noted that gaps had been made in the British wire. Despite this, however, the general feeling among the Germans was that the attack was still not yet imminent. Furthermore, although an enormous volume of shell fire was being directed against the German line, the casualties suffered by the *55th Reserve Regiment* between 24 - 30 June were reported as only five killed and 46 wounded. The shelling had destroyed trenches and managed to cut some of the buried telephone cables, but it had clearly failed in its other task of collapsing enemy dugouts and killing their sheltering occupants.

The men of the LRB had trained, practised and rehearsed their attack for nearly a month and were confident that they and the other units of the 56th Division would achieve their objectives. The LRB was the left flank of the division, with the Queen Victoria's on their right and the London Scottish and the Rangers of 168 Brigade further over. Once the lodgement in the German lines had been achieved, the Queen's Westminsters were to pass through their comrades of 169 Brigade and link up with the North Midlanders in Gommecourt who would be approaching the village from the north. Any remaining German resistance in the park could then be pinched out. There was no intention of then advancing further into German-held territory so no reserves were available - the British line would merely have been straightened by eliminating the German salient. The obvious worry, to anyone privy to the full plan, was how the two divisions attacking the north-west and south-west shoulders of the salient would fare once it became obvious to the Germans that there were to be no attacks immediately to the north and south of those British divisions. All available German artillery would then be brought to bear to fire both frontally and in enfilade on those two formations and would cut them off in what would have become a salient of their own making. However, according to the greater plan, this was not important because the German concentration on this attack would divert their attention particularly from the attack towards Serre by the 31st Division. In other words, the 46th and 56th Divisions could, if necessary, be sacrificed for the good of the overall plan.

The LRB was to advance in six waves, with 'A' 'C' and 'D' Companies up, and with the officers carrying rifles and conforming to the movements of their men. The principal objective of the first wave - which would lie down 150 yards in front of their own line three minutes before zero - was to clear any remaining wire and then consolidate. 'A' Company, on the extreme left, would cover the rest of the battalion from attacks through the wood which would remain under British shell fire for a further three hours. 'D' Company, on the right, was instructed to link up with the Queen Victoria's. (Map 4) Despite Bates's protests to Brigade, the troops were to be burdened down with tools, bridges, ladders, sign posts, extra ammunition and bombs. They were warned not to leave any dugouts uncleared as they advanced and also warned against any looting. Orders were made for the despatch of prisoners back to the British lines and in case of casualties, two stretcher bearers per company were detailed to go forward without their stretchers. The provision of only eight bearers, armed solely with field dressings, for 800 attackers, as well as the extra weight and equipment to be carried across in the advance, does not seem to have unduly worried the men:

> *We were given all sorts of ridiculous things to carry but we were very*
> *confident and in high spirits because we'd been told there was nothing*
> *to worry about. My Company Commander had said we were better*
> *trained and equipped than the Germans and that the artillery would*
> *have killed them all anyway. We imagined ourselves brewing up in the*
> *German lines while the later waves passed through.* (B. Houle)

The men had an unexpected day's rest from their digging and training when the attack was postponed for 48 hours. The *War Diary* noted that it was not known whether the delay was a consequence of the bad weather and the condition of the trenches, or for some other reason. Whatever the reason, the rest at Souastre was 'much appreciated' by the troops. The battalion had not enjoyed one day's complete rest during the month of June and was already utterly exhausted. If divisional and regimental morale had not remained so high there might have been questions asked as to whether it could undertake such a strenuous and hazardous operation in view of the exertions during the month. But, still confident and anticipating success, the LRB moved up through the fine but cloudy night of 30 June to the assembly trenches and relieved the 2nd Londons in 'Y' Sector before Hebuterne.

The LRB was to advance next day with 803 men and 23 officers. It had been decided by higher authority that the Second in Command, Ralph Husey, five other officers, the RSM, CSMs and ten other senior NCOs should stay at the Transport lines to provide the nucleus on which to rebuild the battalion should 'large casualties occur'. Characteristically, Husey protested so vigorously on being left out of the attack that, in order to appease him, he was designated the division's Liaison Officer to the 48th Division lying to its south. Although still disappointed at not being allowed to direct the battalion's work from the German side of No Man's Land - this task was to be performed by Capt Somers-Smith - it did allow Husey to be where he could see some action. Of the sergeants who were to be left out, only two had come originally from the 3rd Battalion. Among the longer-serving NCOs joining them in the battle surplus were Tom Burroughs and Charles Bradford, both of whom were waiting to be re-called to England and take up commissions.

Encouraged by the ferocity of the bombardment on the German lines, the men who had gone forward to the assembly trenches settled down as best they could for the night. The fire ceased at 23.00 hours to allow 2Lt Pogose to go out with a small patrol to inspect the German wire; Pogose reported back that it was sufficiently well cut in front of the LRB objectives not to need the Bangalore Torpedoes. The signallers and runners, including Graham Williams and Arthur Hollis, had been designated their tasks and positions, and they spent the time re-checking the cables and telephones. Sunny Jessop, now happily returned to 'A' Company, passed the night chatting to his old friend Sgt Lilley and his platoon commander and former colleague from the ranks, 2Lt 'Shumery' Doust. Arthur Schuman had said farewell to his friend of long-standing, Barney Griew, one of the runners. Griew had written to his parents in Hackney the day before apologising for his latterly irregular correspondence. He blamed it simply on 'circumstances' and because, 'there is not much to write about'. Schuman and seven others of his platoon listened to 'Bessie' Slaughter happily predict that 'this time tomorrow we'll be pushing up daisies'. Graham Williams, in more optimistic vein, promised his fellow signaller L/Cpl Deane (who had been detailed to go over with the first wave), that he would see him in Gommecourt village the next night.

As Victor Hember marched away from camp with 'C' Company the evening before the attack, he had waved a 'cheery *au revoir*' to his fellow 'Clubite', Gerald. A little later, Hember passed and received a word of encouragement from his old Colour-Sergeant, now Captain and Adjutant, Dick Wallis. Wallis was to remain at battalion headquarters with Lt Col Bates throughout the course of the day, and was often the first man to greet the survivors as they struggled back to their own lines the following night. After taking up the rations and still more equipment to the RE dumps lying just inside the British lines, Aubrey Smith and Kimbo Vallentine-Warne returned to the Transport lines. Their initial role in the attack was now complete. The sergeants of the battalion's nucleus personnel stood beside the transport men and, with mixed feelings, watched the battalion march off. They had collected the letters and personal effects of men in their companies for safe keeping, or if the need arose, despatch. One such letter, written by Rifleman Joseph McGrath of 'C' Company and typical of its type, was destined to be sent after the attack. McGrath, from Hendon, was the usual type of LRB man, having joined the 3rd Battalion with a few friends early in 1915. All these youths had refused to apply for commissions, electing instead to stay and serve together. This 24 year old wrote to his parents:

> *Well, the moment has at last come, and everybody hopes the London Rifle Brigade is going to add to its list of honours and make a great name for itself...There will be casualties, probably very heavy judging by the nature of the work...[but we are all]..in the best of spirits and eager...There is not one who would shirk going into the charge..I have not the least fear of death, all through, this life has been more like a huge sport to me.*

These sentiments were reflected in the thoughts of other men as they waited for the dawn and then the hour of attack. Williams recalled that 'many were actually looking forward' to it and that the number of men reporting sick had fallen markedly. 'We all wanted the LRB once again to distinguish itself and to be there when it did so'.

Over their heads the bombardment screamed and thundered. As 'Z' Hour approached, the gunners sweated and strained to increase its volume and intensity. In the trenches, conversation dropped off as men isolated themselves in their own thoughts, dozed, or checked their equipment one more time. Officers and NCOs moved up and down the trenches, encouraging and calming some of the men, and a liberal ration of rum was doled out shortly before the advance. German fire remained desultory during the night, but at 04.00 a more intense bombardment began to sweep the British front trenches. This continued until 06.25 when the German guns concentrated on counter-battery work. Then, almost as if they knew the precise moment of the infantry assault, they switched again to the assembly positions and front trenches. So accurate was the fire that the first wave were relieved when, under cover of smoke, they climbed out of their trenches and advanced a little way into No Man's Land. Here, on the tapes put out the night before, they laid down for three minutes and waited for the whistles to order them forward. One man of 'A' Company, however, did not even get this far. Lancelot 'Sunny' Jessop, who had successfully managed to wangle himself back to his old company, was hit in the leg by shrapnel while still in the trench. Capt Cholmeley took one look at the wound and ordered him back to the battalion aid post. Jessop's 'final' letter home was eventually retrieved from his sergeant - but he was one of the lucky ones.

CHAPTER VII

Annihilation

Here lies a clerk who half his life had spent
Toiling at ledgers in a city grey,
Thinking that so his days would drift away
With no lance broken in life's tournament.
(H. Asquith, *The Volunteer*)

The initial advance by the LRB was executed as practised so many times over the replica trenches at Halloy. (Maps 4 and 5) The smoke discharge was actually commenced five minutes before schedule, and by the time the first wave rose from the tapes in No Man's Land, the smoke was dense along most of the battalion front. The Germans, huddled in their dugouts and waiting for the intensified shell fire to lift onto the rear areas, would then race up the steps in the hope of reaching the parapet before the British infantry. The shelling of the last hour had succeeded in blowing in many of the entrances to the dugouts, had flattened the trenches and destroyed most of the wire. Furthermore, the front trench was enfiladed from Fonquevillers and the British fire was sufficiently accurate to drop shells precisely in the trench thus making its occupation impossible.

The first wave crossed the 250 yards of open ground and beat the Germans in the race to the parapet. The enemy had decided correctly that there was to be no direct attack against the front of their salient and the troops manning the shoulders were particularly concerned to get up to their parapet directly the enfilade fire moved beyond the parados. Unfortunately for the Germans, the LRB arrived above Fir and Fen almost simultaneously as the barrage lifted and many prisoners were immediately despatched back across No Man's Land. They passed some British dead and wounded as the crossing had not been totally unopposed and some of the troops in the following waves began to suffer from the fire of German machine guns and the counter-bombardment which had begun to crash down on No Man's Land.

Tom Short,[204] one of the newest arrivals to the battalion, remembered that despite the order that they should carry rifles, officers waved revolvers in case anyone defaulted. But his more poignant memory was of being 'raked with machine gun fire' while his friends dropped all around him. As a Lewis gunner, Short should have gone over with the third or fourth waves, and another in that group, suffering from a similar volume of fire, was Arthur Schuman:

> *Officers led the way, most of them dropped immediately. Machine guns seemed to crackle from every direction. I kept my head as low as possible, helmet tilted to protect my eyes, but I could still see men dropping all around me...the din was terrific, stifling any screams..[there was] just one opening on which the German fire was rapid and most accurate. Not many of us got through.*

The divisional report on the operation mentions little opposition coming from the enemy trenches and of only one machine gun, which was firing high, operating at this stage. Schuman and Short were on the left of the LRB front and probably suffered from that gun, while L/Cpl Foaden, in the centre of the attack with 'C' Company, also ran into difficulty from machine gun fire once his wave emerged from the thinning smoke. Harold Morgan thought it was 'uncanny, men were falling down around us', and although Henry Russell, a veteran of Plugstreet and Ypres, saw many of his colleagues drop, 'this somehow didn't seem to worry me'. Russell leapt into a shell hole alongside Lt Wallace who shouted something like 'must go on', stood up and was immediately 'riddled with bullets'. Russell too rose to carry on, but was also hit and fell back into the hole where he was destined to stay throughout the bombardment of the long day.

On the other hand, Basil Houle, the sniper, advancing only a 150 yards further over to the right than L/Cpl Foaden, experienced little difficulty in getting across:

> *Some of the smoke didn't work because, I heard later, some of the chaps got a bit tight on the rum, but we got over without much trouble. It was a beautiful morning and we were weighed down with those signposts and things but there wasn't much response from Jerry while we were going across. In fact I only saw one chap get hit and that was Sgt Olorenshaw and one of our men helped him forward into the German trench.*

Similarly, 2Lt Petley, on the right with 'D' Company, talked of his men shaking out in No Man's Land, forming up and then advancing across against little opposition as they 'might have done on Wimbledon Common'. The wire had been well cut in front of the battalion's objectives, but it had been so thick that it did still provide something of an obstacle. 'Punch' Hughes followed Petley with the fifth wave and talked of 'easy progress', not under fire from artillery or machine guns, and crossing at a steady 'walking pace'. But the men of Hughes's wave, like those of the earlier ones, were now thoroughly mixed, and although the advance continued to the German third line - Eck Trench - where consolidation began, difficulties were beginning to hamper the operation.

The men of 'A' Company in particular were finding it hard to establish exactly where they were. Their left flank and consequently that of the division was Point 94, where Firm and Fir Trenches met at a virtual right-angle on the edge of the wood. 2Lt 'Shumery' Doust was shot and killed very soon after reaching this point. A Lewis gun was immediately set up at this junction and another was established at Point 16, 100 yards further along Fir where it met Fen. Point 94 was vital to the whole attack as it was to be the base from where 'B' Company would launch their assault on the wood three hours after Zero. Meanwhile the Signallers had been detailed to set up a visual station and run duplicate telephone lines there from the Report Centre in 'Z' Hedge. The problem was that these German trenches on the edge of the wood had been flattened by the bombardment - so much so that Tom Short was convinced that they were in fact dummy trenches to fool the British aerial observers. Those trenches inside the park, having been sheltered by trees, had suffered little from the British fire. Troops from these systems soon brought a heavy fire to bear upon 'A' Company. Desperately, they began to deepen and extend the remains of the enemy trenches; 'We literally did not know which way to face...we were being fired on from all directions'.

Overall, the first half hour of 169 Brigade's infantry assault had proved a success. All the LRB's objectives had been reached and the men were busy putting up wire, clearing dugouts and waiting for the next stage of the operation. The battalion had linked up with the Queen Victoria's on their right and Capt Somers-Smith had set up his advanced HQ where Fen Trench met Exe. 2Lt Jerry Pogose, with some of the scouts and a section of battalion bombers under 2Lt 'Curley' Boston, had congregated with Somers-Smith, while another bombing section had taken up position at Point 16. It was now up to the Queen's Westminsters to pass through and link up with the North Midlanders in Gommecourt village.

The Germans meanwhile had been busily assessing the extent and objectives of the attack. Once it became clear that there was no attack developing immediately to the south of the front occupied by the 56th Division or to the north of the 46th Division, they began to concentrate their resources on isolating the British troops already established in the German lines. The failure of the North Midlanders to penetrate the German trenches also added to the difficulties of the Londoners because the enemy soon realised that the main threat came from the southern shoulder of the salient. The majority of their local artillery, as well as that to the north of Gommecourt opposite the 37th Division, began to bring its fire to bear on No Man's Land above and below the park. Providing the assaulting troops could be cut off from their reserves and fresh supplies, there was no immediate need to launch large-scale infantry counter-attacks on the new British positions. Thus, German fire concentrated on providing an impenetrable curtain of high explosive and shrapnel to fall between the attackers in their lodgements and assistance from their old positions.

By 09.30 hours the enemy barrage falling on No Man's Land had begun to achieve its ends. Along the front of the 56th Division, carrying parties and reinforcements from the old British lines either attempted to penetrate this wall of fire, and were savagely mauled in the attempt, or were ordered to shelter in the British trenches in the hope it might ease. The Londoners on the other side of the barrage soon began to notice the approach of German bombing parties working their way down several trenches. Snipers were also active, picking off men as they struggled to throw up bomb blocks and deepen trenches. The first significant group pushed down Ems trench from the civilian cemetery about 12.30 hours. By this time both brigades of the 56th Division had already reported that they were short of grenades, but local commanders realised the impossibility of any parties crossing No Man's Land to bring fresh supplies. German dugouts were scoured and those boxes already brought across, doled out. Each rifleman had brought two Mills bombs with him during the advance and company commanders had been instructed to collect them from the men as soon as the situation permitted. The men themselves had been ordered not to throw these bombs 'except in a grave emergency' - but, as the Germans marshalled their resources, something which could be described as an emergency, and one that was growing graver by the minute, was rapidly becoming apparent.

The men of 'D' Company in Eck trench were in danger of being cut off by Germans coming down Ems. These were then expected to cut along Female and thus behind Eck. A party of company bombers was despatched by Capt de Cologan to intercept the Germans where Female met Ems. These bombers, under L/Cpl Dennis, had already fought their way along Ferret and then up Exe, but were so outnumbered by the enemy that they were forced to fall back along Female. They were joined shortly by de Cologan who was ordered by Somers-Smith at 13.30 to withdraw to the original German front trenches. This order to withdraw had not reached 2Lt Petley, who, with about 40 men, had temporarily managed to halt the German bombers approaching further along Eck. Eventually, at 18.00, he ordered Signalling Sergeant F.S. Robinson to take the men, who included Schuman and the Ebbetts twins, down to de Cologan while he and Sgt Austin tried to bring down the wounded Sgt Sidney Olorenshaw. Robinson had struggled up from the advanced HQ with the news that most of the battalion had been ordered to fall back on the German first line. The order, although gratefully received, was by no means easy to execute.

Petley and Sgt Austin soon realised they would have to leave Olorenshaw to the mercy of the Germans and concentrated instead on trying to fight a rearguard against four separate enemy bombing parties. The rest of the 'C' and 'D' Company survivors dashed back towards the former German trench above ground, avoiding obstacles, shell holes and wire as best they could. Basil Houle was lying in the area between Female and Ferret, potting away at any German head he saw;

> Sometime in the afternoon an officer came crawling along looking for grenades which annoyed me a bit because I was quite happily concealed with my rifle and I thought he would give my position away. Anyway he left me to it but I crawled to a different shell hole near the German second line and shot two German grenadiers in the trench below me. Bombs started coming over but I was in that wonderful state when I could have killed anybody. Then another officer fell into my shell hole and ordered me to head back.

The officer ordering Houle to withdraw was probably either Petley, who had separated from Sgt Austin in the second line, or 2Lt Smith of 'D' Company. These two young subalterns fell back into Fen and Ferret and began to organise their defence.

Another man now manning the remains of Fen's parados was L/Cpl Foaden of 'C' Company. He and others had fought their way up to the company's objective of The Maze and now expected the Queen's Westminsters to pass through and continue the advance. Some Westminsters had arrived later in the morning but as it was clear that the attack on the park had not materialized, and since they realised that if they advanced further their left flank would be in the air, they stayed where they were. They had with them a Lewis gun and several packs or buckets of ammunition. The time was spent trying to fill sandbags and consolidate their position while suffering continually from a group of German snipers operating from in or near Erin trench. Around 16.00 hours Victor Hember fell into the trench. Hember ordered Foaden's group to retreat to Fen in accordance with the rest of the battalion, but Foaden insisted that any withdrawal would be impossible until dusk. Initially Hember agreed, but as the Germans were now approaching in force and there were only two grenades among 16 men, the Lewis was rendered useless and the withdrawal began. Hember and five others were immediately wounded when one of the two grenades exploded prematurely. He was left behind while the remainder eventually found their way back to Fen. Here they reported to de Cologan, Harvey and Petley.

On the extreme left of the attack on the edge of the park, Tom Short and Rfn Reynolds were still firing their Lewis guns into the wood and across the lane leading up to the village. In preparation for the assault by 'B' Company three hours after Zero, the British barrage had continued to fall as scheduled on the wood. It was clear to all that the attack could not take place while German fire on No Man's Land remained so intense. 'A' Company was also heavily involved in a bombing fight, and had been further handicapped by sending many of its reserve supply of bombs across to 'D' Company in the afternoon. Following the death of Doust and the departure of Capt Cholmeley and Lt Pocock, Sgt Lilley, with whom Sunny Jessop had wiled away the previous night, assumed command of the company. He kept the Lewis guns firing from some sort of protected positions (it had proved impossible to build the intended strong point at Point 94) but pressure from the German bombers gradually forced them back. Unhindered by excess equipment, carrying their grenades in sandbags and further assisted by the still dense undergrowth of the park, the enemy bombers pressed forward. At about 18.00 hours, having heard nothing from Somers-Smith for some time and observing British troops withdrawing from the German lines, Lilley decided he had better find out what was happening on the broader front and set off to find de Cologan.

De Cologan knew that the Germans were closing in from all directions on the remaining groups of LRB fighting to hold on to their lodgements in the German lines. In fact, the situation was becoming increasingly desperate. Ammunition was low and a continually growing number of wounded were arriving to swell the ranks of those already sheltering in the German dugouts. On the other side of No Man's Land, Lt Col Bates and Capt Wallis had received only sketchy information during the course of the day. Owing to the smoke and German barrage, communications between themselves and the attacking companies had immediately run into difficulties. Battalion HQ was sited between the original and the recently dug British front lines and by 09.00 had received two written reports from Somers-Smith in the advanced HQ. These reported that 'C' and 'D' Companies had reached their objectives, but as 'A' was having a fierce fight in the wood, he had ordered forward two platoons of 'B' to assist . Both platoons did begin the journey, but as Wallis later recalled, 'not a man got more than a few yards'. However, amidst the smoke and confusion of battle, Bates was unaware that these platoons had not gone across, and, shortly after, he ordered the remainder of 'B' to cross with their loads as planned; the runners carrying the orders were both hit *en route* so the instructions never arrived. This did not make a great deal of difference as, all morning, small parties of 'B' Company did try to render help to their hard-pressed comrades on the other side of No Man's Land. It was all to no avail for they were either driven back by the continuing shell fire or became casualties themselves.

The riflemen and NCOs manning the Report Centre in 'Z' Hedge had kept watch on Point 94 hoping to pick up some sort of visual signals. The duplicate telephone lines had been severed immediately and the volume of fire ensured they could not be repaired. The watching signallers, themselves subject to the intense shelling, saw nothing from the other side until after 13.00 hours - and then it came not from Point 94, but further along to the right where it was more difficult for them to spot. It was Rfn Nitz who first saw the Venetian Shutter, later discovered to have been operated by L/Cpl Fowle. The message was simple: 'S.O.S. Bombs'. The signal was immediately passed down to HQ, where Bates reluctantly acknowledged that there was nothing that could be done. This was the first information he had received from his own battalion for over two hours. Reports had come in from Brigade, who had relied on aerial observation, and another arrived from the Queen Victoria's. This message had been brought over from the German lines by Rfn Charles Hudson, the former student who had only recently returned to the battalion following his wounding at Ypres. Shouting that he had two messages Hudson collapsed, badly wounded, into a trench where an officer of the Queen Victoria's was stationed. The officer endorsed them, learnt that Hudson was the third man to attempt the crossing with the message, and then detailed one of his own men to assist the young rifleman down to the aid post. The message, and later a report praising Hudson's courage and determination, was passed on to the LRB.

Bates could do little except hope that more precise information on the whereabouts of his men in the German lines would come in. He ordered the barrage to be put down north of Maze and Eck at 13.10 hours, believing that all the LRB must have evacuated that area. Through his glasses he could see men being forced back into the German first line and the wounded beginning the attempt to cross back to the British front. Arthur Hollis and another runner waiting at Battalion HQ were then ordered to take a message over to Somers-Smith or de Cologan. The pair scurried off down the sunken road towards Fen. Shells and bullets hissed and exploded around them, wounding Hollis's partner. Hollis pressed on alone and succeeded in passing his message to a sergeant in the German trench. After recovering his breath, he then returned the way he had come, sustaining a wound on the way.

Others attempting the return journey from the German lines were not so lucky. Arthur Holmes also went over from the British lines carrying a message that it was 'Everyman for himself'. He passed a young boy of his own company badly wounded in the stomach, who called to him for assistance. Holmes could not stop to help but ran on to the German lines and delivered his message. He watched as men began to leave the trench and begin the crossing, only to be mown down by machine gun fire as they bunched together. Holmes decided to wait in a shell hole until dark before making his attempt. Arthur Schuman made a dash for it. Running faster than he believed possible, through the shelling and machine gun fire, he reached the British line safely and was congratulated by Wallis and RSM MacVeagh. 'Punch' Hughes also made an immediate run for it and succeeded in reaching safety. Basil Houle left the shell hole from where he had sniped at the enemy but, in his dash back to the German first line, was hit by what he thought was British shrapnel. He took what cover he could and lay on a corpse which, somewhat disconcertingly began to moan and hiss; Houle studied his companion, decided the man was dead as 'he didn't have any guts', and promptly fell asleep.

All along the former German front line, men began to crawl or run back to the British side while others waited for the night to shroud their withdrawal. On the left, Tom Short decided to wait a little longer as he thought the British would renew the attack. In fact General Snow ordered his reserve battalions to hold themselves in preparation for a night attack to support one proposed by VIII Corps on Serre. By the time darkness fell, the men of the London Division were in no position to help anyone but themselves. With ammunition exhausted and the majority wounded, the withdrawal continued. As parties made their escape from the German lines, 2Lts Petley and Smith and about a dozen men remained in Fen to form a rearguard. Further to the left Sgt Lilley, now returned from his foray to find de Cologan, and Sgt Frost, also of 'A' Company, passed the time in making the wounded as comfortable as possible. Having held out all day against determined German attacks coming through the wood, they eventually led a party of exhausted men back to the British lines. Other men of 'A' Company, including Tom Short, failed to get away and surrendered when surrounded by Germans. Short was saved from a German bayonet by a rasping order of 'Halt' from an officer who appeared just in the nick of time. The officer then said in perfect English, 'Come along you men. You've done enough for one day. Get down this dugout before you get hit'. Short and his companions then learnt why their efforts during the day had met with such frustration; during a two hour long British bombardment they sheltered with complete safety in the 20 foot-deep German dugout.[205]

Basil Houle awoke as a group of Germans approached, but on trying to stand up his legs gave way and he flopped down again, 'cursing everything and everyone'. He and several others were rounded up and sent along a communication trench into Gommecourt village. Here they assembled with a party of about 60 men from a mixture of London regiments. Meanwhile back in No Man's Land, groups of men were still trying to reach the comparative safety of their own lines. Having lain wounded in a shell hole just in front of the German first line all day long, Henry Russell finally decided on an attempt to crawl back. Throughout the long hours of daylight, with German shells falling incessantly around him, Russell had pondered on three options; he could blow himself up with a Mills bomb - but that was merely what the Germans were already trying to do; administer an over-dose of morphine - but he had forgotten to bring the tablets; or finally, the course he decided upon, to drink the contents of a Worcester Sauce bottle filled with rum and fall asleep. Coming to after dark, he crawled back to the British trenches and was soon on his way to the casualty clearing station. The runner, Arthur Holmes, also fell into the trenches occupied by the 2nd London. Further out, in No Man's Land, other groups were desperately trying to drag their wounded comrades across the shell holes and through the tangled wire to safety before daylight revealed them to the German sentries.

One such group comprised Cpl Waddington, Rfn Elleson and L/Sgt William Marlborough. These men had been sheltering in a shell hole just in front of the German first line, waiting for darkness, when a grenade burst in the hole wounding all three. Marlborough took the worst of the blast and passed out, but the others roused him about midnight and began the crawl across No Man's Land. Elleson helped Marlborough while Waddington, wounded some twenty times himself, followed painfully behind. Progress was slow and, by the time they had cleared the German wire, Waddington instructed Elleson to go on ahead and try to return with some stretcher bearers. Elleson did as he was told and shortly came across Capt Wallis out looking for wounded. Wallis told him it was impossible to get any bearers and told the rifleman to do what he could to help. Bravely, Elleson returned to the German wire and spent three hours searching for his comrades until the approach of daylight and German sentries forced him back. Waddington had meanwhile decided to leave the unconscious Marlborough, and managed to get back to the British line where he was soon picked up and sent down to the casualty clearing station.

Inside the British trenches there was constant activity as runners passed up and down, officers tried to establish platoon strengths, wounded were brought in, trench walls rebuilt and manned, and the dazed and exhausted survivors struggled to regain their shattered senses. Instead of an expected German counter-attack, however, a local truce was declared and as the early dawn broke soldiers from both sides went into No Man's Land to bring in the wounded. Arthur Schuman was amongst the searchers who saw Wallis and the battalion's padre talking to a German officer. The *Official History* notes there was 'ceremonial saluting on both sides but no fraternization'. Save for the bundles of discarded equipment and the crumpled remains of several hundred dead, within two hours No Man's Land was again empty.

While the unwounded troops tried to take stock of their own survival, those who had not taken a direct part in the battle came up to rejoin the battalion or bring up fresh supplies and rations. Victor Hember's friend Gerald drove one of the ration limbers up before the 'truce' had commenced, and later described the front zone as an inferno of flame and shells. He began to question those he knew on the fate of friends and colleagues. Apart from their own immediate experiences, however, the survivors could tell Gerald and the other inquirers little. Their number was so pitifully low that the picture soon began to emerge of a wholesale slaughter. It rapidly became apparent that the casualties for this one day affair at Gommecourt far exceeded those of the entire Ypres battle. Those members who had fought in the Salient in 1915 soon realised that this latest engagement would have a deeper and more extreme impact upon the regiment than Fortuin and Weltje had done. The utter exhaustion and haggard faces told their own stories. The non-participants immediately realised that those who now manned the firestep or huddled asleep in the trench funk holes had witnessed the virtual annihilation of the battalion. It would be years before the final fatalities would be known - indeed the statistics are not completely reliable seventy years on - but it was clear to all members of the Transport and nucleus personnel that those numbed and silent surviviors were but a fraction of those who had marched away from Souastre the previous night.

Some idea of the extent of the losses had been assimilated by Lt Col Bates earlier in the afternoon. At 17.00 hours, in reply to a Brigade request for information, Bates reported that there were only two officers and 87 other ranks unwounded in the

LRB's lines. An hour later he reported that those numbers were now 'very much less'. His account of the operations was written on 8 July and was a more detailed and specific resume than the one found in the *War Diary*. The Diary itself explains that recounting the operational and move orders had been greatly complicated by the 'very numerous alterations in disposition and formation of the battalion'. These and other amendments, it was claimed, had resulted from the original postponement of the attack. However, two tables attached to the Diary do provide a detailed breakdown of the casualties sustained during the attack. These tables vary in total by one, and make an arithmetical error in the addition of columns. Using corrected addition, one of the tables gives: killed or died of wounds, 55; wounded but within the British lines, 234 (this included 29 shell-shocked victims who returned to duty by 11 July); 69 wounded and missing; 210 missing - a total of 568 casualties or 71% of the 803 other ranks who had assembled in the front area shortly after midnight on 1 July.

The distribution and extent of these casualties is further broken down into totals sustained by each of the separate companies; 'C' in the centre suffered worst with 178, followed by 'A' with 162 and 'D' with 144. In other words, of those troops who advanced across No Man's Land in the first six waves, exactly four out of five became casualties. Perhaps not surprisingly 'B', the reserve company, experienced the lowest overall number of casualties although it did also have the lowest number of shell-shocked returning to duty within two weeks. This could presumably have been because these men had been exposed to the terrible effects of the German counter-bombardment throughout the entire day. Unlike their comrades inside the German lines, who could at least do something in retaliation against the enemy bombers and snipers, these men could do nothing except huddle in their own trenches or wait apprehensively for an order to send them into the inferno of No Man's Land. Finally, the casualty rate amongst the NCOs and riflemen of the three assaulting companies shows a degree of uniformity; 75% of sergeants, 70% of corporals, 96% of lance-corporals and 80% of riflemen. The overall casualty rate amongst the commissioned men was 83%, with Captain Cholmeley being the only officer going over the top whom Lt Col Bates saw again that day.

Calculating from the official *Soldiers Died* lists, a total of 266 LRB men were killed on 1 July - 33% of those who went over the top or stayed in the British trenches with 'B' Company. The Regimental History states that on the night of 2 July the battalion marched away from 'Y' Sector with 183 other ranks, i.e. 23% of the attackers. If the number of slightly wounded and shell-shocked known to have returned to the battalion by 23 July is added to the 183, a total of 224 is reached. Thus the impact of the one day attack had meant that only 28% of those who took part in it were again back, or still serving with the battalion three weeks later. To develop the analysis further, by subtracting the 266 killed and the 183 who marched away from the 803, the total of the men wounded and captured is 354. Furthermore, another 24 men are known to have died during the remainder of July: one of those was a 3rd Battalion recruit dying in England, one was killed on 2 July at Bayencourt and two were killed when the battalion next went into the trenches. This means that another 20 soldiers died of wounds received during the attack of 1 July. So, the total figures for the consequences of that day read; 286, or 36%, fatalities, and 41% non-fatalities or prisoners.

The fatalities also indicate how few members of the original August 1914 battalion assembled in the trenches for the attack. Hember, Williams and Jessop were of course there, but of the 266 immediate fatalities, only a tiny proportion, 6% or 17 men, were pre-war or August 1914 men. A similar picture emerges for the original 2nd Battalion men; only 45 or 16% of the total deaths were of these men drafted out to the 1st Battalion before Second Ypres. The great majority of deaths were, therefore, of men despatched from the 3rd Battalion between August 1915 and May 1916 - 224 or 78% of the total.

Three out of four LRB men to die that day have no known grave and their names appear on the Thiepval Monument which towers above the Somme uplands. Most of them died within the German lines and the enemy in the Gommecourt sector later reported the burial of over 1400 British troops. Some of these bodies were later recovered and reinterred in the large cemetery established on the old British front lines, Gommecourt Number 2. In this cemetery lie the identified remains of 45 LRB men and over 20 others who are also known to have belonged to the regiment. One of those who was identified is L/Sgt William Marlborough.

Immediately it received notification that he was 'missing', Marlborough's family in Ilford began to make enquiries as to his fate. Letters were written to various members of the LRB, until eventually, replies were received from Cpl Waddington and Rfn Elleson, apparently the last two men to see Marlborough alive. These two, themselves recovering from wounds, related their stories of how they had made the vain attempt to get the sergeant back to the British lines, but could add no more information as to his eventual fate. Neither could a letter from the War Office dated January 1917 shed any more light on the matter. The issue of the LRB's 'missing' was then raised in the Commons the following month by Mr. Joynson Hicks (Brentford) who was informed that: 'It is feared that the only conclusion that can be drawn is that they are now dead and steps will be shortly taken to accept the deaths officially'. The War Office followed this with a letter to the family in April, stating that their son was now presumed 'Dead'. A further family enquiry to the Territorial Force Records Office in May brought the reply that no articles of private property belonging to Marlborough had been received in the office. Despite these discouraging letters the man's family had not yet given up all hope. In August 1917 they next wrote to the Red Cross. This organisation sent the standard duplicated reply to all such LRB enquiries which stated that the soldiers of the regiment posted as 'missing' could not have survived and that they were reluctantly giving up all hope of hearing anything of Marlborough's fate. Another letter, this time from the Infantry Records Office, arrived only a week after that from the Red Cross. This one informed the family that the body had been found and buried in Gommecourt Number 3 Cemetery. This information extinguished any lingering hope of survival the family may have retained over the previous 14 months and it was further informed in February 1921 that the body had been exhumed and re-interred in Gommecourt Number 2. This was a standard and frequent procedure as remains in many smaller battlefield cemeteries were in the the process of being concentrated into larger ones by the Imperial War Graves Commission. The family was assured that 'every measure of care and reverence' had been taken during a properly conducted re-burial service. The final chapter to the distressing story came in 1927 when Marlborough's now widowed mother paid 8s.2d. to the Imperial War Graves Commission for the inscription on the gravestone of: '*In the Midst of life We are in death*'.

Although L/Sgt Marlborough's family could perhaps have gleaned some comfort from knowing that their son had eventually received a proper burial, there was no such satisfaction for the families of the majority who died on 1 July. Marlborough's body had been found following the voluntary withdrawal made by the Germans from the Gommecourt salient in 1917. Others lying in No Man's Land had been recovered after the battle, and one of the men detailed for this grisly task was John Morris. A previous mention of Morris noted that after a chance meeting in September 1914 outside the Queen's Hall, a recruiting sergeant had persuaded him to enlist. Much had happened to Morris in his short Army career since joining the LRB, the most important being his commission to the Leicester Regiment. Now, as an officer in the 46th (North Midland) Division, he later described the area over which the men of his division and the LRB on their right attacked, as stinking like a cess pool - a factor that had prevented recovery of corpses for longer than a week. When the Germans did eventually withdraw, it helped to clear up the question of what had happened to some individuals. Graham Williams visited the area and discovered the rotting remains of a haversack containing a book known to have been circulating amongst the signallers about the time of the battle. L/Cpl Dean, whom Williams had promised to meet in Gommecourt village on the night of 1 July, was the last known possessor of the book. To Williams it seemed, 'pretty obvious that this was the last trace of L/Cpl Deane...Our supposition that he had been blown to bits must have been correct'.

Following the disappearance of Victor Hember, and long before the German withdrawal, Gerald had assumed the task of writing to the 'Club'. In his first letter he described how Hember had been left behind, wounded in the enemy line, and how he believed that he would have been quickly picked up by the Germans when they reoccupied their trenches:

> *Vic did well and all who are left of his crowd speak very highly of the way he conducted himself and the good work he did before he was wounded. He knew what they were going into, he had been through severe fighting before and faced the prospect cheerfully. I hope and trust that he will recover and that before long we shall hear that he is having not too bad a time in Germany. He deserves a rest from the turmoil'.*

As events later proved, Gerald's hopes that Hember had been picked up by the Germans were misplaced. The body of 300041 Sgt Hugh Victor Hember, aged 27 years, pre-war member, veteran of Plugstreet, survivor of Ypres, erstwhile lengthy and frequent correspondent to friends at home, was never identified and his name is engraved on the Thiepval Monument.

Among the other 206 LRB names from this battle found on the Thiepval piers are Sgt 'Bunny' Austin, who had fought the rearguard with 2Lt Petley, Harry Dods from Denmark Hill who had rejoined on the outbreak, one of the two Ebbetts twins, Joseph McGrath, the writer of the 'farewell' letter quoted above, 'Bessie' Slaughter who had joked with Schuman about 'pushing up daisies', and young Harold Wonter - rejected by ten regiments on the grounds of defective eyesight. He died while daily expecting his commission in the Yorks and Lancs Regiment to come through. Other names are those of Bleaden, the employee at the Patent Office who had been gassed at Ypres and then seconded to recruiting duties at the depot, and Stanley Terraneau. Terraneau, grandson of a former major in the 10th Madras Native Infantry, had abandoned his theatrical career in order to enlist with his brother Cecil in the 2nd Battalion in September 1914. He arrived at the 1st Battalion in August 1915, and according to his CSM became, 'One of the most popular members of a fine Company...one of the finest soldiers in the Regiment'.[206] (Meanwhile Cecil had taken a commission in the RNAS and was killed in East Africa two months before his brother). Finally, another name mentioned before, is that of L/Cpl Stanley Wagstaff formerly of the Employers' Liability Assurance. The Wagstaff brothers had enlisted together in the 2nd Battalion and were drafted out together in 1915; John was killed at Ypres and Gommecourt saw the death of Stanley, who, like his brother has no known grave.

The name of Arthur Schuman's friend, Barney Griew, one of the six battalion runners to die from the action of that day, also appears on the Thiepval Monument, even though he actually died of wounds in Germany. Griew, classified as B2, but 'determined to do his bit on the HQ Staff'[207] is unusual because most of those captured by the enemy but subsequently dying from wounds, received a recorded burial. Another LRB man who was also later buried by the Germans, was Sgt Sidney Olorenshaw. It will be remembered that following their rearguard action, 2Lt Petley and Sgt Austin had decided to abandon the wounded Olorenshaw, and he was subsequently picked up by the Germans. Nearly three weeks later Olorenshaw, (who, incidently, is incorrectly listed in *Soldiers Died* as Oldrenshaw), died of his wounds in a field hospital and was buried along with several other men from the 56th Division in the military cemetery at Le Cateau.

The wounded of Third Army who managed to get themselves back to the British lines were probably better catered for than their colleagues in Fourth Army to the south. The latter's resources for care and evacuation were stretched to breaking point, whereas the 46th and 56th Divisions, being the only two divisions taking offensive action in Third Army, had all the resources of that Army to call upon.[208] Consequently, the evacuation of men from the Gommecourt area was efficient and effective. Sunny Jessop, hit fifteen minutes before zero, was quickly innoculated for tetanus at the casualty clearing station and then, just as the first wounded were beginning to arrive, was taken by ambulance down to the Base. Three days later he was back in England. Some of Jessop's colleagues, though, were not as fortunate: two succumbed to their wounds in the casualty clearing station beside the railway at Warlincourt, two more a little further down the line at Doullens and another four at the huge Base Hospitals on the coast. These included the young student Charles Hudson, who had courageously delivered the message to the officer of the Queen Victoria's. His unselfish bravery was never recognised by any award. Four more died in German hands and lie buried in cemeteries along the German lines of communication, while two others survived long enough to reach England, only to die of their injuries there.

Many of the wounded, like Jessop, treated in the Base or stationary Hospitals, were then returned to the Territorial Base Camp and thence, once they had recovered, back to the regiment. One man who managed to avoid a return to the trenches was the former 'miner' attached to the RE in Ypres Wood, and latterly a company runner, Arthur Hollis. His wound, received when making the return dash across No Man's

Land after delivering a message, necessitated his leaving the battalion. While at the Base, he received a letter from Capt Wallis that well illustrates the 'family' atmosphere that the regiment had worked so hard to develop both in the training and service battalions. Athough Hollis had not been a long established pre-war member - in fact he had only reached the 1st Battalion in December 1915 - and was not even a NCO, the Adjutant wrote to him in familiar and informal vein. Joking that he supposed Hollis was finding it 'a bit slow without shells' at the Base, Wallis went on to complain, 'We have just had a supply sent over which annoyed me very much - bad luck to them'. He then requested that this mere rifleman visit the sister of 2Lt Pogose and express Wallis's commiserations on the death of her young brother. It is not recorded whether Hollis did go round to Acre Lane, Brixton, but the fact that the request was made and was not considered in any way unusual emphasises the easy relations between officer and other ranks noted earlier.

2Lt 'Jerry' Pogose, whom Wallis thought 'no words could praise too much', was one of the nine officers to die in, or from wounds received during the battle. Wallis had a particularly high opinion of this young intelligence officer who, like Hollis, had only been with the LRB for a year. Wallis went out into No Man's Land on the night of 1 July to look for the subaltern. Pogose was found, badly wounded and died the next day. Another 2Lt, Edward Thomas, crawled around No Man's Land for three days blinded in both eyes and was eventually brought in. 'Curley' Boston, one of the early Commissions in the Field, was, like Thomas, shortly afterwards invalided out of the Army, while Petley, Rose, Smith and Bobby Lydall, another Plugstreet veteran, would all recover and rejoin the regiment. Apart from Pogose, four other subalterns died that day: Balkwill - wounded as a sergeant at Ypres, Benns - a 1909 entrant from the Commercial and Dominion Line and whose employers had presented him with his sword on commission, and Charles 'Shumery' Doust of 'A' Company. Lt Col Bates wrote to Doust's father in fairly typical manner describing his son as 'most trustworthy and capable'. Capt Cholmeley, Doust's company commander and therefore better acquainted with his work, went further and described him as an 'asset to the Mess with his graphic and humorous descriptions of his experiences in the trenches...absolutely tireless...and always seemed to be helping somebody'.[209] The Doust family had long been associated with the LRB and Shumery's brother had enlisted with him in August 1914. The last of the four subalterns was Archibald Warner who was killed in a shell hole which he had shared with the wounded Henry Russell. Considerably older than the others at 32 and also, untypically, married, Warner was an ex-Whitgift G.S. and Cambridge man and a qualified solicitor. He had enlisted in the Artists in June 1915 and had then joined the LRB, where one of his three brothers was still serving. It will be remembered that the eldest brother, Sgt Evan, had been one of the first LRB casualties in Plugstreet.

Lt Clode-Baker, aged 22 from Beddington and a Freeman of the Merchant Taylor's Company, never made it back across No Man's Land. He was later found and buried in Gommecourt Number 2, while the two captains to die, Bernard Harvey, late of Malvern College and Oxford, and Somers-Smith who commanded the battalion on the other side of No Man's Land, are both commemorated on the Thiepval Monument. Finally, the one LRB officer taken prisoner that day was Captain Arthur de Cologan, formerly of Queen's College, Oxford and the Somali Camel Corps.

It appears that de Cologan either left it too late to make a bolt across No Man's land, or although unwounded, decided to stay with those similarly trapped. Basil Houle thought that the officer was still down a dugout when the Germans called upon him to surrender, but did not actually come across him until the British captives were standing under close guard in Gommecourt village:

> When we arrived, there was a loud argument proceeding between one of our officers and the German sergeant in charge. The Captain, a hot-headed Irishman, furious that he had been caught in a dugout without the opportunity of firing a shot, was insisting on walking in front of us, while the Jerry sergeant wanted him in the ranks with the other prisoners. Eventually - and just when we were wondering if he would get us all shot with his silly argument, he got his way and we proceeded in a slow-moving, straggling disorder to their headquarters, where the wounded were examined by a doctor and injected against tetanus. The red-tabbed officer in charge of us had his photo taken with us and now separated from those unwounded, we were loaded onto farm carts and conveyed to a railway station and put on a hospital train, one carriage for us and one for the German wounded, complete with nurses and all comforts and transported to Minden town, in Westphalia.

It seems likely that 56 non-commissioned LRB ranks were captured that day with de Cologan, including Tom Short, Basil Houle and several others who will be mentioned again: Ernest Evanson - of whom a German officer inquired on seeing his LRB badges, 'I suppose you are a City man?'; Riflemen Sidwell and Rippengale and L/Cpl Carle. Their experiences of two years' captivity will be discussed later, but for now, attention will turn to consider how their comrades, still with the battalion, and the several subsequent reports, viewed their experiences and efforts of that tumultuous July day.

These men felt an immediate and justifiable pride in what the battalion had achieved that day, but it was a pride tinged with regret at what the operation had cost and disappointment that they had not been able to hold on to the gains made in the German lines. Graham Williams thought the entire battle had been a failure, 'even though we realised that it was by no means our fault'. This understandable human reaction of apportioning blame to someone else runs through the memoirs and official records: Williams blamed the 46th Division, Gerald those on either flank, Arthur Holmes, the French on their right, and Husey, the lack of success by the 46th Division and the inability of the reserve company to get across with fresh supplies of bombs. Reflecting on the failure some time later, the Regimental History of the 4th London Regiment, like many other such accounts, considered the failure was a consequence of four factors: the deep German dugouts, insufficient attention paid by the British to counter-battery work, lack of bombs, and, what it believed to be the most important cause, the German counter-barrage.[210]

When assessing the Gommecourt battle from their point of view, the German reports praise their own artillery and one succinctly explains that, 'The enemy's barrage frequently failed'.[211] They also emphasise the excellence of their deep dugouts which had allowed the troops to endure the seven day bombardment without, 'depreciation of their fighting power' and then meet the infantry assault with 'vigour and energy'. Morale had been maintained by holding the trenches most exposed to the bombardment with the minimum strength required for immediate defence, and by ensuring that ample rations were dumped in the front areas. This foresight provided sufficient food for the garrisons even when the bombardment prevented rations being brought up from the rear.

The enemy specifically criticised the British artillery in the pre-assault phase for only firing upon the German rear areas during the afternoons. This extraordinary inflexibility in the bombardment's timetable allowed the Germans to replenish their guns' ammunition stocks so that not one battery 'ran the least danger of exhausting its ammunition supply'. The *Official History* also criticises the role played by the British artillery during the afternoon of 1 July when it failed to fire upon the German guns ranging on No Man's Land: 'Good counter-battery work...might now have relieved the situation'.[212]

Although the Germans were clearly not greatly impressed by the British artillery, it should be remembered that this was the first real battle fought by the Territorial and New Army gunners. It is generally regarded that artillery require a longer period of time than infantry to prepare and perfect their skills, and the batteries on the Somme certainly needed a larger proportion of heavy calibre guns than was available. Nevertheless, and despite these handicaps, the Germans acknowledged that the British equipment and preparations for the battle were 'magnificent'. The local report gave fulsome praise to the ample British provision of machine guns, Lewis guns, mortars, ladders etc. and of the maps and photographs carried by the officers which included every recent detail of the German trenches. The enemy meticulously recorded every item of equipment discarded by the British in their trenches, even down to ten knobkerries and 3880 loose cartridges, but in particular the report stresses the 'disturbing effect' that British aerial supremacy had had on their men both before and during the assault.

The work performed by 8 Squadron RFC was also acknowledged in the divisional report of 18 July. In addition the report praises the 'energy and zeal displayed by all ranks...in their effort to complete the preparations against time and under very adverse conditions of weather', and explains that the 'success' of the operation was in no small measure attributable to the hard work of the Divisional Staff. But whether the operation had been a 'success', and indeed how that 'success' might be defined or assessed, were questions on the lips of many who had survived the slaughter. In terms of making a lodgement in the German lines and then holding it against enemy counter-attack, the Gommecourt battle had been an utter failure. Yet even if that had been an intention - and at best it was only a secondary one - it did not necessarily mean that the primary objectives of containing and killing Germans would have been achieved. If these two vital elements - the two principal motives behind the Gommecourt attack - are taken separately, it becomes clear that the two assaulting divisions failed to achieve their intended aims.

The British expectation was that the attack on Gommecourt would force the Germans to divert men and guns away from the main assault further south. As far as can be ascertained, the only German troops involved in repelling the assault were men of the two German divisions already deployed in the Gommecourt area. Their 13 reserve and support companies were all that were needed to throw back what had, to all intents and purposes after 07.45 hours, become an attack by only one division. Not one German soldier was moved from either the section of front facing the 48th Division - where it soon became obvious to the enemy that there would be no attack - or, more importantly, from further south where the principal assault was taking place. Even if the enemy did not have to re-deploy any of its infantry, GHQ and Fourth Army believed that the Germans would have to use a significant proportion of their artillery around Serre to fire upon the 56th Division. This, it was hoped, would have the effect of depleting the number available for use against the 31st Division forming the northern flank of the real offensive. Here again, the British plan failed to achieve its objective of containing Germans, not because the plan was essentially flawed, but because the attack by the 31st Division was over virtually before it began. The men of the Pals battalions of Yorkshire and Lancashire were decimated in No Man's Land, initially by machine gun and rifle, rather than artillery fire, and although small parties of men fought their way through the German wire, they were eventually isolated and overwhelmed. German artillery ranged upon the British assembly trenches and rear areas for the rest of the day but the threat from the 31st Division was over as many of its battalions had more or less ceased to exist. This assault had been repelled by the German infantry and artillery facing the British on that sector, and there had been no need for any local commander to request additional help from the divisions to the north. Thus, the diversionary attack had again failed to achieve its objective. Ironically, there is evidence to suggest that German guns in the Puisieux area - in theory intended as support to those nearer Serre - did fire upon the Gommecourt sector simply because there was no need for them to target on the 31st Division.

As for the other twin objective, killing Germans, the facts appear straightforward. The *55th Reserve Infantry Regiment* returned several differing totals for its casualties. If the highest is taken - 13 officers and 578 other ranks - and compared to that of the 138 and 3716 of the 56th Division's three infantry brigades, the balance can clearly be seen to favour the Germans. Attackers would be expected to lose more heavily than defenders, but not at the rate of 6.5:1. The stratagem employed in the attack was the classic pincer movement, which might have proved successful if the assault had not taken place upon an area held for two years by an industrious and efficient enemy. Significantly, they saw their defences not as a springboard for future offensives but as a permanent system of defence in depth. There was nothing wrong with the concept of the Gommecourt attack, but there was in the place chosen to execute it.

With hindsight and access to the official papers, it is easy to criticise the intention and objectives of the diversionary attack, but to the men of the LRB and their colleagues in the other London battalions, they were not so simple to unravel. At least one LRB soldier remained confused and critical over the affair into the 1980's:

> *Looking at the whole affair afterwards, it was clearly a ridiculous*
> *piece of planning, worked out in complete ignorance of conditions.*
> *Not surprising, when nobody above a Colonel ever visited the front*
> *line. As for a diversionary attack, we were never told that and neither*

*was it explained to us that we weren't expected to hold on in the
German line.* (B. Houle)

Houle, of course, had been captured and was not party to the various
congratulatory speeches issuing from the pens and mouths of generals as July
progressed. Gerald soon realised it had been only intended as a diversion because on 20
July he wrote: 'Apparently, the main objective of the attack was attained, *viz.* to cause
the Germans to bring up reserves and attract them from other attacks which we are
making elsewhere'. He was probably basing this upon the communique issued by
General Snow which read: 'Although Gommecourt has not fallen into our hands, the
purpose of the attack, which was to contain and kill Germans, was accomplished'. In
almost identical vein, GOC 56th Division praised the 'splendid way' in which 169
Brigade had captured the German trenches until forced by lack of ammunition and
grenades to retire, and was 'satisfied that the main task of the division in containing and
killing Germans was most thoroughly accomplished'. Upon later reflection, Williams
felt that not enough was done to explain this at the time: 'Long after, it was made known
that Gommecourt had not been a failure at all. It seems a pity that we could not have
been told this immediately after the event...This explanation (that the battalion had
succeeded in all it was intended to do) would at least have helped to dissipate the gloom
we felt'.

One man who remained gloomy and despondent about the attack for years was
the Adjutant Dick Wallis. Understandably, he did not take kindly to General Snow's
comments when addressing the survivors: '...and when I heard you had been driven
back, I did not care a damn. It did not matter whether you took your objectives or not'.
As the troops looked around their shattered ranks and thought of friends and colleagues
lying dead in the German lines, these less than tactful remarks, made to a brigade that
had lost about 69% of its attacking strength, probably did little to restore their morale.
So bitter was Wallis over what he considered to be the 'sacrificing' of the division, that
he wrote a long criticism on the whole concept of the operation. He believed that most
of what he called the eight principles of war - objective, offensive, security, mass,
economy of force, movement surprise and cooperation - were broken or ignored. The
time of the attack, the numbers involved and the training undertaken were all of British
choosing and their supplies and armaments apparently inexhaustible. The morale of
every battalion in the division was excellent, obstacles had largely been destroyed and
communications had been arranged to meet all eventualities. Yet, despite these
advantages, Wallis reflected, the day was lost. He claimed 'security was left to
luck..(and).. offensive without security is merely delayed suicide'. In his eyes the
greatest sin was the failure to conceal the preparations. However, given the stated
purpose of the Gommecourt battle, to achieve surprise would have defeated the very
object. Wallis also simplifies the problems experienced with communications and
cooperation between the infantry and artillery, but overall his criticism is pertinent, and,
on the whole, justified. It should also be remembered that these were the thoughts of a
man whose adult life had revolved around the LRB and who had witnessed the virtual
annihilation, while at its pinnacle of fitness and efficiency, of the regiment he loved.

For, after Gommecourt, the 1st Battalion LRB was never to be the same again.
On 1 July all members were volunteers, soldiers in a unit they had deliberately chosen to

join and prepared to pay 25 shillings for the honour. All had spent a minimum of six months in the army, came very largely from the commercial classes of London, and with the great majority having already experienced active service in the trenches around Ypres. Regimental morale and enthusiasm were beyond question and there was an absolute faith in the ability of the battalion, and of this fine London Division as a whole, to achieve all that would be asked of it. Unfortunately, what the men had not appreciated as they rose to assault the German lines on that sunny, Saturday morning, was that GHQ regarded them as expendable.

CHAPTER VIII

Controversy and the First Great Transition

Unbeknown to the survivors of the LRB as they trudged dispirited and exhausted towards the safety of St Amand, they were shortly to be confronted by the consequences of a controversy that had been gathering momentum at home for the previous six months. The arguments over the strategy and the tactics employed on that tragic Saturday would rage for decades, but of more immediate concern to the officers and men of the shattered battalions of 169 Brigade was how rapidly they would be brought up to strength and plunged again into battle. That they would be reinforced almost immediately was not in doubt. It was the means and methods by which these reinforcements were to be allocated and allotted to the various battalions that were to cause so much heated argument and complaint.

The recent War Office policy of posting men to battalions overseas irrespective of their regiment of enlistment, completely and often irreversibly changed the whole character and composition of units. Despite its long and proud history, the LRB was not to be excluded from the effect of this policy. However, before looking at the consequences this practice was to have on the regiment in July 1916, it is first necessary to trace the history of the dispute back to its early origins in the House of Commons. Parliamentary papers and other documentary evidence reveal how the issue had arisen in the first instance, and the impact that it had already had on the men serving in the 2nd and 3rd Battalions at home.

The method employed in supplying reinforcements to the serving battalions and of keeping the second and third line units still at home up to something resembling full strength was an extremely contentious one for members of the Territorial Force. During 1915 and 1916, emotions ran high, both inside and outside of Parliament, as it became obvious that the War Office was reneging on earlier promises by allowing the transfer of men from one Territorial unit to another as the need or expediency arose. The Territorial County Associations embarked upon a campaign of resistance to the new arrangements and petitioned the War Office in an attempt to reverse the policy. The basis of their argument was that the War Office was openly breaking faith with the Territorials who had already emphatically demonstrated their commitment, patriotism and ability to the nation. Furthermore, the Territorials believed that such an insensitive policy was particularly damaging to regimental *esprit*, and thus to general efficiency.[213]

The first surviving reference made by the LRB to the issue is a *War Diary* entry of January 1916. Following a brigade order, several of the battalion were detached to form part of 8 Brigade's Machine Gun Section. A protest was entered on the grounds that, as these men were members of the Territorial Army, they could not legitimately be transferred elsewhere, especially, it could be added, to the Regular Army of which 8 Brigade was part. The protest was again submitted when the LRB left the 3rd Division in February 1916, but apparently to no avail. 2Lt E.E. Pool, an original 2nd Battalion man, and 2Lt L.M. Pullen, who had been commissioned in the 3rd Battalion, had both only been with the 1st Battalion for a month. Both were destined to serve throughout the war in the Machine Gun Corps. The fate of the other ranks who had comprised the LRB's Machine Gun Section - four gun crews and drivers - is not known for certain, although it appears probable that they, like their officers, did not return to the battalion when it left to form part of 169 Brigade.

Evidence also suggests that some men had already been experiencing some difficulty in actually arriving at the 1st Battalion without having first to serve a period in some other overseas unit. Arthur Hollis was drafted from the 3rd Battalion at Tadworth in October 1915 and, after a spell at the Base Camp in Rouen, was sent down to the Ploegsteert sector. A week later, 'having heard that there was a draft leaving', he applied for a posting and joined the 1st Battalion at Poperinghe. How widespread this practice was with regard to LRB men is hard to determine, but it is known that some troops in other London Regiments were first posted to entrenching battalions before joining their own battalion. Hollis even seems to suggest that there was an element of choice as to where the members of the draft might go although this is certainly overstating the case. It is more likely that the draft was only temporarily attached to one of the digging detachments, while its eventual destination was already pre-determined.

According to the Regimental History, a total of 1,466 men had been sent overseas by May 1915 and of that total, all but 58 had actually reached the 1st Battalion.[214] No sources are cited for the figures and it is probably safe to assume that the 58 who never arrived would have been retained at the Base on administrative work, been taken ill, or might have suffered mishap while training. A very few, perhaps, might have been transferred elsewhere. Personal memoirs and serial numbers of men in the 1st Battalion by mid-1916 suggest that all but a minute number were in fact LRB enlisted and trained. In this respect the regiment was perhaps a little fortunate as the Queen's Westminsters, for example, had already received a draft of 223 men from the disbanded 2/2nd London in May 1916.[215] So, although some of the 1st Battalion men might have been aware of the controversy raging at home, its actual effect on the serving battalion had been, in the pre-Gommecourt period, non-existent.

The War Office had originally promised that if sufficient men from a unit opted to undertake foreign service they would be sent out together as a draft. When it became apparent that in several cases this assurance was not always being observed, the matter was raised in Parliament by a Colonel Yates in June 1915. In response to the question as to whether he would take steps to prevent such occurrences happening in the future, Tennant, the Under-Secretary of State for War, asked that Yates use his influence to encourage men to accept the principle that they might be drafted to regiments other than of their own choosing. He went on to praise what he called the 'really fine characteristic of our men' as being their willingness to 'take up service in whatever capacity is most desired and most wanted'.[216]   As events were to demonstrate within the next few months, the men were perhaps not quite as 'willing' as Tennant had assumed. By the time the 2/2nd London had arrived at the Queen's Westminsters immediately before the opening of the Somme offensive, the transfer of men from one unit to another was becoming an increasingly widespread and bitterly resented aspect of life in the Territorial Force.

There was something of a Parliamentary lull over the issue for the next few months, but in January 1916 an MP asked Tennant whether, under the Military Service (No.2) Bill then under discussion, men in the Territorial Force could be transferred to the Regulars or the New Army. Tennant replied that men could not be 'transferred', but could be 'attached' for duty to the Regular battalions. Neither, he continued, did the Bill give power to send abroad any member of the Territorial Force who had not undertaken the Imperial Service Obligation.[217]   Two months later, the pace hotted up when Mr. Bryce, quoting the relevant sub-section of the Territorial Forces Act, 1907, declared no man could be transferred to the Regulars without his consent. If that was the case, he questioned, why was a Territorial battalion of the Cameron Highlanders being merged with a Regular battalion of the same regiment?[218]

The response by the official spokesman clearly shows the insensitive attitude that both the Government and the War Office were adopting towards the controversial issue, and why the War Office, in particular, had thought nothing of transferring the LRB's Machine Gun Section to 8 Brigade. Mr. Long explained that there was no intention of destroying the Territorial battalion of the Camerons, and then went on to say that he found it, 'difficult to appreciate the Honourable Gentleman's complaint because after all, if it had been finally absorbed, it had been absorbed into a battalion so famous, it would be a fact about which nobody need grumble'.[219]   This statement demonstrated that Long, on behalf of the Government, totally failed to appreciate or understand the fire and the motivation that had driven men to enlist in particular Territorial battalions, or, the inestimable *esprit de corps* that had been built up within them. It was this failure to recognise the importance of unit morale and *esprit* that was to arouse such great resentment on the part of the men and their regiments.

Other MPs began to press the Under-Secretary of State on the issue of transfers and also on the position of those men in Territorial battalions who had not originally signed for foreign service. Until February 1916 such men had often been induced to accept 'foreign' by the offer of one month's leave but, as the majority had since fallen under the provisions of the Military Service Act, the offer had been withdrawn. Trying another avenue of approach, some MPs pursued the matter of whether those men serving in the so-called provisional battalions, and who had opted for foreign service before 2 March 1916, would still be able to choose to go, as the War Office had originally promised, to the 2nd or 3rd Battalions of their own regiment. Several cases, principally those of members of London Regiments, demonstrated that the War Office had apparently gone back on its earlier assurance, and these instances were subsequently raised in Parliament.[220]   For example, men of the 2nd Provisional Battalion (Queen Victoria's) had requested to be sent to their own battalion, but instead had been posted to the London Irish. Similarly, men of the HAC and Artists, who had signed for foreign service before 2 March had, despite protests, been sent to the Kensingtons. Tennant repeatedly answered these questions by declaring that the troops remained free to join whichever battalion or unit they wanted, unless the Army Council decided it had a need for them elsewhere.[221]

Not satisfied with this obvious catch-all expedient of the War Office, Mr. Nield raised the matter again in April on behalf of, amongst others, some LRB men. He quoted Army Council Instruction No 301 of 6 February 1916 which catagorically stated that if men agreed to accept foreign service before 2 March, they would stay in the Corps into which they had enlisted. If this was the case, Nield enquired, why had men from the LRB been transferred to other units? He finished with a flourish by declaring that a more recent Army Council Instruction[222] completely ignored the earlier promise. He was followed later by another Member who declared that as a consequence of the Army's utilitarian dictates, there was a growing feeling of discontent amongst a 'very large number of men.[223]

Among this 'very large number of men' was a sizeable contingent of LRB men currently training with the 3rd Battalion, and other members of the regiment who had been posted to the 101st Provisional Battalion. This unit was stationed at Southwold and consisted chiefly of former 1st and 2nd Battalion men who, on account of age or unfitness, had been unable to sign for foreign service. All this group, some still being underage, had undertaken the foreign service obligation in December 1915 and had been informed a month later that they would be transferred to the 2nd Battalion, then stationed at Ipswich. At the last moment and 'much to their chagrin' the proposed move was stopped and they were attached to the 2/23rd London. The Staff at Bunhill Row tried in vain to get these men back from Sutton Veny, but, as one of the number recalled, a concession was granted in that they were allowed to choose which regiment in their new division they wished to join.[224]

Another group of LRB volunteers, those in 'F' Company of the 3rd Battalion, were also transferred to the new 60th (London) Division. This batch of 300 had enlisted in November 1915 and had trained with the 3rd Battalion at Fovant from January 1916. By June of that year, instead of following the usual path of earlier training companies in being despatched to the 1st Battalion, the company had been split up and attached to the 2/13th, 2/21st and 2/22nd London stationed at Warminster.[225] Like their counterparts from the Provisional Battalion, these men were transferred to the 60th Division. In response to Nield's inevitable question in the House on 13 April, Tennant insisted that they had been 'attached' to a London Division and further stressed that it was 'not alien in character' to the regiments from which they had been posted. He claimed that they had not been transferred against their will, but again concluded his comments by re-emphasising that the Army Council reserved the power of attachment.[226] When pressed on the subject again a few days later, Tennant expanded on this by declaring that the Army Council Instruction No 552 of 11 March 1916 allowed the attachment of men in English provisional battalions, who had undertaken the Imperial Service Obligation before the appointed date, to be attached to units in three Territorial Divisions, including the 60th.[227] That appeared to be game, set and match to the War Office. To get itself out of difficulties, it could now, seemingly, at will, issue any Instruction containing any retrospective element it wished.

To the men of the LRB in the process of being moved from Southwold and Fovant to Warminster, and from a unit in which they had specifically enlisted to one in which they had probably specifically chosen not to, the thrusts and parries in the House of Commons were probably moot points. After all, soldiers probably soon learnt that the Army moved in mysterious, if not downright illogical, ways. The Under-Secretary of State was, however, becoming increasingly wearied by the whole issue. In May 1916, in response to yet another question on the transfer of men from a provisional battalion, he replied in exasperation that as he had already answered at least 20 such questions, 'I may, I think, therefore say that my attention has been drawn to it'. Before sitting down, he again declared that in this case, as in the others, the Army Council had exercised its power of attachment in accordance with the requirements of the Army.[228] To him, the matter was finished, and because the Military Service Act replaced any earlier promises or agreements, he could breathe a sigh of relief and assume that the controversy was over. Besides, within six weeks the matter of transferring men from various home battalions to other home units with similar characteristics, was to fade into virtual insignificance because the losses on the Somme necessitated filling up serving battalions with men from vastly different and varied regimental origins. In this respect, the men of the LRB mentioned above were fortunate, for, as Tennant explained, the units to which most of them were being sent were not markedly different from their own regiment.

The 60th Division had formed in 1915 but had since been 'bled white'[229] to provide drafts for another London Division, the 47th, which had gone overseas in March 1915. Numbers were further depleted when Home Service men had gone to their respective regimental 3rd Battalions in August, and by the end of the year the strongest infantry battalion in the division could muster only some 300 men. However, the War Office promised that after December 1915 the division would not have to provide any further drafts and, as was noted earlier, the battalions were brought up to strength by the transfer of men from third line units. On the arrival of these men, including the 300 from the LRB, the Divisional General was immediately impressed by their 'extraordinary quickness, intelligence and alertness'. As an officer used to commanding Regular troops he found the difference in the levels of intelligence very noticeable.[230] Initially, most of the LRB men would not have felt much out of place in their new units: 100 went into the Kensingtons, and those from 'P' Company, 101st Provisional Battalion, chose mainly to go into the London Scots, the Queen's Westminsters, and the principal South London battalion, the 2/23rd.[231] All but the latter had very similar histories and backgrounds to the LRB, but with the arrival in May 1916 of about 3000 men from Yorkshire and the Midlands, the 'London Division' became more 'London' in name than reality. Nevertheless, the *Official History* described the division as containing 'excellent material' when it went into the line near Neuville St Vaast in June 1916.[232] Although the division was not to undertake anything more than line-holding and a trench raid during its short stay in France, several of the LRB men posted to it lie in cemeteries to the West and North of Arras.[233] In November the division moved to Salonika and then in June 1917, on to Alexandria. The LRB men who travelled with it perhaps saw more exotic sights and varied conditions of warfare than their comrades who remained with the 3rd Battalion, yet athough their designations and buttons may have changed, one of the former 'F' Company men cherished and appreciated his short time in the LRB: 'The spirit of fellowship fostered at Fovant was ever strong, and we were always merely 'attached', not 'transferred' to the other regiments '.[234]

Meanwhile, in France the rank and file of the 1st Battalion probably knew little of the arguments and debates at home. Following the Gommecourt attack, they were expecting drafts from their own 3rd Battalion to bring them up to strength. This was what had happened after 2nd Ypres in 1915, and again while the 56th Division had assembled at Halloy. What did in fact occur came as an unexpected surprise, because in place of the anticipated draft of LRB men, the battalion was to accept its first great influx of men from a totally different regiment. Furthermore, not only was it a different regiment, but it was also one of a decidedly inferior social composition.

At the end of June 1916 there were possibly as many as 500[235] LRB men at the Base Camp in Rouen waiting to be posted up the line. These men had enlisted and been trained as LRB, had been imbued with the spirit of the regiment's discipline and *esprit de corps*, and had naturally been anticipating being posted to their own 1st Battalion. Similar expectations and aspirations were experienced by the men from the other London Regiments also awaiting posting. The fact that so many of these men were not to reach their anticipated destination caused indignant and vigorous protests from many of their respective commanding officers. So loud and scornful were the complaints that when the war was over the War Office published an attempted justification for its policy.

Many of the regimental histories of the London Regiments record their dissatisfaction with War Office policy, although they do allow that the Base was working under extreme pressure and difficulties. Similarly, they concede that as the battalions of the division had to be filled up again as soon as possible, it would have been impracticable to await reinforcements from their original units.

What was seen by contemporaries as being both indefensible and incomprehensible though, was why, when drafts of men were available for posting to their own regiments, they were not being despatched to them. This led in the LRB to accusations of 'lack of interest' and 'lazy stupidity' on the part of the Base staff,[236] and in other units of feelings of discouragement and dissatisfaction.

There is an unsigned paper in the LRB *War Diary* dated 27 July 1916 which specifies the origins of the drafts that did arrive at the battalion and which also offers a few pertinent comments on the process as a whole. It begins by pointing out that the newspapers were making much at the time of the supposed chaotic state of the German Army. The Germans were, it was claimed, so short of men that they were desperately having to throw regiments into the line irrespective of their normal brigade or divisonal allocations. The LRB paper then goes on to explain that conceit or complacency on the part of the British Army was somewhat misplaced. The LRB was originally informed by Brigade that, amongst others, it would soon be receiving a total of 61 men from the 1st London, 78 from the Civil Service Rifles and 260 from the 1/7th Middlesex; none of these men was subsequently to arrive. Battalion HQ was also told to expect 355 other ranks and 3 officers from the 2/7th Middlesex. When the men arrived, there were no officers, and 80 of the 364 who actually turned up, then had to be transferred to the Queen Victoria's. The German Army certainly did not have the monopoly on chaos or bureaucratic muddle.

The last draft to arrive at the battalion, on 16 July, consisted of LRB men, but far from being the 'large draft from the 3rd Battalion' that Graham Williams remembered, they amounted to a total of 16, and 15 of those had originally been detailed to go to the Queen Victoria's! The whole of the 56th Division was full of men busily changing buttons, shoulder flashes and cap badges, and others, trying on kilts or swopping kilts for trousers. The Queen's Westminsters had to place ammunition boxes on the fire step for its draft of 'Bantams' to stand on,[237] and the Commanding Officer of the Queen Victoria's had to get used to running a battalion comprising men from 17 different regiments.[238]   Dick Wallis, the Adjutant of the LRB, complained that detachments of men from 'dozens' of battalions were arriving, and that he was prohibited from trying to exchange London Scottish troops for LRB men who had been posted to the Scottish. The Divisional History notes the contemporary grumbling and adds that General Hull did make an attempt to get the system altered or amended.[239] There appear to have been some small successes when, for example later in the month, the Queen Victoria's managed to send 63 assorted men back to their own units. Furthermore, in August, the Westminsters succeeded in sending men from three London Regiments back down to the Base in exchange for a draft of their own men.[240] However, in the final analysis, the LRB appears to have come out of the disruption reasonably well for, by the time the small LRB detachment arrived, the battalion was up to a fighting strength of around 800.   Instead of being composed of men from many different regiments, the table in the *War Diary* shows that it consisted principally of men from the 2/7th Middlesex, the Post Office Rifles, and the 200-odd LRB survivors of the Gommecourt attack.

So, for the first time, the LRB was no longer the LRB of old. The controversy over the transfer of Territorial Force men against their will had resulted in the creation of an increasingly hybrid London Division. The County Associations had lost their battle with the War Office, which was, after the slaughter of the 1 July, even more determined to avoid large numbers of men from the same locality dying on the same day. Dispersion was to be the order of the day for New Army and Territorials alike. The consequences and impact that these new drafts had on the composition of the battalion will be discussed later, but what is important to stress here is that, unhappy as the regiment was with the way the drafts had been posted to them, it was not unhappy with the soldierly qualities of the new arrivals. The trouble that some of the men went to in order to get themselves drafted overseas underlined their keenness, and it is unlikely that there were any unwilling conscripts within the new drafts. As the consequence of their service in the desert, the *War Diary* records that the Middlesex were 'very good men and looked very well', but despite them being 'excellent in every way', in the words of the Adjutant, they were 'NOT LRB'.

CHAPTER IX

Drowning on the Somme and Freezing in Laventie

The newly constituted LRB, which returned to the trenches north of Gommecourt a week after the disaster of 1 July, was thus a very different battalion from that which had gone into the battle. The LRB-trained men had been swamped by the new arrivals and, although it was still very much a London battalion, the great majority of these newcomers were from Tottenham, an area from where the LRB had traditionally attracted few recruits. The men drafted from the Post Office Rifles bore a close similarity to the usual LRB man, but the men from the Middlesex Regiment were of a different type altogether. Before Gommecourt the LRB had been largely but not exclusively drawn from the commercial classes. Exceptions to this were, for example, Arthur Holmes, a decorator, and Will Hefford, a butcher, but these men had been very much in the minority. Now, for the first time, the battalion was composed of largely non white-collar workers and who came, principally, from North London.

The 7th Middlesex had been one of the few Territorial units near full strength when war broke out, and its reserve, the 2/7th battalion, began recruiting at Hornsey on 4 September. By the end of the month the battalion had moved to Barnet and, by the beginning of 1915, training had made sufficient progress for it to be considered capable of acting as a garrison battalion.[241] Consequently, it moved to Gibraltar in February and there relieved its own parent battalion. The second line unit despatched about a third of its strength to the 1/7th in August, and these volunteers were replaced by a draft from home just before the unit moved to Egypt. After a sojourn of ten weeks in Cairo, the battalion then went out into the desert west of Alexandria to fight the Senussi as part of the Western Frontier Force. Casualties had not been particularly severe, and so what really amounted to still very much the original battalion arrived at Marseilles in May 1916. On disembarkation, it was promptly incarcerated in a typhus quarantine camp for three weeks. By the middle of June the battalion heard the disappointing news that it was to be disbanded. To sweeten this bitter pill a little, it was announced that some of the men would be sent to join the first line unit in 167 Brigade. Most of the remainder subsequently arrived at St Amand and joined what was left of the LRB.

There had also been changes, although less dramatic, amongst the LRB's officers. The unit had soon been brought back up to strength by the appearance of four officers from the Finsbury Rifles and by eight direct commissions from the ranks. Rifleman C.H. John had enlisted in August 1914, and L/Cpl R.D. Poland had come out with the September 1915 draft from the 3rd Battalion. The remaining direct commissions were all sergeants; three, including E.G. More, one of the many men to join the LRB from Christ's Hospital, had been pre-war members and *Chyebassa* men, two were early draftees from the 2nd Battalion, while the last, A.P. Sharman, had come back to England from West Africa to enlist. Sharman had served as a trooper in the South African War, and for a second lieutenant had reached the relatively advanced age of 37 years. The four company commanders were all LRB men of long-standing while Wallis, Husey and Bates continued to fill the three senior positions. The only significant difference between the officers serving before Gommecourt and those at Fonquevillers was that now only one of the battalion's 30 officers, Capt Charles Long, who was soon to be invalided out anyway, was an Oxbridge man.

These men commanded what Aubrey Smith called the 'motley collection of drafts',[242] almost all of whom were of course unaccustomed to the LRB method of discipline. Not having come from a Rifle regiment, the Middlesex men were also unaccustomed to the LRB's orders of command and its 140 paces to the minute march. This soon became apparent at the medal parade for the Gommecourt battle. As he jogged along at the unseemly pace, one sweating and confused former Middlesex man whispered out of the corner of his mouth to Graham Williams, 'You calls this a march? I calls it a **** jig!'. The Middlesex men also soon came across the regiment's obsession with route marching. A three-day march in very trying conditions left many men of the brigade lying by the road sides. The LRB does not seem to have suffered from these stragglers as much as some other units and the men who did fall out were apparently from the new drafts. This did not go down well with Husey who, by August was in command of the battalion. He gave the new men a severe lecture on the pride the regiment took in its marching and stressed how he, for one, was not prepared to let the established standards fall. The less than subtle warning appears to have been sufficiently heeded by the newcomers.

A change in attitude by the officers towards the men under their command was apparent to the remaining original LRB men. Having been used to a system in which they were consulted and treated with a degree of laxity befitting intelligent men, they did not enjoy the new, more typical Army regime. At the same time, however, they understood its necessity and appreciated the fact that Husey made it clear to them that he sympathised with their changed, uncomfortable predicament. Yet even though the original LRB men might be able to recognise a more militaristic relationship between officers and men, the new arrivals still considered that their new regiment operated in a different, more relaxed way:

> We noticed the difference in the style of command and relationship of
> officers and men. It seemed to be more of a kind of matey, chummy
> kind of approach. The Warrant Officers weren't the Guards-type, they
> were more like father figures. It was unlike the strict discipline of the
> old County Regiments where one had to stand to attention to speak

even to a Lance-Corporal. Also there appeared to be less 'bull' about the state of the camp and billets than with us who were constantly kept busy with pointless tasks like painting stones and scrubbing floors. (S. Amatt)

Sid Amatt was not in fact from the Middlesex Regiment but had arrived with a draft of about 70 men from the Essex in September. After hearing about the heavy casualties of 1 July, some of these men had made great efforts to get themselves posted overseas. Amatt, from Walthamstow, had enlisted under age in the 2/7th, a Territorial battalion of the Essex Regiment, in December 1914. Then, having opted for foreign service almost immediately, he and his fellow volunteers grew increasingly frustrated at the time the Authorities were taking to post them to France. The battalion continued its training at Thetford and then in April 1916 moved to Harrogate, where news of the opening of the Somme offensive reached them:

Being young and high spirited we were fed up with the normal routine and were chaffing at the bit so a group of us who had soldiered together since the beginning held meetings in our tents to decide how we could help the lads in France. Well one 'bright spark' suggested we write a Round Robin asking the C.O. to post us to the front for service. We signed it in the shape of a circle so no-one could be seen as the leader, gave it to the Orderly clerk and threatened him with dire destruction if he didn't put it in front of the C.O. next morning. We never heard anything for a couple of days, we thought it was ominous then we were told to parade together in front of the C.O. So we did, about 16 of us and he laid down the law, quoting King's Regulations at us and then congratulated us on having the spirit to volunteer and promised to help all he could. (S. Amatt)

The squad immediately began intensive training, and after a couple of weeks, were kitted out, given a slap up meal by the officers, presented with nickel-plated cigarette cases by the officers' wives, and then put on a train for Southampton. After an uneventful crossing to Le Havre and its Base Camp, the group were put through more training - which did not go down well with the men - and then, after taking five days to reach Meaulte near Albert, they joined the LRB. Here the men were addressed by several officers of the regiment who quickly told them of the traditions of the LRB, including the Brighton March, explained that they were about to join a regiment which had already earned fame and glory for itself, and was sure to do so again in the near future. The Essex men felt great pride at being posted to this battalion, and although they did not consider themselves in any way superior to the New Army battalions, they did regard themselves as being a little 'special'. After having gone to all the trouble of getting themselves posted overseas, they were pleased at having ended up in what they knew to be an elite unit.

The orignal LRB survivors were hugely outnumbered by the various drafts and, as if to increase the feeling of virtual alienation within their own regiment, some appear to have been further put out by the natural rivalry which existed between the Middlesex and the Essex men. The new arrivals do not seem to have easily lost their former regimental identities, and instead, retained their old affiliations with a sort of detached relationship with the remaining LRB personnel. Amatt and his friends felt that they were not easily accepted by the LRB men and that there was something nearing resentment, but also resignation, that these labouring men would have to be tolerated for the sake of the emergency. It seems possible that this divide between the classes was never totally eradicated from the older members of the LRB, but the younger recruits who joined later took a different view and mixed in well with those from the non-commercial classes. One of these younger, newer members was Archie Groom, who arrived at the battalion just after it had left the Somme. Although Smith believed the approach had changed,[243] Groom did not notice any real difference in the methods of discipline in the 1st Battalion compared to those he had experienced while training with the 3rd Battalion. Groom considered himself fortunate that he had been drafted to the parent battalion where *esprit* was the basis of the relationship between officers and men, and thought that the system did not change until 1918. Then, following the disappearance of most of the LRB-trained men, he believed the more usual disciplinary methods were introduced.[244]

Although in many ways a typical LRB recruit, Groom and his colleagues joining the regiment in 1916 differed in one important respect They, like those enlisting before them, had actually volunteered to join the LRB, but unlike the 1914 and 1915 men, the decision was not completely of their own volition. In October 1915, in a final attempt to stave off the introduction of full-scale conscription, the Government accepted a proposal of the Secretary of State for War, which became commonly known as the Derby Scheme. This idea still encouraged men between the ages of 18 and 41 to volunteer, but those who did not want to enlist immediately could attest and then wait to be called-up in age groups. In theory, at least, this scheme allowed men the opportunity to join a regiment of their preference.[245] However, when Archie Groom presented himself in March 1916 at the White City, after having attested the previous October, he was told that he would be posted to the Regular army. Surprising himself at his own persistence, he insisted that as he had volunteered, he was entitled to join a battalion of his own choice. By a certain amount of wrangling he managed to overcome Authority's obstacles and reach the LRB's 3rd Battalion. Here, at Fovant he met with the other 30 odd members of his training platoon. Groom described his colleagues as a good mixture of young and old and with about one third of them married. Sharing fairly similar attitudes and backgrounds, the units soon became a congenial and happy group.

Groom's platoon was one of the few drafted overseas during the Somme offensive fortunate enough to actually reach the 1st Battalion. He did not go overseas with his friends, but later rejoined those who had survived the September and October battles and would stay with the battalion until March 1918. Another of the platoons to reach the 1st Battalion at the end of September was the 27th Training Platoon, 'The Fovant Scottish'. One of its instructors at Fovant had been Sergeant Maurice Howard, now recovered from the effects of the gas he had received at Ypres in May 1915. One draft of 45 men arrived in the charge of L/Cpl Wood, originally from the same City office as Smith, and another of the men wounded at Ypres. Smith, now of course an experienced member of the Transport section, considered that Wood was lucky not to have been sent up the line to join something unpleasant like the '17th Hackney

Harriers'. Despite this good fortune, Smith considered that it must still have been 'very depressing' for him to arrive in a company where every man was now a stranger.[246] The LRB youngsters arriving with Wood and similar drafts contrasted with the Essex and Middlesex men already with the battalion in both their accents and education. Sid Amatt thought that most of his friends from the Essex were largely illiterate boys who had left their council schools at fourteen to take labouring jobs. Having been an apprentice in a silk spinning factory, Amatt considered himself to be a 'little bit above the run of things', although still nowhere near as literate or well-spoken as the LRB boys.

Some of the reinforcements arrived when the battalion was actually in the line at Fonquevillers. A major problem for Battalion HQ was to post the men to companies, reorganise the specialist sections, and try to make a quick assessment of the abilities and experience of those men arriving at the battalion already wearing NCO stripes. Some LRB survivors of 1 July were promoted, including Arthur Schuman, who was made up to sergeant, and those senior NCOs who had been part of the nucleus personnel rejoined. One of those sergeants, Tom Burroughs, had recently returned home for a commission, and another equally experienced man, Bradford, was killed early in July. Sgt Charles Bradford, (possibly a *Chyebassa* man, but certainly out since January 1915), had earlier received the Military Medal for recovering a wounded colleague. He was about to return to England and the 3rd Battalion for a commission when he was killed by a Lewis gun. Second-Lieutenant William Gardiner and Bradford had led a raiding party into No Man's Land one night and sections within the party somehow managed to end up bombing each other. Much to the enjoyment of the Germans, who happily observed the spectacle,[247] the raiders ran into further trouble when regaining their own trenches and a Lewis gun caught both Bradford and Gardiner just in front of their own lines.

Throughout the rest of July and the month of August, casualties were in fact very light. There were plenty of working parties to be found, but the greatest problem was probably the acclimatisation of the Middlesex men who, coming from the heat of the Western Desert, were now wading and splashing through water waist-deep in the trenches around Foncquevillers. Mid-way through July the weather changed for the better. The trenches dried out as the temperatures soared. Medal parades and shorter periods in the line allowed a little time for men to write home and reassure anxious relatives and interested employers. Rifleman Frewer, formerly a clerk in the Counting House of Shaw & Sons, printers of Fetter Lane, replied, seemingly without much enthusiasm, to such an inquiry from his firm:

> *Many thanks for your kind inquiries about me; we are having a very busy time and we were in the July 1st advance. I am in the best of health and I find that I feel much better after this outdoor life. The weather has got very hot now and is getting almost unendurable, but we are able to stick it. We have been moving about a lot lately but we are resting now, although I have to go on fatigue every night from 5 to 2 o'clock next morning and then parade again about 9.30. We have just had a General Inspection and medals were presented to officers and men for the July 1st affair. The Lord Mayor of London came and inspected us about a month ago.*[248]

It was during this period that the LRB first had experience of the new British weapon that was hoped would break the stalemate of the Western Front. While at Canchy, 169 Brigade made several practice attacks with tanks but, according to Wallis, the LRB were more impressed by a lecture from a certain Colonel Campbell on the "Spirit of the Bayonet" than with Britain's new secret weapon. Apparently, at the beginning of the talk, the battalion was wearing a 'bored and dissatisfied look', but by its close, 'everyone was licking his lips and gloating in anticipation of bayoneting "fat Germans"'. Arthur Schuman thought that many of the men now in the battalion were woefully lacking in the necessary arts of war. Although badly affected himself by the experience of Gommecourt, and 'simply resigned to whatever was in store for me', Schuman tried to inspire the more recent recruits with the confidence that he himself now seemed to lack. Many of the 'Derby men', and later the conscripts, had been prematurely rushed out to France to fill up battalions destroyed by the offensive as it continued to crawl, trench by trench, vaguely in the direction of Bapaume. Most had therefore, undergone only the barest period of training. However, compared with the amount of actual *fighting* time that many of these men would experience - often simply *minutes* - their twelve week training stints were positively lengthy.

The LRB was to be hurled into the maelstrom of shrieking metal and fetid wastes twice in the space of four weeks and would stagger out on both occasions as a shadow of the battalion that had gone in. The experience of the Somme saw the battalion at a depth of despair and depression not witnessed again until it had struggled and drowned in the swamps of Glencorse Wood a year later. The battalion came close to breaking point in the confusion of Leuze Wood and the muddy craters before Les Boeufs, but on both occasions regimental *esprit* and the sheer doggedness of the British infantryman carried it through these traumas. Subsequently, another rebuilt battalion, would recover its composure and energies before then enduring the vagaries of generals and the icefields around Laventie and Neuve Chapelle.

The first of the two slaughterings took place in and around Leuze Wood during the September attacks towards Combles. The village lay at the foot of the so-called Combles Ravine - a slope falling about 60 feet in approximately 900 yards. The French had captured the bottom of the Ravine to the south of the village and the 56th Division were to make an attack, in cooperation with their allies, with the intention of establishing defensive flanks on both sides of the Ravine. This would allow Combles itself to be pinched out as other British attacks progressed. The LRB moved from Canchy and bivvied in the inappropriately-named Happy Valley to the north of Bray on 4 September.

The battalion arrived at this destination soaked through. It then endured the thunderstorms of the following night, either sheltering beneath ground sheets, a handful of bell-tents, or huddled in a few water-logged slit trenches. As the move had been conducted in a rush, no hot food was provided at the end of the fourteen-mile march. Throughout that uncomfortable night, an air of severe and extreme depression, as heavy as the storm clouds above, hung over the morose battalion. The weather improved the following day, and then, on 6 September, the battalion slithered across the mud to the support trenches in Chimpanzee Valley. Here it witnessed a ferocious and prolonged barrage from the British guns. Hampered by ammunition limbers and the impedimenta of war, the battalion continued forward to the area of Falfemont Farm a thousand yards to the south-west of Leuze Wood. The final stage of this trek provided a gruesome education for most of the men: blackened British and German dead lay sprawled in grotesque attitudes over the ground and in the ruined trenches, many of them victims of phosphorus grenades. Except for the relatively tranquil period of line holding during July and August, this was the first real experience of war for many of the new arrivals. Even the hardened Arthur Schuman was stunned at the horribly disfigured bodies. Evidence of the ferocity and brutality of the recent fighting was clear for all to see. Unfortunately, so too was the obvious obscurity of where the British line ended and the German one began.

The battalion's bombers were first into action, forcing the Germans out of 200 yards of Combles Trench. This ran south-east down the slope from Leuze Wood towards the village. The success was short-lived as the Germans counter-attacked, but the main LRB attempt went in on 9 September. From the start it was clear that the situation in front of the objective of Loop Trench was totally confused. The Kensingtons and the London Scottish were also assembling in this heavily shelled and overcrowded sector of the wood, so Major Husey, characteristically commanding from the front, managed to sort the companies into some kind of order, and then sent out a patrol under 2Lt Slade to try to ascertain where the Germans lines were. Slade eventually returned, having dodged the continuous shelling and floundered around in the mud of the shattered wood for several hours, with the news that the trenches that the LRB were supposed to be occupying were still in German hands. Brigade's original orders were for the battalion to hold on to the north-east and north-west corners of the wood, and it had further insisted that frequent and reliable messages be passed back to Brigade HQ. It was all very well for the Staff to order that regular despatches be sent, but another matter completely, as to whether they would actually arrive at their destination. Once the attack began, the messages coming from the company commanders inside the wood, and from the captured parts of Loop Trench to Battalion, and thence to Brigade, painted a desperate picture. Most of them were succinct and took the form of requests for information on the position of supporting battalions, reports of failures to secure objectives, complaints about the impossibility of continuing the attacks because the men were exhausted, requests for immediate relief because numbers were so low, and frantic declarations that what few troops remained were demoralised and incapable of further action. Brigade ordered the attacks to continue but the local commanders had largely lost touch with all but the troops sheltering in the immediate shell holes. Machine gun fire and intense shelling were answered by only a weak and spasmodic British barrage. By late afternoon it was clear to Brigade that the attack had faltered and crumbled against these impossible odds. What remained of the LRB and 169 Brigade was relieved by a composite battalion from 16 Brigade.

Nothing had been achieved that day except the death, mutilation and wounding of nearly 50% of those taking part. Between 6-10 September, 105 LRB men were killed or would die from wounds received in that period. When the roll was called on 11 September, fighting strength amounted to a mere 19 officers and 324 men. The dejected remnants rested and cleaned up as best they could at The Citadel - a large tented encampment above Carnoy. Wallis surveyed them as they half-listened to the divisional band playing during the squally afternoon, and pondered on the similarity of the scene and of Nero's fiddling while Rome burned. A draft of 95 arrived to swell the ranks before the LRB, as Divisional Reserve, again moved up to Chimpanzee Trench. Carrying parties were in constant demand and what remained of the battalion's bombing section was sent to help the 2nd London's attack against Loop Trench. Most of these soon became casualties. Further unnecessary demoralising losses were sustained when the rest of the battalion was heavily shelled by British artillery. This was the final straw for Husey who sent several complaints down the line towards the gunners and the Brigade Major, but all to no avail. In desperation and anger he despatched another to Brigade: 'I shall be glad to hear the matter has been investigated, as it is quite intolerable that my men should be subjected to shelling by our own guns, and so persistently'. Arthur Schuman was on the receiving end of the British guns and afterwards thought it further demonstrated that the BEF was, 'getting into a rather chaotic state'.

The battalion attacked again on 18 September, and once again, the weather was atrocious. The men were halted by heavy machine gun fire coming from a gun hidden in a sunken road leading into Combles. The bombers fought their way closer to the gun, eventually silencing it, while the rest of the battalion continued the attack down Combles Trench the following day. The Germans made a counter-attack which was partly fought off, but late in the evening of the 20 September, the battalion was relieved by the equally exhausted Westminsters who, having struggled up to the line through the incessant downpour and desolation of the old trench systems, arrived long after they were due. While the troops grabbed a few hours sleep in Angle Wood, another large draft of 230 arrived. The respite was short-lived for the men had once more to drag themselves from their stupor to provide carrying and burying parties. The battalion returned to the line on 24 September in preparation for another attack but, as the promised two tanks never arrived at the start line, the attack was called off. Later that day Brigade sent down information extracted from a captured German officer that the enemy was thought to be evacuating the village of Combles. Patrols sent forward to test the accuracy of the report were halted by trench mortar fire and showers of grenades. Not surprisingly Husey thought the battalion had reached the end of its endurance. He had begun despatching desperate appeals for relief five days earlier, but until now they had fallen on deaf ears:

> *My bombers are non-existent - few of them are now good at bombing and still fewer men know how to fire the No.23 Rifle Grenade...(we are) really very tired and exhausted, also I have a considerable number of men whom I have refused to allow to leave the trenches, who are very sick chiefly from chill and exposure. I much regret to say that I do not think this battalion is now capable of an active offensive.* [249]

Fortunately, relief was now, at last, about to arrive. On 26 September the LRB entered Combles and joined up wth the French who had penetrated from the south. A large haul of enemy weapons and equipment was collected and, after the appearance of the 8th Middlesex, the LRB marched, or more correctly, slithered and slipped its exhausted way back to Meaulte. Here, Wallis remembered, it arrived 'whacked to the wide world'.

The experience of Combles had been severe and costly. Brigade was equally concerned over the losses and reported to Division that: 'Battalions have now no bombers, few Lewis Gunners, few officers of experience of standing and the class of officers arriving as drafts is very poor'.[250]   More officers did arrive at the LRB's Transport Lines during this short period of rest, and during the month a total of 413 non-commissioned men were drafted to the battalion.   The battalion had been at full strength when it first moved to Falfemont Farm, so these men replaced the recorded total of 447 casualties it had incurred during the month.   Of these 136 had been killed or had subsequently died of wounds.   The final draft was no sooner posted to companies when, after only one day to bathe and clean up, the battalion with a fighting strength of 542 once again moved into trenches. This time the destination was a little further north, near Guillemont Station.

The incessant demand for carrying parties occupied the battalion for the first two days of this tour.   This occupation provided the most recent arrivals with their first experience of shellfire and the carnage that the offensive was producing.   The boys from the Essex Regiment had missed the engagements of September and were now collecting the corpses littering the approaches to Trones Wood:

One day just after dinner we had been gathering all these bodies together when we heard a shell coming so we all ducked and hit the ground, but it landed just by the side of the road where there was a convoy of limbers pulled by mules. I saw the cart, mules and driver all go up in the air, lifted the whole lot right up and threw them down in bits yards away - this was very enlightening to me. (S. Amatt)

The battalion itself continued to suffer casualties from the German shelling and machine gun barrages.   Arthur Schuman, for example, was leading a patrol to investigate some German wire when a bullet killed his friend Cooke.   They had been drafted together in June 1915 and Schuman had first talked to Cooke as the latter stood alone on Waterloo Station waiting for the draft train.   They had subsequently developed a close friendship, and had been two of the fortunate few to regain the British lines unwounded on the night of 1 July.   Cooke was posted 'Missing' but Schuman was able to confirm the death of his friend and return his watch to the grieving parents a few weeks later.   Schuman had lost his 'best pal', Barney Griew, on 1 July, and now with the death of Cooke his depression seemed overwhelming.   He was finally wounded himself four days later and returned to England, to be invalided out of the Army in April 1918.

The weather was so bad that reliefs of the front trenches usually took place every other day.   The men were up to their knees in water, in trenches that bore little resemblance to the field manual examples, and were continually exposed to German bombardments.   The reliefs over the devastated ground, water-logged shellholes and congested roads, took hours longer than scheduled.   After one such relief, the LRB struggled back to dugouts between Trones and Bernafay Woods, amidst optimistic rumours that it had finished with the Somme.   The authorities thought differently, however, and, after two days of shovelling liquid mud from the roads, the battalion was warned to parade and move off to relieve the London Scots shortly after midnight on 8

October. The three-mile trek, done in single file, throughout a filthy night and along roads cratered and strewn with obstacles of all descriptions, lasted until daylight. The London Scots, who had been cut up badly in an attack the previous day, staggered rearwards, vacating the slit trenches and connected shellholes to the north-east of Les Boeufs to the LRB. Fortunately, the German gunners took little notice of the operation, despite the daylight and the sluggishness of the overburdened infantry as they struggled to carry their trench equipment over the glutinous ground. Brigade sent down orders that the battalion, in cooperation with the Queen Victoria's and the French (although no-one seemed to have any idea when or where their attack would go in) would advance towards Le Transloy and seize the objectives 167 Brigade had failed to secure during their assault of the previous day. Company orders were written hastily, and objectives decided without the aid of maps. More tools, bombs and ammunition had to be brought up before the attack began. By now, the Germans were aware of the impending action and shells crashed down on the LRB's assembly trenches:

> *During the morning a shell landed in our bay and took off the head of one man and wounded several others including a Corporal who had one hand and a foot almost severed. Then they brought round a rum issue at 1.00 pm. and told us we were going over the top at 3.00 pm. We had 100 rounds in pouches and they gave us two 50-round bandoliers and two Mills to put in our pockets. All that equipment and we were supposed to be fighting men! Anyway we tried following a five minute creeping barrage. We only got about 100 yards because the machine gun fire was terrible so me and my pal Ted Freeman dropped in a shell hole to shelter. After he was shot through the heart and I felt him shudder before he fell back dead. After this things seemed all messed up and then after dusk I found myself plodding back to find the regiment. I remember I fired at a German getting out of a trench. But what chance have you got of hitting a man 100 yards away; you've got all that equipment on, you've been bogged down all night trying to get into the trench then cramped up once you're there, and you're standing up with shells, shrapnel and bullets flying around and a bayonet stuck on the end of your rifle - what chance have you got?* (S. Amatt)

This attack and the few days which preceded it cost the lives of 16 of the Essex men. Their fate was typical of many who joined weak battalions in between battles. They barely had time to adjust to their changed surroundings and colleagues, before disappearing when their new battalion tried another advance across the wastelands of the Somme. The LRB's advance had bogged down in the mud and although the companies almost reached their objectives, their flanks were exposed. After dusk the few survivors were ordered to retire to their original start line. They had been halted by the same machine guns, sited in abandoned field gun pits, that had swept through the ranks of the London Scots and three other battalions before them. After nightfall the battalion was relieved by the 1st Royal Warwick and moved back to the same trenches between Bernafay and Trones Woods that it had left the night before. Expecting the LRB to do what four previous battalions had failed to accomplish was, the incensed Wallis believed, 'simply murder'. He criticised the Staff for ordering fatigued men, who had already been stood down for the night, and who were also suffering from acute stomach disorders, to begin a march in a thunderstorm and intense darkness, towards the front. Wallis believed this was the, 'worst if not the hardest march ever accomplished' by the battalion and by the time it was relieved, the whole division had been, 'worked to the utmost limit of human endurance'. Certainly, the LRB was not in any shape to take further offensive action in the immediate future; of the 542 men and 21 officers who had made their way up to Guillemont Station on 1 October, only 108 and two respectively were able to answer the roll nine days later.

Sid Amatt was the only member of 'B' Company actually to answer his name at that roll call, although several others did turn up later that day. 'A' and 'B' Companies had been the first two waves and subsequently had suffered the worst casualties. In total, the number of dead or died of wounds for the ten day tour and attack of October is 164, or 30% of the attacking force. During the two months of September and October, the battalion had therefore lost exactly 300 killed or died of wounds, and somewhere around 520 more wounded or captured. The two months had seen 101 of the former 494 Middlesex men and 23 of those 96 drafted from the Post Office Rifles killed - 20% and 24% respectively. These two regiments had comprised a majority in the battalion for four months, and although there were still survivors of both, they were in turn to become a minority when fresh drafts brought the battalion back up to strength.

Seven of their number had won a medal or Divisional Card and nine of the original 1914 LRB men were also awarded honours. These figures seem a little disproportionate in view of the small number of the originals still actually serving, but the majority of the medals given to these men following the two Somme actions, were not for specific gallantry in those engagements. They were awarded, instead, for continued application and devotion to duty since going overseas. An exception was the award of a DCM to Sgt Roulston. Described as a 'fiery Irishman', Roulston was the son of a Wesleyan Minister. He had single-handedly rushed down a trench during the Combles attack, killing 30 Germans 'methodically, one after another'. His own luck was soon to run out and he was later killed at Les Boeufs. One of the former Middlesex men also won the DCM during the September battles. L/Cpl Taylor surprised two German officers as they sat eating a meal in a dugout; he knocked them out and then blew them up with their own grenade.

Inevitably the two months thinned the already depleted ranks of the pre-war and 1914 members even further. Eight of those men died including Sgt Birt, whom Maurice Howard had carried away from Ypres, and L/Cpl Chapman, the son of a doctor and three times previously wounded. Similarly there were so few of the original 2nd Battalion men still with the battalion, that only five were killed during this period. Several long-serving officers also died during these months. 2Lt Horace Smith had only rejoined the battalion after the Combles affair, having recovered from his wound received at Gommecourt. Norman Baldwin, a *Chyebassa* man, from the Royal Masonic School, was killed at Les Boeufs and another *Chyebassa* man, Arthur Sedgewick, who had been one of the first to be Commissioned in the Field and whom Wallis described as 'an old and very popular member of the Regiment', died of wounds in a casualty clearing station at Corbie. The Intelligence Officer, Edward Bantoft, a solicitor and former Musketry Instructor in the 3rd Battalion, who had volunteered for overseas service following the Gommecourt affair, also died of wounds in Corbie. George Taylor, who had served in the ranks since 1907 and who took a commission having returned from Plugstreet with frost bite, was also killed in October. Another of the many Haileybury College men, James Dewar (who had been with the battalion precisely seven days) and Captain M. Maynard, a Brighton marcher and ranker on the *Chyebassa*, were also presumed dead after 8 October. Two other young subalterns from the LRB died, as did three from the Finsbury Rifles who had been attached to the regiment since July.

Besides those already mentioned, 14 LRB officers had been detached for duties with other regiments of the 56th Division: of these, two were killed and only five were fit enough to rejoin the battalion in mid-October. Many other officers, 17 in total, had been wounded or invalided out of the battalion during those two months; nine of them had been rankers on the *Chyebassa* and included John Stransom, the former lance-corporal who had run the full-time wiring party at Plugstreet. Another casualty was the lance-corporal who had been in charge of the battalion's runners on the day Sgt Belcher had won his VC. Others wounded during this period were the long-serving Arthur Read, a Colour-Sergeant on the *Chyebassa*, and Captain Gilbert Nobbs. Nobbs had been a pre-war member but emigrated to Canada shortly before the outbreak. Rejoining the regiment in 1914, he was only posted to the 1st Battalion in August 1916 and was then blinded in both eyes in Leuze Wood. Captured by the Germans, he was repatriated the following year and would later write a book of his experience.[251]

Only five of the LRB non-commissioned dead from 1 July had home addresses from outside the London postal area and, despite the change in composition since then, only nine of the September and October dead have non-London domiciles. The principal difference between the Gommecourt and Somme dead lies in the areas of London from where they originated. Because the majority of the battalion was composed of former Middlesex men, the working-class streets of small terrace houses or tenement blocks of North London are far more frequently represented than the areas from where the LRB traditionally recruited.

Sixty-nine percent of the dead, a fraction less than the July figure, have no known grave, and their names are beside those of the Gommecourt missing on the Thiepval Monument.[252] Of those bodies that could be identified, 11 of the September dead are buried in the two cemeteries in Combles, and five of the October men who died of wounds in the dressing stations are buried in Grove Town Cemetery, high above Meaulte on the wind-swept uplands. A few other identified remains are scattered around the larger Somme cemeteries where they were re-interred after the war, and others lie beside the casualty clearing stations concentrated in the old town of Corbie. The remainder are buried near the Base Hospitals in Rouen and Etaples.

Those men still with the battalion took what rest they could and cleaned up. Their immediate future was still uncertain, although they could expect to be made up to strength and hurled once more into the battle. Their plight appeared pitiful; exhausted to the utmost degree of endurance, they had struggled like automatons along the pitted roads away from Les Boeufs, encased in slime, and with bowed heads sunk deep on their wearied chests. *Esprit* had for the moment disappeared as each man was lost in his own numbed thoughts. It would return, given rest, food and baths, but experience had shown that the authorities were prepared to use, replenish, and use again a brigade destroyed twice over. The men could not afford to be optimistic. Yet, on 11 October, Aubrey Smith, Kimbo Vallentine-Warne and the rest of the Transport began a move towards Amiens. The next day Graham Williams, Sid Amatt and the rest of the battalion trudged from Mansel Copse to Treux, and embussed for Picquigny, where Archie Groom and more reinforcements were waiting to join. For 169 Brigade and the LRB, the long, bewildering and anguished experience of the Somme was at last over.

The men who had joined the battalion during the bloody months of September and October, and who had survived, were now to experience a quieter but by no means comfortable form of warfare. New drafts had arrived, and although it is not absolutely clear, the majority of the men joining appear to have been LRB-trained. There were certainly some from other London Regiments, although it is difficult to spot recruits from the County Regiments. The battalion was by no means at full strength during the next few months, but the character of the LRB was beginning to re-assert itself. The Middlesex and Essex men were still a fairly distinct group, but with the appearance of some younger recruits, as well as the 'Derby men' and conscripts, the battalion was again becoming more of a homogenous unit.

A.V. Polhill was fairly typical of the type of man joining the battalion while it recovered its strength in the months between the battles of the Somme and Arras. A product of an educational system that painted Germany as the bogey man of Europe, Polhill believed that she was responsible for the outbreak of the war and in the pre-war years had been unreasonably threatening to Britain's maritime supremacy. A witness to the anti-German demonstrations of the early weeks of the war, Polhill left the Stationers' Company School in August 1915 to begin work with an insurance firm. Concerned at the quizzical looks he was attracting from women in the streets of London, he joined the Derby Scheme aged 18, in order to get the khaki armlet that signified attestation. He was far from a heroic young man, but felt it was his duty to enlist and disliked the idea that someone else might have to make a sacrifice on his behalf. Polhill signed for the Derby Scheme at Mill Hill School at the same time as his friend Bert Acomb. After being rejected by the Honourable Artillery Company because, like Groom, he wore glasses, the young pair opted for the LRB because, 'most of the young chaps went for it'. It was boys such as Groom, Polhill and Acomb who were to be the backbone of the regiment as it prepared for the Arras offensive in the Spring of 1917.

For the time being, however, ideas of a renewed offensive on the Western Front had to be postponed until the weather improved. So, until Spring arrived, the 56th Division could do nothing except begin a long march from Picquigny northwards to the Richebourg L'Avoue sector near Neuve Chapelle, where, it was hoped, it could lick its substantial wounds. The LRB marched well - Husey was not forced to repeat his earlier lecture to the Middlesex men - and on 28 October the battalion moved into the breastworks to relieve the 8th Worcester. The new area was almost entirely flat and, like the Ypres sector further north, once the drainage ditches had been destroyed by shellfire, the shallow water table prevented trenches being dug. Sandbag breastworks had been constructed but had been allowed to fall into a fairly advanced state of dilapidation. Furthermore, the protecting wire was in places almost non-existent. Wallis, immediately found fault with the neglected state of things. Another, and perhaps more important factor which also made Wallis take an instant dislike to the sector, was that it appeared very quiet. After the incessant pounding on the Somme, many of those less aggressively inclined than Wallis appreciated this relative peace and quiet. Rifleman Frewer had received another parcel of food from his former employers and wrote back:

> *We are all pegging along in spite of the cold weather...but one good thing is that we are not having much rain. We have been having a very busy and hot time since I last wrote, but a month ago we moved right out of it and are in a quiet part of the line. Before we came here we used to be moving practically every other day, with mud inches deep and continually dodging shell-holes; but now it is so quiet that we would not know that there was a war on, except for a few guns going off occasionally.*[253]

Wallis and Husey, however, decided that this happy situation should not be allowed to continue. Consequently, the LRB and the other battalions of the division began to liven things up.

A trench mortar scheme upon the German lines brought a fairly prompt response: it delighted Wallis even though it 'knocked the British front line to blazes'. To him, the physical damage did not matter a great deal, more importantly, the German response confirmed that, 'progress had certainly been made'. The Adjutant continued to grow happier with each tour that passed. The fire from both sides grew in intensity as the Germans retaliated against every British attempt to 'stir up the sleeping Hun' and within a few weeks, Wallis could happily record that the sector was in a 'satisfactory state of war'.

The battalion spent most of its time repairing the trenches and putting up wire. During the first few weeks after coming off the Somme, the weather had become colder but the ground was still sufficiently sodden for the men to be reduced to wading through communication and front line trenches. The main concerns of the troops were to prevent the collapse of the breastworks and dodge the Minnies and aerial torpedoes. The Germans accepted the gauntlet thrown down by the 56th Division and concentrated their heaviest barrages on the front and support lines at night. The British artillery was frequently called on to bombard suspected Minnie emplacements. This would usually quieten things down, but only for sufficient time to allow the Germans to reposition their weapons and commence firing again. Despite this almost constant activity during the six day trench tours, the actual casualties were fairly light; in November five were killed and 11 wounded, while December saw no fatalities and only seven wounded. Patrols went out almost nightly and although most did not get into the enemy trenches, 'gathered much useful information'. [254] One such patrol from another battalion had captured a prisoner who revealed that the German officers were planning a large Christmas dinner in certain dugouts known to the British. The 56th Division prepared an elaborate programme for the artillery and trench mortars, partly to welcome the officers to their dinner and also to prevent the enemy making any attempt to leave their trenches with the intention of fraternising. The planned shoot was executed at 21.30 hours - the time the Germans were supposed to be assembling. In reply, the British suffered from a massive and prolonged retaliation on New Year's Day when the billeting areas to the rear were saturated with German shells.

Before beginning their first trench tour, the new arrivals to the battalion would usually spend two weeks training in the assembly areas to the rear. When out at rest, units used the relatively undamaged buildings of Merville, the largest town nearby, while closer to the line, the billets were in some former racing stables at Laventie. Polhill and Acomb were still together and along with the rest of their draft were greeted on arrival by Sgt Moore of 'A' Company. Moore is described by Polhill as a 'real pukka soldier with a Guardsman-type cap', who impressed upon the new men the need to be keen on drill. He is a type of figure that does not appear anywhere else in the recollections - the more usual LRB NCO being smart, but wearing the typically altered Field service cap. The reason for the difference was perhaps the fact that Moore had come to the LRB from the Middlesex Regiment. The new draft was later addressed by an officer who told them of the the battalion's part in 2nd Ypres and 1 July, before parading before Husey. Both Groom and Polhill were hugely impressed with him; 'a complete picture-book fighting soldier - handsome with a Kaiser William moustache, five wound stripes and a black polo pony'.[255] Husey gave them a lecture on *esprit* by explaining that they had joined the finest regiment in the British Army and insisting that the only good German was a dead one. Having gained the impression that the regiment did not take prisoners, the men were then posted to platoons and went up the line.

Several old faces re-appeared in different guises during this period, including two former *Chyebassa* sergeants, now officers, Arthur White and John Calder. Eric Rose, wounded on 1 July rejoined in November, and another of the Warner brothers of Croydon, Bertram, arrived in December. Like his brothers, Archie and Evan, Bertram had been to Whitgift Grammar School before then going on to study agriculture in Evesham. He had elected to enlist in the Worcesters and went to France with them before returning for a commission in the LRB in September 1916. Two other new officers were Tom Burroughs, who had been in the nucleus personnel on 1 July and a recipient of a letter from the Marlborough family, and John Godward who had also missed the Gommecourt battle. Although several other LRB men wounded during the stay on the Somme rejoined, the regiment was not to regain its pre-Gommecourt character of being officered solely by LRB men, for seven officers arrived from other London Regiments.

January's weather continued to be appalling: breastworks collapsed and the flooded rear areas hampered training and the movement of working parties. The Germans suffered equally as badly and decided to evacuate their front lines and withdraw down their communication trenches to their reserve line sited on the lower slopes of Aubers Ridge. This gave their troops a slightly drier existence but also gave the Staff of the 56th Division what it considered was an opportunity to demonstrate the unit's fighting spirit and aggression. Orders were issued that the former enemy front line should be occupied by British troops who would make them into defensive posts and hold them against anticipated German attempts to re-take them. In later years, the subsequent operations by the LRB and fellow battalions of the division brought forth an out-pouring of anger and invective against the cupidity of the Staff.

By advancing into the German line, the garrisons had to move across the flat expanse of the former No Man's Land while under observation from the Germans on the higher ground. This journey was exceptionally difficult as the ground was flooded; by mid-January the swampy expanse had been transformed into a sheet of ice and snow. The posts were relieved every twenty-four hours so the frozen troops, who had to endure 20 degrees of frost and no possibility of hot food, struggled across the icy wastes to spend a freezing period under the continual gaze of the watching Germans. Whatever the real purpose of the exercise may have been, it was lost to the soldiers who had to carry out the orders. The Brigade order said that the posts should be sited where they could give the best observation on the western exits of the three principal German communication trenches. Those three trenches ran up to the posts and afforded the enemy protection when advancing upon them for one of their periodic raids. The garrisons in the posts, 350 yards in advance of their own line, were completely cut off from their support platoons in the British line. These unfortunate troops held themselves in readiness to cross the open area should the Germans raid the posts. The 2nd London's Regimental History acknowledges that it does not really know why the Staff ordered the posts to be established, but the episode at least demonstrated that, despite the enemy and the weather, the division was capable of holding them.[256] Polhill put it down to 'some sort of devilry' on the part of the Staff, while Groom calls it simply, 'Operation Bloody Senseless'.[257] Whatever the motive - and the Corps Commander recorded it as being merely another example of the policy of harassing the enemy by all possible means - it was a job hated by the men who had to carry it out.

Crouched in what amounted to shell holes immediately above the former German line the posts, about 500 yards apart, were impossible to consolidate owing to the iron-hard ground. The garrisons had to put up with regular artillery bombardments which had their range to the inch, and frequent bombing raids by German infantry creeping unobserved along their communication trench. The artillery fired *around* the posts rather than *upon* them in order to prevent any support reaching them from the British line. Once isolated, the German infantry then showered them with grenades and trench mortars. The garrisons fought stubbornly to drive the attackers off, but it is clear that the Germans had no intention of actually capturing the posts. They had no need or desire to do so. Having voluntarily evacuated them, they were content to merely harass the beleagured British troops, inflict as many casualties upon them as possible, while keeping their own to a minimum. They knew that the British would attempt to reinforce the posts and that there would be another garrison for them to attack next night, either at that post, or another a few hundred yards away.

One such raid took place on Enfield and Barnet Posts when they were being held by parties of the LRB. The Germans advertised their intent by putting gas shells into the posts during the afternoon of 24 January and then followed them up with a box barrage to protect the infantry assaults at 21.00 hours. A soldier in Barnet had spotted the Germans assembling for the attack before the barrage came down, and the NCO in the post sent a runner back to the British lines requesting the immediate support of the platoon standing by for such an emergency. These troops rushed across to the posts and arrived just as the isolating box barrage came down. With these additional troops, during the space of a few frenetic minutes, the LRB fought off the German raiders with, according to the *War Diary*, 'considerable casualties'; Groom, on the other hand, gloomily recalls that all *he* could see next morning were two abandoned bloodstained great coats[258] - but at least the rest of the day was quiet.

Major-General Haking, the Corps Commander, congratulated the battalion on repulsing the raid and singled out in particular the two newly returned officers, Rose and Prior for their work during the night. The raid had cost the LRB 14 wounded, two dead and another who would die two days later from wounds received. The dead were recovered and buried in Laventie, but the survivors had to endure the biting cold and nervous strain of nightly expecting another German raid. Furthermore, most of them probably held sentiments similar to those of Groom in that they were extremely fed-up and little comforted by the praise handed down to them by Haking a few days later. The communique referred to the 'fine military spirit' displayed by the officers and men and that other 'formations' had been so encouraged by the way the division had held these advanced posts, that they too had adopted a similar policy. Groom was not impressed and later wrote a long critical account of the whole policy in general, and the Corps Commander's remarks in particular. He especially expressed his distaste at the platitudes offered to the troops who suffered from the mis-conceived plan.[259]

Other accounts show a similar hostility to the policy of occupying the posts. The 'History' of the London Scots praises the Germans for showing greater wisdom than the British in evacuating them in the first place,[260] while that of the 2nd London thought the Germans must have gained a great deal of satisfaction in seeing the British occupying these inadequately protected posts.[261] They were of very small tactical or strategic value to either side, and their occupation exposed the unfortunate troops to frequent and very accurate bombardments. Even Wallis, not usually the most critical of the Staff, thought the posts 'cost a lot of lives and achieved nothing'. Eventually even the Staff themselves came to realise the excessive strain the posts were causing and the effects this was having on the morale of the men holding them. The *War Diary* of 169 Brigade recorded in late January that, 'Garrisons feel that they are occupying a shell trap; battalions are on the defensive and not offensive, the morale of the men is suffering'. The outcome was that Division decided that the posts should be evacuated on 29 January. The commander of the Queen's Westminsters, Colonel P. Harding, who had long considered the posts untenable and compared them to bait on a hookless fishing line, was consequently delighted when he received the order from the Divisional Commander. The general expressed his regret at having to sanction a withdrawal just when the men 'had got their tails up'. Harding replied by assuring the commander that, 'no order had ever been obeyed with such alacrity';[262] in the LRB, according to Wallis, 'everybody gave a sigh of relief' that the distasteful experiment was over.

One man who had managed to avoid the worst of the Fauquissart experience was Sid Amatt. Just before Christmas it was discovered that he was not yet 19 and was despatched first back to Merville, where he was employed as a mess orderly, and then on down the line to become a cook at the Base Camp. While he enjoyed himself in the relative warmth and safety, his friend 'Dicko', also formerly of the the Essex Regiment, and two newer pals, the Loftus brothers from the Middlesex drafts, occupied themselves trying to keep warm. The sergeants lived in cosy little dugouts with charcoal stoves, while the officers and warrant officers were, according to Polhill, never around. That is possibly an exaggeration, but the officers were probably more comfortable than the non-commissioned men who, although not expected to be 'on parade' when in the trenches, had to shave daily and keep some sort of hygiene amidst the intense cold of the confines of the trench walls. When not in the front line, working parties were found but owing to the condition of the ground, apart from carrying fatigues, there was little they could do. The officers were reduced to ordering the men to break up an unresponsive heap of frozen gravel with pick-axes and perform other similar time wasting duties. Some were occasionally detached to work for the RE - the job usually involved pushing waggons along the light railway - while on another occasion, the battalion had to spruce itself up for a general's inspection and stand around in the freezing cold for some time. When the general did eventually appear, he rode by with barely a glance in their direction. With the penetrating cold and the futility of the posts, morale does appear to have suffered. Groom describes the period of one when the deep reserves of regimental *esprit* had to be plundered to prevent letting the regiment down or admitting to those in authority that morale really was sinking.[263]

Although the posts had been abandoned, normal trench routine continued. Once the enemy had re-occupied his front line, patrols were again sent out to gather information on his identity and activity. On 2 February, after it had just come out of the line and moved to Laventie as reserve, Brigade asked the LRB to present a scheme for a raid on the German lines. As this was to be the first such operation undertaken by the battalion since the unfortunate affair when Sgt Bradford and 2Lt Gardiner had been killed by fire from their own lines, training was begun immediately. Special emphasis was put on the role to be played by the battalion's bombers. It was a new experience for all those detailed to take part - 'B' Company having been selected to conduct the raid - including the three officers who were to command the enterprise. They were Captain Crews, the former Municipal Secondary School boy Commissioned in the Field just before Gommecourt, 2Lt Perowne, whose ten years in the Norfolk Yeomanry had probably not prepared him too thoroughly for a trench raid, and the newly arrived former *Chyebassa* private, but now subaltern, John Godward.

Once the battalion moved back into the trenches, patrols were sent out to reconnoitre the ground and approaches to the German lines. It had been decided to raid the two posts known as Devil's Jump and Hampstead, but the success or failure of the exercise depended upon the weather staying cold and the shell holes and ditches remaining frozen. Any thaw would seriously hamper the efforts of the men crossing No man's Land and penetrating the German trenches. John Godward led a small patrol to investigate the former British posts of Barnet and Enfield during the night of 14 February; the former was empty but a German party in Enfield inflicted wounds on all but one of the British patrol. One soldier, Corporal Watson, an original 2nd Battalion man was killed, but a greater worry to Battalion was the injury sustained by Godward. This meant that another officer, who would not have time to adequately reconnoitre the ground beforehand, had now to be detailed to lead one of the raiding parties. While Godward had been leading one patrol, another went out under Perowne to see what was going on in Hampstead. The Germans were discovered to be working hard, and further patrols on the next two nights confirmed that the enemy was busy putting up new wire and sending out as many patrols as the LRB. This activity and the onset of the thaw convinced Battalion that the raid should take place on the night of 17-18 February, before the ice grew any thinner and the mud more impassable. 2Lt Prior, who had been one of those congratulated by the Corps Commander for helping to 'repulse' the German raids on Barnet and Enfield in January, was chosen to replace the wounded Godward and lead the party attacking Hampstead.

On the way - Brighton Marchers, 1913. (HU65444)

Arriving at Brighton. The new record of 14 hours 23 minutes for the 52.5 mile march was often used in later years to build regimental *esprit* and pride in new recruits. (HU65446)

Eastbourne Camp beneath Beachy Head, August 1914. The annual camp was brought to an abrupt halt following Britain's declaration of war. (HU65447)

On board the SS *Chyebassa*. The 1st Battalion on its way to France, 4th November 1914. (HU65479)

The Brewery, Ploegsteert. The LRB used it as a bathhouse until the owner complained. It was soon reduced to a shelled ruin. (HU65483)

"Tootsie" Hands' kitchen, Ploegsteert Wood, 1914/15. "Tootsie" is standing on the right. (HU65449)

LRB HQ, Ploegsteert Wood, 1914/15. (HU65451)

Keeping, Castle, Pumphrey, Stannard and Carter with an imitation
gun in the snow of Ploegsteert. (HU65497)

Clerks from the Sun Fire Insurance office serving in 'C' Coy in 1915.
They are wearing their recently issued goatskin jackets. Left to
right: Sgt Adams, Gibson, Annsted, Richardson, Stannard, Denton,
Harding, Warwick, Cpl Henshaw. (HU65495)

"Uncle" Dick Wallis in a Ploegsteert dugout. (HU65411)

Experimenting with a rifle grenade. From left to right: Earl Cairns, Col-Sgt Over, Staff Sgt Adams and Capt. Oppenheim. (HU66184)

Part of No.13 Platoon at a Ploegsteert estaminet, February 1915. The three Dixon brothers are; Bill (back left), Walter (left front), and Squib (right front). A fourth brother would join the LRB in 1920. Henry Williamson's friend, Baldwin, is second from right, back row. (HU66185)

The souvenir hunter Cpl Pothecary (centre with rifle) and Gardiner,
Hobson, unknown, unknown and Hollis. (HU65455)

The LRB plot in the cemetery which bears the Regiment's name. The
earliest LRB burials took place in January 1915.(Author's collection)

Roll call in Elverdinghe Wood, April 1915. (HU65416)

Although he is not wearing his VC ribbon this photograph of Sgt D.W. Belcher is thought to have been taken after the 2nd Battle of Ypres. (HU65423)

Sgt D.W.Belcher VC, R.H.Stonnill and John Stransom DCM, taking a break in Ploegsteert Wood. (HU65456)

Cpl Victor Hember in the Maison Electrique, Armentieres. (HU65490)

Russell Latham. (HU65428)

'Q' Coy draft from 2nd Battalion just before leaving Haywards Heath (January 1915). (Author's collection)

Punch Hughes.

Sgt 'Punch' Hughes MM. Hughes survived the Gommecourt attack, but lost a leg in Glencorse wood, the action in which he won his Military Medal. (HU65464)

Rfm Aubrey Smith MM and Bar. (HU65449)

Chilcott, Harbord, Charles, Smith and Raynor of the Transport Section. (HU65457)

L/Cpl Maurice Howard and unknown recruit at Tadworth. (Author's collection)

"Wheatley's lambs" at Tadworth. 2Lt Fletcher Wheatley is in the
centre wearing a tie. (Author's collection)

Members of A10 Training Platoon at Blackdown, October 1917. John
Sutton, who was being posted with this group of Aiv boys, is bottom
left. (Author's collection)

The "Fovant Scottish" Platoon, July 1916. According to some reports the London Scottish appeared to be winning the war on its own. Claiming that they would save the War Office money by providing their own kilts, bagpipes, sporans etc., these LRB recruits of 'F' Coy, 3rd Battalion, demanded a transfer to that august Territorial unit. (Author's collection)

LRB prisoners captured on 1 July 1916. Left to right: Houle, Whitehouse, Honeywell, Rippingale, Evanson (sitting), Dean, Chrisfield, Sidwell. (Author's collection)

Gommecourt No.2 Cemetery. This cemetery contains the graves of at least 45 LRB men who fell on 1 July 1916. L/Sgt William Marlborough's grave is fourth from right, second row of the plot immediatel in front of the camers. (Author's collection)

1st Battalion in reserve in Chimpanzee Trench, 7 Sept 1916. (HU66183)

The officers of the LRB as they prepared to leave the Somme for Laventie, October 1916: standing - John, QM Kelly, Perowne, Stransom, Poland, Lankaster, Gordon, Rev Horley-Smith, sitting - Crews, Wallis, Husey, MacOwan, Tait (RAMC). (LRB collection)

The LRB's officers taken shortly before they went back in the line for the final time: Back row - Belither, Cockerell, Bradley (RASC), Finch, Reid. Middle row - Chodale (RAMC), QM Denny, Darrington, King, Barnes, Stevens (18/London), Scott (12/London), Rev Johnston, Terry. Sitting - John, Hancocks, Wallis, Brunell, Crews, Tabberer (9/London) Front row - Mills (7/London), Coles, Grimwood. (Author's collection)

The whole operation proved to be an unfortunate experience for those taking part. Not only had the ice thawed considerably, but heavy rain was falling and a thick ground-mist hampered the raiders as they crossed No Man's land. Direction was lost and it proved almost impossible to identify their objectives as the German lines were simply flooded shell holes with all vestiges of trenches having been obliterated. There were very few Germans about in these advanced positions and it became clear, even in the murky darkness, that once the thaw had begun, the enemy had evacuated these positions for the relative comfort of those further back. No machine gun emplacements or identity papers were discovered, and then to spread further gloom and disappointment, the British artillery opened up on the party led by Lt Perowne. This barrage resulted in the wounding of Perowne and the death of one of his men. The unhappy episode was brought to an end when Captain Crews, waiting with the supports in the British front line, ordered the buglers to sound the withdrawal. The Germans were content with the LRB's failure to discover anything worthwhile or take a prisoner, and stopped their artillery fire once the raiders were back in their own lines.

The unfortunate man killed by the British guns was Rifleman Overy and another man, Hemmingway, died of wounds later that night in the British lines. Apart from Perowne, four other men were wounded during the action which had not succeeded in securing prisoners, gaining any information, or apparently even killing any Germans. The only thing it did achieve was to confirm the belief that the Germans had sensibly withdrawn to drier ground. Although it was not as embarrassing as the fiasco near Fonquevillers the previous July, and with the acknowledgement that the elements had proved a severe handicap, this was the second time that a raid by the LRB had gone quite badly wrong. It was not the fault of the officers and men taking part, but the foolishness of authority in ordering such an operation once the thaw had commenced and the rain had began to fall in torrents. In view of the difficulties the raiders had had to overcome, it was perhaps fortunate that the 72 troops had not suffered even more severely.

The remainder of the month was spent undertaking the usual trench tours and working parties. One more man, Rifleman Angold, a Gommecourt survivor was to die during that period. The men realised that a major move was about to be made when troops of the 8th West Yorks, 49th Division relieved them on 1 March. With the end of their unpleasant although relatively unbloody, sojourn in the Laventie sector, the LRB and the other battalions of the 56th Division were about to embark on yet another, albeit shorter, but equally uncomfortable and exhausting experience of war.

When young recruits such as Polhill and Acomb arrived at Laventie they had been hardened up during their two week stint in the 56th Division Training Battalion before being posted to the battalion in the line. Approximately 200 such men followed that route to the battalion and, once they had joined their comrades in the trenches, there was little room for further training. Their fitness, and in particular their feet, suffered during the trench tours, yet these men were probably in a better condition than those who had marched away from the Somme. Despite regular rubbing with whale oil, their feet had become soft from the constant immersion in the water-logged trenches, and now those feet were to begin a march of 96 miles across broken, snow-covered roads.[264]

The first three days were not too bad; the men were carrying full packs and had hoped to put other souvenirs and accoutrements on the cookers and Lewis gun carts.

This plan however was adandoned when the NCOs announced that extra kit could not be carried in this way although the Lewis gun teams themselves managed to secrete some extras on their carts. Aubrey Smith, Kimbo Vallentine-Warne and the rest of the Transport had no problems with their kit, but the remainder of the battalion simply had to trudge along, weighed down as pack animals. On the fourth day the column arrived at Le Boisle. It was supposed to stay here for a few weeks to carry out training for what the Divisional Staff had described, somewhat optimistically, as the 'open warfare' that would follow the Spring offensive. As the men settled into their billets to tend their feet and ease their aching bones, orders were received that the march would re-commence before dawn. The next three days saw the division endure blizzards and freezing temperatures until, finally, it arrived at a camp of Nissen huts in Fosseux. The *War Diary* records with obvious pride that not one man was lost through falling out and only six were evacuated to hospital with, measles or influenza. The 2nd London admitted to three falling out,[265] but Polhill remembered that the reason why the LRB arrived intact was partly to do with regimental *esprit* and partly to the attitude of the Medical Officer:

> *Some tried to fall out, and just as we were getting into the suburbs of*
> *Arras, some were really crawling. The M.O. came along on his horse*
> *and got them up - more or less jumped on these chaps with his horse.*
> *I felt like shooting him....it was a very sad time.*

The men had suffered badly from the effects of the weather and the lack of fitness for such a march. The 96 mile trek formed the shape of an unenclosed circle - the direct route from start to finish being nearer 20. The question of whether it was a deliberate plan to get the men back to some sort of fitness, or whether it was simply an example of Staff bungling, was open to some speculation. However, the arrival of the division, now back under the command of General Snow, its old Corps Commander of the Gommecourt days, in the rear areas of the Arras sector, presaged the opening of another bitter battle. The consequences of this move were to signal yet another change in the composition of the LRB.

CHAPTER X

The Agony of Attrition

By 1917, Arras was very much a city in the front line of war. Its magnificent cathedral and other medieval buildings lay partially ruined, but in the cellars and tunnels beneath the cobbled streets various departments of Third Army's administrative machinery revolved incessantly to plan and prepare for the coming offensive. The voluntary German withdrawal in March had thrown the combined Anglo-French plan into some confusion, but amendments were made to take account of the more advanced British lines and the stronger German front system of trenches. The enemy had withdrawn to some high ground further east, to lines that protected the still-unfinished part of the Hindenburg Line which eventually ran down to Lens. This section was known to the British as the Drocourt-Queant switch. Despite the incomplete state of the main German defensive system, the sections Third Army were preparing to assault were still extremely formidable.

The LRB moved into trenches to the south of Arras near Achicourt, and immediately began to sustain casualties from the intensive German shelling. One of the first to die was another of the 1914 *Chyebassa* men, Sgt Edwin Howard, and he, like most of the other casualties, was buried in the nearby cemetery. The battalion was attempting to dig new communication trenches between the old British and the recently abandoned German front system and, at the same time, to convert the former enemy ones, which had, of course, originally faced west, to now face east. The chalk ground made digging difficult and the parties were continually exposed to the German guns, which had the ranges to a nicety. Despite the change to 'Summer Time' on 26 March, the weather was dreadful. Mud clogged the cratered roads, and other parties were constantly employed attempting to fill the holes. Troops and limbers were continually passing up and down carrying stores and equipment for the offensive, or marching to new sectors.

The villages of Beaurains, Agny and Achicourt, to the south and south-east of the city, were a favourite target for the German guns. Carrying parties were continually shelled as they approached the cross roads and junctions of the village. While going up and burdened with their loads, the troops could do little except trudge on and pray. The return journey, on the other hand, was a mad dash through the ruined village centres and out to safety on the other side. On the evening of 7 April, while driving his ration limber towards Agny, Aubrey Smith and the rest of the convoy were halted by a line of wagons waiting to pass through the village. Initially, the centre of the village came under shellfire, but soon the German gunners extended their ranges and shells began landing on the road where the convoy waited. Amidst the close-packed wagons and cookers, the shells took their toll, and Smith's closest friend since the day of their enlistment was killed. Claude 'Kimbo' Vallentine-Warne, aged 27 years from Kingston Hill, was buried nearby in Agny Military Cemetery alongside others of the London Division killed that night. Smith was devastated, for 'Kimbo's' death was not only a severe personal loss, but also a blow to the regiment; it represented the disappearance of yet another of the survivors of Ypres and Gommecourt.

The death of a few more Londoners could not, of course, delay the intense preparations being made for the forthcoming offensive. Four tanks were allocated to the 56th Division and when the assault began, fire from massed machine guns would sweep down the Cojeul Switch and into the German-held village of Neuville-Vitasse. The battalions of the division were in the process of being reorganised along the lines laid down by the authorities, whereby platoons were intended to become self-contained units of one rifle, one Lewis gun, one bombing and one rifle grenade section each. Meanwhile, the British guns, wheel to wheel along the roads, kept up a continual bombardment on the German lines all over the Easter weekend. The date of the infantry assault was, however, postponed for twenty-four hours as heavy rain, and then snow, fell on Good Friday. The surplus personnel, which for the first time included Graham Williams, amounted to 113 men under the command of Captain Arthur White. These men were ordered to join the Divisional surplus personnel battalion on 5 April, and on the following day, Good Friday, a battalion Church Parade was conducted. The men knew they were not to go over with the first assault on Easter Monday, 169 Brigade being divisional support - but the tension amongst the assembled battalion was great. With the possible exception of 40 men who had arrived in March, the rest of the battalion had at least had the experience of modern warfare in the Neuve Chapelle sector. There were still, of course, men who had been at Gommecourt, Leuze Wood and Les Boeufs - men who had taken part in several offensives, and had seen each of them go wrong, usually to a greater, rather than a lesser degree. This attack was to take place against similarly strongly entrenched German positions on higher ground, and with the possibility of a snow storm to hamper movement. Why this one should succeed, where the others had failed, was an open question.

Despite the pessimism in some men's minds, the infantry assault on 9 April was successful and, according to the *Official History*, must be considered one of the 'great days of the War'.[266] It goes on to describe it as, 'the most formidable and at the same time most successful British offensive hitherto launched'.[267] Certainly, as far as the 56th Division was concerned, it was successful. All objectives had been reached and secured by the two attacking brigades, and at 16.00 hours the LRB moved forward to occupy trenches nearer the front. Packs had been dumped in Achicourt the previous night and bombs, rifle grenades, flares and tools drawn. On 11 April the battalion was ordered further east to relieve the 8th Middlesex and it was during this operation that the young Polhill saw his first dead British Tommies, 'which gave us a bit of a shiver'.

Earlier Polhill had also watched as the cavalry advanced against the village of Monchy. Monchy stands above the battlefield in a commanding position, and was 'looking lovely in the sunshine - we thought it was the end of the war'. Similarly, when Figg of the Transport went up to a dump nearer the line, one LRB man seemed genuinely delighted at the progress made and remarked to Figg, 'Isn't it a jolly fine war, eh?'[268] The optimism of these men was a little premature. The cavalry was soon cut to pieces in front of the German wire, and the threatened snowstorm, which had held off during the initial attack, now began. The troops, assembling in largely derelict and still very muddy trenches, had been ordered to dump their greatcoats before moving off and were therefore exposed to its full fury; two men, Riflemen Herink and Gilruth, subsequently died of exposure.

Strong bombing parties were ordered to attack up Nepal Trench, part of the Wancourt-Feuchy Line, until they met the Queen Victoria's who were supposed to be working their way down. The operation was successful and was then continued down Heninel Trench towards Rum Jar Corner. (Map 6.) It was here that the third of the Warner brothers from Croydon was to die; Bertram, the former agriculturalist and member of the Worcester Regiment, led two abortive attacks along Heninel Trench before falling on the third but successful attempt. The advance on the village of Wancourt continued when Peter Titley and 2Lt Reed led patrols into it, only to find it deserted. The Germans had only recently evacuated their dugouts and the patrols pushed on over the almost dry Cojeul river and up the grassy slopes towards Wancourt Tower. Polhill had seen one of his Fovant companions, Robert Nye, wounded in the bombing attacks and followed behind Titley who was leading the advance armed only with a shooting stick. A machine gun fired on them from Guemappe, which prompted Dredge to suggest they should wave their arms and legs about in order to try to get a 'Blighty'. Polhill was not impressed, and joined the rest of his platoon in a huge crater on the slope east of Wancourt. Here they were ordered to halt and hold themselves in readiness to support an attack going in on their left against Guemappe. Looking back on the day's activity, Polhill later reflected on this, his first experience of what had almost amounted to 'open warfare':

> *I had all sorts of feelings like wishing the people at home could see you in this situation...it was exciting and you were with all your friends. If you were on your own it would be very frightening...but you didn't get much opportunity to enquire as to what had happened to whom - you were too busy and sections kept pretty much to themselves'.*

In fact there were not many casualties for Polhill and others to enquire about. The battalion had attacked in accordance to the Brigade order of keeping about 200 yards between the widely extended lines and, consequently, losses had been very light during the advance. Although several more soldiers were evacuated during the night suffering from the effects of gas, the entire operation had been remarkably painless - only eight deaths since 9 April. A day's rest at Rum Jar Corner allowed some cleaning up, but the weather was still atrocious, and as the battalion had been on the go since 9 April, the pause, although welcome, was hardly sufficient to revive it fully. The respite was only to be short-lived as at 02.00 hours HQ received orders that the battalion was to support an attack timed for 05.30 by the Westminsters and Victoria's. The troops were awakened from their uneasy and uncomfortable slumbers and moved off at 03.45. What followed was a period of utter confusion; Brigade orders were vague as it did not know at what time divisions on either flank were going to advance. This difficulty was compounded when three battalions of the Durham Light Infantry were given the wrong assembly co-ordinates and so became hopelessly mixed up with the advanced battalions of the 56th Division near Wancourt Tower. When the muddled attack began, the mass presented a magnificent target for the German machine gunners in Guemappe. They poured such a volume of fire into at least six separate battalions concentrated in a small area of about 1,000 yards square, south of the demolished Tower, that the advance crumbled. The Queen Victoria's were all but annihilated. The LRB, in support, were more fortunate, sustaining only a further five deaths, four of whom were former Middlesex men. The Germans made a determined counter-attack which necessitated the LRB despatching its HQ details to protect Brigade HQ. By the early hours of 15 April though, the battalion had been relieved by the London Scottish and had marched, extremely wearily, to rest in Neuville-Vitasse.

So far, the Battle of Arras had not made a great impact on the battalion - the *War Diary* recorded 17 killed, 55 wounded and eight missing. The final number of dead, including those who died of wounds such as Polhill's friend, Nye, amounted to 23. Of these only three were not later identified, and their names appear on the Arras Memorial to the Missing on the Faubourg d'Amiens. On paper, therefore, the battalion's numbers should not have been affected too greatly since it left Vielle Chapelle, apparently at full strength, in March. The reality was, however, somewhat different. When it came out of the line, the battalion's 'effective strength' was 972, but its 'fighting strength' amounted to only 14 officers and 488 other ranks. The missing 484 were accounted for by 104 men of the Transport, 114 in the surplus personnel, 16 on courses, 24 training with the Depot Battalion, 99 'detailed', 44 serving with the Field Ambulance and 78 listed as 'casualties'. Perhaps the most revealing statistic was that the remainder, a total of only five men, were away on leave.

Two of the fortunate men to miss the battle were Archie Groom, who had received orders to report for a Lewis gun course just before the battle began, and Sid Amatt, formerly of the Essex Regiment. Since being sent down as under age from Vielle Chapelle, Amatt had been enjoying himself at the Base, but Authority finally decided it was about time he rejoined the LRB. He was sent up with a draft of non-LRB men towards the battalion, but some of the group were side-tracked in Arras and ordered to report to a nearby Field Ambulance. Amatt was 'very willing and able' to take on this new role; the roar of battle, a few miles away, had already begun, and the twelve-hour shifts tending the wounded, plus the promise of regular hot food, seemed infinitely preferable to huddling in freezing trenches. Groom was to be back with the battalion before it rejoined the battle in early May, but Amatt's luck held and he remained with the Field Ambulance until the end of the month.

When he left the Base, although unaware of it himself, Amatt had been given a new regimental number. The re-numbering of personnel was part of an important, rationalising change taking place within the Territorial Force during this period. When Amatt, along with the other Essex volunteers, had first joined the LRB, they had been given an 'LRB' number by the Base authorities. The problem for the administrators at

Le Havre was that they did not know precisely how far the regimental numbering sequence had reached at the home depot. In fact, those joining the 3rd Battalion in June and July 1916 were receiving numbers in the 5000's. In order to give themselves a clear gap between any subsequent arrivals from the training battalion, and those coming, like Amatt, from other regiments, the authorities in France started the Essex members' sequence at 10000. Although these 70 odd men actually arrived at the battalion *after* the large drafts from the Middlesex, 7th London and the Post Office Rifles, these groups were given *higher* regimental numbers than the Essex men. These larger groups may have been given their numbers, which start at 10500, before the Essex volunteers were allocated theirs. Then, perhaps the authorities realised they had left too large a gap between those being issued at home and those in France and used Amatt and his friends to help close the gap.

This system had worked satisfactorily, for once the 1st Battalion had left the Somme most of the drafts joining it were from the 3rd Battalion and were bringing their own regimental numbers with them. However, the Army decided - possibly as part of a scheme to make the transfer of men from the Regular to the Territorial Force and vice versa less contentious - to re-allocate and issue new numbers. Each unit of the London Regiment was given a start and finish figure - the LRB's could eventually run from 300000 to 319000 - and the clerks and orderlies at home immediately began to work out new numbering for those men still serving with the regiment. The lowest numbers were decided by seniority and then by order of enlistment. The work was begun early in the year and was back-dated to include all those who had fought and died at Gommecourt. The difficulty of the task was exacerbated by the large numbers of men still officially posted as 'missing' from the period on the Somme. To be on the safe side, all men not confirmed to be dead, (and also, in fact, some who were), were given new numbers. Those drafted into the 1st Battalion in July 1916 were slotted in after those who had enlisted in the 3rd Battalion in October of that year. In order to avoid any duplication, the orderly clerks at Le Havre and Rouen numbered men coming from other regiments, but who were about to be posted up the line to the 1st Battalion LRB, with a sequence starting at 315000. This meant that there were still nearly five thousand numbers available for use by recruits to the 3rd Battalion before the series might again run into trouble.

The 60 men who left the Base with Amatt *en route* for the 1st Battalion were mainly from the training battalions of the Queen Victoria's, the Finsbury Rifles and a sprinkling of recruits from the Rangers. The majority of these men were conscripts rather than volunteers or Derby Men, and they joined the battalion while it was out of the line on rest during the last week of April. Eight LRB men also returned to the regiment after recovering from wounds. Another important arrival was its new Commanding Officer, Major Burnell. Wallis had been in command during the opening stages of the battle because Husey had again been in hospital. Wallis stepped down on the return of a man who, like himself, had been a member of the LRB since the previous century. Burnell and the new men had a few days to get accustomed to their changed surroundings before an order arrived on 28 April instructing the brigade to move to divisional support west of Wancourt. As a further indication that the battalion would again soon be in action, the surplus personnel were ordered to be detached and sent to billets in Arras. So, with a fighting strength of probably somewhere around 500, the LRB once more marched towards the front.

On 1 May the battalion relieved the Westminsters in the front line east of Guemappe. The company commanders had been up to have a look at the area the day before, and had decided that the next two days should be spent digging assembly trenches immediately to the rear of the front line. The situation was fairly quiet, but the British were about to launch an attack on a broad front and the enemy put over gas and 5.9-inch shells from time to time. The men knew they were to be on the right of the brigade's attack. They were given no information as to their real objectives, other than they were to take a chalk pit and the ruins of a sugar-beet factory either side of the main Arras-Cambrai road. (Map 7). They were ignorant of what they were supposed to do if they reached and consolidated those positions. The junior officers and presumably the senior NCOs were privy to the plan, but Groom and Polhill, with their respective Lewis gun teams, simply knew the direction of the intended advance.

An issue of hot rum and tea was served at 02.00 and the infantry went over the top at 03.45 on 3 May. It was still dark but the attackers were silhouetted by a moon behind them and German fire was immediately heavy. Polhill, in the second wave, went over 'excited and elated,' and soon a few Germans began surrendering. The attack faltered in front of The Pit, the most advanced troops only getting within 30 yards of this heavily defended position. St Rohart's Factory was similarly strongly held and the LRB squashed into shell holes and the former German front trench for protection. To make life even more uncomfortable, British guns began firing upon them, although this stopped after a flare had been fired to draw the attention of a spotter plane. Without officers and NCOs, the men stayed where they were until dusk by which time it was clear that the attacks on either flank had failed. The troops of 167 Brigade had in fact barely clambered from their trenches before the German bombardment came down, and those who struggled on towards the German line were swept away by small arms fire. The LRB thus had the frustration of having to fall back, with nothing to show for their efforts and casualties. They retreated only as far as a trench where the ferocious Sgt Moore was holding a revolver and threatening to use it on anyone who wanted to withdraw any further. The troops stayed here until 01.15 hours on 4 May when they were ordered to retire to the original British front line. Here they were soon relieved by the Westminsters. The *War Diary* makes no mention of any German counter-attack, whereas the *Official History*, which bases its account of them on German sources, is scathing about the British response to these enemy attacks. Groom also believed that the Germans launched a counter-attack at about 22.00 hours but, by the time the LRB withdrew, the line had settled down and the shelling had become only desultory,

This brief attack had not produced the same sort of casualty figures as those on the Somme but the losses were still substantial. Fifty-six men were killed or would subsequently die from wounds received between 1 - 4 May. This represents the smallest proportion of deaths to attackers yet experienced by the battalion. The *War Diary* records a total of 169 casualties and even using a low estimate of a fighting strength of 500, this amounts to only 34% of the attackers - again the lowest proportion in any battle so far. Not surprisingly, Polhill remembered that 'morale was very good' and it rose further when for the next few days the battalion cleaned up, trained and salved in the area known as The Harp, near Tilloy. Two long-serving members of the regiment died during the offensive: Sergeant Needell of 'A' Company, a member for eight years, and Edmund Parker, an articled clerk from Primrose Hill, who had joined in January 1912. None of the dead were from the original 2nd Battalion, so the great majority were men like Uden, another of Polhill's draft, from the 3rd Battalion. Another five of the dwindling band of Middlesex men died and six from the latest draft to arrive at the battalion just before the attack were also killed. A higher than usual proportion of the dead were identified, so only 32, or 52% of them are commemorated on the Arras Memorial to the Missing. Six were buried in Duisans British Cemetery, to the west of Arras, after having died in the nearby casualty clearing stations, and several others later died of wounds in Etaples.

To swell the depleted ranks of the battalion a little, three drafts amounting to 73 men arrived in the last days of May. One group arrived at the same time as Ralph Husey returned from his most recent stay in hospital. Wallis recorded in his diary that 'immediately the news spread, and his reception by the cheering battalion was immense'. The return of his old friend made more of an impression on Wallis than America's entry into the war - an event he had recorded in April but then forgotten until after Husey's reappearance. Another man who returned to the battalion was Sid Amatt, fresh from his duties at the Field Hospital. There were others, however, who were travelling in the opposite direction. Two men, who had been without leave for nineteen and eighteen months respectively, were given the much sought-after passes and left for England.

June, a relatively quiet month, allowed time for the new drafts to settle in and have a gentle introduction to war. Line holding and working parties took up a lot of the time but there was still opportunity for company training and bombing tests in the hot sun and intermittent thunderstorms. Sid Amatt had only been back with the battalion two weeks before he and several others fell victims of trench fever. Amatt was evacuated to England, while others who were suffering from various blood disorders and boils, ascribed to the poor diet and lack of vegetables, had to remain at duty. Graham Williams spent a leisurely six weeks at Third Army's Signalling School, during which time he revisited the Gommecourt battlefield and discovered L/Cpl Dean's haversack. Yet, quiet as the Guemappe sector was, several casualties were evacuated following an attack by the Germans on 17 June. This left 'A' Company with five dead and 18 wounded. Two nights later, the indefatigable Husey, now a lieutenant-colonel, decided to lead a patrol consisting of himself, Wallis and Tom Burroughs into No Man's Land. Moved by the breaking of a beautiful dawn, Husey insisted upon singing a sloppy popular song with a chorus of, *In the summertime, she holds your hand and you hold hers, etc.* before returning to their own lines. The Germans seemingly were not too impressed with the trio's choral efforts and promptly opened fire.

At several parades attended by generals and their staffs, awards won during the recent fighting were distributed. These included a DCM for Sgt Moore and a Military Medal for Sgt Hammond, a medical orderly who had come out with one of the 2nd Battalion drafts before Ypres. Twenty-five Divisional Cards were awarded, but some of these, for example that awarded to L/Sgt Baker, were later up-graded to Military Medals. Two *Chyebassa* men also received recognition for their service; Sgt Munday, who had been the Orderly Room Sergeant since November 1914, was awarded the MSM, and Sgt Swan was Mentioned in Despatches. Finally, a Divisional Card was given to one of the most recent arrivals, Rfn Hyland; he had landed in France as a soldier in the Queen Victoria's, but was transferred to the LRB before being posted up the line.

With Husey's return and Burnell now becoming the Second-in-Command Wallis, temporarily, again became the commander of his old 'B' Company. He used this opportunity to get the men smartened up and then drilled them to such an extent that they gave a two-hour demonstration to the rest of the battalion, a demonstration that Wallis himself described as, 'The most perfect exhibition I have witnessed outside of Wellington Barracks'. Proud as he undoubtedly was of the skill and appearance of the men under his command, Wallis was concerned that the life the battalion was leading was becoming too easy. Attention was paid to ensuring morale stayed high. This included the first full bathing parade for two months, and a series of lectures on the regiment's sporting history and earlier exploits. These were delivered to instil regimental *esprit* into the new drafts arriving from a variety of units. Battalion and brigade sports were held in the grounds of the local chateau and included such bizarre events as mounted musical chairs. The greatest emphasis, though, was put on training the men in new methods of assault. It had already been realised that the Germans were no longer holding their front lines in strength. Instead, they were relying more on small garrisons fighting in concrete pill-boxes while keeping strong numbers of counter-attack troops to the rear. The newest troops had received little training in methods of attacking these positions, so much of their time was spent in rehearsing these tactics. The men were also well-occupied with the inevitable route marches. The Westminsters, like the LRB, had long prided themselves on their march discipline and were consequently concerned when large numbers of their recent drafts fell out whilst on these marches. Their answer was to order extra marches during the hours that the estaminets were open, and the problem was resolved.[269] The LRB method was to have the recently formed bugle and drum band play to keep the pace, while Husey rode up and down the column on his pony, Lynch, alternately haranguing and praising the men.

While the sun shone, and while their period of rest continued, Wallis considered that the men were, 'almost hating the thought of going back to war'. Groom agreed. In a lengthy passage on this period he stresses how the troops were determined to make the most of this very pleasant experience, for they knew that it could not last forever.[270] Wallis noted in his diary: 'Trench holding was too quiet for the 56th Division. We were to be fattened up'. Confirmation of a move came on 20 July, and by a series of marches and train journeys, the division arrived in Fifth Army area behind Ypres. The weather was wet and on the day the Third Battle of Ypres began, the LRB was listening gloomily to a lecture from the Divisional Gas Officer on the hazards of mustard gas. This melancholy individual put so much feeling into the dangers of this pernicious weapon that in the end Husey cut him short by proposing a hearty vote of thanks and expressing the hope that the officer would be able to deliver another comic turn at the battalion's next concert.

It was of course clear to all that the battalion was about to go into the line and take its turn to do an attack. Training was intensified and marches were undertaken with the troops wearing respirators. Kit inspections became increasingly frequent and on 11 August the nucleus personnel were detached. Among these fortunate few were Polhill, chosen as a reward by CSM Bamford for offering to collect bodies following the attack on St Rohart's factory, and Cpl Babington, a *Chyebassa* man and friend of Graham

Williams from the Signals. Among those who remained at Palace Camp an air of gloom and despondency spread. Smith remembered it as being the counterpart of that miserable night in Happy Valley just before the Combles attack.[271] Groom's Lewis gun team was 'moody and apprehensive', but Wallis, on the other hand, believed morale was good and that no-one had given a second thought to the 'prospective hell we were going to'. Since the end of its part in the Battle of Arras, the battalion had received drafts amounting to at least 300 men, and others had returned having recovered from wounds. The battalion must therefore have been very close to what by that time, in mid-1917, was considered 'full strength' - i.e. about 800 men.

New officers had arrived and included three from other London Regiments. Four more came from the LRB, one of whom, Francis Ball, was a graduate of Canadian and American universities and a former sergeant in the Princess Patricia's Canadian Light Infantry. Another university man, and more of a throw back to the pre-war LRB officer, was William Butcher. Son of a Member of the Royal College of Surgeons and late of Eton and Trinity, Butcher had been a member of Cambridge OTC before being commissioned to the 2nd Battalion in October 1914. By 1916, aged 24, he had been promoted to captain, and although this was his first time out, he was put in command of 'A' Company when he joined the battalion in June. By contrast, from a more humble background, came Bernard Pocock. A pre-war member of the Civil Service Rifles and pupil of Emanuel School, Woodford Green, Pocock was an employee of The Northern Assurance Company in the City. The company had almost 60 of its nearly 400 male staff serving in the Territorials or Naval Reserve when war broke out and, until 1915, it continued to pay full salary to those who were given permission to enlist once war was declared. Then, the company decided that army pay and allowances would be taken into consideration; half-salary would continue to be paid, while any deficiency on the full salary would be made good when the soldier returned to the position kept open for him. This qualification was probably made to try to ensure that a man would not continue to receive full pay for the duration and then decide not to return to the company. It was also designed to ease the financial burden on the firm, for by January 1917, 210 of its employees were serving in the forces.[272]

Pocock had survived Gommecourt, but had spent much of the time since on duties away from the battalion. He rejoined it in June 1917, just as another member of the Northern was leaving and another was wondering if he would be sent home for a commission before the coming battle. Harold Moseley, from the Foreign Fire Department, had served with the regiment in the early years of the century and was then called up from the National Reserve in December 1914. The regiment used him at home for two years as a drill instructor with the 3rd Battalion before sending him out in December 1916. He won a mention in Despatches for the attack on St Rohart's factory, but then suffered some sort of accident which necessitated his spending three months in hospital. He was thus fortunate in missing the Ypres battle. The other employee was Percy Hills, a much younger member from the Accounts Department and a man who had done well in the shooting and marching competitions while training with the 3rd Battalion. Hills had been drafted to France in September 1916. Instead of being sent to the battalion, he had been put into 169 Brigade's trench mortars. There he remained until applying for a commission in June 1917. Following the usual procedure, he was then taken out of the line. However, instead of returning home, he was sent to join the battalion the day it moved up to the start line near Glencorse Wood.

Hills and the rest of the battalion moved up to the dugouts in Half Way House north-east of Zillebeke on 14 August. On arrival at this desolate spot, Lt Col Husey was immediately badly wounded. 2Lt Sellon of the Finsbury Rifles became Adjutant in place of Wallis, who once again became the Commanding Officer. Wallis called a conference of officers and senior NCOs and impressed upon them all to remember that the coming attack was to be a 'day of slaughter'. Their one hope was to 'kill, kill, kill', and neither ask nor expect any mercy. Wallis was none too confident about the coming battle and later recorded that he had heard the Divisional General say that if any such scheme had been set at Sandhurst, the officer responsible would have been asked to 'seek fresh pastures of thistles on which to graze'. The preparations had been far from ideal. Apart from a very brief and unsatisfactory visit by some officers to the Queen Victoria's (who were then holding the front line) where the party suffered a heavy gas bombardment, the ground over which they were to attack was unreconnôitred. Thus, the troops had no actual experience of the ground, or of the conditions underfoot. In fact the 'ground' was no more than a swamp, where hundreds of shell holes, brimming with water, merged into a seemingly boundless expanse of water and slime. The battalion, as right flank, was meant to advance from this cratered ground into the shattered stumps of Glencorse Wood, trying to avoid the 'lake' near Nonne Bosschen, and then press on into Polygon Wood. The troops would be caught in a murderous fire not only from the Germans sheltering in the numerous concrete pill boxes directly to the front, but also from the several machine guns known to be in Inverness Wood on their right.

Brigade had decided that movement over the sodden, shelled ground would be easier for small columns than extended lines. Wallis adopted this tactic for all but the first two waves, who were instead to advance on a four platoon front. Brigade had told commanders that if any wave did not reach its objective, they should reinforce the attack and push on. The LRB were given the help of two machine guns and a trench mortar from Brigade, as well as 'B' Company of the Queen Victoria's who were to mop up and allow the LRB to continue the advance. After the LRB had moved up to the tapes laid in front of the inappropriately-named Surbiton Villas, this unfortunate company were to stay in the line while their regimental comrades passed to the rear. (Map 8)

Battalion HQ was in the gloomy dark of Hooge Tunnel. Here, beneath the Menin Road, Graham Williams and the other signallers were regaled with 'improper stories' by Nitz. These men were, for the time being, in relative safety, but their comrades in the companies moved up under an intense German bombardment and suffered at least 50 casualties before reaching the start line. Once there, they lay out all night in the sodden ground as the German fire continued. The stench of the decaying corpses of those who had already tried to take Glencorse Wood filled their nostrils. As dawn broke and the mist cleared, the troops advanced towards the remains of the wood under a clear, sunny sky. The first objectives, a line of pill boxes in a sunken track inside Glencorse Wood, were taken, but as they pressed on, the LRB, and the 2nd London on their left, having become bogged down by the German gunfire and the soft ground, lost their own barrage. Some men did manage to get into Polygon Wood, and from this advanced position, Captain Butcher despatched a carrier pigeon which managed to reach Battalion HQ The message was succinct: 'We are surrounded'. This was the last news of 'A' Company. Exhausted from struggling over the broken and flooded ground, they were overwhelmed by counter-attacks from German reserve companies. These had been held further back in the wood, and with others that emerged from Inverness Copse, joined in halting the stuttering British advance.

Archie Groom and his Lewis gun team had suffered casualties before the advance began. These, combined with those of the platoon's bombers and rifles sections, caused their badly-shocked officer, 'Armstrong', to mumble repeatedly that half his platoon consisted of three men.[273] Groom himself had advanced as far as the eastern edge of Glencorse Wood, but fell back with a few other survivors to their original start line. Here they sheltered, and until relieved by the Qeen Victoria's, numbly tried to take stock of their situation. When the Victoria's arrived, the LRB stumbled back in the dark to Half Way House. Later the same day, 17 August, the remnants trudged back to the Cafe Belgé and then by lorries to Abeele, where they were billeted in farm buildings.

The casualties had been enormous. At Half Way House the battalion amounted to 20 men; after the reserve company had been located, the number swelled to almost 80. The nucleus personnel rejoined on the 19 August and the next few days were spent in trying to reorganise the survivors into some sort of military order. It seems as though the temptation to reduce companies to only two platoons was resisted, but the numbers could certainly have justified that action. The *War Diary* recorded a total of 361 casualties, slightly higher than the other attacking battalion of 169 Brigade, the 2nd London, who had gone into the attack with just over 400 men. The actual number of LRB in the front line of 14 August is not known but, as the battalion was supposedly at 'full strength', the number of attackers must have been somewhere around 500. The *War Diary* has only 42 men killed between 14-16 August. It also has 147 listed as missing, and although very many of these were in fact dead, confirmation only came later. By analysing the figures issued after the war, the engagement cost a total of 145 men killed or died of wounds. The greatest proportion came from 'A' Company, which penetrated most deeply into the German lines, and includes three of its number who died in German hospitals. By looking further at the list of the dead and their regimental numbers, the composition of the battalion on the eve of the attack can be more precisely determined. This is made easier because the former regiments of many of those who were drafted to the battalion before the battle are recorded in the *Soldiers Died* lists.

The picture emerges of a hybrid regiment, but one in which the majority, 59%, were LRB-trained. Although it is impossible to be absolutely precise because men were not necessarily drafted to France in the sequence in which they enlisted, the regimental numbers of the dead suggest that 19 of them could have been at the Gommecourt battle, and another 50 might have been present during the rest of the time on the Somme. This implies that perhaps roughly 40% of those taking part in this attack had undergone a similar experience in the period before the Battle of Arras. Survivors from that battle, like Groom and those of Polhill's draft, were also in the front line at Glencorse Wood, but their numbers are more difficult to assess. Whatever the precise figure, the regimental numbers of the men show that all the LRB men had been in the Army at least since the previous November.

Of course not all of those who had been with the battalion from the period before Arras were LRB-trained. Eleven of the dead were those from the Middlesex and Essex drafts of July 1916, including the redoubtable Sgt Moore, DCM. Of more importance to the make-up of the battalion before the Ypres battle were the men who had joined since Arras. These men are fairly easy to identify because they were issued with their LRB regimental numbers in France and, consequently, are of a series distinct from that issued by the home depot. It is apparent that the relationship between the LRB and the Finsbury Rifles, which had seen so many of their officers attached to the LRB, was continued, presumably more by good luck than design, with respect to the other ranks. It was from this regiment that the largest draft arrived after Arras, followed by sizeable numbers from the London Irish and the Rangers. There had also been men arriving in ones and twos from a number of other London regiments, such as the 31st (County of London), a provisional battalion composed of former Home Service personnel. Other battalions from within the London area, such as the West Kents, had also supplied a proportion of the reinforcements. Although such a large proportion of the battalion were therefore not LRB men, the battalion was still overwhelmingly a London battalion - only three of the dead were from outside the capital's postal area. The impact of the battles since Gommecourt would thus have brought in men from differing employment and social backgrounds. This change in composition was forcibly brought home to Smith when, during a battalion concert in June, he was rather put out by the enthusiastic applause received in response to a 'comic' song.[274] However, although many of the men might have been from the inner areas of London, and were Derby men and conscripts rather than volunteers, they were at least, for the time being, still Londoners.

Of the dead, 69% were not recovered or identified, and their names were later engraved on the Menin Gate. A dozen were later found and buried in the massive Hooge Crater Cemetery, while another six died in the clearing stations at Brandhoek on the Poperinghe road. Other casualties were taken to the facilities at Wimereux on the coast, and Lijssenthoek and Mendinghem nearer the line. The Germans buried those who died soon after their capture in Ghent, while one lone LRB man, Rfm Chenoweth, possibly of 'A' Company, was buried near his objective in Buttes New Cemetery on the edge of Polygon Wood. Only two of the dead, Sgts Merton and Saunders were of the original battalion - and they had been August 1914 entrants - Merton still being only 21 years old. Information on many of the others is sparse. Percy Hills from Harringay, would not be returning home for his commission; Skinner from Catford, was a 40 year old confectioner, and Clem Golding had recently resigned his commission in the Suffolk Cyclist Battalion. Another fatality was the 18 year old brother of a *Chyebassa* man, Alan Gibson, but the biggest difference between those dying in this, as opposed to earlier battles, is the higher proportion of married men. It is not possible to put any figure on this as the marital status of many men is not specified, but a subjective estimate suggests that perhaps as many as 40% were married. Similar dificulties occur when trying to assess the average age of the dead. Most of those whose ages are recorded are in their late twenties, but as we would expect from a battalion then largely composed of non-volunteers, there was certainly a number of young 18 and 19 year olds. Furthermore, there was a good sprinkling of men in their thirties and forties, which thus increases the average age considerably. There had been, of course, long-serving and thus slightly more mature men on the *Chyebassa*, but the large number of very young boys who enlisted in August 1914 kept the average age down to twenty-two.

A very small number of officers actually took part in the attack, so the casualties amongst them, although high in proportion, 75%, were, in fact, only 12. Two of the dead were Captain Arthur White, a former sergeant on the *Chyebassa*, and the recently joined Captain William Butcher. The newly appointed Adjutant, 2Lt Sellon of the Finsbury Rifles, died from wounds received while at HQ, and Edward Boland, later to become Physician Emeritus to Guy's Hospital, was wounded at the assembly area. Peter Titley, who had advanced into Wancourt with a walking stick, was badly wounded, so too was Sworder, an alumnus of the same school as Pocock and also formerly of the Northern Assurance. Pocock himself had not taken part in the attack, remaining behind at the Transport lines with the two long serving members Tom Burroughs and Frederick Crews. One of the three officers who took part and emerged physically unscathed from the attack was Groom's platoon officer, the Canadian Francis Ball; he was not, however, to remain much longer with the battalion, being invalided home in November.

The number of wounded given in the *War Diary* for those three days in August is 160 although several of these were certainly later to die from their wounds. 'Punch' Hughes, one of the few men of 'D' Company who had survived Gommecourt unscathed, lost a leg in Glencorse Wood, but one man who reached England safely and made a full recovery was L/Cpl Graham Williams. Williams, the enthusiastic pre-war Territorial from Aldenham College, witness to the 1914 truce, survivor of Second Ypres, Gommecourt, Combles and Les Boeufs, was finally wounded as he sheltered in Hooge Tunnel. Despite the shrapnel in his elbow he took a message up to the signal station where he was told by his former pre-war colleague Sgt Robinson to get himself down to the Aid Post. There his wound was dressed by another long-time member, Pioneer Sgt Wortley. Next he boarded a train to the casualty clearing station at Poperinghe, then another to a general hospital at Wimereux, before finally arriving in a converted Cardiff school. There he convalesced until fit enough to be posted to the 3rd Battalion.

While Williams and the other wounded were being evacuated down the line to safety, the remainder of the battalion, now joined by the battle surplus, were reorganising at Abeele. Although Polhill was relieved to see Buggs, the man whose place he had been given in the nucleus personnel amongst the survivors, he soon realised the toll that the disaster had reaped. At least another four of his Fovant draft were dead. Despite this realisation, his strange recollection was that despite the battalion having been 'smashed to bits, morale seemed alright'. This observation is at variance with that of Aubrey Smith and the account of the subsequent events of the next few days remembered by Wallis. Groom mentions a 'mutiny' by the men in July when they were forced to work twelve-hour shifts for French farmers who paid the Army for the labour. The troops worked for three days and then refused to do any more. They considered that troops out on 'rest' should not be forced to work in the fields, especially as they were not receiving the money paid by the farmers to the Army.[275] No other source mentions this incident and Groom's recollections are frequently challenged by Polhill. What is clear, however, is that a more serious example of discontent emerged when the remnants of the battalion were at Abeele.

Smith recalled that he and his comrades were 'stupified' to learn that following the attack the whole division was being withdrawn. They would assume that the 2nd London and the attacking battalions of 167 Brigade had also suffered severely, but it was not so much the losses that caused the disquiet, as the way those losses had been sustained. In a survey of the attacks carried out by the LRB during the course of the war, Smith blamed their failures on a variety of circumstances. When considering the latest affair in Glencorse Wood, the culmination of all those previous failures, he asked, 'How could all these dashed hopes fail to dishearten us? After seeing the pitiful remains of the battalion...something like disgust with the British tactics made itself felt'. To reinforce this opinion, he went on to quote a passage from a later history which also concluded that a strong sense of discouragement appeared during the battle amongst the men who felt that they were being uselessly and callously sacrificed.[276]

A similar analysis of the state of morale within the regiment was recorded by the normally optimistic Wallis. He recalled that the failure had spread a cloud of severe depression over the battalion. In a long critical passage he blamed the disaster on the lack of adequate preparation and faulty Staff work on the part of Gough's Fifth Army. He continued the discourse by recounting that Orderly Sergeant Munday approached him while the battalion rested to warn him of the prevailing sentiments of a growing lack of confidence, of uncertainty and discontent that were manifesting themselves in the battalion. Munday suggested that as the feelings were so strong in the LRB, Wallis should order a battalion parade in an attempt to diffuse and explain the situation. So:

> Under the quiet shade of the trees in an orchard at Abeele...I carried
> out his suggestion, realising at once that regardless of discipline or
> Field Service Regulations this feeling of distrust must be 'nipped in the
> bud' at once. The LRB owes a great debt of gratitude to Sergeant
> Munday...especially as I agreed completely with their opinion of
> General Gough and his Staff...Until the end of the War, the 56th
> Division never lost confidence in their Divisional Commander, Brigade
> or Regimental officers...and this blind trust carried them through to
> the end...We were fortunate enough never to be again under the
> command of General Sir Hubert Gough and his Staff.

It is difficult to imagine that such an incident could have happened in the LRB in the earlier years of the war. But there lies the dichotomy of the regiment and the impact that the war had made upon it. The volunteers of 1914-15 had not experienced the numbing, demoralising effect of repeated offensives and, consequently, had looked on the slaughter at Ypres in May 1915 as being an honourable episode. They were proud that they, mere amateurs, had parried the violent thrusts of a professional army. But, by 1917, even the most enthusiastic and dedicated of those volunteers were affected by the seemingly endless and pointless slaughter. That men like Smith and Wallis, whose loyalty to the LRB and their country was beyond question, should feel that things had gone so horrendously wrong, underlined the depth of discontent that must have been felt by the conscripts. Few men in the regiment could see the worth of sacrificing such enormous numbers of men and accepting the consequent loss of morale and allied problems, which might emanate from such a policy, for the sake of taking the blasted and devastated Passchendaele ridge.

However, the brief but violent stay in the Salient was over. The 56th Division was to be transferred to Third Army, which necessitated forced marches and interminable train journeys back down to the Somme. The division crossed the devastated battlefields of the 1916 engagements and moved on into those areas whence the Germans had voluntarily withdrawn the following year. The regions had been laid waste by the enemy, but once the LRB arrived at Lebucquiere in the Louverval sector, the trials of the last month were soon forgotten. Depressed and disillusioned they might be, but the men soon grew re-accustomed to the quieter routine of trench life. This new sector faced the apparently impregnable Hindenburg Line in front of Cambrai, and on the British side of the lines, the conditions had been made as comfortable as possible by the troops stationed in the area. The battalions out on rest could enjoy billets which seemed positively luxurious compared with those of previous occupation. There were neatly laid out huts, some with hanging vegetation to obscure them from aerial observation, with carefully attended gardens attached. The Transport lines offered the animals proper brick standings and covered shelter, while the *piece de la résistance* was the railway named after Honorary Lieutenant and Quartermaster John Peterson. Peterson had served continuously since 1896 and had been RQMS when granted the honorary commission in 1914. Although he was soon to return home in order to take over the running of the family business, Peterson continued to serve in the LRB until reaching the upper age limit in 1925. His narrow gauge railway wandered between the huts and buildings, carrying food and fodder to the stores and stables and with even a small branch line going off to the midden. Here were the conditions where the LRB could physically and mentally recover from its latest mauling, rebuild its morale and prepare itself for the next endeavours.

The battalion that could so enjoy the changed environment was still, however, a very weak one. Numbers are a little vague but the Divisional History records that the strength of the four battalions of 169 Brigade in September amounted to 1,921, i.e. an average of below 500, and also that the strengths remained about the same for October.[277] The LRB had received a small draft of 35 before it left the Salient, and was to receive a total of another 143 before it went into action at the Battle of Cambrai. Only four of these drafts came in groups of 20 or more, so just under a half arrived in small parties from the Base. This makes it very difficult to determine from which regiments they originated, but at least some, possibly as many as 60, came indirectly from the 3rd Battalion. Arthur Magnus of A2 Training Platoon had arrived in France in August and, although some of his friends had been sent almost immediately to the battalion, Magnus and others were kept behind at Rocquigny.[278] They were in turn warned for a draft and eventually joined the regiment in mid September while it was out on rest at Lebucquiere.

The remainder of the replacements seem to have been collected in small groups from a variety of units, although, significantly, not only from those of the London Regiment. There were certainly small groups of men who came from the Durham Light Infantry and the Northumberland Fusiliers. To complicate the issue further, some men, who had fought with the LRB in Glencorse Wood, had retained the numbers issued by their previous regiments. This makes it difficult to give a completely accurate picture of the total casualties sustained by men fighting as part of the LRB because those casualties will appear in the fatality rolls of their original unit. Similarly, with the coming battle at Cambrai, where the LRB *War Diary* mentions men with 10th London and Post Office Rifles' numbers. It seems likely that a high proportion of the drafts arriving before Cambrai was made up of these men, who, although appearing on the LRB's strength, kept, as many of their colleagues were to do during the following year, their original regimental numbers.

Polhill thought that many of these drafts were from the Middlesex Regiment. In later years he recalled that compared with the LRB, whom he considered to be 'picked men...and more cultured', these new men were not 'quite the same class'. There is no trace of any former Middlesex man (other than those with numbers that indicate they had arrived with the July 1916 draft) being killed, so it is probable that Polhill is confusing what he believed were new men with those who were already there. But, one former Middlesex man of the July 1916 draft, who did make a re-appearance at Battalion HQ in September, was Herbert Higham. Higham, from Islington, had been wounded at Combles and, on recovery, had taken a commission. Now, as one of the 17 new officers who arrived between September and November, he was the first of the veterans of the Senussi campaign in the Western Desert to serve as an officer in his adopted regiment. Eight of the new officers were men attached from other regiments, largely London ones, but also included the new second in command, Major Cheshire of the Lancashire Fusiliers. The trend towards giving commissions to men who had not been to the public schools continued, and two such men, Thomson and Renwick from Whitgift Middle and Ilford County Schools respectively, also joined before Cambrai. Thus, the essential change caused by these new arrivals was that by November 1917 the battalion was being led by officers of whom nearly half were not actually from the regiment itself.

Several familiar officers were still serving; Husey (in between his many spells in hospital to recover from wounds) was officially the CO; Wallis spent most of the time as acting CO; Captain Calder and four more *Chyebassa* men, Frederick Crews, Thomas Prior, John Godward, (now recovered from his wound received in March) and the Transport Officer, Albert Gordon were still there. Tom Burroughs remained as Bombing Officer and another of the older members was commissioned to replace QM Peterson. Addison Denny had first joined the regiment in 1896 and, as a sergeant after 2nd Ypres, had written to the home depot reporting the losses and discussing the uses his company alone could make of the draft rumoured to be on its way. With Peterson's return to England, Denny was made Honorary Lieutenant and Quartermaster. He was to continue in the post until the cadre returned in March 1919.

Besides these men, there were still possibly as many as 40 or 50 other *Chyebassa* men serving with the battalion. At the third anniversary of its landing in France, 70 men attended a dinner in the Cinema Hall at Lebucquiere. Aubrey Smith was one of the diners so not all of them were actually men who had sailed on 4 November 1914. Furthermore, several others serving in other regiments or units were also present. The greatest number of these originals, probably 26, were in the Transport section, while HQ personnel comprised the next largest proportion. The remainder were dotted around elsewhere with at least two in the Signals and another three serving with the companies. Whatever the actual total of men on the roll - and the alternatives are

799 'effective strength', 691 'ration strength' and 471 'fighting strength' - this handful of original men represents only a tiny proportion of the battalion about to enter the Battle of Cambrai. Smith, whose morale does not seem to have recovered fully since the death of Vallantine-Warne and the departure of other old friends, reflected sadly that, 'every old hand that departed left a gap that no new-comer could adequately fill'.[279] Yet, however gloomy the current state of the battalion appeared to him, the essential thing to Smith was the fact that, because there was still such a disproportionately high number of old faces remaining with the Transport, they continued to be treated in the 'traditional' LRB manner by the new Transport Officer. This came as a pleasant surprise for he arrived at the Transport with the reputation of having been a strict company commander. The concession and acceptance that *esprit* could replace more formal regulations meant that these men could still feel that, whatever was happening in the companies, the Transport section was still the LRB of old. For this reason the old hands had elected to stay together as long as the Army would permit them. It did not matter to them that many of the originals were still waiting for their first stripe three years into the war; the sense of unity and the *esprit* that comes from belonging to a small, close-knit community existing within a larger, changing mass was sufficient for them to resist applying for commissions or accepting other, less hazardous occupations.

The positions occupied by the troops in the front zone were simply posts connected by trenches, rather than the more usual front and support fire trenches. This necessitated the positioning of more posts lying further out as the width of No Man's Land was in places over 2000 yards. Those troops detailed to man the forward slit trenches spent uncomfortable nights peering anxiously into the dark whilst trying to hear the clink of equipment or footfalls of any approaching German patrol. Neither the main line posts nor the forward ones were adequately wired against German raids and once the activity in preparation for the coming offensive began, half the garrisons, rather than the usual two sentries, stood to during the night. While out on rest, the hours of darkness were spent in assisting the divisional Pioneers in widening the Bapaume-Cambrai road and then in carefully camouflaging their work before dawn broke. The advantages of secrecy learnt at Messines were applied to the approaching battle which, despite the pleading of the Tank Corps, was rapidly taking on the dimensions of a major offensive rather than the original concept of a large raid.

The troops realised something big was about to happen but, as usual, were told nothing of the coming operation. The commanding officers had learned of the broad outline of the scheme at a brigade conference on 4 November and the men first had their suspicions confirmed on 12 November when they were warned that, 'in the event of an advance', they should consider it a point of honour to leave their trenches clean and sanitary, with nothing that could be classified as salvage lying about. Company officers were instructed to polish up the knowledge of their platoon commanders and NCOs in the principles of open warfare, and commanders were told to warn their troops that, if the Germans voluntarily withdrew from their front positions, they should be wary of booby traps. Arrangements were also made for the nucleus personnel to be detached. For the first time, the *War Diary* is very specific about who should be left behind and thus be available to rebuild the battalion in the event of heavy casualties. The total amounted to 85 NCOs and riflemen taken from HQ personnel and the four companies.[280]

The LRB was not too involved in the battle on its momentous first day, but moved up as close support on the 21 November. The objective of the 56th Division was to take Tadpole Copse and support the attack of the Ulster Division on the village of Moeuvres. The Germans soon recovered from their initial surprise and concentrated many counter-attacks upon the British positions where Archie Groom and his colleagues were furiously firing off buckets of Lewis gun ammunition and frantically throwing bombs to halt the advancing hordes. Groom, although a section commander, had no knowledge of the overall plan, nor of his particular part in it, having not been issued with any map or information.[281] All he and the rest of the companies could do was hold their particular positions until relieved. HQ was suffering too. Subjected to severe gas bombardments and shelling in their former German dugout, which now faced the wrong way, almost the entire Orderly Room staff and practically all the signallers, runners, police and other details had, by late on 30 November, been evacuated to the Field Ambulance. Most of the survivors, Wallis, Poland, the MO and a handful of other ranks were exhausted, suffering from temporary blindness and near collapse, when Rfn Cowley staggered into the dugout with the news that Wallis's wife had given birth to their first son.[282] This announcement helped to brighten the atmosphere for a time, as did the arrival of the surplus personnel whom Wallis had sent to come up from the Transport lines. Although the battalion's strength on 1 December was reputed to be 40 officers and 730 men,[283] it was so weak in the line that the deployment of the surplus was necessary if it was not to be overwhelmed in another counter-attack. Tom Burroughs had been congratulating himself on his luck at being left out of the battle, but now, as one of those reporting to HQ, he arrived in the middle of a severe bombardment. According to Wallis, Burroughs found his new situation somewhat amusing, and proceeded to 'laugh till he cried'.

The weak and very tired battalion remained in the line until it was relieved by the 9th Royal Scots at 21.30 hours on 2 December. According to the *War Diary*, part of the previous three days had been spent in digging a communication trench, under almost continual shelling, between the former British front line and the German trenches now in British hands. Groom, too, refers to this task and claims that the battalion staged a mutiny by refusing to dig the trench unless they received some food.[284] This is the second such occurence mentioned by Groom and was supposed to have been sparked off when it was rumoured that a neighbouring battalion had received hot food. The companies had been living on biscuits for eight days, despite Smith's assertion that every scrap of bread received by the stores was sent up to them[285] and the consequence of the rumour was that the LRB downed tools for an hour in protest. There are no other references to this incident in any of the extant sources. Groom infers that the whole affair was deliberately hushed up because the consequences of allowing news to leak out of a mutiny by a regiment with the traditions and *esprit* of the LRB would be too dreadful to contemplate. It is of course possible that such a protest did take place, as 1917 was a year of unrest and failure for the Allied armies in general, but the Regimental History puts great emphasis on the fact that the rations only failed to get up on one night during the entire war - and that was at Arras.[286] The conditions at Cambrai, although by no means easy, were not that fluid so as to make it seem impossible for the battalion to be found and rations dumped.

The battalion was back at Lebucquiere by 02.00 on 3 December and at 09.00 marched the four miles to Fremicourt and entrained for Berneville. The following day was spent cleaning up, re-equipping and taking stock of the losses and experiences. The casualties during the time since leaving the Salient and the opening of the Cambrai battle had amounted to just one man - Rfn Lea who was accidently killed when a dugout collapsed - and those sustained during the actual battle were surprisingly light. The *War Diary* gives a total of one officer and 12 non-commissioned men killed between 20 November to 3 December. The officer was 2Lt Leslie Thompson, a 35 year old married man who had only been out since September. 12 deaths among the other ranks are quite easy to identify, but as one of the men named in the *War Diary* was from the 17th London, who did not have a LRB number, 12 might not be quite the complete picture. Of the non-commissioned soldiers who clearly did die in the battle whilst serving with the battalion, five were commemorated on the Cambrai Memorial to the Missing. One of these is probably Groom's Sgt 'Benson' whose body lay on the parapet for five days before burial. As his name appears on the Memorial to the Missing, his grave was presumably later lost.[287] In the cemetery attached to the Memorial lies Sgt Radford, who had been in the surplus personnel at Gommecourt, and who was killed when a shell landed on a bivvy occupied by several sleeping sergeants. None of the dead were from the original 1st or 2nd Battalions, but five more *Chyebassa* men were among the wounded. Signalling Sgt Robinson was evacuated as a gas casualty, as was Gernat, another signaller who had left the battalion with injured feet during 2nd Ypres. Aubrey Smith also lost his old office friend Whittle and two more originals from the Transport section. The officers, too, had been lucky, for apart from the death of Thompson, there was only one other casualty. Of the 14 officers who went into action, only four were actually LRB men. It was in fact, one of these non-LRB officers who was to provide the regiment with one of its most celebrated incidents.

Second-Lieutenant Maginn, born and bred in Cork, had been posted to the LRB from the London Irish and had acquired a reputation of being an 'average' officer with perhaps a tendency to exaggerate slightly his patrol reports. When the 36th Division were driven out of Moeuvres on 22 November, Maginn's platoon, which was in support but constituted the flank of the 56th Division, was almost surrounded. Leaving his platoon, which included Groom, in the hands of his sergeant, Maginn went over to see what 'Ulster' proposed to do about the situation. On being told that the 36th Division would not be launching a counter-attack for a few hours, he decided to lead an immediate attack himself. The LRB platoon knocked out three or four machine guns and released several British prisoners taken by the Germans from the 36th Division, but because he had left the division's flank under the command of a sergeant, Maginn's action was immediately questioned by the authorities. It was later decided, however, that that aspect of the operation could be ignored and he was recommended for the MC. Not content with that one reckless attack, Maginn went out a few days later to rescue a wounded officer of the Irish Rifles. Besides bringing in the officer, he took time out to snipe a few Germans, an act which Polhill ascribed to a surplus of rum. Finally, on the day the battalion was relieved, Maginn's luck ran out and he went 'beserk' when a shell landed nearby and killed two men. He was evacuated and on recovery spent the rest of the war with the 3rd Battalion. While serving with the Training Battalion papers from the 36th Division arrived which recommended him for the Victoria Cross. The order for his MC was therefore cancelled but instead of a VC he was awarded a DSO. This was an unusual event in itself as General Hull, commanding the 56th Division, did not approve of that medal going to other than Regular officers.[288]

The billets provided in Berneville for troops coming straight from eight days of battle and in the depths of winter were appalling, and Husey (who had only that day rejoined the battalion from hospital) immediately organised scrounging parties. The following day the Town Major lodged a complaint with Divisional HQ that several wooden signs - including his own 'Town Major's Office' - had disappeared; his loss did at least provide some succour to the cold, weary troops. The stay at Berneville was brief, but long enough for the battalion to hear a speech by the brigadier and a congratulatory message from the C-in-C which praised the division for its 'magnificent defence'. These parades were commonplace and did nothing to lift the gloom felt by the battalion. The men were clearly frustrated by the eventual failure to exploit the initial success of the battle and, had they known the findings of the Court of Inquiry which sat to discover why the German counter-attacks had been so successful, they would probably have been gloomier still. The Inquiry and Haig's subsequent report to the War Office both laid the blame on the 'feeble resistance' of some of the infantry.[289] Had the troops been aware of this condemnation, they might in their disillusion have simply dismissed it as yet another example of how the Staff failed to understand and appreciate the problems faced by the PBI. A further and perhaps more graphic illustration of the insensitivity of authority was soon to appear. For the time being though, 56th Division was now to take over the Gavrelle sector, east of Arras, where it could at least find comfortable rest billets in Ecurie Wood.

There was plenty of work for the men to do making barbed wire concertinas and improving the defences - work urged upon the battalions by the Army and Corps Commanders who were becoming increasingly uneasy about the possibility of a major German Spring offensive. Only three men had arrived to replace the casualties of November and December, which in total must have been considerably in excess of 80, so the battalion must have been very short of men in the line and on working parties. Cambrai itself had not had a great impact on the number of men on the strength, but it had affected morale. The chance of a major success and an opportunity to shorten the war had been squandered, and all the men could look forward to was another seemingly endless winter of freezing trenches and numbing routine. The only bright spots were the shooting down of an enemy plane by a Lewis gun team and the appointment of Lt Col Husey to temporary command of 169 Brigade. This certainly pleased the longer-serving members of the battalion, who realised that it was still unusual for a Territorial officer to be promoted to such a position; it was probably not so appreciated by the more recent arrivals as it meant the LRB's turnout and appearance had to be better than ever. On his return from three days at the Base, Wallis once more took command of the battalion. He was unhappy at the state of the sector's defences, but not downhearted at the mood he found in the regiment. To Wallis, although perhaps a little behind schedule, everything was still going according to plan and he dismissed the rumours of the anticipated German offensive heard at the Base, as being merely rear echelon 'wind':

> *The further one got from the war, the more horrible, dangerous and*
> *nerve-wracking it appeared to be. On rejoining the battalion, it was*

pleasant to see the cheery optimism of everbody. Neither the officers
nor the men cared twopence for the fat Bosches or their new horrors.

Although Wallis might not have appeared too concerned, those at the Base and in Higher Command were convinced that the Germans were bound to launch an offensive when the weather improved. The German commanders knew that their next effort would have to be the last desperate gamble to try to secure a victory in the West. By utilising the troops released since the ceasefire on the Eastern Front, Ludendorff hoped to drive a wedge between the British and French armies and force a decision in the West before the Americans arrived in sufficient number to swing the balance irreversibly in favour of the Allies. To counter the anticipated onslaught, the BEF had, in common with the other combatant armies, adopted a new system of defence in depth. It was into one of these sectors, still under construction, that the 56th Division had moved.

The different elements comprising this new system were known by a variety of names, but for our purposes they will be referred to by the following terms. The trenches nearest the German lines were the forward section of the Forward Zone, but the 'lines' were a series of posts up to 1000 yards apart. Posts, such as Towy, Bird and Mill were garrisoned by up to company strength; their purpose was not to *halt* a determined attack by the enemy, but slow it down. They were protected to the front by belts of wire and connected to the rear by communication trenches leading to the Marine-Naval Line. This continuous trench was also in the Forward Zone and lay about 800 yards behind the posts. Battalion HQ was sited here and this zone was meant to further slow down, and if possible halt, the attack which the posts had previously disrupted. If the attack was not halted at the Marine Line, the Battle Zone (or Red Line), sited a 1000 yards further back and covered by the guns firing from behind Vimy Ridge, would then be expected to perform the task. Further back still, on high ground overlooking the Forward and Battle Zones, was a final line of defence. If the enemy could penetrate this far and fight their way through this Rear Zone, the way to the coast was open.

The Commander of XIII Corps, General Horne, ordered that, as the posts were a little too far forward from effective support from the guns on Vimy Ridge, they should not be expected to fight out a battle. Consequently, they were held more thinly than their counter-parts in Fifth Army further south.[290] Third Army's emphasis was on ensuring that the Battle Zone should not fall; while the Marine-Naval Line was held in strength and covered more effectively by the artillery than the forward posts, the main battle was expected to be fought 1000 yards to their rear.

Apart from the still unfinished state of the British Zones, and many of the rear-most Green Lines existed on paper only, the High Command was equally concerned over the shortage of men to defend them. Many in the BEF believed that Lloyd George was responsible for the retention in Britain of what they considered to be an inordinately high number of trained men. In reality, the policy actually belonged to Field-Marshall Sir William Robertson, Chief of the Imperial General Staff, although the Prime Minister was perfectly happy to support the idea. Lloyd George reasoned that if Haig was deprived of sufficient troops, he would not be able to indulge in what the PM considered to be further pointless and futile offensives. The High Command's response to the manpower shortage was to conduct a major re-organisation of the BEF which involved the reduction of infantry brigades from four to three battalions. This meant that *battalions* were now stronger than they had been for some time, but that *brigades* were weaker. In all 141 battalions disappeared and the programme affected the LRB in three significant ways. The greatest blow to regimental morale came with the disbanding, after only one year on foreign service, of the 2nd Battalion. Secondly, the transfer of their friendly rivals in the Queen Victoria's to the 58th Division had an effect on both regimental and divisional morale.[291] Finally, and of more immediate concern to the LRB, was how to cope with the influx of nearly 300 men posted to it from the Rangers.

The 1/12th County of London (Rangers) had, like the LRB, been created as a Territorial unit from a Volunteer battalion under the Haldane reorganisation of 1908. It had achieved some notoriety in 1893 when, despite some opposition from the War Office, the Colonel bought two Nordenfeldt five-barrel guns and thus claimed to be the first infantry battalion in the British Army to use a machine gun.[292] In its Territorial days, there seems to have been one company recruited from students attending the London Polytechnic, while another regular source of men was the London Gas, Light and Coke Company. Although most of its recruits do appear to have come from the working classes, by the time the battalion landed in France on Christmas Day 1914, it contained a fairly large contingent of clerks. The unit had seen heavy fighting at Ypres and had been one of the three battalions that formed the composite battalion along with the LRB after the battle. When the 56th Division formed in 1916, the Rangers had gone into 168 Brigade and had suffered like the rest of the division in the battles on the Somme and beneath the Passchendaele Ridge. In 1918 it was the unfortunate unit of 168 Brigade to be disbanded and, while many of its men went to join the second line battalion, the remainder were absorbed by the LRB. The regiment had ceased to be a unit composed exclusively of actual Rangers after 1 July 1916, and by 1918 it was, like every other battalion in the division, a hybrid. This did not make its disappearance any easier for the men to take. Wallis remembered that hundreds of men, whose morale and *esprit* had been shattered, no longer had any interest in the war or the Allied cause. As it seemed incomprehensible that any of the old loyal Volunteer units, with their long and proud traditions, could be deliberately disbanded by the Army, Wallis recalled that at first no-one could actually believe the order. Memories of Gommecourt, the Somme and Glencorse Wood (which to him now seemed 'useless sacrifices'), coupled with this latest example of insensitivity, severely shook Wallis's confidence in the Corps and Army commanders. Smith wrote that the men were 'furious' over the decision to disband the Rangers, and it seems that it was only because of the tact and sympathy shown by Husey, in welcoming them as fellow 'black-buttoned bastards', that the men became reconciled to their new unit.[293] The actual composition of the draft of 288 men from the Rangers will be discussed later, but Polhill at least looked upon the influx as something to be welcomed. He considered its arrival gave him the opportunity to discover, 'fresh friends and angles on things, which cheers you up'.

Besides the non-commissioned men, the Rangers also had eight of their officers attached to the LRB. These, combined with another two from other London regiments as well as those from the LRB itself, soon brought the battalion back up to strength. Several of these officers had themselves been attached from their original regiments to the Rangers, and before the March offensive began, three of them were to be posted elsewhere. Of the six officers who arrived in January and February from the 3rd Battalion, only two had been in the regiment for all of their army careers. Kite-Powell was a *Chyebassa* man and had been at home since being wounded at Voormeezele in February 1916, while Jones had enlisted in the reserve battalion in February 1917. The remaining four new second lieutenants had all seen active service, and one of them, Harrington, had fought with the London Yeomanry in Gallipoli and Palestine. These men had roughly eight weeks to acquaint themselves with their platoons and to familiarise themselves with their posts and the procedures of withdrawal from the Forward to the Battle Zone. Trench warfare made some of them casualties before the Germans launched their offensive and two LRB-trained men - the elderly Francis Fass, the last of the Charterhouse men, and John Godward - returned home on courses before the attack came. New to the LRB as many of the officers were, there was, nevertheless, a great deal of experience within their ranks. They were helped in their settling in process by the longer-serving officers such as Dick Wallis, Tom Burroughs, Frederick Crews, John Calder, Frank Hancocks, Thomas Prior and, the apparently invincible Ralph Husey.

The months of February and March were spent in digging and improving the defences. The men of course knew that a German offensive was expected and, by the beginning of March, bets were being placed as to who would be in the posts when it actually came. One of the former Rangers men wrote in early February that there was a 'general feeling of wind up' and that the 'waxy, anxious and uneasy look' on the faces of the visiting Staff officers was making everyone nervous.[294] Drafts continued to arrive - in all, a total of 127 men - but it is difficult to be certain from which units they were coming. There were certainly some from the 3rd Battalion, both new recruits like Frank Keep, and also former sergeant instructors. Groom, for example, remembers meeting up with his old Fovant platoon sergeant. Following the established procedure, and until he gained some battle experience, this NCO was now again a mere rifleman. Rather than sending out the *whole* unit *en masse* at the same time, these replacements appear to have come from several different training platoons of the 3rd Battalion. For example, many of Keep's platoon were kept behind in England and were later sent to the King's Royal Rifles and the 15th London.[295]

There were also several returned wounded arriving back at the battalion in March. The irrepressible Sid Amatt, having gone home with trench fever in June 1917, was now sent out again with a small draft of about ten recruits and his old friend from the Essex days, Dickins. Amatt and 'Dicko' had served time in the Woking 'glasshouse' for repeatedly going AWOL from the 3rd Battalion at weekends. The final straw came at Christmas 1917, when all the young recruits who had never been out, were given leave, while the older hands were confined to camp. Amatt and Dickins resented this apparently unreasonable distinction and caught the train up to London. On capture and in front of the CO, they were told that they were a disgrace to the regiment. After a suprisingly easy time at the Woking punishment barracks, they were put on the next available draft. On its way to the battalion this group must have combined with another slightly larger one also *en route* for the Gavrelle sector. This swollen, but much needed draft, arrived on 22 March - one day after the massive German offensive against Fifth Army had opened to the south.

Another man on this draft was Herbert Borrett, a former employee of the *Watford Observer*. Borrett had had an unhappy time since joining the Queen Victoria's as a Derby recruit in 1916. He had been invalided home after an operation in November, and then later failed a five month officer training course in 1917 on the grounds that, because he had never been an NCO, he could not command men. Never in robust health - his letters home frequently complain of him suffering from the 'old complaint' - Borrett was then drafted to France, where he was transferred to the LRB and sent up the line. Another LRB man also suffering from illness but more fortunate than Borrett was Albert Snell. Instead of being sent back up the line, Snell was retained at the Base and spent the next few days anxiously wondering whether his brother serving with 'D' Company would survive the coming attack.

At the same time as the battalion was being brought back up to strength, Lt Col Husey returned from commanding the brigade. He discovered that because the battalion had made so many moves since his departure, he was now without a bed. Sid Partridge and three of his friends decided that this situation was incompatible with a man of Husey's popularity and stature. They promptly 'borrowed' the brigadier's, and then dumped it in Husey's dugout. The crime, and the bed, were discovered and the four were paraded before Husey, who had to go through the charge routine. Before dismissing the case, he delivered a very solemn and admonishing lecture upon the dangers of bed-stealing. Trivial though the incident was, it serves to illustrate the esteem in which Husey was held by the men in the battalion. Polhill and Groom[296] both tell a similar story, but set at different times, of how Husey raised himself above the parapet in broad daylight to have a quick look at the condition of the wire. The gesture was obviously designed to instil confidence into the sentries and impress upon them that he was not the sort of CO who stayed safely in the rear, merely content to rely upon reports from the troops in the trenches.

The Germans maintained an almost constant barrage of large and small calibre shells and mustard gas upon the Forward and Battle Zones. Respirators were frequently worn for hours at a time and for three days in early March hundreds of gas shells drenched the area just behind the ruins of Gavrelle. Many men took themselves down to the aid station, and Polhill too, although he had not really suffered from its effects, joined the group debouching from the disused gun pits known as Gavrelle Post. This was the first occasion that Polhill had reported to the MO and he was really expecting just a day away from the line and the opportunity to have a brief rest. To his surprise, he was sent down to a Canadian Field Hospital and thus missed the German attack. Polhill later recorded that he thought many of the men who went down with him had been deliberately lax in putting on their masks - a situation described by Lord Moran as indicative of a battalion where morale had been allowed to sag.[297] It is possible that some of the men felt that they had done their bit and were trying to get out of the line before the full fury of the expected attack developed. The war had been going on for a long time and as there still did not appear to be any prospect of an early Allied victory, the opportunity to get away with an honourable wound must have been a strong incentive. However, the total number of wounded for the entire month of March was 175. Bearing in mind the severity of the German artillery barrages before the infantry assault developed, if a proportion of the men *did* feel that there was insufficient *esprit* to keep them in the front line, it must have been a fairly insubstantial percentage.

The Staff were anxious to discover which enemy regiments were opposite the divisional front. Consequently, the LRB was selected for the dubious honour of carrying out a raid with the intention of capturing prisoners or identifying German units. While their comrades worked on making wire concertinas, carrying parties or practised manning the Rear Zone, members of 'C' Company rehearsed the proposed raid. Under the command of John Calder, a total of 73 all ranks trained to get through the wire obstacles under the protection of a trench mortar barrage and capture a live German. The force was divided into three waves; the first under the command of the newly arrived 2Lt Kite-Powell, and the second under 2Lt de Moyse Bucknall, an officer attached to the LRB from the Inniskilling Dragoons. The last wave would be brought over by Calder himself. However, when the raiders crawled through their own wire in front of Gavrelle's civilian cemetery on the night of 16 March, and dashed across No Man's Land, they found the German wire still very much intact. A period of some confusion followed. As bombs were exchanged, the men tried to hack their way through the three belts of wire, but Calder, realising that the covering barrage would soon be lost, ordered the men back to their own trenches. No German was captured, but it was discovered, to the raiders' cost, that the enemy trenches were very strongly held and that his wire was very thick. Several other raids by different battalions also failed to grab a prisoner. Fortunately, the cost to the LRB of their latest escapade was not too great; all the raiders returned, bringing with them their 13 wounded - one of whom was Frank Keep.

The LRB's final tour of duty in the Forward Zone before the attack, began on the night of 21 March. The companies and platoons relieved the 7th Middlesex during a bombardment that was to continue, in varying degrees of intensity, for most of the following seven days. Some of the posts were badly blown in and the communication trenches were soon impassable. The men settled down as best they could and for the next few days, during any lull in the shelling and registration by the German guns, they worked on digging out the shattered trenches and putting up more wire. Upon their return Sid Amatt and Dickins had been posted to different platoons of 'B' Company, the bulk of which was deployed in Mill Post. However, Amatt and a weak platoon, were later sent further out into an advanced trench where they were to remain for five nights holding a front of 400 yards. The tension among the men was great as they knew the attack was coming. They had also heard disquieting rumours that the Germans had chosen big athletic men to form snatch squads trained to conduct raids on the British outposts. Sentries patrolled up and down the trench on a beat of about 100 yards, and although they did receive some hot food, the nervous anticipation, shelling and general debilitation, made them increasingly drowsy. To prevent himself from falling asleep on duty and being 'awoken' by a German cudgel, Amatt discovered that if he stuck his rifle between his feet, the bayonet just reached the underside of his steel helmet; if his head dropped forward he was prodded awake.

A hundred yards to the rear of Amatt's platoon was Mill Post. (Map 10). This lay on the highest point of the line, a few feet above the flat plain, to the north of the village. The redoubt comprised a circular dugout with several, very steep entrances. Wooden props supported the stairwells and coils of wire protected the approaches from the front and flanks. Its great disadvantage was that, as it was easily visible from the German lines, it attracted a disproportionately high percentage of German shells. The

German gunners had all the shelter's entrances registered to a nicety and were continually dropping 'Minnies' and higher calibre shells on and around it. Save from the largest calibres, the men housed beneath were relatively safe, but the almost certain knowledge that they were either going to be killed, captured or wounded, did little to inspire them with confidence. Furthermore, the activities of the German patrols also helped sap their faith in their chances of survival. Frequently, enemy squads approached the British trenches to capture or kill sentries, and the LRB lost one man in such a raid during the early hours of 26 March. However, the Germans too lost men during these raids. One prisoner of 25 March told his British captors that the attack from two divisions recently transferred from the Riga Front was imminent.

The hours of darkness were thus the most tense. The sky was lit with the flames of exploding ammunition dumps, while the roads and assembly areas in the rear zones suffered from remorseless heavy shelling. The guns of the 56th Division, housed in concrete shelters on the eastern side of Vimy Ridge, were withdrawn to the western side during the night of 27-28 March, and so escaped the final bombardment which destroyed the shelters. The early hours of darkness of 27 March were in fact abnormally quiet, and it was during this lull that a message arrived ordering Archie Groom to report immediately to company HQ. On presenting himself to the CSM, Groom was astonished to learn that he was to depart at once for the Army's Gas Warfare School in Doullens. Groom could not believe his luck and, by the time the final bombardment began, he was a safe 30 miles away to the rear.[298] His less fortunate colleagues received a final exhortation from brigade. This order confirmed that the enemy attack was expected next morning and had finished with a declaration that they were all now in the hands of the Almighty. Shortly after, the companies were suddenly jolted into feverish activity by the arrival of an order instructing the LRB to extend its front further north towards Oppy Wood. Division had decided that more troops should be withdrawn from the Forward Zone in order to provide a counter-attack force should the Germans break through. So, in addition to those already occupied, the LRB now had to re-deploy several of its platoons to garrison Bird and Bradford Posts. These moves were only completed by 03.00 hours on 28 March.

Back at the Transport lines, Wallis records that a draft of some 'two or three hundred' reinforcements arrived at dusk on the 27 March. As they paraded before him, Wallis was distressed to discover that most were only 18 and 19 years old. With only some six months training, he reflected sadly, these youngsters were to be thrown straight into the heat of battle. Strangely, the *War Diary* makes no mention of this draft, and it is impossible to identify from their Army numbers any men arriving at that time. Wallis is probably confusing this group with one which had arrived a few days earlier and which was intended as reinforcement for the whole brigade, rather than just the LRB. Yet no matter to which battalion these boys were posted, their baptism of fire and introduction to modern warfare were much the same. As the German 'battering train' began its most intensive period of fire, the darkened horizon erupted into a continual and unprecedented blaze of explosions and searing sheets of flame. These young, inexperienced boys were about to be thrown headlong into this shrieking inferno.

Just as the LRB was completing its re-deployment, the British artillery positions were covered with mustard gas. An hour later, the Germans shifted their fire forward to the HQ positions in the Marine Line, and at 05.00 hours, began the most intense fire yet upon the posts. The heavy calibre guns were joined by seemingly hundreds of trench mortars and the wire and posts were obliterated. Amatt and his colleagues in the advanced trench had so far been largely ignored by the German batteries, but now they could see the enemy calmly setting up their trench mortars both in front of and behind their front trenches:

> *Soon they started coming over and we were shouting, 'Minnie left' and 'Minnie right' and we were running around like a bunch of scared chickens. They demolished our trench, blew up our hand grenades and there was a hell of a muddle. Some blokes were shouting out because they'd been buried up to their necks in loose earth. Anyway, I don't know if we ever had an order to retire, but those of us who were left all did. We charged back to Mill Post where there was a sergeant and an officer of the MGC with a Vickers on top of the dugout. They told us to get down inside the post as they fired a few rounds off.*

Once the final stage of the bombardment began, all communication with HQ in the rear of the Forward Zone was immediately severed. Some wounded from the front positions struggled back bringing reports of the damage and the virtual annihilation of the defenders. The Lewis guns and trench mortars had been destroyed in the fury of the bombardment and the wounded from Bradford Post claimed that the entire garrison, including Captain John Calder were dead. The German infantry came over at 07.00 when the barrage again shifted onto the Marine Line. They advanced in huge numbers, with rifles slung, blankets and spare boots tied on their packs and rations for six days. To the amazement of those British able to observe their activities, German horse-drawn artillery unlimbered in the open just behind the infantry. Standing in the trench beside Mill Post, Victor Rushton stared in astonishment at the sight of the advancing infantry. As he took up a kneeling position and began firing into this amazing target, he was wounded in the face by one of his colleagues firing from behind him. On going down into the dugout to get it dressed, he was surprised to see so many men still sheltering there. These men, whether wounded or not, had little opportunity to respond to the sentry's cries of 'Germans in the trench!' before the enemy troops were upon them. Rushton's tumble down the steps of the dugout was followed by a bouncing hand grenade and a German voice shouting down the entrance. A LRB man yelled, 'Kamarad' in response and the voice ordered them to take off their packs, leave their rifles in the dugout and climb the steps with their hands above their heads. Rushton was the first out and saw about a dozen of his platoon lying dead where they had fallen. He was followed by the long-serving CSM Bamford, and Sid Amatt

> *Well, I was highly delighted when I was captured. I thought, 'Well, that's me out of it in any case'. I didn't have any feeling of shame, in fact I was very happy at the thought of being a prisoner because I knew we treated their blokes OK and I thought, 'That will do me.' It was just one of those things. Before the attack during the shelling I had got to such a state that I didn't care what had happened to me, but now I was happy. Anyway, what can you do if a big bloke sticks a*

Luger in your ribs? - the first thing you do is say 'Kamarad' and hope for the best.

The Germans pushed on through the posts and as they approached the rear of the Forward Zone, presented a perfect target for the British guns and the men of the HQ details in the Marine Line. The enemy slowed as they encountered difficulties in crossing the area of old trenches where there was still wire to provide an obstacle, and soon lost their barrage. Other parties chased the retreating LRB men down the trenches, showering grenades after them, while the British desperately tried to establish bombing blocks to slow the advance. Lt Col Husey watched the enemy come over the open ground to the north of Gavrelle village in five waves:

> *The enemy appeared to have got through the Front Line system without much difficulty and very shortly he was seen...advancing in great numbers on Marine Line. Every single man of Battalion HQ thereupon manned the parapet and opened a heavy rifle fire on the advancing masses who offered a wonderful target. I took up a firing position myself near the two machine guns in Marine trench and can confidently state that great execution was done by machine guns and rifles.* (War Diary)

Tom Burroughs rallied a few men and threw up a succession of bomb blocks all of which were either stormed or out-flanked by the Germans. He withdrew down the communication trench towards the Marine Line, where he met Wallis calmly firing a rifle into the advancing hordes. Wallis mentions that for the second time, (the first being the occasion when Burroughs arrived at HQ during a severe strafe at Cambrai), the young officer laughed repeatedly as he retold how all his blocks had been overwhelmed and that now he had run out of bombs. Wallis, who also seems to have been enjoying himself immensely, handed Burroughs a rifle with no bayonet and asked him if he would like to lead a 'determined bayonet charge, consisting only of himself'. Burroughs apparently declined and the two men set off happily down the trench to join Husey in the Marine Line. The relief at actually having something to do, after enduring days of shelling, had probably induced this light-headed reaction, but they both realised the seriousness of the position. The HQ details were all that remained of the battalion in the front area and they were now in danger of being outflanked and attacked by overwhelming numbers. In an attempt to save what little of the battalion remained, Husey ordered a gradual withdrawal down the communication trench which led to the Battle Zone. Here, the four officers and 64 men of the LRB reorganised and joined with the 2nd London to continue the battle.[299] It was still only 10.30, but the German effort was largely spent, and the order that had been sent down to the Transport lines warning about 50 men from the stores, surplus personnel etc. to stand by, was cancelled. Although by 13.00 both forward brigades of the 56th Division had fallen back to the Battle Zone, they had managed to keep the line with the 4th Division on their flank intact. The enemy made further tentative efforts to attack the Battle Zone, but were always halted by the combined infantry and artillery fire. By dusk, patrols and listening posts were pushed out in front of the British wire. The Germans were quiet and made no more attempts to dislodge the defenders.

It had been a day of slaughter on both sides. German dead lay in their hundreds above ground, while the British were for the most part buried beneath their collapsed trenches and dugouts. By nightfall the LRB's strength amounted to seven officers and 64 men; this from a morning total of 18 and 564 respectively. The survivors were relieved by the 7th Middlesex the following day and marched back to billets in Roundhay Camp. Here the battalion was immediately reorganised into two fighting platoons and a HQ platoon. Having arrived at the Gas School only to discover it had closed, Archie Groom returned from Doullens and rejoined the battalion while it reorganised. He found the whole situation, with so many of his old comrades having disappeared, all rather depressing and when the drafts of reinforcements arrived, Groom questioned the wisdom of putting all the Gavrelle survivors into the same company.[300] In contrast to Groom's depression, however, Wallis thought that the survivors were all in the 'best of spirits'. He attributed this strange remark to what he called the 'infantryman's greatest wish gratified' - i.e. the opportunity to fire 15 rounds per minute at an enemy target not 150 yards away.

The total number of LRB dead is a little difficult to determine, as again, some of the recent draftees retained their own Army numbers. An exhaustive search of the cemeteries, memorials and of the casualty rolls of regiments known to have supplied drafts before the battle, gives a total of seven such dead on the 28 March. These would presumably have been included on the strength of the LRB and so would have been counted in the casualty figure supplied by the LRB to Brigade. Six of these men were from the Post Office Rifles, a unit which had supplied the LRB with a fairly large draft of mixed ages in early March. This might not be the complete total of those who still retained their own numbers but, if these are added to the known number of LRB dead, a total of 89 men died on either the 28 or 29 March. Again, it is difficult to be precise about how many died from wounds received that day because the members of the disbanded 2nd Battalion were also in the thick of the German offensive, and it is not always possible to determine which of the dead were from that battalion. The position of their graves can give an important, but by no means decisive, clue. Some of the registers in the cemeteries near the Bases can give further help by indicating, for example, that a man died from wounds 'received at Gavrelle'. However, for the purposes of accuracy, only those men who can be positively identified as belonging to, or being attached to the 1st Battalion, are included in the following analysis.

Only one of the dead was an original 1st Battalion man. Frank Idle enlisted on the outbreak and had been out continuously since November 1914. A travelling salesman from South Norwood in civilian life, he had become one of the company cooks and, in this capacity, had become a good friend of Aubrey Smith. Similarly, L/Cpl Gore from Blackheath and Bert Rolfe, a 25 year old clerk with Minchener, Hodson & Co. in the City, were the only men from the original 2nd Battalion to die that day. Altogether 42 of the dead, or slightly less than 50% of the total, had spent their army career solely in the LRB. The remainder comprised another seven of the Middlesex draft of July 1916, but as it seems that Amatt and Dickins were the only two of the Essex volunteers still with the battalion, and both of those survived, the only other death from the immediate post Gommecourt intake was a man from the Post Office Rifles.

Four more of the dead had come from the Queen Victoria's just before the Battle of Arras, and 24, or 27% of the total are those who were transferred from the Rangers. The analysis of those men shows that only 12 of them had actually been trained in the Rangers, so it is clear that the regiment had received a substantial intake of men from a variety of London and Middlesex battalions some time before the unit was disbanded.

If the number and origins of the dead were reflected in the same proportion to the composition of the March 1918 battalion - and there is no evidence to suggest that it was not - Smith's assertion that he did not know many of the men because they were 'largely ex-Rangers' is thus slightly over-stated. He certainly might not have known many of the men manning the Forward Zone, but this was because there had been so many personnel changes since he moved to the Transport in August 1915, that he had little idea of who had arrived, and when. He is nearer the mark however, when he states that there were hardly any men left in HQ personnel to remind him of the 1916, let alone the 1914 battalion, and also when he remarks that the Transport section was the only one whose rank and file bore any vague resemblance to the Plugstreet days.

The Transport had been little affected by the German attack, and in fact Idle was only the third man of the section to die since it had been reformed in 1915. There were still several men like Chrisp and Connibeer who had served right through with the battalion, but they had both, also, spent some time back with the companies. Although there were others who had joined the section in 1915 and who were still there in March 1918, only three men had actually retained their driving job for over two years. (One of those, Tubby Butt, had in fact been on a draft to another regiment on recovering from wounds, but by some fortunate chance managed to finish up back with the LRB.) The only other section to have retained a good proportion of its pre-Gommecourt character was the Regimental Aid Post. There had been several MOs since then, but the NCOs had been together for two years. They all fell into German hands on 28 March.

Compared with earlier battles, far more of those killed in the March engagement have no known grave. No fewer than 92% of the dead have their names commemorated on the Arras Memorial to the Missing. Five identified men are buried in Orchard Dump Cemetery and there are also many other graves known to belong to LRB soldiers. One of the known graves is that of an ex-Ranger who at 37 was among the oldest to die, and another is that of Reginald Carter, a young boy with a Peruvian mother, who had come back to England to enlist in the LRB. So complete and violent was the German bombardment that it must have prevented a large number of wounded from being evacuated. Some were; for example, Albert Snell's brother Ernest, managed to get away with a wound in his hand. While still at the Base in France, Albert received a postcard from Ernest in England declaring that he was safe and well on the way to recovery. But others were not so fortunate. The German infantry arrived so soon at the entrances of the British front line dugouts and captured so many men, that a good proportion of LRB troops who died in German hands during the next few months will have been those who succumbed to wounds received that day.

At the beginning of January 1918. a total of 107 LRB men were notified as being prisoners of the Germans, and this figure rose to 250 in early April. Between May and September, the number increased to over 400[301] - a figure which undoubtedly included men from the 2nd Battalion who had been captured while serving with the Artists Rifles. It is difficult to know how many men were captured from Mill and the other posts, but the March entry in the *War Diary* gives a total of 437 missing. Some of these can be accounted for by men who were later confirmed to be dead, but that still leaves a total of over 360 possible prisoners. That large numbers of men were taken is confirmed by Sid Amatt and Sid Partridge. Amatt ended up in a camp with many fellow-LRB.s, although, by contrast, after Rushton had emerged from Mill Post, he never saw another LRB man again. Among others who were captured that day were the ailing Herbert Borrett of the *Watford Observer*, and CSM Bamford, who was taken with Amatt and Rushton at Mill Post.

Thirteen officers serving with the regiment were also captured, eight of whom had been attached from other units. The LRB officers included the *Chyebassa* man and winner of the MC for his work during the raid of a few days earlier, Kite-Powell. Another was the only man from the Middlesex intake to be given a commission in the LRB, Herbert Higham. Three officers were wounded, and these included Tom Burroughs, but his wound was not serious enough to take him any further than a nearby aid post. He took on the duties of Adjutant immediately upon his return. Remarkably, only two officers died that day: Captain Eric Rose, wounded at Gommecourt and with the battalion as Transport Officer for most of the time since, was actually recalled from the leave boat at Boulogne and was killed while firing a rifle beside Wallis. His death was keenly felt by Smith who thought that another link with the old battalion had been broken. The other was the former August volunteer, one time CSM and schoolmaster from Wanstead, John Calder. The luck of several other long-serving members continued to hold: Frank Crews, Thomas Prior, Frank Hancocks and of course Wallis and Husey survived unscathed. Husey was shortly to leave the battalion to take command of a brigade, and Wallis was to return home in April for a long over-due rest. The remainder of the officers, and the few surviving senior NCOs, were about to surmount an altogether different problem from one that any had experienced before. They were about to try to weld a group of several hundred hugely assorted men, from all regiments and all parts of the county, into a fighting unit which would be ready within two weeks to take its place in the line. If that was not difficult enough, they still had to try to maintain something of the traditional character of the LRB within this newly consitituted battalion. Earlier battles had resulted in the regiment undergoing quite dramatic changes in personnel, but the annihilation at Gavrelle altered it from what had been still very much a London regiment to one that bore a closer resemblance to a battalion of the Northumberland Fusiliers.

CHAPTER XI

'Loungers Round Britain': The Second Battalion

It was the exigency of war that caused the 2nd Battalion of the LRB to be created in 1914, and, similarly, it was the demands of war that caused its demise 40 months later. The intervening period saw the battalion strive against enormous difficulties to equip and train itself for war, a short but hectic period of only 12 months active service, and then, after it had endured an appalling few months in the Salient, the final blow of its disbandment. Because it was born of the war, and in view of its difficult and somewhat chequered history, it is easier to look at its existence and experiences in one section rather than attempt to fit them in chronologically with the war as a whole, or with the 1st Battalion in particular. Clearly, its history and the impact that the war had upon the battalion cannot be seen in isolation from external factors, but for convenience it is necessary to return from the German offensive of 1918 to the period following the outbreak of war in 1914.

An account and analysis of the types of men who joined the battalion when recruiting began in September 1914 and of their motives for enlisting, has already been made.[302] Furthermore, it will be recalled that several hundred of the initial battalion had gone to join the first line unit before and after the Second Battle of Ypres. However, little mention has yet been made of the problems facing the new battalion, or of its early experiences, as it attempted to create a unit able to take its place in the line. And the problems were immense. Some of the more unfashionable Territorial battalions had to struggle that much harder than their more glamorous counter-parts in the New Armies for what few facilities and little equipment existed. For example, because the Kitchener battalions were short of drill instructors and officers, many Territorial units were denuded of trained, experienced men who were sent to train the service battalions. Although, as far as can be ascertained, no LRB member left the regiment to join a Kitchener battalion in the early weeks of the war, there was an acute shortage of qualified instructors to teach the recruits of the 2nd Battalion.

Many former members did return to Bunhill Row and offer their services. These, along with the few NCOs who had not opted for foreign service with the 1st Battalion, formed the nucleus of the training personnel. Insufficient in number, aged and perhaps somewhat vague or rusty on drill, these men did offer the LRB a distinct advantage over the service battalions as they were rejoining a regiment in which they had served. They understood the regiment's traditions and the way the command structure operated, and knew the type of men who were enlisting. Compared with the New Armies, the creation of this new battalion, in spite of the equipment shortages, was probably a little easier because the framework of the organisation already existed. The flesh could be put on the bones as and when further provisions became available. Once the 1st Battalion had moved off to Bisley, the facilities within the Drill Hall became more readily accessible, and although the men continued to live at home and mess separately, the beginnings of regimental *esprit* were developed along the foundations already laid and well-known to the 1st Battalion.

The growth of *esprit* was made the more easy by the re-appearance of the retired members to serve as NCOs, and by the appointment of various officers who knew the regiment and its traditions. These men were to supervise the birth of the new unit and although few of them were still with it by the time it sailed overseas, their experience and knowledge saw the battalion through its first, unsettled few months. The CO, Major G. Tod, was a former Adjutant in the early years of the century, and as the regimental rules required, a Regular officer. The Second-in-Command, George Harvest, related to the Lintotts of Horsham, had enlisted as a private before being commissioned in 1892. He retired as a Captain in 1905 but rejoined in September 1914, and was awarded the rank of Major. These two senior officers were joined by five other former members including Captain H.G. Nobbs who was to be blinded in Leuze Wood with the 1st Battalion - and three who came back from the 1st Battalion. Several more officers were posted to the battalion by the War Office, and commissions were also given to some NCOs from the first line unit. Again, when compared with some of the service battalions who often had to appoint keen, but old, soldiers wearing campaign ribbons from the Ashanti and Zulu Wars, the battalion was also fortunate in having one of the current permanent Staff of Bunhill Row appointed to the key post of sergeant-major.

The selection of junior NCOs was a little more difficult as only a few of the new recruits had had any sort of military experience. There is a fairly widely-held belief that one of the eight companies actually elected its own NCOs, while other men were given a stripe because they had had some experience of drill in the Boys Brigade or Scouts. Drill was about the only thing that the men could do in the early days. The diary of one of the new men, Jack Terry, a former clerk in Waterloo Station, records with consistent regularity, 'Drill at Charterhouse'. The amount of time that the men spent on this occupation was in fact fairly brief. They were ordered to muster at Bunhill Row at 10.00, march to Charterhouse or one of the other school yards used for the purpose and were usually dismissed at 11.00. The afternoons and evenings were spent in visiting friends, taking young ladies for walks, the occasional parade and, in Terry's case, instructing the boys at the local Church Lads' Brigade meetings. Maurice Howard spent much of his spare time mixing with his new friends and going on long walks to try to harden his feet in preparation for the route marches which would inevitably come.

By the third week of its existence the battalion was sitting through the occasional lecture and had discerned which of the school yards were best and worst for drill - the City of London and Cowper Street respectively. Twenty days after joining the Army, some of the recruits also fired their first rifle on the miniature rifle ranges in the

City. Open and close order drill still occupied most of their time but some of the men also began to learn the science of semaphore and other specialist skills. Further preparation for overseas duty also entailed them having to endure the uncomfortable experience of being vaccinated by the Army method. Battalion route marches through London also began in October, but the men did not regard themselves as soldiers until uniforms began to arrive later that month. The pace of life began to increase, and gradually the men were ordered to attend for full-day sessions. Then in November, when the first of those who had volunteered for foreign service, such as the young Richard Lintott, had already been transferred to the 1st Battalion, the battalion travelled down to billets in Haywards Heath.

The next few months in the Sussex countryside really saw both the beginning and end of the original 2nd Battalion. Although it saw little of the brigade's other three battalions, the 2nd LRB was officially part of the 2/2nd London Infantry Brigade. Furthermore, the companies were dispersed over the small town which made messing for the officers and men somewhat difficult. There was a definite emphasis put on the development of *esprit* but the basic problem in trying to weld the companies into a battalion was that the unit was continually contracting. It has already been noted that some 600 men had been transferred to the 1st Battalion by September 1915, and this loss created huge difficulties at a time when there were very few recruits arriving to replace them. The second line battalions became Cinderella-like formations as the majority of men enlisting were sent to their regimental 3rd Battalions. As the months passed, the shortage of men and the status of the 2nd Battalions were recurrent themes of questions in the House of Commons. MP's expressed their concern at the diminished numbers and the consequent decline in the efficiency and effectiveness of the training. Severe deterioration in morale was stressed, and the House heard that the men were becoming increasingly disheartened and discouraged.[303] Some of the fears were allayed by the introduction of the Derby Scheme because it was assumed that large numbers of the forthcoming influx would be directed into the second line formations rather than the third line ones. The need for this action was stressed by one speaker who claimed he had information that a second line Territorial division had received orders to proceed to France in three months time, but at the time of speaking, he declared, the 12 infantry regiments were only 400-strong.[304]

The problems of the second line units were further exacerbated by the fact that when they began recruiting they were ordered to enlist men for both foreign and home service in equal numbers. Although there is no hard evidence to confirm that this order was deliberately disobeyed in the LRB, there are several sources which suggest that the men were asked to state whether they were prepared to accept foreign service before they attested. This might have been the experience of some men - and the fact that over 600 went overseas within 12 months suggests that it was perhaps quite widespread - but there were still plenty of recruits admitted who had clearly not intended to volunteer for foreign service. For those men who wanted to join the army for patriotic or other motives, but who for family or business reasons could not undertake the foreign service obligation, the Territorial Army was the obvious choice. The New Army battalions were being created for overseas service, so no-one with the intention of staying in Britain would volunteer for such a unit. The LRB certainly did have an unspecified number of men who had joined with that intention. Many of them later changed their mind and actually went overseas.

So, the decreasing number of men and the continuing shortages of equipment, combined with the difficulty of training for war a battalion which contained men who, at the time, were unlikely to volunteer to go overseas, made the period of training at Haywards Heath an awkward one. Route marches to and from the firing ranges at Crowborough and Jarvis Brook, still armed with largely antiquated rifles, became more frequent. Battalion Orders of December highlighted the persistent shortages; marching order for NCOs and men meant 'full valises, side arms and rifles. Those who have no equipment will carry greatcoats 'en banderole', haversacks and rifles'. On one such march, Billy Chandler collected several bets because he wagered that he would remember the registration numbers of all cars which passed the column on the way to Brighton. Chandler was also renowned as something of a comic. On one occasion he cheerfully agreed with 2Lt Wilkinson when the latter suggested that there was rather too much dirt in Chandler's rifle barrel, while another of his witticisms later earned a mention in *Punch*.[305] The battalion was sometimes visited and inspected by various generals who usually managed to congratulate it (and just about every other battalion), on its 'steadiness on parade'. What that over-used expression actually means is open to differing interpretations but, during a particularly cold January day in 1915, the LRB decided that it was because no-one had actually collapsed during the hour-long wait before the inspection began. When he arrived, General Ian Hamilton expressed astonishment at the size of the men, believing they were more suited to the Brigade of Guards than Riflemen. Unknown to him, the men had taken precautions against the anticipated legendary lateness of generals and were wearing three sweaters under their greatcoats.[306]

The battalion was deployed several times to resist 'invaders' in the vicinity of the Downs, and in May 1915, the LRB and the rest of the 2/2nd London Brigade, moved to Norwich. In the following month, those who had accepted the foreign service obligation moved to Ipswich while those who had opted for home service were sent to the 101st Provisional Battalion for coast defence. The Ipwich sojourn was remembered as being one of pleasant memories and the gradual over-coming of the burdens and problems associated with bringing the battalion up to some sort of readiness for active service. The battalion's already weak strength was reduced still further though when another 97 men were sent to the 1st Battalion. No accurate figures are available, but the number of men still with it after the first 12 months of its existence must have been only somewhere around 300. The Regimental History claims that there were 600 in 'the autumn' - 100 of whom had arrived in June and another 100 a short time later.[307] Whatever the precise total, what is clear is that the quality of the training remained very limited. The *War Diary*, by way of a 'Statement' talks of it as having progressed 'satisfactorily', with particular attention being paid to the use of the bayonet, digging, night work, P.T. and care of feet. This description disguised the fact that there was little alternative as the Lewis gun section possessed only one gun, there were no live grenades available and no anti-gas measures could be practised because there were no gas masks. Most of the time was occupied in route marches and with parties of men sharing rifles on the ranges at Bawdsey. However, soon after the New Year, things began to improve. A draft of 244 recruits from the 3rd Battalion arrived in early

February and then, despite the vicissitudes of the War Office, 23 men who had originally opted for home service only, but had now signed form AFE 624, arrived safely from the 101st Provisional Battalion. Raised hopes that the entire division might now be sent overseas were tempered by the knowledge that the 60th Division appeared to be enjoying priority of men posted from the training battalions, and also by the continuing exchanges in the House. The Under-Secretary of State cheerfully expressed the view that the initial difficulties of the second line units had now been virtually overcome and that the brigades were being trained for overseas service or, more discouragingly, 'where they may be most required'.[308] Sir J. Walton MP, then suggested that, as the third line system had 'broken down absolutely', the Territorial battalions overseas should be reinforced from the second line battalions at home because their men were better trained than those of the third line. Tennant darkly responded that the War Office had used that method before and that 'it might have to be done again in the future'.[309]

While their immediate prospects of going overseas as an integral part of a complete division were thus somewhat distant, the men were cheered in March by the arrival of 600 Lee Enfields. Musketry began to take on a more serious aspect, but there were other activities too. The battalion put on several concerts at its various locations for the local residents, and as well as the usual brigade sports - where Bert Ives usually took the distance prizes[310] - there were many Zeppelin and invasion alarms. There were continual departures of men going away on courses. Jack Terry, for example, now a sergeant, was sent to the Gas School at Porton - and a handful of the originals also seem to have gone off for commissions at this time.

By July 1916 the 58th Division occupied the camp at Sutton Veny, near Warminster, recently vacated by the 60th Division. As a consequence of its prolonged nomadic existence in England, it was about this time that the battalion acquired its acrostic title of "Loungers Round Britain". There was an immediate intensification of the training schedule although there were still huge deficiencies in rifles and Lewis guns. The extra training was especially needed for a group of raw recruits who came direct to the battalion to make up numbers once those who were deemed medically unfit had been weeded out. Why these 70 completely new entrants - probably conscripts rather than Derby men - instead of trained soldiers from the 3rd Battalion were drafted in was a question only the War Office could answer. The essential point to note is that the 903 non-commissioned men who were to sail from Southampton on 24 January 1917 were all in the LRB either because they had chosen to enlist in that regiment or, because having fulfilled the usual LRB requirements, they had been accepted as members by the regiment.

Although it knew its experience in some aspects of warfare was very limited, the battalion was a happy and confident one. Regimental *esprit* had been deliberately and successfully fostered, made easier by the fact that there had been no drafts from any other regiments to make up numbers:

> *We were a very contented bunch of chaps and glad that we were at last*
> *going to have a crack at the Germans. We had trained hard and*
> *because many of us had enlisted together in 1914 we made good*
> *friends. I spent much of the time in the Orderly Room and there was*

very little crime ever reported. In fact I can only remember one case of a chap over-staying his leave. We all loved the LRB and naturally thought it was the best battalion in the division so we didn't want to let it or our friends down by doing anything that might bring discredit upon us. (J. Terry)

Apart from the 70 men who had joined a few weeks before the battalion sailed, the rest of the men had had sufficient time to get to know each other and to shake down into an efficient and enthusiastic unit. Terry, in 'A' Company, became close friends with three other original members, all of whose army careers were to develop along similar lines. Of the four, only Cockerell had attended a grammar school, Belither had been to the institution that had turned out so many future LRB members, the Coopers' Company School, while Terry and Wright had both attended local council schools. By the time the battalion sailed, all four were sergeants and would eventually serve together as officers in the 1st Battalion. Another original member, A.E. Thain, a former student of Cowper Street School, had, like the four sergeants, been retained by the 2nd Battalion as an instructor to the later recruits. Among the recipients of these men's newly acquired skills were those posted from the 3rd Battalion in the summer of 1915. Two of this group were recruits who in mid-1915 had stood beside each other in the queue to enlist. Adam Macpherson, aged 24 from Westminster School, and the 21 year old Graham Foster of Thornton Heath, would remain firm friends from that time until the latter's death near von Tirpitz Farm in September 1917.

The actual number of men who had joined the battalion in September 1914 and went with it as non-commissioned men in 1917 cannot be fully determined. Eighteen of them can be identified easily because these men were to die during the battalion's twelve months on the Western Front. Added to this group, others who can be identified from lists of awards and other sources, take the total of originals up towards 250. This means that when the battalion sailed nearly a third of it were soldiers who had been in the army for about twenty-seven months. Approximately another 200 had served for eighteen months, and the remainder for just under a year. Thus, when compared with many of the units already overseas and who since the latter half of 1916 had been receiving drafts with as few as eleven weeks training, the battalion could be deemed to be composed of men who had received a thorough and lengthy period of instruction. The scope of the training may not have been as extensive as the purists might have wished; for example, owing to the chronic shortages of equipment, there were clear deficiencies in the Lewis gun teams trained by Thain and his colleagues. But for that stage of the war, the battalion could be described as being more fully and efficiently trained than many of its counter-parts in France. Neither was it completely ignorant of the type of war now being fought as there were a number of men in the ranks who had already seen active service. Again, the precise number is not known, but at least ten had been among the drafts sent out to the 1st Battalion before 2nd Ypres, and had, on recovery of wounds, been sent from the training battalion to the second line unit.

Meanwhile in July 1917, the parent battalion had undergone its transformation to one that bore a closer resemblance to a unit of the Middlesex Regiment, and although by January 1917 it was again more recognisable as the LRB, the 2nd Battalion was, of the two, perhaps a purer version of the regiment. This applied not only to the non-commissioned ranks, but also to the officers. The 30 commissioned men who left for France in January closely reflected the type of officer who had sailed on the *Chyebassa*, but who had virtually disappeared from the battalion by June 1915. There had been many changes in the establishment since the unit's formation, but twenty-six months later ten of the 30 were still pre-war LRB members. Amongst these were some very long-serving men and others, such as Major Harvest, were those who had long since retired but re-enlisted on the outbreak. Two others had seen service elsewhere - Naylor in the Montgomery Yeomanry and Harrison Jones in the Ceylon Planters Rifle Corps - while four young subalterns had served as privates in other regiments since the war started. The long-serving officers knew the traditions of the regiment thoroughly and were thus in a good position to instruct and advise the newcomers in how to handle the men according to the usual methods of discipline. Two of the younger officers had actually enlisted in the 2nd Battalion, and another eight had been commissioned into it while it trained at home. Others, like Richard Lintott's cousin Gordon Harvest, and Sidney Legg, had been overseas with the 1st Battalion as non-commissioned soldiers. In total, ten of the officers had served for some period with the parent battalion before they were later commissioned into the second line unit.

Furthermore, although there were clearly officers with a great deal more experience of active service than their 1914 counterparts of the 1st Battalion, there was a great similarity in the schools which the two groups had attended. England's foremost public schools such as Eton, Repton, Rugby, Harrow, Winchester, were all well represented and, although the total of university men was fewer than had sailed on the *Chyebassa*, seven had been to Oxbridge and had served in their respective OTCs. Finally, another similarity among the senior officers of the two battalions was their somewhat advanced age. The war had not yet had the impact on the reserve battalions which might have prevented men who would find the exacting demands of lengthy active service too strenuous from being sent overseas.

None of the Warrant Officers or senior NCOs had had any active service experience. At least the RSM, J.E. Maguire, was a Regular, and two very senior members of the regiment who had not gone with the 1st Battalion, Smiles and Schonewald, were respectively the CSM and CQMS of 'B' Company. Those holding similar positions in the other three companies were all men who enlisted in September 1914 and had since been promoted. These men and their company commanders were at the heart of the hectic preparations thrust upon the battalion in the first weeks of January. The necessities of war arrived at the stores and were then showered upon troops still ignorant of their future destination. A short period of draft leave was permitted to some of the men and then the entire battalion, as part of the 58th Division, embarked upon three very dubious looking vessels riding uneasily beside Southampton's bustling quays.

*   *   *

The frenzied activity had begun on New Year's Day 1917 and was to continue until the battalion left Sutton Veny at 07.30 hours on the 24 January. Amongst the dignified panic, a reflective Grahame Foster found time to write a final letter to his family in Thorton Heath before leaving camp:

> *On the eve of my departure for overseas I have decided to write you this letter as my mind is full of 'the future'...After many months of training, our turn has come to take our share of the fighting, and I pray we shall prove our worth when the time comes. It is said children cannot appreciate the feelings of their parents when they are wrenched from them. Believe me, I can fully realise your thoughts, and the terrible strain of worry it must cause you, and for this I love you more than ever...If I should be one of the many who will never return home, remember that I leave my life in the hands of our Heavenly Father, and trust in him to help me. I hope you will try and comfort yourselves with the words of my favourite hymn 'Fight the good fight' - these glorious words will always be uppermost in my mind...I write this with the absolute trust that God will bless you all and comfort you in the years to come.*[311]

Foster and the rest of the battalion climbed aboard two trains which carried them to Southampton and then, after idling around in the freezing dock-side sheds for six hours, were split into parties to embark upon three vessels. Two of them reached Le Havre safely that same night, but the Colonel and 450 other ranks on the *Caledonia* had a disquieting introduction to overseas active service. Posted prominently around the handrails and bulkheads were signs declaring that the vessel should not be taken outside the three mile limit. When darkness fell and the convoy steamed silently towards the open Channel, the reasons for the warnings became apparent. Once clear of the Solent the ships struck some very rough weather. With the troops hunched over the rails, the vessels struggled on into the gale for about twelve miles before the *Caledonia*'s skipper decided discretion was the better part of valour and turned his heaving ship back to port. Most troops disembarked and provided a dock-side working party before going on board again at 15.00. This time the *Caledonia* made a successful crossing and the troops went ashore at Le Havre around midnight. Aleady tired and feeling the effects of the voyage, they began the gruelling trudge up the cobbled hill to the camp. At 03.00, on a snowy January morning, the exhausted men rolled into the canvas tents and were allowed to sleep until 08.00.

There was little opportunity to explore the bleak surrounds of the Havre camp as the battalion paraded at 16.30 and commenced the by now traditional journey up the line. The thirty hour experience in the well-ventilated French troop train, while the temperature fell to 20 degrees of frost, was well remembered by the participants. On arrival at Auxi-le-Chateau the men then had to slog four miles along wind-swept and snow-covered roads at the dead of night, until the village of Rougefay loomed through the murk. Only here could blankets be drawn, and then 'A' Company had to march another cold and slippery mile until billets were found in Bachimont. Here the weary sergeants moved into a very dirty, but reasonably comfortable French cottage, and proceeded to establish a mess.

By a strange coincidence the battalion had been attached to the 46th (North Midland) Division in front of Gommecourt Wood for its initial period of trench instruction. The 6th and 8th Sherwood Foresters had been on the left of the LRB's 1st Battalion at Gommecourt, and now, with 10-20 degrees of frost, the 2nd Battalion began to learn the arts of trench survival in the same sectors and dugouts that the 1st Battalion had held in August 1916. The unfriendly climate had already begun to take its toll: Capt Johnston had been evacuated to hospital and another nine sick had only made it as far as Rougefay. German patrols were also very active during the next few nights and on one such bombing raid the battalion suffered its first casualty. Cpl Cornelius Adams was wounded and died from his injuries four days later at Warlincourt. The troops underwent the unpleasant experience of the extreme temperature, intermittent shellfire and static trench warfare for the next seven weeks and then, on receipt of a message which suggested that the Germans had withdrawn, patrols were pushed forward to discover that the enemy opposite had indeed disappeared. Fires were observed in the German front lines and the light of burning villages and exploding ammunition dumps in the rear areas illuminated the eastern sky. As Terry and Potter carried the dixies of hot tea along the shallow communication trench to their company HQ, the uncanny silence and blazing horizon struck Terry as being a 'rather sad sight'. The next day the two forward companies moved into the deserted German trenches. A quick souvenir-hunting expedition produced practically nothing of value and then the troops were ordered to follow the retreating Germans. A hard march across the scorched, ravaged ground ended near to what once had been the village of Boyelles. Here the lines settled down again with the enemy firmly entrenched in his newly constructed defensive system. Billets were found or created from groundsheets in the razed landscape, but it was soon discovered that over-sized rats, unlike the Germans, had not deserted the area.

Fatigues in the shattered areas of the Somme were soon added to the experience of line-holding in the flooded, icy trenches of the Foncquevillers and Boisleux sectors. Furthermore, the experience of war had sharpened Grahame Foster's appreciation of his home and family and enhanced the realisation that he might not see either again. In late March he wrote home from the wilderness of the devastated zone:

> *As one never knows if it is their turn to pay the price for this War of Freedom against tyranny and oppression, I write just a few words should I fall as to comfort you in your sorrow.*
>
> *Since I have been out here my thoughts have been from morn till eve, ever been of you and my desire to get a closer touch with our Heavenly Father. I see life in a totally different way than hitherto but have convinced myself beyond doubt that God will ever guard and guide me during all dangers that I meet with. So should I never return to you on this earth I trust that what I have written will console you to a degree. I have asked Him to shield and bless you through years to come and know that he will never turn a deaf ear to an earnest prayer.[312]*

Foster's work during the next few weeks was to earn him a Military Medal. This allowed at least a temporary re-union with his family as he was accorded a civic reception at Croydon Town Hall in May.

The battalion worked hard on road repairs during the wet months of March and April and on Good Friday, after finishing an eight-hour stint rebuilding a railway line near Mailly-Maillet, four sergeants of 'A' Company sloshed their way along the valley of the Ancre. Their wanderings took them towards St Pierre-Division where they witnessed the signs of the titanic struggles that had taken place among the flooded river flats and the shell-torn escarpments. The sight of derelict tanks sinking slowly into the viscid morass, of the foetid, decaying corpses of animals and the serried ranks of wooden crosses marking the muddy graves of hundreds of British soldiers, made a deep impact upon the small group of friends. The following day, the whole battalion traversed the pitted landscape by way of Beaumont Hamel and Miraumont to Bihucourt. Bivvies were erected in what was euphemistically called a 'camp' and the battalion again set to work trying to lay roads and railways across the muddy wastes.

As far as battle casualties were concerned, the first 14 weeks of active service made a fairly gentle impact - six killed and about 12 wounded - but the ice, the subsequent thaw and the demands made by the working parties had made in-roads on the battalion's strength. There are no actual reports of men contracting trench foot, but the constant exposure to flooded trenches and the biting winds must have caused the departure of many men to the field and base hospitals. Two drafts, amounting to 102 men, had arrived to replace these sick and wounded and the first, of 15 men, came from the LRB itself. Some of them, such as Charles Miles, a young junior clerk from the City who had been invalided home with trench feet from the 1st Battalion in March 1916, were returned wounded. It is possible that at least a proportion of the larger, second group of arrivals had also come from the 3rd Battalion, although it is clear that it was a mixed group of men drawn largely from several units of the London Regiment. Seven new officers also came up from the Base. They were required to replace not only Ernest Johnson, a veteran of the South African War, but also the equally aged Second-in-Command, George Harvest and Colonel Tod, both of whom returned to England.

The new CO was, as the regimental rules still in theory required, a Regular. Yet, as the new commander of a Territorial regiment, Lt Col P.D. Stewart had something of a peculiar background. He came to the LRB from the 3rd Dragoon Guards and, to make his new duties even more difficult, he arrived at a battalion dispersed over several locations and one which had been unable to carry out any concerted training since its arrival in France. Temporary relief from the drudgery of working parties was, however, near at hand for the whole division was withdrawn in early May and underwent some intensive preparations for its first real bloody encounter later that month.

The 7th and 62nd Divisions had been hammering away for days at the German fortress among the ruins of Bullecourt and now the 58th Division was deployed to make its attempt against what was fast becoming a charnel house. A witness quoted in the *Official History* remarked that he never saw a battlefield where those still alive lived in such close proximity to the unburied dead.[313] The LRB was to lead the assault against the south-west face of the village and following a bombardment, astoundingly violent in intensity but short in duration, 'A' Company with platoons of 'B' and 'C' swept forward from the railway cutting and secured the area known as the Red Patch. The Post Office Rifles then worked across the LRB's front and occupied the entire village. The two assaulting battalions were fortunate in that their attack took place against an enemy who was preparing to evacuate the village. Consequently, casualties were remarkably light. Eleven soldiers - only one of whom has an identified grave - and one non-LRB officer were killed, while 36 were reported wounded. After the war, the Brigadier of 174 Brigade described the attack as 'brillant' and thought that 'rarely had new troops ever been put to a severer test than those who received their baptism of fire at Bullecourt'.[314] The success of this first real test of the battalion was also admired by those who had made the attempt on the village and failed: the OC commanding the Regular 7th Division sent a note to the OC of the London Division congratulating him and his men on this, their first experience of an assault against an entrenched and fortified position.[315]

The Bullecourt battle was followed by a steady but undramatic drain on battalion strength (including six unfortunate men wounded by shellfire while bathing) during subsequent operations in warm weather against the Hindenburg Line in the Croisilles area. In July the whole division moved into some magnificent trenches near Havrincourt Wood and in August entrained at Arras for Poperinghe. The deep, well-constructed trenches to the south-west of Cambrai were to be replaced by the muddy shellholes lying beneath the Passchendaele ridge. As the train of assorted cattle wagons and carriages pulled into the sidings at Godwaesvelde and the men detrained before marching forward to Poperinghe, it was clear to all that the 58th Division was about to take its turn in the ferocious battles to the east of Ypres.

There had not been any great overall change in the battalion's composition during these first eight months abroad, but there had of course been several important changes among the senior personnel. Besides the officers already mentioned, two young subalterns died as a result of wounds received at Bullecourt - Lawrence Forbes from the Artists OTC and Richard Lintott's cousin and one-time private on the *Chyebassa*, Gordon Harvest. Four others, including another *Chyebassa* man Frank Barry, had gone home to England with severe wounds. RSM Maguire had also returned to England to be replaced by the former CSM of 'A' Company, Bottomley. He, in turn, was replaced by another September 1914 man, CSM Caines. The four sergeants of 'A' Company: Terry, Cockerell, Belither and Wright, all survived the early fighting. Terry had been lucky to be sent on a rifle grenade course at Warloy while the Bullecourt action was on and then had been away on leave during the June engagements. Similarly Thain, Macpherson and Foster had all survived unscathed, the latter having been promoted to sergeant. Among the officers, Capt Geoffrey Kitching, a subaltern on the *Chyebassa*, was the only one of the four company commanders of January 1917 still with the battalion. Most of the officers were LRB men, but there were at least five, and possibly six, lieutenants from the St Pancras battalion of the County of London Regiment.

There had also been new arrivals among the ranks of the non-commissioned men to replace the 51 dead and 178 wounded. Among the dead was Bert Nelki, a friend of Jack Terry, and Sidney Trim, whose brother Leonard had been killed serving with the 1st Battalion five weeks earlier. Twenty-nine of the dead were killed during one three-day trench tour in the Hindenburg Line in June, and of these dead, only one has a known grave. During this hazardous few days, patrols frequently became dispersed and lost and the constant shelling and sniping had also underlined the steady drain that the war of attrition could exact during mere trench-holding periods. In the months of June and July 123 men arrived at the battalion of which one group of 34 aroused particular interest. These men had actually come directly from the 3rd Battalion. It was thus universally decided that the infamous Practical Joke Department of Whitehall had somehow managed to lose touch with reality and had, after all, proved fallible.[316] The draft was made up of conscripts, with a number of married men among them, in their 20's and 30's. Judging from their Army numbers they only enlisted in May and so had received only a minimal amount of training. They were joined a few days later by a larger draft which, like the one that arrived before Bullecourt, was composed mainly of men from the London Regiment. The majority probably came from the Poplar and Stepney Rifles, but there is evidence to suggest that there was at least one man from the LRB and probably several others. When Aubrey Smith was down at the Havre Base in June 1917, there were several wounded 2nd Battalion men there whom he remembered from his Haywards Heath days. One of them was 'Elsie' Collins. Collins left the 1st Battalion in April 1916, and had been wounded later at Bullecourt. According to Smith, Collins was posted back to the 2nd Battalion in July.[317]

The men posted from other units as well as those who had originally enlisted in the LRB, moved up to relieve the Post Office Rifles in the line north of St Julien on the night of 8 September. Immediately, the battalion began to sustain casualties from the German shelling which was concentrating largely upon the approaches and disintegrating banks of the Steenbeke. British patrols went out at night to inspect the enemy's wire, but during the day there was little to do except shelter beneath what breastworks had been erected, or in the shell holes. Although not yet flooded, these were becoming increasingly unpleasant. By the time it was relieved on the night of the 12 September, the battalion had lost ten dead and 26 wounded. One of the wounded was Sgt Jack Terry, hit by a piece of shrapnel sufficiently badly to give him a nice clean 'Blighty'. He was carried down the line, evacuated to a casualty clearing station at Hazebrouck and then to the 53rd General Hospital at Wimereux. He and the others wounded during that first tour were really the lucky ones for they were not only to miss the battalion's attack on the 20 September, but also the long agonizing last few months of the year which were spent working, fighting and suffering in the icy, cratered landscape.

The next six days were spent training at Reigersburg while the seventh, 'Y' Day, was devoted to genuine rest. With 108 surplus personnel already detached, at 22.45 on the 19 September, a very dark and rainy night, 16 officers and 452 other ranks paraded and began the slippery and tiresome march towards Vancouver crossroads. Making their way along the duckboard track as far as the dismembered trees of Kitchener Wood, and then heading across the broken ground, the leading company finally arrived at the tapes laid earlier by 2Lt Reeve, at 03.40. Twenty-five minutes later the whole of the assaulting troops were in position and were allowed to sleep until a sandwich ration was passed along the lines at 05.20. The slumbering troops were roused from their nerve-induced sleep to find that the gradually lightening skies revealed rain-laden clouds being driven along by a gusting wind. The men were soaked through and the night's incessant rain had turned the already boggy ground into a quagmire. The weeks of shell fire had cut the lower ground into areas of impassable swamp and, in order to try to by-pass the worst of this, and equally important, to avoid a frontal assault upon the German strong-points on the western end of the Gravenstafl ridge, the battalion had been ordered to pivot and attack south-east up the more gently rising ground. This would allow them to take the German pill-boxes in the flank and rear, while the 173rd Brigade on the lower ground to the right, was attacking its objective of Schuler Farm.

At 05.40 under a covering barrage of smoke, high explosive and machine gun fire, the battalion rose from the shell holes and began the advance. The featureless landscape meant that the flanks of each company were instructed to advance on a compass bearing. As the company officers became casualties and the identifiable features on the ground were at a premium, it became increasingly difficult for the men to maintain direction. There appeared to be concrete blockhouses everywhere and the fire emanating from their low slits, combined with the enemy barrage which played backwards and forwards across the line of advance, took a heavy toll of the heavily-laden attackers. The fire from one pillbox to the west of Hubner Farm was particularly devastating and, as the troops took what shelter they could, they discovered that they were sharing the shell holes with Scots of the 51st Division. In that featureless landscape, the Scots had mistaken Hubner Farm for one of their own objectives. The right flank company made better progress but came under fire from German machine guns manned in the open. Gradually, the troops pushed forward and finally took the pill-boxes from the rear. Large numbers of Germans surrendered, and once an objective had been reached and taken, runners were sent to the rear with 'message maps'. Few of the runners actually completed the journey back to Battalion HQ, and because there were so few officers left, those men who took an objective and then began to consolidate, usually had little idea of where they actually were. An irregular line was eventually established by the LRB running to the east of von Tirpitz and Stroppe Farms. Later in the day the 6th London passed through to continue the advance up the slope to the south-east and took the site of Wurst Farm.

If any LRB man had known where he actually was and if he had studied the engagement or spoken to the survivors of the 1st Battalion who had fought at Ypres in 1915, he might have realised that the battalion was now manning the same positions as the Germans had held when they launched their gas attack on 2 May 1915. Below the right shoulders of the British troops lay the Hanebeke and on the other side of the valley, only 2000 yards from where they now sheltered, was the position held so desperately and fatally by men such as Albany Featherstonehaugh, Sydney Legg and Arthur Pigden. However, for the men of the 2nd Battalion, there was little time for reflection. Around 18.00 the enemy could be seen massing for a counter-attack in the Stroombeke valley and as the columns began to advance, Lewis gun and heavy machine gun fire was brought to bear upon them at a range of about 1500 yards. Rifle fire was opened at about 650 yards and then, as the remaining Germans struggled to within 150 yards of the scattered British posts, the barrage crashed down and destroyed the attack. The few suvivors went to ground or tried to re-cross the shell-swept zone and regain their own lines. They tried again the following day, but met with a similar annihilation.

The LRB were relieved by the Hackney Rifles on the night of 21-22 September and trudged back to Reigersburg and later Brake Camp. Of the 452 non-commissioned men who made that journey up to the jumping-off tapes, 179 made their weary way back. During the course of the attack 99 other ranks had been killed or were to die from wounds, representing 22% of the attacking force, and another 173, or 38%, were wounded. When the surplus personnel rejoined on 25 September, the battalion's fighting strength rose to 287. Some respite, however, was on the way and later that same day a draft of 141 arrived to swell the depleted ranks.

Among the dead of 20 September was the young bank clerk from Thornton Heath, Sgt Grahame Foster, MM. His great friend Adam Macpherson survived safely and was later to marry Foster's twin sister.[318] Several of the draft of 34 from the 3rd Battalion whose arrival had been greeted with so much incredulity had died, and so had the junior clerk Charles Miles who had only recently returned from yet another stay in hospital. Sixty-eight of the bodies were never recovered or identified, and the names of the men were later put along side those from the 1st Battalion on the Menin Gate. Other bodies were recovered after the war and were concentrated in a few scattered cemeteries, particularly Tyne Cot and New Irish Farm. Six more men died at the casualty clearing stations at Dozinghem and Mendinghem, and another in the Base Hospital at Etaples. Frederick Caines, promoted to CSM of 'A' Company after Bottomley had become RSM, was killed, as was CQMS Saul Schonewald, the longest-serving non-commissioned officer on active service with either battalion of the LRB. Instead of staying in the rear, as he was entitled to do, Schonewald went forward to the jumping-off tapes with his company and was killed later in the day. As the third most senior member of the regiment, he had been allotted number 300003 when the new series was introduced in May 1917; his experience in the traditions and ways of the regiment had in the early days done much to weld the September 1914 recruits into a unit.

Casualties among the officers had also been heavy. The former Charterhouse man, Capt Frederic Furze was the most senior officer to die and his name, along with those of Lieutenants Sharman and Ticehurst, who had been wounded with Capt Nobbs in Leuze Wood, appears on the Menin Gate. Four other LRB junior officers and two attached from the St Pancras battalion also died that day. In total, of the 16 involved in the attack, nine died and the remainder were wounded. Yet, despite heavy casualties, the operation had been a remakable success. The *Official History* was fulsome in its praise, and believed that the success was a consequence of the thoroughness of the preliminary training.[319] The creeping barrage was considered to have been excellent, a belief supported by the *War Diary* which also praised the extent and density of the smoke screen. Standing barrages and gas had been put down on likely approaches from the German rear areas and these were thought to have demoralised the Germans in the forward positions. The flank attack had secured the higher ground around Wurst Farm and any Staff Officer reading his map in the comfort of Montreuil might have considered that an important advance had been achieved. The reality was somewhat different as, although the troops of 174 and 173 Brigades had achieved all that had been asked of them, the advance had been of little strategic value. The British had fought their way to the crest of the Gravenstafl ridge, only to now come under direct observation from the one on which the village of Passchendaele stood. True, they could overlook the German positions in the Stroombeke valley to the north and east, but any advance up that flooded area would be observed by the Germans on the higher ground from both of those directions. However, the battle of attrition which the troops were fighting on Haig's behalf, would not be halted for mere strategic reasons. In effect, the British and Colonial troops were slogging their way deeper into more of a salient than had existed at the commencement of the offensive. Haig, however, persisted in the belief that the state of the French army made it politically impossible to halt the advance and consolidate for the winter months on the higher ground now in Allied possession.

The British offensive thus had to continue through the autumn rains of 1917. The LRB and the 58th Division were withdrawn from the Salient for three weeks at the end of September, although they were to return to spend the last few months of the year in that wilderness of flooded shellholes. During its time at Licques the battalion paraded to witness the presentation, to the survivors, of the 26 Military Medals and six Distinguished Conduct Medals earned during September. When it left Brake Camp on 25 September, the battalion's strength was about 428. The return of the surplus personnel, the Transport and HQ details, had swollen the ranks of the company men who had survived the attack on von Tirptiz Farm, and to this figure, a draft of 141 non-commissioned ranks must be added. Unfortunately, it is unclear from which unit these men arrived. The *War Diary* gives no clue but the Regimental History records that 'amongst other reinforcements' an unspecified, but 'large' number of men from the Army Service Corps arrived while the battalion trained at Licques.[320] This could be the same draft as the 141 who were waiting at Brake Camp, or an additional one which went unrecorded in the *War Diary*. Little is known of the ASC men, except that the History praises them for their 'efficiency and cheerfulness'. What little evidence there is from the serial numbers, suggests that the actual number of them was probably only about 30. Although unlikely, it could be that these men had not been issued with new LRB numbers but had retained their old ones. Alternatively, it might be simply that the 'large' draft was really quite a small one. These troops might have tended to stand out more than the other reinforcements because, unlike them, they had not been trained as infantry.

Whatever the precise impact these drafts had made on the battalion's strength, the LRB was back in the crater zone and manning the shell-holes behind Poelcapelle by the end of October. The weather was very cold and the rain fell in torrents as the companies took up positions in Pheasant and Rose Trenches. The situation was still obscure following an attack up the water-logged valley of the Lekkerboterbeke by the 6th and 8th London, and the LRB was ordered to send out patrols to attempt to ascertain where the enemy line was. The patrols found the going impossibly difficult. Stretcher bearers suffered particularly as they struggled through the adhesive and clinging mud, liable to be picked off by snipers or become victims of the rolling shell-fire. Germans manned fortified shell-holes and guns from within their concrete mebus sprayed the patrols as they picked their way through the morass and slime. Casualties mounted during the three-day tour and the earlier three days spent performing carrying parties around the canal bank. The total of killed and missing in the *War Diary* amounts to 35, while the Regimental History gives 36. However, the number listed in the later official roll for the same period only amounts to 15, with another two dying of wounds at Dozinghem on 1 November. The difference between the totals is significant as it can either demonstrate the inaccuracy of the *War Diary* in recording casualties - for example it gives 20 killed on 27 October while the *Soldiers Died* list has only two - or, it implies that their was a large number of men serving with the battalion who do not appear as LRB casualties. The names of the men who died during the battles of October and November and have no known grave are inscribed on the panels of the Tyne Cot Memorial to the Missing, and of the 14 LRB names listed, at least four were certainly serving with other units. It is likely, therefore, that there were men fighting with the LRB who appear in the casualty lists of their former regiment and thus it becomes increasingly difficult to establish accurate casualty figures within a particular unit. A further example of this difficulty can be seen from the *War Diary* entry of 4 November. It records that two men were killed while on a working party, but there are no LRB deaths indicated in the later roll for several days either side of that date. The fact that there were men from other regiments with the battalion has already been suggested, and this is confirmed by a mention in the *War Diary* of the award of a Military Medal to L/Cpl Hernberg. Hernberg has a serial number which clearly indicates that he was a member of the Poplar and Stepney Rifles.

During the course of November at least another four men were killed. Battalion strength was now so low that it was decided to amalgamate platoons so as to give each company two strong platoons, each supported by a Lewis gun team Two drafts did arrive that month, and the first, of 84 men, had come from the 3rd Battalion. This was a group of men who clearly had not been posted overseas in sequence of enlistment as many men with higher serial numbers were already dead. Although it is difficult to be exact, the majority of the group seem to have been young 19 year olds like Charles Taylor. They left England and arrived at the battalion only six days later, unlike the second draft, which endured a much more round-about route. There is no mention of this second draft in the *War Diary*, but again, they were certainly men from the 3rd Battalion who left England in October. On arrival at Havre, Honour, Yates, Kinsella and an unknown number of their colleagues were transferred to the Post Office Rifles before later returning to the LRB. After wandering around the rear areas for some days, the party finally discovered the LRB at Herzeele. Then, following some stiff daily marches, the battalion bivvied in Huddleston Camp behind Ypres. Three weeks training at Huddleston and later at Lottinghem allowed the drafts of October and November to become absorbed in the battalion and also provided the opportunity to fill the gaping vacancies among the Lewis gunners and rifle grenadiers

The entries in Honour's diary for the next three weeks record the demoralising and debilitating experience that working in the front areas could have upon men. The LRB and the remainder of 174 Brigade were detailed to provide working parties while the division's other two brigades held the line. Accommodation at Huddleston Camp was basic in the extreme, with two companies being allocated flooded and collapsing sandbag dugouts. Working parties went out daily on timber fatigues, salvaging and often arrived at some dark, snowy rendezvous, only to discover that the duckboards they were supposed to carry forward, had been dumped somewhere else. Some parties were attached to the RE and had to slog and slip their way back and forward to Langemarck carrying barbed wire and piquets. Guard duty in howling snow storms, interspersed with about two hours sleep, could last for 24 hours, and on their way to and from Eagle Dump, frequent gas bombardments necessitated the wearing of energy-sapping respirators. Despite the atrocious weather and the constant attention of the enemy, casualties were suprisingly light. During the entire month of December there seem only to have been two killed, Rfn Jones and Manning, both buried in Cement House Cemetery, and seven wounded. A draft of 19 men and seven officers also arrived which brought the battalion's total strength by the end of the month to 899 and ration strength to 628. Compared to the beginning of the month, this was a reduction of 29 and 207 respectively. The large difference between the figures for ration strength is explained by 90 men being 'detached', 50 on leave, ten on courses and 25 sick. The total strength of 899 was, for that stage of the war, a high figure. However, when the Transport, HQ details and surplus personnel are deducted from the ration strength, it means that only about 450 men would be available for duty in the line - about the same number as attacked on 20 September.

According to the *War Diary*, only two more men were wounded before the battalion left the front zone around Poelcapelle on 9 January and marched back to Road Camp at Proven. Other men had returned to England to take up commissions. Amongst others who can be identified were the three sergeants of 'A' Company, Cockerell, Belither and Wright. Meanwhile the battalion stayed at Proven for ten days, during which time Archibald Lintott, the former CIV man and Richard Lintott's uncle, was presented with the MC for his work in getting the rations up every night. In all, 19 Military Medals and three Distinguished Conduct Medals were awarded for the actions during September and October. Among the recipients were RSM Bottomley, H.B. Hooson, one of that large group of trainee teachers who joined in September 1914, and the brother of the pianist at many of the 3rd Battalion's concerts, Timberlake. The time spent at Proven also gave the opportunity for what is described as 'useful training' in PT, the use of the bayonet and Lewis gun firing. Classes for runners, bombers and junior NCOs were also held. Training continued at Moreuil after the battalion had made the long journey south, and a hint of the blow that was about to fall came with Lt Col Stewart's announcement that he was leaving the battalion to take command of the 58th Division's Machine Gun unit. Three days later, amid increasing speculation and rumour about changes in the structure of the BEF, a letter arrived from the authorities announcing that the 2nd Battalion of the LRB was to be disbanded.

In terse, official language, the letter simply announced the end of a battalion of London's oldest volunteer regiment. The notification went on to state impassively that the men were to be posted to the London Irish, the Artists and the 2nd Hackney Rifles, serving respectively in the 47th, 63rd, and 58th Divisions. The men of the battalion were devastated and could not understand how the authorities could be so insensitive as to disband a unit with such a famous pedigree. When details of the great changes which were taking place within the BEF became known, in some cases, bewilderment turned to anger. There was a draft of LRB men at the Base waiting to be posted up the line, but instead of going to the 1st Battalion, they were sent to the Artists to join the 450 arriving from the 2nd Battalion. This might have been easier to accept had it not been known that most of the Rangers in the 56th Division were being posted to their own second line unit in the 58th Division. Why, therefore, if the system allowed transfer between the same regimental units in the two London Divisions, as was apparent in the case for the Rangers, could it not be done for the LRB? The administrative arrangements seemed all the more callous because instead of transferring the 300 disbanded Rangers to the 1st Battalion LRB, the authorities could just as easily either have used men from the 2nd Battalion or those LRB men waiting at the Base. There was, however, one small crumb of consolation; because the number of officers and men transferred from the LRB to the Artists was so large, for the time being, the Artists became the LRB in all but name.

The physical disappearance of the battalion came about very quickly. In the space of three days, the three groups destined for their new regiments had been addressed by the OC 174 Brigade and the GOC 58th Division and then departed for their new battalions. The brigadier 'impressed upon all ranks that they should at all times maintain the high standard of discipline and efficiency of the 2nd LRB', while the general congratulated them on their 'achievements' whilst serving with the division.[321] A remnant of officers and men remained to tidy up the final loose ends for a few more days and to despatch onward men returning from courses and leave. However, by the end of January, the demands of war had ensured that the 2nd Battalion was no more.

On its disbandment battalion strength was 35 officers and 850 men. Remarkably, only four of the officers were not actually LRB men. Of the original officers who had sailed in January 1917, three had been invalided home, five had been posted to other units sometime during the year, five had been so severely wounded that they were still recovering in England, six had been killed or died of wounds, and ten were still with the battalion awaiting posting. Two of these ten, Claude Furze and Vere Welch, were to die during ensuing battles and another two, Wilkinson and Legg, platoon commanders in January 1917, were both later to command the Artists Rifles.

Of the non-commisioned men, at least 179 had been killed while serving with the battalion in France. The great bulk of them were LRB trained, but there were also two of the July 1916 Middlesex draft to the 1st Battalion who died while fighting with the 2nd battalion. There are also fatalities from other London units, the RAMC and the ASC, but as was shown above, recent drafts had confused the nature and composition of the battalion. It is possible to distinguish certain individuals, such as Francis Radford, who enlisted in September 1914 and served all the way through until disbandment. Such men, however, probably numbered less than 50. There were also some pre-war LRB members like Archibald Hansen and V. Woodman serving with the 2nd Battalion who were to be posted elsewhere in January. But what of the remainder of the original enthusiatic 964 men who had enlisted in September 1914?

The war had made a severe impact for, by its conclusion, 23% of these volunteers were dead. Five of these were either killed or died while serving as non-commissioned men in other regiments and another 30 were killed while holding commissioned rank. Despite the fact that so many of them had been killed relatively early in the war at Ypres in 1915, 26% of the originals were given commissions during the war. The majority served in other units of the London Regiment, while 26 were commissioned into the LRB itself. Another seven went into the RFC or RNAS (D.G. Cooke and B. de Roeper for example, were both credited with five 'kills' while serving with 20 Squadron and the RNAS respectively). The number gaining commissions clearly reflects the quality and education of these volunteers. Although of course by no means unique, the original 2nd Battalion represented the cream of London's clerical classes, a group of young sportsmen intensely patriotic and with an over-riding sense of duty. They transferred the loyalty and *esprit* they had developed in their clubs, societies, training colleges and offices, to a different kind of community. This new community consisted of a group of young men from largely identical backgrounds and upbringing who had been inspired to enlist in a regiment of their own choice by similar motives. The allegiance and loyalty to that new community was to survive its demise, and continue long after the war had ended.

Once their initial anger had subsided, the prevailing sentiment amongst the men waiting to be transferred was one of quiet resignation. Although they might no longer be serving with the LRB, they were being posted elsewhere largely by companies which meant that they would still be with their friends. That was at least something for which they could be grateful. Charles Taylor, one of the draft of 84 which had arrived in November, recalled that 'our draft was distressed when parted from the regiment and always considered ourselves LRBs',[322] a fact that was reflected on the headstones of many of Taylor's colleagues who were later killed. Those who were posted to the Artists had a terrible time with the Naval Division during the German offensive, and their graves are found along the line of retreat from Ytres to Albert. Unlike their former comrades who were sent to the Hackney Rifles, these men have 'London Rifle Brigade' on their headstones and appear in the LRB section of *Soldiers Died*. One such example is that of CSM Frederick Clarke who had come to the LRB from the Kensingtons, and was then posted to the Artists. His grave, along with those of three other former LRB men who fell in early April 1918, nestles inside Aveluy Wood, the scene of their bitter rearguard action.

The arrival of the 450 2nd Battalion men at the 1/28th London was observed with some distaste by at least one of the Artists himself. 'Private X' thought the LRB men 'hated coming to us almost as much as we hated their coming', but later conceded that they soon mucked in together with no ill-feeling. He was quite content with 'his new CSM and platoon commander, but disliked his new company commander:

> *He knew exactly how an officer ought to behave because he had once seen one impersonated in a musical comedy. He was foul-mouthed and used to encourage the men to sing smutty songs on the march...he had about as much brains as a demented louse. Subsequently he was taken prisoner on the March retreat, and it served the Germans damned well right.*[323]

Another draft from the LRB's 3rd Battalion appears to have joined the Artists just before the German offensive of March and, by the Armistice, at least 55 of the former LRB men had died. By that time, only some two officers and 80 other ranks of the 18 and 450 remained with the Artists.

The men who had been posted to the London Irish in the 47th Division fared little better. Jack Terry's friend Albert Thain was on leave when the battalion was broken up and eventually joined the London Irish, only to be separated from them again during the retreat. Re-united once more, in May he took part in the attacks over the ground lost in March. Near the ruins of Albert, he and his colleagues discovered their battalion's post bags containing letters and newspapers from relatives at home applauding the unit's tenacity during the March battles. At least 39 of Thain's comrades were to die before the end of the war. Many of their names are inscribed on the Arras Memorial to the Missing, while the known graves are scattered around the Bouzincourt region above Albert.

Those troops sent to the 2/10th London suffered a similar casualty rate as the war progressed. They were certainly not so heavily involved in the March fighting, but this is a more difficult group of men to identify positively. They appear in the LRB list of *Soldiers Died*, but the roll gives no indication that they were transferred out of the LRB. However, an analysis of their dates of death and the memorials, or parts of the front where the known graves are located, suggests that a minimum of 29 of the former 150 members of 'A' Company were later killed. In addition to these soldiers, there are also several men who might have served for some time in the 2nd Battalion, but who died while members of the Post Office Rifles, which was, like the 2/10th London, a unit of the 58th Division. Alternatively, it is possible that these men could have been posted direct from the 3rd Battalion currently training at Blackdown Camp.

Although the 2nd Battalion no longer existed, the third line unit retained its name as the Third Battalion LRB and, as has been shown, since 1916 had been sending out trained soldiers who had little chance of actually reaching either the 1st or 2nd Battalions. During the course of its short existence, the 2nd Battalion had received somewhere around 800 volunteers and conscripts from the home unit. It is to a study of the character and training of the third line, which had made such a significant contribution to the history of the 2nd Battalion, that attention will now turn.

CHAPTER XII

'Send that man at once to 130 Bunhill Row!'

Like the 2nd Battalion, the Third, or Training Reserve Battalion was a product of the war. The third line units were, of course, never intended to be sent overseas as complete battalions, their purpose instead was to be the provision of replacements for the two service battalions. Reference has already been made to the birth of the battalion in November 1914 and to its early experiences. It has already been noted that, despite the predictable problems of acquiring sufficient equipment and instructors, it had sent out its first large draft of recruits from Tadworth at the end of August 1915. This draft had successfully reached the 1st Battalion, but there was understandable concern as to how extensive and thorough its training had been. In fact, the 3rd Battalion had been more fortunate in respect of instructors than the Second mainly because the wounded from the First were sent down to Tadworth rather than Haywards Heath before being despatched overseas again. The training battalion could therefore call upon and utilise the practical experience of these men in the type of warfare being conducted in France and, equally importantly, retain those who would make the best instructors. Many of these men, labelled B1 were sent on courses for drill and musketry and, when qualified, replaced the 3rd Battalion NCOs who were then drafted out. By this means Harding and Maurice Howard became attached to the training battalion and started their new careers as instructors.

Although they had fought in the trenches of Plugstreet and Ypres, these youngsters had little real idea of the duties or skills of instructors. Enthusiasm and pride in the regiment counted for a lot, but it did not fill in the genuine gaps in their military knowledge. The RSM, the long-serving ex-Clr-Sergeant Whittingham and another former Clr Sergeant, but now Second Lieutenant, George Vaile, knew the regulations thoroughly. They had not only to guide men such as Howard through the intricacies of *King's Regs*, to instil into them the necessary methods of handling men, but also instruct them both in military technique and how to turn raw recruits into LRB soldiers in what, for the present, was an indeterminate period of time:

We were given a first stripe and the Drill Instructors gave us a rough idea and told us to study King's Regs., and then before you could say 'Jack Robinson', we were given a second stripe, and then the third, until we had the cream job of Drill Sergeant. Then the Army in its wisdom decided that no Drill Sergeant or Warrant Officer could remain an Instructor until they'd been through a course of drill at the Coldstream's barracks, Chelsea. That I did, a month's course. It began with a CSM asking each of our squad of about 20 what we knew about drill instruction. I replied, 'I know nothing' and he replied, 'That's what we want. We'll learn you all you've got to know'. In my opinion it was time wasted, although I did have a good holiday. (M. Howard)

Later in the war, junior NCOs were sent to Southern Command's NCO School at Tidworth, where among other things they were futilely taught the more usual Army calls of command, means of carrying weapons and pace of march.

The system of training devised in the 3rd Battalion is frequently recalled as being identical to the method of education most of the recruits had experienced at their public schools. Its inception was credited to Major King but was, in fact, by no means unique among units of the London Regiment.[324] The scheme was designed so that the battalion represented the school, the companies the houses and the platoons the individual forms. The platoons were taught the curriculum by masters who were grouped into specialist subjects and each faculty was allocated a specific time within the timetable. Each platoon also had its own form master and senior monitors, the platoon officer and 'marching' NCOs, who took the students to their subject class and usually sat with them. If the platoon officer knew the subject sufficiently well, he could be excused and spend his time in some other useful instruction. This sensible idea was later spotted by the brigadier who promptly ordered that all parties of 50 men must be under the command of an officer. This seemingly pointless decree was easily circumvented in the LRB by simply dividing any such party into two groups of 25, each under a corporal.

Such a system allowed young boys like Basil Houle and his friends in 'Wheatley's Lambs' to settle down quickly into army life. With the support of a helpful and sympathetic man like Fletcher Wheatley, they could identify closely with one another and develop a strong sense of belonging and *esprit*. Polhill too remarked upon the attitude of the officers and NCOs who, he said, treated the recruits without harshness or bullying, and 'more or less as equals'. By the end of their training, he claimed that his platoon 'almost worshipped our officers because they were so nice'. Fierce rivalry existed between the training companies and even between platoons within the same company:

We were individually convinced that our regiment was the cream of the London Brigade and that our platoon was undoubtedly the best in the regiment. As a platoon we were immensely self-critical and the roughest of judgement was meted out to any member who was considered to have lowered the standard by slackness or ill-discipline. (R. Angel)

From this inter-platoon rivalry sprang the strong Regimental *esprit*, a factor which was recognised both at the time and in later recollections. The nurturing was helped too by the attachment of corporals and sergeants of the 'Overseas Company' to the training platoons. These NCOs were in theory awaiting posting abroad again but, in practice, many of them stayed with one platoon from its creation to its departure. While these veterans might have taken the opportunity to regale the innocents with 'soldiers' tales', their accounts of the engagements fought by the battalion appeared to have the desired effect:

> *We had a young corporal attached to our platoon who had gone with the 1st Battalion but had been wounded at Ypres. He made our hair stand on end with some of his stories about the mud and blood, but he also told us what a good life it was for most of the time and how well our regiment had done along side the Regulars. We were complete amateurs but we felt a great deal of pride and couldn't wait to get out there ourselves.* (B. Houle)

Another inception made while the battalion trained at Tadworth was the creation of a special class for potential NCOs and officers. Candidates for commissions had formerly been required to spend time in the trenches before their application could be considered but, as the demand for officers increased, applications from recruits in the 3rd Battalion were also considered. This class of about 30 men was initially under the command of Lt Beard (who was later killed at Les Boeufs), and he was succeeded in turn by 'Johner' Johnston after he had recovered from his pre-Gommecourt wound. The officers were assisted by two veteran stalwarts of the regiment, Sergeants Malone and Harriss. Tom Malone was by all accounts a remarkable man. He had been a Regular and after serving his time had joined the LRB as Sergeant-Major in 1897. He retired from that position ten years before the war and on its outbreak, aged 50, was offered the post of RSM at the Rifle Brigade depot in Winchester. Declining this position, he re-enlisted in the LRB as a private and sailed on the *Chyebassa*. He was finally persuaded to return home to the 3rd Battalion in May 1916 on the grounds that his experience would be of immense use to the recruits. The 1st Battalion apparently lined the road and cheered as he departed. On arrival at Tadworth he refused the offer of a commission, arguing that, as a sergeant, he would be freer to act as philosopher and guide to both new recruits and senior officers alike.[325]

The NCO/Officer class normally ran for three weeks before the candidates then appeared individually in front of Colonel King. Equipped with reports from Johnston and Malone, who had during the period got to know the individuals well, King decided whether the candidate should be sent to an Officer Cadet Battalion. On return, as a subaltern, these men were next usually appointed as commanders to each of the training platoons, a practice which sometimes threw up strange coincidences. Norman Catlow, for example, had originally been a raw recruit in one of Sgt Maurice Howard's training platoons. Then, after having passed through the special class and an Officer Cadet Battalion, he returned to command another of Howard's platoons. Their subsequent relationship seems to exemplify the spirit and form of discipline within the LRB.

Catlow assured Howard that the latter would inevitably make his platoon the best in the company and offered a cheque if his prediction proved correct. By the time Howard finished training the platoon, Catlow had been posted overseas. Nevertheless, he enquired from France whether a cheque should be sent. Howard replied in the affirmative and so the platoon enjoyed some celebratory drinks at Catlow's expense.

The role of NCOs such as Howard in the training battalion was crucial. They can be a unit's strength, but also, if badly chosen, its greatest weakness. That the form of discipline in the LRB was far removed from the more traditional army methods has already been noted, and it was on this discipline that morale in the training, as well as the overseas battalion, was founded. If the NCOs had not been sympathetic to and thoroughly immersed in this method of discipline, then the whole system would not have worked; recruits would either take advantage of the supposed easiness, or sadistically-minded NCOs could exploit the apparent lack of close supervision by officers. The recurrent theme of several of the memoirs is the close relationship between the platoon NCOs and their charges. To take two examples: Maurice Howard received many letters sent by his former recruits after they were posted to France and to other units. Their tone is informal, frequently beginning, 'Dear old Sgt.', and sufficiently chatty to indicate an easy, sincere relationship. Similarly, when 'Cherub' Angel and the rest of A13 platoon were posted, saying farewell to their sergeant was, 'rather an emotional experience. Stan Baker had been our guide and friend since he had first arrived...getting to know each one of us thoroughly and teaching us many things not to be found in any training manual...In particular he taught us that life in the Army is largely what the soldier himself makes of it'.

It is clear from the accounts that those who decided how the training should be conducted in the regiment, realised that a bullying or heavy-handed approach would never draw out the best in any recruit. Unfortunately though, this more tactful and less martial approach was not always appreciated in the manner intended by all of its recipients:

> *One of the recruits in my platoon was the son of a school friend of my mother's. He had a sleeping out pass for himself and his wife and one Sunday afternoon another sergeant and I saw the fellow walking with his webbing thong dangling between his legs. We couldn't allow that because he would be picked up for being improperly dressed. I didn't want to embarrass him in front of his wife so I called him to one side and hooked it up. He hated it and never had a good word to say about me and in fact my mother told me that he had told his mother that Sgt Howard drinks too much!'.* (M. Howard)

In January 1916 the battalion moved by train to Dinton and then marched a few miles to occupy a newly hutted camp at Fovant near Salisbury. Constructed at the foot of the rolling hills, the facilities were still primitive, but gradually a drainage system was dug and the roads and duckboards laid. While the battalion was establishing itself at Fovant, it received its first batch of Derby recruits, and although the facilities were better than at Tadworth or Sutton, the heterogeneous nature of the new intake created additional problems with training schedules and schemes. These difficulties were further exacerbated by the necessity of having to turn these civilians into soldiers in what amounted to about eleven weeks. The pressure on the training battalions to furnish replacements for those lost during the Somme offensive was immense. It just was not possible to conduct homogenous training as the age, physical ability and temperaments of the men differed so greatly. Polhill's 38 Platoon, for example, consisted of 18 year olds such as himself, as well as older men of 35-40. Despite having originally been classified as A1, some of the latter had to be discharged owing to trouble with their feet. However, the LRB had one great advantage over the New Army reserve battalions who were also admitting men under the Derby scheme. Even after the payment of the regimental subscription had been abolished by Parliament, the regiment could still pick and choose the recruits it would accept under the scheme. This privilege applied not only to the Derby men like Groom and Polhill, but also to that new phenomenon of 1916, the conscript.

By attesting under the Derby scheme, many of the men called-up under the Military Service Act of 1916 had already indicated their willingness to serve. This applied to both single and married men - the latter originally having been assured that they would not be called upon until the bachelors had gone. So, from January 1916 the LRB had begun accepting single men aged between 18 and 41 who were technically conscripts, but in effect were still really Derby men. They were to be followed in May of the same year by their married counterparts. These batches of men arrived at the 3rd Battalion, which, despite the loss of so many men to the 1st and 2nd Battalions, was still described as 'strong'. Recruitment too, having picked up a little in previous months, was reported as being 'very brisk' when the Derby men began to arrive. In the course of the next twelve months, another 2,000 of these men would be despatched overseas, but although the regiment was able to decide which of these new men it would accept for training, inevitably some of the 1916 members were of a different social class from the usual type of LRB man. One such group was somewhat disparagingly nicknamed the 'Stratford OTC'[326]. However, the majority of the recruits seem to have come from the areas of London and the sort of occupations from which the LRB had traditionally recruited.

The Derby men and conscripts arrived at a camp which consisted of rows of dreary, uninviting, huts centred around the large, often windswept square. Yet, one man who experienced it felt that despite the monotony and drudge of the daily routine, few who were there could not look back at it without some affection: 'For there was a spirit of comradeship there which links up the dreariness into pleasant recollections'.[327] Polhill's platoon semed to enjoy the life so much that they frequently joked that when the war was over, they would return to Fovant for a month's training. Pleasant or not, the training was necessarily intense for these men were urgently required for the mincing-machine of the Western Front. Their knowledge of affairs military was nevertheless somewhat patchy and after the battalion had moved once again, this time to Dawlish in Devon, the conscripts were joined by yet another type of recruit. This new sort consisted of boys of 18 years who had volunteered six months before they were due to be called up. By enlisting prematurely they were entitled to join a regiment of their own choice; if they waited, they ran the risk of being posted to any unit ready to absorb another intake. The idea was that these boys, classified as Aiv, all physically fit and enthusiastic, would have a much longer period of training than the norm, and thus make better soldiers. Rather than the usual three months, these recruits would have a full year of training because they could not, in theory, be sent overseas until they were 19 years old. Depending upon when their eighteenth birthday fell, they were grouped into platoons of about 40 and stayed together for their entire period of training. When they attained the statutory age, they were then posted overseas, usually as a complete unit. Unlike the training platoons composed of conscripts, these new ones were given an experienced NCO as mentor and guide. Training, which became increasingly strenuous and demanding as their physiques developed, was carried out with a great deal of inter-platoon rivalry.

Typical of these new trainees was John Sutton of Paignton. Chaffing at not being old enough to enlist, Sutton spent the time between leaving school and his eighteenth birthday working in the family printing business. His mother had already intercepted and withheld his application form for the RFC, but in October 1916, three months before the scheme officially became operable, he was accepted by the LRB and later reported to Regimental HQ along with others whose eighteenth birthdays fell in the same month. Boys such as Sutton and Angel had been greatly concerned by the introduction of conscription because they feared that, 'the pride of being a volunteer was no longer attainable and that our eventual embodiment as fighting men would have no merit about it'. Delighted at now having the opportunity to volunteer, these boys seem to have been inspired, like their 1914 volunteer counterparts, by a mixture of patriotism and a desire to get away from home and to embark upon what they believed to be the 'great adventure'. Believing that conscripts were by definition non-patriotic, or at least, less patriotic, they were eager to be accepted by one of the elite regiments as soon was legally practicable. The advantage to the LRB and other units permitted to enrol such youths was that they received boys of what they considered to be the correct social class, and who, furthermore, had elected to enlist in those regiment because they really wanted to.

These teenagers were certainly of the same type as those who joined the LRB, Post Office Rifles and Civil Service Rifles in the pre-war days.[328] Furthermore, they were prepared to spend a great deal of time and money to ensure that they joined a regiment of their own choice. Harold Phillips, from rural Oxfordshire, was urged by his father to write to a contact in London in the hope that this Mr Light could get him into a 'superior class' regiment. One of his friends had already spent £4 on several journeys to London, applying to one regiment after another, but all to no avail. Mr Light replied that Harold should come up to London immediately, try for the LRB, be prepared to enter at once and, if he were accepted, stay. Despite these efforts though, the young man ended up elsewhere.[329]

The class battalions of the London regiment had generally been able to cock a snook at the official recruiting office when it had tried to send down to the respective headquarters men whom the regiments were unwilling to accept. The depots could argue that their training battalions were full and were thus unable to accept another intake. However, in early 1918, this seemingly ideal position ended and authority exacted its revenge. The War Office decided that regiments could no longer pick and choose their own recruits and, to celebrate the new regime, the Finsbury Recruiting Officer despatched a 'specially selected batch [to the LRB] with instructions that they were to be fed for several weeks and than medically examined to see if they could be fit for training'. These men were from the poorest areas of London and the first thing to be done was to get them clean. Accordingly, Captain Fergusson instructed Corporal Chippingdale to issue them with soap and towels and ordered them to scrub each other in the showers. Harding recalls that within a fortnight the men were filling out and doing so well on LRB food that they commenced a full training schedule. Yet even after it had been decided that the LRB should accept any recruit sent to it authority, on occasions was not without *some* compassion. Harry Richmond was called-up to Hounslow Barracks in April 1918 and created a sensation by demanding to be sent to his brother's regiment, the LRB. The Sergeant-Major, temporarily taken aback by this impudence, recovered and bellowed, 'You can't join that posh mob now - you're a b.... conscript!' Richmond persisted, the Sergeant-Major swore, and an officer, assuming that the Sergeant-Major had turned up another conscientious objector, appeared, to investigate what the row was about. When the spluttering Warrant Officer managed to blurt out an explanation, the officer rasped 'Send that man at once to 130 Bunhill Row'.[330]

The life led by these young conscripts, as well as their more elderly companions, was hard and intense. Visits to the wet canteen by the Aiv boys were frowned upon but, as few of them had started drinking, to the majority this was no real hardship. In their spare time they contented themselves by experimenting with pipes and going on runs and bicycle rides, often accompanied by their platoon sergeant. Bunhill Row also sent down some of the pre-war School of Arms equipment and the boys were encouraged to fence with sabres and spring-bayonets. They were also provided with running kit from regimental funds. Unusual as this may have been, the characteristic which made the LRB stand out from the New Army and Regular battalions, as well as from many other Territorial ones, was the quality of the food in the messes. The LRB was obliged to drop its existing means and to adopt the prescribed methods of army messing in 1916, but this did not lead to a reduction in either the quantity or quality of the rations provided. Men from other units were constantly surprised at the food put in front of them:

> *At the end of 1917 we were given a number of sergeants from other battalions to share our training. At dinner one day a sergeant from one of the Middlesex units said when dinner was served, in his Cockney voice, 'Blimey, do you always eat like this?' Our Quartermaster and President of the Regimental Institute didn't have any money going into their own pockets they devoted it all to the troops. It was always hinted that there was corruption in other units, but all I can say is, having had experience of food in the Sergeants' Mess of the Brigade of Guards, well, you've heard the expression 'dog's dinner'.* (M. Howard)

Harding believed that when the visiting men returned to their own units, they complained about the quality of their own messes, and consequently, higher authority conducted an investigation into the provision made in the LRB. The outcome of the enquiry apparently proved that the Quartermaster's section, under Lt Kelly and Staff-Sgt Soman, did not overspend but, unlike many of its counterparts in other regiments, was merely efficient.

Apart from the provision of the soldiers' more immediate needs, the battalion also organised regular concerts and revues. There was a garrison theatre at Deepcut where touring companies performed and the large dining hut also doubled as a ready-made auditorium for battalion performances. The pre-war Bandmaster, P.S. Robinson, was transferred from the 2nd Battalion in 1916 and managed to collect together a bugle band from men who were unfit for foreign service. Other musicians formed a string band who gave performances in their own right and doubled as supporting turns in the comedy revues. Complete with professionally printed programmes, a great deal of effort and planning went into these events which were usually held to boost regimental funds or the Prisoner of War Fund. At times though, a certain amount of subterfuge was needed to keep the troupe and its producers together. Maurice Howard had taken such a prominent role in their organisation that, when he paraded before the Medical Board reviewing his fitness category, the RSM had a quiet word with the Chairman. The Chairman apparently replied, 'If you want him, keep him'. The band and players also often performed for local charitable concerns and it was after one such outing that Howard lost his position as the Major Domo of the concert party. Howard took a troupe to a local hospital without first obtaining the colonel's permission. His role was assumed by his former colleague in the Plugstreet wiring party, John Stransom.

In addition to their basic training, some of the Aiv boys were sent away on various courses and given other duties. One of the most common tasks was the unloading of hospital trains and acting as medical orderlies. Others were given a short period of instruction on how to act as bearers and firing parties at military funerals. If the need was urgent, this training could be condensed into a few hours on a Saturday morning. Emphasis was put on acquiring what was allegedly prescribed in the manual as the essential demeanour for such melancholy duty - 'a h'aspect cheerful but subdued'.[331] In lighter moments when for example the bitter winter of 1917-8 occasionally brought training to a halt, inter-platoon snowball fights on a massive scale took place: 'the fighting was tough and bitter and prisoners usually ended up being stuffed into snow drifts'.[332]

With the hordes of self-enlisted 18 year olds as well as the conscript intakes, by the time it left Blackdown Camp in April 1917, the battalion had swollen to about 1600 men. Aisne Barracks provided the best facilities yet enjoyed by the battalion and besides now having the opportunity to practise wiring and more extensive digging, the battalion could also concentrate on that aspect of infantry training which had been neglected for two years; musketry. Since the Somme many soldiers had been drafted to France without any real knowledge or experience of musketry other than their basic firing course. Consequently, complaints from the units receiving these drafts had been frequent and bitter and there were stories of men not bothering to resist enemy attacks until they were within bombing range. At Blackdown the battalion apparently did so well in musketry returns that Aldershot Command began to disbelieve the scores submitted. The returns showed that training platoons were producing 70-75% First Class shots. To verify the accuracy of these scores, two platoons on their way down to fire their course at Pirbright were intercepted by a detachment of Guards. The Guards ordered all the LRB staff and officers back to camp and assumed command of the platoons. Their subsequent report confirmed that 80% of the men had qualified as First Class Shots and no more was heard from the higher echelons of Aldershot.[333]

The large square at Blackdown also permitted daily parades by the whole battalion - something that had been impossible at the earlier camps. With the Aiv boys as well as the many other classifications of men waiting to be posted, these parades could involve six or seven training companies of as many as five platoons each. If sufficient officers were available, the unifying and *esprit*-building experience of company drill was even possible. Regimental history was taught to the boys as part of the unofficial curriculum, usually by their platoon sergeants during wet afternoons or evening sessions, while the constant theme recurrent in the more formal lectures and drills was the fostering of regimental spirit. By emphasising the traditions of the LRB the regimental system showed itself capable of taking the underprivileged and even the reluctant conscript, and of transforming him into an efficient soldier by encouragement, cajoling or, if necessary, bluster. The 3rd Battalion at Blackdown, however, was not the battalion it had been, for like the 1st Battalion in France, its composition had undergone a significant change. To the casual observer it was still the LRB and because it had the opportunity to mould men from the start of their army careers, it had an advantage over the parent battlion which had to persuade men brought up under different regimental traditions to adopt the ways of the LRB. The Regimental History stresses how well the intakes to the training battalion responded to the teaching of regimental *esprit* and how they became, apart from their accents, indistinguishable from the more usual LRB recruit. However, the difference was there. Except for the platoons of 18 year olds, the training companies contained a higher percentage of married men than before, the occupational spread would therefore have been greater and the enthusiasm to learn the trade perhaps less committed. Here again, the attitude of the NCOs in particular was vital. They had to foster the comradeship of regimental spirit which helped men from increasingly different backgrounds to live and work together, to adapt themselves and overcome what might have begun as outright hostility to the army. Roots could be established and nurtured which would set the men in good stead no matter to which unit they were later posted. When they compared themselves with new colleagues from other battalions, the LRB men believed that their training had provided them with a greater all-round expertise and thus a greater confidence in themselves as soldiers. When Harold Pratt was transferred to the Machine Gun Corps he found that, 'My training in the LRB was invaluable compared with training shown by men transferred from other regiments. Although we had all spent about the same amount of time in training, I thought that which I had had in the LRB had prepared me more thoroughly'. Howard agreed: 'We wanted to teach them self-reliance as well as pride in their regiment. Many of them were officer material - the sort of man who would easily adapt to whatever demands were made upon them'. Other regiments apparently continued to send their potential officers and NCOs to Blackdown to sample the LRB system. What so many of the LRB men must have found difficult to understand was why, after so much emphasis had been laid on making them LRB men, were they then shunted off willy-nilly to any regiment needing a draft? To the ordinary Tommy, the Army moved in mysterious if not malicious ways.

The Aiv platoons trained for six months and then 'passed off the square', although there was still field training and engineering to be learnt. The other training companies followed a similar, although shorter period of instruction. Following new orders, from August 1917 all categories of men had to undergo a final two weeks of intensive training when they were taken off all other fatigues and duties. A specialist staff was formed of two officers and five NCOs whose job it was to supervise this final period of live firing, living in trenches, night schemes etc., all of which were done in fighting order. Platoons that had finished their last intensive two weeks were then despatched overseas as the need arose. Drafts continued to be sent throughout the winter of 1917-18, but the impact of the German offensive launched the 3rd Battalion into a frenzy of activity. John Sutton's platoon of Aiv boys had already gone in February, posted virtually *en masse* to the Post Office Rifles, but Sutton himself had accidently injured his foot and was kept behind. At the beginning of March he was ordered to parade with a collection of recovered wounded and instructors, none of whom he knew, and was sent over to France. They were all lucky to join the 1st Battalion as it recovered from the mauling at Gavrelle. Unfortunately, the experience of Sutton's friends in A10 Platoon was pretty much the norm during these eventful days for most of those being sent from Blackdown ended up in other regiments. 'Cherub' Angel and his friends in A13 Platoon, for example, would not be nineteen until June, but as they were as fit as they were ever likely to be, they were given innoculations, loaded down with more and more equipment, much of it very new and very stiff, and paraded for departure. They were amazed to see sergeants and instructors, whom they had considered to be permanent fixtures of the training battalion, parading in full equipment too. The boys realised that if these God-like creatures were being sent out, the Army's need must indeed be great.

It was not only the recent recruits and permanent drill staff who were being rushed out to France. Graham Williams, having recovered from his wound received near Glencorse Wood, was in 'G' Company with other veterans of the 1st Battalion. Unless they particularly asked to be, these men were normally unlikely to be put on a draft. Some had gone, but others had been dissuaded by the knowledge that the likelihood of them actually rejoining the 1st Battalion was fairly remote. Harding recounts a story of two corporals at the Base, one from the LRB and one from the London Scottish, being ordered to exchange clothing before going up the line. He assumed that the policy of mixing up drafts was deliberate, while Williams, unsure whether it was merely some 'pip squeak of a junior subaltern, in a safe clerical job, anxious to show a little brief authority', or from higher authority, recommended courts martial for those responsible. If he had been sure of getting back to the Signalling section of the 1st Battalion, Williams would have volunteered to have been put on a draft. Instead, he applied for a commission. Others in a similar position also followed the same path when, in July 1918, all category Bi men (fit for garrison duty abroad) were up-graded to Ai. Colonel King ordered some of the old 1st Battalion men to apply for commissions, which they did, and then heard no more.[334]

Some of 'G' Company and a number of sergeant-instructors did volunteer to be included on a draft after having asked for an assurance that they would be sent to the 1st Battalion, or to the battalions to which the disbanded second line unit had been attached. Some of those going just before the German attacks of March did in fact arrive at the battalion before the Gavrelle battle. Unfortunately, others, such as Harold Moseley of the Northern Assurance, continued to be posted elsewhere. Although drafted at a different time, Moseley actually joined up with the youths of Sutton's A10 Platoon in the Post Office Rifles and, like several of those, was killed in August. The final destination of the platoons as they left Blackdown was uncertain, but although the majority did not reach the 1st Battalion, many joined battalions with traditions similar to those of the LRB. Two platoons of Aiv boys were posted to the Civil Service Rifles. This gave rise to a theory that an attempt was being made to match up some of the drafts with divisions that were at least territorially similar to their training units, or to units which had similar characteristics. Thus, A10, A12 and A13 Platoons were all sent to the 47th London Division, while A11 ended up in a Regular battalion of the Rifle Brigade. The experiences of the boys when being posted and sent to their new battalions bear remarkable similarities. Most thought that the sorting out process at the Base was quick and efficient and although they felt it regrettable, the boys seem to have accepted that the urgency of the military situation precluded their reaching their own regiment. There is also a consensus in the remaining evidence that their troubles only really started once they had been posted up the line.

Those young men of A9, posted to a battalion of the West Yorkshire Regiment, spent three weeks tramping around from place to place trying to catch up with their new unit, and after detraining at Warloy, members of A12 and A13 began what was to become a terrible march of endurance. They formed part of a column of about 600 men, some of whom were NCOs and riflemen of the Civil Service Rifles returning to their own battalion. These and the LRB boys contrived to keep together in a compact body, encouraging and helping each other as the march lengthened and the weather deteriorated. The LRB members were determined to march together and make a good impression upon the men of their new regiment. By the time the march ended, they were the only formed body remaining. The actual number of reinforcements allotted to the CSR was too great for the battalion to absorb, so with stragglers from the column still arriving two days later, the CO accepted the two LRB platoons *en bloc* and divided them between two companies.

These young 18 year olds were relieved to he accepted as a group, and pleased to discover that their new regiment was one with similar traditions and social make-up to the LRB. Although they still felt pangs of regret when exchanging their LRB badges for Prince of Wales feathers, these were nothing compared to the initial disenchantment experienced in another part of the line by their former colleagues of A9 Platoon. These youths were exchanging their badges for 'hefty racehorses as big as our heads', and were 'frightfully annoyed' at having been posted to what Eric Green described as a battalion of 'giddy Yorkshire lads'. They also found the discipline very different:

> *If only Sergeant Butler were here, it would turn his hair grey. We stroll on parade (on such occasions as we do parade) with our hands in our pockets, smoking, and usually assume a recumbent position on the command, 'Stand at ease' - six months confined to barracks at Blackdown at least.*[335]

Things began to improve with the arrival of another batch of reinforcements, mainly from other units of the London Regiment, and also when the LRB boys began to have stripes showered upon them from Battalion HQ. Green, for example, became a

Lewis gun instructor, Dennis acted as 'interpreter' to the American MO and so many other former LRB members were made lance-corporals that, by the end of their first month, only one of the draft had failed to land a 'posh job'. Despite the fact that he had not yet been given a stripe or a job at HQ, Keep still thought that the LRB draft had made 'quite a good impression on the Yorks crowd', and that they had done their best to keep up the traditions of their former regiment. On the other hand, Eric Green felt that he had risked dragging the regiment's name through the dust for being charged with impudence to a Redcap: 'Thank goodness, though, my actions are attributed elsewhere to the Yorks rather than the jolly-old LRB'. While A9 Platoon had been taken aback by the lax discipline in the West Yorks, A11 in the 3rd Rifle Brigade found that of the Regulars equally disconcerting. The attitude of the officers and NCOs to the men was very different from that which they had experienced at Blackdown. Soon after being posted, Collingwood wrote that the more formal discipline was not going down well with the platoon. Later letters show that the group did in fact adapt, settle in and, like the men of A9, were soon promoted.

The regimental histories of those units permitted to enrol these adolescents stress that the period of time they had for training, coupled with their enthusiasm, made them good soldiers. A10's new CO in the Post Office Rifles praised them for their determination and powers of endurance in the face of the heavy fighting they experienced during the Allied counter-offensives. Lt Col Derviche-Jones admired their intelligence and the confidence held in their own ability. These features, he considered, made the London Territorial about the best fighting material in the British Army.[336] On the other hand, Siegfried Sassoon, admittedly writing about an earlier phase of the war, thought that the boys under twenty seemed to be less able to put up with the mud, boredom and discomfort.[337] Similarly, Sid Amatt, at the advanced age of twenty, thought that the youngsters captured with him during the German offensive endured the privations of a prisoner of war with a great deal less stoicism than he mustered:

> The LRB boys at the camp we was in, well I can only describe them as
> 'Mummy's boys'. They were from good homes and had been fussed
> over, so weren't fitted for the tough life of a soldier in those days.
> They'd led sheltered lives and were raw and they lost heart because
> everything seemed to be going against them. They lost the will to live,
> and with a starvation diet and the circumstances we was in you soon
> succomb to dysentery and pneumonia. Also there was no news and
> that lowered their morale still further. They just died of broken hearts
> and a loss of spirit. I thought, 'I'm not going to let this get me down'.
> Blow that, I wanted to survive.

A similar condemnation of the fighting quality and powers of endurance of these young soldiers was made by a man serving in the Artists Rifles. When it was disbanded, about half of the 2nd Battalion was posted to the Artists to join several drafts of LRB Aiv boys who were already attached to them. The writer described these boys as being 'nearly all unspeakably bad soldiers', thought that the clerks were 'terribly deficient in guts' and suggested that they would have been better off staying at home.

He stresses though that he was not blaming the boys themselves and insists that he was grateful not to have been forced to endure the same terror when he was only nineteen.[338]

Critical as these few examples are, there is no doubt that the great majority of the young boys sent over to France to resist the German onslaught and then turn the tide and force the enemy back towards his own frontiers, did a remarkable job. In the heat of summer they fought and slogged their way over the wilderness of the old Somme battlefields, and then endured open warfare in the wet and cold of winter against a determined and still resilient enemy. Between March and October 1918, the 3rd Battalion of the LRB sent 876 men and boys to the Bases in France. Few of these actually fought with the 1st Battalion, but made their contribution to the final victory with other units. Active and positive recruiting at home aimed at a particular type of man had ensured that the training battalion remained for most of its existence much as it had originally been constituted. The War Office, in egalitarian mood, had decreed that it should, like all other units of the London Regiment, become socially indistinguishable from any other regiment and thus it was forced to accept men of a type that would not have joined it in the earlier years of the war. Yet although Bunhill Row had to enrol any group of men the recruiting offices sent down to it, there is evidence to show that the LRB did still continue to receive its more familiar type of recruit. Boys such as Stephen Forrow, who had spent over seven years in the London Diocesan Church Lads' Brigade, a recognised cadet unit, could then be called up to the LRB aged 18 years 5 months. In April 1918, after having attained the rank of sergeant in the CLB, Forrow was recommended by his former commander to the LRB for his 'integrity and perseverance'. After seven months training he was then sent overseas.[339] Forrow and some of his colleagues of the 1918 intakes were fortunate to join the 1st Battalion, and of course the battalion itself was delighted to receive them. It would have been equally delighted to have received the boys of the Aiv platoons from the 3rd Battalion after the annihilation at Gavrelle, rather than the hugely mixed bag of recruits it did absorb in April 1918. If it had been possible to post the majority of the drafts despatched from Blackdown to the first line unit, it would have made the task of rebuilding the broken battalion that much easier. However, the BEF still insisted upon dispersion and, it is to the varied collection of Durham coal miners, ex-cavalry men and under 19 year olds assembling at St Aubin, that this study should now return.

CHAPTER XIII

The London and North-Eastern Rifle Brigade

After the 64 survivors of the German attack on Gavrelle were pulled out of the line on 29 March, they marched north-west to the village of St Aubin. The Staff work was excellent because here, while the men took a hasty dinner, a draft of 399 men arrived to join the battalion. Three days later another 226 turned up, and during the course of the four weeks following Gavrelle, a total of 854 men joined. In common with the other battalions of the 56th Division, the LRB had to accept men from a wide diversity of regiments, but the recollections of the remaining LRB men were that the newcomers were from the Durham Light Infantry or Northumberland Fusiliers. The impression given by Smith is that they were from a battalion of Durham miners which had been broken up to provide drafts. He talks of them having a 'mutinous air' because they had not been posted to one of their 'Doorham Divisions' and complains that their marching discipline was not that expected in the LRB. Wallis too believed that the first 400 were practically all Durham miners and that they were among the last of the men to be called up under the Derby Scheme. In reality though, the composition of the new battalion was more complicated and complex than these rather simplistic recollections imply.

Archie Groom, who had been fortunate to miss the attack on 28 March, was nearer the mark. He certainly remembered some of them as northerners, but also says that there were youngsters only just called up, instructors out for the first time, as well as a number of troops who had been in France. This final group were accompanied by their own regimental NCOs. This coincides with the view taken by the Regimental History of the Queen's Westminsters. The Westminsters received men who had actually been fighting with various north country regiments during the preceding weeks, but who had been wounded and sent down to the Base. On recovery, they arrived at the Westminsters complete with wound stripes, service chevrons and good conduct badges.[340] The 4th London's camp in 168 Brigade was apparently transformed into a 'mild imitation of the Tower of Babel'. The London Scottish received men from the

Gordons, Royal Fusiliers and Home County regiments.[341]   According to Smith, the 'London Division' was London only in name.[342]

It is impossible to get a precise picture of the 'new' LRB because many of the men posted to it again retained their old army numbers.   However, by a study of the casualties and the awards lists, it is possible to identify various groups.   There are certainly men from the Post Office Rifles, the Poplar and Stepney Rifles, the Blackheath and Woolwich battalions, and the Hackney Rifles.   There were also about 50 youngsters of an Aiv platoon from the Civil Service Rifles and some men from the London Cyclists Battalion.   Undoubtedly, however, the majority of the new men, the 399 who joined on 30 March, came from the Rifle Brigade.   This again is only half the story.   These men had been posted from whatever their original regiments had been, to a Territorial unit of the Rifle Brigade only a short time before they were drafted overseas.   A total of 59 of them were to die before the Armistice, and from the information given in *Soldiers Died* and the CWGC registers a fuller analysis of this draft can be made.   Twenty-two of the dead came from the DLI and eight had come from the Northumberland Fusiliers.   As they were all in their twenties or thirties, some of these soldiers may well have been former miners whose call-up had been deferred, while others may have been like Rfn Hardy, who had come from the disbanded 2/8th Battalion of the DLI.   Besides these men, there are others who were a lot younger and were clearly joining the LRB at the beginning of their active service.   These troops, who, like their colleagues from Northumberland and Durham had been issued with and kept their Rifle Brigade numbers, came from the RASC, the Cavalry and the 13th Training Reserve.   These boys tended to come from the Midlands rather than the far North, although to the genuine LRB men this geographical difference was probably academic.   To complete the impression of a battalion of north country men, the out-numbered LRB-trained soldiers might have realised that apart from the accents originating from the towns of Tyne and Wear and the Black Country, there was also a smattering of Yorkshire from men who had been posted *via* the Rifle Brigade from the West Yorkshire Regiment.

This second major transformation of the LRB in respect to its non-commissioned men was thus completed within a month, but what of the officers sent to command this heterogeneous battalion?   Perhaps the most obvious qualification was that any commander should be something of a polyglot and one who had the ability to understand and treat men who were very untypically LRB.   Groom and Smith immediately noticed the difference in the way the senior officers reacted to their new charges, although Smith also remarked that once Husey had lectured the troops on his expectations of them, they changed for the better.   Twenty-one officers joined the battalion during April and May, and remarkably, only three of them were not from the LRB.   John Godward rejoined after taking an Instructor's course in England and C.H. John returned from serving briefly with III Corps' School.   Former Clr-Sgt George Vaile, commissioned into the 2nd Battalion before being transferred to the 3rd, was also drafted to the 1st Battalion in May.   These men knew the ways and traditions of the LRB, and another four of the new arrivals had also served with the regiment in France.   These included the first of the four former sergeants of 'A' Company of the 2nd Battalion, Wisbey Wright.   Eight of the remainder had enlisted as riflemen in the 3rd Battalion in either 1916 or 1917, and had been commissioned into it - products of 'Johnner' Johnson and Tom Malone's Officer Class.   One other young subaltern, H.B.

Waters had served overseas with the 6th Sussex until being commissioned and posted to the LRB, while the final junior officer to join the battalion, was Leslie Gyton. Gyton enlisted in January 1914 as a 16 year old bugler, but when mobilisation began, being under age, he was posted first to the 2nd Battalion and then to the 101st Provisional Battalion. In 1916 he moved to the 3rd Battalion and was commissioned the following year. These newly-arrived 2nd Lieutenants were all young men and came from a variety of schools, some of which had already produced many officers for the LRB. The outstanding characteristic of the group is that none of them appeared to have attended any of the principal public schools; council schools and the company schools were the norm, although one man, Thiede, had attended university in America.

As these men arrived to take up their duties, the battalion bade farewell to two of its most popular and respected officers. In May, Ralph Husey was promoted to Brigadier-General and appointed to command 25 Brigade in the 8th Division. It was still a fairly rare occurrence for a Territorial officer to be promoted to such a rank, especially in a Regular division, so it was with a great deal of trepidation and diffidence that Husey left to take up his new command. The genuine LRB members of the battalion and those who had served for any time under Husey knew that the regiment was losing an exceptionally brave and gallant officer. His contribution to the life and welfare of the regiment, both before and during the war, was immense, and his departure, while being viewed as an honour to the regiment he had served so assiduously, was also tinged with genuine and profound regret. Husey's new command fell victim to the renewed German offensive near the Chemin des Dames at the end of May and he died from wounds received while rallying men of his brigade's shattered battalions from his usual position of command - the front. This quiet, but inspirational, determined and skilled soldier died in German hands on 30 May 1918. After being the driving force behind the record-breaking Brighton March, Husey started the war as Captain of the old 'A' Company. He was wounded seven times during the war and was awarded the DSO and Bar, the MC and mentioned in despatches four times. His position as OC the 1st Battalion was taken by his old friend and former stockbroker, Charles Burnell.

Before his departure, Husey wrote a compassionate and sympathetic letter to Dick Wallis. Wallis was torn between accepting the offer of returning to England to take a place on a Senior Officers course, or staying with the regiment he so loved. He was clearly reluctant to leave the battalion, but appears to have been persuaded by Husey's concern for his health:

> *God knows no C.O. in the B.E.F. ever had a better Adjutant or Second in Command, but I did honestly feel that it would be a damned shame if I didn't get you a rest, as I know and know that you know that you are not fit, and if you ever cracked, you would crack so badly that you would be an invalid for years...Honestly Dick, if you don't take your full six months you will be a fool, and I consider an ungrateful fool, and I should feel really hurt if you attempted to rejoin the battalion or any other unit before your time was up.* [343]

Wallis was convinced and received a extremely complimentary report on his abilities and suitability for command on completion of the course. Like Husey's departure, Wallis' also dealt a great blow to the morale of the few remaining originals. He shook each of the Transport section by the hand because to him they were the only few representatives of the battalion that had travelled with him on the *Chyebassa* and who had endured and survived the tumultuous experiences of the succeeding three years. Although his technique in handling men was different from Husey's, Wallis had made a significant impact and impression upon the battalion through his efficiency. The keeness to impart to all newcomers his knowledge and love of the regiment's traditions did much to weld the varied and diverse drafts to the battalion rapidly into an efficient and unified unit.

A rare and vital glimpse of the composition of a company in the newly constituted battalion in mid-1918 is provided by a lengthy report of a trench raid found in the LRB papers. The report, written in a service notebook, lists the objectives, details of the covering barrage and other such information vital to the success of the raid and, of more importance to us, it also gives the names of the men of 'D' Company who were to undertake the operation.

The purpose of the raid, on German trenches lying immediately south of the main Arras-Cambrai road near Tilloy, was identification of enemy units by securing, if possible, live prisoners. One of the new officers, Capt Cecil Tabberer, who in 1914 had landed in France as a private with the Queen Victoria's, led a patrol out into No Man's Land during the night of 5-6 June. This was followed five nights later by another night reconnaissance under the command of 2Lt J.P. Gee. There is no comment on HQ's reaction to the order to conduct a raid, but it is probably safe to assume that as daylight raids demanded by Brigade or Division were normally dreaded by battalions, it would hardly have been received with alacrity. Nevertheless, it was decided that 'D' Company, with Lieutenant F.D. Hancocks commanding, should undertake the raid and that it would take place on 12 June. Hancocks was an experienced company commander and had enlisted in the LRB in May 1914 after having served for a short time in the Cheshire RFA (T.F.). He crossed in the *Chyebassa* as a private, was commissioned in France following the devastation on the Somme in October 1916 and, as one of the few survivors of the battalion after the 28 March, was promoted Lieutenant in April 1918. As OC he was to remain at the raid HQ with seven men, including CSM Maskell. Maskell must have been one of the NCOs mentioned by Archie Groom who arrived in April with a draft from their own regiment - in this case the Blackheath and Woolwich Battalion.

The attacking force was divided between Numbers 13, 14 and 15 Platoons. The first two groups would consist of two runners, two stretcher bearers and 22 raiders, while 26 men of Number 15 Platoon would constitute the third party. Covering fire while the raiders were in the German trenches would be provided by the Lewis gun platoon of nine men, with another four forming a 'nucleus garrison' and a further four Lewis gun men attached to Number 13 Platoon. The names and numbers of the men are all recorded in the *Army Book 152*, and, by using the serial numbers as the guide, a detailed picture of what by June 1918 must have been a typical company of the LRB can be drawn.

Only one member of the group, the OC, Hancocks, had been a pre-war soldier of the regiment, while only another seven had enlisted as, and been trained as, LRB men. The longest serving of these was Rfn S. Bailey, Hancock's batman, who had joined the 3rd Battalion early in 1915; three others had been with the battalion in France since mid-1917. The bulk of the raiders are what Smith would have categorised as 'Doorhams', but their origins were a little more complicated than that. Most were certainly from the disbanded DLI and Northumberland Fusiliers battalions who had been posted *via* the Rifle Brigade to the LRB. But there were also several who came from other regiments. There were, for example, a couple of men from the West Riding Regiment and another, Rfn Dawes, who had come with the draft from the RASC. The remainder were a hugely assorted bunch. Some were certainly men who had been wounded while serving with other units of the London Regiment, while there were also just under a dozen of the 18 year olds from the Civil Service Rifles rushed out from their 3rd Battalion after the March offensive. They were part of the group drafted to the LRB at the same time as Rfn Angel and his comrades of A13 Platoon from Blackdown were despatched to join the CSR. Finally, two men, Sgt Lovett and Rfn Durrant, had been posted from the Post Office Rifles and had retained their original numbers.

The second lieutenants detailed to lead the platoons were very inexperienced men as all three had only joined the battalion in France as recently as April. Having enlisted in 1917, 2Lt H.G. Coles was one of the young officers commissioned from the 3rd Battalion and was destined later to become the 1st Battalion's intelligence officer. John Gee, from the Grocers' Company School, had been commissioned from the Inns of Court OTC in November 1917, a month earlier than Coles. The third subaltern, Edgar Thiede, had attended Princetown University before enlisting in the 3rd Battalion in October 1915. He had been commissioned at the same time as Gee and was later to be wounded near Angreau five days before the Armistice.

During the frenetic action of the raid these officers would be relying on the more experienced NCOs to execute their orders and keep the men moving. Numbers 13 and 15 Platoons would have four each and Number 14 two. Preparations had been thorough and extensive, each of the officers and the NCOs having reconnôitred their ground and the route to their particular objectives at least twice. The British trenches offered no effective ground observation over the German lines so all information on the enemy had to be gathered from patrols and aeroplane photographs. In preparation for the operation Lt Hancocks sent down for 94 'raid jackets' and, at the same time, queried with the Adjutant the point of leaving the mens' identity tags behind when every man's box respirator had the name, number and often even the regiment of its owner written on it. Hancocks proposed instead that the raid should be conducted without the gas masks, but that they should be left in the front line ready for the raiders' return.

The assault went over in daylight at 15.00 hours on 12 June under cover of a box barrage and plenty of smoke. Two German machine guns were brought to bear on them, one firing very erratically while the other was soon silenced by the barrage. The German wire proved no obstacle and, on entering the German trenches, the raiders spotted one particularly large and deep dugout, with four entrances. A lot of discarded digging equipment lay around which suggested that the Germans had been working when the barrage fell. During the course of the raid the enemy in fact remained below ground - 'not coming out to fight' as the report later stated, although 24 bodies were counted. It was later thought that six of them had been killed by grenades thrown by the raiders, while the remainder appeared to have been caught by the shelling. The corpses were identified as members of the 23rd Pioneer Battalion, 2nd Reserve Company. Unable to find a live German and having bombed all available targets, the British evacuated the German lines and returned to their own through a very sparse German counter-barrage.

Brigade HQ was clearly pleased with the effort, praising the preparatory work achieved by the patrols and accepted that the failure to secure any prisoners was a consequence of the deep dugout. The report went on to describe the stunt as a 'complete success as the enemy's losses were undoubtedly very grave'. *The Times* of 14 June carried a report of a 'successful daylight raid' and in a later piece mentions Hancocks by name. The Corps Commander rounded off the proceedings by sending a message through Brigade offering his 'congratulations on success...Another time they must remember that live Boches are of value to us'.

But what of the men who undertook the operation? The initial report stated the following casualties: three killed, eleven wounded and one missing. From the *Soldiers Died* list the actual total ended up as seven killed or died of wounds, including two of the youngsters from the CSR, which thus leaves seven wounded. The men initially reported as missing was the former RASC man, Rfn Dawes who, according to a later report by Sgt Frudd, appeared to have been wounded by a British shell. He was carried back to the British wire but, despite a later patrol led by 2Lt Thiede and Sgt Frudd, his body was not recovered. Eight men were recommended for awards for their part in the operation; both Rfn Bailey and Rfn Elleray were eventually awarded the Military Medal. Bailey received his for bringing in four wounded under fire, while Elleray's was for showing 'great initiative and boldness' by bringing back a German Light Trench Mortar. Sgt Lovett, formerly of the POR, was given a 'Mention', and was later to receive the Military Medal for his work during the crossing of the Honelle in November.

For a proportion of the troops, and perhaps even the majority, this was their first taste of offensive action. Despite their very disparate military backgrounds, this assorted group of original volunteers, Derby men and conscripts had rehearsed and executed a well prepared and difficult operation. Once its success became known, the return to even this limited form of active warfare should have done much to develop unit morale. This was particularly important at a time when the battalion was beginning to suffer from the appearance of another insidious killer, influenza. Furthermore the affair should have confirmed to Brigade and Divisional HQs that only two months after its virtual annihilation at Gavrelle, and having had little opportunity to reorganise and absorb its new men, the LRB was again a unit capable of undertaking the risky business of a daylight raid. As a postscript, however, by the Armistice, another seven of those who took part in the operation would be dead.

The months since the battle at Gavrelle had been occupied with trench tours and working parties in the area to the south and south-east of Arras. One of the men from the Rifle Brigade had been killed as early as 5 April, but on the whole, casualties had been light with only two killed and 23 wounded in the space of two months. Two officers had also left with wounds and were replaced by Cecil Tabberer and the former Adjutant of the 2nd Battalion, Lt Cope. By June, RSM Bottomley who had gone to the 1st Battalion in the same capacity when the 2nd Battalion had been broken up, had also gone home for a time and was replaced by A/RSM Barrett. Barrett was one of the few remaining of the July 1916 draft from the 7th Middlesex and it is a mark of how far the battalion had changed, as well as the extent of the integration of the Middlesex into the regiment, that one of these men should be promoted to the highest non-commissioned rank. Barrett was awarded the DCM in June and another recipient of an award that month was RQMS Hamilton. As the senior non-commissioned member of the regiment, he was given the honour of receiving the first regimental number of the new series in May 1917. In recognition of his twenty-five years unbroken service to the regiment, Hamilton was awarded the MSM.

June was also the month when the battalion once more began to sustain a significant number of casualties. John Sutton, the young member of A10 Platoon who had been separated by injury from his colleagues when they were posted, lost one of his new friends, Alan Hudson. Hudson was one of the very few men from the north-east to enlist in the 3rd Battalion and was killed when a lone shell exploded near to a group as they lay sunbathing some way behind the line. Archie Groom had been gassed in May and went back to England, a fellow member of his old 26 Platoon from Fovant took over his Lewis gun team. This man, Charles Heather, was killed with three others of his team during a German raid on the Kensington's trenches. The battalion's Lewis guns had a notable success in the middle of the month when they brought down two enemy aircraft but on a less happy note, when the troops returned from that tour to the camp at Berneville, large numbers of them went down with 'flu'. Smith talks of the 'majority' being affected and that to 'many' of them it ultimately proved fatal.[344] Most were apparently treated in the camp but the *War Diary* records that over 200 were sent off to the hospitals in the space of five days. None of the deaths in June or July of men serving in the battalion are stated as being a consequence of 'flu', although one, Rfn Baker, died of pneumonia in Le Havre. All the others are specified as either being killed in action or dying from wounds. Thus it is difficult to substantiate Smith's claim. What is clear, though, is that it would be a considerably under-strength and decidedly ill battalion which moved back into the front line at the end of June.

In total the losses for June had been 19 killed and 23 wounded. This was followed in July by another four deaths. Once the impetus of the German offensives had been contained these summer months saw a period of consolidation and then preparation on the part of the Allies. The LRB's experience was one of routine: training, marching, concert parties and baths occupied its time but it was clear that this reasonably peaceful existence could not last for ever. Those men of the disbanded 2nd Battalion who had remained with other units of the 58th Division took part in the opening of the Allied offensive in front of Amiens on 8 August, and their former colleagues in the 47th Division joined in a few days later. The other London Division currently in France, the 56th, was to begin its contribution to the advance in the sector formed by the triangle of the old Roman roads from Arras and Bapaume which coverged on Cambrai.

As the troops of the LRB marched in very warm weather, to Saulty on 21 August, they were unaware that they and the rest of 56th Division were being transferred to Byng's Third Army. They were now part of a growing force gathering to throw the Germans from the high ground roughly along the Bapaume-Arras road. The division's first objectives were the villages of Boyelles and Boiry Becquerelle and the German reserve trenches which lay to their east. A huge force of artillery was collected to help the infantry, who would also be supported by the RAF and III Tank Brigade.

However, the troops of 56th Division had had no opportunity to reconnôitre the ground and neither had the divisional artillery had the chance to register its guns. The infantry of 168 Brigade, who were to lead the attack, had a tiring march from St Amand to Blairville during the afternoon of 22 August, and then had to slog another three miles during the night to their forming up positions. The LRB and 169 Brigade were still some miles behind, but following the successful attack by the 4th London, the Kensingtons and the London Scottish, the battalion moved to the former German trench which lay to the east of the two villages on 24 August. The attack was held up in several places by the fire from German machine guns and, once the objectives had been secured, the enemy drenched their former positions with mustard gas. The LRB suffered from this during the night of 24-25 August, and then had to withstand violent shelling during the following day. It was to remain in its present position while the attack continued. This time the assault was led by 167 Brigade towards Summit Trench, a northern extension of the St Leger Reserve. Once more, the infantry were supported by tanks and stormed Summit Trench but could press on no further. Machine gun fire from the village of Croisilles, the broken ground and belts of uncut wire broke up the attempt by the 8th Middlesex, but the division was ordered to continue the attack the following day. Major-General Hull protested that, as there were by now no tanks available for support and because the area was still very strongly held, the likelihood of advancing very far was decidedly remote. Corps HQ took cognisance of Hull's remarks and amended its orders to instruct the division to take Croisilles and a trench beyond it running up the valley of the Sensee towards Fontaine les Croisilles. Croisilles village was an outlying section of the Hindenburg Line and thoroughly organised for an all-round defence. Patrols sent out by 167 Brigade found that the wire was deep and that any approach over the crest from Summit Trench immediately brought heavy fire down upon it. Consequently, 167 Brigade was ordered to remain facing the village while a new attack by 169 Brigade would try to out-flank to the north.

The LRB received its orders during a short lull in the shelling and was instructed to relieve the 7th Middlesex in Summit Trench. The battalion moved up and the relief was complete by 20.30 hours on the night of 26 August. Casualties had so far been light but from zero hour, only 30 minutes after the relief had been made, German fire immediately began to take its toll. On emerging from the trench, the two attacking companies shook out into artillery formation and advanced for 400 yards until machine gun fire from front and flanks forced them to take cover in a sunken road north-west of Croisilles. Darkness fell, and at 03.30 the men were ordered to withdraw back up the slope to their start line and re-group for a frontal attack in the morning. The enemy seemed to anticipate the attack and laid an intense barrage down upon Summit Trench from 09.00 to 11.00 hours. The British artillery opened its barrage ten minutes before the infantry went over at 09.36 and immediately the leading company, 'A', began to draw fire from the village and the trenches to the north. Again, the advance wilted in the face of heavy casualties and orders were received in the afternoon to try again. This attempt was made further north by two companies who used the cover of former German trenches to reach the Sensee before they too were held up by uncut wire and machine gun fire. Tom Burroughs took part of his company across the road linking Croisilles and Fontaine to join up with the 2nd London and the rest of the battalion came up at dusk.

These two days had seen the LRB make its first real attacks since the Battle of Cambrai nine months before, and thus the activity witnessed during the period had been a new experience for the large majority of the participating troops. The tactics used were still those of the earlier years of the war because, although the battalion had advanced about 1700 yards, the ground over which they had fought, and the resistance put up by the enemy, was reminiscent of previous battles of attrition. This was not yet quite the period of open warfare. The ground was a labyrinth of disused trenches and wired obstacles and there was also the sobering knowledge that these villages were merely the outposts of the Hindenburg Line. The main defences remained skulking menacingly a little further to the east. It was against this deep defensive barrier that the LRB were to attack the following day.

On this occasion, the attack was to be launched by the Westminsters with the LRB in close support. 'A' Company, which had been unable to move since the attack of the day before, had now rejoined the battalion, but overall the strength of the attacking companies must have been very weak. The *Official History* records that the 2nd London had only 11 officers and 193 other ranks, of whom 35 were with Battalion HQ.[345] The LRB had certainly lost four officers, while 'A' Company, under the command of the former 2nd Battalion man Vere Welch, is known to have been only 60 strong. Nevertheless, the Westminsters attacked south-eastwards towards the ruins of Bullecourt, scene of the 2nd Battalion's blooding over a year earlier, and immediately ran into trouble. The supporting creeping barrage was effective, but the troops came across huge belts of wire strung longitudinally between the trenches of the Hindenburg Line. In an effort to get around these obstacles, the companies veered to the north with the left companies of the LRB following in support. The three companies of the Westminsters took up position in trenches north-west of the village of Hendecourt, which lay about a mile to the north of Bullecourt. Here they were joined by about half of the LRB. The right companies moved up over the open ground, using the trenches for direction, and had arrived correctly in front of Bullecourt. However, in the face of intense machine gun fire from the village and sniping from Germans, who had emerged from dugouts once the barrage and attackers had passed over them in their rear, the attack faltered. Attempts to out-flank the machine guns failed until Tom Burroughs, with the help of a trench mortar battery and two companies of the Kensingtons, led an attack which took and consolidated a line of trenches about 1200 yards to the north-west of the village. Night was beginning to fall and back at Battalion HQ signaller John Sutton was aware that Colonel Burnell had little real idea of what had happened during the day:

> *The situation was all very confused. We kept getting runners coming in with messages from 'C' and 'D' Companies that they were taking up position in grid reference such and such. But the colonel kept saying that they were in front of the wrong village and had been mixed up with another division. He spent ages on the 'phone to Brigade trying to find out if they knew anything, but they seemed to be just as confused as us. Eventually we learnt that two of our companies were in fact in the right place and then we received orders that we were to continue the attack the next day. Well, the colonel said a few choice*

> *words about how was he going to do that when his battalion was*
> *spread all over the globe, and then began to issue orders which would*
> *get the men sorted out and into some sort of order.*

The two LRB companies, with the troops of the Westminsters and 2nd London in front of Hendecourt, had in fact ended up in the area allocated to 57th Division. Zero for the attack on 24 August was put back until 13.00 hours in the hope that the battalions could have sorted themselves out by that time. When the hour arrived, however, there had been no accurate news of the whereabouts of 'C' and 'D' companies. So, 'A', 'B' and Battalion HQ moved up to the assembly positions which, owing to a German withdrawal during the night, was now about 300 yards in front of Bullecourt. The London Scottish of 168 Brigade led the attack up the gentle slope towards the village, supported on their left flank by the 325 men who constituted the entire attacking strength of 169 Brigade. These troops, amounting to a weak battalion rather than a brigade, pressed on into the ruins and took the village in the face of stiff opposition and were relieved by 167 Brigade during the night. Even then, their troubles were not over. German high explosive and gas shells escorted them as they stumbled wearily down the valley towards Croisilles, Boisleux au Mont and then rest.

This period of fighting had constituted a severe test for the LRB and its sister battalions in the division, and one which had made a deep impact upon their respective strengths. The LRB's ration strength at the beginning of the month had been 35 officers and 989 men; by the end of August it had fallen to 25 and 669. Probably no more than two-thirds of these totals were actually available for fighting, so by looking at the casualties sustained during the period, some indication of how weak the battalion was, after this its first offensive action for eight months, can be made.

The *War Diary* gives two lists of casualty figures for the month of August. The later, revised one, gives 54 killed, 17 died of wounds, 226 wounded and two missing among the non-commissioned men, with three officers killed and 13 wounded. It seems likely that there had been only one death in the 1st Battalion, that of 18 year old Arthur Lane, formerly of the CSR, before it moved up to its assembly area on 22 August. Calculating from the *Soldiers Died* lists, there were a further ten deaths between 21-26 August while the battalion was waiting to move up to the attack, which leaves the bulk of the 79 known deaths to have occurred between the 27-29 August. This total breaks down further into 32 men who enlisted in the LRB, 23 with LRB numbers but who were posted into the regiment from elsewhere, and 24 who came from the Rifle Brigade. Within the first two groups, 11, the highest proportion yet, have non-London residential addresses and, as might be expected, the majority of the men from the Rifle Brigade came from the North-East and Yorkshire. In total, 31 men or 39% of the dead who had served in this *London* battalion, within a *London* division, came from outside the capital. Furthermore, only four out of ten had actually enlisted in the LRB.

Among those who died were two former Rangers and survivors of the Gavrelle battle, and one of the Middlesex draft of July 1916. Another four young members of the Aiv Platoon from the CSR died, as did two of the men who had arrived with CSM Maskell from the Blackheath and Woolwich battalion. Rfn J. Harris, from Bethnal Green, had also joined the battalion since April. He had served with the Ox & Bucks Light Infantry in the South African War and was then later transferred from the Queen

Victoria's to the LRB. He was 37 years old, while Cyril Franklyn, who died of wounds at Ligny St Flochel, was a mere 19. Franklyn was probably a member of A14 Platoon at Blackdown, but missed being transferred with the rest of the platoon to the 3rd Rifle Brigade and, instead, ended up in the 1st Battalion LRB in June or July. The inscription on his headstone, *Soon, soon, to faithful warriors cometh rest*, was all too apt. CSM Price was one of the men from the 3rd Battalion rushed out to France in April. Another employee of the Northern Assurance, Price had re-joined the LRB in November 1914 and spent three and a half years as a musketry instructor. A married man from Forest Gate, aged 35 years, he was killed on 29 August. Two further original members of the 1st Battalion, Wilfred Chappell and Leo Cousin were killed, while Fred Gorner and Bernard Freeman, original 2nd Battalion men, but who were now serving with the 1st, both died of wounds received during the battle.

Twenty-seven men, or 34% of the total, have no known grave and their names were later inscribed on the Vis Memorial to the Missing, built about five miles to the north of where most of the men died. Twelve of the dead, including CSM Price were buried in the HAC Cemetery at Ecoust, eight in the large Bucquoy Road Cemetery near Boisleux St Marc and another four at Bac du Sud on the Arras-Doullens road. The latter two cemeteries were made by the several casualty clearing stations that were sited in the localities. Three more men died of wounds and were buried in Bagneux British Cemetery which lay near four other casualty clearing stations at Gezaincourt, just south of Doullens. Other men who died in the battle lie in a number of cemeteries dotted around the contested zone and the rear areas.

If the *War Diary*'s total of 299 casualties is accepted and that only two-thirds of the ration strength were available for fighting purposes, it means that the battalion had suffered about 45% casualties. While not as high a proportion as was sustained at Gommecourt, Glencorse Wood or Gavrelle, it was sufficiently large to have a significant impact upon fighting strength. The battalion was to receive only 30 reinforcements during September, so that when the nucleus personnel, Transport etc. had been removed, the number of men capable of undertaking the next operation must have been no more than 350. When 'B' Company and what few men of 'A' could be found attacked on 29 August, only about 100 men could be mustered. Capt Wilfred von Berg, the Adjutant, underlined the extent of the casualties when he wrote to a fellow officer in England. Von Berg complained that there were few men left who could tell the tales of individual gallantry performed during the operation. He then went on to emphasise that, despite the stiff fighting, the troops had stuck it well, and that 'morale has never been better'.[346] Furthermore, divisional morale had apparently soared because it had advanced further than any other in the same time. Von Berg, at least, found this new type of warfare 'awfully exciting' and was 'quite looking forward to the next 'binge'.[347]

Von Berg also praised the qualities of the junior officers, but their ranks were severely depleted during the month; two subalterns had been killed and another seven wounded, although two of the nine were attached from other regiments. 2Lt E. Frey had been a runner with the 1st Battalion before being wounded in September 1916 and, on recovery, was granted a commission. He died on 26 August and four days later, Vere Welch, late of the 2nd Battalion, was also killed. Welch, from Harrow School, and the only son of a colonel, had been wounded in June 1917 and died as he led his men of 'A' Company towards the enemy machine gun nests in the ruins of Bullecourt.

Still only 21 years old, Welch was buried alongside some of his men in the HAC Cemetery. Two other captains who were wounded were the former Clr-Sgt George Vaile, who left the battalion just before completing his nineteenth year in the LRB, and Tom Burroughs. Apart from three months in 1916, when he was attending Officer Cadet School, Burroughs had served with the 1st Battalion since January 1915 and had been rifleman, sergeant, bombing officer and adjutant. Now, as a company commander, he was badly wounded in the abdomen while directing the local attack of 'B' company, the Kensingtons and the trench mortars against the Germans on 29 August. He was evacuated but never fully recovered from his wound and died in 1920.

Finally, earlier in the year, two officers had returned to England to train as RAF personnel. One of them, L.G. Hummerstone, still officially a member of the regiment, had returned to France as an observer with 12 Squadron. He was killed on 21 August and was buried in the same cemetery as other members of the LRB who died later that same month.

On 1 September the nucleus personnel rejoined the battalion as it rested and cleaned up at Boisleux au Mont. The first three weeks of that month was relatively quiet, the time being taken up with reorganising, training, and trench holding. Despite some persistent shelling, casualties did not make any significant impact upon the already depleted strength, and on 21 September, just before the battalion was about to undertake another attack, a draft of 13 officers arrived. Three of the subalterns were from other units of the London Regiment, but the remaining ten came from the LRB itself. Three of them were the former sergeants of 'A' Company of the 2nd Battalion; Terry, Cockerell and Belither. They were now rejoining the fourth of the group, Wisbey Wright, who arrived in April. Another of those 'one pippers' who assembled at the Transport lines on 21 September was Lancelot 'Sunny' Jessop. Since recovering from the wound he received immediately before zero on 1 July 1916, Jessop had been with the 3rd Battalion. He subsequently applied for a commission and began his training at Number 1 Officer Cadet Battalion, housed in Alston Hall, Newton Ferrers in Devon. Jessop was posted to 'B' Company - the same one as Jack Terry and Donald Cockerell. The 145 cadets in the Company were divided alphabetically into four platoons and were immediately thrown into a hectic six months of training and sports. Inter-platoon games and competitions encouraged *esprit* and team work and, in July 1918, the three LRB cadets were commissioned and sent back to the 3rd Battalion at Blackdown to await posting abroad.[348]

On 16 September the new second lieutenants received orders that they were to proceed overseas and were granted two days embarkation leave. Terry, who spent those days shopping and saying farewell to his family and fiancee, disembarked with the others at Boulogne at 04.30 on 19 September. Two days were spent 'messing around' at Etaples, before they moved up to the 56th Division's Reception Camp at Etrun. The night was spent in a comfortable chateau and the following day they moved first to the Transport lines, and then to Battalion HQ which was housed in a huge cave system known as the Schmidthohle. The battalion had moved the short distance from Vis to this position, which lay to the south of the Arras-Cambrai road near Dury crossroads, in preparation for the attempt to cross the Canal du Nord. Terry was posted to 'C' Company and welcomed the renewal of the great friendship he had formed with Wright since the early days of the 2nd Battalion. There was opportunity to develop the friendship further during the next three days as the battalion trained and rehearsed its part in the coming attack. On the dark, drizzly night of 25-26 September it relieved the 21st Battalion Canadian Infantry in the line and made final preparations for the attack.

The conditions at the front were very poor. The line was a series of largely unconnected, waterlogged shell holes and the role of the LRB was to rise from these brimming pools and mop up northwards along the Agache valley. If the main attack further east was successful, the twin villages of Sauchy-Cauchy and Sauchy-Lestree, lying to the east of the Canal du Nord, would then be cleared and consolidated. The Canadians on the right flank would lead the initial assault and they would be followed in turn by the Westminsters. The latter's fighting strength for the operation amounted to a mere 15 officers and 318 other ranks - probably a similar total to that of the LRB. Despite this paltry number of men, however, the subsequent attack was 'the most successful operation in which the QWR took part during the whole war'.[349] The LRB too found the going relatively easy. Zero was delayed for an hour because the Canadians had been temporarily held up at Marquion, but 'B' Company cleared the west bank of the canal and the remainder crossed almost without opposition. A good many Germans were captured and new positions were taken up in the enemy's former pill boxes and dugouts.

The next five days were spent being severely bumped and gassed. The LRB tried to establish a continuous line with the battalions on either flank, but German patrols were very active and sectional positions were frequently raided. A week of rest near some magnificent former German baths in Sauchy-Cauchy was spent in salving, training, concert parties and a never-ending search for canteens which could supply supplements to the rations. This happy interlude ended with a return to the 'line'; dismal positions comprising dripping brick-lined culverts and dank funk holes in the canal bank. The shelling remained heavy, and at times it became impossible for the officers to visit their posts owing to the intensity of the enemy machine gun fire. Jack Terry's diary, which at its most lucid is barely even laconic, dryly records the unpleasantness of the positions but does brighten up when detailing the occasional evening walks and talks with Wright and Tabberer, his company commander. Similarly, when the companies were relieved by the 46th Canadian Battalion and marched back to Sauchy-Lestree, the later experience of lorry jumping was described as 'good fun'. On the other hand, this enjoyment was tempered by the soreness of raw flesh on his inner thigh consequent upon his experimentation with horse-riding.

When considering the importance and nature of the objectives taken, the losses during September and October had not been severe. Three of the subalterns who joined the battalion earlier in September, Adams, Cross and Keep, were killed, along with probably 14 other ranks. The picture is somewhat complicated by the deaths of some 14 soldiers listed as LRB, but who were fighting with a battalion of the Rifle Brigade in the near vicinty. These were young troops from an Aiv platoon of the 3rd Battalion whose bodies were later removed to a cemetery further over to the east of the battlefield. The number of wounded during the two months is not recorded in the *War Diary*, but it does give a figure, 53, for September alone. If the fighting strength of the LRB was similar to that of the Westminsters, then the men available for the next operation, if no significant number of reinforcements arrived, must have dropped to well below 300. Officially, the ration strength at the beginning of October was 32 officers and 603 other ranks, so the arrival of a pamphlet recently issued by the General Staff, caused some wry amusement at Battalion HQ. Designed to deal with the decreasing strength of units, OB/1919 laid down that 21 officers and 642 men should be kept for 'fighting'; 90 other ranks for 'administration' and 10 and 50 for the nucleus personnel. This would then allow 118 for what was called 'supplies for reinforcements'. The grand total of these various groups amounted to 33 and 900, which meant that there was a minimum of 732 other ranks for fighting and administration alone! In other words the actual fighting strength of the battalion was at least 50%, and probably a great deal more, below its supposed establishment.

As the troops of the London Division made their way back to Haute Avesne, those who had been in France for any length of time, might have reflected on what had been a new experience. The crossing of the canal had revealed a hitherto unknown characteristic of the German soldier: his apparent willingness to surrender in large numbers. Of course Germans had surrendered in previous battles, but only after putting up a fierce and spirited resistance. In the villages east of the canal, the British were surprised to find the Germans readily prepared to give themselves up to the very weak London battalions. This was the first time that the division had witnessed what amounted to a moral collapse of the enemy - an observation from which they took great succour.

The period of rest during the last two weeks of October were spent in miserable weather. Practice on the ranges, inter-company football, church parades and for the officers, censoring mail and the occasional 'rag' in the Mess, passed the time. Company dinners were held and the officers were invited to the Sergeants' Mess for meals on a number of occasions. Overall, there was an air of subdued expectancy amongst the men. They knew that they would have to fight again, but at the same time, there was the feeling that the Germans were, at last, on the run. The Transport had even been reorganised into two sections to take account of the new type of warfare. One of the echelons was to act more as a flying column, carrying SAA and grenades, to keep up with the advance of the infantry. The other group would follow with the less immediate needs.

The Transport section had in fact suffered a severe blow on the night of 25 September. The Transport lines were pitched near Upton Wood, just to the south of the Arras-Cambrai road, when German planes came over and bombed the camp. At least six of the section were sufficiently badly wounded, or burned in the subsequent fire, to be sent down the line. Four of them were men who joined the section when it was reformed in 1915, and another was one of the two Transport Officers, W.A. Chrisp. Chrisp enlisted in August 1914 and served continuously, being promoted to 2nd Lieutenant in June 1918. His departure made a profound impact upon the section, for while he had remained its essential core or fulcrum had appeared secure. Now, with Chrisp's evacuation, the departures over the years of the other older hands, previously not so noticeable, suddenly appeared in sharp reality. Although there were still at least eight 1915 men, only two original members of the Transport remained; Cpl Charles and Connibeer. So many of the group of friends who had decided in 1915 to stick together in the section and not seek commissions, had by now disappeared home with wounds, that Conniber no longer felt that the obligation binding. Consequently, he applied for a commission and left in October 1918. Of the other old hands, QMS Hurford had been burnt in the bombing, but remained with the battalion, and Gerrish was soon to return to England as a gas casualty. Aubrey Smith probably still had a dozen colleagues in the section who had served with him since the Voormezeele days, but the night's bombing had really finished off his immediate close circle of friends.

For the former Aiv boy, John Sutton, changes in personnel had not affected him as severely. As a signaller in Battalion HQ, he knew very few of the men in the companies and really only came across linesmen and runners when they reported at HQ. Living therefore in semi-isolation, Sutton's 'circle' was even more immediate than Smith's. It seems that the men in the various HQ details were largely, if not exclusively, from the London area as Sutton could not later recall that so many of the contemporary battalion were from the North-East. During the next few heady days of the great advance across open ground, Sutton was to be kept very busy:

> *I remember them as being very exciting days. We seemed always to be*
> *moving forward and shifting positions almost from day to day. Even*
> *for me, who had only been with the battalion since April, the change in*
> *what we were doing was tremendous. I suppose as a signaller I was in*
> *a better position than most to know what was going on, but somehow,*
> *I don't really think I ever knew where we were or how the advance in*
> *general was going.*

By the time the LRB moved back to the front, the Allied advance in the Corps' sector had passed well to the east of Cambrai. Buses and lorries carried the battalion to billets in Lieu St Amand on 31 October, and it spent the next day resting and tidying up. The next day, Saturday, battle equipment was drawn at Maing and the troops resumed their march across open rolling country to relieve the 6th Duke of Wellington's near Famais. Major Dick Wallis had returned from his six month Senior Officers' course and was attached to his old battalion with no specific job other than as a roving observer. This was a position he relished for he could move about the lines at will. Another familiar face that had just returned from other duties was Frederick Crews. He had come back from a sixteen month assignment at GHQ Lewis Gun School and was now one of only two men serving with the battalion who had spent their entire war in France or Belgium. Crews and Wallis rejoined a battalion which was, however, still severely understrength. A draft of 24 arrived but the ration strength still only amounted to 631 other ranks.

On receipt of news from Brigade that the Westminsters had discovered a German withdrawal along the entire front, the battalion moved off early on 3 November. The cold, wet and very dark night was spent in Saultain, a village still occupied by civilians, and on the following day the LRB supported a successful attack by the Westminsters against Sebourg. The German artillery pounded the village in retaliation and an uncomfortable night was passed in cellars and sunken roads. At 04.00 hours on Guy Fawkes' Day, the sodden troops assembled in a lane to the east of Sebourg for an attack on Angreau. Under cover of a creeping barrage the attack went in at 05.30. Jack Terry led his platoon into the village - the first non-captive English man that the civilians had seen - and the village was secured. When the attempt was made to resume the advance later in the day, the troops were held up by heavy shell and machine gun fire coming from the east bank of the Honnelle and the woods beyond. The LRB sheltered in the previously undamaged houses and cellars of the village, and to add further to their discomfort, were treated to a liberal number of Yellow Cross gas shells.

During the night orders arrived instructing the battalion to continue the attack at dawn. Once the company officers were informed of the objectives and time, the platoon officers briefed their NCOs and men. Terry spent a few minutes talking with his platoon and warned them that the attack was bound to be difficult. The Germans he explained, were well dug in amongst the wooded slopes and still held the village of Angre on their left flank. The weather, a constant and penetrating drizzle, did not encourage the men who were also told they would have to wade across the three-feet deep Honnelle.

> *After I had finished telling the chaps that it would not be an easy task,*
> *there was a bit of a silence. Then this was broken by one of the*
> *Geordies who simply said: 'Ha'wae. Let's gann kill the boogers'. We*
> *attacked under the creeping barrage and crossed the river. Some of*
> *the Germans bolted from their cover, and one tripped up some wire*
> *and fell into a shell hole. His foot was still trapped in the wire and he*
> *was hanging headfirst down the hole. One of my men took very careful*
> *aim at him from about ten yards and fired. It was just like potting c*
> *rabbit.* (J. Terry)

So weak were the two attacking companies, that they advanced with gaps of about 20 yards between each man. The Germans allowed them to push on into the edge of the woods before they counter-attacked in an effort to close the pocket of the salient which the advance had created. The attack on the LRB's right flank had failed which meant that the battalion's own success was now to cause it problems. The officers realised they were in danger of being surrounded and ordered their men to retreat to the west bank of the river. Terry organised a Lewis gun team to fight a rearguard and gave the other men covering fire as they re-crossed the river before then withdrawing themselves. Most of the men regained the west bank safely but, during the subsequent shelling, Donald Cockerell was killed. Terry's sadness at the loss of his old friend from the 2nd Battalion was compounded when his batman, Tom Denham, was killed by shrapnel as they marched back to Sebourg. Denham, from Gravesend, was one of the Aiv draft to arrive from the Civil Service Rifles in April. Although they had known each other for only a matter of seven weeks, Terry had been touched by the young man's concern for his comfort and welfare. Cockerell and Denham were buried in Angreau Communal Cemetery two days later with 12 other men of the battalion who fell in early November. Among them were CSM Walker of 'B' Company who had come from the Bedford Regiment, a 1st Battalion original, Sgt John Frost from Denmark Hill and the last of the July 1916 Middlesex draft to die, L/Cpl Arthur Valentine. As far as the LRB was concerned then, the crossing of the Honnelle had been a bloody and unsuccessful operation. Thirty-three other ranks were killed or later died of wounds received during those early days of November, and somewhere around 120 more were wounded. Apart from Cockerell, 2Lt Barnes, attached from the 18th London, had been killed and four other junior officers wounded. The actual fighting strength of the battalion must have reached a new post-Gavrelle low of some 250 rifles. However, with a timely sense of irony, the battalion was to receive its largest draft of reinforcements since April - after it had withdrawn from the line for the final time.

Unknown to the men, the attack on 6 November was to be the last offensive action taken by the LRB. The armistice came into effect when the battalion was resting in billets at Erquennes. Terry's diary entry for that day was its usual succinct self: 'Did nothing. Hostilities ceased; troops very bucked. Rather cold'. The note that the troops seemed animated runs contrary to other contemporary accounts, which tend to record that the event was acknowledged in a less than sanguine manner. The *War Diary* merely mentioned that hostilities were to cease at 11.00, that the brass band played at guard mounting for first time and that the battalion was employed on road mending. Wallis observed the reaction when the order of cessation was posted outside the Orderly Room: 'No crowd collected to read and discuss...The first man to pass, read the order and then sauntered away; later two came along, stopped, read, spat on the road and left - no interest no enthusiasm'. The *War Diary* of the neighbouring 4th London recorded a similar reaction: 'Everybody appeared to be too dazed to make any demonstration. Men were much less cheerful than they had been for some days'.[350] Some, like John Sutton, clearly believed that the signing of the armistice did not necessarily mean that the war was actually over:

> *We knew nothing and certainly did not know that our advance was so important. The first indication I had of it was seeing the Colonel standing on the street corner at Erquennes and saying, 'Abdication of the Kaiser'. We certainly did not realise the significance of the word 'armistice' which according to my school days indicated a pause and not necessarily the end of war. 11 November was a quiet day for me and a few others and the absence of gunfire was odd. As far as I can remember it took the surrender of the German Navy to convince us that the war was really over as far as the fighting was concerned.*

Back in England, the 3rd Battalion at Blackdown Camp celebrated Armistice Night with a huge bonfire. E.B. Harding, still with the Training Battalion along with Maurice Howard as an instructor, recalled that the fire was so large that other units in the camp imagined that the LRB had mutinied. Further north at Duxford aerodrome, Graham Williams viewed the celebrations and the armistice itself as something of an anti-climax. Having left the 3rd Battalion to take a commission in the RAF, Williams reflected gloomily:

> *How very much I wished that I could have been with the LRB in France...This prospect (i.e. release from the trenches) must have given them great cause for rejoicing, and I would very much have preferred to be there, with the LRB instead of here at Duxford, among men who were comparative strangers, compared with those of the LRB, with whom I had shared so many varied experiences.*

If Williams had actually been with the battalion in France, he would have been hard put to find many of his old friends still there. For the few remaining older hands, as well as the more recent arrivals, the experience of war was over and the impact of peace about to be felt. This was not quite as simple a transition as might have been anticipated and, for the time being, the soldiers still had a job to do. Army discipline had to be maintained to ensure that when the thorny problems arising from what appeared to some to be an unfair and discriminatory system of demobilisation raised their contentious heads, the battalion would not disintegrate morally, as well as physically.

CHAPTER XIV

Captivity and Demobilisation

The Armistice on the Western Front not only brought peace to the troops in the opposing lines, but also signalled the end of captivity to those who had been taken prisoner in earlier engagements. In fact, very few LRB men - probably less than a dozen - had been captured until the Gommecourt attack of 1 July 1916. It seems likely that 56 other ranks and Capt de Cologan were taken by the Germans that day, and a Regimental Prisoner of War Fund was established in September 1916 to help alleviate the hardships endured by the prisoners. Most of those captured at Gommecourt, such as Basil Houle, Ernest Evanson, H.C. Sidwell and F.S. Crisfield, eventually ended up in the same prison camp for at least some part of their captivity. However, before they were reunited in the camp, they had first to recover from any wounds received that day.

When the train carrying the wounded Basil Houle arrived at Minden in Westphalia, he and the other British casualties were put into the annex of the main hospital. There were no nurses to greet them, only paper bandages to bind their wounds, and to the dismay of the British they found that the wards were already occupied by all sorts of men suffering from an assorted variety of diseases and injuries. These included a Russian dying of syphilis, another emaciated compatriot, and a mad Frenchman who was continually trying to escape dressed only in his cotton pyjamas. Fortunately medical help did eventually arrive. After three weeks the British had their uniforms returned, and those with only slight wounds were transferred to the main camp on the outskirts of Minden and put on light work.

The camp was very large and laid out in square sections with one for the British, one for the French and one for the Russians. There was also an extensive German military camp near the main gates as well as the usual machine gun towers and barbed wire. In the centre of the British square, which was bounded by the sleeping huts, was a bathhouse containing showers and coal-fired water heaters. There were also some primitive stoves where the captives could heat anything they might have to cook. The camp was mostly occupied by Regulars and some Territorials who had been taken in the early stages of the war. The Regulars especially were a very hard-bitten bunch who, the new arrivals were told, had endured a terrible first few months of captivity. Stories were told of how they were detailed to clean out cavalry stables while the Germans threw scraps of bread into the horse muck and laughed as the starving British scrambled to retrieve them. They were extremely bitter, refusing to salute German officers and stubbornly took the subsequent punishments. Conditions had improved since the Red Cross had begun to look after the welfare of prisoners, but the new captives were surprised to note that there were no British NCOs in the camp above the rank of corporal.

The explanation given for this unusual state of affairs was that the junior ranks had rebelled against the senior NCOs and forced the Germans to move them to a separate camp. The Regular sergeants and warrant officers had apparently acted in the same way *after* capture as they had before, except that they were now taking orders from German rather than British officers. The starving British prisoners were allegedly paraded in the snow - wounded and unwounded together - and put through physical drill and bellowed at in the same manner as on the barrack square at Aldershot. The story continued that as soon as the other ranks acquired some regular food through the Red Cross and recovered their strength, they revolted and chased the senior NCOs from the camp. Those old sweats who remained took the 1916 arrivals to their hearts and, by sharing out their own food parcels, made sure that all had one reasonable meal a day. Once relatives at home had been informed that their men-folk were captives, food parcels began to arrive. The men divided themselves up into groups of five or six so that should any delay in the receipt of one man's parcel occur, the others in the group could keep him supplied. Basil Houle's section consisted of himself, Sidwell and Brown from the LRB with Morris of the Victoria's and Hughes of the Westminsters. Evanson, Rippingale, Hoddinott and Crisfield and the remaining LRB men were scattered about in several other groups.

Life for the prisoners in Minden Camp was not unpleasant and the light work at least saved them from suffering the extremes of boredom. In March 1917 this relatively relaxed existence was replaced by one of hard and monotonous work. Approximately 250 British troops, including, it seems, all the LRB who had been at Minden, were transferred to Camp JO 32. This camp was, in reality, a coal mine at Westerholt. There were already about 2000 prisoners working in the mine and when the new men arrived at the gates, some of the original men came out of their huts to greet them. Houle and the others watched in amazement and then anger, as the latter group were immediately driven back with kicks and rifle butts. The new arrivals joined in the general pandemonium, and for a few minutes something of a minor riot occurred. Eventually the German guards restored order, but the party of 250 had already decided to refuse to draw mining clothes and stood fast when the Germans ordered them to do so:

> *The Germans then began to get stuck in amongst us, and after a few of*
> *us had been knocked out with rifle butts there were bodies with bloody*
> *heads lying about all over the parade ground. The Feldwebel, through*
> *one of the British who could speak German, said that he wasn't*
> *interested in what we did or didn't do underground. His orders were*
> *to see that we went down the mine and he would carry out these*
> *orders. He said we could please ourselves whether we went down*

conscious - but go down we would. When we saw he wasn't bluffing,
we gave in and drew our mining clothes. (B. Houle)

Life underground was hot and hard. The British were teamed with German miners and there were always armed guards moving around. The common language used by all prisoners was a broken German; a man purporting to come from the Queen Victoria's acted as interpreter when any lengthy communication needed to be made. There was little spare time, but Sundays were days of rest. Many Sunday afternoons were spent listening to a band formed largely by bandsmen taken during the Retreat. They had somehow obtained a reasonable variety of instruments and according to Houle 'played beautifully'. Most of the prisoners apparently settled down to make the most of what little comforts could be enjoyed, but it seems that the older, married men with families found the adjustment most difficult. Some men never settled at all and were contiually planning to escape. A few managed to get away four or five times, but were usually soon caught and then spent their time in the punishment cells planning their next attempt. The majority of the men, however, were so tired after their eight-hour shift down the mine, that all they wanted to do was find something to eat and go to bed.

After they had been beaten up by a group of German guards, Houle and about 20 others, decided upon an escape attempt. This party had been transferred from underground work to surface jobs and, as a consequence, their bread ration was cut. The British struck in protest and were marched into the colliery boiler room. As they entered, guards armed with solid rubber truncheons attacked them and then left them to cook for twenty-four hours. At the end of the period they were offered water and then agreed to go back underground if their bread ration was restored. Despite their complete lack of knowledge of tunnelling and with no facilities for disposal of spoil, the men then decided to dig a tunnel. The intention was that once they had made their escape along the tunnel, the entire British contingent could follow. After a few week's hard digging, the tunnel was betrayed to the Germans by the man who claimed to come from the Queen Victoria's [351] After a period in the punishment cells, the group were put back to work underground.

Although that attempt failed, others were more successful. Evanson and Sidwell escaped and were free for five days until recaptured. These two LRB men and an Australian named Gardiner were in what the Germans called the 'Bad Men's Party'. Evanson and Gardiner teamed up for their next escape and crossed into Holland in February 1918. They travelled on to Rotterdam where Evanson tracked down the branch office of the London firm of accountants for whom he had worked. The two men were put on a ship for England and Evanson spent the rest of the war as RQMS with the 3rd Battalion at Blackdown.

The month before Evanson's escape, Houle was moved to work on a farm in Westphalia. Here he was well-treated by the elderly owner and his wife, food was more plentiful and he was even allowed to cycle around the countryside visiting local taverns. He was certainly luckier than the LRB men captured at Cambrai. At a fund raising rally for prisoners' benefits held in July 1918, Major-General Sir Frank Lloyd, commanding the London District, claimed that for the approximately 400 LRB in German hands, the 'horrors of war had been accentuated fifty times' by the way the enemy treated their prisoners. Captain Nobbs, who had been repatriated following his blinding and capture at Leuze Wood, spoke after Lloyd and explained how a LRB men captured at Cambrai had been put to work with 168 other British captives behind the lines: 'They were kept there for three months, working from 6am to 7pm unwashed, unshaved and in rags during the cold of November and December...beaten with butt-ends...food consisted of black bread and watery soup...At the end of three months they were taken away in a state of collapse. Out of the 168 men, 12 were dead and 90 admitted to hospital'.[352] It seems unlikely that any of the reported dead were LRB men as all those who died during the three or four months after Cambrai can be accounted for as having died of wounds, killed in action or died of disease in England. However, when the Armistice came, six LRB prisoners remained unaccounted for and no trace was later discovered of their fate.

At the beginning of January 1918 there were reported to be 107 LRB prisoners in Germany and 14 interned in Switzerland.[353] The number rose following the German offensive in March, not only by those taken at Gavrelle, but also by a number of former 2nd Battalion men captured while serving with the Artists. It was explained earlier that the actual number of LRB captured at Gavrelle cannot be accurately determined - it could have been as many as 360, although the Germans officially notified the Red Cross that they had taken 250. This was certainly an under-estimate as several men are known not to have been on the list of names provided, and in fact were never reported as actually having been captured. The extent and speed of the German advance, and the number of British they captured, cleary caused administrative difficulties to the Germans. Men from the same regiment and captured in the same place were often split into different parties as they marched away from the front. Victor Rushton, as we know, never saw another LRB man again, although CSM Bamford and CSM Diplock, also captured at Mill Post, did later end up in the same camp. Smith believed that two LRB men escaped from Douai soon after capture and re-crossed the lines,[354] while another account of what is probably the same story, suggests that at least one of the men, a sergeant, was one of the former Rangers.[355] Sid Amatt spent a few days salvaging equipment and waste near Douai, sleeping in brick ovens and eating sauerkraut and black bread, both of which played havoc with his digestive system. His twentieth birthday was spent huddling for warmth in a half-built cottage *en route* for a another village that was to be 'home' for the next few weeks.

This village was used as a staging post for German troops as they moved up or from the line. Amatt and a group of about 15 men from various regiments were detailed to keep the billets clean, sweep the roads, load and unload trucks and railway wagons. They had a reasonable amount of liberty and could wander about fairly freely provided they were available when needed. Eventually, this rather pleasant existence was ended when the party were transferred to the large camp run mostly by the East Yorks. It was here that Amatt came across the young boys from the LRB whom he considered could not take the hard life of a prisoner particularly well. The camp was not far from Conde, north-east of Valenciennes, and the men were employed loading barges on the nearby canal. On one occasion they were marched down to the canal in the usual way and then told to dig a trench which had been marked out by tapes:

> *Well, there was a lot of murmuring, lots of Scots who said, 'We can't*
> *have this, it's against the Geneva Convention'. The Unteroffizer*
> *ranted and raged, threatened us with dire extinction. Then he lined up*

30 guards who loaded their rifles and said that if we didn't start digging he'd shoot every tenth man. So we had to line up, jockeying for position, but before he got far with his numbering sequence, a mounted officer with a black patch over his eye came up and struck the Unteroffizer with his whip and ordered the British to march back to the camp and to get double rations. (S. Amatt)

The sound of the Allied guns could be heard thundering away in the distance. In October the British prisoners were divided into groups and told they were to begin a march, *via* a very round-about route, which would take them to Germany. Being very weak and undernourished, the pace was slow, and on the second night the exhausted British were billeted in the church at Peruwelz. Amatt and another took their chance while the guards relaxed, and escaped. The two men risked knocking on the door of a nearby house, and the owner, a Belgium doctor, gave them food before taking them upstairs where they found another three British soldiers. These men had been hiding there for some time, and after two weeks of a cramped existence in the attic, half a platoon of British cyclists were spotted passing through the town. The cyclists were followed shortly by a troop of Canadian cavalry, to whom the captives gave themselves up, and were eventually transported back to Calais.

One man who was not so fortunate in his experience of captivity was the far-from-robust, former employee of the *Watford Observer*, Herbert Borrett. Mrs Borrett had received a letter from Husey dated 31 March 1918 which 'regretted' that her husband was reported missing. Possibly fearing the worst, her hopes would have been revived a few days later when a POW card arrived from Borrett himself. Various letters and cards followed, written in such a tiny hand and densly packed lines that the German censor instructed Mrs. Borrett to tell her husband 'not to write so closely'. The letters frequently requested his family to send soap, socks, cigarettes and clothes etc. Although his letters were reaching Watford, as late as 25 July Borrett had still heard nothing from home. Any parcels that had been sent had thus clearly not arrived at their destination. Borrett was probably in the same camp near Conde as Amatt, because in early August, the 34 year old died in Conde Hospital and was buried in the nearby communal cemetery. A letter from a fellow prisoner to his widow explained that the nursing sister who had looked after Borrett said that he had died from heart failure. The sister had also apparently bought some flowers for the funeral and attended it herself. The epilogue to the sad affair came in September 1919 when Mrs Borrett and her young son Cyril were eventually granted £19 2s.8d. by the War Office as a War gratuity.

Herbert Borrett was one of the 18 LRB men to die in captivity. By November 1918 there were at least 484 LRB men reported to be prisoners in German hands[356] and the regiment had made increasing efforts during the year to try to ensure that they were supplied with parcels from home. Since the creation of the Regimental POW Fund in 1916, money had been raised by concerts given by the 3rd Battalion's orchestra and donations made through, for example, the LRB Old Member's Club. But the great increase in the number of prisoners after March 1918 had meant that the monthly sum required to provide individual parcels had risen from £268 13s. to £1,345 10s.[357] Parcels were despatched regularly, but when the men taken in March were repatriated, they told the regiment that they had not been in the camps they were supposed to have been in, and consequently never received the parcels. Similarly Basil Houle, despite being a prisoner for over two years, was adamant that he never received a parcel from the LRB. However, the two CSMs taken at Gavrelle, Bamford and Diplock did both receive regimental parcels. Initially a letter arrived from a young girl written in a form of code which told them to watch out for something special arriving shortly in a parcel. When the package appeared, it contained a tin of Keating's Powder, inside which was secreted a complete series of maps showing the area between their prison camp and the Swiss border.

In January 1920 the *LRB Record* claimed that six men had escaped from captivity and managed to get home. Unfortunately, the article failed to specify who the men were. Evanson has already been mentioned; Carle is supposed to have swum the Danube, while Rippingale is also acknowledged to have made a complete escape. The two men who made it back through the lines from Douai brings the total to five, but it has not been possible to identify the sixth man.

When Houle heard that the war was over he made his way back from the farm to a camp at Friedrichsfeld. Scenes of near-anarchy greeted him on arrival: German sentries smoked on duty and as there was no German officer to be seen, the entire camp was under the perilous command of German NCOs. The British spent the next week threatening to burn the camp down if the Germans did not provide transport. Eventually a train was arranged which dropped them about a mile from the Dutch border. Most of the 460 LRB who were repatriated appeared to have arrived home in either December or early in the New Year. Once back in England, Amatt was given two month's leave and went home to Walthamstow where his mother had hung a black-trimmed photo of her young son in uniform.[358] Tom Short, who had been saved from a German bayonet by the shout of an officer after dusk on 1 July, arrived home on New Year's Day, while Basil Houle was at his parent's house in Hendon for Christmas.[359] The men's demobilisation generally came through while they were still officially on leave and they only had to report to the Crystal Palace for the procedure to be completed. Their experience in getting out of the Army was relatively easy; for their former colleagues still serving with the LRB in Belgium, the task was not always as straight forward.

The end of hostilities finally came so quickly that there had been little preparation or thought given to how the men should be occupied once the fighting was over. The principal objective of most was to get out of the Army as soon as possible and try to re-establish themselves in civilian life. The expectation was that demobilisation would be set in train almost immediately, and that the fairest way would be to release those whom had served longest first. Wallis realised that it would not be quite as simple as that and believed the men did not appreciate that several million men, all with an expectation of employment, could not all be thrown onto the commercial and industrial world at the same time. In fact it was to be late December before the first LRB man was sent home for demobilisation.

The important thing as far as the officers were concerned was to keep the men occupied in, preferably, useful work and thus avoid any discontent from setting in. Fourteen officers joined the battalion after the Armistice, but only four of them were actually from the LRB. However, three of them had served with the battalion in France before, and the other, Captain Cecil Marriott, had spent most of the war with the 3rd Battalion. Harold Crisp was on the *Chyebassa* as a runner and was commissioned in

July 1916. After having been in the surplus personnel for the Gommecourt attack, he was wounded in Leuze Wood, and on recovery went first to the 2nd Battalion and then in January 1918 to the London Irish. Second Lieutenants Crane and Hood had both served abroad for some months, and the former had been wounded during the August fighting around Bullecourt. These men thus knew the ways of the LRB, but the other ten new officers did not. In view of the fact that the LRB was still comprised of a large proportion of men from the Rifle Brigade, on paper, this might not have seemed too much of a problem because nine of the subalterns were actually from various units of the Rifle Brigade. However, as most of the other ranks who had come from the Rifle Brigade had spent so little time in that regiment, there had been only a minimal chance of them developing any sense of identity with it. Should there be any long delays in getting the demobilisation scheme under way, as platoon commanders, these new young officers, together with their more experienced colleagues like Terry, Jessop and Wright, would be in the fore-front of defusing any potentially disruptive element within the ranks.

A scheme of route marches, road mending and PT was worked out, and the inevitable inter-company football tournament began. In preparation for the forthcoming general election, some attention was paid to education, explanations to the men on how the democratic system worked, and lectures on how the demoblisation procedure would operate. There is a possibility that there may have been some reaction to the apparent delay in demobilisation because on 3 December, Jack Terry's diary makes a reference to 'D' Company trouble'. The *War Diary* makes no mention of the incident, nor of any special meetings of officers, but Terry's entry for 4 December says that the early parade was cancelled and that the later one was addressed by Colonel Burnell. The next evening this was followed by an officers' conference and during the evening of 6 December, Terry held what he calls a 'pow-wow' with his own platoon. It is difficult to know whether this activity was a consequence of any discordant element in the ranks complaining about delays - and John Sutton who was still at Battalion HQ does not recall any untoward incidents - or whether it was a combination of factors. The weather had been very wet, the men's billets were not particularly good, several parades for presentation of medals had been washed out, and it was a long march to the nearest baths. The fact that Terry, a man who dearly loved the LRB, recorded these entries in what is normally a very succinct and mundane diary, suggests that they did hold some special significance for him. It might not be purely coincidental that from the second week in December, there was a lot more football being played and Captain Cecil Tabberer lectured frequently to the troops on topics such as the 'Rise and Fall of Great Empires', the 'Rise of the Muslem Faith' and the 'Early History of Rome'.

Working parties were still found, largely to clear snow or mud from the roads, but all work was suspended on Christmas Day. The officers drank champagne after the morning church parade and then waited on the troops at dinner. A 'rag' in the nearby chateau occupied the officers during the afternoon and then some of them visited the homes of local civilians. The next stop was for a drink in the Sergeants' Mess and then the sergeants were in turn invited back to the Officers' Mess. The day was rounded off with 'a sing' in Wisbey Wright's billet. However, the obvious enjoyment and good spirit of Christmas was rudely shattered a few days later by an incident at the battalion concert. On Boxing Day, the first man from the battalion - a miner from the Leeds area with only two months active service - was sent down to the Base *en route* for demobilisation. When the Transport section heard the news they were incensed and decided upon a protest. There were still at least a dozen men in the section like Aubrey Smith who had been in France since early 1915, and they resented priority in demobilisation going to men who had only just come out. The protest took the form of a constant barracking by the section throughout the concert and ended with the officers, who were the main performers, leaving the 'stage', 'choleric with rage'.[360]

There is no record of any disciplinary action following the demonstration, perhaps because the LRB officers, although deploring the protest, could sympathise with the men's frustration. Smith says that the disorderly element was kept well in check and that the reputation of the regiment was never actually blemished during this period. There are no further references to any similar incidents and the battalion seems to have spent January attending concerts, pantomimes, playing sports and finding the odd working party. Tug-of-war, football and boxing matches meant that teams frequently travelled into Mons, where Guinness was available, and for the officers, soirees and dances at the Hotel de Ville helped to pass the time. Naturally, as the demobilisation machine gathered momentum there was a continual reduction in the numbers of men and officers available for the teams and outings. By the end of February, nine officers and 442 other ranks had disappeared home, although there had also been drafts of 109 and 89 arriving in November and December. These were very largely young boys like Stephen Forrow, late of the London Diocesan Church Lad's Brigade: some of them were despatched in March and April to the Queen's Westminsters who were to form part of the Army of Occupation. Fortunately, John Sutton was not among this party. Instead, he was posted to the signalling staff of 169 Brigade and spent a fair proportion of the next four months sight-seeing in Brussels.

Meanwhile, the old-established faces of the LRB continued to disappear from the battalion. Dick Wallis had left in December to command the Kensingtons for a time, and Jessop returned in late January, about the same time as Smith. When looking back on his war experience, Smith considered that it was only because he had belonged to a regiment which employed a sensitive method of discipline and actively fostered regimental *esprit*, that he had kept his sanity and nerve. Of his draft from the old 'Q' Company of the 2nd Battalion, only he and Sgt Munday - the man who had possibly averted a crisis after Glencorse Wood - remained with the battalion until the Armistice.[361] Jack Terry took a group of men through the demobilisation machinery in February and, having discharged his responsibilites, spent the next two weeks at home going to shows and visiting relations. He returned to the battalion and a lunch in Mons with Wright for only five days before being told he was off for demobilisation the next day. After a hectic few days he eventually caught the 06.30 from Fovant, arrived home at Waddon and, as something of an anti-climax following his four and a half years of service, spent the afternoon unpacking and writing letters.[362]

The drain on the strength continued until what was left of the battalion moved to Antwerp. By a strange quirk of coincidence, as several of the officers wandered around the quays, they spotted the *Chyebassa* tied up along side. Hopes that they might sail home on the same vessel which had taken them to France and active service, proved unfounded, and on 24 May 1919 the cadre embarked with 3 officers, 27 other ranks and 40 wagons on two vessels, the *Arbroath* and the *Hunsclyde*. After four and a half years in France and Belgium, the 1st Battalion was returning to England with only three of the men that had sailed with it on 4 November 1914.

The regiment had just one more official duty to perform before it reverted fully to its peacetime role - an official parade past the Mansion House. About a thousand former members turned up to take part in the parade, including Graham Williams, Maurice Howard and Jack Terry, but only three *Chyebassa* officers are thought to have taken part - Burnell, Hugh Johnston and Addison Denny. Despite the supreme professionalism shown by the regiment during its long and distinguished war service, its final parade in its war-time condition allowed the alleged amateurism, for which the Territorials had been so ridiculed in the pre-war period, to re-assert itself. As Lt Col Burnell led the column past the Lord Mayor, the leading company commander - perhaps a little over- awed by the grandeur of the occasion - gave the command, 'Right wheel! - No! Left wheel! - No! Right wheel! - Oh damn it - go down Princess Street!'[363]

Aftermath

The immediate post-war period was one of uncertainty for the entire TF and thus also for the LRB. It was not until February 1920 that the regiment's future was confirmed, and once permission had been given, the battalion began to re-form along very much the same lines as it had existed before the war. The subscription of 25/- was reintroduced, and many former members came back to Bunhill Row to re-enlist. The attraction of rejoining the regiment and serving again with friends and colleagues from the war years was strong enough to persuade at least 36 former officers to relinquish their commissions and re-enlist as riflemen. However, after the initial burst of enthusiasm, recruitment slowed and numbers remained low throughout the 1920's. There were sufficient members though to make the annual camp and training weekends of military worth.

As the 1920's gave way to the '30's and the fascist dictators began to threaten again the precarious peace of Europe, the democracies gradually turned their attention to re-armament. Following Hitler's occupation of Prague, War Office permission was given for the Territorial Army to duplicate their 1st Battalions. When the LRB announced that it would again form a 2nd Battalion sufficient recruits enlisted to fill the new unit within 20 hours - quicker than the original 2nd Battalion had done in September 1914. Several of its officers from the First World War were still with the regiment, and to underline further the theme of continuity of service, when war broke out in September, amongst the other ranks were two 1914 men - CSM Rob Lydall and Rfn Maurice Wray. On embodiment, the 1st Battalion became the 7th Rifle Brigade, and the 2nd Battalion, the 8th Rifle Brigade. During the course of the war, the two battalions were to serve in Africa, Italy and Central Europe. Several 1914-18 members, such as 'Cherub' Angel fought in the war, while other former members, now too old for active service, performed duties as air raid wardens and Home Guard troops while daily working at their office desks.

Several post-war reorganisations again gave cause for concern about the regiment's future. Eventually, the LRB became one company of the newly formed 4th Royal Green Jackets and, following 'Options for Change', it has been re-roled as part of the Allied Reaction Corps - one of only eight from the entire Territorial Army. Although this role may seem far removed from its original purpose as a home defence volunteer rifle unit, many of the traditions developed since 1859 have continued and remain intact. Soldiers of the serving regiment are invited to the annual reunion, and former members are encouraged to make visits to the present HQ to watch the men train and take advantage of the facilities themselves.

Many of the former members joined one of the several veteran's associations formed after 1918. The traditional *Chyebassa* dinner, which had begun during the war, continued to be held annually on 4 November. At the 1922 dinner, 29 of the 129 diners were still serving with the regiment, and the highest post-war attendance was achieved in 1931 when 171 *Chyebassa* men turned up. So important was the anniversary that Harding organised a Calcutta branch of the *Chyebassa* Club, and there were other off-shoots in South Africa and New Zealand. This club remained exclusively for men who had sailed with the 1st Battalion in 1914 but, as early as 1924, John Stransom had suggested that membership should be opened to all former LRB men. His proposal elicited several hostile replies to the *LRB Record*, and a consensus finally emerged that the *Chyebassa* reunion should be retained, but that there should also be a full annual regimental dinner.

The 2nd Battalion Club continued to hold a separate annual dinner until well into the 1960's and there were also regular reunions of former Fovant and Blackdown training platoons. There were sometimes one-off reunions too, for example, the 25 Year Anniversary of the Brighton March. The war had taken its toll of the original men, but 42 survivors turned up for a dinner in April 1939. They calculated that when the war ended, there were three lieutenant-colonels, six majors, 17 captains, seven lieutenants, two subalterns and three riflemen of the original 60 marchers still serving in the army. However, as the years passed and the numbers attending each of the reunions dwindled, it was decided that the *Chyebassa* Club and the 2nd and 3rd Battalion Clubs should amalgamate to form the LRB Veterans Association. Today the Association also includes those men who had fought as 'LRB' during the Second World War. These men meet annually to renew friendships formed during their war experience, and although theirs was a different war from that of the earlier generation, the bonds of friendship and pride in their regiment are just as strong. They have inherited the sense of brotherhood, an identity and a loyalty that provided the men of 1914-18 with a unity of purpose and a comradeship which lasted throughout their lives. Its essence and significance was summed up after the war by John Stransom:

> [If the enemy] *had seen to it that none of the human machinery for enforcing discipline remained, there came in that hour to each and every man...esprit de corps. Its power was absolute and stronger than the strongest discipline, for it bound every man by the simple expedient of belonging to every man, so that he fought to retain his own, and saw to it that his comrade did the same.* (LRB Record, 1924)

Seventy years after demobilisation, Maurice Howard also reflected on his long association with the regiment and the Veterans' Club:

> *Perhaps I tend to romanticise, after all it was a long time ago, but I can't imagine serving with a better bunch of chaps. You knew you could rely on them and if you were ever in trouble and you spotted someone wearing a LRB tie, you knew you were 'quids in'. I suppose the LRB is just in my blood, and always will be.*

FOOTNOTES

The full title of printed sources and details of authors will be found in the section entitled 'Sources'. Except in cases of possible confusion, only the author's name will be given here. Similarly, the full title and catalogue references of unpublished sources held by the Public Record Office, Imperial War Museum, National Army Museum and Peter H. Liddle's archive, will be found in the earlier section.

1	Haldane, R.B., p.185.
2	Spiers, E.M., p.95.
3	ibid. p.162. In October 1907 the King met the Lord Lieutenants at Buckingham Palace and urged them to put the weight of their local influence behind the work of the county associations.
4	City of London Territorial and Auxiliary Forces Association Committee minutes, 1908-39. Guildhall Library, MSS 12,606/1. 5/3/1908. See Appendix Vl for a break down of the London Regiment.
5	ibid. 16/6/1908, and C of LT and AFA Recruiting Committee minutes, 1908-1939. Guildhall MSS 12,613,1 28/4/1908.
6	Harding.
7	C of LT and AFA Committee, op. cit. 5/7/1908 and 18/7/1911.
8	C of LT and AFA Recruiting Committee, op. cit. 9/10/12 and 8/1/13.
9	LRB company year books.
10	Williams, H.G.R.
11	In common with other rifle regiments, the LRB always referred to the bayonet as a 'sword'.
12	Sellwood, A.V., p.109.13 LRB Regimental History, hereafter cited as Regt. Hist.
14	Spiers, p.163.
15	Regt. Hist., p.52.
16	Price, R., p.228.
17	C of LT and AFA Recruiting Committee, op.cit. 14/4/08, and Committee, 2/11/10.
18	Cunningham, H., *The Volunteer Force* (Croom Helm, 1974). Cited in Spiers, p.92.
19	Williamson, H. *How dear is life,* p.60. Williamson's *Chronicles of ancient sunlight is* a semi-autobiographical account of his life. His main character, Phillip Maddison, of the Moon Insurance Co. enlisted in the 'London Highlanders'. Williamson himself worked for the Sun Fire Insurance Co. and joined the LRB in January 1914.
20	Green, H., p.37.
21	C of LT and AFA Recruiting Committee, op. cit. 10/6/14.
22	Ford, T. Murray, p.186.
23	Speech made by Dick Wallis to the London Scottish Veterans' Association. Reported in the *London Scottish Gazette,* May 1933.
24	Ford, T. Murray, p.185.

25   Myer, H.D.

26   For example, in 1909 the 2nd London decided that as they had exhausted the pool of potential recruits from North Lambeth and Pimlico, they would trawl for recruits in Kilburn and Willesden - areas untouched by any other TF unit. Grey, W.E., p.xxxiii

27   C of LT and AFA Recruiting Committee, op. cit. 13/11/12 and 8/1/13.

28   Another incentive for young men in business to join may have been the existence of the regiment's Freemason's Lodge which had been founded in 1882.

29   C of LT and AFA Committee, op. cit. 22/4/13.

30   ibid., 17/10/11.

31   Guildhall Library, 9386.

32   Official mobilisation instruction, LRB Collection.

33   Williams. A former milk-cart pony apparently broke the leg of Capt Lintott, the machine gun officer.

34   This appears to have been common-place among the London regiments.

35   Williamson, H., *How dear is life;* Williams also mentions the toilet doors.

36   Latham, R.

37   ibid.

38   Regimental histories of the respective London units.

39   Myer.

40   Letter dated 19.8.14 found in P. le May's papers, P.H. Liddle's archive. By 27/8/14 1600 men had enlisted in the 10th Royal Fusiliers.

41   There was a long tradition of sons following fathers into the LRB. For example, when F.S. Clark joined he was the third generation of his family to do so, and the sixth member to enlist.

42   Fry, W., p.11-12.

43   For example the Northern Assurance Co. The numbers of employees enlisting must have proved something of a financial strain on many companies.

44   *Official History 1914*, Vol. II, p.2-3. The footnote states that five units whose men had signed the general service obligation were the Northumberland Yeomanry, the Dorset Fortress Company, RE, 6th East Surrey and the 7th and 8th Middlesex. However, the figure of over 17,000 men seems high for those still actually serving with or who could be expected to rejoin these five formations in the event of an emergency.

45   ibid.

46   According to Esher, Kitchener had realised by 13 August 'that he will be forced to make use of the Territorials for foreign service while his new armies are in the course of formation'. Quoted in Simkins, P., p.44. See Spiers, E.M., p.185 for a discussion on Kitchener's initial reservations about using the TF abroad.

47   WO 162/23, Mobilisation 1914. The C of LT and AFA op. cit.

claimed on 25/8/14 that all its units were in possession of the required clothing and equipment.

48   *Official History 1914.* Vol. II, p.6.

49   French, Viscount J., p. 292.

50   Ian Hamilton to LRB Record Nov. 1928. The first TF division to go overseas and into action as a complete division, was the 42nd (East Lancs.) .

51   Lindsay, J.H., p.20.

52   Wheeler-Holohan, A. and Wyatt, G., p.19.

53   LRB Record, Aug. 1924.

54   Henriques, J.Q., p.8.

55   Savery later gained a commission in the Middlesex Regiment.

56   LRB *Newsletter* Nov. 1964.

57   Jessop, L. Letter to author.

58   Fry,W.,p.13.

59   ibid. p.15.

60   Latham, R.

61   Myer claims that 90 of his men in the 6th London were not fit to march and had to travel by train.

62   Both Williams and Harding praise Tootsie Hand's abilities.

63   Latham, R.

64   WO 159 19 X/L 00829, no date but probably written in November 1914. These rounded figures correspond fairly closely to those supplied by the Adjutant-General's Office. This source (WO 162/3) is generally considered to be more reliable than those supplied by the War Office.

65   Montague, C.E., p.10.

66   Published version of Lloyd George's speech in the Queen's Hall, 19/9/14.

67   Morris, J., p.6.

68   The 33,204 men who enlisted on 3/9/14 created the largest single daily total of the war, and from then on the figures declined. However, 12,527 enlisted on 11/9/14 and even though the daily average of the following week fell to just over 6,000, this was still too many for the system to cope with. So, in the second week of September, the height qualification was raised to 5' 6". Numbers enlisting then decreased to an average of about 2,500 a day. WO 159 19 X/L 00829 and WO 162/3.

69   LRB Record 1948. Two companies of 2/2nd London were recruited at about the same time from Westminster Training College. Grey, p.14.

70   Regt. Hist., p.69.

71   Latham, R.

72   Wallis.

73   Regt. Hist., p. 70.

74   Latham, B., p. 17.

75   Regt. Hist., p. 71.

76   Fry, p. 7.

77   Regt. Hist., p. 72.

78   ibid., p. 82.
79   Wallis quotes from General Seeley's book *Adventure* where the
        purpose behind the attack is explained.
80   Williamson, H., IWM tape.
81   ibid .
82   Roache is buried in the same plot in Rifle House Cemetery as men of
        the Rifle Brigade who were killed on 19-20 December.
83   Regt. Hist., p.85. Smith also remembered that many of the local
        people were pleased to discover that many of the LRB could speak
        French.
84   Williams.
85   Regt. Hist., p.70.
86   French, p.264
87   *Evening Times,* 27/3/15.
88   Williams.
89   Fry, p.22.
90   Williams.
91   Latham, R.
92   Fry, p.30.
93   LRB Record, 31/1/35.
94   Letter from Bobby Lydall printed in *Manchester Guardian,* 1/1/15.
95   Latham believes that there was one large hole, while Wallis thought
        that the dead were returned to their respective front lines.
96   Bates correspondence, quoted in Brown, M. and Seaton, S. *Christmas
        Truce* (Cooper, 1984) p.68.
97   Fry, p.30.
98   Williamson, H. IWM tape.
99   Operational orders, LRB Collection.
100   Latham, R.
101   Frank and Maurice Wray.
102   Latham, R.
103   ibid.
104   Fry, p.30.
105   The Germans put up lights in their parapets during the night before
        Good Friday, 1915. Rifleman Abery remembered that some
        conversation took place until the Germans threw over two grenades.
        (Letter to the BBC deposited in the IWM). Latham says that when the
        enemy suggested a truce, 'we weren't having any'.
106   Latham, B., p.25.
107   It seems likely that a 'live and let live' system did operate from time to
        time. M. Howard far preferred the Saxons, who were 'kindly and
        quiet', to the 'savage, troublesome' Bavarians. Occasionally the
        Saxons would fire off a few dozen M.G. rounds and shout out, 'Only
        making tea Tommy'.
108   Latham, R.
109   LRB *newsletter,* 1962.
110   Barrie, A. No sources given for the information.
111   Latham, B., p.21.

112 LRB *newsletter,* 1962.

113 ibid.

114 In 1973 Gadsdon remembered that the weather was 'on the whole dry', but later recollections and even contemporary descriptions of the weather can be deliberately or accidentally erroneous: e.g. one day when Captain Mason of the 4th King's was censoring letters, he discovered that one soldier had written: 'Its been raining and the weather's been awful and we've had a little snow'. Another man wrote: 'The weather is fine, and just lately it has been just like summer'. (P.H. Liddle archive).

115 LRB *newsletter,* 1973.

116 LRB Record, November 1919. It should be remembered that 11 Brigade was comprised of five battalions - viz. the four regular ones and the LRB.

117 Whitehead diary, 25/12/14.

118 Latham, R.

119 ibid. In 1962 Latham claimed that a professional actor in the LRB called Cunliffe wrote *The madamoiselle from Armentières,* and that he later joined the the 'Follies'. The Wray brothers did not accept Latham's claim, and there is no trace of a Cunliffe in the LRB during the Plugstreet period.

120 Regt. Hist., p.72.

121 Latham, R.

122 Whitehead letter 7/2/15.

123 Latham, R.

124 Harding.

125 Regt. Hist., p.75. On 7 January the LRB, for the first time, took sole responsibility for their own portion of the line. Their original stretch of line extended from the River Warnave south to the Estaminet - the trench being known as Essex Trench. It had one company in the line, another with its platoons divided between a farm 300 yards south-east of the Brewery, London Farm, Mountain Gun Farm and Red House and the third company formed part of the brigade's composite battalion. The fourth was in Armentières. See map 1 forthe locations of the farms.

126 The shortage of officers meant extra duties for those who were fit. There was little time for relaxation although the LRB did sign the 'Card' sent to *The Field* of 24/1/15 for the three hunt meetings held by the 4th Division.

127 Latham, R.

128 In the 1980's BBC TV used the IWM MSS to serialise the life of Willett in a programme entitled *Wilfred and Eileen.*

129 Harding.

130 Latham, R.

131 War Diary 11/4/15.

132 Canadians of the Saskatchewan and Manitoba battalions and men of the 46th (North Midland) Division had received their initial trench instruction from the LRB.

133	Williams.
134	Extract from an unnamed letter of 15/5/15 found in the Whitehead papers.
135	Williams.
136	Regt. Hist., p.91. That memories of the march figure so prominently in the recollections is not really surprising as peoples' earliest memories are often the best remembered.
137	Pocock .
138	Latham, R.
139	Whitehead diary.
140	ibid.
141	Latham, B., p.28.
142	Hember, V.
143	ibid.
144	Smith, A., p.43.
145	Latham, R.
146	Smith, p.47 and M. Howard.
147	Hember, V.
148	Williams.
149	Lance-Corporal 'Curley' Boston, shortly after being commissioned in the field, was awarded the DCM for organising and leading the wiring party.
150	Hember, V. and Wallis.
151	Hember, V.
152	ibid.
153	*Official History 1915.* Vol. I, p.295.
154	Whitehead diary.
155	Hember, V.
156	Whitehead.
157	Smith, p.57.
158	Wallis.
159	Herbert, A.P., *After the battle;* 'And we shall have the usual Thanks Parade, The beaming general and the soapy praise. '
160	Hember, V.
161	Whitehead.
162	Hember. V.
163	Wray, M. *Newsletter,* Nov. 1960.
164	*Official History 1915.* Vol. I, p.333.
165	*Newsletter,* Sept. 1983.
166	Belcher was later commissioned into the Queen Victoria's and survived the war. He died in 1953.
167	Williams.
168	*Newsletter,* Nov. 1960.
169	Hember, V.
170	*Official History 1915.* Vol. I, p.340.
171	`Official history 1915.* Vol. I, p.299.
172	ibid p.356.
173	Fry, p.24.

174 *A short history of the LRB,* p.46.
175 Harding's salary was £40 per year and this, with rises, was paid to him for the duration.
176 Williamson, H.W., *How dear is life,* p.61.
177 Wheeler-Holohan, A. and Wyatt, G., p.253.
178 *Daily Graphic,* 6/3/15.
179 *Daily Chronicle,* 12/5/15.
180 Latham, B., p.37.
181 Recruitment handbill in LRB Collection.
182 Wheeler-Holohan and Wyatt, p.253.
183 Letters to the author.
184 At least one man, Vivian Woodward, an international footballer, left the 2nd Battalion in order to take up a commission in the 10th Middlesex as soon as it began to recruit.
185 WO 159 19. X/L00829, 26/5/15H.
186 Hansard, 1915. 72.1651.
187 ibid.
188 Morgan's letter is attached to Schuman's account found in the National Army Museum.
189 Rev 'Tubby' Clayton speaking at the Regimental Memorial Service at St Botolph's Church. *Newsletter,* Nov. 1955.
190 This extract is taken from a letter signed by 'Gerald' found amongst the V. Hember papers. It is impossible to decide precisely who 'Gerald' was as there are several possibilities. Neither is it ever clear to what type of 'club' Gerald, Hember, Rivers etc. actually belonged. It is most likely to have been a local church group or a mixed sporting club.
191 An article in *The Sunday Times* of 20/5/73 by Bob Mainwood, a veteran of the London Scottish, claimed that discipline in the Scottish was stricter than in any other regiment and that it was largely administered by the men themselves.
192 Moran, Lord, p.175.
193 Manning, F., p.229.
194 Herbert, A.P., p.165.
195 Smith, p.247. Smith still uses the rank of 'Private' in 1916, despite the fact that the regiment had adopted the rank of 'Rifleman' in 1915.
196 Dixon, N.F., p.197.
197 Williams.
198 Smith, p.143.
199 Wallis.
200 Middlebrook, M., p.170.
201 *Official History 1916.* Vol. I, p.454.
202 ibid. p.456-7.
203 The German account is reproduced in the LRB's Regimental History.
204 The account of events on 1 July has been compiled from the War Diary, later reports, personal memoirs and reminiscences in the LRB Collection and other archives.

205	The incident of Rifleman Short's capture is described in Middlebrook, p.237.
206	*City Press*, 15/7/16.
207	A note attached to Griew's papers in P.H. Liddle's archive.
208	For a longer discussion on the care of the wounded see Middlebrook, p.230-1.
209	*City Press*, 15/7/16.
210	Grimwade, F.C., p.167.
211	Regt. Hist., p. 390.
212	*Official History 1916*. Vol I, p.472.
213	Guildhall MSS 12,606/2. Minutes of C of LT and AFA Committee.
214	Regt. Hist., p.128.
215	Henriques, W.H., p.81.
216	Hansard 1915. 72,1788.
217	ibid., 78, 1071.
218	ie. Part II, clause 7, sub section 4 (4). Hansard 1915. 81, 315.
219	Hansard 1915. 81, 322.
220	ibid., 81, 756 and 81, 1367.
221	ibid.
222	ACI No. 552.
223	Hansard 1915. 81, 2190.
224	LRB Record, March 1920.
225	ibid., Feb. 1920.
226	Hansard 1915. 81, 1978.
227	ibid.
228	ibid., 82, 1516.
229	Dalbaic, P.H., p.34.
230	ibid., p.35.
231	LRB Record, Feb. 1920.
232	*Official History Macedonia*. Vol. I, p.227.
233	Mainly Louez Military and Ecouvres Cemeteries.
234	LRB Record, Feb. 1920.
235	Wallis, but a little later he revises the figure to 400.
236	Wallis.
237	Henriques, W.H., p.102.
238	Mention in LRB War Diary.
239	Dudley Ward, p .50.
240	Henriques, W.H., p.108.
241	King, E.J., p.309.
242	Smith, p.153.
243	ibid., p.157.
244	Groom, A., p.160.
245	This was a concession won by the Director-General of the TF, Major-General Bethune. He wanted to ensure that the TF was kept up to strength and had also been petitioned to give special consideration to the class of men allotted to units like the LRB and HAC.
246	Smith, p.l78.

247   ibid., p.154.
248   Shaw & Sons, *Pro patria,* p.222.
249   War Diary.
250   Brigade Order cited in LRB War Diary.
251   Nobbs, G. *English Kamarad.* In his memoirs Wallis recorded that a new officer arrived with the draft on 6/9/16. Wallis names this officer, and alleges that he immediately reported, although unwounded, to a casualty clearing station. Battalion HQ requested that he should be court-martialled on a charge of cowardice, but a shell hit divisional HQ and the papers were lost. By the time the second request was submitted, the eye-witnesses had all been killed or evacuated wounded. To Wallis's disgust, the officer was awarded the OBE for work done 'in the safety of the War Office.'
252   These include John Sharp, a cousin of E.B. Harding who had recently arrived from the Artists.
253   Shaw & Sons. Frewer was invalided home shortly afterwards with trench fever. After a two month stay in hospital, he was selected to go to America to help train the U.S. Army - a job which lasted over 12 months.
254   Mason, R.J., says that prizes of leave were offered as inducements to go on patrol - medals apparently were not considered sufficient.
255   Groom, p.74.
256   Grey, W.E., p.157-8.
257   Groom, A., p.74.
258   ibid., p.79.
259   ibid., p.80-82.
260   Lindsay, J.H., p.138.
261   Grey, p.157.
262   Henriques, W.H., p.136.
263   Groom, A., p.83.
264   Bert Acomb was invalided home after a scratch on his leg turned septic. He eventually became a musketry instructor with the 3rd Battalion.
265   Grey, p.170.
266   *Official History 1917.* Vol. I, p.201.
267   ibid.
268   Smith, p.220
269   Henriques, J.Q., p.164.
270   Groom, p.97-99.
271   Smith, p.264.
272   *The War Record of the Northern Assurance Co. Ltd.*
273   Groom, p.115. Groom's '2Lt Armstrong' was 2Lt F. Ball.
274   Smith, p.241.
275   Groom, p.103.
276   Smith, p.273-4. Smith quotes from Nelson's *History of the War.*
277   Dudley Ward, p.168.
278   References to A.V. Magnus come from his diaries in the IWM Dept. of Documents and letters in the LRB Collection.

279   Smith, p.291.
280   Details of the nucleus personnel were as follows: 2 CSMs; A/RSM;
      the intelligence and bombing sergeants; 2 HQ runners; 2 LG
      instructors; 2 HQ pioneers; 6 HQ signallers; 1 sergeant, corporal,
      lance-corporal, signaller and runner from each company; 1 from each
      of the four sections of a platoon.
281   Groom, p.143.
282   Rfn Cowley was blinded in 1918, but met up with Wallis again at a
      regimental reunion in 1939. '2nd Battalion Club List', 1939.
283   Dudley Ward, p.209.
284   Groom, p.147.
285   Smith, p.288.
286   The night of 14/15 April. The rations were finally dumped only a few
      hundred yards from the battalion's position. Regt. Hist., p.195.
287   Groom, p.144. 'Benson' is almost certainly Sgt C.J. Barrett.
288   At the rear of his book, Wallis describes the sequel to Maginn's
      activities. At a dinner given in his honour, Maginn sat next to de
      Valera who offered Maginn command of a battalion of Sinn Feiners
      once the war was over. Maginn accepted this and returned to France.
      When demobbed from the British Army, he returned to Ireland to take
      up his new post. However, on the way he met some officers of the
      Royal Irish Constabulary who talked him into becoming an officer in
      the Black and Tans! Six weeks later he was killed by Sinn Feiners in a
      Dublin street fight. According to Wallis, 'It did not matter to Maginn
      on which side he was fighting as long as he was in the fight!'
289   *Official History 1917*. Vol. III, p.298.
290   *Official History 1918*. Vol. II, p.62-3.
291   Some of the Queen Vic's were transferred to the Queen's
      Westminsters. The latter's Regimental History claimed it had probably
      never received a better draft of men.
292   Wheeler-Holohan and Wyatt, p.7.
293   Smith, p.303.
294   Meecham, A.G.
295   Keep's brother was killed in October 1918 while serving with the 18th
      KRRC. He is buried in Hooge Crater Cemetery.
296   Groom, p.158.
297   Moran, Lord, p.87. The London Scots lost over 100 gas casualties in
      the Red Line during early March. Lindsay, p.169.
298   Groom, p.158.
299   The 2nd London had not suffered very severely, with only 1 officer
      and 23 other ranks killed, 2 and 69 wounded, and 15 missing. Grey,
      W.E., p.323.
300   Groom, p.160.
301   LRB Record, January 1920.
302   See Chapter II.
303   Hansard, 1915. 77, 536.
304   ibid. 77, 563.
305   Obituary for Billy Chandler in a '2nd Battalion Club List of

Members'.
306 ibid. 1939.
307 Regt. Hist., p.265.
308 Hansard, 1916. 80, 1948.
309 ibid., 80, 2434.
310 Bert Ives became an international athlete and President of the English Cross Country Union. He died in 1975.
311 Foster, G.M. Letter dated 10/1/17.
312 ibid. Letter dated 24/3/17.
313 *Official History 1917*. Vol.I, p.497.
314 Brigadier-General C. Higgins, cited in LRB Record, Nov., 1919.
315 Cited in Regt. Hist., p.287.
316 LRB Record, Dec. 1920.
317 Smith, p.256.
318 Adam Macpherson eventually became Assistant Chaplain General to the Forces. He died in 1987.
319 *Official History 1917*, Vol. II, p.286.
320 Regt. Hist., p.301.
321 War Diary.
322 Charles Taylor, *Newsletter* 1977.
323 ' Pte X', *War is War*, p. 198. In reality, ' Pte X' was Pte A. Burrage.
324 In early 1916 the London Scots were apparently criticised by a staff officer who accused them of trying to run the battalion on public school lines.
325 Obituary of Tom Malone in LRB Record, Feb. 1923.
326 Regt. Hist., p.324.
327 Nobbs, G., p.23
328 *History of the POW Civil Service Rifles*, p. 375
329 Phillips, G. Papers in P.H. Liddle archive.
330 *Newsletter*, Oct. 1955.
331 Angel, R.L.
332 ibid.
333 Harding.
334 Among the diners at the *Chyebassa* dinner on 5/11/18, were almost 90 other ranks who had sailed on 4/11/14 and were now serving with the 3rd Battalion.
335 This, and the following quotations, come from a series of letters written by members of a training platoon to their former sergeant, Maurice Howard. Private possession and loaned to author.
336 Quoted in Messenger, C., p.129.
337 Sassoon, S. *Memoirs of an Infantry Officer*, Faber and Faber edition, 1982, p.32.
338 'Pte X' . p.198.
339 Forrow, S. Papers.
340 Henriques, J.Q., p.237.
341 Grimwade, F.C., p.407, and Lindsay, J.H., p.174.
342 Smith, p.332.
343 Letter attached to Wallis's book of recollections.

344   Smith, p.338.

345   *Official History 1918.* Vol IV,, p.335.

346   Regt. Hist., p.240.

347   ibid.

348   Information culled from *The Star-less Knight,* journal of 4th 'B' company, No 1 OC Bn Feb-July 1918. Private possession.

349   Henriques, J.Q., p.275.

350   Grimwade, p.503.

351   After the war, by a strange quirk of coincidence, Basil Houle came across the soldier from the Queen Vic's while they both travelled on a bus along Regent Street. Houle accosted the man who admitted that he had betrayed the plan to the Germans, but in his defence, claimed that the enemy had threatened to harm some of his German relatives if he did not co-operate.

352   Reported in the *Daily Telegraph,* 17/7/18.

353   Regt. Hist., p.338.

354   Smith, p.337.

355   Mason, R.J. This story must refer to Sgt Pullen and Rfn Barker who escaped after being captured at Gavrelle. However, they overcame their escorts in the former German front line rather than several miles to the rear in Douai. The Army numbers of the two men show that they certainly did not come to the LRB from the Rangers when the latter was disbanded in January and it is more likely that they arrived with a very mixed draft from a variety of mainly London Regiments in late February or early March.

356   Regt. Hist., p.338.

357   ibid.

358   Amatt returned to the silk factory, but could not settle. On hearing a rumour that work was about to begin on a channel tunnel, he went to Dover. Next he applied to join the Black and Tans but was rejected because he had gone AWOL from the Army. Finally he enlisted in The Tank Corps. During the the Second World War he served in an anti-aircraft battery in England. He died in 1989.

359   Houle decided not to go back to office work and went up to Felling, Co. Durham, to work as a miner. When the Second World War broke out he went back to London and tried to join the LRB. De Colgan was sitting on the opposite desk, and told Houle he would not have him in his regiment. Houle was later commissioned and spent the war tunnelling with the RE in the Middle East. He died in 1988.

360   Smith, p.404.

361   ibid., p. 408.

362   Jack Terry returned to his job with the L & SW Railway. He died in 1986.

363   *Newsletter,* Sept. 1964.

LRB Fatalities

The whole issue of casualties sustained during the war aroused a fierce controversy in the years following. Statistics and counter-statistics were bandied about by historians and writers in attempts to prove their respective arguments as to whether the Allies or Germans lost more heavily in the set-piece battles. Seventy years on there is still little agreement and, consequently, it is virtually impossible to decide upon an accurate or definitive figure for the number of men from the LRB who were killed, died of wounds or died during the war years. Throughout this work, constant reference has been made to figures determined from the *Soldiers Died* lists, which is probably the source most historians would accept as being closest to accuracy. The total number of non-commissioned men listed as 'LRB' in that source, amounts to 1,664, and in the sister publication, the names of 80 officers are recorded. In his work of recollection Dick Wallis gave the totals as 1,580 and 91 respectively, a total of 1,671, which coincides exactly with the figure inscribed on the Roll of Honour housed in St. Botolph's Church, Bishopsgate. Wallis also gives a figure of 4,882 as wounded and missing, and points out that among that figure there would be 'several hundred' who should be included amongst the killed. The same figure of 91 officers is found in the register of the LRB Cemetery at Plugstreet. The note was attached to the register when Lieutenant General Sir H.F.M. Wilson, formerly GOC, 4th Division, unveiled a tablet in 1927 commemorating the dedication of the cemetery by the Bishop of London on Easter Sunday 1915. The total of other ranks given in that same source is 1,831. Finally, another figure is given in the programme printed for the reunion of November 1919 to celebrate peace and the Sixtieth Anniversary of the creation of the regiment; this source gives the lowest totals of any; 76 officers and 1,494 other ranks.

Thus, there is plenty of room for diversity of opinion and scope for misinterpretation of the available fatality figures. The War Diary cannot be taken as an accurate source for it rarely includes those who died of wounds once they had been evacuated. Neither can the 1919 programme mentioned above, for it was printed too soon after the events to have tapped all the sources. Yet even the LRB list in *Soldiers Died* includes men who were no longer serving with the regiment and ignores completely, in the sections covering the London Regiment, the 60 deaths of the men who joined from the Rifle Brigade in late March and early April 1918. Their names are found in a separate section within the Rifle Brigade list.

There appears to be no real logic in the way by which some men are listed in *Soldiers Died*. For those men who died while fighting in the two service battalions of the LRB there is no problem, but there are anomalies in cases of soldiers who were transferred from the regiment. It is understandable to find the names of those who were sent to the Artists and units of the 58th Division when the 2nd Battalion was broken up, for having fought with the LRB, they still regarded themselves as 'attached' rather than 'transferred' to their new regiments. Nevertheless, even in these cases, there are complications. Those who went from the 2nd Battalion to the Artists, 2/10th London and the Post Office Rifles, are listed in the LRB roll with their LRB numbers, but those who went to the London Irish appear in its roll with London Irish numbers. Thus, while the 55 who died with the Artists, and 29 with the 58th Division were still regarded as LRB, their 38 colleagues who died fighting with the London Irish in the 47th Division were not accorded that honour.

Besides those troops despatched *en masse* from the 2nd Battalion, there are several instances of individuals who were posted out of the regiment, but whose names still appear in the LRB roll. For example Corporal R. Wood, one of the men who joined the LRB from the 7th Middlesex in July 1916, was killed in September 1918 fighting with another unit, while Bertie English died serving with the 3/3rd King's African Rifles in Mozambique. At least in English's case the roll acknowledges that he died in Africa, but the entry for Henry Gullen has 'killed in action, France and Flanders'. Why Gullen is even in the LRB list is something of a mystery for he was one of the men transferred to units of the 60th Division in 1916 and is buried in Ramleh War Cemetery, Israel. Another inconsistency concerns men posted to battalions of the Rifle Brigade. Those men who went in 1917 and 1918 and who were killed are usually found in the LRB list. For some reason however, a group of Aiv boys, who were transferred to one of the Regular battalions of the parent regiment, are included in that battalion's roll rather than the LRB's.

The controversy surrounding the transfer of large numbers of men from the training battalions of the London Regiment to the 60th Division early in 1916 has already been discussed and, although the men seem to have considered that they were still really LRB, the names of the dead appear in the lists of their adopted battalions. Of the 300 odd LRB men so transferred, at least 94 were to die either during the division's short stay in France, or in the subsequent Balkan and Egyptian campaigns. These men are generally fairly easy to identify for in the *Soldiers Died* lists of their new regiments, their names are usually followed by a statement such as, 'Formerly 5 CLR.' Yet, there are, as in Gullen's case, exceptions. Alfred Frith was killed in September 1916 with the 2/17th London, but his name, like Gullen's, appears in the LRB list. However, not so easy to identify are men who were transferred to units not already mentioned. There are known to have been deaths from among the occupants of one hut of Aiv boys when some of the platoon were posted to the Machine Gun Corps in 1918. In all, something like 320 LRB appear to have been sent to the MGC, during the war, but its list in *Soldiers Died* does not specify the dead men's former regiments and neither is it possible to spot them from their Army numbers. On the other hand, the dead of the Aiv boys from 'Cherub' Angel's platoon who were transferred to the Civil Service Rifles in April 1918, are found in the LRB list. There are other units to which recruits to the LRB are known to have been posted, but like that of the MGC the rolls of those regiments do not always give the origins of men posted to them. For example, Harry Hughes was sent with a draft, via the 2nd Canadian Entrenching Battalion, to the 17th KRRC in August 1916. Unfortunately, it cannot be determined from information in that battalion's roll as to whether any of the draft were later killed. Later LRB drafts to the KRRC are similarly only identified by occasional reference to the men's former regiments in the cemetery registers or other incidental sources.

In the same way that the LRB list contains names of men who were no longer serving with the regiment, other regimental lists have the names of their men who died while fighting with the LRB. However, to confuse the issue a little more, these entries do not always state that fact. Among other examples, there were men from the Post Office Rifles with the LRB at Gavrelle, although their names are recorded in the POR's list. Again, they can only be identified as men fighting with the LRB from coincidental references in the memorial and cemetery registers. A stranger case than those is that of Rifleman Stanley Holder. Holder was killed at Gavrelle and his name is engraved on the LRB panels on the Arras Memorial to the Missing. In the memorial's register he has a number indicating that he belonged to the 7th London, but he appears in the LRB *Soldiers Died* list with a LRB number low enough to suggest he must have joined the regiment in 1915. It is possible that Holder was transferred from the LRB to the 7th London and then back again, but the issues of regimental numbering and also regimental identification from cemetery headstones raise further problems. Those LRB men who went to the Artists again pose no difficulty; they all have the LRB badge engraved on the headstone. There is, however, a LRB badge above the grave of S.J. Cook who died of wounds at Ligny St Flochel in September 1918 while serving with the 1st Battalion. This is despite the fact that he retained his Post Office Rifles number and appears in that regiment's list of dead in *Soldiers Died*.

Another interesting case of a man who enlisted in the LRB but was posted elsewhere, is that of Rifleman John Westbrook. Along with a group of perhaps 30 other LRB men, as well as parties from several other London Regiments, Westbrook was posted to the 12th Royal Irish Rifles in early 1917. He had not served overseas with the LRB and was killed in March 1917 whilst definitely serving with the Irish Rifles. However, unlike those of his former colleagues from the LRB who also died while serving in the Central Antrim Battalion, his headstone was inscribed with a LRB badge, rather than that of the Irish Rifles. Furthermore, on the headstone he is described as 'Royal Irish Rifles and London Rifle Brigade' - an unusual occurrence for a 1917 grave.

It is more common to find the badge of a man's original regiment on the graves of soldiers who died in 1918. For example, except for Rifleman G. Dixon, who has an LRB badge and an inscription which acknowledges that he had been transferred from the Rifle Brigade, the men who came to the LRB from the Rifle Brigade in 1918, have the badges of their former regiment on their headstones. Yet, as a final example of these inconsistencies, Rifleman John Smart - recruited directly into the LRB in early 1917 and buried in Grass Lane Cemetery on the Somme - has a Rifle Brigade badge above his grave!

It also appears that not all of the next of kin or even the authorities who provided the information for the entries in the cemetery registers knew exactly in which unit the dead soldier had served. For example, many of the Aiv youths killed with the 3rd Rifle Brigade have '3 Bn. LRB' or '5 Bn. LRB' (a unit which never existed) in the register, and no mention at all of the fact that they were fighting with the Rifle Brigade. One entry even goes a step further by claiming that the dead man was a member of the '3 Bn. attached 5 Bn. LRB'. Some of those posted to the London Irish have '2 Bn. LRB' beside their names and one man even has his LRB number despite the fact, as mentioned above, he would have been issued with a London Irish one. One man, who is known to have been attached to the Post Office Rifles, has simply 'LRB', while Frederick Outen, formerly of the POR's but who joined the LRB in July 1916, is stated in the Thiepval register as belonging to the 1st Rifle Brigade. Another of the somewhat strange examples is that of Fred Williams, buried in Sunken Road Cemetery, Villers-Plouich. The headstone has a LRB badge, number and inscription. The register, on the other hand, makes no mention of his LRB membership recording instead that, although he died of wounds while serving with the Artists, he actually belonged to the London Irish Rifles.

Finally, the *Soldiers Died* list does not include all those non-commissioned men who were actually serving members of the LRB when they died. Corporal G. Lintott of the 2nd Battalion died from acute septicaemia in the 1st Eastern General Hospital in June 1915, but is not listed. Neither are G. Gough, who was killed in Glencorse Wood and is buried in Hooge Crater Cemetery, or Rifleman Wiles, who appears to have arrived with the draft of Rifle Brigade men in 1918. Wiles was killed in August, yet his name is not in either the LRB roll or the RB one which contains the names of his colleagues from the same draft. A similar case is that of Rifleman A. Balchin, buried in Lievin Communal Extension Cemetery. Although probably fighting with the Post Office Rifles at the time of his death, Balchin has a LRB number but is not mentioned in any London Regiment's list in *Soldiers Died*. Although there are omissions in the *Soldiers Died* rolls, this source also names seven LRB men as having been killed, but of whom the Commonwealth War Graves Commission has no trace.

Identifying LRB officers who were killed is not as difficult as spotting the non-commissioned men. However, arriving at a precise total of the dead is just as problematical. The LRB's own roll deposited in the Imperial War Museum has a total death toll of 172 men who were commissioned from the ranks of the regiment. These men are in addition to those officers posted directly on commission into the regiment, or who were already serving in it when war was declared and who were later killed. Thirty-eight of the 172 died while serving in the LRB, the remainder died while fighting with other units. However, this figure does not coincide with the 80 names given in the *Officers Died* list. That roll includes 19 officers who are recorded as 'LRB', but certainly died while they were attached to other regiments. Again, it is understandable that the five who died after being transferred to the Artists in 1918 should be included, but it is not clear why others who were sent to various battalions of the London Regiment should be, especially as they do not have the LRB badge on their headstones. If those 19 are subtracted from the total though, the remaining 61, who were certainly killed while serving with the 1st or 2nd Battalions, should in turn, be supplemented by 15 others who had been attached from their particular regiments and died with the LRB.

The *Soldiers Died* list provides the names of some, but by no means all of the LRB men who died after the Armistice. At least two died in early 1919 while serving with the battalion overseas, but because they had not sustained their injuries or wounds before 11 November, they were not included as official war casualties. Furthermore, it is safe to assume that there must have been many others who, like Major George Harvest and Tom Burroughs, died after the war from injuries sustained during it. Complications such as these make any accurate total of LRB men dying as a consequence of the war impossible. Neither, as was pointed out earlier, is it possible to determine precisely even those who died during it. However, if the number of those fatalities who are known to have enlisted and trained with the regiment, but who were later transferred elsewhere, is added to the LRB list in *Soldiers Died*, as well as the 60 from the Rifle Brigade, the figure for non-commissioned men would certainly rise from 1,664 to at least 1,886. This figure still of course excludes two major groups; those former LRB men who died while serving with the KRRC, the MGC, the Labour Corps and several other units, as well as the men who died after they were posted into the LRB, but who retained their original regimental numbers throughout their LRB service.

APPENDIX II

Commissions

Throughout the preceding pages, frequent reference has been made to men of the regiment who were either commissioned into one of the three battalions, or, who went from the LRB to other units. One regimental source states that a total of 12,642 other ranks served in the LRB during the war and, of these, 1,339 were commissioned. This represents 11% of the total, which is quite a remarkable proportion when considering that the LRB, unlike the Artists, never became an OTC. The figure is even more impressive when it is remembered that the 1st Battalion sustained 505 fatalities between November 1914 and July 1916. In view of the educational and social background of the majority of these men, it could be assumed that, had they survived Ypres and Gommecourt, perhaps most of them would have been considered suitable for commission.

It has already been noted that over 400 *Chyebasse* men were to apply for and receive commissions, and also that 26% of the original 2nd Battalion became officers. The percentage of suitable men may have fallen once conscription began to have an effect on the composition of the 3rd Battalion, but a consistently high number of men continued to be sent annually to the Officer Cadet Battalions. The majority of these would-be officers received their initial training in Sergeant Tom Malone's class at Fovant or Blackdown, and were then posted back to the 3rd Battalion after they had passed through the OCB. The 3rd Battalion thus became something of a holding unit for subalterns awaiting despatch overseas. During the course of the war, 195 such men were posted to the battalion on their first commission.

Of the 1,339 men commissioned from the ranks, 174 were retained by the regiment itself. Many of the remainder went into the infantry regiments of the British Army - including the Guards - while others went into the Artillery and Service Corps. Fifty-four joined the Royal Flying Corps and Royal Air Force on their first commission, but it is known that others, such as Willie Fry, first became officers in a line regiment, and then went into the RFC. For some unexplained reason, a relatively large number of LRB men, 17, were commissioned into the Royal Naval Air Service. The majority however, served in less glamorous units. Not surprisingly perhaps, the largest number, 283, joined other battalions of the City and County of London Regiment, while 87 joined one of the other local regiments, the Middlesex.

In all, 172 or 13% of those commissioned, were killed, including 38 of those who served in the LRB itself. Their names contribute to the officially listed total of 80 dead LRB officers - the fourth largest total in the entire Territorial Force.

Commanding Officers and Adjutants of the LRB, 1908-1919

Commanding Officers; 1st Battalion

1908: Col Lord Bingham (Rifle Brigade)
Commanded 1st London Territorial Brigade 1912-16

1912: Lt-Col Earl Cairns, CMG (Rifle Brigade)
Invalided home sick April 1915

February 1915 - August 1916: Lt-Col A.S. Bates, DSO
Invalided home. Commanded 3/5th Lancashire Fusiliers
and took them to France in February 1917

August 1916 - August 1917: Lt-Col R.H. Husey, DSO
Wounded and home

August 1917 - December 1917: Lt-Col F.H. Wallis, MC
Home to attend Senior Officers School

December 1917 - May 1918: Lt-Col R.H. Husey, DSO
Left to command 25th Brigade, 8th Division

May 1918 - May 1919: Lt-Col C.D. Burnell, DSO
Brought back cadre of Battalion

Adjutants; 1st Battalion

1909: Capt A.C.H. Kennard (Rifle Brigade)
Retired, then commanded 2/1st and 1/1st London
Regiment until 1916 and later a Labour Group

1909 - 1912: Capt J.A.W. Spencer (Rifle Brigade)
Served as General Staff Officer in several theatres
of operations. Lt-Col 1919

1912 - May 1915: Capt A.C. Oppenheim DSO (KRRC)
Home, wounded May 1915. Second in command of 2nd KRRC
until May 1917 (wounded), then to Sandhurst as
Instructor

May 1915 - April 1916: Capt H.L. Johnston, MC

Wounded June 1916. To France and 6th London June 1918
Rejoined 1st LRB February 1919

April 1916 - September 1916: Capt F.H. Wallis, MC

September 1916 - March 1917: Lt D. McOwan
Invalided home March 1917 and out of the Army June
1919

March 1917 - May 1917: Capt J.H. Stransom, DCM
Invalided home and to 3rd Battalion

May 1917 - August 1917: Capt F.H. Wallis, MC
Assumed command of 1st Battalion

August 1917 : 2Lt B.H. Sellon (11th London)
Died of wounds

August 1917 - May 1919: Capt W.C. von Berg, MC
Came home with cadre

Commanding Officers; 2nd Battalion

September 1914 - April 1917: Col G.R. Tod
Invalided home April 1917 and then commanded 23rd Royal
Welch Fusiliers

April 1917 - December 1917: Lt-Col P.D. Stewart, DSO
(3rd Dragoon Guards)
Left to command 58th Division M.G. Battalion

December 1917 - February 1918: Lt-Col C.E. Johnston, MC
Commanded 8th London and later 7th London

Adjutants; 2nd Battalion

September 1914 - June 1915: Capt C.G.H. Macgill, MVO
Staff Officer at home

June 1915 - July 1917: Capt F. Furze
Killed in action 20 September 1917

July 1917 - January 1918: Lt R. Cope
Adjt. III Corps Reinforcement Camp and later
joined 1st Battalion

Commanding Officers; 3rd Battalion

November 1914 - May 1915: Col H.C. Cholmondeley, CB
        Left to command 173rd Bde. 58th Division

June 1915 - August 1919: Brevet Col N.C. King, TD

Adjutants; 3rd Battalion

November 1914 - August 1918: Capt J.F.C. Bennett
        Joined the RAF

August 1918 - March 1919: Capt G.C. Chambers

March 1919 - April 1919: Capt.J.H. Stransom, DCM

APPENDIX IV

1st Battalion LRB Order of Battle, 1914-1919

When the LRB began its mobilisation in August 1914, it was part of the 2nd, London Infantry Brigade, 1st London Division. The division's three infantry brigades were all composed of either City or County of London Battalions. The 1st Infantry Brigade contained the four Royal Fusilier battalions of the City of London, the 2nd Brigade had the LRB, the 6th and 7th London, and the Post Office Rifles. Finally, the 3rd Brigade was made up by the 9th London (Queen Victoria's), 10th London (Hackney), 11th London (Finsbury Rifles) and the 12th London (Rangers). The division's mounted troops were the 2nd County of London Yeomanry (Westminster Dragoons) and the artillery was provided by the 1st City of London and the II, III, and IV County of London Brigades. The other supporting arms were all from the London area.

However, the division soon began to break up under the demands of war, and in early September 1914 the 1st London Infantry Brigade embarked for Malta. In November three battalions were transferred to the 4th London Infantry Brigade, 2nd London Division, and between November 1914 and January 1915, another three battalions, including the LRB were despatched to France. What remained of the division was sent to join the 2/1st London Division, which later became the 58th (2/1st London) Division. In April 1915, these two remaining original battalions of the 1st London Division, the Hackney and the Finsbury Rifles battalions, were transferred to the East Midland Brigade, East Anglian Division. (This formation was soon to become the 54th (East Anglian) Division.)

Meanwhile, the LRB had been despatched to France, and on 17 November 1914 the battalion joined 11 Brigade, 4th Division. While serving with this brigade of Regulars, the LRB took part in:

25 April - 4 May   **Battle of St. Julien** (Second Army)
8 May - 13 May   **Battle of Frezenberg Ridge** (Second Army)

On 19 May 1915 the battalion was transferred to GHQ troops until it joined 8th Brigade, 3rd Division. When the LRB joined this brigade, the other three battalions in it were the 2nd Royal Scots, 4th Middlesex and 7th King's Shropshire L.I., but by the time it left it in February 1916, the 4th Middlesex had been replaced by the 8th East Yorks.

In January 1916 the Army Council had authorised the re-formation of the 1st London Division and consequently the 56th (1st London) Division began to assemble in the Hallencourt area in February 1916. However, of the original twelve pre-war infantry battalions, only seven were to form part of the re-born division.

56th (1st London) Division: June 1916

167th Inf. Bde. 7th Middlesex, 8th Middlesex, 1st London (RF), 3rd London (RF)
168th Inf. Bde. 4th London (RF), 12th London (Rangers), 13th London (Kensingtons), 14th London (London Scottish)
169th Inf. Bde. 2nd London (RF), 5th London (LRB) 9th London (QVR), 16th London (QWR)

Each brigade had its respective machine gun company, and light trench mortar battery. There were at this time four brigades of field artillery, supplemented by three medium and one heavy trench mortar batteries. There were also three field companies of engineers, (1st Edinburgh, 2/1st London and 2/2nd London) and three field ambulances, (2/1st London, 2/2nd London and 2/3rd London). The 5th Cheshire as Pioneers, the Divisional Signal Company, the Divisional Ammunition Column and the Mobile Veterinary Section completed the establishment.

By the beginning of March 1918 the division had been reorganised:

56th (1st London) Division: March 1918

167th Inf Bde - 7th Middlesex, 8th Middlesex, 1st London
168th Inf Bde - 4th London, Kensingtons, London Scottish
169th Inf Bde - 2nd London, LRB, Queen's Westminster Rifles

Each brigade lost its own machine gun company, (their fire power being provided by No 56 Bn MGC), but the three infantry brigades retained their light trench mortar batteries. The artillery had been reduced to two brigades and there were only two medium trench mortar batteries. The 5th Cheshire remained as the Pioneer battalion but the field companies of engineers had lost their names and had been numbered the 416th, 512th and 513rd. Apart from the appearance of a Divisional Employment Company, the 247th, the other supporting arms remained as they had been in June 1916 and the division was to stay in this form until it began its demobilisation after the Armistice.

Battles and Major Engagements fought by the 56th (London) Division

1916

Battles of the Somme

1 July	Gommecourt (Third Army)
9 September	**Battle of Ginchy** (Fourth Army)
15-22 September	**Battle of Flers-Courcelette** (Fourth Army)
25-27 September	**Battle of Morval** (Fourth Army)

1-9 October	**Battle of the Transloy Ridges** (Fourth Army)

1917

14 March-5 April	**German Retreat to the Hindenburg Line** (Third Army)

Battles of Arras

9-14 April	**First Battle of the Scarpe** (Third Army)
3-4 May	**Third Battle of the Scarpe** (Third Army)

Battle of Ypres

16-17 August	**Battle of Langemarck** (Fifth Army)
21 November -2 December	**Battle of Cambrai**

1918

First Battles of the Somme

28 March	**First Battle of Arras** (First Army)

Second Battles of the Somme

23 August	**Battle of Albert** (Third Army)

Second Battles of the Arras

26-30 August	**Battle of the Scarpe** (Third Army)

Battles of the Hindenburg Line

27 September -1 October	**Battle of the Canal du Nord** (First Army)
8-9 October	**Battle of Cambrai** (First Army)
9-12 October	**Pursuit to the Selle** (First Army)

The Final Advance in Picardy

4 November	**Battle of the Sambre** (First Army)
5-7 November	**Passage of the Grande Honnelle** (First Army)

APPENDIX V

2nd Battalion LRB Order of Battle 1914-1918

The authorisation to begin the creation of the Reserve, or second-line units of the Territorial Force was granted on 31 August 1914. Gradually, the 2/1st London Division began to take shape, but it was handicapped by the loss of the 2/1st London Infantry Brigade to Malta between December 1914 and February 1915. The 2/1st was then replaced by the 3/1st London Infantry Brigade. In August 1915 the 2/1st London Division became known as the 58th (2/1st London) Division, and its three infantry brigades became the 173rd, 174th and 175th Brigades.

58th (2/1st London) Division: June 1917

173rd Inf Bde - 2/1st London, 2/2nd London, 2/3rd London, 2/4th London

174th Inf Bde - 2/5th London (LRB), 2/6th London, 2/7th London, 2/8th London (Post Office Rifles)

175th Inf Bde - 2/9th London (QVR), 2/10th London, 2/11th London, 2/12th London

These brigades were supported by the 214th, 198th and 215th Machine Gun Companies, three batteries of light, three of medium and one heavy trench mortar batteries, and two brigades of field artillery. There was no pioneer battalion, but three field companies of engineers, the 503rd (2/1st Wessex), 504th (2/2nd Wessex) and 511th (1/5th London), three field ambulances (all Home Counties) and the other usual supporting arms completed the establishment. Until it was disbanded in January 1918, the 2nd LRB, as a unit of the 58th (2/1st London) Division, took part in the following battles and engagements:

1917

17-28 March	**German Retreat to the Hindenburg Line** (Third Army)
4-17 May	**Battle of Bullecourt** (Fifth Army)
20 May-16 June	**Actions of the Hindenburg Line** (Fifth and Third Armies)

Battles of Ypres

20-25 September	**Battle of Menin Road Bridge** (Fifth Army)
26-27 September	**Battle of Polygon Wood** (Fifth Army)
26 October- 10 November	**Second Battle of Passchendaele** (Fifth and Second Armies)

APPENDIX VI

The London Regiment

When the Territorial Force was formed in 1908 the old Volunteer units were organised into City or County Battalions of the London Regiment. Each of the battalions was affiliated to one of the Regular Army Regiments - for example, the LRB was affiliated to the Rifle Brigade, while the Westminsters and Victoria's were affiliated to the King's Royal Rifle Corps.

The missing 26th and 27th Battalions were originally allocated for use by the Honourable Artillery Company and the Inns of Court, but these two historic regiments objected to their high numbers and were allowed to retain their old titles. The LRB had objected to being numbered the 5th Battalion, but in its case the authorities were not prepared to sustain the objection.

During the war, most of the battalions formed their own Second and Third Line units and in 1917 another six battalions, numbered the 29th-34th County of London Regiment, were formed and affiliated either to the Royal Fusiliers, The Rifle Brigade or the King's Royal Rifle Corps.

BATTALION	OFFICIAL NAME	FAMILIAR NAME
1st	City of London	Royal Fusiliers
2nd	City of London	Royal Fusiliers
3rd	City of London	Royal Fusiliers
4th	City of London	Royal Fusiliers
5th	City of London	London Rifle Brigade
6th	City of London	Rifles
7th	City of London	HQ = Sun Street
8th	City of London	Post Office Rifles
9th	County of London	Queen Victoria's Rifles
10th	County of London	Hackney
11th	County of London	Finsbury Rifles
12th	County of London	Rangers
13th	County of London	Kensington
14th	County of London	London Scottish
15th	County of London	POW Civil Service Rifles
16th	County of London	Queen's Westminster Rifles
17th	County of London	Poplar and Stepney Rifles
18th	County of London	London Irish Rifles
19th	County of London	St. Pancras
20th	County of London	Blackheath and Woolwich
21st	County of London	First Surrey Rifles
22nd	County of London	The Queen's
23rd	County of London	HQ = Clapham
24th	County of London	The Queen's
25th	County of London	Cyclist Battalion
28th	County of London	Artists Rifles

APPENDIX VII

The 1st Battalion of 1914

The names below form an incomplete list of the NCO's and privates who sailed with the 1st Battalion on the *Chyebassa* in November 1914. These men were eligible for the '1914 Star' as they were within range of German guns by 22 November 1914. The information given is in the following sequence: Name, original Regimental Number, original Company (ie. in the 8 Company system), date of enlistment or re-enlistment if applicable, residence (if known), occupation or place of work (if known), rank in November 1914 (the rank 'Private' was not replaced by 'Rifleman' until May 1915), if commissioned, the regiment to which they were commissioned, date of death, regiment he was serving with if not the LRB, grave or memorial if still serving with the LRB and, finally, rank and age at death.

Abbott, E.T., 8535, 0, February 1909, Shooters Hill, L/Corporal, Died 1978.

Adams, J., King's Royal Rifle Corps, attached LRB on Permanent Staff, Citation for MM in *The London Gazette* 11 November 1916:
For conspicuous devotion to duty especially during the Second Battle of Ypres when he took over the duties of R.S.M. He was with the Battalion the whole time and of inestimable value during that period. Since then he has both, while the Battalion has been in the trenches and out, carried out his duties and more with marked ability and an entire disregard of danger.
He was awarded the DCM in June 1917:
This WO has been with the battalion in France since November 1914. He became acting RSM in April 1915 during the Second Battle of Ypres where he gained the MM for gallantry in the field. He has at all times shown himself cool and collected in action and has been of the very greatest use in instructing the NCO's of the Battalion, setting them the finest example of good discipline.

Alexander, H.J., 9322, A, November 1911, Westcliffe-on-Sea, Private, 7th London, 25 July 1918 (2Lt. 7th London).

Andrew, E.J., 9290, G, June 1911, 1 Marlborough Avenue, Hull, (b. London), Private, Engineer, East Yorkshire Regiment, Killed in Action, 23 March 1918, (Lt. 10th East Yorkshire).

Appleton, H.W., 9714, G, March 1914, Leytonstone, Private, Killed in Action, 11 February 1915, LRB Cemetery.

Aris, J.W., 9513, P, February 1913, Norwood, Brighton March, Private. Several cartoons published from the Front in *News of the World* May 1915, RASC and 2/6th London, Died 1977.

Ashby, H.H., 9395, D, March 1912, Balham, Private, Middlesex Regiment, Killed in Action, 28 September 1915 (2Lt. 23rd Middlesex).

Atkins, N., 9668, Q, December 1913, Yew Tree House, Penn, (Bucks.), Private, Died of Wounds, 7 December 1914, Bailleul Communal Cemetery, Age 19.

Atkins, H.B., 9567, P, June 1913, 77 Brighton Road, Stoke Newington, Private, Killed in Action, 1 July 1916, Thiepval Memorial, Corporal, Age 27.

Austin, W.G.S., 9978, E. August 1914, Tottenham, Private, Killed in Action, 1 July 1916, Thiepval Memorial, Sergeant, Age 27.

Babington, W.A., 9522, G, March 1913, 113 Woodside, Wimbledon, Private, Lloyds. Served for most of the war in France. Wounded once. Mentioned in Despatches:

For consistent good work, especially during the operations at Arras in April 1917 and Ypres, August 1917. He was N.C.O., in charge of telephone lines and displayed great courage and coolness at all times.
Died 1967.

Baker, E.C., 9809, G, August 1914 (probably re-enlisted), Wealdstone, Private, Wounded April 1915, 2Lt. LRB, served at home.

Baldwin, E.W., 9397, Q, April 1912, Wimbledon, Private, Killed in Action, 3 May 1915, Menin Gate, Age 32.

Balkwill, C.V., 125, H, August 1914, Catford, Private, Wounded April 1915 as Sergeant LRB. Re-joined 1st Battalion, May 1916, Killed in Action, 1 July 1916, Thiepval Memorial.

Barker, H.C., 8965, G, April 1909, 102 Kenilworth Road, Wandsworth, Private, commissioned in LRB at Ypres April 1915, MG Section, Attached to MGC, October 1916. Served with 186 Company, MGC, in Mesopotamia.

Bassingham, A.R., 9230, O, November 1910, 120 Lordship Lane, Stoke Newington, Private, Killed in Action, 24 December 1914, Ploegsteert Wood Cemetery, Age 21.

Bate, F., 6389, H, 1895, Clr.-Sergeant Former CIV, Left after 2nd Ypres RASC.

Bedford, T.C., 9499, D, February 1913, Ilford, Private, Died of Wounds, home 15 March 1915.

Belcher, D.W., 9539, O, April 1913, 6 St. Andrews Road, Surbiton, Furniture salesman, Lance Sergeant, awarded Victoria Cross for bravery at 2nd Ypres, *London Gazette* 23 June 1915:

On the early morning of 13 May 1915, when in charge of a portion of an advanced breastwork south of the Wieltje - St. Julien Road, during a very fierce and continuous bombardment by the enemy, which frequently blew in the breastwork, L.-Sergeant Belcher, with a mere handful of men, elected to remain and endeavour to hold his position after the troops near him had been withdrawn. By his skill and great gallantry he maintained his position during the day, opening rapid fire on the enemy, who were only 150 to 200 yards distant, whenever he saw them collecting for an attack. There is little doubt that the bold front shown by L.-Sergeant Belcher prevented the enemy breaking through on the Wieltje Road, and averted an attack on the flank of one of our divisions.

Douglas Belcher was later commissioned into the QVR but rejoined the LRB in 1922. He died in 1953.

Bell, C.M., 9215, P, October 1910, 210 Wightman Road, Harringay, Thompson and Company (Shippers), Private, Wounded December 1914. Returned to 1st

Battalion March 1915, Died of Wounds, 27 April 1915, Bailleul Communal Cemetery Extension, Age 22. Had a brother (Corporal) in the 2nd Battalion.

Bell, D.H., 8351, P, April 1908, Catford, Lance Corporal, Cartoon of Plugstreet Wood published in *Evening News* February 1915. Left for commission March 1915, Cameron Highlanders and RFC.

Benns, A.L., 9148, P, April 1910, New Cross, Christ's Hospital and Aske's Schools, Commerce and Dominion Line, Lance Corporal, Wounded March 1915, LRB rejoined 1st Battalion, March 1916, C Company, Killed in Action, 1 July 1916, Second Lieutenant, Thiepval Memorial.

Bevan, R.V., 9291, Q, June 1911, East Sheen, Medical student, Private, Died of Wounds, 12 December 1915, Bailleul Communal Cemetery, Age 21.

Blunden, A.E., 8647, P, August 1914 (re-enlistment), Leytonstone, Gresham Life Assurance, Sergeant. Lost an arm May 1915. Died 1978.

Boston, G.G., 9497, A, February 1914, Purley, Lance Corporal, Commissioned in Field 8 May 1915, Awarded DCM, for conspicuous bravery during 2nd Ypres, Bombing Officer and recommendation for award sent in after Gommecourt:

This officer behaved with the utmost gallantry and organised all the bombing attacks in Gommecourt Park which materially helped the companies who were endeavouring to consolidate there. He personally compelled the enemy to collect and supply him with a large number of their own bombs which were used with good effect by our men. He was severely wounded in two places.

'Curley' Boston was gazetted out of the Army in 1918.

Bradley, E.J., 140, G, August 1914, Suckley (Worcs.), Solicitor, Private, Died of Wounds, 5 December 1914, Bailleul Communal Cemetery, Age 22.

Brown, P.G.M., 9704, H. February 1914, 4 Styles Way, Park Langley, Beckenham, County of London Electric Supply Company, Private, Killed in Action, 3 May 1915, Menin Gate, Age 18.

Chambers, G.C., 8329, G, November 1911, Manor Park, Served continuously. Severely wounded 6 May 1915. Commissioned into the 3rd Battalion LRB. Assistant Adjutant July 1916 - August 1918 when he assumed the duties of Adjutant.

Chrisp, W.A., 9486, Q, August 1914 (probably re-enlisted) Kennington Park, Private, Transport Section, Served continuously, Promoted 2Lt. September 1918 and wounded. Mentioned in Despatches January 1917:

Transport Corporal. For the last six months and particularly during the last month he has shown great ability, tireless energy and an unfailing devotion to duty. On several occasions he has rendered invaluable assistance in the performance of transport duties both for the Regiment and the Brigade proving himself always both resourceful and courageous with a marked determination to serve his Regiment to the utmost of his power. That the battalion has never suffered through the failure of its transport arrangements is largely due to the splendid work accomplished by this NCO.

Coleman, J.D., 9472, Q, December 1912, 3 Station Road, Faversham. Resided in the City, J. Howell & Co. (City), Private, Killed in Action, 3 May 1915, Menin Gate, Age 20.

Collcott, A.W., 9428, Q, September 1912, Streatham, Clerk with Vacuum Oil Company, Private, wounded at 2nd Ypres. Discharged age 20 from 3rd Battalion July 1916.

Cooper, H.C., 9796, O, August 1914, New Cross, Prudential Assurance, Private, Battalion runner, Killed in Action, 27 April 1915, Menin Gate.

Crews, F.H., 9144, A, April 1910, London, Private, Direct commission to LRB January 1916. Spent 16 months as Instructor at GHQ, Lewis Gun School, LRB LG Officer from October 1918 and acting Second-in-command after Armistice. Served in France continuously from November 1914 - January 1919. Awarded MC *London Gazette* 25 November 1916:

This officer was in charge of the reserve company during the attack on Hazy Trench from Lesboeufs on the afternoon of 8 October 1916 and behaved in a most gallant way throughout the day. On being ordered forward to re-inforce he led his company through heavy shellfire most skilfully and on reaching the advanced line found that the Battalion had suffered severe losses and that he and one of his subalterns were the only remaining officers. He immediately organised the remaining men and dug in on a good line. At dusk he reconnoitred the ground in front of his line and personally captured an enemy MG which he brought back.

Daniel, A.A., 35, H, August 1914, Blackheath, Private, Died of Wounds, 25 January 1915, LRB Cemetery, Age 20. One of three brothers who enlisted in August and sailed on the *Chyebassa*.

Daphne, A., O, May 1909, 9 Roseleigh Avenue, Highgate, Accountant, L/Corporal, Killed in Action, 13 December 1914, Lancashire Cottage Cemetery.

Dawson, J.W., 9444, Q, November 1912, 'Mayville', Churchfield Avenue, Finchley, J. Howell & Company (City), Private, Killed in Action, 13 May 1915, Menin Gate, Age 19.

Dixon, H.S., 9730, P, March 1914, 145 Albion Road, Stoke Newington, Private, Killed in Action, 3 May 1915, Menin Gate, Age 18. One of three brothers who sailed: one, Walter, Died of Wounds, at Wimereux on 10 May, 1915 and a fourth joined the LRB in 1917.

Elliot, C.J., 9395, P, April 1912, Dulwich, Gresham Life Assurance, Private, Died of Wounds, 27 April 1915, Vlamertinghe Military Cemetery. Recommended for award.

Eustace, F., 8698, H, February 1909, Sydenham, Served in South African War, Brighton March, Private, QM's batman and thought to have served throughout in France.

Featherstonehaugh, W.R., 7437, G, January 1900, 14 Denmark Avenue, Wimbledon, Served in South African War, Corporal, CQMS in 3rd Battalion 1916, and in post-war Battalion. T.F. Efficiency Medal and Clasp.

Frank, G.L., 7183, G, April 1899, 26 Denton Road, Twickenham, Union Castle Line, Sergeant, Killed in Action, 3 May 1915, Menin Gate, Age 33 as CSM, Pre-War Entertainments Committee, 17 years service.

Gardiner, J.P., 9312, Q, October 1911, Hornsey, J. Howell & Company (City), Private, Killed in Action, 16 February 1915, Menin Gate, Age 20.

Gibson, G.M., 8723, G, February 1909, 14 Dingwall Road, Thornton Heath, Lance Corporal, Commissioned to Essex Regiment. His brother Alan was killed while serving with the LRB in 1917. Gilbert died in 1976 and had served as a Colonel in the Rifle Brigade during World War II.

Hall, C., 9752, O, May 1914, London, Private, Wounded February 1915, 2Lt October 1915 and to an Entrenching Battalion. To 1st Battalion September 1916. Wounded October 1916 and then to 2nd Battalion. Attached 18th London and wounded March 1918. Assistant Adjutant, 3rd Battalion RQMS, in LRB in 1930 and was embodied with the 2nd Battalion LRB (8th RB) in September 1939.

Harding, E.B., 9717, P, February 1914, Ealing, Sun Fire Assurance, Private, Wounded April 1915 and served in 3rd Battalion for remainder. Rejoined LRB February 1920 and from 1921 as a Private in the Calcutta Horse, Died 1990.

Jarvis, H.S., 9547, H, April 1913, Winchmore Hill, Messrs Chaney and Bull, Private, Inval, Home December 1914. Rejoined March 1915, Killed in Action, 3 May 1915, Menin Gate, Age 20.

Jessop, L., 9861, A, August 1914, Hampstead, Haileybury College OTC, Insurance Company, Private, Wounded July 1916, Corporal with 3rd Battalion until commissioned. Rejoined 1st Battalion September 1918. Rejoined LRB as Rifleman post-war ARP, Warden and Army Liaison Officer with Civil Defence 1939-45. Died 1989.

John, C.H., 9987, E, August 1914, Ealing, Private, Wounded May 1915, Direct commission to LRB July 1916. Stayed in France continuously from November 1914 to December 1918. Citation for MC:

For conspicuous gallantry, coolness and determination during operations near Angreau 4-6 November 1918. When the attack was held up on 4 November, he organised a strong defensive flank superintending the work and encouraging his men by his fearless behaviour under heavy M.G. fire. On the following day his Company was leading wave, he organised and led parties to clear out the M.G.s holding the village. On both days he was slightly wounded. On 6 November he again led the attack and did specially fine work reaching his first objective and when compelled to withdraw, he withdrew fighting. He was again slightly wounded by shellfire, his pack being destroyed whilst on his back. His fearless behaviour and complete disregard of danger was a splendid example to all his men.

John died in 1980.

Kelsey, S.G., 9270, Q, March 1911, 53 Westfield Road, Hornsey, Private, Signaller, Killed in Action, 2 May 1915, Menin Gate, Age 26.

Latham, E.B., 9609, P, September 1913, Buckhurst Hill, Family business, Private, Wounded 26 April 1915, MM 3rd Battalion, recruiting team until commissioned to 17th London. Mid-1917 to Indian Army. Died 1980. Brother of Russell Latham.

Legg, J.F., 8021, O, October 1904, St. Martin's, Kingston Road, new Malden, Lance Corporal, May 1915 CSM Commissioned into LRB and out with 2nd Battalion, January 1917. Transferred to Artists and temporarily in command of them September 1918, RAF, 1939-45.

Lydall, R.F., 9690, P, January 1914, Dulwich, Student Borough Poly, Private, Home January 1916 and commissioned into LRB. Rejoined 1st Battalion June 1916, Wounded July 1916. Overseas with 2nd Battalion until March 1918, then with 3rd Battalion, CSM of 'C' Company, LRB 1930 and embodied in 1st Battalion, LRB, (later 7th RB) as CSM in September 1939.

Manbey, B.K., 8488, H, February 1909, Southend, Corporal. Badly wounded as CSM, May 1915, Commissioned and into RAF, by October 1916.

McOwen, D., 8752, D, re-enlisted June 1913, London, Sergeant, Wounded April 1915. Commissioned into LRB and rejoined 1st Battalion July 1916, Adjutant September 1916-March 1917 when invalided. Mentioned in Despatches, CSM, A Company, LRB 1930.

Ovington, C.E., 9662, D, November 1913, Tottenham, Brighton March, Private, Wounded April 1915. Commissioned into LRB August 1915. Rejoined 1st Battalion March 1916 and seconded to 169 Brigade MG Company. Second in command of 56th Battalion MG Company, January 1919. Served in every engagement in which the 56th Division took part.

Paxton, E.G., 9411, A, May 1912, 3 Sydney Road, West Ealing, Asiatic Petroleum Company, Private, Killed in Action, 13 May 1915. Menin Gate, Age 22.

Pearse, C.N., 5, H, August 1914, 8 Eldon Park, Norwood, Accounts Clerk, Private, Died of Wounds, 27 November 1914, Bailleul Communal Cemetery, Age 26.

Peppiatt, W.H., 9556, G, May 1913, 'Maglona', Derby Road, Woodford, LNWR, Brighton March, Private, Died of Wounds, 5 February 1915, LRB Cemetery, Age 26.

Petley, R.E., 9263, G, February 1911, Beckenham, Private. Home for commission in LRB January 1916. Rejoined 1st Battalion May 1916. Severely wounded 1 July 1916. To 2nd Battalion, December 1917, transferred to Artists and captured March 1918. Severely wounded.

Pigden, A.B., 9563, G, May 1913, 39 Connaught Road, Stroud Green, Accountant, Private, Killed in Action, 3 May 1915, Menin Gate, Age 21.

Pocock, F.A., 9544, Q, April 1913, Walworth, Private, Signaller. To 3rd Battalion as Lance Corporal, Signal Instructor, CQMS, LRB in 1930 and embodied in 2nd Battalion, (8th RB) in September 1939. Died 1977.

Read, A., A, January 1900 and served continuously, London, Clr Sergeant, Wounded April 1915, September 1915 LRB, rejoined 1st Battalion, September 1916. Wounded October 1916 and then with 3rd Battalion.

Rice, E.F., 9983, H, August 1914, Wandsworth, Private, Lance Corporal of Plugstreet Wiring Party. Wounded May 1915. Commissioned into LRB August 1916 and rejoined 1st Battalion September 1916. Attached Trench Mortar Battery, November 1916 and killed 18 February 1917.

Rowe, H.J.C., 9471, O, December 1912 (with his brother), 27 Esmond Road, Bedford Park, Private. One of Belcher's group, MM as Lance Corporal in September 1916. Commissioned into Cheshire Regiment.

Sceats, D.B., 7957, P, May 1902, London, CQMS, Mentioned in Despatches June 1918 as never being absent from duty through wounds or sickness since 1914.

Schultz, L.H., 8331, H, re-enlisted May 1914, London, Brighton March, Corporal, Sergeant April 1915, Wiltshire Regiment, Killed in Action, October 1915 as 2Lt. 2nd Wiltshire.

Sell, C.H., 8298, O, May 1907, Purley, Lance Corporal, wounded April 1915, LRB and rejoined 1st Battalion January 1916 and severely wounded September 1916 by a simultaneous explosion of two 5.9 shells, one each side of him. With 3rd Battalion. Rejoined LRB as Sergeant and served 1920-1931. Died 1955.

Slade, E.H., 9412, E, May 1912. Forest Hill. Went with Battalion, but soon detached for map work at 4th Division HQ. Awarded MM gazetted with Direct Commission July 1916. Joined 169th Brigade, HQ as Intelligence Officer November 1916-February 1918. Awarded MC for carrying out several reconnaissances in Glencorse Wood on 16 August 1917. Rejoined 1st Battalion but home (sick) June 1918 and to 3rd Battalion.

Smith, A.H., 9735, O, April 1914, Surbiton, Accountant, Private, Wounded and home, February 1915, Leicestershire Regiment, July 1915, Killed in Action, July 1916 with 9th Leicestershire.

Sparks, F.E., 8380, O, September 1908, 54 Croydon Road, Beckenham, Lloyds, Pre-War Entertainments Committee, Lance Corporal, M.G. Section, Killed in Action, 13 May 1915, Menin Gate, Age 30.

Stonnill, R.H., 9137, O, April 1910, 19 Ranelagh Gardens, Barnes, Battalion Scout, Lance Corporal. Recommended for award May 1915, MM for September 1916. Commissioned into King's Own Royal Lancashire and to Salonika. Then RFC as Flying Instructor. Died 1977.

Stransom, J.H., 75, D, August 1914, Private, Wounded 28 April 1915 two days before being gazetted. LRB 3rd Battalion. Rejoined 1st Battalion September 1916. Invalided May 1917 to 3rd Battalion. Adjutant March-April 1919, Editor of *LRB Record* in 1920's and 1930's. Embodied with 2nd Battalion (8th RB) in September 1939.

Swann, W.F., 9496, Q, January 1913, Dalston, Brighton March, Private, Mentioned in Despatches as Sergeant, May 1917. Citation for Belgian Croix de Guerre February 1918:

This N.C.O. has been in France and Flanders since 5 November 1914 during which time he has fought at Ypres in 1914, 1915 and 1917. During the recent operations near Moeuvres he was acting C.S.M. He has on all occasions shown conspicuous courage and set an excellent example.

It is thought that Swann remained a member of the LRB after the war and was certainly CSM, of 'B' company, in 1930.

Taylor, G.O., 8335, H, January 1908, Chiswick, Pre-War Entertainment Committee, Brighton March, Corporal. Home with frost-bite March 1915, Commissioned into LRB September 1915 and rejoined 1st Battalion September 1916, Killed in action, 8 October 1916, Thiepval Memorial and Serre Road No. 2 Cemetery. Age 28.

Thomas, G.D., 8616, Q, 1911, London, Brighton March, Sergeant, Killed in Action, 27 April 1915 as CSM, Menin Gate, Age 27.

Titley, P., 7562, Q, 1900, Leatherhead (?), CIV, Sergeant, Wounded, March 1915. Commissioned into LRB June 1915 and rejoined 1st Battalion January 1916. Wounded June 1916 and to 2nd Battalion until rejoined 1st Battalion November 1916. Badly wounded August 1917, Died 1923.

Wallis, F.H., 8852, O, January 1899 to January 1907. Re-enlisted March 1909 and served continuously. 8 St John's Road, Hendon, Manager of

Greenshields and Company, London office, from 1911, Clr-Sergeant and CSM when Commissioned in Field February 1915. Served continuously as Lieutenant to Lieutenant-Colonel and commanded 1st Battalion on occasions until home March 1918 to attend Senior Officers School. Then commanded 1/13th London after Armistice. Demobilised 1919 and joined Head Office staff of Greenshields in Montreal. Became associated with Royal Montreal Regiment. MC for Gommecourt: Bar to MC for Third Ypres and a second Bar awarded December 1918:

In the operations near Sebourg and Angreau, this officer by his great gallantry and resource was of the greatest help. On 5 November, he went forward to reconnôitre. He found the Battalion had just captured Angreau but had got somewhat disorganised. He sent back a valuable report on the situation and helped to organise the forward companies. This work was done under extremely heavy M.G. and shellfire. His utter disregard of danger was a splendid example to the men and undoubtedly it was largely due to his work that the Battalion was able to hold the village though both its flanks were exposed.

Ward, E.J., 68, H, August 1914, Ashford, Bank Clerk, Private, Killed in Action, 8 December 1914, Rifle House Cemetery, Age 23.

Weeks, R.S., 9624, O, October 1913, 37 Dalmore Avenue, Dulwich, Lloyds Bank, Private. Was in Belcher's group and wounded May 1915. Commissioned into Middlesex Regiment, Killed in Action, 9 October 1916, 2Lt. 10th Middlesex attached Rifle Brigade.

Whitehead, J.E., 9884, A, August 1914, Crouch End, Law, Russell and Company, Stuff Merchants, Private, Wounded, 13 May 1915, Middlesex Regiment, August 1915, 2Lt. 7th Middlesex, Killed in Action, 15 September 1916.

Williamson, F., 7928, A, May 1902, London, Sergeant, Invalided home early 1915, LRB and 3rd Battalion until demobilised for a time to work in munitions. Joined 2nd Battalion May 1917. Posted to Artists and killed 24 March 1918. Age 33.

Wortley, J.H., 9223, A, November 1910, Norbury, Awarded DCM in Half Yearly Honours List January 1917:

This N.C.O. has been with the Battalion in France since November 1914 and since October 1915 he has been Battalion Pioneer Sergeant in which capacity he has always shown great devotion to duty and untiring zeal in his work. While the Battalion was at Hebuterne he worked on trenches and dugouts incessantly, often under heavy shellfire, and during the present operations on the Somme he has always behaved in a most exemplary and gallant manner and in addition to his ordinary duties as Pioneer Sergeant has practically performed those of the B.S.M. while in the line. He has at all times been of the very greatest service to me.

Wray, M., 9292, O, June 1911, 24 Kingsmead Road, Tulse Hill, Brighton March. Sergeant. Commissioned in Field May 1915. Seconded to Rifle Brigade from March 1916 and served in Salonika. Rejoined LRB post-war as Rifleman and was embodied in 1st Battalion (7th RB) in September 1939.

The Original Second Battalion

Frequent reference has been made throughout these pages to the personnel of the LRB's second line unit which began recruiting in September 1914. The incomplete list below shows what happened to some of the original non-commissioned members of the battalion during their Army service. As all these men enlisted in September or October 1914 there is little point in detailing the actual date of attestation, so the information runs as follows: name, original regimental number, residence, occupation or place of work and then any additional details:

Atkinson, H.J., 165, Dulwich, Westminster Bank, Croydon. Commissioned to 8th KOYLI, Killed in Action, August 1916, Age 22.

Appleyard, E.J., 427, Stoke Newington, Simpkin, Marshall, Hamilton and Company (City). Went with 2nd Battalion, Posted to Artists, Died of Wounds, 2 June 1918, Bagneux British Cemetery, Age 26.

Bartlett, D.B., 160, Streatham, Cluttons (Westminster), Posted to 1st Battalion, Killed in Action, 3 May 1915, Menin Gate, Rifleman, Aged 21.

Bartlett, L.F., 1077, Leytonstone, Credit Lyonnais, Posted to 1st Battalion, March 1915. Killed in Action, 13 May 1915, New Irish Farm Cemetery, Rifleman, Age 20.

Bleaden, L.A., 690, 71 Northbrook Road, Ilford, Patent Office, Posted to 1st Battalion and home with (gas) wounds May 1915. On recruiting duties in London until rejoined 1st Battalion May 1916. Killed in Action, 1 July 1916. Thiepval Memorial, Rifleman, Age 20. His brother was killed serving with the Royal Fusiliers seven days later, and another brother served in the Honourable Artillery Company.

Bradford, C.W., 789, Kensington, native of Eastbourne, Bank Clerk, Posted 1st battalion, possibly *Chyebassa*, MM at 2nd Ypres. Killed accidentally just before returning home for commission 20 July 1916. Hannescamps New Cemetery, Sergeant, Age 29.

Brown, L.V., 605, 102 Teignmouth Road, Cricklewood, London and South West Bank, Posted to 1st Battalion, March 1915, Killed in Action, 27 April 1915. Menin Gate, Rifleman, Age 21.

Burge, L.G., 228, Stroud Green, Commercial traveller, Posted to 1st Battalion, February 1915, Killed in Action, 3 May 1915, Menin Gate, Rifleman.

Burroughs, T.E., 235, London, Posted to 1st Battalion, January 1915. Returned home for commission as Sergeant in July 1916. Rejoined 1st Battalion January 1917. At times Bombing Officer and Adjutant. Citation for MC in *London Gazette* 22 June 1918:

For conspicuous gallantry during the German attack near Gavrelle 28 March. This officer organised the remnants of Battalion HQ personnel and established in succession five bomb blocks. He personally held three and in no case did he withdraw until his bombs gave out. As soon as fresh supplies were picked up in the trenches a further stand was made. On nearing the Red Line a block was established and this line was held finally. He showed a complete disregard of danger and his high spirits and cheerfulness were an excellent example.

He was later awarded a Bar to his MC:

Throughout the whole period 26-30 August 1918 in which the Battalion was attacking from East of Boyelle to Bullecourt this officer showed great skill in handling his Company and always kept HQ informed of actual situations often under very difficult circumstances. On 28 August his Company was detached to clear a picket of machine guns and form a defensive flank for the advance of the Brigade on Bullecourt. When he found he could not get on he sent back for a T.M., organised his attack and led it himself capturing six machine-guns with their teams, thus saving a very critical situation.

The strain of his wartime service was generally thought to be the cause of Tom Burrough's early death in 1920.

Butcher, H.T., 317, Purley. Commissioned to Rifle Brigade, Killed in Action, 18 February 1916. Essex Farm Cemetery, Age 25.

Butler, E., 171, 'Calcutts', North Hyde, Heston, Land agents, Tring. Posted to 1st Battalion, Killed in Action, 3 May 1915, Menin Gate, Rifleman, Age 23.

Calder, J.S., 656, Wanstead, London University, Schoolmaster, Posted to 1st Battalion and sailed on *Chyebassa*, Wounded May 1915 as Corporal, CSM by February 1916 and home for commission into 3rd Battalion. Rejoined 1st Battalion, November 1916, Killed in Action, 28 March 1918, Arras Memorial, Age 30.

Chamberlain, E.J., 791, Thornton Heath, LCC Education Department. Commissioned into Rifle Brigade, Killed in Action, 6 October 1917, Age 24.

Claridge, A.A., 316, Gerards Cross, Brechmeyer, (Holborn Viaduct), Posted to 1st Battalion, Killed in Action, 13 May 1915, Menin Gate, Corporal, Age 32.

Claridge, A.B., 322, Ilford, Oppenheimer, ((Holborn), Posted to 30/London (Home Service Battalion), then to 26/Royal Fusiliers. Killed in Action, 20 September 1917, Age 27. Enlisted with his brother.

Cooke, A., 830, Islington, LGC, Education Department, Posted to 1st Battalion, March 1915, Wounded May 1915, Killed in Action, 1 July 1916. Thiepval Memorial, Rifleman, Age 24.

Darrington, H.E., 296, Commissioned to 9th Middlesex May 1915, Killed in Action. In RFC, 20 November 1917.

Davis, S.J., 381, Wallington, Samuel Kid, (City). To France with Battalion January 1917 as Battalion MG Sergeant. Home for Commission June 1918 to LRB. Died 1962.

Day, W., 174 Goodmayes, Burberry's (London). To France with Battalion, Died of Wounds, 9 October 1917, Etaples Cemetery, Lance Sergeant, Aged 22.

Elkington, H.J., 572, Romford, Continental Type Company. Posted to 1st Battalion and wounded while serving with MG Section May 1915. Home to 3rd Battalion. Helped to make the LRB Badge on the hill above Fovant. Died 1959.

Ebbetts, S.A., 784, 30 Wormholt Road, Shepherds Bush, LCC, Education Department. Posted to 1st Battalion, September 1915, Killed in Action, 1

July 1916. Thiepval Memorial, Corporal, Age 25. His twin brother enlisted at the same time and survived the war.

Emerson, F., 961, London, To France with 2nd Battalion and invalided home April 1917. Commissioned in 3rd Battalion, May 1918. To France and posted 2/2 London, Killed in Action, 26 August 1918.

Freeman, B., 812, Tottenham, Tottenham Education Department. Posted to 1st Battalion, Died of Wounds, 28 August 1918. Buried Neiderzwehren Cemetery, Cassel, Germany.

Garton, E., 1047, Blackheath, Local business. Posted to 1st Battalion, January 1915. Died of Meningitis, 9 March 1915, Longuenesse Souvenir Cemetery, Bugler, Age 20.

Gower, H.W., 582, Cricklewood, Insurance Clerk. To France with 2nd Battalion, Wounded May 1917. To 3rd Battalion on recovery as Sergeant Musketry Instructor, Company Commander in 5th Bucks Home Guard 1940-45.

Gumprecht, E., 790, King's Oak Hotel, High Beech, Loughton, Pearl Assurance. Posted to 1st Battalion, January 1915, Killed in Action, 3 May 1915, Menin Gate, Rifleman, Age 21, B.Sc. (London).

Harvey, H.F., 847, New Barnet, C, Williamson (City), Posted to 1st Battalion, March 1915, Died of Wounds, 23 May 1915, Buried Christ Church, Barnet, Rifleman, Age 21.

Haseldine, N.W., 314, Clapham, London and S.W. Bank, Posted to 1st Battalion, March 1915, Killed in Action, 3 May 1915, Menin Gate, Rifleman.

Hewitt, T.A., 617, Letchworth, Solicitor of Supreme Court. Posted to 1st Battalion, January 1915, Killed in Action, 3 May 1915, Menin Gate, Rifleman, Aged 26. Parents lived in Australia. LL.B. (London).

Hodson, W., 298, London, Draper, Posted to 1st Battalion, January 1915, MG Section, Died of Wounds, 22 May 1915 in Wandsworth Military Hospital. Age 23.

Hooson, H.B., 816, Highhams Park, LCC Education Department. To France with Battalion. Into Insurance after the war and helped to set up the City Branch of the British Legion. Died 1961.

Howard, M., 739, Hove, Salesman, Posted to 1st Battalion, January 1915. Wounded May 1915 (gas) and home. Instructor in 3rd Battalion, Civil Defence Officer 1939-45.

Howells, F.J., 1011. To France with 2nd Battalion. Awarded MM at Bullecourt. Home for commission October 1917, Second Lieutenant May 1918. Back to France in August and posted elsewhere.

Johnson, A.B., 589, 112 Choumert Road, Peckham. Native of Westcliffe-on-Sea, Colonial Bank, Posted to 1st Battalion, Killed in Action, 1 July 1916, Thiepval Memorial, Rifleman, Age 22.

King, G.Z., 951, Norwich, Posted to 1st Battalion, D Company, Killed in Action, 1 July 1916, Thiepval Memorial, Sergeant, Age 42.

Lane, H.V., 829, Kensington, LCC Education Department. Out with 2nd Battalion. Posted to Artists, Died of Wounds, 29 March 1918, Mons Communal Cemetery, Corporal, Aged 30.

Light, J., 1063, Brighton, Sewell, Edwards and Neville (City). Posted to 1st Battalion, Killed in Action, 3 May 1915, Menin Gate, Rifleman, Age 26.

Linzell, H.H., 717, Finchley, Posted to 1st Battalion, March 1915. Home for commission Border Regiment, Killed in Action 3 July 1916, 7th Border, Danzig Alley Cemetery, Age 21. MC.

Madder, R., 465, Carshalton. On staff of P & O Line, Commissioned 1915 to Gloucester Regiment, Killed in Action, 20 July 1916. Treasurer of the London Shipping Orchestral Society.

McVeagh, A.J., 709, London. Had been a Corporal in the City Imperial Volunteers. In LRB 1908-10. Re-enlisted September 1914 and posted to 1st Battalion almost immediately. *Chyebassa*. Served continuously in France until demobilisation in March 1919 as CSM. Mentioned in Despatches April 1916. Citation for Belgian Croix de Guerre, awarded February 1918:
This W.O. has served continuously in France and Flanders since November 1914 during which time he has fought in the vicinity of Ypres in 1914, 1915 and 1917. During the recent operations near Moeuvres he was acting Battalion Sergeant-Major. He has on all occasions shown an excellent example and displayed great courage.

Metcalfe, J.H., 439, Forest Gate. Out with 2nd Battalion, January 1917. Home for commission to LRB. To France August 1918 and posted to 2/17th London.

Morris, P.D., 180, Hendon, Posted to 1st Battalion, Died of Wounds, 2 July 1916, Walincourte Halte Cemetery, Lance Corporal, Age 22. One of seven sons; five were serving, four had passed through the LRB.

Newell, J.G., 282, 3 Breakspears Road, St. Johns (SE4). Family paper-making business. Posted to 1st Battalion, early 1915, Killed in Action, 28 April 1915. Menin Gate, Rifleman, Age 21.

Noel, A., 836, Highbury, Jewellers in the City. Commissioned to 2nd London and Killed in Action, 3 May 1917. Had enlisted with his brother.

Parker, R.M., 984, Clapham, Articled clerk. Posted to 1st Battalion, March 1915, Wounded 2 May 1915 and then to 3rd Battalion. Commissioned to ASC, October 1915 and served with it until October 1917. Then re-trained for infantry with 3rd Battalion, LRB. To France March 1918 and posted to 2/10th London. Wounded 12 August 1918. Home Guard 1940-45.

Patrick, J.J., 1092, Battersea, Accounts Department, Kilburn Town Hall, Posted 1st Battalion, Wounded May 1915. Home for commission to 2/10th Middlesex. Out to Egypt, Died 1980.

Pearman, C.V., 401, Finchley, British and Dominion Insurance Company. Posted to 1st Battalion, August 1915. Died of Wounds (received at Gommecourt) 18 July 1916 in Cambridge Hospital, Aldershot, Lance Corporal.

Powell, W.F., 408, London, Draughtsman. Posted to 1st Battalion, March 1915. Wounded May 1915, July 1915 to November 1917 with Signal Section 1st Battalion, then left LRB to become topographical draughtsman at IV Corps HQ. Died 1982.

Radford, F.S., 529, Lee (Kent). Out with Battalion and then posted to 18th London when disbanded, Killed in Action, 21 March 1918. Sergeant. Age 31.

Rhodes, M.J., 575, 'Crossways', Little Kimble, Bucks. Resided in Balham. Commercial Union (Cornhill). Out with 2nd Battalion, Killed in Action, 20 September 1917. Menin Gate, Corporal, Age 37.

Rimington, E.W., 246, South Norwood, Leary and Company (City), Posted to 1st Battalion, January 1915, Died of Wounds, 30 April 1915. Bailleul Communal Cemetery Extension, Rifleman, Age 23.

Rowlatt, W., 658, Putney, Buenos Ayres and Pacific Rail Company (City), Posted to 1st Battalion, August 1915, C Company, Killed in Action, 1 July 1916, Thiepval Memorial, Rifleman, Age 37.

Sanders, W.F., 781, Harlesden, Willesden Education Department, Posted to 1st Battalion, August 1915, Killed in Action, 1 July 1916, Thiepval Memorial, Rifleman, Age 24.

Schaeffer, E., 395, The Thatched House, Muswell Hill, Family business, Posted to 1st Battalion, January 1915, B Company, Killed in Action, 13 May 1915, Menin Gate, Rifleman, Aged 25. His brother enlisted at the same time and was wounded at 2nd Ypres. On recovery he was commissioned into the KRRC.

Searle, A.E., 285, Ware, City and Midland Bank. Posted to 1st Battalion, 1915, Killed in Action, 1 July 1916, Thiepval Memorial, Corporal, Age 23.

Slater, F.M., 9902, Muswell Hill, Lloyds Bank, Enlisted August 1914 in 1st Battalion. Posted to 2nd Battalion and then to 34th London, Killed in Action, 24 August 1918, Lance Corporal.

Smith, A.M., 145, London, Office clerk. Posted to 1st Battalion, January 1915. Transferred to Transport Section, August 1915. Served continuously, Citation for MM:

During the operations of 14-16 August 1917 this rifleman showed gallantry and courage when employed on the Brigade transport. When bringing up ammunition etc for the attack his limber sank in the mud. Under heavy shellfire and without assistance he unloaded the front half and was then able to get out of the mud. He reloaded and proceeded to the Dump. He then returned for the front half limber which he dealt with in the same way - the whole time under shellfire.

Smith was later awarded a Bar to his M.M.:

During operations near Sebourg and Angreau on 4-6 November 1918, this rifleman was in charge of the T.M. limber. He spent the whole time under heaviest fire taking up his limber to foremost positions. It is due to his courage and determination that it was possible for hostile machine-guns to be silenced by T.M. fire. He was quite fearless and carried out his duties with great courage under trying conditions.

Terry, J.W., 275, Godson Road, Thornton Heath. Clerk in London and South Western Railway. To France with 2nd Battalion. Wounded September 1916 and home for commission. Posted to 1st Battalion, September 1918. MC for the crossing of the Honnelle, November 1918.

For conspicuous gallantry on 5 and 6 November near Angreau. He was in charge of leading patrol to enter Angreau and conducted a successful mopping up expedition in the village. On 6 November he showed excellent leadership and it is largely due to this officer that the Company, extended to

20 paces, reached its first objective, although the advance was across a river and through a wood under heavy machine-gun fire.

Returned to work at the London and S.W. Railway. Died 1986.

Thain, A.E., London, Solicitor's clerk. Lewis Gun Instructor and went with 2nd Battalion, A Company. Served right through until disbanding and posted to London Irish. Demobilised as Sergeant 1919. Home Guard 1940-45. Died 1988.

Thomas, E.G., 457. Commissioned September 1915 and then to 3rd Battalion. To 1st Battalion, May 1916. Severely wounded 1 July 1916 and invalided out blind 1917.

Townend, C.R., 196, Croydon. Insurance broker. Posted to 1st Battalion, January 1915. Died of Wounds, 23 June 1915 (received at Ypres) in Charing Cross Hospital. Buried Shirley (Surrey), Rifleman, Age 25.

Ward, J., 978, Brentwood, Royal Exchange Buildings. Out with 2nd Battalion. Then posted to Artists. Died of Wounds, 29 March 1918. Etaples Cemetery. Corporal. Age 23.

West, W.F., 823, Southall, LCC Education Department. Posted to 1st Battalion, 1915, Died of Wounds at home 12 May 1915. Buried City of London Cemetery, (East Ham), Rifleman, Age 25.

Williamson, E.R., 33, Vincent Road, Croydon. Posted to 1st Battalion, January 1915. Commissioned in LRB February 1915 and home March 1915. Rejoined 1st Battalion January 1916 and posted to 169 LTM Battery, April 1916, Killed in Action, 10 September 1916. Thiepval Memorial, Age 22. Citation for MC:

For conspicuous bravery at Gommecourt on 1 July 1916 whilst employed in the 169 Infantry Brigade T.M. Battery. He took charge of a section which had lost its officer and did fine work in reconnoitring, bombing and rallying straggling men.

Wilkinson, H.G., 904, Radley College. Commissioned to LRB February 1915. To France with 2nd Battalion as Lieutenant. Attached to Artists February 1918. Commanded them April-August 1918 until severely wounded.

APPENDIX IX

Awards to Officers, NCOs and Riflemen Serving with the LRB

The rank and the Regimental or Army Number given is usually that held by the NCO or rifleman at the time of the award, but this number is not necessarily the one with which the man finished the war. The sources for the men with numbers before their names are the War Diaries, (whose awards entries are known to be incomplete) and a note book found in the LRB Collection, *The Regimental History* and other, official, sources have been used for the men without numbers. This list does not include men who were either trained in or commissioned into the LRB and then later posted to other regiments. The date given can refer either to the date of the event for which the award was given, or when it was gazetted. The great majority of those NCO's and riflemen without numbers or dates for their awards will have belonged to the 2nd Battalion. This battalion's War Diary mentions the number of Military Medals awarded after various actions, but apart from the rare exception, not the names of the individual recipients; for example, 26 MMs were awarded following the 20 September 1917 battle, and a further 19 in January 1918.

VC = Victoria Cross
MC = Military Cross
MM = Military Medal
DSO = Distinguished Service Order
DCM = Distinguished Conduct Medal
MSM = Meritorious Service Medal

Only British, French and Belgian Awards are listed:

Name, Regimental/Army Number, Rank, Award and Date, Former Regiment, Date if killed:

Adams, E.A., 6968, Sergeant, DCM, 30 June 1915.
Adams, J., 1867, A/RSM, DCM, 9 July 1917, MM, 6 May 1916.
Alesbury, R.E., 372456, Rifleman, MM, 6 November 1918, 8th London.
Allison, R., 318351, Rifleman, MM, 27 October 1918, West Surrey.
Andrews, L.W., Rifleman, MM.
Atkinson, W.L., Rifleman, MM.
Bailey, S.E., 300853, Rifleman, MM. June 1918.
Baker, G.G., 304885, Rifleman, MM, 6 November 1918.
Baker, H.G., 304093, Sergeant, DCM, 18 July 1917.
Baldock, W.T., 371297, Rifleman, MM, September 1918, 8th London.
Banks, W., 741561, Rifleman, MM, 6 November 1918, 25th London.
Barker, H., 318076, Rifleman, DCM, 26 June 1918, Unknown.
Barker, H., 371206, Lance Corporal, MM, April 1918, 8th London.

Barrell, A.H., 304084, A/RSM, DCM, 21 October 1918.
Barrett, A., 45143, Sergeant, MM, 6 November 1918, Rifle Brigade.
Barry, F.P., Captain, MC, May 1917.
Bates, A.S., Lieutenant-Colonel, DSO 23 June 1915, French Croix de
                    Guerre (with Palm).
Bazire, A.E., Rifleman, MM, 20 September 1917.
Beauchamp, W.S., Lance Sergeant, MM, 20 September 1917.
Belcher, D.W., 9539, Lance Sergeant, VC, 13 May 1915.
Bell, M.J., Rifleman, MM.
Berry, W.H., 300991, Rifleman, MM, 6 November 1918.
Billington, W.L., 9921, Sergeant, MM, 13 May 1915.
Bishop, W.S., 304745, Rifleman, MM, 16 August 1917.
Blumson, W.J., Lance Corporal, MM.
Bolton, F.H.M., Rifleman, MM, 12 September 1917.
Bone, R.G., Lance Corporal, MM, 12 September 1917.
Boston, G.G., 9497, Lance Corporal, DCM, 11 March 1916.
Bottomley, C., 300437, RSM, DCM, 6 February 1918.
Bouverie, C., 302078, Sergeant, MM, June 1917.
Box, J.H.G., Rifleman, MM, 20 September 1917.
Bradford, C.W., 787, Sergeant, MM, 2 May 1915, Date killed 19 July 1916.
Branch, S.O., 9482, Lance Corporal, MM.
Bridges, E.L., Lance Corporal, MM.
Brock, F.H., 300708, Sergeant, DCM, 6 February 1918.
Buck, H.G., 1124, Lance Corporal, MM, 27 October 1916.
Burnell, C.D., Lieutenant Colonel, DSO, 3 June 1919.
Burningham, C., Rifleman, MM.
Burroughs, T.E., Captain, MC, 22 June 1918, Bar, August 1918.
Burton, J.A., 300417, Sergeant, MM, May 1917.
Bushell, W., 315235, Rifleman, DCM, 26 January 1918, 18th London.
Buxton, P., 45136, Rifleman, MM, 5 November 1918, Rifle Brigade, Date
                    killed 11 December 1918.
Calder, J.S., Captain, MC, December 1917, Bar, 16 March 1918, Date
                    killed 28 March 1918.
Carpenter, C., 305186, Lance Corporal, MM, 6 November 1918.
Charles, P.D., 300184, Lance Corporal, DCM, 3 September 1919.
Chart, H.B., 303156, Rifleman, MM, 16 August 1917.
Chodak, H.A., (RAMC), Lieutenant, MC.
Clarke, H.G., Rifleman, MM.
Clarke, R.S., 8896, Rifleman, DCM, 11 March 1916.
Cowley, J., 304138, Rifleman, MM, 16 August 1917.
Cowley, W.J., Sergeant, MM.
Crews, F.H., Captain, MC, 25 November 1916.
Crisp, H.J.C., 9298, Lance Corporal, MM, 10 September 1916.
Crocker, F.A., 1289, Rifleman
Crockford, A.H.J., Sergeant, MM.
Cross, S.H., Second Lieutenant, MC, 14 June 1917.
Cruwys, L.E., Sergeant, MM, 12 September 1917.
Cutting, H., 318218, Lance Corporal, DCM, January 1919, London Regiment.

Davies, T., 304148, Rifleman, MM, 16 August 1917.

Deacon, W., 45425, Lance Corporal, MM, September 1918, Rifle Brigade.

Dearing, C., 300335, Corporal, MM, 2 December 1917.

Dickson, J.E., 315389, Sergeant, MM, 5 November 1918, Durham L.I.

Doughty, C., Corporal, MM.

Ducker, R.F., 301180, Rifleman, MM. 16 August 1917.

Dunk, H.W., 2516, Rifleman, MM, 10 September 1916.

Dunnett, W.E., 92, Rifleman, MM.

Durant, A., 370367, Rifleman, MM, 6 November 1918, 8th London.

Dyer, P.T., 660, Sergeant, MM, 2 August 1916.

Ebbetts, R.F., 776, Corporal, MM, 1 July 1916.

Edington, A., 2822, Rifleman, MM, 1 September 1916.

Evanson, E., 1495, A/RQMS, MM, 1918.

Ewins, V.B., 302300, Rifleman, MM, May 1917.

Feather, E., 45325, Rifleman, MM, 6 November 1918, Rifle Brigade.

Feeley, P.F., 315229, Lance Corporal, MM, 16 August 1917, London Regiment.

Foaden, J.H., 1621, Lance Corporal, MM, 1 September 1916.

Foster, G.E., 301666, Lance Corporal, MM, May 1917, Date killed 20 September 1917.

Fowle, V.L., 1220, Lance Corporal, MM, 1 September 1916.

Foxall, A.T., 371955, Corporal, MM, 23 November 1917, 8th London.

Freemont, L.T., Rifleman, MM.

Frentzel, W.N., 301519, Corporal, MM, 20 September 1917, Date killed 9 November 1918.

Frost, A.A., 300110, CQMS, MSM, 1918.

Gant, F.A., 300609, Rifleman, MM, 16 August 1917.

Gates, W.R., Rifleman, MM.

Gee, J.P., Second Lieutenant, MC, 27 August 1918.

Gibson, C.G., Lance Corporal, Belgian Croix de Guerre.

Godsmark, P., 9535, Corporal, MM. 27 October 1916.

Golton, L., 305098, Rifleman, MM, 5 November 1918.

Goodall, A., 300560, Rifleman, MM, 16 August 1917.

Gordon, A., 9435, Sergeant, DCM, 21 June 1916.

Gordon, G., 9457, Rifleman, MM, 27 October 1916.

Gordon, S., 496, Sergeant, MM, 18 April 1917.

Grain, G.W., 318050, Sergeant, MM, September 1918, London Regiment.

Grainger, P.T., 302894, Rifleman, MM, November 1918.

Gration, J., 302774, Sergeant, DCM, 21 October 1918, Date killed 24 March 1918.

Gray, A., 301633, Rifleman, MM, Date killed 10 August 1918.

Greene, F.N., 300504, Rifleman, MM, December 1917.

Greenfield, P., Corporal, MM, 20 September 1917.

Grimwood, P.L., Second Lieutenant, MC, 6 November 1918.

Hamilton, W.G., 300001, RQMS, MSM, June 1918.

Hammond, S.A., 818, Lance Sergeant, MM, April 1917.

Hancocks, F.G., Captain, MC, June 1918.

Hands, G., 150, Sergeant, DCM, 13 February 1917.

Harvest, G.L., Lieutenant, MC, May 1917, 20 June 1917.

Hawthorn, W., 10535, Rifleman, MM, 9 September 1916, 8th London.

Hayes, J., 304070, Lance Corporal, MM, 16 August 1917, 8th London.

Haylock, J.O., 9899, Sergeant, MM, 27 October 1916.

Helsham, G.D., 35216, Rifleman, MM, September 1918 Rifle Brigade.

Hernberg, D., 570282, Lance Corporal, MM, 20 September 1917, 17th
London.

Hilay, E.J., Rifleman, MM.

Hilling, J.A., 370437, Lance Corporal, MM, April 1918, 8th London.

Hoadley, V.S., 301252, Corporal, MM, 16 August 1917.

Hodges, H.W., Sergeant, MM.

Hodgkinson, E.W., 161, Rifleman, MM, 27 October 1916.

Holland, E., 302586, Rifleman, MM, 16 August 1917.

Holtorp, P., 305442, Sergeant, MM, 16 August 1917.

Hood, D., 2Lt., MC, 3 May 1917.

Hooson, H.B., Sergeant, MM.

Hotz, R.C., 300880, Corporal, DCM, 6 February 1918.

Houghton, H.R., 300858, Rifleman, MM, 16 August 1917.

Houston, J., 302597, Corporal, MM, 16 August 1917.

Howells, J., 300640, Sergeant, MM, May 1917.

Hughes, E., 300449, Sergeant, MM, 16 August 1917.

Hunter, T.W., 9587, Rifleman, MSM, May 1915.

Husey, R.H., Brigadier General, DSO, 1 January 1918, Bar 22 June
1918, MC May 1915, Date killed 30 May 1918.

Imber, E.A., Rifleman, MM, 20 September 1917.

Ingle, F., 43770, Rifleman, MM, September 1918, Rifle Brigade.

James, A.E., 574021, Rifleman, MM, 29 August 1918, 17th London.

James, F.A., Rifleman, MM.

Jarvis, O.V., Lance Corporal, MM.

John, C.H., Captain, MC, 6 November 1918.

Johnston, C.L., Lieutenant Colonel, DSO, 7 November 1918.

Johnston, H.L., Captain, MC.

Keele, F.C., 10835, Sergeant, MM, 10 September 1916, 7th Middlesex,
Date killed 21 June 1917.

Kench, E.L., 10039, Rifleman, DCM, 25 November 1916, 7th Essex.

Kench, W., 304237, Sergeant, MM, 16 August 1917, 7th Middlesex,
Date killed 28 March 1918.

Kent, H.J., Q.M. and Lieutenant, MC, January 1918.

Kibby, D., Rifleman, MM, 20 September 1917.

Kingsbury, T.A., 300792, Corporal, DCM, 6 February 1918.

Latham, E.B., 9609, Rifleman, MM, May 1915.

Lee, G.M., Sergeant, MM.

Leech, R., 45271, Rifleman, DCM, 10 January 1920, Rifle Brigade.

Lewis, S.H., 300416, Sergeant, MM, 6 November 1918.

Libby, F.T., 302391, Lance Corporal, MM, Date killed 4 May 1917.

Lilley, W.M., 515, Sergeant, DCM 22 September 1916, Belgian Croix
de Guerre, 1917.

Lindsay, J.S., 1006, Rifleman, DCM, 11 March 1916.
Lintott, A.J.C., Lieutenant, MC, January 1918.
Lockhart, W.E., 9597, Rifleman, MM, 27 October 1916.
Lovett, G., 370142, Sergeant, MM, 5 November 1918, 8th London.
Lowe, H.S., 303197, Lance Corporal, MM, Bar, Date killed 5 April 1918.
Mackay, D., 129, Sergeant, MSM, May 1915.
Maginn, F.J., Second Lieutenant, DSO, 5 July 1918.
McLoughlin, M.N., 300135, Rifleman, MM, 16 August 1917.
McVeagh, A.J., 300516, CSM, Belgian Croix de Guerre, February 1918.
Marlone, T., Sergeant, MSM.
Martin, A.G., 24, Lance Corporal, MM, 23 November 1917.
Martin, A.J., 370151, Rifleman, MM, December 1917, 8th London.
Maskell, L.S., 315296, CSM, DCM, 11 March 1920.
Mason, W.G., 1131, Sergeant, MM, 21 December 1916.
Milcovich, M., 301580, Sergeant, MM, 1918.
Miller, F.W.M., Rifleman, MM.
Moore, G.G., 304265, Sergeant, DCM, 18 July 1917, 7th Middlesex, 15
                    August 1917.
Moore, N.C., 45349, Rifleman, MM, 6 November 1918, Rifle Brigade.
Mortimore, P.J., Sergeant, MSM.
Morton, J.F., Lance Corporal, MM.
Munday, H.W., 300467, Sergeant, MSM, June 1917.
Murrell, S.A., Sergeant, MM.
Newell, W.H., 304392, Rifleman, MM, 16 August 1917, 7th Middlesex.
Newman, C., 300057, Rifleman, MM, 16 August 1917.
North, F., 304283, Lance Corporal, MM, 16 August 1917, 7th Middlesex.
Otter, F.L., Captain, MC, 20 September 1917.
Over, E., Sergeant, MSM.
Parslow, R., 762, Lance Sergeant, MM, 21 December 1916.
Parsons, A.R., 301687, Rifleman, MM, June 1917.
Payne, H., 302994, Rifleman, MM, 16 August 1917.
Pearson, R., 302117, Rifleman, MM, 16 August 1917.
Pembroke, J.A., Corporal, MM.
Penney, G.C., 9239, Lance Sergeant, MSM.
Petley, R.E., Second Lieutenant, MC, 1 July 1916.
Pilley, F., Rifleman, MM.
Porter, H.R., 301720, Lance Corporal, DCM, 6 February 1918.
Pothecary, W.F., 9338, Sergeant, DCM, 30 June 1915.
Potter, C.G., 300912, Sergeant, MM, May 1917.
Pratley, L.A., 318046, Sergeant, MM, September 1918, London Regiment.
Prike, L., Lance Sergeant, MM, 20 September 1917.
Pringle, E., 7015, Sergeant, MSM.
Pullen, C., 318048, Sergeant, DCM, 26 June 1918.
Raines, C., Rifleman, MM.
Reeve, G.R., Second Lieutenant, MC, April 1918.
Riddell, J.W., (RAMC), Captain, MC, 1917.
Richmond, W.J., Sergeant, MM.
Rippingale, C.G., Corporal, MM.

Robinson, F.S., 300042, Sergeant, MM, December 1917.

Rogers, R., 300933, Corporal, MSM, September 1918.

Ross, R., 315372, Rifleman, MM, 6 November 1918, Durham L.I.

Roulston, W.A., 9995, Sergeant, DCM, 14 November 1916, Date killed
        8 October 1916.

Rowe, H.J., 9471, Lance Corporal, MM, 27 October 1916.

Rowe, W.T., Rifleman, MM.

Russell, R., Captain, MC, 1915.

Sceats, D.B., 300012, CQMS, MSM.

Sears, H., Lance Sergeant, MM, 20 September 1917.

Simmonds, W.H., 300171, Sergeant, MM, 16 August 1917.

Slade, E.H., 9412, Sergeant, MM, 27 October 1916, 2Lt, MC, 16 August 1917.

Slade, J.H., Lance Corporal, MM.

Small, A.E., 301043, Lance Corporal, MM, April 1918.

Smith, A.M., 300281, Rifleman, MM, 16 August 1917, Bar 6 November 1918.

Smith, F.A., Lance Corporal, MM.

Somers-Smith, J.R., Captain, MC, 1 July 1916, Date killed 1 July 1916.

Spettigue, P.R., Second Lieutenant, MC, 30 August 1918.

Stapeley, T.W., 300788, Sergeant, DCM, 6 February 1918.

Stewart, P.D., Lieutenant Colonel, DSO, 27 October 1917, Dragoon Guards.

Stock, C., 302951, Rifleman, MM, September 1918.

Stockdale, H., 315358, Rifleman, DCM, 15 November 1918, Unknown.

Stonnill, R.H., 9137, Lance Corporal, MM, 27 October 1916.

Stow, H., 304355, Lance Corporal, MM, September 1918, 7th Middlesex.

Straker, S.E., 9777, CQMS, MSM.

Stransom, J.H., 75, Lance Corporal, DCM, 30 June 1915.

Sullivan, L.J., Staff Sergeant, MSM.

Swann, W.F., 300108, Sergeant, Belgian Croix de Guerre, 1917.

Tabberer, C.O., Captain, MC, November 1918, QVR.

Tatterton, W., 45202, Rifleman, MM, September 1918, Rifle Brigade,
        Date killed 5 November 1918.

Taylor, C., 11003, Lance Corporal, DCM, 6 February 1918, 7th Middlesex.

Taylor, H., Second Lieutenant, MC, 16 August 1917.

Terry, J.W., Second Lieutenant, MC, 6 November 1918.

Thomas, A.C., 147, Rifleman, MM, 27 October 1916.

Thomas, A.J., Rifleman, MM.

Thompson, L., 303930, Rifleman, MM, 3 May 1917.

Thompson, W.A., Second Lieutenant, MC, November 1918.

Thurnall, C.G., 301362, Lance Corporal, MM, 16 August 1917.

Timberlake, S.H., Lance Corporal, MM, 20 September 1917.

Todd, R.V., 8541, Sergeant, DCM, 5 August 1915.

Trehern, F.M., 300086, CSM, MM, 27 October 1918.

Trenow, G.F., Second Lieutenant, MC, May 1917, Date killed 20 September
        1917.

Trevelyan, C.W., Captain, MC.

Turner, H., 9289, Lance Corporal, MM, 27 October 1916.

Turner, T., 45391, Lance Sergeant, MM, 27 October 1918, Rifle Brigade.

Vaizey, G.R., Lance Corporal, MM, 20 September 1917.

Virgo, S.R., 132, C/Sergeant, MSM.

Von Berg, W.C., Captain, MC, 1918.

Wade, G., 315360, Rifleman, MM, September 1918, Unknown.

Wade, W., 304392, Rifleman, MM, 16 August 1917, 7th Middlesex.

Wallis, E.S., Corporal, MM.

Wallis, F.H., Lieutenant Colonel, MC, 1 July 1916, Bar, 16 August 1917, Bar, 11 December 1918.

Ward, A.R., 300054, Rifleman, MM, 16 August 1917.

Waugh, E.A., QMS, MSM.

Weston, C.J., Lance Corporal, MM.

White, A.Y., 301644, Lance Corporal, MM, 20 September 1917, Date killed 20 September 1917.

Williams, W.W., Rifleman, MM.

Williamson, E.R., Lieutenant, MC, 10 September 1916, Dated killed 25 August 1918.

Wilson, P., 301624, Sergeant, MM, June 1917.

Woodward, S.J., CQMS, MSM.

Wortley, J.H., 9223, Sergeant, DCM, 13 February 1917.

Wright, T.F., 301491, Rifleman, MM, May 1917.

Wynne-Williams, T.H., 302186, Rifleman, MM, 23 November 1917.

APPENDIX X

Medal Citations

Below is a selected list of the medal citations and Mentions in Despatches given to men serving with the LRB. Several such examples have already been included in previous appendices and as it would be impracticable to give the citations for all some 260 individual LRB medal winners and another almost 200 'Mentions', this list concentrates more on officers and those other ranks who were not members of the original 1st and 2nd Battalions.

372456 Alesbury, Rifleman P.E., MM.
On 5 November 1918 this rifleman voluntarily remained with a wounded comrade, in a position of danger and under heavy fire, pressing an artery which had been severed in the wounded man's leg. He stayed with the wounded man for an hour until help came and undoubtedly saved his life.

318351 Allison, Rifleman R.R., MM.
On 27 October 1918 this man's company was holding the forward outpost line, North of the Arras-Cambrai road. On 3 occasions he volunteered for and succeeded in getting through the enemy's bombardment to the forward posts, thus enabling his Company Commander to keep in touch and get to the Canal crossing at the right moment which was of vital importance to the subsequent proceedings.

300117 Babington, Corporal W.A. *Mention in Despatches, January 1918.*
For consistent good work, especially during the operations at Arras in April 1917 and Ypres August 1917. This corporal was NCO in charge of telephone lines and displayed great coolness and courage at all times.

304093 Baker, Lance Sergeant H.G., DCM.
On 3 May 1917 this NCO showed conspicuous gallantry especially in hand to hand fighting. During the advance he observed an enemy MG in action. With 3 men he charged the position and personally bayoneted the Germans and captured the MG which was brought in at night. Our left flank being exposed he established a strong point and used the captured MG with good effect on the Germans.

304084 Barrell, CSM, A.H. DCM.
This WO is my best CSM, and a most splendid and efficient type. He has at all times behaved in a most gallant and exemplary manner, and has always proved of the very greatest assistance to his company commander.

45143 Barrett, Sergeant A., MM.
Showed great courage during operations near Sebourg and Angreau 4-6 November, 1918. He was in charge of one of the mopping up parties in Angreau and by his good leadership and courage two MGs were silenced and the enemy

captured. On 6 November his section captured one officer and seven men and he afterwards helped to establish a forward post. Although badly wounded in the mouth he remained in charge of his section until dusk and his cheerfulness was a splendid example to all.

9921 Billington, Sergeant W.L., MM. *London Gazette, 27 October 1916.*
For conspicuous gallantry during the 2nd Battle of Ypres and more especially on 13 May 1915. His efforts to tend the wounded under the heaviest fire were unsparing. On the night of 13 May he rendered my MO and OC Trench invaluable assistance in finding, digging out, collecting and tending the wounded under continuous fire directed at stretcher parties and a relief which was taking place. Since this date he has been consistently attentive to all his duties under all circumstances.
(This recommendation was sent in to the authorities on 6 May 1916.)

304745 Bishop, Rifleman W.S., MM.
During the attack on the Polygon de Zonnebeke on 16 August 1917 this rifleman was in the first wave and showed complete disregard of danger. When the company stretcher bearers had become casualties he was detailed to act as SB. He carried out these duties attending to wounded the whole time under heavy MG fire. He arranged for walking wounded cases to help one another and it is due to his efforts that a large number of wounded were got back from the foremost wave to our lines.

300991 Berry, Rifleman W.H., MM.
During the operations near Angreau on 6 November 1918 this rifleman showed conspicuous gallantry whilst working as a linesman. During the entire day under the heaviest shellfire he continued to work without ever seeking cover, endeavouring to repair the telephone wires as fast as they were broken by shellfire.

305186 Carpenter, Lance Corporal C., MM.
This NCO showed conspicuous gallantry and initiative during operations near Angreau on 6 November 1918. The advance on his right was checked by MG fire and he at one realised the position and with one man pushed forward a Lewis Gun and silenced the enemy MG. His position was well in front of our line and he held this post until he was shelled out and forced to withdraw. His bravery undoubtedly helped the Company, on his right to reach their objective.

300184 Charles, Lance Corporal P.D., DCM.
During operations near Angreau on 5 November 1918 this NCO was in charge of 2 ration limbers. It was impossible to find carrying parties and he therefore took his limber to within 300 yards of the outpost line under the heaviest shell fire. On completion of his work he returned at the request of the Company Commander and brought up SAA and delivered same at Company HQ - the whole time under extremely heavy shell fire.

302074 Collins, Corporal C.
On 29 August 1918, near Croisilles, this NCO showed great courage and initiative in breaking down nests of enemy machine-guns and volunteered to bring in wounded under heavy machine-gun fire. On 30 August after all the officers and sergeants of his company had fallen, he took command and showed great initiative in leading the company to the attack.
(This recommendation was submitted for the award of a DCM, but Corporal Collins appears neither to have received that medal, nor even a Military Medal.)

9298 Crisp, Lance Corporal H.J.C., MM. *London Gazette, 27 October 1916.*
During the attack from Leuze Wood on 10 September 1916 he behaved in a most gallant and capable manner in getting reinforcements across the open ground under heavy fire. By his good leadership he was able to get his men through with a minimum of loss and by his coolness and courage was at all times an example to his men.

1289 Crocker, Rifleman F.A., MM.
September 1916; A Battalion runner. He carried several messages at all times of the day and night from Battalion HQ to the firing line. He was sent with an important message by day to the front line and was badly wounded leaving the trench. He however continued, delivered the message and returned in an exhausted condition with the reply. He previously received a card from the Divisional General for gallant conduct during the attack on Gommecourt on 1 July 1916.

Cross, Second Lieutenant S.H., MC.
For conspicuous gallantry on 3 May 1917. During the attack on Lanyard Trench he was acting as a company commander. With a small party of men he captured a machine-gun from the enemy. Over 1000 rounds were fired from this gun with good effect and numerous casualties were inflicted on the Germans. Afterwards he organised the consolidation of the position and handed over the machine gun to the 2nd London who occupied the north end of the trench. His coolness and courage under fire was a splendid example to his men.

318218 Cutting, Lance Corporal H., DCM.
During operations on 6 November this NCO showed conspicuous gallantry. On receiving a message from the first wave he acted promptly and successfully tackled a M.G. which had held up the advance and captured the garrison of 9 Germans. He was completely alone when he carried out this important work, his section all having become casualties.

300335 Dearing, Corporal C. MM.
During operations, near Moeuvres, on 2 December 1917 this NCO showed conspicuous courage. Under intense bombardment he worked in the open repairing lines and keeping the communications open between the front line and Battalion HQ. Regardless of danger he carried on his work throughout the day and after the Battalion was relieved he remained behind for several hours

repairing the lines in order to hand over 'communications' to the relieving Battalion. His devotion to duty and courage were excellent.

2516 Dunk, Rifleman H.W. MM.
As a S.B. he worked all day and night of 5 July 1916 without any thought to his own safety - volunteered for all the most difficult tasks and latterly, although wounded himself, still continued to work.
September 1916 - for conspicuous gallantry on 10 September. he worked throughout the day and night with the utmost coolness and courage attending to the wounded lying out in No Man's Land. In full daylight he carried a man on his back for 800 or 900 yards across the open and brought him into our lines under heavy shell fire, although he was wounded himself.

315229 Feeley, Lance Corporal P.F. MM.
During the attack on the Polygon de Zonnebeke on 16 August 1917 this NCO went forward alone when the advance was checked by MG fire, killed the enemy and captured the gun. With the aid of a Corporal in the 2nd London this NCO fired the gun into formations of the enemy as they approached. When compelled to withdraw, the gun was disabled. He also captured and killed 2 German snipers. During the whole day he set a magnificent example and showed great courage and gallantry.

Grimwood, Second Lieutenant P.L. MC.
During operations near Sebourg and Angreau 4-6 November 1918 this officer showed conspicuous gallantry. On 5 November the attack was held up by MG fire. This officer crawled forward and cleated these MGs and by skilful handling of his platoon, the MGs were silenced and the enemy captured or killed. On 6 November during a German counter-attack he rallied his men and held his position, inflicting casualties on the enemy until ordered to withdraw.

305098 Golton, Rifleman L.G. MM.
For conspicuous gallantry whilst on patrol near Angreau on 5 November 1918. His NCO was badly wounded and he crawled up with a comrade to render first aid. His comrade was also his, Rifleman Golton continued and got his NCO into dead ground and then crawled out again and got his comrade in. He brought back accurate information regarding the location of the MG position and finally assisted in silencing same.

300504 Greene, Rifleman F.N. MM.
Transport Driver; Near Moeuvres, on night of 2-3 December 1917, this rifleman was in charge of a Lewis Gun limber. A shell exploded near him, badly wounding him in the thigh, killing one of his horses and wounding the other. With great pluck and resource he cut loose his dead horse, gave another driver the harness to replace the harness that had been damaged by the same shell and finally brought back his wounded horse to the Transport Lines. He showed an excellent example to all drivers.

300001 Hamilton, RQMS, W.G. MSM. *London Gazette 17 June 1918.*
This Warrant Officer has acted as RQMS, since 1915 and has always carried out his duties in a most efficient and zealous manner. During the recent operations on the Cambrai front he acted as QM, and owing to his untiring work the Battalion was always catered for in the most satisfactory manner. This WO has served with the Battalion in France since November 1914 continuously and has never been absent from duty through illness or wounds.

818 Hammond, Acting Sergeant S.A. MM. *14 December 1917.*
For conspicuous gallantry and devotion to duty. This NCO is the Medical Officer's Orderly and displayed untiring energy during the whole period the Battalion was in action. On the night of 14 April [1917] when the Battalion was relieved he searched the ground and attended to a large number of wounded of several battalions although the ground was under shell and machine gun fire. He superintended the stretcher bearers and his courage was an example and encouragement to all he came in contact with.

Hancocks, Lieutenant F.G. MC.
For successfully organising and carrying out a daylight raid upon enemy posts east of Tilloy on 12 June 1918. The success of the raid was very largely due to this officer's skill and enterprise in preliminary reconnaissance, also to the excellent morale and fighting spirit of his men and engendered by his keenness, cheerfulness and ability as a leader.

150 Hands, Sergeant G. DCM. *New Year's Honours List, 1917.*
This NCO has been with the Battalion in France since November 1914. He came out as Cook-Sergeant and has served in that capacity ever since. Since May 1916 while the Battalion was at Hebuterne and during the recent operations on the Somme, this NCO has always, in the face of great difficulties and heavy fire, kept his cookers at work and has never failed the Battalion at all. His devotion to duty has been worthy of the highest praise.

35216 Helsham, Rifleman, G.D. MM.
Throughout the fighting from 26-29 August 1918, near Croisilles, this Rifleman never spared himself in attending to and bringing in the wounded. On the night of 28 August he went out single handed in front of our own lines - all this work was done under heavy MG fire.

370437 Hilling, Lance Corporal J.A. MM. *London Gazette 12 June 1918.*
During the German attack on 28 March 1918, near Gavrelle, this NCO held a bombing block with his section. When the attack developed down the trench, he held the enemy up with rifle fire and bombs, inflicting many casualties. His supply of bombs becoming exhausted he continued to delay the advance by manning the parapet with his section. He set an excellent example and showed good leadership.

Hood, Second Lieutenant D. MC.
For conspicuous gallantry during the attack on 3 May 1917. This officer did specially good work leading a bayonet fight. He was with the 4th wave and found a trench occupied by about 60 Germans and a MG which the earlier waves had passed by. He at once led a charge with 20 of his men, smashed the MG and after killing between 20 and 30 Germans, took the remainder prisoner. His example was magnificent and not only encouraged his men but largely helped to make the surviving Germans surrender.

300449 Hughes, Sergeant E. MM.
During the attack on the Polygon de Zonnebeke on 16 August 1917 this NCO was shot through the leg on leaving the trench in front of the Battalion Assembly Area. He continued the advance, cheering his men, encouraging them to overcome the marshy obstacles. He set a magnificent example. His wound compelled him to give up and he crawled back to our lines. During the whole time he displayed great coolness and courage.

Husey, Acting Lieutenant Colonel R.H. Bar to DSO. *London Gazette 22 June 1918.*
For conspicuous gallantry and devotion to duty during an enemy attack. When the enemy approached close to his battalion headquarters he held the forward end of a communication trench with the personnel of his headquarters and a few other men, and largely assisted in breaking up the enemy's attack. He used a rifle himself at close range, and inflicted many casualties on the enemy. He then conducted an obstinate withdrawal to the next line of defence, where the enemy were finally held up. He set a magnificent example of courage and determination.
(Ralph Husey died of wounds in German hands on 30 May 1918. He was originally buried in the village of Le Thour but was re-interred after the war in Vendresse British Cemetery.)

10039 Kench, Rifleman E.L.. DCM. *London Gazette 25 November 1916.*
With his Lewis Gun team he went with the first wave of our assault (8 October 1916) and on reaching the objective with only 3 of his team left, took up a position in an enemy sniper's post occupied at the time by 2 of the enemy who they killed. Then Rifleman Kench noticed parties of the enemy trying to work round our right flank. He brought his gun into action against large patrols and shot several parties with his rifle, thus preventing the enemy getting round our right flank. Later his remaining comrade was killed. When it became necessary for the two to withdraw, he brought his Lewis Gun with him.

304327 Kench, Sergeant W. MM.
During the attack on the Polygon de Zonnebeke on 16 August 1917 this NCO was acting SSE. All the officers of his company were killed or wounded and Sergeant Kench assumed command of the company. He made most determined efforts to maintain the ground won in the face of enemy counter-attacks. When the line was forced back he reorganised all the men he could find, put them in shell holes and gave fire orders. This position he held until the enemy fired at

him from both flanks. He withdrew in an orderly manner, 2 men at a time, and reported with his men to an officer of the QVR.

370142 Lovett, Sergeant G. MM.
During operations near Angreau on 5 November 1918 this NCO was a platoon commander and showed conspicuous gallantry and ability in handling his platoon. In the face of heavy MG fire he led his platoon and held his objective in spite of the fact that over half his platoon were casualties and he himself was wounded but carried on. He remained with his men for the attack on the following day and his courage was magnificent and an example to all.

Maginn, Second Lieutenant J.F. DSO. *London Gazette 5 July 1918.*
For conspicuous gallantry and devotion to duty. When an officer of another Regiment was very severely wounded and was unable to move he rushed forward with his stretcher bearers under heavy machine-gun and sniper fire and sniped the enemy for 15 minutes, covering the stretcher bearers, who were thus able to bring the wounded officer back. He showed splendid courage and resource.

304265 Moore, Sergeant G.G. DSM.
For conspicuous gallantry. On 11 April 1917 he led the bombing attack up Nepal Trench and established a block at the junction of Nepal and Heninel Trenches. The same night he cleared Heninel Trench up to the junction with Cojeul Trench. He held this important junction until all bombs available were thrown and his section had practically all become casualties. He then withdrew to Sunken Road and remained there until a fresh supply of bombs was obtained. He again energetically attacked and joined up with the 2/London at the junction of Heninel and Cojeul Trenches. 15 Germans were killed and 2 severely wounded in these attacks. Later he bombed a MG killing 2 men. The third man managed to get away with the gun.
(George Moore was killed near Glencorse Wood on 15 August 1917. His name appears on the Menin Gate.)

300467 Munday, Sergeant H.W. MSM. *June 1917.*
This NCO has been Orderly Room Sergeant since September 1915 and has invariably shown himself most capable and hardworking. During the recent heavy fighting, working often under the most trying and difficult circumstances, he never once got behind with his work and by his devotion to duty kept all his records up to date.

304583 Newell, Rifleman W.H. MM.
During the attack on the Polygon de Zonnebeke on 16 August 1917 this rifleman was a Company runner. Although wounded in the left shoulder he continued the advance with his Company Commander. Later his Company Commander was severely wounded. Whilst attending to him he was captured by 2 German snipers. Before his capture he had taken the personal effects from his Company Commander including his revolver. The Germans took his rifle and SAA etc from him but overlooked the revolver. He was made to lie down between the Germans whilst they continued firing, during which time he killed one German

and made his escape, reaching our lines at 11 pm the same night, with the revolver still in his possession.

300057 Newman, Rifleman C. MM.
During the attack on the Polygon de Zonnebeke on 16 August 1917 this rifleman displayed conspicuous gallantry. He was employed as a Stretcher Bearer and showed untiring energy in getting wounded up to the time of the German counter-attack. When the Germans heavily shelled our assembly position before zero he attended to and assisted wounded regardless of danger.

301687 Parsons, Rifleman A.R. MM.
Stretcher Bearer. This rifleman has already received 3 Divisional Cards for good work in previous actions. On 3 May 1917 he again showed conspicuous gallantry and carried out his duties quite regardless of his own safety. He commenced attending to the wounded in the foremost waves from the moment the advance was held up and for over 24 hours under heavy MG and shell fire he continued getting the wounded into shell holes and carrying them down at night. His knowledge of the ground and the position of the men proved of great assistance and helped guides and runners to deliver their messages.

302117 Pearson, Rifleman R. MM.
During the attack on the Polygon de Zonnebeke on 16 August 1917 this Rifleman became the only remaining man of a LG team. During the rear guard fighting he mounted his gun on a concrete emplacement which had been previously cleared of the enemy. From this position he provided covering fire which enabled the remainder of the platoon to be extricated and prevented the enemy from cutting them off. He collected panniers which had been dropped by casualties in the advance and thus maintained a useful volume of fire when ammunition was running short. His energy, initiative and resource probably prevented the capture of the remnant of his platoon.

318038 Pullen, Sergeant C. DCM.
For conspicuous gallantry during the German attack on 28 March 1918, near Gavrelle. He was in charge of a bombing block which was finally surrounded and he and one of his men became prisoners. A German officer and NCO formed his escort and took them back to the old German lines. Owing to the escort moving in front of their prisoners, the latter were able to pick up 2 German bombs with which they killed both the officer and the NCO and escaped to our own lines, bring back very valuable information.
(Pullen's partner, 318076 Rifleman, H. Barker, also received the DCM.)

9995 Roulston, Sergeant W.A. DCM. *London Gazette 14 November 1916.*
This N.C.O. did excellent work whilst leading a bombing attack down a German Communication Trench. (September 1916) He undoubtedly killed over 30 of the enemy with his rifle. After his Platoon Commander had been wounded and all his senior M.C.C. had become casualties he led his platoon with great gallantry and gained his objective. His courage was magnificent and he set a splendid example.

(Sergeant Roulston was killed at Les Boeufs on 8 October 1916 and is buried in Caterpillar Valley Cemetery.)

300171 Simmonds, Sergeant W.H. *Mention in Despatches, 25 May 1917.*
This NCO is Transport Sergeant and has been with the Battalion since its arrival in France in November 1914. He has invariably proved himself a thoroughly capable and energetic NCO and has been of the utmost assistance to his Transport Officer. It has been greatly owing to his wide knowledge of horses that they kept in good condition during the trying weather and hard work.

Sergeant Simmonds was then awarded the MM in September 1917.

During the operations near Hooge 14-16 August 1917, this NCO was entirely responsible for bringing up the rations to the Battalion and acted as Transport Officer. He came up each night with the transport under shell fire and it is due to him that rations, water etc reached the Battalion each night. By carefully reconnoitring routes personally in advance of his transport he was able to get the rations up to Battalion HQ, with practically no casualties to men or horses.

Slade, Second Lieutenant E.H. MC. *London Gazette 18 October 1917.*
During an attack (16 August 1917) he carried out many reconnaissances under heavy fire and furnished very valuable information as to the progress of the operations.

Stewart, Acting Lieutenant Colonel, P.D. DSO. *London Gazette 18 March 1918.*
For conspicuous gallantry and devotion to duty. He led his battalion with great skill in an attack, capturing all the objectives and holding them against several counter-attacks. By his example and training he inspired all ranks in his battalion with a very fine fighting spirit.

315358 Stockdale, Rifleman H. DCM.
On 26 August 1918, near Croisilles, during a night attack this rifleman was very active in carrying messages under heavy MG fire. On 27 August he volunteered to go forward and cut gaps in the wire under heavy MG fire. On the following day he showed splendid courage and determination volunteering for a bombing party in which he took an active part. It was during this attack that he was severely wounded. He set a splendid example to his comrades.

11003 Taylor, Lieutenant Corporal C. DCM. *London Gazette 11 November 1916.*
This NCO was particularly gallant in hand to hand fighting. (September 1916) He managed his bombing section particularly well in clearing enemy trenches and dug-outs, using German bombs after his English bombs had all been thrown. At one point he met 2 German officers and 3 men, when only 2 of his section were left. The first officer he killed with a blow on the head with a German bomb, knocked the second officer down and put a bomb under him, chased the 3 Germans down the trench and disposed of them by hooting. He repeatedly tried

to force his way down the communication trench until he himself was wounded. Before the attack he had personally reconnoitred the ground on both sides of the communication trench.

45202 Tattering, Rifleman W. MM.

On 27 and 28 August 1918, near Croisilles, this Stretcher Bearer displayed great courage bringing in our wounded under very difficult circumstances. At one time he became separated from the other SBs but carried on heedless of very heavy and accurate MG fire, in his work of dressing the wounded and getting them back to our lines. By his initiative and resource he undoubtedly saved the lives of many, doing a lot of the work single handed.

(Tatterton was killed near Angreau on 5 November 1918 and was buried in the village's Communal Cemetery.)

Taylor, Second lieutenant H. MC. *London Gazette 18 October 1917.*

During the attack on the Polygon de Zonnebeke on 16 August 1917 this officer showed conspicuous gallantry especially in hand to hand fighting. East of Glencorse Wood a strong point was met and with a handful of men the entire garrison numbering over 30 of the enemy were killed. He entered the strong point and killed the occupants and practically reached his objective. His Company Commander being wounded and his Company being reduced to small numbers, he reorganised the remaining men and established himself in an advanced position. This point was held until his available men were reduced to 15 when the enemy counter-attacked in force. During his withdrawal, by skilful handling of his men he inflicted further casualties on the enemy.

Thomson, Second Lieutenant W.A. MC.

On 27 October 1918, north of the Arras-Cambrai road, this officer was in command of a Company detailed to cover R.E. working parties and the crossing of the Canal by the LRB and QWR. They came under heavy fire, 2 of the officers being wounded. By skilful handling he succeeded in getting his Company to the Canal Bank with hardly any delay and his fearlessness under heavy fire was a splendid example to his men. The arrival of the Brigade at its Assembly place and its subsequent success would have been greatly jeopardised if any delay had been caused in these operations.

300086 Threaten, CSM. F.M. MM.

This Warrant Officer came out to France in November 1914 as a Rifleman and served continuously until wounded as Sergeant in December 1915. He rejoined the Battalion in January 1918 since when he has done most valuable work as Battalion Lewis Gun Sergeant. He has consistently displayed great gallantry in action and shown himself to be a soldier of the highest merit. Owing to his position as Lewis Gun Sergeant he did not take part in the recent fighting (August 1918) and consequently had no opportunity of distinguishing himself.

304392 Wade, Rifleman W. MM.

During the attack on the Polygon de Zonnebeke on 16 august 1917 this rifleman was a platoon runner and showed conspicuous bravery by continually crossing the open, although swept by M.G. fire and bringing back reports as to how the line was held. During the withdrawal he got his platoon officer out of a bog and helped wounded back. He was quite fearless.

300054 Ward, Rifleman A.R. MM.

During the attack on the Polygon de Zonnebeke on 16 August 1917 this rifleman acted as runner. At all times of the day and night he carried important messages to the companies and displayed great coolness and courage under the heavy fire of the enemy. He never failed to deliver any messages entrusted to him.

301624 Wilson, Sergeant P. MM.

During the attack on 3 May 1917 this NCO showed conspicuous bravery. He was in charge of the 3rd wave which suffered severe casualties. His advance was temporarily stopped by a trench full of the enemy. He rallied his remaining men and took up a position in shell holes and inflicted several casualties on the enemy by rifle and rifle-grenade fire. Later, re-inforcements arrived and the advance was resumed. Between 20-30 Germans were then disposed of by bayonet fighting and several prisoners taken. Sergeant Wilson set an excellent example and it was due to him that the attack on this trench was successful. He was badly wounded.

302186 Wynne-Williams, Rifleman T.H. MM.

During the attack near Moeuvres on 22 November 1917, he acted as a runner and displayed conspicuous bravery. On 2 occasions his comrades were killed whilst accompanying him but he never failed to keep pushing on until he delivered his message - under fire the whole time. On 24 November during a German counter-attack he was sent with another runner to deliver an important message. His comrade was killed and he was badly wounded near Battalion HQ. He crawled the remainder of the distance and delivered his message before reporting to the Aid Post.

MAPS

The accompanying maps are based on trench maps produced during the war. In order to help the modern visitor locate the scenes of the actions and battles discussed within the text, certain amendments have been made. With a few exceptions (on Map 10), roads marked in bold lines are those which appear on the Michelin 51 and 53 sheets (1 cm = 2 km or 1:200,000). Some of those marked as dotted lines represent, in some instances, roads which have reverted to their pre-1914 use. Many of the surfaced roads, especially in the Ypres area, are suitable for cars and the tracks can be walked generally without difficulty. The absence of fences in the area east of Arras also means that the tracks can be cycled, providing the bike is equipped with 'all-terrain' tyres. The construction of new roads has complicated the picture somewhat and in order to keep the maps as clear as possible, the following roads and motorways have been omitted:

Map 3   A19 where it ends abruptly opposite Buffs Road Cemetery.

Map 6   A1 which passes immediately to the west of Wancourt civilian cemetery.

Map 8   A19 as it passes in a cutting between Nonne Bosschen Wood and the Polygon de Zonnebeke.

Map 10   The construction of the Gavrelle by-pass to the north of the village and the motorways which pass to the south and east have altered the road system quite radically. The road running east-west through the village on Map 10 (N50) still exists, but access to the D49 to Bailleul is now via the by-pass. The D33 heading north from the centre of the village to Oppy now runs in a straight line and passes under the by-pass about 150 yards north of the village before rejoining its original line near the electricity station. However, apart from the 40 yards where it is bisected by the cutting carrying the by-pass, the original road, marked on Map 10, can still be followed.

As a further aid to identifying the locations, the Commonwealth War Graves Commission cemeteries have also, where appropriate, been drawn.

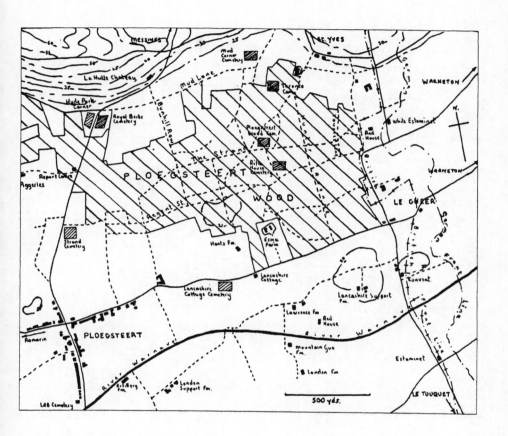

MAP 1. PLOEGSTEERT WOOD : DECEMBER 1914 - APRIL 1915

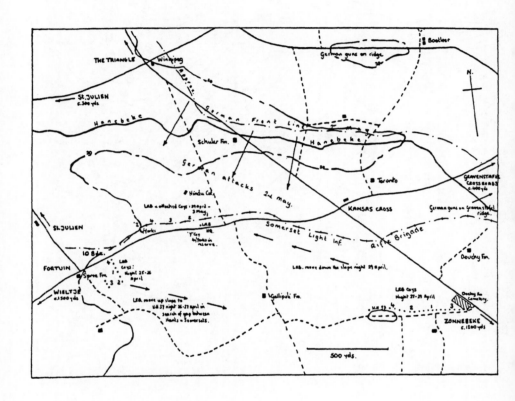

MAP 2. BATTLE OF ST JULIEN : 25 APRIL - 4 MAY 1915

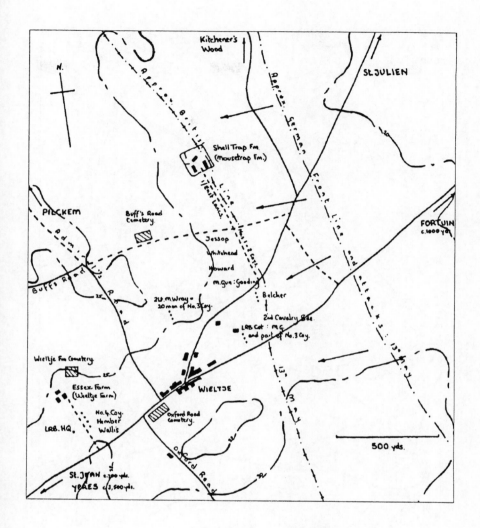

MAP 3. BATTLE OF FREZENBERG RIDGE

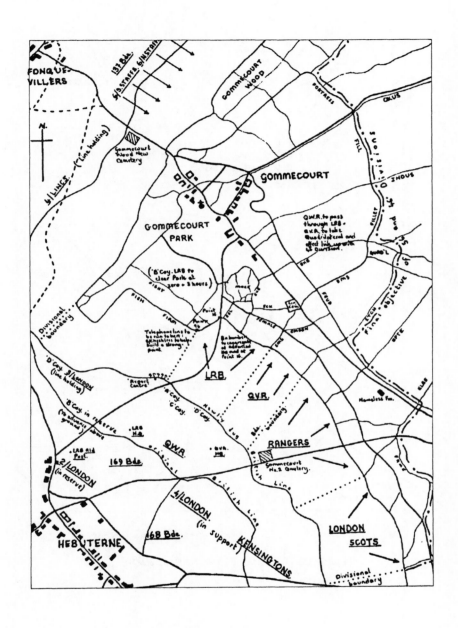

MAP 4. GOMMECOURT : THE PLAN

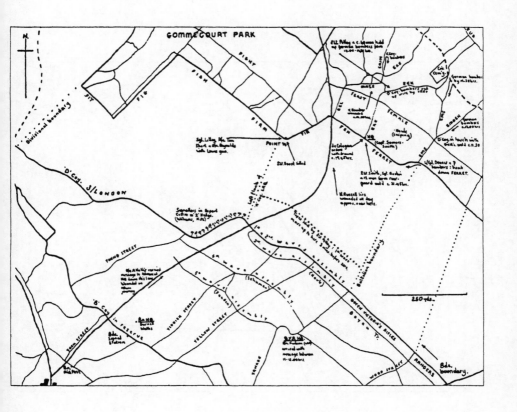

MAP 5. GOMMECOURT : THE ATTACK 1ST JULY

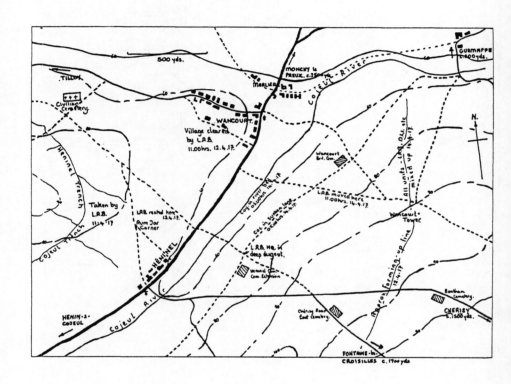

MAP 6. FIRST BATTLE OF THE SCARPE : 9 - 14 APRIL 1917

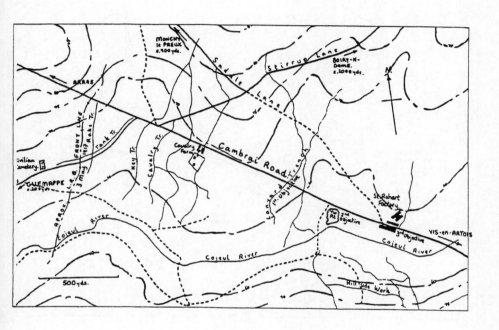

MAP 7. THIRD BATTLE OF THE SCARPE : 3 - 4 MAY 1917

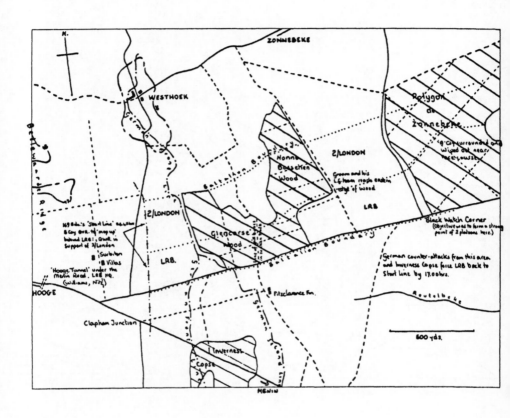

MAP 8. BATTLE OF LANGEMARCK : 16 AUGUST 1917

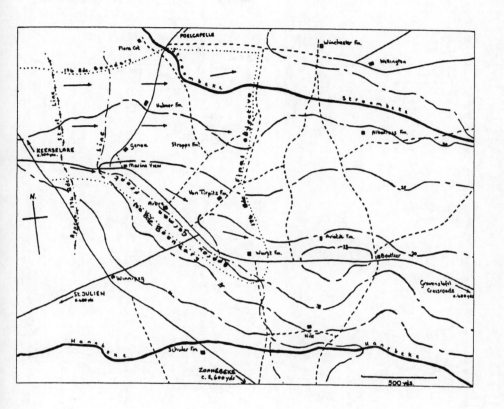

MAP 9. BATTLE OF MENIN ROAD : 20 SEPTEMBER 1917

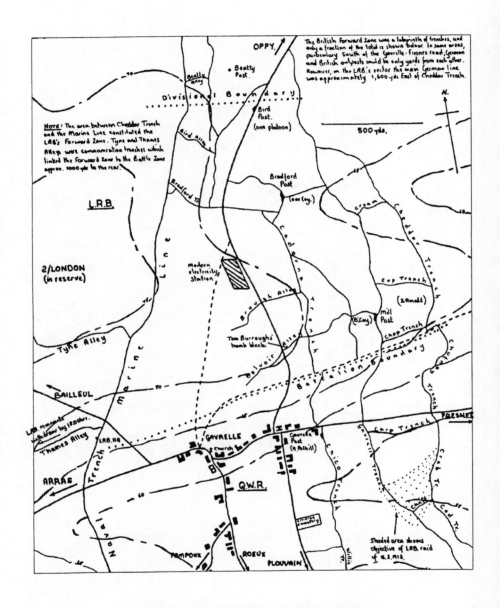

The British Forward Zone was a labyrinth of trenches, and only a fraction of the total is shown below. In some areas, particularly South of the Gavrelle-Fresnes road, German and British outposts could be only yards from each other. However, in the LRB's sector the main German line was approximately 1,600 yds East of Cheddar Trench.

OPPY

• Beatty Post.

Beatty Alley

Division al Boundary

Bird Post. (one platoon)

500 yds.

NOTE: The area between Cheddar Trench and the Marine Line constituted the LRB's Forward Zone. Tyne and Thames Alleys were communication trenches which linked the Forward Zone to the Battle Zone approx. 1000 yds to the rear.

Bird Alley

Bradford Tr.

Bradford Post (one coy.)

L.R.B.

Cedar Tr.

Cream

Cheddar Trench

2/LONDON (in reserve)

Modern electricity station

Brough Alley

Cup Trench

(½ Amalt)

mill Post

(B Coy)

Chop Trench

Tom Burroughs' bomb block

Belvoir Alley

Battalion Boundary

Carp Trench

Tyne Alley

Marine Line

Carp Trench

BAILLEUL

Thames Alley

LRB remnants withdrew by 1800 hrs.

LRB. HQ.

B

GAVRELLE

Gavrelle Post (½ Amhill)

Carp Trench

FRESNES

Chico Tr.

church

ARRAS

London Trench

Q.W.R.

Willis Tr.

Cod Tr.

incendiary something

Shaded area shows objective of LRB raid of 16.3.1918.

TAMPOUX

ROEUX

PLOUVAIN

N.

MAP 10. GAVRELLE : 28 MARCH 1918

STILL

21
DESIGNS
by
Kim Hargreaves

CREDITS

DESIGNS & STYLING
Kim Hargreaves

EDITOR
Kathleen Hargreaves

MODELS
Angharad Hunt
Charlotte Stacey
Naomi Vergette-D'Souza

HAIR & MAKE-UP
Diana Fisher

PHOTOGRAPHY & EDITORIAL DESIGN
Graham Watts

LAYOUTS
Angela Lin

PATTERNS
Sue Whiting & Tricia McKenzie

© Copyright Kim Hargreaves 2014.

First published in 2014 by Kim Hargreaves,
Intake Cottage, 26 Underbank Old Road, Holmfirth,
West Yorkshire, HD9 1EA, England.

British Library Cataloguing in Publication Data.
A catalogue record for this book is available from
the British Library.

ISBN–10   1-906487-21-8
ISBN–13   978-1-906487-21-8

CONTENTS

SO STILL

With an ease and a quiet **CONFIDENCE** the collection has an
AURA *that is hard to resist, hushed tones enhance the* **MOOD***,
while deep cables and* **SUBTLE** *ribbing complete the story.*
The **SENSUALITY** *of sheer fabrics and the* **SIMPLICITY**
of clean lines have no **DESIRE** *to seek the limelight*
but can't fail to **COMMAND** *attention.*

Naomi wears **COSY** an Oversized V-neck Sweater
knitted in Brushed Fleece, worn with **MIST** a Slouchy Ribbed Hat,
knitted in Mohair Haze & Fine Lace

This page, Angharad wears **CHILL** a Rib & Drop Stitch Scarf, knitted in Brushed Fleece. Opposite; Naomi wears **MIST** a Slouchy Ribbed Hat, knitted in Mohair Haze & Fine Lace

Charlotte wears **COMFORT** *a Soft Ribbed Cardigan*
knitted in Kid Classic & Kidsilk Haze, worn with **MIST** *Slouchy Hat,*
knitted in Mohair Haze & Fine Lace

Angharad wears **COLD** a Cosy Understated Sweater Dress, knitted in Brushed Fleece

Naomi wears **SILENCE**
a Classic Sweater with
Low Scooped Back,
knitted in Kidsilk Haze
& Fine Lace

17

Angharad wears **COLD** an Understated Tunic
worn with **CHILL** a Ribbed & Drop Stitch Scarf,
both knitted in Brushed Fleece

Angharad wears **DARK**
a Sweater with Funnel Neck,
worked in Shaded Stripes
& knitted in Kidsilk Haze

21

Opposite, Angharad wears **DARK**
Sweater worked in Shaded Stripes
& Knitted in Kidsilk Haze, and
this page **DARKNESS** a Hooded Coat,
knitted in Brushed Fleece

23

Opposite Naomi wears **MIST** a Slouchy Hat knitted in
Kid Classic & Kidsik Haze and this page **DARKNESS**
a Hooded Coat, knitted in Brushed Fleece

Charlotte wears **HUSHED** *a Pretty Cropped Cardigan worn with* **MIST** *Hat, both knitted in Mohair Haze & Fine Lace*

This page Naomi wears **MIST** a Slouchy Hat knitted in Kid Classic
& Kidsilk Haze, Opposite, Angharad wears **TEMPERATE** a Fitted Sweater
with Frill Edgings, knitted in Mohair Haze & Fine Lace

Angharad wears **BLACK**
a Sleeveless Sweater with
Funnel Neck, knitted
in Brushed Fleece

Angharad wears **TRANQUIL**
a Relaxed Tunic worked in
Bobbles & Cables, knitted
in Kid Classic

Angharad wears **GENTLE** a Delicate Scarf
worked in Classic Garter Stitch, knitted in Kidsilk Haze Stripe

Angharad wears **GENTLE**
a Delicate Scarf worked in
Classic Garter Stitch, knitted
in Kidsilk Haze Stripe

Angharad wears **FOND** an Edge to Edge Jacket
worked in Rib with Cable Trim,
knitted in Cocoon

Naomi Wears **MILD** a Classic Cardigan
worked in Cables & Bobbles
& knitted in Cocoon

Angharad wears **LIGHT** a Button Through Sweater,
worked in a Pretty Lace & knitted in
Kidslk Haze & Fine Lace

Charlotte wears **QUIET** a Ribbed Cardigan with Lace Trim, knitted in Lima,
worn with **MIST** a Slouchy Hat, knitted in Kidsilk Haze & Fine Lace

Angharad wears **HUSHED** a Pretty Cropped Cardigan,
knitted in Mohair Haze & Fine Lace

Charlotte wears **INTENSE** a Fitted Dress
with Ribbing details, knitted in Lima, worn with
MIST a Slouchy Hat, knitted in Kidsilk Haze

Charlotte wears **MIST** *a Slouchy Hat,*
knitted in Kidsilk Haze & Fine Lace, with **INTENSE**
a Fitted Dress with Ribbing Details, knitted in Lima

Angharad wears **HONOURED**
an Elegant Peplum Jacket worked in Tweed Stripes
& knitted in Felted Tweed

This page, Naomi wears **MIST** a Slouchy Ribbed Hat, knitted in
Kid Classic & Kidsilk Haze, Opposite, Angharad wears **FLATTER**
a Body Conscious Skirt, knitted in Lima

Angharad wears **FLATTER** a Body Conscious Skirt
which features Ribbing Detail, knitted in Lima

Naomi wears **SHADOW** a Classic Tweed Jacket worked in Subtle Stripes,
Knitted in Felted Tweed & Felted Tweed Aran, worn with **MIST**
a Slouchy Hat, knitted in Kid Classic & Kidsilk Haze

THE
END

COMFORT
Shawl collared jacket in soft ribbing

Recommendation
Suitable for the knitter with a little experience
Please see pages 12 & 13 for photographs.

	XS	S	M	L	XL	XXL	
To fit bust	**81**	**86**	**91**	**97**	**102**	**109**	**cm**
	32	34	36	38	40	43	in

Rowan Kid Classic and Kidsilk Haze
Kid Classic

	11	12	13	14	14	15 x 50gm

Kidsilk Haze

	7	8	8	9	9	10 x 25gm

Photographed in Kid Classic in Pumice with
Kidsilk Haze in Steel

Needles
1 pair 4mm (no 8) (US 6) needles
1 pair 4½mm (no 7) (US 7) needles
1 pair 5mm (no 6) (US 8) needles

Tension
21 sts and 28 rows to 10 cm measured over
pattern using 5mm (US 8) needles and one
strand each of Kid Classic and Kidsilk Haze
held together.

Special note: We found it preferable to knit
the two yarns together from separate balls
rather than winding them together.

BACK
Cast on 101 (107: 113: 117: 123: 131) sts
using 4½mm (US 7) needles and one strand
each of Kid Classic and Kidsilk Haze held
together.
Row 1 (RS): K0 (3: 2: 0: 3: 3), P1, *K3, P1,
rep from * to last 0 (3: 2: 0: 3: 3) sts, K0
(3: 2: 0: 3: 3).
Row 2: K2 (1: 0: 2: 1: 1), P1, *K3, P1, rep
from * to last 2 (1: 0: 2: 1: 1) sts, K2 (1: 0:
2: 1: 1).
These 2 rows form patt.
Cont in patt for a further 8 rows, ending with
a WS row.
Change to 5mm (US 8) needles.
Cont in patt until back measures 48 (48: 50:
50: 50: 50) cm, ending with a WS row.
Shape raglan armholes
Keeping patt correct, cast off 8 (7: 6: 8: 7: 7)
sts at beg of next 2 rows.
85 (93: 101: 101: 109: 117) sts.
Size XS only
Next row (RS): (P1, K3) twice, P1, patt to last
9 sts, P1, (K3, P1) twice.
Next row: K2, P1, K3, P1, K2, patt to last 9 sts,
K2, P1, K3, P1, K2.
Next row: (P1, K3) twice, P2tog, patt to last
10 sts, P2tog tbl, (K3, P1) twice.
Next row: K2, P1, K3, P1, K2, patt to last 9 sts,
K2, P1, K3, P1, K2.
Rep last 4 rows once more. 81 sts.
Sizes M, L, XL and XXL only
Next row (RS): (P1, K3) twice, P2tog, patt
to last 10 sts, P2tog tbl, (K3, P1) twice.
Next row: K2, P1, K3, P1, K1, K2tog tbl,
patt to last 10 sts, K2tog, K1, P1, K3, P1, K2.
Rep last 2 rows – (-: 3: 1: 3: 6) times more.
- (-: 85: 93: 93: 89) sts.
All sizes
Next row: (P1, K3) twice, P2tog, patt to last
10 sts, P2tog tbl, (K3, P1) twice.
Next row: K2, P1, K3, P1, K2, patt to last 9 sts,
K2, P1, K3, P1, K2.
Rep last 2 rows 22 (27: 23: 26: 26: 24) times
more. 35 (37: 37: 39: 39: 39) sts.
Next row (RS): (P1, K3) twice, P2tog, patt to
last 10 sts, P2tog tbl, (K3, P1) twice.
Next row: K2, P1, K3, P1, K1, K2tog tbl, patt
to last 10 sts, K2tog, K1, P1, K3, P1, K2.
Cast off rem 31 (33: 33: 35: 35: 35) sts.

POCKET LININGS (make 2)
Cast on 25 (25: 25: 29: 29: 29) sts using
5mm (US 8) needles and one strand each
of Kid Classic and Kidsilk Haze held together.
Row 1 (RS): P1, *K3, P1, rep from * to end.
Row 2: K2, P1, *K3, P1, rep from * to last
2 sts, K2.
These 2 rows form patt.
Cont in patt for a further 38 rows, ending
with a WS row.
Break yarn and leave sts on a holder.

LEFT FRONT
Cast on 63 (66: 69: 71: 74: 78) sts using
4½mm (US 7) needles and one strand each
of Kid Classic and Kidsilk Haze held together.
Row 1 (RS): K0 (3: 2: 0: 3: 3), P1, *K3, P1,
rep from * to last 2 sts, K1, P1.
Row 2: (P1, K1) twice, P1, *K3, P1, rep from *
to last 2 (1: 0: 2: 1: 1) sts, K2 (1: 0: 2: 1: 1).
These 2 rows set the sts – front opening edge
4 sts in moss st with all other sts in patt.
Cont as set for a further 8 rows, ending with
a WS row.
Change to 5mm (US 8) needles.
Work a further 40 rows, ending with a WS row.
Place pocket
Next row (RS): Patt 12 (15: 18: 16: 19: 23) sts,
slip next 25 (25: 25: 29: 29: 29) sts onto a holder
and, in their place, patt across 25 (25: 25: 29:
29: 29) sts of first pocket lining, patt rem 26 sts.
Cont straight until left front matches back to
start of raglan armhole shaping, ending with
a WS row.
Shape raglan armhole and front slope
Next row (RS): Cast off 8 (7: 6: 8: 7: 7) sts,
patt to last 16 sts, P2tog tbl (for front slope
dec), patt 14 sts. 54 (58: 62: 62: 66: 70) sts.
Working all front slope decreases as set by last
row and all raglan armhole deceases as set by
back raglan armhole, cont as folls:
Work 3 (1: 1: 1: 1: 1) rows.
**Dec 1 st at raglan armhole edge of next 1 (1:
9: 5: 9: 15) rows, then on 1 (0: 0: 0: 0: 0) foll
4th row, then on foll 21 (25: 21: 24: 24: 22) alt
rows **and at same time** dec 1 st at front slope
edge of 3rd (5th: 5th: 5th: 5th: 5th) and 1 (4:
4: 7: 5: 4) foll 6th rows, then on 4 (2: 2: 0: 2:
3) foll 8th rows. 25 sts.
Work 1 row, ending with a WS row.

Next row (RS): Patt 8 sts, P3tog, patt 14 sts. 23 sts.

Cont in patt as set on these 23 sts only (for back neck collar extension) for a further 46 (48: 48: 50: 50: 50) rows, ending at front opening (moss st) edge.

Next row: Patt 16 sts, wrap next st (by slipping next st from left needle onto right needle, taking yarn to opposite side of work between needles and then slipping same st back onto left needle - when working back across wrapped sts work the wrapped st and the wrapping loop tog as one st) and turn.

Next row: Patt to end.

Next row: Patt 8 sts, wrap next st and turn.

Next row: Patt to end.

Work 1 row across all 23 sts.

Break yarn and leave sts on a holder.

RIGHT FRONT

Cast on 63 (66: 69: 71: 74: 78) sts using 4½mm (US 7) needles and one strand each of Kid Classic and Kidsilk Haze held together.

Row 1 (RS): P1, K1, P1, *K3, P1, rep from * to last 0 (3: 2: 0: 3: 3) sts, K0 (3: 2: 0: 3: 3).

Row 2: K2 (1: 0: 2: 1: 1), P1, *K3, P1, rep from * to last 4 sts, (K1, P1) twice.

These 2 rows set the sts – front opening edge 4 sts in moss st with all other sts in patt.

Cont as set for a further 8 rows, ending with a WS row.

Change to 5mm (US 8) needles.

Work a further 40 rows, ending with a WS row.

Place pocket

Next row (RS): Patt 26 sts, slip next 25 (25: 25: 29: 29: 29) sts onto a holder and, in their place, patt across 25 (25: 25: 29: 29: 29) sts of second pocket lining, patt rem 12 (15: 18: 16: 19: 23) sts.

Cont straight until right front matches back to start of raglan armhole shaping, ending with a WS row.

Shape raglan armhole and front slope

Next row (RS): Patt 14 sts, P2tog (for front slope dec), patt to end.

Keeping patt correct, cast off 8 (7: 6: 8: 7: 7) sts at beg of next row. 54 (58: 62: 62: 66: 70) sts.

Work 2 (0: 0: 0: 0: 0) rows.

Complete to match left front from **, reversing shapings.

SLEEVES (both alike)

Cast on 49 (51: 53: 57: 59: 59) sts using 4½mm (US 7) needles and one strand each of Kid Classic and Kidsilk Haze held together.

Work in patt as given for back for 10 rows, ending with a WS row.

Change to 5mm (US 8) needles.

Cont in patt for a further 10 rows, ending with a WS row.

Next row (RS): Patt 9 (8: 7: 9: 8: 8) sts, M1, patt to last 9 (8: 7: 9: 8: 8) sts, patt 9 (8: 7: 9: 8: 8) sts.

Working all increases as set by last row, keeping edge 9 (8: 7: 9: 8: 8) sts correct as set and taking inc sts into patt between these sts, cont as folls:

Inc 1 st at each end of 10th and 2 (3: 4: 5: 6: 7) foll 10th rows, then on 8 (7: 6: 5: 4: 3) foll 8th rows. 73 (75: 77: 81: 83: 83) sts.

Cont straight until sleeve measures 44 (45: 46: 47: 48: 49) cm, ending with a WS row.

Shape raglan

Keeping patt correct, cast off 8 (7: 6: 8: 7: 7) sts at beg of next 2 rows.

57 (61: 65: 65: 69: 69) sts.

Working all raglan decreases in same way as back raglan armhole decreases, dec 1 st at each end of next and 12 (11: 9: 10: 10: 11) foll 4th rows, then on foll 1 (4: 8: 7: 9: 8) alt rows. 29 sts.

Work 1 row, ending with a WS row.

Keeping raglan decreases correct as set, cont as folls:

Left sleeve only

Dec 1 st at each end of next row, then cast off 9 sts at beg of foll row. 18 sts.

Dec 1 st at beg of next row, then cast off 9 sts at beg of foll row.

Right sleeve only

Cast off 10 sts at beg and dec 1 st at end of next row. 18 sts.

Work 1 row.

Cast off 10 sts at beg of next row.

Work 1 row.

Both sleeves

Cast off rem 8 sts.

MAKING UP

Press all pieces with a warm iron over a damp cloth.

Join all raglan seams using back stitch or mattress stitch if preferred. Graft together both sets of 23 sts for back neck collar extensions, then sew one edge in place across top of sleeves and back neck.

Pocket tops (both alike)

Slip 25 (25: 25: 29: 29: 29) sts from pocket holder onto 4½mm (US 7) needles and rejoin one strand each of Kid Classic and Kidsilk Haze held together with RS facing.

Work in patt as set for 6 rows, ending with a WS row.

Cast off in patt.

Sew pocket linings in place on inside, then neatly sew down ends of pocket tops.

Join side and sleeve seams.

Belt

Cast on 11 sts using 4mm (US 6) needles and one strand each of Kid Classic and Kidsilk Haze held together.

Row 1 (RS): K2, (P1, K1) 4 times, K1.

Row 2: K1, (P1, K1) 5 times.

Rep these 2 rows until belt measures 155 (160: 165: 170: 175: 180) cm, ending with a WS row.

Cast off in patt.

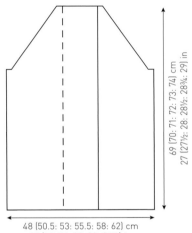

48 (50.5: 53: 55.5: 58: 62) cm
19 (20: 21: 22: 23: 24½) in

69 (70: 71: 72: 73: 74) cm
27 (27½: 28: 28½: 28¾: 29) in

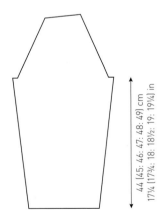

44 (45: 46: 47: 48: 49) cm
17¼ (17¾: 18: 18½: 19: 19¼) in

Recommendation

Suitable for the knitter with a little experience
Please see pages 8 & 9 for photographs.

	XS	S	M	L	XL	XXL	
To fit bust	**81**	**86**	**91**	**97**	**102**	**109**	**cm**
	32	34	36	38	40	43	in

Rowan Brushed Fleece

	8	8	9	9	10	11 x 50gm

Photographed in Crag

Needles

1 pair 6½mm (no 3) (US 10½) needles
1 pair 7mm (no 2) (US 10½/11) needles

Tension

12½ sts and 19 rows to 10 cm measured over stocking stitch using 7mm (US 10½/11) needles.

COSY
Oversized V-neck sweater

BACK

Cast on 67 (71: 75: 77: 81: 85) sts using 6½mm (US 10½) needles.
Row 1 (RS): K1, *P1, K1, rep from * to end.
Row 2: P1, *K1, P1, rep from * to end.
These 2 rows form rib.
Work in rib for a further 14 rows, dec 1 st at end of last row and ending with a WS row. 66 (70: 74: 76: 80: 84) sts.
Change to 7mm (US 10½/11) needles.
Beg with a K row, now work in st st throughout as folls:
Cont straight until back measures 48 (48: 49: 49: 49: 49) cm, ending with a WS row.
Shape raglan armholes
Cast off 4 sts at beg of next 2 rows.
58 (62: 66: 68: 72: 76) sts.
Work 2 rows, ending with a WS row.
Next row (RS): K1, K2tog, K to last 3 sts, K2tog tbl, K1.**
Working all raglan armhole decreases as set by last row, dec 1 st at each end of 4th and 4 (4: 2: 3: 2: 1) foll 4th rows, then on foll 10 (11: 15: 14: 17: 20) alt rows.
26 (28: 28: 30: 30: 30) sts.
Work 1 row, ending with a WS row.
Cast off.

FRONT

Work as given for back to **.
Work 1 row, ending with a WS row.
Divide for front neck
Next row (RS): K25 (27: 29: 30: 32: 34), K2tog tbl, K1 and turn, leaving rem sts on a holder. 27 (29: 31: 32: 34: 36) sts.
Work each side of neck separately.
Working neck and raglan armhole decreases as set by back raglan armhole, dec 1 st at raglan armhole edge of 2nd and 4 (4: 2: 3: 2: 1) foll 4th rows, then on foll 6 (7: 11: 10: 13: 16) alt rows **and at same time** dec 1 st at neck edge of 2nd and foll 7 (8: 8: 9: 8: 7) alt rows, then on 3 (3: 3: 3: 4: 5) foll 4th rows.
5 sts.
Work 1 row, ending with a WS row.
Next row (RS): K1, sl 1, K2tog, psso, K1. 3 sts.
Next row: P3.
Next row: K1, K2tog.
Next row: P2.

Next row: K2tog and fasten off.
With RS facing, rejoin yarn to rem sts, K1, K2tog, K to end.
27 (29: 31: 32: 34: 36) sts.
Complete to match first side, reversing shapings.

SLEEVES (both alike)

Cast on 29 (31: 33: 33: 35: 37) sts using 6½mm (US 10½) needles.
Work in rib as given for back for 12 rows, ending with a WS row.
Change to 7mm (US 10½/11) needles.
Beg with a K row, work in st st throughout as folls:
Work 2 rows, ending with a WS row.
Next row (RS): K3, M1, K to last 3 sts, M1, K3.
Working all increases as set by last row, inc 1 st at each end of 6th and every foll 6th row to 47 (47: 39: 45: 45: 45) sts, then on every foll 8th row until there are 51 (53: 53: 55: 57: 59) sts.
Cont straight until sleeve measures 46 (47: 48: 49: 50: 51) cm, ending with a WS row.
Shape raglan
Cast off 4 sts at beg of next 2 rows.
43 (45: 45: 47: 49: 51) sts.
Working all raglan decreases in same way as raglan armhole decreases, dec 1 st at each end of 3rd and 4 foll 4th rows, then on every foll alt row until 13 sts rem.
Work 1 row, ending with a WS row.
Left sleeve only
Dec 1 st at each end of next row, then cast off 3 sts at beg of foll row. 8 sts.
Dec 1 st at beg of next row, then cast off 4 sts at beg of foll row.
Right sleeve only
Cast off 4 sts at beg and dec 1 st at end of next row. 8 sts.
Work 1 row.
Rep last 2 rows once more.
Both sleeves
Cast off rem 3 sts.

MAKING UP

Press all pieces with a warm iron over a damp cloth.
Join both front and right back raglan seams using back stitch or mattress stitch if preferred.

Neckband

With RS facing and using 6½mm (US 10½) needles, pick up and knit 9 sts from top of left sleeve, 35 (37: 37: 39: 41: 43) sts down left side of front neck, place marker on needle, pick up and knit 35 (37: 37: 39: 41: 43) sts up right side of front neck, 9 sts from top of right sleeve, and 24 (26: 26: 28: 28: 28) sts from back. 112 (118: 118: 124: 128: 132) sts.

Row 1 (WS): *P1, K1, rep from * to within 2 sts of marker, P2tog, slip marker onto right needle, P2tog tbl, **K1, P1, rep from ** to end. This row sets position of rib as given for back. Keeping rib correct, cont as folls:

Row 2: Rib to within 2 sts of marker, K2tog tbl, slip marker onto right needle, K2tog, rib to end.

Row 3: Rib to within 2 sts of marker, P2tog, slip marker onto right needle, P2tog tbl, rib to end.

Row 4: As row 2.

104 (110: 110: 116: 120: 124) sts.

Cast off in rib (on **WS**), still decreasing either side of marker as before.

Join left back raglan and neckband seam.

Join side and sleeve seams.

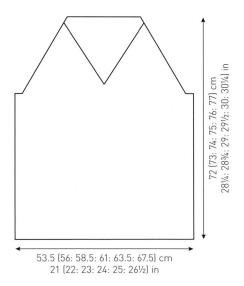

72 (73: 74: 75: 76: 77) cm
28¼ (28¾: 29: 29½: 30: 30¼) in

53.5 (56: 58.5: 61: 63.5: 67.5) cm
21 (22: 23: 24: 25: 26½) in

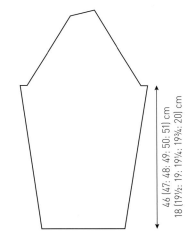

46 (47: 48: 49: 50: 51) cm
18 (19½: 19: 19¼: 19¾: 20) cm

SILENCE
Classic sweater with low scooped back

Recommendation
Suitable for the knitter with a little experience
Please see pages 16 & 17 for photographs.

	XS	S	M	L	XL	XXL	
To fit bust	**81**	**86**	**91**	**97**	**102**	**109**	**cm**
	32	34	36	38	40	43	in

Rowan Kidsilk Haze and Fine Lace
Kidsilk Haze
        4   5   5   5   6   6 x 25gm
Fine Lace
        2   3   3   3   3   3 x 50gm
Photographed in Kidsilk Haze in Shadow with
Fine Lace in Cameo

Needles
1 pair 2¾mm (no 12) (US 2) needles
1 pair 3¼mm (no 10) (US 3) needles
2¾mm (no 12) (US 2) circular needle

Tension
23 sts and 31 rows to 10 cm measured over
stocking stitch using 3¼mm (US 3) needles
and one strand each of Kidsilk Haze and Fine
Lace held together.

Special note: We found it preferable to knit
the two yarns together from separate balls
rather than winding them together.

FRONT
Cast on 116 (124: 132: 138: 146: 156) sts
using 2¾mm (US 2) needles and one strand
each of Kidsilk Haze and Fine Lace held
together.
Row 1 (RS): K2 (1: 0: 3: 2: 2), P2, *K3, P2,
rep from * to last 2 (1: 0: 3: 2: 2) sts, K2 (1: 0:
3: 2: 2).
Row 2: P2 (1: 0: 3: 2: 2), K2, *P3, K2,
rep from * to last 2 (1: 0: 3: 2: 2) sts,
P2 (1: 0: 3: 2: 2).
These 2 rows form rib.
Work in rib for a further 21 rows, ending with
a **RS** row.
Row 24 (WS): P2 (1: 0: 3: 2: 2), K2tog, *P3,
K2tog, rep from * to last 2 (1: 0: 3: 2: 2) sts,
P2 (1: 0: 3: 2: 2).
93 (99: 105: 111: 117: 125) sts.
Change to 3¼mm (US 3) needles.
Beg with a K row, now work in st st throughout
as folls:
Cont straight until front measures 39 (39: 40:
40: 40: 40) cm, ending with a WS row.
Shape armholes
Cast off 4 (4: 5: 5: 6: 6) sts at beg of next
2 rows.
85 (91: 95: 101: 105: 113) sts.
Dec 1 st at each end of next 1 (3: 3: 5: 5: 7)
rows, then on foll 4 (4: 5: 5: 6: 6) alt rows,
then on foll 4th row.
73 (75: 77: 79: 81: 85) sts.
Work 15 (17: 15: 13: 15: 17) rows, ending
with a WS row.
Shape front neck
Next row (RS): K22 (22: 23: 24: 25: 27)
and turn, leaving rem sts on a holder.
Work each side of neck separately.
Cast off 3 sts at beg of next and foll 2 alt rows.
13 (13: 14: 15: 16: 18) sts.
Dec 1 st at neck edge of next 3 rows, then
on foll 3 (3: 3: 4: 4: 4) alt rows, then on foll
4th row.
6 (6: 7: 7: 8: 10) sts.
Work 3 rows, ending with a WS row.
Shape shoulder
Cast off.
With RS facing, rejoin yarns to rem sts, cast off
centre 29 (31: 31: 31: 31: 31) sts, K to end.
Complete to match first side, reversing
shapings.

BACK
Work as given for front until 22 rows less have
been worked than on front to start of armhole
shaping, ending with a WS row.
Shape back neck
Next row (RS): K39 (41: 44: 46: 49: 53)
and turn, leaving rem sts on a holder.
Work each side of neck separately.
Cast off 3 sts at beg of next and foll alt row.
33 (35: 38: 40: 43: 47) sts.
Dec 1 st at neck edge of next 3 rows, then
on foll 5 alt rows, then on foll 4th row.
24 (26: 29: 31: 34: 38) sts.
Work 1 row, ending with a WS row.
Shape armhole
Cast off 4 (4: 5: 5: 6: 6) sts at beg of next row.
20 (22: 24: 26: 28: 32) sts.
Work 1 row.
Dec 1 st at armhole edge of next 1 (3: 3: 5:
5: 7) rows, then on foll 4 (4: 5: 5: 6: 6) alt rows,
then on foll 4th row **and at same time** dec
1 st at neck edge of next and 2 foll 4th rows,
then on 0 (1: 1: 1: 2: 2) foll 6th rows.
11 (10: 11: 11: 11: 13) sts.
Dec 1 st at neck edge **only** on 2nd (6th: 4th:
2nd: 8th: 6th) and 1 (0: 0: 0: 0: 0) foll 6th row,
then on 3 (3: 3: 3: 2: 2) foll 8th rows.
6 (6: 7: 7: 8: 10) sts.
Work 5 (9: 9: 11: 15: 19) rows, ending with
a WS row.
Shape shoulder
Cast off.
With RS facing, rejoin yarns to rem sts,
cast off centre 15 (17: 17: 19: 19: 19) sts,
K to end.
Complete to match first side, reversing
shapings.

SLEEVES (both alike)
Cast on 46 (48: 50: 52: 54: 56) sts using
2¾mm (US 2) needles and one strand
each of Kidsilk Haze and Fine Lace held
together.
Row 1 (RS): K2 (0: 0: 0: 1: 2), P2 (0: 1: 2: 2:
2), *K3, P2, rep from * to last 2 (3: 4: 0: 1: 2)
sts, K2 (3: 3: 0: 1: 2), P0 (0: 1: 0: 0: 0).
Row 2: P2 (0: 0: 0: 1: 2), K2 (0: 1: 2: 2: 2),
*P3, K2, rep from * to last 2 (3: 4: 0: 1: 2) sts,
P2 (3: 3: 0: 1: 2), K0 (0: 1: 0: 0: 0).
These 2 rows form rib.

Work in rib for a further 36 rows, inc
1 st at each end of 19th of these rows
and ending with a WS row.
48 (50: 52: 54: 56: 58) sts.
Change to 3¼mm (US 3) needles.
Beg with a K row, now work in st st throughout
as folls:
Work 2 rows, ending with a WS row.
Next row (RS): K3, M1, K to last 3 sts, M1, K3.
Working all increases as set by last row,
inc 1 st at each end of 8th (8th: 8th: 10th:
8th: 8th) and 4 (2: 1: 0: 3: 1) foll 8th rows,
then on every foll 10th row until there are
70 (72: 74: 76: 80: 82) sts.
Cont straight until sleeve measures 47 (48: 49:
50: 51: 52) cm, ending with a WS row.
Shape top
Cast off 4 (4: 5: 5: 6: 6) sts at beg of next
2 rows. 62 (64: 64: 66: 68: 70) sts.
Dec 1 st at each end of next 3 rows, and foll
3 alt rows, then on 2 foll 4th rows.
46 (48: 48: 50: 52: 54) sts.
Work 1 row.
Dec 1 st at each end of next and every foll
alt row until 40 sts rem, then on foll 7 rows,
ending with a WS row.
Cast off rem 26 sts.

MAKING UP
Press all pieces with a warm iron over
a damp cloth.
Join both shoulder seams using back stitch
or mattress stitch if preferred. Place markers
either side of all cast-off sts at base of front
neck, and all cast-off sts at base of back neck
(this includes the sets of 3 cast-off sts either
side of the centre set).
Neckband
With RS facing, using 2¾mm (US 2) circular
needle and one strand each of Kidsilk Haze
and Fine Lace held together, pick up and knit
17 (17: 17: 19: 19: 19) sts down left side of
front neck, 50 (51: 51: 51: 52: 53) sts from
front between markers, 17 (17: 17: 19: 19:
19) sts up right side of front neck, 66 (70: 70:
72: 76: 78) sts down right side of back neck,
29 (30: 30: 32: 33: 33) sts from back between
markers, and 66 (70: 70: 72: 76: 78) sts up
left side of back neck.
245 (255: 255: 265: 275: 280) sts.
Round 1 (RS): *P2, K3, rep from * to end.
Rep this round 12 times more.
Cast off in rib.
Join side seams. Join sleeve seams.
Insert sleeves into armholes.

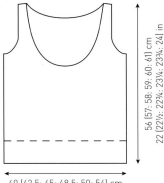

56 (57: 58: 59: 60: 61) cm
22 (22½: 22¾: 23¼: 23¾: 24) in

40 (42.5: 45: 48.5: 50: 54) cm
15¾ (16¾: 17¾: 19: 19¾: 21¼) in

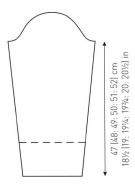

47 (48: 49: 50: 51: 52) cm
18½ (19: 19¼: 19¾: 20: 20½) in

HUSHED
Classic cropped cardigan

Recommendation
Suitable for the knitter with a little experience
Please see pages 27, 46 & 47 for photographs.

	XS	S	M	L	XL	XXL	
To fit bust	**81**	**86**	**91**	**97**	**102**	**109**	**cm**
	32	34	36	38	40	43	in

Rowan Mohair Haze and Fine Lace
Mohair Haze
	8	9	9	10	10	11 x 25gm

Fine Lace
	2	2	3	3	3	3 x 50gm

Photographed in Mohair Haze in Nest with Fine Lace in Cameo

Needles
1 pair 3mm (no 11) (US 2/3) needles
1 pair 3¾mm (no 9) (US 5) needles

Buttons – 6

Tension
23 sts and 30 rows to 10 cm measured over stocking stitch using 3¾mm (US 5) needles and one strand each of Mohair Haze and Fine Lace held together.

Special note: We found it preferable to knit the two yarns together from separate balls rather than winding them together.

BACK
Cast on 92 (98: 104: 110: 116: 124) sts using 3mm (US 2/3) needles and one strand each of Mohair Haze and Fine Lace held together.
Row 1 (RS): K0 (0: 1: 0: 0: 0), P1 (0: 2: 2: 1: 1), *K2, P2, rep from * to last 3 (2: 1: 0: 3: 3) sts, K2 (2: 1: 0: 2: 2), P1 (0: 0: 0: 1: 1).
Row 2: P0 (0: 1: 0: 0: 0), K1 (0: 2: 2: 1: 1), *P2, K2, rep from * to last 3 (2: 1: 0: 3: 3) sts, P2 (2: 1: 0: 2: 2), K1 (0: 0: 0: 1: 1).
These 2 rows form rib.
Work in rib for a further 10 rows, ending with a WS row.
Change to 3¾mm (US 5) needles.
Beg with a K row, now work in st st throughout as folls:
Cont straight until back measures 22 (22: 23: 23: 23: 23) cm, ending with a WS row.
Shape armholes
Cast off 4 (4: 5: 5: 6: 6) sts at beg of next 2 rows.
84 (90: 94: 100: 104: 112) sts.
Dec 1 st at each end of next 1 (3: 3: 5: 5: 7) rows, then on foll 3 (3: 4: 4: 5: 5) alt rows, then on foll 4th row.
74 (76: 78: 80: 82: 86) sts.
Cont straight until armhole measures 17 (18: 18: 19: 20: 21) cm, ending with a WS row.
Shape shoulders and back neck
Cast off 7 (7: 7: 7: 7: 8) sts at beg of next 2 rows.
60 (62: 64: 66: 68: 70) sts.
Next row (RS): Cast off 7 (7: 7: 7: 7: 8) sts, K until there are 10 (10: 11: 11: 12: 12) sts on right needle and turn, leaving rem sts on a holder.
Work each side of neck separately.
Cast off 4 sts at beg of next row.
Cast off rem 6 (6: 7: 7: 8: 8) sts.
With RS facing, rejoin yarns to rem sts, cast off centre 26 (28: 28: 30: 30: 30) sts, K to end.
Complete to match first side, reversing shapings.

LEFT FRONT
Cast on 54 (57: 60: 63: 66: 70) sts using 3mm (US 2/3) needles and one strand each of Mohair Haze and Fine Lace held together.
Row 1 (RS): K0 (0: 1: 0: 0: 0), P1 (0: 2: 2: 1: 1), *K2, P2, rep from * to last 9 sts, K9.

Row 2: K7, *P2, K2, rep from * to last 3 (2: 1: 0: 3: 3) sts, P2 (2: 1: 0: 2: 2), K1 (0: 0: 0: 1: 1).
These 2 rows set the sts – front opening edge 7 sts in g st with all other sts in rib.
Cont as set for a further 10 rows, ending with a WS row.
Change to 3¾mm (US 5) needles.
Row 13 (RS): Knit.
Row 14: K7, P to end.
These 2 rows set the sts for rest of left front – front opening edge 7 sts still in g st with all other sts now in st st.
Cont as now set until left front matches back to start of armhole shaping, ending with a WS row.
Shape armhole
Cast off 4 (4: 5: 5: 6: 6) sts at beg of next row.
50 (53: 55: 58: 60: 64) sts.
Work 1 row.
Dec 1 st at armhole edge of next 1 (3: 3: 5: 5: 7) rows, then on foll 3 (3: 4: 4: 5: 5) alt rows, then on foll 4th row.
45 (46: 47: 48: 49: 51) sts.
Cont straight until 18 (18: 18: 20: 20: 20) rows less have been worked than on back to start of shoulder shaping, ending with a WS row.
Shape front neck
Next row (RS): K29 (29: 30: 31: 32: 34) and turn, leaving rem 16 (17: 17: 17: 17: 17) sts on a holder (for neckband).
Dec 1 st at neck edge of next 4 rows, then on foll 4 (4: 4: 5: 5: 5) alt rows, then on foll 4th row. 20 (20: 21: 21: 22: 24) sts.
Work 1 row, ending with a WS row.
Shape shoulder
Cast off 7 (7: 7: 7: 7: 8) sts at beg of next and foll alt row.
Work 1 row.
Cast off rem 6 (6: 7: 7: 8: 8) sts.
Mark positions for 6 buttons along left front opening edge – first to come level with row 13, last to come level with start of front neck shaping and rem 4 buttons evenly spaced between.

RIGHT FRONT
Cast on 54 (57: 60: 63: 66: 70) sts using 3mm (US 2/3) needles and one strand each of Mohair Haze and Fine Lace held together.

Row 1 (RS): K7, *K2, P2, rep from * to last 3 (2: 1: 0: 3: 3) sts, K2 (2: 1: 0: 2: 2), P1 (0: 0: 0: 1: 1).
Row 2: P0 (0: 1: 0: 0: 0), K1 (0: 2: 2: 1: 1), *P2, K2, rep from * to last 5 sts, K5.
These 2 rows set the sts – front opening edge 7 sts in g st with all other sts in rib.
Cont as set for a further 10 rows, ending with a WS row.
Change to 3¾mm (US 5) needles.
Row 13 (RS): K2, K2tog, yfwd (to make a buttonhole), K to end.
Making a further 4 buttonholes in this way to correspond with positions marked for buttons on left front and noting that no further reference will be made to buttonholes, cont as folls:
Row 14: P to last 7 sts, K7.
These 2 rows set the sts for rest of right front – front opening edge 7 sts still in g st with all other sts now in st st.
Complete to match left front, reversing shapings and working first row of neck shaping as folls:

Shape front neck
Next row (RS): K2, K2tog, yfwd (to make 6th buttonhole), K12 (13: 13: 13: 13: 13) and slip these 16 (17: 17: 17: 17: 17) sts onto a holder (for neckband), K to end.
29 (29: 30: 31: 32: 34) sts.

SLEEVES (both alike)
Cast on 44 (46: 48: 50: 52: 54) sts using 3mm (US 2/3) needles and one strand each of Mohair Haze and Fine Lace held together.
Row 1 (RS): K1 (0: 0: 0: 1: 0), P2 (0: 1: 2: 2: 0), *K2, P2, rep from * to last 1 (2: 3: 0: 1: 2) sts, K1 (2: 2: 0: 1: 2), P0 (0: 1: 0: 0: 0).
Row 2: P1 (0: 0: 0: 1: 0), K2 (0: 1: 2: 2: 0), *P2, K2, rep from * to last 1 (2: 3: 0: 1: 2) sts, P1 (2: 2: 0: 1: 2), K0 (0: 1: 0: 0: 0).
These 2 rows form rib.
Work in rib for a further 26 rows, inc 1 st at each end of 13th of these rows and ending with a WS row. 46 (48: 50: 52: 54: 56) sts.
Change to 3¾mm (US 5) needles.
Beg with a K row, now work in st st throughout as folls:
Work 2 rows, ending with a WS row.
Next row (RS): K3, M1, K to last 3 sts, M1, K3.
Working all increases as set by last row, inc 1 st at each end of 8th (10th: 10th: 10th: 10th: 10th) and every foll 10th row to 68 (68: 68: 66: 78: 76) sts, then on 0 (1: 2: 4: 0: 2) foll 12th rows. 68 (70: 72: 74: 78: 80) sts.
Cont straight until sleeve measures 47 (48: 49: 50: 51: 52) cm, ending with a WS row.

Shape top
Cast off 4 (4: 5: 5: 6: 6) sts at beg of next 2 rows. 60 (62: 62: 64: 66: 68) sts.
Dec 1 st at each end of next 3 rows, and foll alt row, then on 4 foll 4th rows.
44 (46: 46: 48: 50: 52) sts.
Work 1 row.
Dec 1 st at each end of next and every foll alt row until 36 sts rem, then on foll 7 rows, ending with a WS row.
Cast off rem 22 sts.

MAKING UP
Press all pieces with a warm iron over a damp cloth.
Join both shoulder seams using back stitch or mattress stitch if preferred.
Neckband
With RS facing, using 3mm (US 2/3) needles and one strand each of Mohair Haze and Fine Lace held together, slip 16 (17: 17: 17: 17: 17) sts from right front holder onto right needle, rejoin yarns and pick up and knit 23 (23: 23: 26: 26: 26) sts up right side of front neck, 34 (36: 36: 38: 38: 38) sts from back, and 23 (23: 23: 26: 26: 26) sts down left side of front neck, then K across 16 (17: 17: 17: 17: 17) sts on left front holder.
112 (116: 116: 124: 124: 124) sts.
Row 1 (WS): K7, P2, *K2, P2, rep from * to last 7 sts, K7.
Row 2: K9, *P2, K2, rep from * to last 7 sts.
Rep last 2 rows 3 times more, ending with a **RS** row.
Cast off in patt (on **WS**).
Join side seams. Join sleeve seams.
Insert sleeves into armholes.
Sew on buttons.

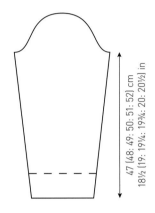

39.5 (42: 44.5: 47: 49.5: 53.5) cm
15½ (16½: 17½: 18½: 19½: 21) in

39 (40: 41: 42: 43: 44) cm
15¼ (15¾: 16: 16½: 17: 17¼) in

47 (48: 49: 50: 51: 52) cm
18½ (19: 19¼: 19¾: 20: 20½) in

Recommendation

Suitable for the knitter with a little experience
Please see pages 38 & 39 for photographs.

	XS	S	M	L	XL	XXL	
To fit bust	**81**	**86**	**91**	**97**	**102**	**109**	**cm**
	32	34	36	38	40	43	in

Rowan Cocoon

	5	6	6	7	7	8 x 100gm

Photographed in Clay

Needles

1 pair 7mm (no 2) (US 10½) needles
1 pair 8mm (no 0) (US 11) needles
Cable needle

Tension

11 sts and 20 rows to 10 cm measured over
pattern using 8mm (US 11) needles.

Pattern note: On every RS row, the number
of sts increases – every st (apart from the first
and last st) has an increase worked into it.
However, on every foll WS row, these extra sts
are decreased, by working the 2 sts together.
All st counts given relate to the basic number
of sts and do NOT include those increased
on RS rows. It is best to only count sts after
WS rows but, if you need to, when counting
sts after a RS row, count each **pair** of sts, or
loops, (this is one increased st and the base
st) as only ONE st. Remember, when casting
off or working neck shaping on WS rows, each
2 loops on needle only counts as one st. To
decrease one st, you will need to work 4 loops
together, and when casting off you will need
to work each pair of loops together for each
cast-off st.

FOND

Ribbed edge to edge jacket

SPECIAL ABBREVIATIONS

C3B = slip next 2 sts onto cable needle and
leave at back of work, inc in next st, slip centre
st of this group of 3 sts back onto left needle
and inc in this st, then inc in st on cable needle;
C3F = slip next 2 sts onto cable needle and
leave at front of work, inc in next st, slip centre
st of this group of 3 sts back onto left needle
and inc in this st, then inc in st on cable needle;
dec2 = (K3tog, K3tog tbl) all into next 3 sts –
2 sts decreased, and the original 3 sts form
2 loops;
inc2 = (K2tog, K2tog tbl, K2tog) all into next 2
loops (these are the 2 loops that make one "real"
st) – 2 sts increased, and 2 loops form 3 sts.

BACK

Cast on 47 (49: 51: 55: 57: 61) sts using
8mm (US 11) needles.
Row 1 (RS): K1, inc once in each st to last
st (see pattern note), K1.
Sizes XS, M and L only
Row 2: K1, K2tog, *P2tog, K2tog, rep from
* last st, K1.
Sizes S, XL and XXL only
Row 2: K1, P2tog, *K2tog, P2tog, rep from
* last st, K1.
All sizes
These 2 rows form patt.
Work in patt for a further 18 rows, ending
with a WS row.
Counting in from both ends of last row, place
markers after 7th (8th: 9th: 9th: 10th: 10th)
sts in from both ends of row.
Row 21 (RS): K1, patt to marker, slip marker
onto right needle, dec2, patt to within 3 sts
of next marker, dec2, slip marker onto right
needle, patt to last st, K1.
Work 11 rows, ending with a WS row.
Row 33: As row 21. 43 (45: 47: 51: 53: 57) sts.
Work 16 rows, ending with a **RS** row.
Row 50 (WS): K1, patt to marker, slip marker
onto right needle, inc2, patt to within 2 loops
(this is one "real" st) of next marker, inc2, slip
marker onto right needle, patt to last st, K1.
Work 9 rows, ending with a RS row.
Row 60: As row 50.
47 (49: 51: 55: 57: 61) sts.
Cont straight until back measures 34 (35: 35:
35: 35: 35) cm, ending with a WS row.

Shape armholes

Keeping patt correct, cast off 2 sts at beg of
next 2 rows. 43 (45: 47: 51: 53: 57) sts.
Next row (RS): K1, patt 0 (1: 0: 0: 1: 0) st,
dec 2, patt to last 4 (5: 4: 4: 5: 4) sts, dec 2,
patt 0 (1: 0: 0: 1: 0) st, K1.
39 (41: 43: 47: 49: 53) sts.
Working all armhole decreases as set by last
row, dec 2 sts at each end of 4th (4th: 4th:
2nd: 2nd: 2nd) and foll 0 (0: 0: 0: 0: 1) alt row,
then on 0 (0: 0: 1: 1: 1) foll 4th row.
35 (37: 39: 39: 41: 41) sts.
Cont straight until armhole measures 18 (18:
19: 20: 21: 22) cm, ending with a WS row.
Shape shoulders and back neck
Keeping patt correct, cast off 3 (3: 4: 3: 4: 4)
sts at beg of next 2 rows.
29 (31: 31: 33: 33: 33) sts.
Next row (RS): Cast off 3 (3: 4: 3: 4: 4) sts,
patt until there are 6 (7: 6: 7: 6: 6) sts on right
needle and turn, leaving rem sts on a holder.
Work each side of neck separately.
Cast off 3 sts at beg of next row.
Cast off rem 3 (4: 3: 4: 3: 3) sts.
With RS facing, rejoin yarn to rem sts, cast off
centre 11 (11: 11: 13: 13: 13) sts, patt to end.
Complete to match first side, reversing
shapings.

LEFT FRONT

Cast on 28 (29: 30: 32: 33: 35) sts using
8mm (US 11) needles.
Row 1 (RS): K1, inc once in each st to last st
(see pattern note), K1.
Sizes XS, M and L only
Row 2: K1, *P2tog, K2tog, rep from * last st,
K1.
Sizes S, XL and XXL only
Row 2: K1, P2tog, *K2tog, P2tog, rep from *
last st, K1.
All sizes
These 2 rows form patt as given for back.
Cont in patt for a further 6 rows.
Now work in cable patt as folls:
Row 9 (RS): Patt to last 4 sts, C3B, K1.
Work 5 rows.
Last 6 rows form cable patt.
Working in cable patt as now set throughout,
cont as folls:
Work 6 rows, ending with a WS row.

Counting in from end of last row, place marker after 7th (8th: 9th: 9th: 10th: 10th) sts in from end of row.
Row 21 (RS): K1, patt to marker, slip marker onto right needle, dec2, patt to end.
Work 11 rows, ending with a WS row.
Row 33: As row 21.
24 (25: 26: 28: 29: 31) sts.
Work 16 rows, ending with a RS row.
Row 50 (WS): K1, patt to within 2 loops (this is one "real" st) of next marker, inc2, slip marker onto right needle, patt to last st, K1.
Work 9 rows, ending with a **RS** row.
Row 60: As row 50.
28 (29: 30: 32: 33: 35) sts.
Cont straight until left front matches back to start of armhole shaping, ending with a WS row.
Shape armhole
Keeping patt correct, cast off 2 sts at beg of next row.
26 (27: 28: 30: 31: 33) sts.
Work 1 row.
Working all armhole decreases as set by back, dec 2 sts at armhole edge of next and foll 0 (0: 0: 1: 1: 2) alt rows, then on foll 4th row.
22 (23: 24: 24: 25: 25) sts.
Cont straight until 10 (10: 10: 12: 12: 12) rows less have been worked than on back to start of shoulder shaping, ending with a WS row.
Shape front neck
Next row (RS): Patt to last 8 sts and turn, leaving rem 8 sts on a holder (for neckband).
14 (15: 16: 16: 17: 17) sts.
Keeping patt correct, dec 1 st at neck edge of next 2 rows, then on foll 2 (2: 2: 3: 3: 3) alt rows. 10 (11: 12: 11: 12: 12) sts.
Work 3 rows, ending with a WS row.
Shape shoulder
Keeping patt correct, cast off 3 (3: 4: 3: 4: 4) sts at beg of next and foll alt row **and at same time** dec 1 st at neck edge of next row.
Work 1 row.
Cast off rem 3 (4: 3: 4: 3: 3) sts.

RIGHT FRONT
Cast on 28 (29: 30: 32: 33: 35) sts using 8mm (US 11) needles.
Row 1 (RS): K1, inc once in each st to last st (see pattern note), K1.
Sizes XS, M and L only
Row 2: K1, *K2tog, P2tog, rep from * last st, K1.
Sizes S, XL and XXL only
Row 2: K1, P2tog, *K2tog, P2tog, rep from * last st, K1.

All sizes
These 2 rows form patt as given for back.
Cont in patt for a further 6 rows.
Now work in cable patt as folls:
Row 9 (RS): K1, C3F, patt to end.
Work 5 rows.
Last 6 rows form cable patt.
Working in cable patt as now set throughout, cont as folls:
Work 6 rows, ending with a WS row.
Counting in from beg of last row, place marker after 7th (8th: 9th: 9th: 10th: 10th) sts in from beg of row.
Row 21 (RS): K1, patt to within 3 sts of marker, dec2, slip marker onto right needle, patt to last st, K1.
Complete to match left front, reversing shapings and working first row of neck shaping as folls:
Shape front neck
Next row (RS): Patt 8 sts and slip these 8 sts onto a holder (for neckband), patt to end.
14 (15: 16: 16: 17: 17) sts.

SLEEVES (both alike)
Cast on 31 (31: 35: 35: 39: 39) sts using 8mm (US 11) needles.
Row 1 (RS): K1, inc once in each st to last st (see pattern note), K1.
Row 2: K1, P2tog, *K2tog, P2tog, rep from * last st, K1.
These 2 rows form patt.
Cont in patt for a further 3 rows, ending with a RS row.
Row 6 (WS): K1, patt 1 st, inc2, patt to last 3 sts, inc 2, patt 1 st, K1.
35 (35: 39: 39: 43: 43) sts.
Work a further 4 rows, ending with a WS row.
Shape top
Keeping patt correct, cast off 2 sts at beg of next 2 rows. 31 (31: 35: 35: 39: 39) sts.
Next row (RS): K1, patt 1 st, dec 2, patt to last 5 sts, dec 2, patt 1 st, K1.
27 (27: 31: 31: 35: 35) sts.
Working all decreases as set by last row, dec 2 sts at each end of 6th and foll 6th row, then on foll 4th row, then on foll 2 (2: 3: 3: 4: 4) alt rows. 7 sts.
Work 1 row.
Cast off.

MAKING UP
Press all pieces with a warm iron over a damp cloth.
Join both shoulder seams using back stitch or mattress stitch if preferred.

Neckband
With RS facing and using 7mm (US 10½) needles, slip 8 sts from right front holder onto right needle, rejoin yarn and pick up and knit 14 (14: 14: 15: 15: 15) sts up right side of front neck **wrapping yarn round needle once after each picked-up st,** 17 (17: 17: 19: 19: 19) sts from back **wrapping yarn round needle once after each picked-up st,** and 14 (14: 14: 15: 15: 15) sts down left side of front neck **wrapping yarn round needle once after each picked-up st,** then patt across 8 sts on left front holder.
61 (61: 61: 65: 65: 65) sts.
Row 1 (WS): K1, P2tog, *K2tog, P2tog, rep from * to last st, K1.
This row sets position of patt as given for back.
Cont in patt for 1 row more, ending with a **RS** row.
Cast off in patt (on **WS**).
Join side seams. Join sleeve seams.
Insert sleeves into armholes.

41.5 (44: 46.5: 49: 51.5: 55.5) cm
16¼ (17¼: 18¼: 19¼: 20¼: 21¾) in

52 [53: 54: 55: 56: 57] cm
20½ [21: 21¼: 21¾: 22: 22½] in

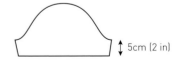

5cm (2 in)

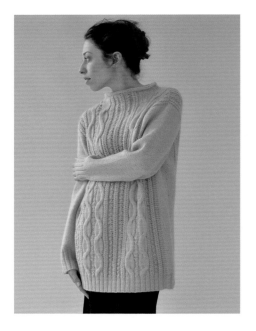

TRANQUIL
Cable & bobble tunic with funnel neck

Recommendation

Suitable for the knitter with a little experience
Please see pages 32 & 33 for photographs.

	XS	S	M	L	XL	XXL	
To fit bust	**81**	**86**	**91**	**97**	**102**	**109**	**cm**
	32	34	36	38	40	43	in

Rowan Kid Classic

	10	11	12	13	14	15 x 50gm

Photographed in Pumice

Needles

1 pair 3¾mm (no 9) (US 5) needles
1 pair 4½mm (no 7) (US 7) needles
3¾mm (no 9) (US 5) circular needle
4½mm (no 7) (US 7) circular needle
Cable needle

Tension

21 sts and 27 rows to 10 cm measured over
stocking stitch using 4½mm (US 7) needles.

SPECIAL ABBREVIATIONS

C8B = slip next 4 sts onto cable needle and
leave at back of work, K4, then K4 from cable
needle; **C8F** = slip next 4 sts onto cable needle
and leave at front of work, K4, then K4 from
cable needle; **MB** = make bobble as folls: (K1,
P1, K1) all into next st, turn and P3, turn and
K3, lift second and 3rd sts on right needle over
first st and off right needle (**Note**: Ensure all
bobbles sit on the RS of the knitting by gently
easing them through the work); **Tw2L** = K into
back of second st on left needle, then K first
st and slip both sts off left needle together;
Tw2R = K into front of second st on left needle,
then K first st and slip both sts off left needle
together.

BACK and FRONT (both alike)

Cast on 135 (141: 149: 155: 161: 171) sts
using 3¾mm (US 5) needles.
Row 1 (RS): K4 (7: 6: 4: 7: 7), P2, *K3, P2,
rep from * to last 4 (7: 6: 4: 7: 7) sts, K4 (7:
6: 4: 7: 7).
Row 2: K4, P0 (0: 2: 0: 0: 0), K2 (0: 2: 2:
0: 0), (P3, K2) 1 (2: 2: 3: 4: 5) times, K5, *P3,
K2, rep from * to last 14 (17: 21: 24: 27: 32)
sts, K3, (K2, P3) 1 (2: 2: 3: 4: 5) times, K2 (0:
2: 2: 0: 0), P0 (0: 2: 0: 0: 0), K4.
These 2 rows set the sts.
Cont as set for a further 17 rows, ending with
a RS row.
Row 20 (WS): K4, P0 (0: 2: 0: 0: 0), (K2tog)
1 (0: 1: 1: 0: 0) times, (P3, K2tog) 1 (2: 2: 3:
4: 5) times, K5, P1, M1, P2, K2tog, P3, K2tog,
P1, M1, P2, (K2, P3) twice, (K2tog, P3) twice,
K2, P3, K2, (P1, M1, P2, K2tog, P3, K2tog)
twice, P1, M1, P2, (K2, P3) twice, (K2tog, P3)
twice, K2, P3, K2, P1, M1, P2, K2tog, P3, K2tog,
P1, M1, P2, K5, (K2tog, P3) 1 (2: 2: 3: 4: 5)
times, (K2tog) 1 (0: 1: 1: 0: 0) times, P0 (0:
0: 0: 0), K4.
126 (132: 138: 142: 148: 156) sts.
Change to 4½ (US 7) needles.
Now work in patt as folls:
Row 1 (RS): K12 (15: 18: 20: 23: 27), P2,
Tw2R, Tw2L, P5, Tw2R, Tw2L, P2, K8, P5, K8,
P2, (Tw2R, Tw2L, P5) twice, Tw2R, Tw2L, P2,
K8, P5, K8, P2, Tw2R, Tw2L, P5, Tw2R, Tw2L,
P2, K12 (15: 18: 20: 23: 27).
Row 2: P9 (12: 15: 17: 20: 24), (K5, P4) twice,
K2, P8, K5, P8, K2, (P4, K5) twice, P4, K2, P8,
K5, P8, K2, (P4, K5) twice, P9 (12: 15: 17: 20:
24).
Row 3: K12 (15: 18: 20: 23: 27), P2, Tw2R,
Tw2L, P2, MB, P2, Tw2R, Tw2L, P2, K8, P2, MB,
P2, K8, P2, (Tw2R, Tw2L, P2, MB, P2) twice,
Tw2R, Tw2L, P2, K8, P2, MB, P2, K8, P2, Tw2R,
Tw2L, P2, MB, P2, Tw2R, Tw2L, P2, K12 (15:
18: 20: 23: 27).
Row 4: As row 2.
Rows 5 to 8: As rows 1 to 4.
Row 9: K12 (15: 18: 20: 23: 27), P2, Tw2R,
Tw2L, P5, Tw2R, Tw2L, P2, C8B, P5, C8F, P2,
(Tw2R, Tw2L, P5) twice, Tw2R, Tw2L, P2, C8B,
P5, C8F, P2, Tw2R, Tw2L, P5, Tw2R, Tw2L, P2,
K12 (15: 18: 20: 23: 27).
Rows 10 to 12: As rows 2 to 4.

Rows 13 to 24: As rows 1 to 4, 3 times.
Row 25: K12 (15: 18: 20: 23: 27), P2, Tw2R,
Tw2L, P5, Tw2R, Tw2L, P2, C8F, P5, C8B, P2,
(Tw2R, Tw2L, P5) twice, Tw2R, Tw2L, P2, C8F,
P5, C8B, P2, Tw2R, Tw2L, P5, Tw2R, Tw2L, P2,
K12 (15: 18: 20: 23: 27).
Rows 26 to 28: As rows 2 to 4.
Rows 29 to 32: As rows 1 to 4.
These 32 rows form patt.
Cont in patt until work measures 51 (51: 52:
52: 52: 52) cm, ending with a WS row.
Shape armholes
Keeping patt correct, cast off 4 (4: 5: 5: 6: 6)
sts at beg of next 2 rows.
118 (124: 128: 132: 136: 144) sts.
Dec 1 st at each end of next 7 (9: 9: 11:
11: 13) rows, then on foll 2 (2: 3: 2: 3: 3)
alt rows.
100 (102: 104: 106: 108: 112) sts.
Cont straight until armhole measures 19 (20:
20: 21: 22: 23) cm, ending with a WS row.
Shape shoulders
Keeping patt correct, cast off 9 (9: 9: 9: 9: 10)
sts at beg of next 4 rows, then 8 (8: 9: 9: 10:
10) sts at beg of foll 2 rows, ending with
a WS row.
Break yarn and leave rem 48 (50: 50: 52:
52: 52) sts on a holder.

SLEEVES (both alike)

Cast on 64 (66: 68: 72: 74: 76) sts using
3¾mm (US 5) needles.
Row 1 (RS): K1 (2: 3: 0: 1: 2), P2, *K3, P2,
rep from * to last 1 (2: 3: 0: 1: 2) sts, K1 (2:
3: 0: 1: 2).
Row 2: P1 (2: 3: 0: 1: 2), K2, *P3, K2, rep
from * to last 1 (2: 3: 0: 1: 2) sts, P1 (2: 3:
0: 1: 2).
These 2 rows form rib.
Cont in rib for a further 19 rows, ending with
a RS row.
Row 22 (WS): P1 (2: 3: 0: 1: 2), K2tog, *P3,
K2tog, rep from * to last 1 (2: 3: 0: 1: 2) sts,
P1 (2: 3: 0: 1: 2).
51 (53: 55: 57: 59: 61) sts.
Change to 4½mm (US 7) needles.
Starting with a K row, cont in st st throughout
as folls:
Work 2 rows, ending with a WS row.
Next row (RS): K3, M1, K to last 3 sts, M1, K3.

Working all increases as set by last row, inc 1 st at each end of 6th and every foll 6th row to 71 (69: 69: 69: 75: 75) sts, then on every foll 8th row until there are 77 (79: 81: 83: 87: 89) sts.

Cont straight until sleeve measures 45 (46: 47: 48: 49: 50) cm, ending with a WS row.

Shape top

Cast off 4 (4: 5: 5: 6: 6) sts at beg of next 2 rows.

69 (71: 71: 73: 75: 77) sts.

Dec 1 st at each end of next 3 rows, then on every foll alt row until 49 sts rem, then on foll 9 rows, ending with a WS row.

Cast off rem 31 sts.

MAKING UP

Press all pieces with a warm iron over a damp cloth.

Join both shoulder seams using back stitch or mattress stitch if preferred.

Collar

With RS facing and using 4½mm (US 7) circular needle, work across sts on front holder as folls: P3 (4: 4: 5: 5: 5), K8, patt 26 sts, K8, P3 (4: 4: 5: 5: 5), then work across sts on back holder as folls: P3 (4: 4: 5: 5: 5), K8, patt 26 sts, K8, P3 (4: 4: 5: 5: 5).

96 (100: 100: 104: 104: 104) sts.

Round 1 (RS): *P3 (4: 4: 5: 5: 5), K8, patt 26 sts, K8, P3 (4: 4: 5: 5: 5), rep from * once more.

Rep last round 7 times more.

Change to 3¾mm (US 5) circular needle.

Next round: Knit.

Rep last round 4 times more.

Cast off.

Join side seams above rib rows.

Join sleeve seams.

Insert sleeves into armholes.

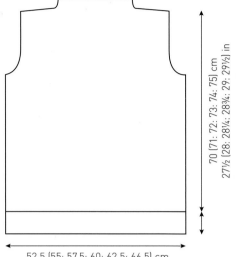

52.5 (55: 57.5: 60: 62.5: 66.5) cm
20¾ (21¾: 22¾: 23¾: 24¾: 26) cm

70 (71: 72: 73: 74: 75) cm
27½ (28: 28¾: 28¾: 29: 29½) in

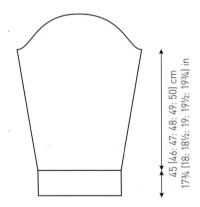

45 (46: 47: 48: 49: 50) cm
17¾ (18: 18½: 19: 19½: 19¾) in

Recommendation
Suitable for the knitter with a little experience
Please see pages 23 & 25 for photographs.

	XS	S	M	L	XL	XXL	
To fit bust	**81**	**86**	**91**	**97**	**102**	**109**	cm
	32	34	36	38	40	43	in

Rowan Brushed Fleece
11 12 12 13 13 14 x 50gm
Photographed in Peat

Needles
1 pair 6mm (no 4) (US 10) needles

Tension
14 sts and 21 rows to 10 cm measured over
stocking stitch using 6mm (US 10) needles.

DARKNESS
Cosy hooded coat

BACK
Cast on 68 (72: 76: 80: 82: 88) sts using
6mm (US 10) needles.
Beg with a K row, now work in st st throughout
as folls:
Work 20 rows, ending with a WS row.
Next row (RS): K2, K2tog, K to last 4 sts,
K2tog tbl, K2.
Working all side seam decreases as set by last
row, dec 1 st at each end of 20th and 2 foll
20th rows. 60 (64: 68: 72: 74: 80) sts.
Cont straight until back measures 55 (55: 56:
56: 56: 56) cm, ending with a WS row.
Shape armholes
Cast off 3 (3: 4: 4: 5: 5) sts at beg of next
2 rows.
54 (58: 60: 64: 64: 70) sts.
Dec 1 st at each end of next 3 rows, then
on foll 1 (2: 2: 4: 3: 5) alt rows.
46 (48: 50: 50: 52: 54) sts.
Cont straight until armhole measures 18 (19: 19:
20: 21: 22) cm, ending with a WS row.
Shape shoulders and back neck
Next row (RS): Cast off 5 (5: 6: 5: 6: 6) sts,
K until there are 10 (10: 10: 10: 10: 11) sts
on right needle and turn, leaving rem sts on
a holder.
Work each side of neck separately.
Cast off 4 sts at beg of next row.
Cast off rem 6 (6: 6: 6: 6: 7) sts.
With RS facing, rejoin yarn to rem sts, cast off
centre 16 (18: 18: 20: 20: 20) sts, K to end.
Complete to match first side, reversing shapings.

LEFT FRONT
Cast on 57 (59: 61: 63: 64: 67) sts using
6mm (US 10) needles.
Row 1 (RS): Knit.
Row 2: K2, P to end.
These 2 rows set the sts – front opening edge
2 sts in g st with all other sts in st st.
Keeping sts correct as set throughout, cont
as folls:
Work 18 rows, ending with a WS row.
Working all side seam decreases as set
by back, dec 1 st at beg of next and 3 foll
20th rows. 53 (55: 57: 59: 60: 63) sts.
Cont straight until left front matches back
to start of armhole shaping, ending with
a WS row.

Shape armhole
Cast off 3 (3: 4: 4: 5: 5) sts at beg of next row.
50 (52: 53: 55: 55: 58) sts.
Work 1 row.
Dec 1 st at armhole edge of next 3 rows,
then on foll 1 (2: 2: 4: 3: 5) alt rows.
46 (47: 48: 48: 49: 50) sts.
Cont straight until left front matches back
to start of shoulder shaping, ending with
a WS row.
Shape shoulder
Cast off 5 (5: 6: 5: 6: 6) sts at beg of next row,
then 6 (6: 6: 6: 6: 7) sts at beg of foll alt row.
35 (36: 36: 37: 37: 37) sts.
Work 1 row, ending with a WS row.
Shape hood
Cast on 15 (16: 16: 17: 17: 17) sts at beg
of next row.
50 (52: 52: 54: 54: 54) sts.
Work 21 rows, ending with a WS row.
Working all hood decreases in same way as
side seam decreases, dec 1 st at beg of next
and foll 10th row, then on foll 8th row, then
on foll 6th row, then on foll 4th row, then
on foll 2 alt rows, ending with a **RS** row.
43 (45: 45: 47: 47: 47) sts.

Now working decreases on edge sts of rows,
dec 1 st at shaped (back) edge of next 5 rows,
ending with a WS row.
38 (40: 40: 42: 42: 42) sts.
Cast off 4 sts at beg of next row, then
5 (6: 6: 7: 7: 7) sts at beg of foll alt row,
then 7 (8: 8: 9: 9: 9) sts at beg of foll alt
row. 22 sts.
(**Note**: To avoid cast-off edge forming
"steps", slip the first st when casting off,
instead of knitting it.)
Work 1 row, ending with a WS row.
Break yarn and leave rem 22 sts on a holder.

RIGHT FRONT
Cast on 57 (59: 61: 63: 64: 67) sts using
6mm (US 10) needles.
Row 1 (RS): Knit.
Row 2: P to last 2 sts, K2.
These 2 rows set the sts – front opening edge
2 sts in g st with all other sts in st st.
Complete to match left front, reversing
shapings.

SLEEVES (both alike)

Cast on 29 (31: 33: 33: 35: 37) sts using
6mm (US 10) needles.
Beg with a K row, work in st st throughout
as folls:
Work 18 rows, ending with a WS row.
Next row (RS): K3, M1, K to last 3 sts, M1, K3.
Working all increases as set by last row, inc 1
st at each end of 12th (12th: 12th: 10th: 10th:
12th) and every foll 12th (12th: 12th: 10th:
12th: 12th) row to 41 (41: 41: 39: 51: 53) sts,
then on every foll 14th (14th: 14th: 12th: -: -)
row until there are 43 (45: 47: 49: -: -) sts.
Cont straight until sleeve measures 49 (50: 51:
52: 53: 54) cm, ending with a WS row.

Shape top

Cast off 3 (3: 4: 4: 5: 5) sts at beg of next
2 rows.
37 (39: 39: 41: 41: 43) sts.
Dec 1 st at each end of next and foll alt row,
then on 4 foll 4th rows.
25 (27: 27: 29: 29: 31) sts.
Work 1 row.
Dec 1 st at each end of next and foll 0 (1: 1:
2: 2: 3) alt rows, then on foll 5 rows, ending
with a WS row.
Cast off rem 13 sts.

MAKING UP

Press all pieces with a warm iron over
a damp cloth.
Join both shoulder seams using back stitch
or mattress stitch if preferred. Graft together
both sets of 22 sts at top of hood, then join
back seam of hood. Sew cast-on edge of
hood section to back neck edge, easing in
slight fullness.
Join side seams. Join sleeve seams.
Insert sleeves into armholes.

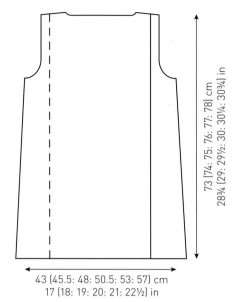

73 (74: 75: 76: 77: 78) cm
28¾ (29: 29½: 30: 30¼: 30¾) in

43 (45.5: 48: 50.5: 53: 57) cm
17 (18: 19: 20: 21: 22½) in

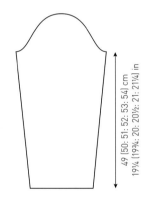

49 (50: 51: 52: 53: 54) cm
19¼ (19¾: 20: 20½: 21: 21¼) in

Recommendation

Suitable for the knitter with a little experience
Please see pages 20 – 22 for photographs.

	XS	S	M	L	XL	XXL	
To fit bust	81	86	91	97	102	109	cm
	32	34	36	38	40	43	in

Rowan Kidsilk Haze

A	Wicked						
	2	2	3	3	4	4	x 25gm
B	Anthracite						
	3	3	4	4	4	5	x 25gm
C	Steel						
	1	2	2	3	3	4	x 25gm

Needles

1 pair 4mm (no 8) (US 6) needles
1 pair 4½mm (no 7) (US 7) needles
1 pair 8mm (no 0) (US 11) needles
1 pair 9mm (no 00) (US 13) needles

Tension

12 sts and 19 rows to 10 cm measured over
pattern using a combination of one 4½mm
(US 7) and one 9mm (US 13) needle and 2
strands of yarn held together.

Special note: We found it preferable to knit
the two yarns together from separate balls
rather than winding them together.

DARK
Shaded sweater worked in an open fabric

STRIPE SEQUENCE

2 strands of yarn are held together throughout
and the shaded effect is created by changing
the colour of one of these strands. Combine
colours as folls:
Rows 1 to 6: Using 2 strands of yarn A.
Rows 7 to 14: Using one strand each of yarns
A and B.
Rows 15 to 20: Using 2 strands of yarn B.
Rows 21 to 28: Using one strand each of
yarns B and C.
Rows 29 to 34: Using 2 strands of yarn C.
Rows 35 to 42: Using one strand each of
yarns B and C.
Rows 43 to 48: Using 2 strands of yarn B.
Rows 49 to 56: Using one strand each of
yarns A and B.
These 56 rows form stripe sequence and are
repeated throughout.

BACK and FRONT (both alike)

Cast on 53 (55: 59: 61: 65: 69) sts using
8mm (US 11) needles and 2 strands of yarn A.
Row 1 (RS): Using a 4mm (US 6) needle, knit.
Row 2: Using an 8mm (US 11) needle, purl.
These 2 rows form rows 1 and 2 of stripe
sequence (see above).
Beg with stripe sequence row 3, cont in stripe
sequence throughout as folls:
Rows 3 to 6: As rows 1 and 2, twice.
Keeping stripes correct, now work in patt
as folls:
Row 7 (RS): Using a 4½mm (US 7) needle,
knit.
Row 8: Using a 9mm (US 13) needle, purl.
Last 2 rows form patt.
Cont straight in patt and stripes as now set
until work measures approx 44 (44: 45: 45:
45: 45) cm, ending after stripe sequence row
28 (28: 30: 30: 30: 30) and with a WS row.

Shape armholes

Keeping patt and stripes correct, cast off 3 sts
at beg of next 2 rows.
47 (49: 53: 55: 59: 63) sts.
Dec 1 st at each end of next 1 (1: 1: 3: 3: 3)
rows, then on foll 1 (1: 2: 1: 2: 3) alt rows,
then on foll 4th row.
41 (43: 45: 45: 47: 49) sts.
Cont straight until armhole measures 18 (19:
19: 20: 21: 22) cm, ending with a WS row.

Shape shoulders and funnel neck

Keeping patt and stripes correct, cast off 3 sts
at beg of next 2 (2: 4: 2: 4: 6) rows, then 2 sts
at beg of foll 4 (4: 2: 4: 2: 0) rows.
27 (29: 29: 31: 31: 31) sts.
Work a further 7 rows (to form funnel neck),
ending with a **RS** row.
Using a 9mm (US 13) needle, cast off purlwise
(on **WS**).

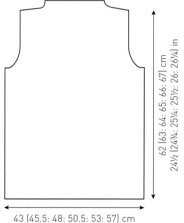

43 (45.5: 48: 50.5: 53: 57) cm
17 (18: 19: 20: 21: 22½) in

62 (63: 64: 65: 66: 67) cm
24½ (24¾: 25¼: 25½: 26: 26¼) in

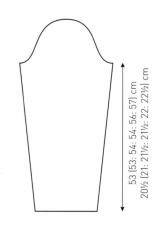

53 (53: 54: 54: 56: 57) cm
20½ (21: 21½: 21½: 22: 22½) cm

Continued on next page...

MIST
Slouchy ribbed hat

Note: The pattern is given for the version in Kid Classic and Kidsilk Haze, followed by the changes for the Mohair Haze and Fine Lace version in square brackets in bold. Where only one set of figures is given, this refers to both versions.

Recommendation
Suitable for the knitter with a little experience
Please see pages 10, 24, 28 & 56 for photographs.

Rowan Kid Classic and Kidsilk Haze

A Kid Classic	2	x 50gm
B Kidsilk Haze	1	x 25gm

Photographed in Kid Classic in Nightly/Kidsilk Haze in Turkish Plum, and in Kid Classic in Spruce/Kidsilk Haze in Forest Green
OR
Rowan Mohair Haze and Fine Lace

A Mohair Haze	2	x 25gm
B Fine Lace	1	x 50gm

Photographed in Mohair Haze in Nest/Fine Lace in Cameo

Needles
Kid Classic and Kidsilk Haze version: 1 pair 4½mm (no 7) (US 7) needles
Mohair Haze and Fine Lace version: 1 pair 3¼mm (no 10) (US 3) needles

Tension
16 [20] sts and 40 [56] rows to 10 cm measured over pattern using 4½mm [3¼mm] (US 7 [3]) needles and one strand each of yarns A and B held together.

Special note: We found it preferable to knit the two yarns together from separate balls rather than winding them together.

Special abbreviations
K1 below = K into next st one row below and at same time slipping off st above.

HAT
Cast on 75 [**95**] sts using 4½mm [**3¼mm**] (US 7 [**3**]) needles and one strand each of yarns A and B held together.
Row 1 (RS): K2, *P1, K1, rep from * to last st, K1.
Row 2: K1, *P1, K1, rep from * to end.
These 2 rows form rib.
Work in rib for a further 8 [12] rows, ending with a WS row. Now work in patt as folls:
Row 1 (RS): K1, *K1 below, K1, rep from * to end.
Row 2: K2, *K1 below, K1, rep from * to last st, K1.
These 2 rows form patt.
Cont in patt until hat measures 26cm, ending with a WS row.
Shape top
Row 1 (RS): K1, *K1 below, P3tog, rep from * to last 2 sts, K1 below, K1. 39 [**49**] sts.
Row 2: K1, *P1, K1, rep from * to end.
Row 3: *K2tog, rep from * to last st, K1. 20 [**25**] sts.
Row 4: P1, (P2tog) 9 [**12**] times, P1 [**0**].
Break yarn and thread through rem 11 [**13**] sts. Pull up tight and fasten off securely. Sew back seam.

DARK – Continued from previous page.

SLEEVES (both alike)
Cast on 23 (25: 27: 27: 29: 29) sts using 8mm (US 11) needles and one strand each of yarns B and B [B: B: B: C: C].
Row 1 (RS): Using a 4mm (US 6) needle, knit.
Row 2: Using an 8mm (US 11) needle, purl.
Beg with stripe sequence row 45 [43: 43: 43: 39: 37], cont in stripe sequence as given for back and front throughout as folls:
Rows 3 to 8: As rows 1 and 2, 3 times.
Keeping stripes correct, now work in patt as folls:
Row 9 (RS): Using a 4½mm (US 7) needle, knit.
Row 10: Using a 9mm (US 13) needle, purl.
Last 2 rows form patt.
Keeping patt and stripes correct, work 6 rows,

ending with a WS row.
Inc 1 st at each end of next and every foll 10th (10th: 14th: 10th: 12th: 12th) row to 31 (31: 39: 31: 41: 39) sts, then on every foll 12th (12th: -: 12th: 14th: 14th) row until there are 37 (39: -: 41: 43: 43) sts.
Cont straight until sleeve measures approx 52 (53: 54: 54: 56: 57) cm, ending after stripe sequence row 28 (28: 30: 30: 30: 30) and with a WS row.
Shape top
Keeping patt and stripes correct, cast off 3 sts at beg of next 2 rows.
31 (33: 33: 35: 37: 37) sts.
Dec 1 st at each end of next and foll alt row, then on 2 foll 4th rows.
23 (25: 25: 27: 29: 29) sts.
Work 3 rows.

Dec 1 st at each end of next and every foll alt row until 19 sts rem, then on foll 3 rows, ending with a WS row.
Cast off rem 13 sts.

MAKING UP
Press all pieces with a warm iron over a damp cloth.
Join both shoulder and funnel neck seams using back stitch or mattress stitch if preferred.
Join side seams.
Join sleeve seams.
Insert sleeves into armholes.

MILD
Boxy cable & bobble cardigan

Recommendation
Suitable for the knitter with a little experience
Please see pages 40 & 41 for photographs.

	XS	S	M	L	XL	XXL	
To fit bust	81	86	91	97	102	109	cm
	32	34	36	38	40	43	in

Rowan Cocoon
7	7	7	8	8	9	x 100gm

Photographed in Jupiter

Needles
1 pair 5½mm (no 5) (US 9) needles
1 pair 6½mm (no 3) (US 10½) needles
Cable needle

Buttons – 7

Tension
15 sts and 21 rows to 10 cm measured
over stocking stitch using 6½mm (US 10½)
needles.

SPECIAL ABBREVIATIONS
C6B = slip next 3 sts onto cable needle and
leave at back of work, K3, then K3 from cable
needle; **C6F** = slip next 3 sts onto cable needle
and leave at front of work, K3, then K3 from
cable needle; **MB** = make bobble as folls: (K1,
P1, K1) all into next st, turn and P3, turn and
K3, lift second and 3rd sts on right needle over
first st and off right needle (**Note**: Ensure all
bobbles sit on the RS of the knitting by gently
easing them through the work); **Tw2L** = K into
back of second st on left needle, then K first
st and slip both sts off left needle together;
Tw2R = K into front of second st on left needle,
then K first st and slip both sts off left needle
together.

BACK
Cast on 71 (75: 79: 83: 87: 93) sts using
5½mm (US 9) needles.
Row 1 (RS): K0 (0: 0: 0: 0: 1), (P1, K1 tbl)
3 (4: 5: 6: 7: 8) times, K3, P2, K1 tbl, P1, K1
tbl, P2, (K1 tbl, P1) 6 times, K1 tbl, P2, K1 tbl,
P1, K1 tbl, P3, K1 tbl, P1, K1 tbl, P2, K1 tbl,
(P1, K1 tbl) 6 times, P2, K1 tbl, P1, K1 tbl, P2,
K3, (K1 tbl, P1) 3 (4: 5: 6: 7: 8) times, K0 (0:
0: 0: 0: 1).
Row 2: P0 (0: 0: 0: 0: 1), (K1, P1) 3 (4: 5: 6:
7: 8) times, K5, P1, K1, P1, K2, (P1, K1) 6 times,
P1, K2, P1, K1, P1, K3, P1, K1, P1, K2, P1, (K1,
P1) 6 times, K2, P1, K1, P1, K5, (P1, K1) 3 (4: 5:
6: 7: 8) times, P0 (0: 0: 0: 0: 1).
These 2 rows set the sts.
Cont as set for a further 15 rows, ending with
a RS row.
Row 18 (WS): Patt 13 (15: 17: 19: 21: 24)
sts, (M1, patt 6 sts, M1, patt 7 sts) 3 times, M1,
patt 6 sts, M1, patt 13 (15: 17: 19: 21: 24) sts.
79 (83: 87: 91: 95: 101) sts.
Change to 6½mm (US 10½) needles.
Beg and ending rows as indicated and
repeating the 28 row patt repeat throughout,
now work in patt from chart as folls:
Cont in patt until back measures 36 (36: 37:
37: 37: 37) cm, ending with a WS row.
Shape armholes
Keeping patt correct, cast off 4 (4: 5: 5: 6: 6)
sts at beg of next 2 rows.
71 (75: 77: 81: 83: 89) sts.
Dec 1 st at each end of next 3 (3: 3: 5: 5: 7)
rows, then on foll 2 (3: 3: 2: 3: 3) alt rows.
61 (63: 65: 67: 67: 69) sts.
Cont straight until armhole measures 18 (19:
19: 20: 21: 22) cm, ending with a WS row.
Shape shoulders and back neck
Cast off 5 (5: 6: 6: 6: 6) sts at beg of next
2 rows. 51 (53: 53: 55: 55: 57) sts.
Next row (RS): Cast off 5 (5: 6: 6: 6: 6) sts,
patt until there are 10 (10: 9: 9: 9: 10) sts
on right needle and turn, leaving rem sts
on a holder.
Work each side of neck separately.
Cast off 4 sts at beg of next row.
Cast off rem 6 (6: 5: 5: 5: 6).
With RS facing, rejoin yarn to rem sts, cast off
centre 21 (23: 23: 25: 25: 25) sts, patt to end.
Complete to match first side, reversing shapings.

LEFT FRONT
Cast on 41 (43: 45: 47: 49: 52) sts using
5½mm (US 9) needles.
Row 1 (RS): K0 (0: 0: 0: 0: 1), (P1, K1 tbl)
3 (4: 5: 6: 7: 8) times, K3, P2, K1 tbl, P1, K1
tbl, P2, (K1 tbl, P1) 6 times, K1 tbl, P2, K1 tbl,
P1, K1 tbl, P2, K5.
Row 2: K7, P1, K1, P1, K2, P1, (K1, P1) 6
times, K2, P1, K1, P1, K5, (P1, K1) 3 (4: 5: 6:
7: 8) times, P0 (0: 0: 0: 0: 1).
These 2 rows set the sts.
Cont as set for a further 15 rows, ending with
a RS row.
Row 18 (WS): Patt 9 sts, M1, patt 6 sts, M1,
patt 7 sts, M1, patt 6 sts, M1, patt 13 (15: 17:
19: 21: 24) sts. 45 (47: 49: 51: 53: 56) sts.
Change to 6½mm (US 10½) needles.
Beg and ending rows as indicated and
repeating the 28 row patt repeat throughout,
now work in patt from chart as folls:
Row 1 (RS): Patt first 38 (40: 42: 44: 46: 49)
sts as row 1 of chart, P2, K5.
Row 2: K7, patt rem 38 (40: 42: 44: 46: 49)
sts as row 2 of chart.
These 2 rows set the sts for rest of left front
– front opening edge 7 sts still in g st with all
other sts now in patt.
Cont as now set until left front matches
back to start of armhole shaping, ending
with a WS row.
Shape armhole
Keeping patt correct, cast off 4 (4: 5: 5: 6: 6) sts
at beg of next row. 41 (43: 44: 46: 47: 50) sts.
Work 1 row.
Dec 1 st at armhole edge of next 3 (3: 3: 5: 5:
7) rows, then on foll 2 (3: 3: 2: 3: 3) alt rows.
36 (37: 38: 39: 39: 40) sts.
Cont straight until 13 (13: 13: 15: 15: 15) rows
less have been worked than on back to start
of shoulder shaping, ending with a RS row.
Shape front neck
Next row (WS): K7, P1, K2tog, P1, K2, patt
to end. 35 (36: 37: 38: 38: 39) sts.
Next row (RS): Patt 23 (23: 24: 25: 25: 26)
sts and turn, leaving rem 12 (13: 13: 13: 13:
13) sts on a holder (for neckband).
Keeping patt correct, dec 1 st at neck edge
of next 4 rows, then on foll 2 (2: 2: 3: 3: 3)
alt rows. 17 (17: 18: 18: 18: 19) sts.
Work 3 rows, ending with a WS row.

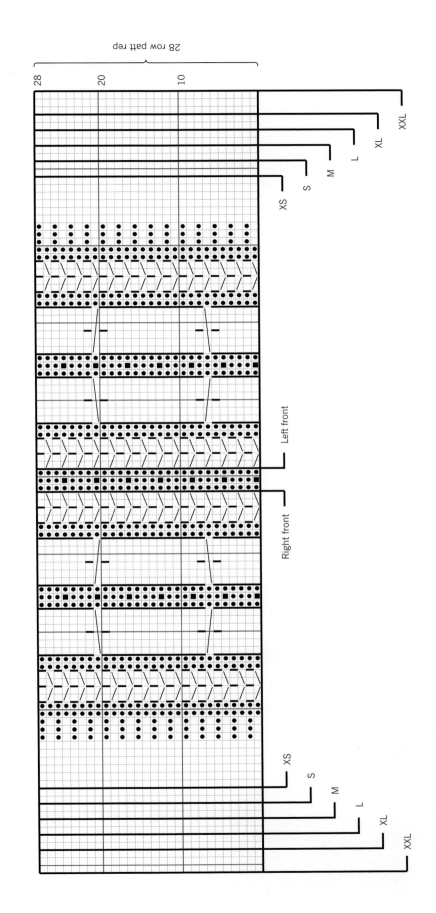

Key

☐	K on RS, P on RS
⊡	P on RS, K on WS
■	MB
╱	Tw2R
╲	Tw2L
╱	C6B
╲	C6F

28 row patt rep

28

20

10

XS

S

M

L

XL

XXL

Left front

Right front

XS

S

M

L

XL

XXL

Shape shoulder

Cast off 5 (5: 6: 6: 6: 6) sts at beg of next and foll alt row **and at same time** dec 1 st at neck edge of next row.

Work 1 row.

Cast off rem 6 (6: 5: 5: 5: 6) sts.

Mark positions for 7 buttons along left front opening edge – first to come level with row 5, second to come level with 17, last to come just above neck shaping and rem 4 buttons evenly spaced between.

RIGHT FRONT

Cast on 41 (43: 45: 47: 49: 52) sts using 5½mm (US 9) needles.

Row 1 (RS): K5, P2, K1 tbl, P1, K1 tbl, P2, K1 tbl, (P1, K1 tbl) 6 times, P2, K1 tbl, P1, K1 tbl, P2, K3, (K1 tbl, P1) 3 (4: 5: 6: 7: 8) times, K0 (0: 0: 0: 0: 1).

Row 2: P0 (0: 0: 0: 0: 1), (K1, P1) 3 (4: 5: 6: 7: 8) times, K5, P1, K1, P1, K2, (P1, K1) 6 times, P1, K2, P1, K1, P1, K7.

These 2 rows set the sts.

Cont as set for a further 2 rows, ending with a WS row.

Row 5 (RS): K1, K2tog tbl, yfwd (to make a buttonhole), patt to end.

Work 11 rows, ending with a WS row.

Row 17: As row 5 (to make 2nd buttonhole). Making a further 4 buttonholes in this way to correspond with positions marked for buttons on left front and noting that no further reference will be made to buttonholes, cont as folls:

Row 18 (WS): Patt 13 (15: 17: 19: 21: 24) sts, M1, patt 6 sts, M1, patt 7 sts, M1, patt 6 sts, M1, patt 9 sts. 45 (47: 49: 51: 53: 56) sts.

Change to 6½mm (US 10½) needles.

Beg and ending rows as indicated and repeating the 28 row patt repeat throughout, now work in patt from chart as folls:

Row 1 (RS): K5, P2, patt rem 38 (40: 42: 44: 46: 49) sts as row 1 of chart.

Row 2: Patt first 38 (40: 42: 44: 46: 49) sts as row 2 of chart, K7.

These 2 rows set the sts for rest of right front – front opening edge 7 sts still in g st with all other sts now in patt.

Complete to match left front, reversing shapings and working first 2 rows of neck shaping as folls:

Shape front neck

Next row (WS): Patt to last 13 sts, K2, P1, K2tog, P1, K7. 35 (36: 37: 38: 38: 39) sts.

Next row (RS): K5, P2, K1 tbl, P1, K1 tbl, P2, K0 (1: 1: 1: 1: 1) and slip these 12 (13: 13: 13: 13: 13) sts onto a holder (for neckband), patt to end. 23 (23: 24: 25: 25: 26) sts.

SLEEVES (both alike)

Cast on 27 (29: 31: 33: 33: 35) sts using 5½mm (US 9) needles.

Row 1 (RS): K1, *P1, K1 tbl, rep from * to last 2 sts, P1, K1.

Row 2: P1, *K1, P1, rep from * to end.

These 2 rows form rib.

Cont in rib for a further 16 rows, inc 1 st at each end of 15th of these rows and ending with a WS row. 29 (31: 33: 35: 35: 37) sts.

Change to 6½mm (US 10½) needles.

Starting with a K row, cont in st st throughout as folls:

Work 6 rows, ending with a WS row.

Next row (RS): K3, M1, K to last 3 sts, M1, K3.

Working all increases as set by last row, inc 1 st at each end of 8th and every foll 8th row to 47 (47: 47: 47: 55: 55) sts, then on 0 (1: 2: 3: 0: 1) foll 10th rows.

47 (49: 51: 53: 55: 57) sts.

Cont straight until sleeve measures 47 (48: 49: 50: 51: 52) cm, ending with a WS row.

Shape top

Cast off 4 (4: 5: 5: 6: 6) sts at beg of next 2 rows. 39 (41: 41: 43: 43: 45) sts.

Dec 1 st at each end of next and foll alt row, then on 3 foll 4th rows.

29 (31: 31: 33: 33: 35) sts.

Work 1 row.

Dec 1 st at each end of next and every foll alt row until 25 sts rem, then on foll 5 rows, ending with a WS row.

Cast off rem 15 sts.

MAKING UP

Press all pieces with a warm iron over a damp cloth.

Join both shoulder seams using back stitch or mattress stitch if preferred.

Neckband

With RS facing and using 5½mm (US 9) needles, slip 12 (13: 13: 13: 13: 13) sts from right front holder onto right needle, rejoin yarn and pick up and knit 14 (14: 14: 16: 16: 16) sts up right side of front neck, 27 (29: 29: 31: 31: 31) sts from back, and 14 (14: 14: 16: 16: 16) sts down left side of front neck, then work across 12 (13: 13: 13: 13: 13) sts on left front holder as folls: (K1 tbl) 0 (1: 1: 1: 1: 1) times, P2, K1 tbl, P1, K1 tbl, P2, K5.

79 (83: 83: 89: 89: 89) sts.

Row 1 (WS): K7, P1, K1, P1, K2, *P1, K1, rep from * to last 13 sts, P1, K2, P1, K1, P1, K7.

Row 2: K1, K2tog tbl, yfwd (to make 7th buttonhole), K2, P2, K1 tbl, P1, K1 tbl, P2, *K1 tbl, P1, rep from * to last 13 sts, K1 tbl, P2, K1 tbl, P1, K1 tbl, P2, K5.

Row 3: As row 1.

Row 4: K5, P2, K1 tbl, P1, K1 tbl, P2, *K1 tbl, P1, rep from * to last 13 sts, K1 tbl, P2, K1 tbl, P1, K1 tbl, P2, K5.

Row 5: As row 1.

Row 6: As row 4.

Cast off in patt (on **WS**).

Join side seams. Join sleeve seams.

Insert sleeves into armholes.

Sew on buttons.

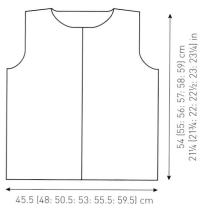

54 (55: 56: 57: 58: 59) cm
21¼ (21¾: 22: 22½: 23: 23¼) in

45.5 (48: 50.5: 53: 55.5: 59.5) cm
18 (19: 20: 21: 22: 23½) in

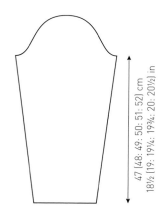

47 (48: 49: 50: 51: 52) cm
18½ (19: 19¼: 19¾: 20: 20½) in

Recommendation
Suitable for the knitter with a little experience
Please see pages 30 & 31 for photographs.

	XS	S	M	L	XL	XXL	
To fit bust	**81**	**86**	**91**	**97**	**102**	**109**	cm
	32	34	36	38	40	43	in

Rowan Brushed Fleece

    4 4 4 5 5 6 x 50gm
Photographed in Peat

Needles
1 pair 5½mm (no 5) (US 9) needles
1 pair 6mm (no 4) (US 10) needles

Tension
14 sts and 21 rows to 10 cm measured over
stocking stitch using 6mm (US 10) needles.

BLACK
Sleeveless sweater with funnel neck

BACK and FRONT (both alike)
Cast on 53 (57: 61: 65: 69: 73) sts using
5½mm (US 9) needles.
Beg with a K row, work in st st throughout
as folls:
Work 8 rows, ending with a WS row.
Change to 6mm (US 10) needles.
Work 14 rows, ending with a WS row.
Row 23 (RS): K3, K2tog, K to last 5 sts,
K2tog tbl, K3. 51 (55: 59: 63: 67: 71) sts.
Work 9 rows, then rep row 23 again.
49 (53: 57: 61: 65: 69) sts.
Work 15 rows, ending with a WS row.
Row 49 (RS): K3, M1, K to last 3 sts,
M1, K3.
Work 13 rows, then rep row 49 again.
53 (57: 61: 65: 69: 73) sts.
Cont straight until work measures 38 (38: 39:
39: 39: 39) cm, ending with a WS row.
Shape armholes
Cast off 3 sts at beg of next 2 rows.
47 (51: 55: 59: 63: 67) sts.
Next row (RS): K3, K2tog, K to last 5 sts,
K2tog tbl, K2, pick up loop lying between
needles and place this loop on right needle
(this loop does NOT count as a st), slip last
st purlwise.
Next row: P tog first st and the picked-up loop,
(P2, P2tog tbl) 0 (0: 0: 1: 1: 1) times, P to last
1 (1: 1: 5: 5: 5) sts, (P2tog, P2) 0 (0: 0: 1: 1: 1)
times, pick up loop lying between needles and
place this loop on right needle (this loop does
NOT count as a st), slip last st knitwise.
Next row: K tog tbl first st and the picked-up
loop, (K2, K2tog) 0 (1: 1: 1: 1: 1) times, K to
last 1 (5: 5: 5: 5: 5) sts, (K2tog tbl, K2) 0 (1:
1: 1: 1: 1) times, pick up loop lying between
needles and place this loop on right needle
(this loop does NOT count as a st), slip last
st purlwise.
45 (47: 51: 53: 57: 61) sts.
Working all armhole decreases as set by last
3 rows and keeping slip st edging correct
throughout as now set, cont as folls:
Dec 1 st at each end of 2nd (4th: 2nd: 2nd:
2nd: 2nd) and foll 0 (0: 0: 1: 2: 3) alt rows,
then on 0 (0: 1: 1: 1: 1) foll 4th row.
43 (45: 47: 47: 49: 51) sts.
Cont straight until armhole measures 18 (19:
19: 20: 21: 22) cm, ending with a WS row.

Shape shoulders and funnel neck
Cast off 3 (3: 4: 3: 4: 4) sts at beg of next
2 rows, then 3 (3: 3: 3: 3: 4) sts at beg of foll
2 rows. 31 (33: 33: 35: 35: 35) sts.
Work a further 6 rows on these sts only (for
funnel neck), ending with a WS row.
Cast off loosely.

MAKING UP
Press all pieces with a warm iron over
a damp cloth.
Join both shoulder and funnel neck seams
using back stitch or mattress stitch if preferred.
Join side seams.

56 (57: 58: 59: 60: 61) cm
22 (22½: 22¾: 23¼: 23¾: 24) in

38 (40.5: 43: 45.5: 48: 52) cm
15 (16: 17: 18: 19: 20½) in

Recommendation

Suitable for the knitter with a little experience
Please see pages 42 & 43 for photographs.

	XS	S	M	L	XL	XXL	
To fit bust	**81**	**86**	**91**	**97**	**102**	**109**	**cm**
	32	34	36	38	40	43	in

Rowan Kidsilk Haze and Fine Lace

Kidsilk Haze							
	5	6	6	7	7	8	x 25gm
Fine Lace							
	3	3	3	4	4	4	x 50gm

Photographed in Kidsilk Haze in Majestic with
Fine Lace in Revival

Needles

1 pair 2¼mm (no 13) (US 1) needles
1 pair 2¾mm (no 12) (US 2) needles

Buttons – 8

Tension

25 sts and 40 rows to 10 cm measured over
pattern **after pressing** using 2¾mm (US 2)
needles and one strand each of Kidsilk Haze
and Fine Lace held together.

Special note: We found it preferable to knit
the two yarns together from separate balls
rather than winding them together.

LIGHT
Pretty lacy button through sweater

BACK

Cast on 123 (129: 137: 145: 153: 165) sts
using 2¼mm (US 1) needles and one strand
each of Kidsilk Haze and Fine Lace held
together.
Row 1 (RS): K0 (1: 0: 0: 0: 0), P0 (2: 2: 1: 0:
1), *K3, P2, rep from * to last 3 (1: 0: 4: 3: 4)
sts, K3 (1: 0: 3: 3: 3), P0 (0: 0: 1: 0: 1).
Row 2: P0 (1: 0: 0: 0: 0), K0 (2: 2: 1: 0: 1),
*P3, K2, rep from * to last 3 (1: 0: 4: 3: 4) sts,
P3 (1: 0: 3: 3: 3), K0 (0: 0: 1: 0: 1).
These 2 rows form rib.
Work in rib for a further 15 rows, ending with
a RS row.
Row 18 (WS): P0 (1: 0: 0: 0: 0), K0 (2: 2:
1: 0: 1), *P2tog, P1, K2, rep from * to last
3 (1: 0: 4: 3: 4) sts, (P2tog) 1 (0: 0: 1: 1: 1)
times, P1 (1: 0: 1: 1: 1), K0 (0: 0: 1: 0: 1).
98 (104: 110: 116: 122: 132) sts.
Change to 2¾mm (US 2) needles.
Now work in patt as folls:
Row 1 (RS): K1 (0: 3: 2: 1: 2), *K2, yfwd, sl 1,
K1, psso, rep from * to last 1 (0: 3: 2: 1: 2) sts,
K1 (0: 3: 2: 1: 2).
Row 2: P1 (0: 3: 2: 1: 2), *P2, yrn, P2tog,
rep from * to last 1 (0: 3: 2: 1: 2) sts, P1
(0: 3: 2: 1: 2).
These 2 rows form patt.**
Cont in patt until back measures 39 (39: 40:
40: 40: 40) cm, ending with a WS row.
Shape armholes
Keeping patt correct, cast off 4 (4: 5: 5: 6: 6)
sts at beg of next 2 rows.
90 (96: 100: 106: 110: 120) sts.
Dec 1 st at each end of next 1 (3: 3: 5: 5: 7)
rows, then on foll 3 (3: 4: 3: 4: 5) alt rows,
then on foll 4th row.
80 (82: 84: 88: 90: 94) sts.
Cont straight until armhole measures
17 (18: 18: 19: 20: 21) cm, ending with
a WS row.
Shape shoulders and back neck
Cast off 7 (7: 7: 8: 8: 9) sts at beg of next
2 rows.
66 (68: 70: 72: 74: 76) sts.
Next row (RS): Cast off 7 (7: 7: 8: 8: 9) sts,
patt until there are 11 (11: 12: 11: 12: 12)
sts on right needle and turn, leaving rem sts
on a holder.
Work each side of neck separately.

Cast off 4 sts at beg of next row.
Cast off rem 7 (7: 8: 7: 8: 8) sts.
With RS facing, rejoin yarns to rem sts, cast off
centre 30 (32: 32: 34: 34: 34) sts, patt to end.
Complete to match first side, reversing
shapings.

FRONT

Work as given for back to **.
Cont in patt until front measures 22 (22: 23:
23: 23: 23) cm, ending with a WS row.
Divide for front opening
Next row (RS): Patt 45 (48: 51: 54: 57: 62)
sts and turn, leaving rem sts on a holder.
Work each side of neck separately.
Next row (WS): Cast on and K 8 sts, patt
to end.
53 (56: 59: 62: 65: 70) sts.
Next row: Patt to last 8 sts, K8.
These 2 rows set the sts – front opening
edge 8 sts in g st with all other sts still in patt.
Cont as now set until front matches back
to start of armhole shaping, ending with
a WS row.
Shape armhole
Keeping patt correct, cast off 4 (4: 5: 5: 6: 6)
sts at beg of next row.
49 (52: 54: 57: 59: 64) sts.
Work 1 row.
Dec 1 st at armhole edge of next 1 (3: 3: 5: 5:
7) rows, then on foll 3 (3: 4: 3: 4: 5) alt rows,
then on foll 4th row.
44 (45: 46: 48: 49: 51) sts.
Cont straight until 24 (24: 24: 28: 28: 28) rows
less have been worked than on back to start
of shoulder shaping, ending with a WS row.
Shape front neck
Next row (RS): Patt 31 (31: 32: 34: 35: 37)
sts and turn, leaving rem 13 (14: 14: 14: 14:
14) sts on another holder (for neckband).
Keeping patt correct, dec 1 st at neck edge
of next 4 rows, then on foll 4 alt rows, then
on 2 (2: 2: 3: 3: 3) foll 4th rows.
21 (21: 22: 23: 24: 26) sts.
Work 3 rows, ending with a WS row.
Shape shoulder
Cast off 7 (7: 7: 8: 8: 9) sts at beg of next
and foll alt row.
Work 1 row.
Cast off rem 7 (7: 8: 7: 8: 8) sts.

Mark positions for 8 buttons along left front opening edge – first to come in 19th row after dividing for front opening, last to come in first row of neck shaping, and rem 6 buttons evenly spaced between.

With RS facing, rejoin yarns to rem sts on first holder and cont as folls:

Next row (RS): K8, patt to end.

Next row: Patt to last 8 sts, K8.

These 2 rows set the sts – front opening edge 8 sts in g st with all other sts still in patt.

Cont as set for a further 16 rows, ending with a WS row.

Next row (RS): K3, K2tog tbl, yfwd (to make a buttonhole), K3, patt to end.

Working a further 6 buttonholes in this way to correspond with positions marked for buttons along left front opening edge, complete to match first side, reversing shapings and working first row of neck shaping as folls:

Shape front neck

Next row (RS): K3, K2tog tbl, yfwd (to make 8th buttonhole), K3, patt 5 (6: 6: 6: 6: 6) sts and slip these 13 (14: 14: 14: 14: 14) sts on another holder (for neckband), patt to end.
31 (31: 32: 34: 35: 37) sts.

SLEEVES (both alike)

Cast on 60 (62: 64: 70: 72: 74) sts using 2¼mm (US 1) needles and one strand each of Kidsilk Haze and Fine Lace held together.

Row 1 (RS): K0 (0: 1: 0: 0: 1), P1 (2: 2: 1: 2: 2), *K3, P2, rep from * to last 4 (0: 1: 4: 0: 1) sts, K3 (0: 1: 3: 0: 1), P1 (0: 0: 1: 0: 0).

Row 2: P0 (0: 1: 0: 0: 1), K1 (2: 2: 1: 2: 2), *P3, K2, rep from * to last 4 (0: 1: 4: 0: 1) sts, P3 (0: 1: 3: 0: 1), K1 (0: 0: 1: 0: 0).

These 2 rows form rib.

Work in rib for a further 25 rows, ending with a **RS** row.

Row 28 (WS): P0 (0: 1: 0: 0: 1), K1 (2: 2: 1: 2: 2), *P2tog, P1, K2, rep from * to last 4 (0: 1: 4: 0: 1) sts, (P2tog) 1 (0: 0: 1: 0: 0) times, P1 (0: 1: 1: 0: 1), K1 (0: 0: 1: 0: 0).
48 (50: 52: 56: 58: 60) sts.

Change to 2¾mm (US 2) needles.

Now work in patt as folls:

Row 1 (RS): K2 (1: 2: 2: 1: 2), *K2, yfwd, sl 1, K1, psso, rep from * to last 2 (1: 2: 2: 1: 2) sts, K2 (1: 2: 2: 1: 2).

Row 2: P2 (1: 2: 2: 1: 2), *P2, yrn, P2tog, rep from * to last 2 (1: 2: 2: 1: 2) sts, P2 (1: 2: 2: 1: 2).

These 2 rows form patt.

Cont in patt, inc 1 st at each end of next and

every foll 10th (10th: 12th: 12th: 12th: 12th) row to 56 (54: 76: 62: 74: 72) sts, then on every foll 12th (12th: 14th: 14th: 14th: 14th) row until there are 74 (76: 78: 80: 84: 86) sts, taking inc sts into patt.

Cont straight until sleeve measures 47 (48: 49: 50: 51: 52) cm, ending with a WS row.

Shape top

Keeping patt correct, cast off 4 (4: 5: 5: 6: 6) sts at beg of next 2 rows.
66 (68: 68: 70: 72: 74) sts.

Dec 1 st at each end of next 3 rows, and foll alt row, then on foll 4th row, then on 3 foll 6th rows.
50 (52: 52: 54: 56: 58) sts.

Work 3 rows.

Dec 1 st at each end of next and foll 4th row, then on every foll alt row until 40 sts rem, then on foll 7 rows, ending with a WS row.

Cast off rem 26 sts.

MAKING UP

Press all pieces with a warm iron over a damp cloth.

Join both shoulder seams using back stitch or mattress stitch if preferred.

Neckband

With RS facing, using 2¼mm (US 1) needles and one strand each of Kidsilk Haze and Fine Lace held together, slip 13 (14: 14: 14: 14: 14) sts from right front holder onto right needle, rejoin yarns and pick up and knit 25 (25: 25: 28: 28: 28) sts up right side of front neck, 39 (41: 41: 43: 43: 43) sts from back, and 25 (25: 25: 28: 28: 28) sts down left side of front neck, then patt across 13 (14: 14: 14: 14: 14) sts on left front holder.
115 (119: 119: 127: 127: 127) sts.

Row 1 (WS): K8, *P3, inc knitwise in next st, rep from * to last 11 sts, P3, K8. 139 (144: 144: 154: 154: 154) sts.

Row 2: K11, *P2, K3, rep from * to last 8 sts, K8.

Row 3: K8, P3, *K2, P3, rep from * to last 8 sts, K8.

Last 2 rows set the sts – front opening edge 8 sts still in g st with all other sts in rib.

Cont as set for a further 5 rows, ending with a **RS** row.

Cast off in patt (on **WS**).

Join side seams. Join sleeve seams.

Insert sleeves into armholes.

Sew cast-on edge of left front opening edge border in place on inside, then sew on buttons.

56 (57: 58: 59: 60: 61) cm
22 (22½: 23: 23¼: 23¾: 24) in

39 (41.5: 44: 46.5: 49: 53) cm
15½ (16½: 17½: 18½: 19½: 21) in

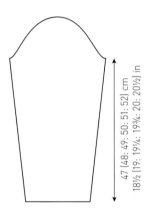

47 (48: 49: 50: 51: 52) cm
18½ (19: 19¼: 19¾: 20: 20½) in

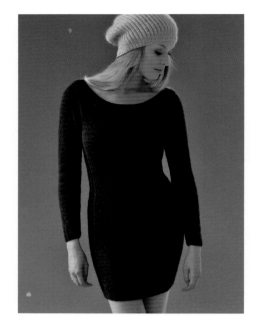

INTENSE
Close fitting dress with scooped back

Recommendation
Suitable for the knitter with a little experience
Please see pages 48 – 50 for photographs.

	XS	S	M	L	XL	XXL	
To fit bust	**81**	**86**	**91**	**97**	**102**	**109**	**cm**
	32	34	36	38	40	43	in

Rowan Lima

10 11 12 13 14 15 x 50gm
Photographed in Paraguay

Needles
1 pair 3¾mm (no 9) (US 5) needles
1 pair 4½mm (no 7) (US 7) needles
3¾mm (no 9) (US 5) circular needle

Tension
22 sts and 30 rows to 10 cm measured over
stocking stitch using 4½mm (US 7) needles.

FRONT
Cast on 74 (78: 83: 88: 93: 103) sts using
3¾mm (US 5) needles.
Row 1 (RS): (K1, P1) 1 (0: 0: 0: 0: 0) times,
(K3, P1) 1 (2: 2: 2: 2: 2) times, K5, *P2, K3,
rep from * to last 8 (10: 10: 10: 10: 10) sts,
K2, (P1, K3) 1 (2: 2: 2: 2: 2) times, (P1, K1)
1 (0: 0: 0: 0: 0) times.
Row 2: (K1, P1) 0 (1: 1: 1: 1: 1) times,
(K3, P1) twice, K1, P2, *K2, P3, rep from
* to last 13 (15: 15: 15: 15: 15) sts, K2,
P2, K1, (P1, K3) twice, (P1, K1) 0 (1: 1: 1:
1: 1) times.
These 2 rows set the sts – 11 (13: 13: 13:
13: 13) sts in textured patt at each end of
row with centre sts in rib.
Cont as now set for a further 4 rows, ending
with a WS row.
Row 7: Patt 11 (13: 13: 13: 13: 13) sts, M1,
rib to last 11 (13: 13: 13: 13: 13) sts, M1,
patt 11 (13: 13: 13: 13: 13) sts.
76 (80: 85: 90: 95: 105) sts.
Working the increased sts in st st (to match
rib of centre section), cont as now set for
a further 3 rows, dec (-: inc: inc: inc: inc)
2 (-: 1: 2: 1: 1) sts evenly over centre rib
section on last of these 3 rows.
74 (80: 86: 92: 96: 106) sts.
Change to 4½mm (US 7) needles.
Row 11 (RS): Patt 9 (11: 11: 11: 11: 11) sts,
K to last 9 (11: 11: 11: 11: 11) sts, patt 9 (11:
11: 11: 11: 11) sts.
Row 12: Patt 9 (11: 11: 11: 11: 11) sts, P to
last 9 (11: 11: 11: 11: 11) sts, patt 9 (11: 11:
11: 11: 11) sts.
These 2 rows set the sts for rest of work – side
seam 9 (11: 11: 11: 11: 11) sts still in patt as
before with all other sts now in st st.
Keeping sts correct as now set throughout,
cont as folls:
Row 13 (RS): Patt 9 (11: 11: 11: 11: 11) sts,
K2, M1, K to last 11 (13: 13: 13: 13: 13) sts,
M1, K2, patt 9 (11: 11: 11: 11: 11) sts.
Working all side seam increases as set by last
row (and taking inc sts into st st), inc 1 st at
each end of 6th and foll 6th row, then on foll
8th row, then on foll 10th row.
84 (90: 96: 102: 106: 116) sts.
Cont straight until front measures 25 (25: 26:
26: 26: 26) cm, ending with a WS row.

Next row (RS): Patt 9 (11: 11: 11: 11: 11) sts,
K2, K2tog tbl, K to last 13 (15: 15: 15: 15: 15)
sts, K2tog, K2, patt 9 (11: 11: 11: 11: 11) sts.
Working all side seam decreases as set by last
row, dec 1 st at each end of 8th and 6 foll 6th
rows.
68 (74: 80: 86: 90: 100) sts.
Work 13 rows, ending with a WS row.
Working all side seam increases as set by
lower section of front, inc 1 st at each end
of next and 3 foll 8th rows, then on 4 foll
6th rows.
84 (90: 96: 102: 106: 116) sts.**
Work 7 rows, ending with a WS row.
(Front should measure approx 63 (63: 64:
64: 64: 64) cm.)
Shape armholes
Keeping sts correct, cast off 4 (4: 5: 5: 6: 6)
sts at beg of next 2 rows.
76 (82: 86: 92: 94: 104) sts.
Dec 1 st at each end of next 1 (3: 3: 5: 5: 7)
rows, then on foll 3 (3: 4: 4: 4: 5) alt rows.
68 (70: 72: 74: 76: 80) sts.
Now working **all** sts in st st, cont as folls:
Work 13 (13: 11: 11: 13: 13) rows, ending
with a WS row.
Shape front neck
Next row (RS): K26 (26: 27: 28: 29: 31)
and turn, leaving rem sts on a holder.
Work each side of neck separately.
Cast off 3 sts at beg of next and foll 2 alt rows.
17 (17: 18: 19: 20: 22) sts.
Dec 1 st at neck edge of next 7 rows, then
on foll 5 (5: 5: 6: 6: 6) alt rows, then on foll
4th row.
4 (4: 5: 5: 6: 8) sts.
Work 3 rows, ending with a WS row.
(Armhole should measure 17 (18: 18: 19:
20: 21) cm.)
Shape shoulder
Cast off rem 4 (4: 5: 5: 6: 8) sts.
With RS facing, rejoin yarn to rem sts,
cast off centre 16 (18: 18: 18: 18: 18) sts,
K to end.
Complete to match first side, reversing
shapings.

BACK
Work as given for front to **.
Work 3 rows, ending with a WS row.

Shape back neck
Next row (RS): Patt 35 (37: 40: 43: 45: 50) sts and turn, leaving rem sts on a holder. Work each side of neck separately.
Cast off 3 sts at beg of next and foll alt row, ending with a WS row.
29 (31: 34: 37: 39: 44) sts.
Shape armhole
Keeping sts correct, cast off 4 (4: 5: 5: 6: 6) sts at beg and dec 1 st at end of next row.
24 (26: 28: 31: 32: 37) sts.
Keeping sts correct as set by front (by working all sts in st st once armhole shaping is complete), cont as folls:
Dec 1 st at neck edge of next 4 rows, then on foll 7 alt rows, then on 3 (3: 3: 4: 4: 4) foll 4th rows, then on foll 6th row, then on foll 8th row **and at same time** dec 1 st at armhole edge of 2nd and foll 0 (2: 2: 4: 4: 6) rows, then on foll 3 (3: 4: 4: 4: 5) alt rows.
4 (4: 5: 5: 6: 8) sts.
Work 7 (9: 9: 9: 11: 15) rows, ending with a WS row.
Shape shoulder
Cast off rem 4 (4: 5: 5: 6: 8) sts.
With RS facing, rejoin yarn to rem sts, cast off centre 14 (16: 16: 16: 16: 16) sts, patt to end.
Complete to match first side, reversing shapings.

SLEEVES (both alike)
Cast on 44 (46: 48: 50: 52: 54) sts using 3¾mm (US 5) needles.
Row 1 (RS): K1 (3: 3: 3: 3: 3), (P1, K3) twice, P0 (0: 0: 0: 1: 2), K2 (1: 2: 3: 3: 3), (P2, K3) 4 (4: 4: 5: 5: 5) times, P2 (2: 2: 0: 1: 2), K2 (1: 2: 0: 0: 0), (K3, P1) twice, K1 (3: 3: 3: 3: 3).
Row 2: (K1, P1) 0 (1: 1: 1: 1: 1) times, (K3, P1) twice, K1, K0 (0: 0: 0: 1: 2), P2 (1: 2: 3: 3: 3), (K2, P3) 4 (4: 4: 5: 5: 5) times, K2 (2: 2: 0: 1: 2), P2 (1: 2: 0: 0: 0), K1, (P1, K3) twice, (P1, K1) 0 (1: 1: 1: 1: 1) times.
These 2 rows set the sts – 9 (11: 11: 11: 11: 11) sts in textured patt at each end of row with centre sts in rib.
Cont as now set for a further 14 rows, ending with a WS row.
Change to 4½mm (US 7) needles.
Row 17 (RS): Patt 9 (11: 11: 11: 11: 11) sts, K2, M1, K to last 11 (13: 13: 13: 13: 13) sts, M1, K2, patt 9 (11: 11: 11: 11: 11) sts.
46 (48: 50: 52: 54: 56) sts.
Row 18: Patt 9 (11: 11: 11: 11: 11) sts, P to last 9 (11: 11: 11: 11: 11) sts, patt 9 (11: 11: 11: 11: 11) sts.

These 2 rows set the sts for rest of work – edge 9 (11: 11: 11: 11: 11) sts still in patt as before with all other sts now in st st.
Keeping sts correct as now set throughout and working all increases as set by row 17 (and taking inc sts into st st), cont as folls:
Inc 1 st at each end of 9th (11th: 11th: 11th: 9th: 11th) and every foll 10th (12th: 12th: 12th: 10th: 12th) row to 50 (66: 66: 64: 58: 76) sts, then on every foll 12th (-: 14th: 14th: 12th: -) row until there are 64 (-: 68: 70: 74: -) sts.
Cont straight until sleeve measures 45 (46: 47: 48: 49: 50) cm, ending with a WS row.
Shape top
Keeping patt correct, cast off 4 (4: 5: 5: 6: 6) sts at beg of next 2 rows.
56 (58: 58: 60: 62: 64) sts.
Dec 1 st at each end of next 3 rows, then on foll 2 alt rows, then on foll 4th row.
44 (46: 46: 48: 50: 52) sts.
Work 1 row.
Dec 1 st at each end of next and every foll alt row until 40 sts rem, then on foll 5 rows, ending with a WS row. 30 sts.
Cast off 3 sts at beg of next 4 rows.
Cast off rem 18 sts.

MAKING UP
Press all pieces with a warm iron over a damp cloth.
Join both shoulder seams using back stitch or mattress stitch if preferred. Place markers either side of all cast-off sts at base of front neck, and all cast-off sts at base of back neck (this includes the sets of 3 cast-off sts either side of the centre set).
Neckband
With RS facing and using 3¾mm (US 5) circular needle, pick up and knit 25 (25: 25: 27: 27: 27) sts down left side of front neck, 36 (38: 38: 38: 38: 38) sts from front between markers, 25 (25: 25: 27: 27: 27) sts up right side of front neck, 51 (54: 54: 57: 59: 64) sts down right side of back neck, 27 (29: 29: 29: 30: 30) sts from back between markers, and 51 (54: 54: 57: 59: 64) sts up left side of back neck. 215 (225: 225: 235: 240: 250) sts.
Round 1 (RS): *P2, K3, rep from * to end.
Rep this round 9 times more.
Cast off in rib.
Join side seams. Join sleeve seams.
Insert sleeves into armholes.

80 [81: 82: 83: 84: 85] cm
31½ [32: 32¼: 32¾: 33: 33½] in

38 (40.5: 43: 45.5: 48: 53) cm
15 (16: 17: 18: 19: 21) cm

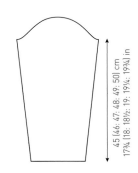

45 (46: 47: 48: 49: 50) cm
17¾ (18: 18½: 19: 19¼: 19¾) in

QUIET
Ribbed cardigan with lace trim

Recommendation
Suitable for the knitter with a little experience
Please see pages 44 & 45 for photographs.

	XS	S	M	L	XL	XXL	
To fit bust	**81**	**86**	**91**	**97**	**102**	**109**	**cm**
	32	34	36	38	40	43	in

Rowan Lima

	8	9	9	10	10	11 x 50gm

Photographed in Paraguay

Needles
1 pair 3¾mm (no 9) (US 5) needles
1 pair 4mm (no 8) (US 6) needles
1 pair 4½mm (no 7) (US 7) needles

Buttons - 6

Tension
22 sts and 30 rows to 10 cm measured
over stocking stitch (or rib when worn) using
4½mm (US 7) needles.

HEM BORDER
Cast on 16 (16: 16: 18: 18: 18) sts using
4mm (US 6) needles.
Work in patt as folls:
Row 1 (WS): Sl 1, K2, yfwd, K2tog, K3 (3: 3:
5: 5: 5), yfwd, K2tog, K2, yfwd, K2tog, yfwd, K2.
17 (17: 17: 19: 19: 19) sts.
Row 2 and every foll alt row: Yfwd, K2tog,
K to end.
Row 3: Sl 1, K2, yfwd, K2tog, K2 (2: 2 4: 4: 4),
(yfwd, K2tog) twice, K2, yfwd, K2tog, yfwd, K2.
18 (18: 18: 20: 20: 20) sts.
Row 5: Sl 1, K2, yfwd, K2tog, K3 (3: 3: 5: 5: 5),
(yfwd, K2tog) twice, K2, yfwd, K2tog, yfwd, K2.
19 (19: 19: 21: 21: 21) sts.
Row 7: Sl 1, K2, yfwd, K2tog, K2 (2: 2: 4:
4: 4), (yfwd, K2tog) 3 times, K2, yfwd, K2tog,
yfwd, K2.
20 (20: 20: 22: 22: 22) sts.
Row 9: Sl 1, K2, yfwd, K2tog, K2 (2: 2: 4: 4: 4),
(K2tog, yfwd) twice, K2, K2tog, (yfwd, K2tog)
twice, K1.
19 (19: 19: 21: 21: 21) sts.
Row 11: Sl 1, K2, yfwd, K2tog, K1 (1: 1: 3: 3:
3), (K2tog, yfwd) twice, K2, K2tog, (yfwd, K2tog)
twice, K1.
18 (18: 18: 20: 20: 20) sts.
Row 13: Sl 1, K2, yfwd, K2tog, K2 (2: 2: 4:
4: 4), K2tog, yfwd, K2, K2tog, (yfwd, K2tog)
twice, K1. 17 (17: 17: 19: 19: 19) sts.
Row 15: Sl 1, K2, yfwd, K2tog, K1 (1: 1: 3:
3: 3), K2tog, yfwd, K2, K2tog, (yfwd, K2tog)
twice, K1.
16 (16: 16: 18: 18: 18) sts.
Row 16: As row 2.
These 16 rows form patt.
Rep last 16 rows 18 (18: 20: 22: 22: 24) times
more.
Cast off (on WS).
Along straight edge, place markers to denote
side seams as folls: counting in from both ends
of strip, miss first 5 (5: 5½: 6: 6: 6½) repeats
and place a marker – there should be 9 (9: 10:
11: 11: 12) repeats between the 2 markers.

BACK
With RS facing and using 4½mm (US 7)
needles, pick up and knit 72 (78: 84: 90: 94:
104) sts along straight edge of hem border
between markers.

Row 1 (WS): P0 (0: 1: 0: 0: 0), K1 (0: 2: 2:
0: 1), (P2, K2) 2 (2: 1: 2: 2: 2) times, place
marker on needle, K2, *P2, K2, rep from * to
last 9 (8: 7: 10: 8: 9) sts, place 2nd marker
on needle, (K2, P2) 2 (2: 1: 2: 2: 2) times, K1
(0: 2: 2: 0: 1), P0 (0: 1: 0: 0: 0).
Row 2: K0 (0: 1: 0: 0: 0), P1 (0: 2: 2: 0: 1),
(K2, P2) 2 (2: 1: 2: 2: 2) times, slip marker
onto right needle, P2, *K2, P2, rep from * to
last 9 (8: 7: 10: 8: 9) sts, slip marker onto right
needle, (P2, K2) 2 (2: 1: 2: 2: 2) times, P1 (0:
2: 2: 0: 1), K0 (0: 1: 0: 0: 0).
These 2 rows set the sts - 9 (8: 7: 10: 8: 9) sts
in rib beyond markers at each end of row, and
centre sts (between markers) also in rib.
Cont as set for a further 5 rows, ending with
a WS row.
Next row (RS): Rib to first marker, slip marker
onto right needle, M1, rib to next marker, M1,
slip marker onto right needle, rib to end.
Working all side seam increases as set by last
row, inc 1 st at each end of 8th and foll 8th
row, then on 3 foll 10th rows, taking inc sts into
rib as set by centre section sts.
84 (90: 96: 102: 106: 116) sts.
Remove markers – rib should now run
smoothly across all sts.
Cont in rib across all sts until back measures
21 (21: 22: 21: 21: 21) cm from pick-up row,
ending with a WS row.
Shape armholes
Keeping sts correct, cast off 4 (4: 5: 5: 6: 6) sts
at beg of next 2 rows.
76 (82: 86: 92: 94: 104) sts.
Dec 1 st at each end of next 1 (3: 3: 5: 5: 7)
rows, then on foll 3 (3: 4: 4: 4: 5) alt rows.
68 (70: 72: 74: 76: 80) sts.
Cont straight until armhole measures
17 (18: 18: 19: 20: 21) cm, ending with
a WS row.
Shape shoulders and back neck
Cast off 6 (6: 6: 6: 7: 7) sts at beg of next
2 rows. 56 (58: 60: 62: 62: 66) sts.
Next row (RS): Cast off 6 (6: 6: 6: 7: 7) sts,
rib until there are 10 (10: 11: 11: 10: 12) sts
on right needle and turn, leaving rem sts on
a holder.
Work each side of neck separately.
Cast off 4 sts at beg of next row.
Cast off rem 6 (6: 7: 7: 6: 8) sts.

With RS facing, rejoin yarn to rem sts, cast off centre 24 (26: 26: 28: 28: 28) sts, rib to end. Complete to match first side, reversing shapings.

LEFT FRONT

With RS facing and using 4½mm (US 7) needles, pick up and knit 44 (47: 50: 53: 55: 60) sts along straight edge of hem border between left side seam marker and end of strip.

Row 1 (WS): P1, (K1, P1) 3 times, *P2, K2, rep from * to last 9 (8: 7: 10: 8: 9) sts, place 2nd marker on needle, (K2, P2) 2 (2: 1: 2: 2: 2) times, K1 (0: 2: 2: 0: 1), P0 (0: 1: 0: 0: 0).
Row 2: K0 (0: 1: 0: 0: 0), P1 (0: 2: 2: 0: 1), (K2, P2) 2 (2: 1: 2: 2: 2) times, slip marker onto right needle, *P2, K2, rep from * to last 7 sts, (P1, K1) 3 times, P1.
These 2 rows set the sts - 9 (8: 7: 10: 8: 9) sts in rib beyond marker at side seam edge of row (this is edge that "meets" back), front opening 7 sts in moss st and all other sts (between marker and moss st) also in rib.
Cont as set for a further 5 rows, ending with a WS row.
Next row (RS): Rib to marker, slip marker onto right needle, M1, patt to end.
Working all side seam increases as set by last row, inc 1 st at beg of 8th and foll 8th row, then on 3 foll 10th rows, taking inc sts into rib as set by centre section sts.
50 (53: 56: 59: 61: 66) sts.
Remove marker – rib should now run smoothly across sts.
Keeping front opening edge 7 sts in moss st throughout, cont in rib across all other sts until left front matches back to start of armhole shaping, ending with a WS row.

Shape armhole

Keeping sts correct, cast off 4 (4: 5: 5: 6: 6) sts at beg of next row. 46 (49: 51: 54: 55: 60) sts.
Work 1 row.
Dec 1 st at armhole edge of next 1 (3: 3: 5: 5: 7) rows, then on foll 3 (3: 4: 4: 4: 5) alt rows.
42 (43: 44: 45: 46: 48) sts.
Cont straight until 18 (18: 18: 20: 20: 20) rows less have been worked than on back to start of shoulder shaping, ending with a WS row.

Shape front neck

Next row (RS): Rib 28 (28: 29: 30: 31: 33) and turn, leaving rem 14 (15: 15: 15: 15: 15) sts on a holder (for neckband).
Keeping rib correct, dec 1 st at neck edge of next 6 rows, then on foll 3 (3: 3: 4: 4: 4) alt rows, then on foll 4th row.
18 (18: 19: 19: 20: 22) sts.
Work 1 row, ending with a WS row.

Shape shoulder

Cast off 6 (6: 6: 6: 7: 7) sts at beg of next and foll alt row.
Work 1 row.
Cast off rem 6 (6: 7: 7: 6: 8) sts.
Mark positions for 6 buttons along left front opening edge – first to come in pick-up row, last to come in first row of neck shaping, and rem 4 buttons evenly spaced between.

RIGHT FRONT

With RS facing and using 4½mm (US 7) needles, pick up and knit sts along rem section of straight edge of hem border between other end of strip and right side seam marker as folls: pick up and knit 3 sts, yfwd, miss point where next st would be picked up (first buttonhole made), pick up a further 40 (43: 46: 49: 51: 56) sts.
44 (47: 50: 53: 55: 60) sts in total (including the yfwd for the buttonhole).
Row 1 (WS): P0 (0: 1: 0: 0: 0), K1 (0: 2: 2: 0: 1), (P2, K2) 2 (2: 1: 2: 2: 2) times, place marker on needle, *K2, P2, rep from * to last 7 sts, (P1, K1) 3 times, P1.
Row 2: P1, (K1, P1) 3 times, *K2, P2, rep from * to last 9 (8: 7: 10: 8: 9) sts, slip marker onto right needle, (P2, K2) 2 (2: 1: 2: 2: 2) times, P1 (0: 2: 2: 0: 1), K0 (0: 1: 0: 0: 0).
These 2 rows set the sts - 9 (8: 7: 10: 8: 9) sts in rib beyond marker at side seam edge of row (this is edge that "meets" back), front opening 7 sts in moss st and all other sts (between marker and moss st) also in rib.
Cont as set for a further 5 rows, ending with a WS row.
Next row (RS): Patt to marker, M1, slip marker onto right needle, rib to end.
Working all side seam increases as set by last row, work to match left front to start of front neck shaping, reversing shapings and making 4 buttonholes to correspond with positions marked for buttons on left front as folls:
Buttonhole row (RS): P1, K1, P2tog, yrn (to make a buttonhole), patt to end.
When right front matches left front to start of front neck shaping, ending with a WS row, cont as folls:

Shape front neck

Next row (RS): P1, K1, P2tog, yrn (to make 6th buttonhole), P1, K1, P1, rib 7 (8: 8: 8: 8: 8) and slip these 14 (15: 15: 15: 15: 15) sts onto a holder (for neckband), rib to end.
28 (28: 29: 30: 31: 33) sts.
Complete to match left front, reversing shapings.

SLEEVES (both alike)

Cast on 38 (40: 42: 44: 46: 48) sts using 3¾mm (US 5) needles.
Row 1 (RS): K1 (0: 0: 0: 0: 0), P2 (0: 1: 2: 0: 1), (K2, P2) 1 (2: 2: 2: 2: 2) times, place marker on needle, K1 (1: 1: 1: 0: 0), (P2, K2) 5 (5: 5: 5: 7: 7) times, P2, K1 (1: 1: 1: 0: 0), place 2nd marker on needle, (P2, K2) 1 (2: 2: 2: 2: 2) times, P2 (0: 1: 2: 0: 1), K1 (0: 0: 0: 0: 0).
Row 2: P1 (0: 0: 0: 0: 0), K2 (0: 1: 2: 0: 1), (P2, K2) 1 (2: 2: 2: 2: 2) times, slip marker onto right needle, P1 (1: 1: 1: 0: 0), (K2, P2) 5 (5: 5: 5: 7: 7) times, K2, P1 (1: 1: 1: 0: 0), slip marker onto right needle, (K2, P2) 1 (2: 2: 2: 2: 2) times, K2 (0: 1: 2: 0: 1), P1 (0: 0: 0: 0: 0).
These 2 rows set the sts – 7 (8: 9: 10: 8: 9) sts in rib beyond markers at each end of row, and centre sts (between markers) also in rib.
Cont as set for a further 8 rows, ending with a WS row.
Change to 4½mm (US 7) needles.

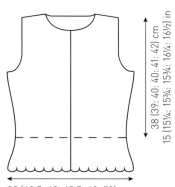

38 (40.5: 43: 45.5: 48: 52) cm
15 (16: 17: 18: 19: 20½) in

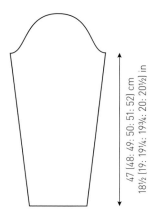

Continued on next page...

89

GENTLE

Pretty scarf worked in classic garter stitch

Recommendation
Suitable for the novice knitter
Please see pages 35 – 37 for photographs.

Rowan Kidsilk Haze Stripe
          2   x 50gm
Photographed in Precious

Needles
1 pair 3mm (no 11) (US 2/3) needles
1 pair 6mm (no 4) (US 10) needles

Tension
18 sts and 32 rows to 10 cm measured over
pattern using a combination of 3mm (US 2/3)
and 6mm (US 10) needles.

Finished size
Completed scarf is 36 cm (14 in) wide and
approx 240 cm (94½ in) long.

SCARF
Cast on 64 sts using 6mm (US 10) needles.
Work in patt as folls:
Row 1 (RS): Using a 3mm (US 2/3) needle,
knit.
Row 2: Using a 6mm (US 10) needle, knit.
These 2 rows form patt.
Cont in patt until almost all yarn has been
used, leaving sufficient to cast off and ending
with a **RS** row.
Using a 6mm (US 10) needle, cast off knitwise
(on **WS**).

MAKING UP
Do NOT press.

QUIET – *Continued from previous page.*

Next row (RS): Rib to first marker, slip marker
onto right needle, M1, rib to next marker, M1,
slip marker onto right needle, rib to end.
Working all increases as set by last row, inc
1 st at each end of 8th (10th: 10th: 10th:
8th: 10th) and every foll 8th (10th: 10th:
10th: 10th: 10th) row to 44 (66: 66: 64:
74: 74) sts, then on every foll 10th (-: 12th:
12th: -: 12th) row until there are 64 (-: 68:
70: -: 76) sts, taking inc sts into rib as set
by centre section sts.
Remove markers – rib should now run
smoothly across all sts.
Cont straight until sleeve measures 47 (48: 49:
50: 51: 52) cm, ending with a WS row.
Shape top
Keeping rib correct, cast off 4 (4: 5: 5: 6: 6) sts
at beg of next 2 rows.
56 (58: 58: 60: 62: 64) sts.

Dec 1 st at each end of next 3 rows, then
on foll alt row, then on 5 foll 4th rows.
38 (40: 40: 42: 44: 46) sts.
Work 1 row.
Dec 1 st at each end of next and every foll
alt row until 30 sts rem, then on foll 3 rows,
ending with a WS row.
Cast off rem 24 sts.

MAKING UP
Press all pieces with a warm iron over
a damp cloth.
Join both shoulder seams using back stitch
or mattress stitch if preferred.
Neckband
With RS facing and using 3¾mm (US 5)
needles, slip 14 (15: 15: 15: 15: 15) sts
from right front holder onto right needle,
rejoin yarn and pick up and knit 21 (21: 21:

23: 23: 23) sts up right side of front neck,
33 (35: 35: 37: 37: 37) sts from back, and
21 (21: 21: 23: 23: 23) sts down left side of
front neck, then patt across 14 (15: 15: 15:
15: 15) sts on left front holder.
103 (107: 107: 113: 113: 113) sts.
Working all sts in moss st as set by front
opening edge sts, work in moss st for 5 rows,
ending with a WS row.
Cast off in moss st.
Join side seams above hem border.
Join sleeve seams. Insert sleeves into
armholes. Sew on buttons.

FLATTER
Close fitting skirt with rib detail

Recommendation
Suitable for the knitter with a little experience
Please see pages 57 – 59 for photographs.

	XS	S	M	L	XL	XXL	
To fit hips	**86**	**91**	**97**	**102**	**107**	**114**	**cm**
	34	36	38	40	42	45	in

Rowan Lima
| | 7 | 8 | 8 | 9 | 9 | 10 x 50gm |
Photographed in Paraguay

Needles
1 pair 3¾mm (no 9) (US 5) needles
1 pair 4½mm (no 7) (US 7) needles

Extras – waist length of 2 cm (¾ in) wide
elastic

Tension
22 sts and 30 rows to 10 cm measured over
stocking stitch using 4½mm (US 7) needles.

BACK and FRONT (both alike)
Cast on 72 (76: 84: 88: 92: 104) sts using
3¾mm (US 5) needles.
Row 1 (RS): K3, (P1, K3) twice, K2, *P2, K2,
rep from * to last 11 sts, (K3, P1) twice, K3.
Row 2: K1, (P1, K3) twice, P1, K1, P2, *K2,
P2, rep from * to last 11 sts, K1, P1, (K3, P1)
twice, K1.
These 2 rows set the sts.
Cont as now set for a further 10 rows, ending
with a WS row.
Row 13 (RS): (Patt 17 sts, P2tog) 1 (0: 1:
0: 0: 1) times, patt to last 19 (0: 19: 0: 0:
19) sts, (P2tog tbl, patt 17 sts) 1 (0: 1: 0:
0: 1) times.
70 (76: 82: 88: 92: 102) sts.
Change to 4½mm (US 7) needles.
Row 14 (WS): Patt 11 sts, P to last 11 sts,
patt 11 sts.
Row 15: Patt 11 sts, K2, M1, K to last 13 sts,
M1, K2, patt 11 sts.
Last 2 rows set the sts for rest of work (edge
sts still in patt as before but centre sts now
in st st) and start side seam shaping.
Keeping sts correct as now set and working
all side seam increases as set by last row, inc
1 st at each end of 14th and 3 foll 14th rows,
then on foll 16th row, then on foll 18th row,
taking inc sts into st st.
84 (90: 96: 102: 106: 116) sts.
Cont straight until work measures 56 (57: 58:
59: 60: 61) cm, ending with a WS row.
Next row (RS): Patt 13 sts, K2tog tbl, K to
last 15 sts, K2tog, patt 13 sts.
Working all side seam decreases as set by
last row, dec 1 st at each end of 8th and foll
6th row, then on 5 foll 4th rows, then on foll
8 alt rows. 52 (58: 64: 70: 74: 84) sts.

Work 1 row, ending with a WS row.
Change to 3¾mm (US 5) needles.
Work a further 14 rows, ending with a WS row.
Using a 4½mm (US 7) needle, cast off **loosely**
in patt.

MAKING UP
Press all pieces with a warm iron over
a damp cloth.
Join both side seams using back stitch
or mattress stitch if preferred. Join ends
of elastic to form a loop that fits comfortably
around waist.
Lay elastic over inside of upper edge of skirt
and secure in place by working herringbone
stitch over elastic (to form a casing).

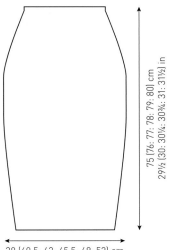

75 [76: 77: 78: 79: 80] cm
29½ [30: 30¼: 30¾: 31: 31½] in

38 (40.5: 43: 45.5: 48: 52) cm
15 (16: 17: 18: 19: 20½) in

HONOURED

Peplum jacket worked in tweed stripes

Recommendation
Suitable for the more experience knitter
Please see pages 52 – 54 for photographs.

	XS	S	M	L	XL	XXL	
To fit bust	**81**	**86**	**91**	**97**	**102**	**109**	**cm**
	32	34	36	38	40	43	in

Rowan Felted Tweed

		XS	S	M	L	XL	XXL	
A	Seafarer	6	6	7	7	7	8	x 50gm
B	Duck Egg	1	2	2	2	2	3	x 50gm
C	Ancient	2	2	2	2	3	3	x 50gm

Needles
1 pair 3mm (no 11) (US 2/3) needles
1 pair 3¾mm (no 9) (US 5) needles

Buttons - 7

Tension
24 sts and 48 rows to 10 cm measured over
pattern using 3¾mm (US 5) needles.

Important note: Please see our information
page (page 102) for tips regarding the tension
for this slip stitch pattern.

Pattern note: When working patt, work all
slipped sts purlwise keeping yarn at **wrong
side** of work – this is **back** of work on RS rows
and **front** of work on WS rows.

STRIPE SEQUENCE
Rows 1 and 10: Using yarn A.
Rows 11 and 12: Using yarn B.
Rows 13 and 14: Using yarn A.
Rows 15 and 16: Using yarn B.
Rows 17 to 22: Using yarn A.
Rows 23 and 24: Using yarn C.
Rows 25 and 26: Using yarn A.
Rows 27 and 28: Using yarn C.
Rows 29 and 30: Using yarn A.
Rows 31 and 32: Using yarn B.
Rows 33 to 38: Using yarn A.
Rows 39 and 40: Using yarn C.
Rows 41 and 42: Using yarn A.
Rows 43 and 44: Using yarn C.
Rows 45 and 46: Using yarn A.
Rows 47 and 48: Using yarn C.
Rows 49 to 54: Using yarn A.
Rows 55 and 56: Using yarn B.
Rows 57 to 62: Using yarn A.
Rows 63 and 64: Using yarn C.
Rows 65 and 66: Using yarn A.
Rows 67 and 68: Using yarn C.
Rows 69 and 70: Using yarn A.
Rows 71 and 72: Using yarn B.
These 72 rows form stripe sequence
and are repeated throughout.

BACK
Cast on 159 (165: 171: 177: 183: 193) sts
using 3¾mm (US 5) needles and yarn A.
Work in patt as folls:
Row 1 (RS): K0 (1: 0: 1: 0: 1), (P1, K1)
11 (12: 12: 13: 13: 15) times, *place
marker on needle, K15, place marker on
needle, K1, (P1, K1) 6 (6: 8: 8: 10: 10)
times, place marker on needle, K15, place
marker on needle*, K1, (P1, K1) 14 times,
rep from * to * once more, (K1, P1) 11
(12: 12: 13: 13: 15) times, K0 (1: 0: 1:
0: 1). 8 markers on needle.
Slipping markers from left needle to right
needle on every row, cont as folls:
Row 2: As row 1, noting that markers are
now slipped from left needle to right needle.
Row 3: K0 (1: 0: 0: 0: 0), P0 (1: 1: 0:
0: 0), K0 (1: 1: 1: 0: 1), P1, (sl 1 - see
pattern note, P1, K1, P1) 5 (5: 5: 6: 6: 7)
times, sl 1 (see pattern note), *slip marker
to right needle, K15, slip marker to right
needle, sl 1 (see pattern note), (P1, K1, P1,
sl 1 – see pattern note) 3 (3: 4: 4: 5: 5)
times, slip marker to right needle, K15, slip
marker to right needle*, sl 1 (see pattern
note), (P1, K1, P1, sl 1 – see pattern note)
7 times, rep from * to * once more, sl 1
(see pattern note), (P1, K1, P1, sl 1 – see
pattern note) 5 (5: 5: 6: 6: 7) times,
P1, K0 (1: 1: 1: 0: 1), P0 (1: 1: 0: 0: 0),
K0 (1: 0: 0: 0: 0).
Row 4: As row 3.
These 4 rows set the sts – 4 panels of g st
between each pair of markers with all other
sts in patt.
Cont as now set for a further 0 (0: 4: 4: 8: 8) rows.
Now starting with stripe sequence row 1
(so that a total of 14 (14: 18: 18: 22: 22)
rows using yarn A are worked before first
stripe in yarn B), cont as set in stripe
sequence throughout as folls:
Work 10 rows.
Next row (RS): Patt to marker, *slip marker
to right needle, P15, slip marker to right
needle, patt to marker, slip marker to right
needle, P15, slip marker to right needle*,
patt to marker, rep from * to * once more,
patt to end.
Next row: Patt to marker, *slip marker to right
needle, K15, slip marker to right needle, patt
to marker, slip marker to right needle, K15,
slip marker to right needle*, patt to marker,
rep from * to * once more, patt to end.
Last 2 rows set sts for rest of peplum – sts
between markers now in rev st st with all
other sts still in patt.
Keeping stripes and sts correct as now set,
cont as folls:
Next row (RS): Work 2 tog, patt to marker,
*slip marker to right needle, P2tog tbl, P to
within 2 sts of next marker, P2tog, slip marker
to right needle, patt to marker, slip marker to
right needle, P2tog tbl, P to within 2 sts of next
marker, P2tog, slip marker to right needle*,
patt to marker, rep from * to * once more,
patt to last 2 sts, work 2 tog.
149 (155: 161: 167: 173: 183) sts.
Working all decreases as set by last row, dec
1 st at each end of 8th and foll 8th row, then
on 6 foll 6th rows **and at same time** dec 1 st
at each side of each rev st st section (between

markers) on 16th and foll 12th row, then on 4 foll 6th rows.
85 (91: 97: 103: 109: 119) sts, and only 1 st in rev st st between each pair of markers.
Work 3 rows, ending with a WS row.
Next row (RS): (Patt to within 1 st of marker, remove this marker and next marker, K3tog) 4 times, patt to end.
77 (83: 89: 95: 101: 111) sts.
Work 1 row, ending with a WS row.
Dec 1 st at each end of next row.
75 (81: 87: 93: 99: 109) sts.
Work 1 row, ending after stripe sequence row 72 and with a WS row.
Using yarn A **only**, work 14 rows, placing markers at each end of 6th of these rows (to denote top of peplum) and ending with a WS row.
Now working again in stripe sequence, starting with row 11 (so there are 14 rows in yarn B between last stripe in yarn B and this next stripe in yarn B), and keeping patt correct, cont as folls:
Inc 1 st at each end of 3rd and 8 foll 8th rows, then on 2 foll 6th rows, taking inc sts into patt.
97 (103: 109: 115: 121: 131) sts.
Cont straight until back measures 20 cm **from markers,** ending with a WS row. (**Note:** Make a note of which stripe sequence row has just been worked to this point so that sleeve stripe sequence can end at same point.)
Shape armholes
Keeping patt and stripes correct, cast off 4 (4: 5: 5: 6: 6) sts at beg of next 2 rows.
89 (95: 99: 105: 109: 119) sts.
Dec 1 st at each end of next 1 (3: 3: 5: 5: 7) rows, then on foll 3 (3: 4: 4: 5: 6) alt rows, then on foll 4th row.
79 (81: 83: 85: 87: 91) sts.
Cont straight until armhole measures 18 (19: 19: 20: 21: 22) cm, ending with a WS row.
Shape shoulders and back neck
Cast off 8 (8: 8: 8: 8: 9) sts at beg of next 2 rows.
63 (65: 67: 69: 71: 73) sts.
Next row (RS): Cast off 8 (8: 8: 8: 8: 9) sts, patt until there are 11 (11: 12: 12: 13: 13) sts on right needle and turn, leaving rem sts on a holder.
Work each side of neck separately.
Cast off 4 sts at beg of next row.
Cast off rem 7 (7: 8: 8: 9: 9) sts.
With RS facing, rejoin appropriate yarn to rem sts, cast off centre 25 (27: 27: 29: 29: 29) sts, patt to end.
Complete to match first side, reversing shapings.

LEFT FRONT
Cast on 89 (92: 95: 98: 101: 106) sts using 3¾mm (US 5) needles and yarn A.
Work in patt as folls:
Row 1 (RS): K0 (1: 0: 1: 0: 1), (P1, K1) 11 (12: 12: 13: 13: 15) times, place marker on needle, K15, place marker on needle, K1, (P1, K1) 6 (6: 8: 8: 10: 10) times, place marker on needle, K15, place marker on needle, (K0, P1) 12 times. 4 markers on needle.
Slipping markers from left needle to right needle on every row, cont as folls:
Row 2: (P1, K1) 12 times, slip marker to right needle, K15, slip marker to right needle, K1, (P1, K1) 6 (6: 8: 8: 10: 10) times, slip marker to right needle, K15, slip marker to right needle, (K1, P1) 11 (12: 12: 13: 13: 15) times, K0 (1: 0: 1: 0: 1).
Row 3: K0 (1: 0: 0: 0: 0), P0 (1: 1: 0: 0: 0), K0 (1: 1: 1: 0: 1), P1, (sl 1 - see pattern note, P1, K1, P1) 5 (5: 5: 6: 6: 7) times, sl 1 (see pattern note), slip marker to right needle, K15, slip marker to right needle, sl 1 (see pattern note), (P1, K1, P1, sl 1 – see pattern note) 3 (3: 4: 4: 5: 5) times, slip marker to right needle, K15, slip marker to right needle, (sl 1 - see pattern note, P1, K1, P1) 6 times.
Row 4: (P1, K1, P1, sl 1 - see pattern note) 6 times, slip marker to right needle, K15, slip marker to right needle, sl 1 (see pattern note), (P1, K1, P1, sl 1 – see pattern note) 3 (3: 4: 4: 5: 5) times, slip marker to right needle, K15, slip marker to right needle, sl 1 (see pattern note), (P1, K1, P1, sl 1 - see pattern note) 5 (5: 5: 6: 6: 7) times, P1, K0 (1: 1: 1: 0: 1), P0 (1: 1: 0: 0: 0), K0 (1: 0: 0: 0: 0).
These 4 rows set the sts – 2 panels of g st between each pair of markers with all other sts in patt.
Cont as now set for a further 0 (0: 4: 4: 8: 8) rows.
Now starting with stripe sequence row 1 (so that a total of 14 (14: 18: 18: 22: 22) rows using yarn A are worked before first stripe in yarn B), cont as set in stripe sequence throughout as folls:
Work 10 rows.
Next row (RS): Patt to marker, slip marker to right needle, P15, slip marker to right needle, patt to marker, slip marker to right needle, P15, slip marker to right needle, patt to end.
Next row: Patt to marker, slip marker to right needle, K15, slip marker to right needle, patt to marker, slip marker to right needle, K15, slip marker to right needle, patt to end.
Last 2 rows set sts for rest of peplum – sts between markers now in rev st st with all other sts still in patt.

Keeping stripes and sts correct as now set, cont as folls:
Next row (RS): Work 2 tog, patt to marker, slip marker to right needle, P2tog tbl, P to within 2 sts of next marker, P2tog, slip marker to right needle, patt to marker, slip marker to right needle, P2tog tbl, P to within 2 sts of next marker, P2tog, slip marker to right needle, patt to end.
84 (87: 90: 93: 96: 101) sts.
Working all decreases as set by last row, dec 1 st at beg of 8th and foll 8th row, then on 6 foll 6th rows **and at same time** dec 1 st at each side of each rev st st section (between markers) on 16th and foll 12th row, then on 4 foll 6th rows.
52 (55: 58: 61: 64: 69) sts, and only 1 st in rev st st between each pair of markers.
Work 3 rows, ending with a WS row.
Next row (RS): (Patt to within 1 st of marker, remove this marker and next marker, K3tog) twice, patt to end.
48 (51: 54: 57: 60: 65) sts.
Work 1 row, ending with a WS row.
Dec 1 st at beg of next row.
47 (50: 53: 56: 59: 64) sts.
Work 1 row, ending after stripe sequence row 72 and with a WS row.
Using yarn A **only**, work 14 rows, placing markers at each end of 6th of these rows (to denote top of peplum) and ending with a WS row.
**Now working again in stripe sequence, starting with row 11 (so there are 14 rows in yarn A between last stripe in yarn B and this next stripe in yarn B), and keeping patt correct,
cont as folls:
Inc 1 st at beg of 3rd and 8 foll 8th rows, then on 2 foll 6th rows, taking inc sts into patt. 58 (61: 64: 67: 70: 75) sts.
Cont straight until left front matches back to start of armhole shaping, ending with a WS row.
Shape armhole
Keeping patt and stripes correct, cast off 4 (4: 5: 5: 6: 6) sts at beg of next row.
54 (57: 59: 62: 64: 69) sts.
Work 1 row.
Dec 1 st at armhole edge of next 1 (3: 3: 5: 5: 7) rows, then on foll 3 (3: 4: 4: 5: 6) alt rows, then on foll 4th row.
49 (50: 51: 52: 53: 55) sts.
Cont straight until 30 (30: 30: 34: 34: 34) rows less have been worked than on back to start of shoulder shaping, ending with a WS row.

Shape front neck

Next row (RS): Patt 33 (33: 34: 35: 36: 38) sts and turn, leaving rem 16 (17: 17: 17: 17: 17) sts on a holder (for neckband). Keeping patt and stripes correct, dec 1 st at neck edge of next 4 rows, then on foll 3 alt rows, then on 2 (2: 2: 3: 3: 3) foll 4th rows, then on foll 6th row.
23 (23: 24: 24: 25: 27) sts.
Work 5 rows, ending with a WS row.
Shape shoulder
Cast off 8 (8: 8: 8: 8: 9) sts at beg of next and foll alt row.
Work 1 row.
Cast off rem 7 (7: 8: 8: 9: 9) sts.
Mark positions for 7 buttons along left front opening edge – first to come just above marked (waist level) row, last to come just below neck shaping, and rem 5 buttons evenly spaced between.

RIGHT FRONT
(**Note:** To keep front opening edge neat, this front is knitted with the fabric reversed – so that RS rows of left front will become WS rows on this front, and all K sts on left front will become P sts on this front, and vice versa. However, all slipped sts **must** still be slipped purlwise with yarn at WS of work as before.)
Cast on 89 (92: 95: 98: 101: 106) sts using 3¾mm (US 5) needles and yarn A.
Work in patt as folls:
Row 1 (WS): P0 (1: 0: 1: 0: 1), (K1, P1) 11 (12: 12: 13: 13: 15) times, place marker on needle, P15, place marker on needle, P1, (K1, P1) 6 (6: 8: 8: 10: 10) times, place marker on needle, P15, place marker on needle, (P1, K1) 12 times. 4 markers on needle.
Slipping markers from left needle to right needle on every row, cont as folls:
Row 2: (K1, P1) 12 times, slip marker to right needle, P15, slip marker to right needle, P1, (K1, P1) 6 (6: 8: 8: 10: 10) times, slip marker to right needle, P15, slip marker to right needle, (P1, K1) 11 (12: 12: 13: 13: 15) times, P0 (1: 0: 1: 0: 1).
Row 3: P0 (1: 0: 0: 0: 0), K0 (1: 1: 0: 0: 0), P0 (1: 1: 1: 0: 1), K1, (sl 1 – see pattern note, K1, P1, K1) 5 (5: 5: 6: 6: 7) times, sl 1 (see pattern note), slip marker to right needle, P15, slip marker to right needle, (sl 1 - see pattern note), (K1, P1, K1, sl 1 – see pattern note) 3 (3: 4: 4: 5: 5) times, slip marker to right needle, P15, slip marker to right needle, (sl 1 - see pattern note, K1, P1, K1) 6 times.
Row 4: (K1, P1, K1, sl 1 - see pattern note) 6 times, slip marker to right needle, P15,

slip marker to right needle, sl 1 (see pattern note), (K1, P1, K1, sl 1 – see pattern note) 3 (3: 4: 4: 5: 5) times, slip marker to right needle, P15, slip marker to right needle, sl 1 (see pattern note), (K1, P1, K1, sl 1 - see pattern note) 5 (5: 5: 6: 6: 7) times, K1, P0 (1: 1: 1: 0: 1), K0 (1: 1: 0: 0: 0), P0 (1: 0: 0: 0: 0).
These 4 rows set the sts – 2 panels of **purl** g st between each pair of markers with all other sts in patt.
Cont as now set for a further 0 (0: 4: 4: 8: 8) rows.
Now starting with stripe sequence row 1 (so that a total of 14 (14: 18: 18: 22: 22) rows using yarn A are worked before first stripe in yarn B), cont as set in stripe sequence throughout as folls:
Work 10 rows.
Next row (WS): Patt to marker, slip marker to right needle, K15, slip marker to right needle, patt to marker, slip marker to right needle, K15, slip marker to right needle, patt to end.
Next row: Patt to marker, slip marker to right needle, P15, slip marker to right needle, patt to marker, slip marker to right needle, P15, slip marker to right needle, patt to end.
Last 2 rows set sts for rest of peplum – sts between markers now in rev st st with all other sts still in patt.
Keeping stripes and sts correct as now set, cont as folls:
Next row (WS): Work 2 tog, patt to marker, slip marker to right needle, K2tog tbl, K to within 2 sts of next marker, K2tog, slip marker to right needle, patt to marker, slip marker to right needle, K2tog tbl, K to within 2 sts of next marker, K2tog, slip marker to right needle, patt to end.
84 (87: 90: 93: 96: 101) sts.
Working all decreases as set by last row, dec 1 st at beg of 8th and foll 8th row, then on 6 foll 6th rows **and at same time** dec 1 st at each side of each rev st st section (between markers) on 16th and foll 12th row, then on 4 foll 6th rows.
52 (55: 58: 61: 64: 69) sts, and only 1 st in rev st st between each pair of markers.
Work 3 rows, ending with a RS row.
Next row (WS): (Patt to within 1 st of marker, remove this marker and next marker, P3tog) twice, patt to end. 48 (51: 54: 57: 60: 65) sts.
Work 1 row, ending with a RS row.
Dec 1 st at beg of next row.
47 (50: 53: 56: 59: 64) sts.
Work 1 row, ending after stripe sequence row 72 and with a RS row.

Using yarn A **only**, work 6 rows, ending with a RS row.
Place markers at each end of last row (to denote top of peplum).
Next row (WS): Using yarn A, patt to last 6 sts, yrn, work 2 tog (to make a buttonhole), patt 4 sts. Making a further 6 buttonholes in this way to correspond with positions marked for buttons on left front and noting that no further reference will be made to buttonholes, cont as folls:
Using yarn A **only**, work 7 rows, ending with a RS row.
Complete to match left front from **, reversing all shapings (by reading K for P and vice versa, and WS for RS and vice versa).

SLEEVES (both alike)
Cast on 47 (49: 51: 53: 57: 59) sts using 3¾mm (US 5) needles and yarn A.
Work in patt as folls:
Row 1 (RS): Using yarn A P1 (0: 1: 0: 0: 1), *K1, P1, rep from * to last 0 (1: 0: 1: 1: 0) st, K0 (1: 0: 1: 1: 0).
Row 2: As row 1.

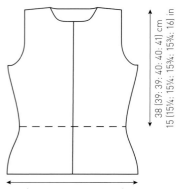

40.5 (43: 45.5: 48: 50.5: 54.5) cm
16 (17: 18: 19: 20: 21½) in

38 (39: 39: 40: 40: 41) cm
15 (15¼: 15¼: 15¾: 15¾: 16) in

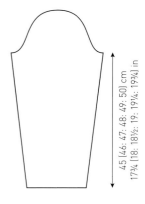

45 (46: 47: 48: 49: 50) cm
17¾ (18: 18½: 19: 19¼: 19¾) in

Continued on next page...

Recommendation
Suitable for the knitter with a little experience
Please see pages 11 & 19 for photographs.

Rowan Brushed Fleece
        4   x 50gm
Photographed in Crag

Needles
1 pair 6½mm (no 3) (US 10½) needles

Tension
14 sts and 20 rows to 10 cm measured over
pattern using 6½mm (US 10½) needles.

CHILL
Rib & drop stitch scarf

Finished size
Completed scarf is approx 25 cm (10 in) wide
and 200 cm (78½ in) long.

SCARF
Cast on 34 sts using 6½mm (US 10½)
needles.
Row 1 (RS): K4, *P2, K2, rep from * to last
2 sts, K2.
Row 2: K2, *P2, K2, rep from * to end.
These 2 rows form rib.
Cont in rib for a further 18 rows, ending with
a WS row.
Row 21 (RS): K4, (P2, K1, yfwd, K1, P2, K2)
3 times, P2, K4. 37 sts.
Now work in patt as folls:
Row 1 (WS): K2, P2, K2, (P2, K2, P3, K2)
3 times, P2, K2.
Row 2: K4, (P2, K3, P2, K2) 3 times, P2, K4.
Rows 3 and 4: As rows 1 and 2.
Row 5: As row 1.
Row 6: K4, (P2, K1, drop next st off left needle
and unravel this st down to yfwd 6 rows below,
K1, P2, K1, yfwd, K1) 3 times, P2, K4.

Row 7: K2, P2, K2, (P3, K2, P2, K2) 3 times,
P2, K2.
Row 8: K4, (P2, K2, P2, K3) 3 times,
P2, K4.
Rows 9 and 10: As rows 7 and 8.
Row 11: As row 7.
Row 12: K4, (P2, K1, yfwd, K1, P2, K1, drop
next st off left needle and unravel this st down
to yfwd 6 rows below, K1) 3 times, P2, K4.
These 12 rows form patt.
Cont in patt until scarf measures approx
190 cm, ending after patt row 11 and with
a WS row.
Next row (RS): K4, (P2, K2, P2, K1, drop
next st off left needle and unravel this st
down to yfwd 6 rows below, K1) 3 times,
P2, K4. 34 sts.
Starting with row 2, work in rib as given
for cast-on edge for 20 rows, ending with
a RS row.
Cast off in rib (on WS).

MAKING UP
Do NOT press.

HONOURED – *Continued from previous page.*

Row 3: Using yarn B (C: A: A: B: A) K0 (1: 0:
1: 1: 0), P1, K1, P1, *sl 1 (see pattern note),
P1, K1, P1, rep from * to last 0 (1: 0: 1: 1: 0)
st, K0 (1: 0: 1: 1: 0).
Row 4: As row 3.
These 4 rows form patt and first 4 rows of
stripe sequence for sleeve.
Keeping patt correct as now set and beg with
stripe sequence row 33 (29: 23: 19: 13: 9),
cont in patt as folls:
Work 12 rows, ending with a WS row.
Keeping patt and stripes correct, inc 1 st at
each end of next and every foll 16th (16th:
16th: 16th: 16th: 18th) row to 71 (69: 65:
63: 61: 81) sts, then on every foll – (18th:
18th: 18th: 18th: 20th) row until there are
– (73: 75: 77: 81: 83) sts, taking inc sts
into patt.
Cont straight until sleeve measures approx

45 (46: 47: 48: 49: 50) cm, ending with same
stripe row as on back to start of armhole
shaping and with a WS row.
Shape top
Keeping patt correct, cast off 4 (4: 5: 5: 6: 6)
sts at beg of next 2 rows.
63 (65: 65: 67: 69: 71) sts.
Dec 1 st at each end of next and foll alt row,
then on foll 4th row, then on 5 foll 6th rows,
then on 2 foll 4th rows.
43 (45: 45: 47: 49: 51) sts.
Work 1 row.
Dec 1 st at each end of next and every foll
alt row until 33 sts rem, then on foll 7 rows,
ending with a WS row. Cast off rem 19 sts.

MAKING UP
Press all pieces with a warm iron over
a damp cloth.

Join both shoulder seams using back stitch
or mattress stitch if preferred.
Neckband
With RS facing, using 3mm (US 2/3) needles
and yarn A, slip 16 (17: 17: 17: 17: 17) sts
from right front holder onto right needle,
rejoin yarn and pick up and knit 22 (22: 22:
24: 24: 24) sts up right side of front neck,
27 (29: 29: 31: 31: 31) sts from back, and
22 (22: 22: 24: 24: 24) sts down left side of
front neck, then patt across 16 (17: 17: 17:
17: 17) sts on left front holder.
103 (107: 107: 113: 113: 113) sts.
Row 1 (WS): P1, *K1, P1, rep from * to end.
Rep last row 4 times more, ending with
a WS row.
Cast off in patt.
Join side seams. Join sleeve seams.
Insert sleeves into armholes. Sew on buttons.

Recommendation

Suitable for the more experience knitter
Please see pages 60 – 63 for photographs.

	XS	S	M	L	XL	XXL	
To fit bust	**81**	**86**	**91**	**97**	**102**	**109**	**cm**
	32	34	36	38	40	43	in

Rowan Felted Tweed Aran and Felted Tweed

A Aran	Stoney						
	12	13	14	14	15	16 x 50gm	
B *FTwd	Ancient						
		2	2	3	3	3	3 x 50gm
C *FTwd	Carbon						
		2	2	2	2	3	3 x 50gm

*Felted Tweed is used DOUBLE throughout

Needles

1 pair 4½mm (no 7) (US 7) needles
4.00mm (no 8) (US G6) crochet hook

5 button frames

Tension

18 sts and 36 rows to 10 cm measured over
pattern using 4½mm (US 7) needles and a
combination of Felted Tweed Aran and Felted
Tweed DOUBLE.

Important note: Please see our information
page (page 102) for tips regarding the tension
for this slip stitch pattern.

Crochet abbreviations

ch = chain; **dc** = double crochet; **ss** = slip
stitch.

SHADOW
Classic jacket worked in tweed stripes

STRIPE SEQUENCE

Rows 1 and 2: Using yarn A.
Rows 3 and 4: Using yarn B DOUBLE.
Rows 5 to 14: Using yarn A.
Rows 15 and 16: Using yarn B DOUBLE.
Rows 17 and 18: Using yarn A.
Rows 19 and 20: Using yarn B DOUBLE.
Rows 21 and 22: Using yarn A.
Rows 23 and 24: Using yarn B DOUBLE.
Rows 25 to 30: Using yarn A.
Rows 31 and 32: Using yarn C DOUBLE.
Rows 33 to 42: Using yarn A.
Rows 43 and 44: Using yarn B DOUBLE.
Rows 45 and 46: Using yarn A.
Rows 47 and 48: Using yarn C DOUBLE.
Rows 49 and 50: Using yarn A.
Rows 51 and 52: Using yarn C DOUBLE.
Rows 53 to 58: Using yarn A.
Rows 59 and 60: Using yarn C DOUBLE.
These 60 rows form stripe sequence and are
repeated throughout. (**Note:** Yarns B and C
are used DOUBLE throughout.)

Pattern note: When working patt, work all
slipped sts purlwise keeping yarn at **wrong
side** of work – this is **back** of work on RS
rows and **front** of work on WS rows.

BACK

Cast on 79 (83: 87: 93: 97: 103) sts using
4½mm (US 7) needles and yarn A.
Work in patt as folls:
Row 1 (RS): Using yarn A P1 (1: 1: 0: 0: 1),
*K1, P1, rep from * to last 0 (0: 0: 1: 1: 0) st,
K0 (0: 0: 1: 1: 0).
Row 2: As row 1.
Row 3: Using yarn B DOUBLE K0 (0: 0:
0: 1: 0), P1 (0: 1: 0: 1: 1), K1 (0: 1: 1:
1: 1), P1, *sl 1 (see pattern note), P1,
K1, P1, rep from * to last 4 (2: 4: 3:
5: 4) sts, sl 1 (see pattern note), P1,
K1 (0: 1: 1: 1: 1), P1 (0: 1: 0: 1: 1),
K0 (0: 0: 0: 1: 0).
Row 4: As row 3.
These 4 rows form patt and rows 1 to 4
of stripe sequence.
Keeping patt correct as now set and beg
with stripe sequence row 5, cont in patt
as folls:
Work 16 rows, ending with a WS row.

Keeping patt and stripes correct, dec 1 st
at each end of next and 2 foll 8th rows, then
on 2 foll 6th rows. 69 (73: 77: 83: 87: 93) sts.
Cont straight until back measures 17.5 cm,
ending with a WS row.
Inc 1 st at each end of next and 4 foll
12th rows, taking inc sts into patt.
79 (83: 87: 93: 97: 103) sts.
Cont straight until back measures 35 (35: 36:
36: 36: 36) cm, ending with a WS row.
(**Note:** Make a note of which stripe sequence
row has just been worked to this point so that
sleeve stripe sequence can end at same point.)

Shape armholes

Keeping patt and stripes correct, cast off
4 (4: 5: 5: 6: 6) sts at beg of next 2 rows.
71 (75: 77: 83: 85: 91) sts.
Dec 1 st at each end of next 1 (3: 3: 5: 5: 7)
rows, then on foll 3 (2: 2: 2: 2: 2) alt rows,
then on foll 4th row.
61 (63: 65: 67: 69: 71) sts.
Cont straight until armhole measures 18 (19:
19: 20: 21: 22) cm, ending with a WS row.

Shape shoulders and back neck

Cast off 6 (6: 7: 7: 7: 7) sts at beg of next
2 rows. 49 (51: 51: 53: 55: 57) sts.
Next row (RS): Cast off 6 (6: 7: 7: 7: 7) sts,
patt until there are 11 (11: 10: 10: 11: 12) sts
on right needle and turn, leaving rem sts on
a holder.
Work each side of neck separately.
Cast off 4 sts at beg of next row.
Cast off rem 7 (7: 6: 6: 7: 8) sts.
With RS facing, rejoin appropriate yarn to
rem sts, cast off centre 15 (17: 17: 19:
19: 19) sts, patt to end.
Complete to match first side, reversing shapings.

LEFT FRONT

Cast on 47 (49: 51: 54: 56: 59) sts using
4½mm (US 7) needles and yarn A.
Work in patt as folls:
Row 1 (RS): Using yarn A P1 (1: 1: 0: 0: 1),
*K1, P1, rep from * to end.
Row 2: Using yarn A P1, *K1, P1, rep from
* to last 0 (0: 0: 1: 1: 0) st, K0 (0: 0: 1: 1: 0).
Row 3: Using yarn B DOUBLE K0 (0: 0: 0: 1:
0), P1 (0: 1: 0: 1: 1), K1 (0: 1: 1: 1: 1), P1,
*sl 1 (see pattern note), P1, K1, P1, rep from
* to end.

Row 4: Using yarn B DOUBLE P1, K1, P1, *sl 1 (see pattern note), P1, K1, P1, rep from * to last 4 (2: 4: 3: 5: 4) sts, sl 1 (see pattern note), P1, K1 (0: 1: 1: 1: 1), P1 (0: 1: 0: 1: 1), K0 (0: 0: 0: 1: 0).

These 4 rows form patt and rows 1 to 4 of stripe sequence.

Keeping patt correct as now set and beg with stripe sequence row 5, cont in patt as folls:
Work 16 rows, ending with a WS row.
Keeping patt and stripes correct, dec 1 st at beg of next and 2 foll 8th rows, then on 2 foll 6th rows. 42 (44: 46: 49: 51: 54) sts.
Cont straight until left front measures 17.5 cm, ending with a WS row.
Inc 1 st at beg of next and 4 foll 12th rows, taking inc sts into patt.
47 (49: 51: 54: 56: 59) sts.
Cont straight until left front matches back to start of armhole shaping, ending with a WS row.

Shape armhole
Keeping patt and stripes correct, cast off 4 (4: 5: 5: 6: 6) sts at beg of next row.
43 (45: 46: 49: 50: 53) sts.
Work 1 row.
Dec 1 st at armhole edge of next 1 (3: 3: 5: 5: 7) rows, then on foll 3 (2: 2: 2: 2: 2) alt rows, then on foll 4th row.
38 (39: 40: 41: 42: 43) sts.
Cont straight until 21 (21: 21: 25: 25: 25) rows less have been worked than on back to start of shoulder shaping, ending with a RS row.

Shape front neck
Keeping patt and stripes correct, cast off 10 (11: 11: 11: 11: 11) sts at beg of next row.
28 (28: 29: 30: 31: 32) sts.
Dec 1 st at neck edge of next 5 rows, then on foll 2 alt rows, then on 2 (2: 2: 3: 3: 3) foll 4th rows. 19 (19: 20: 20: 21: 22) sts.
Work 3 rows, ending with a WS row.

Shape shoulder
Cast off 6 (6: 7: 7: 7: 7) sts at beg of next and foll alt row.
Work 1 row.
Cast off rem 7 (7: 6: 6: 7: 8) sts.
Mark positions for 5 buttons along left front opening edge – first to come level with row 25, last to come 1.5 cm below neck shaping, and rem 3 buttons evenly spaced between.

RIGHT FRONT
(**Note:** To keep front opening edge neat, this front is knitted with the fabric reversed – so that RS rows of left front will become WS rows on this front, and all K sts on left front will become P sts on this front, and vice versa.

However, all slipped sts **must** still be slipped purlwise with yarn at WS of work as before.)
Cast on 47 (49: 51: 54: 56: 59) sts using 4½mm (US 7) needles and yarn A.
Work in patt as folls:
Row 1 (WS): Using yarn A K1 (1: 1: 0: 0: 1), *P1, K1, rep from * to end.
Row 2: Using yarn A K1, *P1, K1, rep from * to last 0 (0: 0: 1: 1: 0) st, K0 (0: 0: 1: 1: 0).
Row 3: Using yarn B DOUBLE P0 (0: 0: 0: 1: 0), K1 (0: 1: 0: 1: 1), P1 (0: 1: 1: 1: 1), K1, *sl 1 (see pattern note), K1, P1, K1, rep from * to end.
Row 4: Using yarn B DOUBLE K1, P1, K1, *sl 1 (see pattern note), K1, P1, K1, rep from * to last 4 (2: 4: 3: 5: 4) sts, sl 1 (see pattern note), K1, P1 (0: 1: 1: 1: 1), K1 (0: 1: 0: 1: 1), P0 (0: 0: 0: 1: 0).

These 4 rows form patt and rows 1 to 4 of stripe sequence.

Keeping patt correct as now set and beg with stripe sequence row 5, cont in patt as folls:
Work 16 rows, ending with a RS row.
Keeping patt and stripes correct, dec 1 st at beg of next row. 46 (48: 50: 53: 55: 58) sts.
Work 3 rows, ending with a RS row.
Row 25 (WS): Patt to last 6 sts, work 2 tog, (yrn) twice, work 2 tog tbl (to make a buttonhole – work twice into double yrn on next row), patt 2 sts.
Making a further 4 buttonholes in this way to correspond with positions marked for buttons on left front and noting that no further reference will be made to buttonholes, cont as folls:
Keeping patt and stripes correct, dec 1 st at beg of 4th and foll 8th row, then on 2 foll 6th rows. 42 (44: 46: 49: 51: 54) sts.
Cont straight until right front measures 17.5 cm, ending with a RS row.
Inc 1 st at beg of next and 4 foll 12th rows, taking inc sts into patt.
47 (49: 51: 54: 56: 59) sts.
Cont straight until right front matches back to start of armhole shaping, ending with a RS row.
Shape armhole
Keeping patt and stripes correct, cast off 4 (4: 5: 5: 6: 6) sts at beg of next row.
43 (45: 46: 49: 50: 53) sts.
Work 1 row.
Dec 1 st at armhole edge of next 1 (3: 3: 5: 5: 7) rows, then on foll 3 (2: 2: 2: 2: 2) alt rows, then on foll 4th row.
38 (39: 40: 41: 42: 43) sts.
Cont straight until 21 (21: 21: 25: 25: 25) rows less have been worked than on back to start of shoulder shaping, ending with a WS row.

Shape front neck
Keeping patt and stripes correct, cast off 10 (11: 11: 11: 11: 11) sts at beg of next row.
28 (28: 29: 30: 31: 32) sts.
Dec 1 st at neck edge of next 5 rows, then on foll 2 alt rows, then on 2 (2: 2: 3: 3: 3) foll 4th rows. 19 (19: 20: 20: 21: 22) sts.
Work 3 rows, ending with a RS row.
Shape shoulder
Cast off 6 (6: 7: 7: 7: 7) sts at beg of next and foll alt row.
Work 1 row.
Cast off rem 7 (7: 6: 6: 7: 8) sts.

SLEEVES (both alike)
Cast on 39 (41: 43: 45: 47: 49) sts using 4½mm (US 7) needles and yarn A.
Work in patt as folls:
Row 1 (RS): Using yarn A P1 (0: 1: 0: 1: 0), *K1, P1, rep from * to last 0 (1: 0: 1: 0: 1) st, K0 (1: 0: 1: 0: 1).
Row 2: As row 1.
Row 3: Using yarn B DOUBLE (A: A: B DOUBLE: B DOUBLE: B DOUBLE) K0 (1: 0: 1: 0: 1), P1, K1, P1, *sl 1 (see pattern note), P1, K1, P1, rep from * to last 0 (1: 0: 1: 0: 1) st, K0 (1: 0: 1: 0: 1).
Row 4: As row 3.

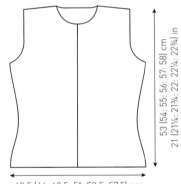

43.5 (46: 48.5: 51: 53.5: 57.5) cm
17 (18: 19: 20: 21: 22¾) in

53 [54: 55: 56: 57: 58] cm
21 [21¼: 21¾: 22: 22¼: 22¾] in

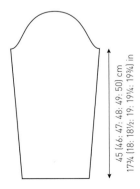

45 (46: 47: 48: 49: 50) cm
17¾ (18: 18½: 19: 19¼: 19¾) in

Continued on next page...

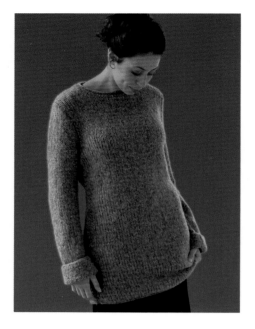

COLD

Understated tunic with turned back cuffs

Recommendation

Suitable for the novice knitter
Please see pages 14, 18 & 19 for photographs.

	XS	S	M	L	XL	XXL	
To fit bust	**81**	**86**	**91**	**97**	**102**	**109**	**cm**
	32	34	36	38	40	43	in

Rowan Brushed Fleece

	7	8	9	10	10	11 x 50gm

Photographed in Crag

Needles

1 pair 5½mm (no 5) (US 9) needles
1 pair 6½mm (no 3) (US 10½) needles
1 pair 7mm (no 2) (US 10½/11) needles

Tension

12½ sts and 19 rows to 10 cm measured over stocking stitch using 7mm (US 10½/11) needles.

BACK

Cast on 56 (60: 64: 66: 70: 74) sts using 6½mm (US 10½) needles.
Beg with a K row, now work in st st throughout as folls:
Work 8 rows, ending with a WS row.
Change to 7mm (US 10½/11) needles.
Work 34 rows, ending with a WS row.
Row 43 (RS): K3, K2tog, K to last 5 sts, K2tog tbl, K3.
Working all side seam decreases as set by last row, dec 1 st at each end of 14th and foll 12th row.
50 (54: 58: 60: 64: 68) sts.
Work 17 rows, ending with a WS row.
Next row (RS): K3, M1, K to last 3 sts, M1, K3.
Working all side seam increases as set by last row, inc 1 st at each end of 14th row.
54 (58: 62: 64: 68: 72) sts.

Cont straight until back measures 60 (60: 61: 61: 61: 61) cm, ending with a WS row.
Shape armholes
Cast off 3 sts at beg of next 2 rows.
48 (52: 56: 58: 62: 66) sts.
Dec 1 st at each end of next 1 (1: 3: 3: 3: 5) rows, then on foll 1 (2: 1: 2: 3: 2) alt rows.
44 (46: 48: 48: 50: 52) sts.
Cont straight until armhole measures 18 (19: 19: 20: 21: 22) cm, ending with a WS row.
Shape shoulders and back neck
Cast off 4 sts at beg of next 2 rows.
36 (38: 40: 40: 42: 44) sts.
Next row (RS): Cast off 4 sts, K until there are 7 (7: 8: 7: 8: 9) sts on right needle and turn, leaving rem sts on a holder.
Work each side of neck separately.
Cast off 4 sts at beg of next row.
Cast off rem 3 (3: 4: 3: 4: 5) sts.
With RS facing, rejoin yarn to rem sts, cast off centre 14 (16: 16: 18: 18: 18) sts, K to end.
Complete to match first side, reversing shapings.

SHADOW – *Continued from previous page.*

These 4 rows form patt and first 4 rows of stripe sequence for sleeve.
Keeping patt correct as now set and beg with stripe sequence row 33 (29: 29: 25: 21: 17), cont in patt as folls:
Work 16 rows, ending with a WS row.
Keeping patt and stripes correct, inc 1 st at each end of next and every foll 16th (16th: 18th: 18th: 16th: 16th) row to 47 (45: 57: 55: 57: 55) sts, then on every foll 18th (18th: 20th: 20th: 18th: 18th) row until there are 55 (57: 59: 61: 65: 67) sts, taking inc sts into patt.
Cont straight until sleeve measures approx 44 (45: 46: 47: 48: 49) cm, ending with same stripe row as on back to start of armhole shaping and with a WS row.
Shape top
Keeping patt correct, cast off 4 (4: 5: 5: 6: 6) sts at beg of next 2 rows.
47 (49: 49: 51: 53: 55) sts.

Dec 1 st at each end of next and foll 4th row, then on 3 foll 6th rows, then on 2 foll 4th rows.
33 (35: 35: 37: 39: 41) sts.
Work 1 row.
Dec 1 st at each end of next and every foll alt row until 27 sts rem, then on foll 5 rows, ending with a WS row.
Cast off rem 17 sts.

MAKING UP
Press all pieces with a warm iron over a damp cloth.
Join both shoulder seams using back stitch or mattress stitch if preferred. Join side seams. Join sleeve seams. Insert sleeves into armholes.
Edging
With RS facing, using 4.00mm (US G6) crochet hook and yarn A, attach yarn to base of left side seam, 1 ch (does NOT count as st), now work one round of dc around entire hem, front

opening and neck edges, working 3 dc into each corner point and ending with ss to first dc, do NOT turn.
Now work one row of crab st (dc worked from left to right, instead of right to left), ending with ss to first st.
Fasten off.
Work edging around lower edges of sleeves in same way, attaching yarn at base of sleeve seam. Using yarn A cover the button frames following instructions on packet. Attach buttons to left front to correspond with buttonholes.

FRONT

Work as given for back until 10 (10: 10: 12: 12: 12) rows less have been worked than on back to start of shoulder shaping, ending with a WS row.

Shape front neck

Next row (RS): K17 (17: 18: 18: 19: 20) and turn, leaving rem sts on a holder. Work each side of neck separately.
Dec 1 st at neck edge of next 4 rows, then on foll 1 (1: 1: 2: 2: 2) alt rows.
12 (12: 13: 12: 13: 14) sts.
Work 3 rows, ending with a WS row.

Shape shoulder

Cast off 4 sts at beg of next and foll alt row **and at same time** dec 1 st at neck edge of next row.
Work 1 row.
Cast off rem 3 (3: 4: 3: 4: 5) sts.
With RS facing, rejoin yarn to rem sts, cast off centre 10 (12: 12: 12: 12: 12) sts, K to end.
Complete to match first side, reversing shapings.

SLEEVES (both alike)

Cast on 34 (36: 38: 38: 40: 42) sts using 7mm (US 10½/11) needles.
Beg with a K row, work in st st throughout as folls:
Work 14 rows, ending with a WS row.
Row 15 (RS): K3, K2tog, K to last 5 sts, K2tog tbl, K3.
32 (34: 36: 36: 38: 40) sts.
Work 19 rows, ending with a WS row.
Next row (RS): K3, M1, K to last 3 sts, M1, K3.
Working all increases as set by last row, inc 1 st at each end of 22nd (24th: 36th: 26th: 36th: 36th) and foll 24th (24th: -: 26th: -: -) row.
38 (40: 40: 42: 42: 44) sts.
Cont straight until sleeve measures 53 (54: 55: 56: 57: 58) cm, ending with a WS row.

Shape top

Cast off 3 sts at beg of next 2 rows.
32 (34: 34: 36: 36: 38) sts.
Dec 1 st at each end of next and 3 foll 4th rows, then on every foll alt row until 20 sts rem, then on foll 3 rows, ending with a WS row.
Cast off rem 14 sts.

MAKING UP

Press all pieces with a warm iron over a damp cloth.
Join right shoulder seam using back stitch or mattress stitch if preferred.

Neckband

With RS facing and using 7mm (US 10½/11) needles, pick up and knit 15 (15: 15: 17: 17: 17) sts down left side of front neck, 10 (12: 12: 12: 12: 12) sts from front, 15 (15: 15: 17: 17: 17) sts up right side of front neck, and 21 (23: 23: 25: 25: 25) sts from back.
61 (65: 65: 71: 71: 71) sts.
Change to 5½mm (US 9) needles.
Beg with a P row, work in st st for 3 rows, ending with a WS row.
Cast off knitwise.
Join left shoulder and neckband seam, reversing neckband seam to allow for cast-off edge to roll to RS. Join side seams. Join sleeve seams, reversing sleeve seam for first 10 cm. Insert sleeves into armholes. Fold 8 cm to RS around lower edge of sleeves (for turn-back).

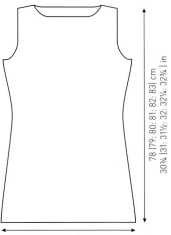

78 (79: 80: 81: 82: 83) cm
30¾ (31: 31½: 32: 32¼: 32¾) in

44.5 (47: 49.5: 52: 54.5: 58.5) cm
17½ (18½: 19½: 20½: 21½: 23) cm

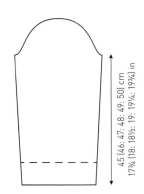

45 (46: 47: 48: 49: 50) cm
17¾ (18: 18½: 19: 19¼: 19¾) in

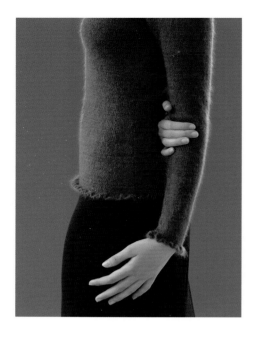

TEMPERATE
Fitted sweater with frilled hems

Recommendation
Suitable for the knitter with a little experience
Please see page 29 for photograph.

	XS	S	M	L	XL	XXL	
To fit bust	**81**	**86**	**91**	**97**	**102**	**109**	**cm**
	32	34	36	38	40	43	in

Rowan Mohair Haze
| | 9 | 10 | 10 | 11 | 12 | 13 x 25gm |
Photographed in Tender

Needles
1 pair 2¼mm (no 13) (US 1) needles
1 pair 3mm (no 11) (US 2/3) needles

Tension
26 sts and 36 rows to 10 cm measured over
stocking stitch using 3mm (US 2/3) needles.

BACK
Cast on 410 (434: 458: 490: 514: 554) sts
using 2¼mm (US 1) needles.
Row 1 (RS): K1, *K2, lift 2nd st on right
needle over first st and off right needle, rep
from * to last st, K1.
206 (218: 230: 246: 258: 278) sts.
Row 2: P1, *P2tog, rep from * to last st, P1.
104 (110: 116: 124: 130: 140) sts.
These 2 rows complete the frill edging.
Change to 3mm (US 2/3) needles.
Beg with a K row, now work in st st throughout
as folls:
Work 20 rows, ending with a WS row.
Next row (RS): K10, K2tog tbl, K to last 12 sts,
K2tog, K10.
Working all side seam decreases as set by
last row, dec 1 st at each end of 8th and
2 foll 8th rows, then on 3 foll 6th rows.
90 (96: 102: 110: 116: 126) sts.
Work 17 rows, ending with a WS row.
Next row (RS): K10, M1, K to last 10 sts, M1,
K10.
Working all side seam increases as set by last
row, inc 1 st at each end of 8th and 4 foll 8th
rows, then on 2 foll 6th rows.
106 (112: 118: 126: 132: 142) sts.
Cont straight until back measures 39 (39: 40:
40: 40: 40) cm **from top of frill edging,**
ending with a WS row.
Shape armholes
Cast off 5 (5: 6: 6: 7: 7) sts at beg of next 2
rows. 96 (102: 106: 114: 118: 128) sts.
Dec 1 st at each end of next 1 (3: 3: 5: 5: 7)
rows, then on foll 3 (3: 4: 4: 5: 6) alt rows, then
on foll 4th row. 86 (88: 90: 94: 96: 100) sts.
Cont straight until armhole measures 18 (19:
19: 20: 21: 22) cm, ending with a WS row.
Shape shoulders and back neck
Cast off 5 (5: 5: 6: 6: 7) sts at beg of next
2 rows. 76 (78: 80: 82: 84: 86) sts.
Next row (RS): Cast off 5 (5: 5: 6: 6: 7) sts,
K until there are 9 (9: 10: 9: 10: 10) sts on right
needle and turn, leaving rem sts on a holder.
Work each side of neck separately.
Cast off 4 sts at beg of next row.
Cast off rem 5 (5: 6: 5: 6: 6) sts.
With RS facing, rejoin yarn to rem sts, cast off
centre 48 (50: 50: 52: 52: 52) sts, K to end.
Complete to match first side, reversing shapings.

FRONT
Work as given for back until 10 (10: 10:
12: 12: 12) rows less have been worked
than on back to start of shoulder shaping,
ending with a WS row.
Shape front neck
Next row (RS): K23 (23: 24: 26: 27: 29)
and turn, leaving rem sts on a holder.
Work each side of neck separately.
Dec 1 st at neck edge of next 6 rows, then
on foll 1 (1: 1: 2: 2: 2) alt rows.
16 (16: 17: 18: 19: 21) sts.
Work 1 row, ending with a WS row.
Shape shoulder
Cast off 5 (5: 5: 6: 6: 7) sts at beg of next and
foll alt row **and at same time** dec 1 st at neck
edge of next row.
Work 1 row.
Cast off rem 5 (5: 6: 5: 6: 6) sts.
With RS facing, rejoin yarn to rem sts, cast off
centre 40 (42: 42: 42: 42: 42) sts, K to end.
Complete to match first side, reversing
shapings.

SLEEVES (both alike)
Cast on 186 (186: 194: 210: 210: 218) sts
using 2¼mm (US 1) needles.
Row 1 (RS): K1, *K2, lift 2nd st on right
needle over first st and off right needle, rep
from * to last st, K1.
94 (94: 98: 106: 106: 110) sts.
Row 2: P1, *P2tog, rep from * to last st, P1.
48 (48: 50: 54: 54: 56) sts.
These 2 rows complete the frill edging.
Change to 3mm (US 2/3) needles.
Beg with a K row, now work in st st throughout
as folls:
Work 8 (8: 8: 10: 8: 8) rows, ending with
a WS row.
Next row (RS): K4, M1, K to last 4 sts, M1, K4.
Working all increases as set by last row,
inc 1 st at each end of 8th (8th: 8th: 10th:
8th: 8th) and every foll 8th (8th: 8th: 10th:
8th: 8th) row to 54 (60: 58: 80: 64: 64) sts,
then on every foll 10th (10th: 10th: 12th:
10th: 10th) row until there are 80 (82: 84:
86: 90: 92) sts.
Cont straight until sleeve measures 48 (49:
50: 51: 52: 53) cm **from top of frill edging,**
ending with a WS row.

Shape top

Cast off 5 (5: 6: 6: 7: 7) sts at beg of next
2 rows. 70 (72: 72: 74: 76: 78) sts.
Dec 1 st at each end of next 3 rows, and foll
alt row, then on 5 foll 4th rows.
52 (54: 54: 56: 58: 60) sts.
Work 1 row.
Dec 1 st at each end of next and every foll
alt row until 44 sts rem, then on foll 9 rows,
ending with a WS row.
Cast off rem 26 sts.

MAKING UP

Press all pieces with a warm iron over
a damp cloth.
Join right shoulder seam using back stitch
or mattress stitch if preferred.

Neckband

With RS facing and using 2¼mm (US 1)
needles, pick up and knit 13 (13: 13: 15:
15: 15) sts down left side of front neck,
40 (42: 42: 42: 42: 42) sts from front,
13 (13: 13: 15: 15: 15) sts up right side
of front neck, and 56 (58: 58: 60:
60: 60) sts from back.
122 (126: 126: 132: 132: 132) sts.
Beg with a K row, work in rev st st for 4 rows,
ending with a **RS** row.
Cast off knitwise (on **WS**).
Join left shoulder and neckband seam.
Join side seams. Join sleeve seams.
Insert sleeves into armholes.

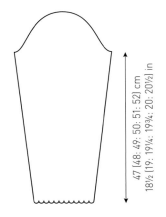

57 (58: 59: 60: 61: 62) cm
22½ (22¾: 23¼: 23½: 24: 24½) in

40.5 (43: 45.5: 48: 50.5: 54.5) cm
16 (17: 18: 19: 20: 21½) in

47 (48: 49: 50: 51: 52) cm
18½ (19: 19¼: 19¾: 20: 20½) in

INFORMATION
A guide to assist with techniques & finishing touches

TENSION

Achieving the correct tension has to be one of the most important elements in producing a beautiful, well fitting knitted garment. The tension controls the size and shape of your finished piece and any variation to either stitches or rows, however slight, will affect your work and change the fit completely.

To avoid any disappointment, we would always recommend that you knit a tension square in the yarn and stitch given in the pattern, working perhaps four or five more stitches and rows than those given in the tension note. When counting the tension, place your knitting on a flat surface and mark out a 10cm square with pins. Count the stitches between the pins. If you have too many stitches to 10cm your knitting it too tight, try again using thicker needles, if you have too few stitches to 10cm your knitting is too loose, so try again using finer needles. Please note, if you are unable to achieve the correct stitches and rows required, the stitches are more crucial as many patterns are knitted to length.

Keep an eye on your tension during knitting, especially if you're going back to work which has been put to one side for any length of time.

SIZING

The instructions are given for the smallest size. Where they vary, work the figures in brackets for the larger sizes. One set of figures refers to all sizes. The size diagram with each pattern will help you decide which size to knit. The measurements given on the size diagram are the actual size your garment should be when completed.

Measurements will vary from design to design because the necessary ease allowances have been made in each pattern to give your garment the correct fit, i.e. a loose fitting garment will be several cm wider than a neat fitted one, a snug fitting garment may have no ease at all.

WRAP STITCH

A wrap stitch is used to eliminate the hole created when using the short row shaping method. Work to the position on the row indicated in the pattern, wrap the next st (by slipping next st onto right needle, taking yarn to opposite side of work between needles and then slipping same st back onto left needle – on foll rows, K tog the loop and the wrapped st) and turn, cont from pattern.

CHART NOTE

Some of our patterns include a chart. Each square on a chart represent a stitch and each line of squares a row of knitting.

When working from a chart, unless otherwise stated, read odd rows (RS) from right to left and even rows (WS) from left to right. The key alongside each chart indicates how each stitch is worked.

PATTERN NOTE FOR HONOURED (page 92) & SHADOW (page 96)

To ensure the firm tension required for this slip stitch pattern, you may need to adjust your needles. Measuring the fabric can be tricky as your knitting may appear slightly long and narrow, it is therefore important to gently pull the fabric into shape and block out to size before pressing.

We recommend that you check the tension every 10 cm or so, pulling your knitting gently to the correct width.

FINISHING INSTRUCTIONS

It is the pressing and finishing which will transform your knitted pieces into a garment to be proud of.

Pressing

Darn in ends neatly along the selvage edge. Follow closely any special instructions given on the pattern or ball band and always take great care not to over press your work.

Block out your knitting on a pressing or ironing board, easing into shape, and unless otherwise states, press each piece using a warm iron over a damp cloth.

Tip: Attention should be given to ribs/edgings; if the garment is close fitting – steam the ribs gently so that the stitches fill out but stay elastic. Alternatively if the garment is to hang straight then steam out to the correct shape.

Tip: Take special care to press the selvages, as this will make sewing up both easier and neater.

CONSTRUCTION
Stitching together

When stitching the pieces together, remember to match areas of pattern very carefully where they meet. Use a stitch such as back stitch or mattress stitch for all main knitting seams and join all ribs and neckband with mattress stitch, unless otherwise stated. Take extra care when stitching the edgings and collars around the back neck of a garment. They control the width of the back neck, and if too wide the garment will be ill fitting and drop off the shoulder. Knit back neck edgings only to the length stated in the pattern, even stretching it slightly if for example, you are working in garter or horizontal rib stitch. Stitch edgings/collars firmly into place using a back stitch seam, easing-in the back neck to fit the collar/edging rather than stretching the collar/edging to fit the back neck.

CARE INSTRUCTIONS
Yarns

Follow the care instructions printed on each individual ball band. Where different yarns are used in the same garment, follow the care instructions for the more delicate one.

Buttons

We recommend that buttons are removed if your garment is to be machine washed.

CROCHET

We are aware that crochet terminology varies from country to country. Please note we have used the English style in this publication.

Crochet abbreviations

ch	chain
ss	slip stitch
dc	double crochet
tr	treble
dc2tog	2 dc tog
tr2tog	2 tr tog
yoh	yarn over hook

Double crochet

1　Insert the hook into the work (as indicated in the pattern), wrap the yarn over the hook and draw the yarn through the work only.
2　Wrap the yarn again and draw the yarn through both loops on the hook.
3　1 dc made

Treble

1　Wrap the yarn over the hook and insert the hook into the work (as indicated on the pattern).
2　Wrap the yarn over the hook draw through the work only and wrap the yarn again.
3　Draw through the first 2 loops only and wrap the yarn again.
4　Draw through the last 2 loops on the hook.
5　1 treble made.

ABBREVIATIONS

K	knit
P	purl
K1b	knit 1 through back loop
st(s)	stitch(es)
inc	increas(e)(ing)
dec	decreas(e)(ing)
st st	stocking stitch (1 row K, 1 row P)
garter st	garter stitch (K every row)
beg	begin(ning)
foll	following
rem	remain(ing)
rev st st	reverse stocking stitch (1 row P, 1 row K)
rep	repeat
alt	alternate
cont	continue
patt	pattern
tog	together
mm	millimetres
cm	centimetres
in(s)	inch(es)
RS	right side
WS	wrong side
sl 1	slip one stitch
psso	pass slipped stitch over
tbl	through back of loop
M1	make one stitch by picking up horizontal loop before next stitch and knitting into back of it
M1p	make one stitch by picking up horizontal loop before next stitch and purling into back of it
yfwd	yarn forward (making a stitch)
yon	yarn over needle (making a stitch)
yrn	yarn round needle (making a stitch)-
MP	Make picot: Cast on 1 st, by inserting the right needle between the first and second stitch on left needle, take yarn round needle, bring loop through and place on left (one stitch cast on), cast off 1 st, by knitting first the loop and then the next stitch, pass the first stitch over the second (one stitch cast off).
Cn	cable needle
C4B	Cable 4 back: Slip next 2 sts onto a cn and hold at back of work, K2, K2 from cn.
C4F	Cable 4 front: Slip next 2 sts onto a cn and hold at front of work, K2, K2 from cn.

THANK YOU!

We would like to thank an amazing group of people who have contributed to this book, firstly Graham for the most brilliant photography and editorial design, Angela for her skills on the page layouts, our three most beautiful & gorgeous models, Naomi, Charlotte and Angharad, Diana for the great hair & make-up, Siobhan and Laura at Coco North hairdressers (www.coco-north.com); as always – Sue and Tricia for their pattern writing & checking expertise, Ella, Glennis, Margaret, Sarah, Alicia, Joan & Betty for all their wonderful knitting, Susan for her patience in finishing the garments, Ann, Vicky, Kate & David at Rowan and finally to Jackie, for yet again stepping in with some much needed last minute help.

You are all fantastic; we couldn't have done it without each and every one of you!

Kim, Kathleen and Lindsay

INDEX